WHY PUNISH PERPETRATORS OF MASS ATROCITIES?

This edited volume provides a comprehensive account of theoretical approaches to international punishment. Its main objective is to contribute to the development of a consistent and robust theory of international criminal punishment. For this purpose, the authors – renowned scholars in the fields of criminal law, international criminal law, and philosophy of law, as well as practitioners working at international criminal courts and tribunals – address the question of meaning and purpose of punishment in international law from various perspectives. The volume fleshes out the various dimensions of a theory of international punishment and highlights the differences between 'ordinary' (domestic) crime and international crimes and their respective enforcement. At the same time, throughout the volume a major focus is on the practical consequences of the different theoretical approaches, in particular for the activities of the International Criminal Court.

Florian Jeßberger is Professor of Law at the University of Hamburg, where he holds the Chair in Criminal Law, Criminal Procedure, International Criminal Law, and Modern Legal History. Before joining the University of Hamburg in 2010, he was the Lichtenberg Professor of International and Comparative Criminal Law at Humboldt-University Berlin. He has held various visiting fellowships, inter alia, in Oxford, Ferrara, and Naples, and is a Member of the Board of Editors of the Journal of International Criminal Justice.

Julia Geneuss is Postdoctoral Researcher and Lecturer in Criminal Law at the University of Hamburg. She holds a Dr. iur. from Humboldt-University Berlin and a LL.M. from NYU School of Law. She has been awarded several prizes for her doctoral dissertation on the prosecution of crimes under international law in Germany, in particular under the principle of universal jurisdiction. She is a member of the Editorial Committee of the Journal of International Criminal Justice.

ASIL Studies in International Legal Theory

The purpose of the ASIL Studies in International Legal Theory series is to clarify and improve the theoretical foundations of international law. Too often the progressive development and implementation of international law has foundered on confusion about first principles. This series raises the level of public and scholarly discussion about the structure and purposes of the world legal order and how best to achieve global justice through law.

This series grows out of the International Legal Theory project of the American Society of International Law. The ASIL Studies in International Legal Theory series deepens this conversation by publishing scholarly monographs and edited volumes of essays considering subjects in international legal theory.

Books in the Series

Why Punish Perpetrators of Mass Atrocities?: Purposes of Punishment in International Criminal Law Edited by Florian Jeßberger and Julia Geneuss

The Challenge of Inter-legality Edited by Jan Klabbers and Gianluigi Palombella

The Nature of International Law Miodrag A. Jovanović

Reexamining Customary International Law Edited by Brian D. Lepard

Theoretical Boundaries of Armed Conflict and Human Rights Edited by Jens David Ohlin

Human Rights in Emergencies Edited by Evan J. Criddle

The Theory of Self-Determination Edited by Fernando R. Tesón

Negotiating State and Non-State Law: Global and Local Legal Pluralism Edited by Michael A. Helfand

Jus Post Bellum and Transitional Justice Edited by Larry May and Elizabeth Edenberg

Normative Pluralism and International Law: Exploring Global Governance Edited by Jan Klabbers and Touko Piipaerinen

The Future of International Law: Global Government Joel P. Trachtman

Morality, Jus Post Bellum, and International Law Edited by Larry May and Andrew T. Forcehimes

Global Justice and International Economic Law: Opportunities and Prospects Edited by Chios Carmody, Frank J. Garcia, and John Linarelli

Parochialism, Cosmopolitanism, and the Foundations of International Law Edited by Mortimer Sellers

The Role of Ethics in International Law Edited by Donald Earl Childress III

The New Global Law Rafael Domingo

Customary International Law: A New Theory with Practical Applications Brian D. Lepard

International Criminal Law and Philosophy Edited by Larry May and Zachary Hoskins

Why Punish Perpetrators of Mass Atrocities?

PURPOSES OF PUNISHMENT IN INTERNATIONAL CRIMINAL LAW

Edited by

FLORIAN JESSBERGER

University of Hamburg

JULIA GENEUSS

University of Hamburg

CAMBRIDGE
UNIVERSITY PRESS

CAMBRIDGE
UNIVERSITY PRESS

University Printing House, Cambridge CB2 8BS, United Kingdom

One Liberty Plaza, 20th Floor, New York, NY 10006, USA

477 Williamstown Road, Port Melbourne, VIC 3207, Australia

314-321, 3rd Floor, Plot 3, Splendor Forum, Jasola District Centre, New Delhi - 110025, India

79 Anson Road, #06-04/06, Singapore 079906

Cambridge University Press is part of the University of Cambridge.

It furthers the University's mission by disseminating knowledge in the pursuit of education, learning and research at the highest international levels of excellence.

www.cambridge.org
Information on this title: www.cambridge.org/9781108465892
DOI: 10.1017/9781108566360

First published 2020
First paperback edition 2021

A catalogue record for this publication is available from the British Library

Library of Congress Cataloging in Publication data
NAMES: Jeßberger, Florian, editor. | Geneuss, Julia, 1979- editor.
TITLE: Why punish perpetrators of mass atrocities? : purposes of punishment in international criminal law / [editd by] Florian Jeßberger, Julia Geneuss.
DESCRIPTION: 1. | New York : Cambridge University Press, 2020. | Series: Asil studies in international legal theory | Includes bibliographical references and index.
IDENTIFIERS: LCCN 2019038182 (print) | LCCN 2019038183 (ebook) | ISBN 9781108475143 (hardback) | ISBN 9781108465892 (paperback) | ISBN 9781108566360 (epub)
SUBJECTS: LCSH: International criminal law. | Punishment. | Atrocities.
CLASSIFICATION: LCC KZ7050 .W49 2020 (PRINT) | LCC KZ7050 (EBOOK) | DDC 345/.0773–dc23
LC record available at https://lccn.loc.gov/2019038182
LC ebook record available at https://lccn.loc.gov/2019038183

ISBN 978-1-108-47514-3 Hardback
ISBN 978-1-108-46589-2 Paperback

Contents

Contributors

Philipp Ambach
Chief of the Victims Participation and Reparations Section in the Registry of the International Criminal Court, The Hague.

Kai Ambos
Professor of Criminal Law, Criminal Procedure, Comparative Law, International Criminal Law and International Law at Georg-August-University Göttingen, and Judge at the Kosovo Specialist Chambers and Specialist Prosecutor's Office, The Hague; *amicus curiae* of the Special Jurisdiction for Peace, Bogota, Colombia.

Jochen Bung
Professor of Legal Philosophy and Criminal Law at the University of Hamburg.

Silvia D'Ascoli
Associate Prosecutor at the Kosovo Specialist Chambers and Specialist Prosecutor's Office, The Hague.

Daniela Demko
Professor of Criminal Law, Criminal Procedure, International Criminal Law, Comparative Criminal Law and Legal Philosophy at the University of Leipzig.

Mark A. Drumbl
Class of 1975 Alumni Professor of Law and Director, Transnational Law Institute, at Washington and Lee University, Lexington.

Aziz Epik
Postdoctoral Researcher and Lecturer in Criminal Law at Humboldt-University, Berlin.

Silvia Fernández de Gurmendi
Judge (2010–2018) and President (2015–2018) of the International Criminal Court, The Hague.

Julia Geneuss
Postdoctoral Researcher and Lecturer in Criminal Law at the University of Hamburg.

Klaus Günther
Professor of Legal Theory, Criminal Law and Criminal Procedure at Goethe-University, Frankfurt am Main.

Jakob v.H. Holtermann
Associate Professor in Legal Philosophy at the Center of Excellence for International Courts of the University of Copenhagen.

Florian Jessberger
Professor of Criminal Law, Criminal Procedure, International Criminal Law and Modern Legal History at the University of Hamburg.

Mordechai Kremnitzer
Professor emeritus of Law at the Hebrew University of Jerusalem, Senior Research Fellow at the Israel Democracy Institute.

Frank Neubacher
Professor of Criminology and Criminal Law at the University of Cologne.

Jens David Ohlin
Professor of Law at Cornell University, Ithaca.

Immi Tallgren
Senior Researcher, Erik Castrén Institute, University of Helsinki and Centre for Women, Peace and Security, London School of Economics.

Harmen van der Wilt
Professor of International Criminal Law at the University of Amsterdam.

Elies van Sliedregt
Professor of International and Comparative Criminal Law at the University of Leeds.

Sergey Vasiliev
Assistant Professor of International Criminal Law at the University of Amsterdam.

Andreas Werkmeister
Postdoctoral Researcher and Lecturer in Criminal Law at Humboldt-University, Berlin.

Gerhard Werle
Professor of German and International Criminal Law, Criminal Procedure and Modern Legal History at Humboldt-University, Berlin.

Alex Whiting
Professor of Practice at Harvard University, Cambridge.

Preface

Why punish perpetrators of mass atrocities? Given the rapid development and advancing consolidation of international criminal law, it seems rather late to ask this question. However, the question of rationales of international punishment is still under-researched and under-theorized, and of relevance for a solid grounding of international criminal law. Therefore, in our view, it was about time to bring together scholars and practitioners from different disciplines and groups of experts: scholars whose research focuses on theories of punishment in general, scholars whose main research interest is international criminal law, and finally lawyers working at international criminal courts or tribunals and concerned with the enforcement of international criminal law. The present volume is the result of these discussions.

Why Punish Perpetrators of Mass Atrocities? Purposes of Punishment in International Criminal Law goes back to a conference on the same topic held at the University of Hamburg in October 2017. Several of the contributions assembled in this volume are edited papers presented at the Hamburg conference. In addition, we asked a number of colleagues to address specific questions that proved to be indispensable in order to approach the issue from a basis as complete as possible. Finally, some colleagues – some who attended the Hamburg conference, and others that did not – were kind enough to submit concise comments on one or more of the longer chapters. With this approach, our aim was to create a 'discursive environment', within which contested issues come to the fore and allow us to sharpen the future research questions.

The conference has been made possible through generous funding from the *Deutsche Forschungsgemeinschaft* and the *Hamburgische Wissenschaftliche Stiftung*.

We would like to acknowledge the assistance of Felix Behnke and Christina Lemke, who contributed to the successful completion of this volume, as well as the support of the whole team of the Hamburg *Lehrstuhl* during the conference. Our gratitude also lies with our publishers, Tom Randall and Gemma Smith, for their valuable support and, in particular, their patience.

All websites cited in this volume have last been accessed on 1 December 2018.

Abbreviations

AC	Appeals Chamber
Art(s).	Article(s)
AU	African Union
BVerfG	*Bundesverfassungsgericht* (German Constitutional Court)
cf.	confer
CPC	*Cour Pénale Spéciale Centrafricaine*
EAC	Extraordinary African Chambers
ECCC	Extraordinary Chambers in the Courts of Cambodia, Khmer Rouge Tribunal
ECHR	European Convention on Human Rights
ECtHR	European Court of Human Rights, European Court
ed.	edition, editor
eds.	editors
e.g.	for example *(exempli gratia)*
et al.	and others *(et alii)*
et seq.	and the following *(et sequens; et sequentes)*
EU	European Union
fn.	footnote(s)
GA	General Assembly
ICC	International Criminal Court
ICCPR	International Covenant on Civil and Political Rights
ICTR	International Criminal Tribunal for Rwanda
ICTY	International Criminal Tribunal for the former Yugoslavia
i.e.	that is *(id est)*
IMT	Nuremberg International Military Tribunal, Nuremberg Tribunal
IMTFE	International Military Tribunal for the Far East, Tokyo Tribunal

KSC	Kosovo Specialist Chambers and Specialist Prosecutor's Office
LRA	Lord Resistance Army
p.	page(s)
para(s).	paragraph(s)
PTC	Pre-Trial Chamber
RPE	Rules of Procedure and Evidence
SCSL	Special Court for Sierra Leone
Sec(s).	Section(s)
STL	Special Tribunal for Lebanon
TC	Trial Chamber
UK	United Kingdom
UN	United Nations
UNAMSIL	United Nations Mission in Sierra Leone
UN Doc.	Documents of the United Nations
US	United States of America
v.	versus
Vol.	Volume

1

Introduction: The Need for a Robust and Consistent Theory of International Punishment

JULIA GENEUSS AND FLORIAN JESSBERGER

I WHY THE 'WHY PUNISH' QUESTION?

Ever since the trial against the major war criminals of World War II before the International Military Tribunal at Nuremberg, the institution of punishment has beenan integral part of the international legal system. Nowadays, a large number of perpetrators and accomplices of crimes under international law – i.e. genocide, crimes against humanity and war crimes – are being sent to jail by international judges. But why and to what aim do we punish individuals for their involvement in mass atrocities? How can we justify punishment by international criminal courts and tribunals vis-à-vis the affected individual? More generally: What are the (realistic) objectives of international criminal law?

The question of meaning and purpose of criminal punishment has been and still is widely discussed in the domestic context. As a result, a differentiated range of theories of domestic punishment exists. In international criminal law, however, despite a number of important writings (listed in the select bibliography), the academic debate on justifications for and purposes of punishment is only beginning. Similarly, in their judgments, international criminal courts and tribunals generallly avoid taking a firm stance on the meaning and purpose of punishment. As a result, the issue is still underexplored and a consistent and robust theory of international punishment has yet to be developed. This lack of research is all the more surprising, given that the debate on theories of punishment in international criminal law is by no means a purely academic exercise, but has various practical consequences. First of all, it touches upon the legitimacy of international criminal law as such. In addition, the question of purposes of punishment is of concrete practical importance and concerns, inter alia, the prosecutor's selection of situations to investigate and cases to prosecute, the decision on the charges and the sentencing decision.

The obvious starting point of the discussion on the purposes of international punishment are the traditional punishment theories – retribution, deterrence, prevention and expressivism – known from the domestic context (the 'domestic analogy' approach). However, given the distinct quality and dimension of the core international crimes, it is questionable whether and to what degree traditional theories of punishment can be transferred to the international level. Crimes under international law form part of macrocriminality, which differs from 'ordinary' criminality, i.e., crimes committed in a domestic context, in many ways. In particular, in contrast to 'ordinary' crimes, crimes under international law cannot be regarded as isolated events, but are typically committed in the context of an overall disturbed society. The crimes are part of collective action; both the perpetrators and victims of crimes, under international law, can generally be characterized by their group membership. In addition, on the part of the perpetrators, different hierarchical levels must be distinguished, for example the 'bureaucratic masterminds' or 'armchair perpetrators' – the 'big fish' – on the one hand and their followers as the direct perpetrators – the 'small fish' – on the other. When developing a rationale for international punishment, these peculiarities, inter alia, must carefully be identified, and the traditional theories must be adapted and modified.

In the present volume, authors inquire into the meaning and purpose of international punishment. While one of the aims of this volume is to contribute to the development of a consistent and robust theory of international criminal punishment, a second, not less important objective is to link the theoretical discussion of purposes of punishment in international criminal law to their practical consequences. Therefore, throughout the volume a major focus is on the practical consequences of the different theoretical approaches, in particular for the activities of the International Criminal Court (ICC).

II STRUCTURE

The volume starts off with an introductory contribution by the former President of the ICC, Judge Silvia Fernández de Gurmendi. In her contribution she highlights the practical importance of theories of punishment in international criminal law in general and the work of the ICC in particular. She particularly discusses three goals of international criminal justice: conflict prevention, i.e., deterrence; reconciliation; and rehabilitation. Regarding the former, much like Frank Neubacher and Harmen van der Wilt in their respective contributions, she sees the impunity gap – which is due to the nature of the crimes and the lack of universality of the ICC's jurisdiction – as the main obstacle to a potent deterrent effect ensuing. As regards the reconciliation, similar to Philipp Ambach in his chapter, she emphasizes the importance of 'ownership', accomplished by victims' participation, and, in this regard, the importance of outreach. Regarding reconciliation, she outlines the elements of restorative justice in the ICC Statute, and the problems connected to reparations and the limited scope of cases. Finally, as a third rationale for punishment, she discusses the rehabilitation of the convicted perpetrators.

The volume is divided into three thematic parts. The first part – *Setting the Framework: Criminological, Historical and Domestic Perspectives* – prepares the ground for the ensuing theoretical and practical debate on rationales of punishment in international criminal law. Frank Neubacher looks at theories of punishment in international criminal law from a criminologist's perspective. He addresses three interconnected issues: the purpose of punishment; the explanation of international crimes; and sentencing. As regards the former, he is a strong advocate of a combination of different preventive theories as rationale for (international) punishment, but adds elements of restorative justice. Regarding the explanation of international crimes, he distinguishes three levels: the macro-, meso- and micro-level, connected to the system, the group, and the individual, respectively. Andreas Werkmeister in his contribution takes up on this differentiation and develops a preventive theory of punishment specifically designed for the meso-level. For Neubacher it is most important to emphasize that collective violence, in which international crimes are being committed, is a situational process. He explains that when it comes to mass atrocities the perpetrator's behaviour is illegal, but socially not deviant – Klaus Günther draws on this insight in his contribution when he develops a theory of 'civic courage'. Finally, as regards the reaction to international crimes, Neubacher explains that for a deterrent effect to ensue, the certainty of punishment is decisive, not the severity. Regarding the sentencing decisions, he sees a disregard of the individual perpetrator's circumstances and proposes a more nuanced model of liability (and, thus, culpability) which takes into account the hierarchical position of the perpetrators as well as his or her discretional power.

Sergey Vasiliev undertakes a thorough analysis of international criminal tribunals' statements on theories of punishment. For the theoretical underpinning of the analysis, he divides the 'why punish' question into two parts. Firstly, why *punishment*? – a non-question that cannot be answered from within by international criminal courts and tribunals. However, from the outside there seems to be a growing criticism regarding the narrow notion of punitive justice. The second part of the 'why punish' question, the *why* do we punish?, is the one addressed by the contributions in this volume. Vasiliev concludes that courts' statements display 'ritualism' and 'monotony', and that due to their 'hypnotic repetition' are of limited practical value. While deterrence and retribution can be identified as the main objectives referred to by judges, the underlying principles and rationales are taken from domestic criminal law doctrine, without ever questioning their suitability in the context of international criminal law. The contents of these goals and objectives are, however, coloured with a reference to the goals set for the establishment of international criminal justice institutions as such. As a result of his analysis, Vasiliev comes to the conclusion that the few statements on theories of punishment by international courts and tribunals are a mere speech act, 'by which courts preach to international criminal law's founding articles of faith'. They say that they punish for retribution and deterrence, but in reality the main purpse of punishment is related to expressivism and didactics. In his view, which seems to be shared by Elies van Sliedregt in her contribution, expressivism emerged as a kind of 'ultimate catch-all objective' and 'meta justification' for punishment, in order to reproduce and reinforce the normative belief system upon which the enterprise of international criminal prosecution rests.

Next, Elies van Sliedregt discusses the 'domestic analogy' and analyzes the differences and similarities between domestic, i.e. 'ordinary', and international criminal justice. First, she distinguishes what she calls the domestic analogy 'proper' and the domestic analogy 'of transplants'. While the former relates to international law and concerns the question of building a world order analogous to the domestic order and includes the question of the authority to punish, the latter refers to criminal law and the (unreflected) application of domestic concepts and theories on the international level. Focusing on the domestic analogy of transplants, she continues to extrapolate the *sui generis* nature of international criminal law, which she discusses in relation to the nature of international crimes, the perpetrators of international crimes and the punishing community. Van Sliedregt determines that today there is a move towards a communicative theory of international punishment, as well as an emphasis on reconciliation and reparations, and makes an argument for a stronger integration of rehabilitation, post-trial justice and reintegration into the international criminal justice system. In addition, she criticizes that in international criminal law there is no consideration for other forms of sanctions aside from incarceration – an issue that is also mentioned by Sergey Vasiliev.

Kai Ambos takes up the question of the domestic analogy 'proper' and raises the question of whether a right to punish can exist without a state, and answers it in the affirmative. When it comes to what Elies van Sliedregt would call the domestic analogy 'of transplants', he is less sceptical: In his view, international criminal law can very well borrow and import concepts from domestic law, albeit it should not be done too schematically and there might be some limits. As regards sentencing, Ambos emphasizes the important of concrete sentencing factors and a transparent sentencing procedure, but in his view theories of punishment have no influence on the outcome. Gerhard Werle and Aziz Epik seem to disagree with this in their contribution.

Referring to the title of the first part of this volume – 'Setting the Framework' – Immi Tallgren explains that there is not one framework in which the 'why punish' question can be asked. Instead, different frames are required to draw attention to the plurality of perspectives that could be taken on international punishment. Thus, in her comments, Tallgren pictures the landscape in which 'why punish' is asked and thereby sheds light on the contexts of that context of knowledge, its production, reproduction and subjectivities. While sketching out these frames – the frame of law, the frame of criminology, the moral frame, the frame of 'fantasmatic logic' and the frame of politics – Tallgren makes visible the outside of the chapters 'setting the framework' and discusses what aspects of the 'why punish' question are missing in this volume, and whose voice is excluded from our debate.

Jochen Bung raises doubts as to the distinctiveness of international criminal law. In his view, there is no need for specific theories of punishment in international criminal law or to develop specific criminological theories addressing international crimes. In his view, we can draw on what we know from the domestic context. While he agrees that there still is guessing and shadowboxing when it comes to the 'why punish' question in international criminal law, he notices that this is equally true when it comes to domestic theories of punishment. What is special though is that international criminal law emerged challenging the classic rules of state sovereignty and non-intervention. For him, this is where the discussion should start, and instead of asking 'why punish', we should raise questions such as: Will international criminal law vanish again? Should we hope it will vanish again? Has it helped to establish a collective memory which will prevent us from experiencing future mass atrocities? Is international criminal law a matter for experts and specialists? Is it sufficiently democratic? Is it a sufficiently universal affair? Or is it just another colonial strategy? Can it get less selective? And: Is international criminal law capable of self-criticism?

The second part of the volume – *Rationales for Punishment in International Criminal Law: Theoretical Perspectives* – turns to the different theoretical approaches regarding the aims and justifications of punishment – retribution, deterrence, prevention, expressivism – and examines their sustainability regarding the international criminal law context.

Jakob v.H. Holtermann addresses the question of whether or not we have reason to believe that the ICC can deter potential perpetrators of international crimes, in particular the crime of aggression and taking the Danish and British involvement in the Iraq War as an example, and he believes we have good reason to do so. As a 'normativist' he criticizes the critics of deterrence, and their, in his view, too demanding burden of proof regarding a deterrent effect: It is not about conclusive evidence, but about levels of probability. And just like in domestic criminal law, we have reason to believe that the threat of international punishment has a deterrent effect. The domestic analogy – of transplants, in Elies van Sliedregt's words – does not break down, despite the differences between domestic, i.e. 'ordinary' and international crimes. In Holtermann's view these differences should not be exaggerated, and, like Bung, he argues that the main difference lies in the absence on the international level of anything resembling a state's monopoly of force. In the end, he argues that the ICC is one preventive measure among others, like a slice of Swiss cheese, i.e. with holes, or one component of a 'broad spectrum' drug, and that taken together – with other slices of Swiss cheese, or other components of a 'broad spectrum' drug – these measures cause a deterrent effect.

In contrast to Holtermann, Mordechai Kremnitzer emphasizes retribution as a rationale of punishment for international crimes, opposing the claim that it should be dismissed or marginalized. While not rejecting deterrence, he brings forward a number of reasons why the retributivist rationale is important. First, for Kremnitzer only punishment based on retribution is morally justified and, in particular from the offender's human dignity, legitimate. Second, retribution helps to secure the principle of proportionality in sentencing in international criminal law and in this way counter the dangerous trend of overpunishing the 'small fish' – in particular 'victimizers-victims', i.e. 'Kapos' or child soldiers, a topic he takes up from Mark Drumbl – while underpunishing the big ones. In this regard, Kremnitzer develops the 'theoretical move' that retributive justice should be implemented by the 'principle of conservation of criminal energy': the 'small fish's' reduced guilt serves as aggravating circumstance to the deeds of the 'big fish'. As a result, the 'big fish' should be in the focus of any prosecutorial strategy of international criminal tribunals, and the problem of (vertical) selectivity due to limited state cooperation should be overcome by (fair) trials in absentia.

Daniela Demko develops the basic features of a comprehensive expressive theory of punishment for international crimes. She highlights the communicative significance of two functions of international punishment: the trust in norm validity and the assignment of responsibility. While focusing on the communicative aspects of international punishment, she also shows how retributive and preventive theories and the specific purposes of punishment in international criminal law – the protection of victims and the rejection of a collective guilt thesis – can be integrated into an expressive theory of international punishment. In addition, Demko identifies the protection of the truth, the protection of victims and the rejection of a collective guilt thesis as criminal purposes specific to international criminal law, and integrates them into the statement of content of international punishment.

In his comprehensive comment on the contributions by Holtermann, Demko and Kremnitzer, Mark Drumbl engages with their respective pleas for a predominance of deterrence, expressivism and retribution. In reference to Kremnitzer's contribution on retribution, he doubts that 'victimizers-victims' deserve punishment. They might deserve something else, but something that is not delivered in a criminal courtroom. While he is sympathetic to the expressivist theory and the communicative function of punishment, as developed by Demko, he doubts that a court room is the best place to host those conversations. He worries that the medium – the court – becomes the message. Similarly, he doubts that the courtroom is the best place to tell the truth. The criminal trial illuminates selectively, not comprehensively. It communicates an incomplete truth that does not shed light on the bystanders and complicity side-standers. Finally, with regard to Holtermann, Drumbl – as one of the critics of deterrence that Holtermann criticizes – remains unconvinced that international punishment has a deterrent effect. For him, deterrence can at best be believed through a combination of anecdote, superimposition and faith. However, he concedes that deterrence might work when it comes to the crimes of aggression and maybe war crimes because they indeed involve more rational actors. While here the ICC could work as a slice of Swiss cheese, one must admit that the ICC is not a big fish court. In the end, his comment is a compelling argument to look beyond criminal law and to move away from courtrooms and jailhouses. Taking up Vasiliev's distinction between the *why* and the *punish* parts of the 'why punish' question, Drumbl has doubts that international punishment is the answer to mass atrocities.

Similar to Demko, also Klaus Günther takes an expressivist approach of international criminal law and considers the contents of the message communicated with international punishment. In his outline of the communicative structure of criminal law in general, he considers the different stages of the communicative sequence and, at the same time, elaborates on the different messages sent at each stage to the offender, the victims and the society. He then asks the question of whether these messages can be transferred from the domestic to the international level, i.e., the domestic analogy of transplants. While a transfer is possible, Günther argues that some modifications are necessary in particular regarding the normative community as addressees. Günther explains that due to the dual status of each individual – as a member of the 'international community' and as a member of the domestic normative community, addressees of international criminal norms at the same time are also always bound by domestic laws. This dual status requires a 'critical reflective attitude' with regard to the human rights legitimacy of the domestic law. And in case of a – direct or indirect – norm collision between domestic law and international law, international criminal law delivers the message to disobey the demands of the domestic system: What is required from the addressee of international criminal law norms is civic courage and the willingness to non-conformist behaviour.

In the remaining two contributions of the second part, the authors develop a specific human-rights centred theory of international punishment. However, while Andreas Werkmeister develops a human-rights based *justification* for punishment, Jens David Ohlin develops from human rights an *obligation* to punish perpetrators of international crimes owed to the victims.

Andreas Werkmeister develops a combined meso preventive theory of international punishment. The underlying perspective of his theory is the legitimacy vis-a-vis the individual and the concept of human dignity is the foundational core. As a result, he highlights the limiting principles of punishment inherent to any punishment theory irrespective of its main purpose. After discussing problems with retribution and expressivism, he argues that a combination of different preventive theories provides for a suitable model for the justification of international punishment. Similarly to Frank Neubacher, Werkmeister differentiates also between macro-, meso- and micro-levels, and makes an argument for targeted meso prevention. This way, the offender is punished to deter others, but is addressed as a member of a case-specific transnational group. In this way, Werkmeister develops a new form of prevention between special and general prevention.

Jens David Ohlin, on the other hand, develops from human rights what he calls a theory of 'expressive retributivism' for international crimes (and other severe human rights violations). Relying on the jurisprudence of the European Court of Human Rights he argues for a state's duty to punish international crimes, a duty that is owed to the victims and based on human rights.

Somehow provocatively, he states that in the context of international criminal law, even mercy is a human rights violation. Ohlin connects his theory of 'expressive retributivism' to the anti-impunity discourse in international criminal law, and argues that, if states do not comply with their duty to punish international crimes, the ICC can step in. The victims' human right to see their perpetrators punished also explains their role and significance in international criminal procedure.

The aim of the third part of the book –*Consequences for the Practice of the International Criminal Court* – is to closely link the theoretical discussion to practical consequences. The theoretical approaches to international punishment are applied to and tested on specific issues from the practice of the ICC, e.g. the selection of situations and cases by the ICC's Office of the Prosecutor and the sentencing decision. In addition, the question is discussed how the selective and asymmetrical enforcement of international criminal law can be reconciled with the different rationales for punishment.

While Sergey Vasiliev in his contribution analyzed, inter alia, statements on theories of punishment that can be found in sentencing decisions of the ICC, Alex Whiting undertakes a similar exercise and thoroughly analyzes the submissions by the ICC Office of the Prosecutor and statements made by the Prosecution. He explains the different approaches of the first and the second Prosecutor: The first embraced a theory of 'disruption and specific deterrence', seeking to intervene in real time to stop ongoing crimes with the Court being a force for diplomacy and peace. The second Prosecutor, on the other hand, focuses on the judicial tasks of the Court, chooses fewer cases, acts slowly and carefully. This way, the Court moved towards an expressive theory of punishment, where investigations and cases are a way of expressing, shaping and enforcing norms. In the end, Whiting concludes that at the ICC's Office of the Prosecutor theory does not dictate practice – it is the other way round: The Office's strategy is reactive to and constrained by the dependency on state cooperation and the limits of the ICC's authority. Only within those constraints can theories of punishment play a role: 'robust theories of punishment are a luxory of actors with power'.

Similar to Alex Whiting, Harmen van der Wilt explains the ICC's and the Rome Statute's 'design selectivity', i.e. the ICC's legal, structural and political limitations as well as its inherent selectivity when selecting 'situations' and 'cases'. He analyzes how the problem of selectivity in international criminal law, i.e. the systematical exemption of entire categories of perpetrators from accountability, creates tensions with traditional theories of punishment. In emphasizing the shift from punishment to trial, he argues that international criminal law's inherent selectivity can best be processed by expressivism.

However, contemporary international criminal law, he concludes, conveys the 'perverse message' that 'criminal responsibility depends on the party or nation one belongs to and the side on which one fights'. For the future, he calls for an approach of 'dauntless perseverance'.

Gerhard Werle and Aziz Epik discuss the impact of theories of punishment on the sentencing decisions of the ICC. In their view, the question of 'why punish' has – and should have – an impact on the 'how' of punishment, i.e. on the sentencing process and its outcome. After a careful analysis of the ICC's sentencing decisions they come to the conclusion that a consistent approach with regard to the sentencing objectives can be detected, but that judges do not elaborate on how these objectives influence and guide the sentencing decisions. In the following, the authors outline a coherent sentencing model that takes into account theories of punishment and the objectives of sentencing. As its most important requirement is to ensure proportionality, Werle and Epik discuss the factors that should be taken into account in determining the gravity of the crime and the culpability of the offender. Within the proportionality framework, in order to ensure special deterrence and rehabilitation, the individual circumstances of the offender can also be taken into account. Expressivism and general deterrence, however, do not play a role.

Silvia D'Ascoli discusses some issues that were addressed in the contributions of Whiting, van der Wilt, and Werle and Epik. She agrees that the objectives and purposes of punishment guiding the sentencing process should be predetermined by the relevant system and not decided by the judges on a case-by-case basis, and is disappointed how little the ICC jurisprudence on sentencing has so far contributed to the development of rationales for international punishment. Similarly, in her view it is a missed opportunity that no clear sentencing guidelines have been determined at the ICC (as was the case at the ad hoc Tribunals), including any expressed weight, from the purposes of punishment. She recalls that the initial Prosecution's proposition of '80 per cent baseline' of the statutory maximum as a starting point to determine sentences was dismissed by the Trial Chamber – and after that the Prosecution did not propose any other approach or solution.

Finally, Philipp Ambach focuses on the victims of crimes under international law. While Jens David Ohlin developed a theory of victim-related *retributive* justice, Ambach's approach is victim-related *restorative* justice. Similar to the introductory contribution by Silvia Fernández de Gurmendi, Ambach explains that victims' participation in international criminal law proceedings lead to an enhanced ownership that moves away from punitive aspects. As a consequence, outreach is of major importance and selectivity is problematic. In sum, and rather in contrast to (or in addition to) Ohlin,

Ambach argues that international criminal justice and international criminal law proceedings have moved beyond mere punishment – or, to put it differently, that from the victims' perspective (retributive) punishment is not enough.

In a concluding contribution by the editors, the threads are being pulled together. The key research questions assessed by the authors of this volume are summarized, with a view to delineating possible elements of a theory of international punishment, or at least to identify some 'themes' that seem to play a more important role than in the domestic context. This is combined with an indication of the issues which remain open, paving the way to new research in the field.

2

The Practical Importance of Theories of Punishment in International Criminal Law

SILVIA FERNÁNDEZ DE GURMENDI*

After almost three decades of efforts to investigate and prosecute perpetrators of the gravest international crimes, it is an appropriate time to go back to the basic question: 'Why punish perpetrators of mass atrocities?' With a rapidly evolving case-law and practice on the matter,[1] a reflection on the purpose of punishment of mass crimes offenders is indeed both timely and relevant. Yet, examining the purpose of punishment of perpetrators of mass atrocities raises a broader, more fundamental question: 'Why international criminal law?' Punishment can indeed not be looked at in isolation – it is only but one of the components of the criminal process. The purpose of punishment is closely tied to the overall goals of criminal justice.

I THE ASSUMPTIONS OF INTERNATIONAL CRIMINAL JUSTICE

The Rome Statute of the International Criminal Court (ICC) expressly contains the assumptions on which the international community relied when establishing the first permanent international criminal jurisdiction. The Preamble of the Rome Statute acknowledges, in the first place, that grave crimes such as those which marked the twentieth century, 'threaten the peace,

* This contribution is drawn from a video-address delivered by the author on 7 October 2017 on the occasion of the symposium 'Why Punish Perpetrators of Mass Atrocities?', held at the University of Hamburg.

1 For instance, at the ICC, sentences have been handed down in the last five years in five cases against eight individuals (Thomas Lubanga Dyilo, Germain Katanga, Jean-Pierre Bemba Gombo – for both core crimes and offences against the administration of justice – Aimé Kilolo Musamba, Jean-Jacques Mangenda Kabongo, Fidèle Babala Wandu, Narcisse Arido and Ahmad Al Faqi Al Mahdi). Sentences have been subject to review in two of these cases (Thomas Lubanga Dyilo and Germain Katanga). In parallel, the ad hoc Tribunals for the former Yugoslavia and Rwanda generated abundant jurisprudence on sentencing of perpetrators of mass atrocities.

security and well-being of the world'.[2] Correlatively, the Preamble regards justice as a means to 'contribute to the prevention of such crimes'.[3] In other words, the Rome Statute assumes that international justice, with its deterrent effect, is a means to achieve lasting peace, security and the well-being of the world.

The ad hoc Tribunals, which preceded the ICC, were established on the same assumptions. As clearly spelled out in the relevant constituting resolutions, the UN Security Council set up the International Criminal Tribunal for the former Yugoslavia (ICTY) and the International Criminal Tribunal for Rwanda (ICTR) based on the belief that an international tribunal could contribute to ensuring that the crimes committed in the former Yugoslavia and in Rwanda would be halted and effectively redressed. These crimes, by their gravity, were deemed of concern to the international community as a whole.[4] It bears recalling that when establishing the ICTY and ICTR, the UN Security Council resorted to Chapter VII of the UN Charter,[5] which empowers the Security Council to take actions with respect to threats and

2 ICC Statute, Preamble paragraph 3.

3 ICC Statute, Preamble paragraph 5.

4 For the ICTY, see UN Security Council Resolution 827 (1993):

> *The Security Council*, [...] *Determining* that this situation continues to constitute a threat to international peace and security, *Determined* to put an end to such crimes and to take effective measures to bring to justice the persons who are responsible for them, *Convinced* that in the particular circumstances of the former Yugoslavia the establishment as an *ad hoc* measure by the Council of an international tribunal and the prosecution of persons responsible for serious violations of international humanitarian law would enable this aim to be achieved and would contribute to the restoration and maintenance of peace, *Believing* that the establishment of an international tribunal and the prosecution of persons responsible for the above-mentioned violations of international humanitarian law will contribute to ensuring that such violations are halted and effectively redressed [...].

For the ICTR, see UN Security Council Resolution 955 (1994):

> *The Security Council*, [...] *Determining* that this situation continues to constitute a threat to international peace and security, *Determined* to put an end to such crimes and to take effective measures to bring to justice the persons who are responsible for them, *Convinced* that in the particular circumstances of Rwanda, the prosecution of persons responsible for serious violations of international humanitarian law would enable this aim to be achieved and would contribute to the restoration and maintenance of peace, *Believing* that the establishment of an international tribunal for the prosecution of persons responsible for genocide and the other above-mentioned violations of international humanitarian law will contribute to ensuring that such violations are halted and effectively redressed [...].

5 UN Security Council Resolution 827 (1993), Preamble ('*Acting* under Chapter VII of the Charter of the United Nations'); UN Security Council Resolution 955 (1994), Preamble ('*Acting* under Chapter VII of the Charter of the United Nations').

breaches of peace. The establishment of the ad hoc Tribunals thus made it clear that armed force is no longer the sole response to conflict and that justice forms part of the arsenal available to address threats and breaches of peace.

The same rationale guided the UN Security Council when supporting the creation of a Special Court for Sierra Leone (SCSL) in 2000.[6] The recent Security Council referrals of situations to the ICC[7] show a continued belief that accountability is part of conflict prevention. The two situations referred to date by the Security Council to the ICC – Darfur[8] and Libya[9] – were deemed to constitute a threat to international peace and security. The recourse to the ICC by the UN Security Council is an acknowledgement that international criminal justice continues to play a key role in halting crimes. The recent establishment of the Mechanism for Syria by the UN General Assembly was also premised on the correlation between justice and peace.[10]

International justice fulfils a second, complementary purpose which extends beyond the reach of conflict prevention. The various resolutions establishing the ad hoc Tribunals and other international criminal mechanisms emphasize the confidence that justice can contribute to *reconciliation* of societies.[11] Criminal justice indeed helps ascertain what happened. If criminal judgments cannot fully satisfy the requirements of history, as criminal justice

6 UN Security Council Resolution 1315 (2000):

> *The Security Council*: [...] *Recognizing* that, in the particular circumstances of Sierra Leone, a credible system of justice and accountability for the very serious crimes committed there would end impunity and would contribute to the process of national reconciliation and to the restoration and maintenance of peace, [...] *Reiterating* that the situation in Sierra Leone continues to constitute a threat to international peace and security in the region [...]

7 Pursuant to Art. 13(b) of the ICC Statute, the UN Security Council, acting under Chapter VII of the UN Charter, may refer a situation to the Prosecutor of the Court.

8 UN Security Council Resolution 1593 (2005): '*The Security Council*, [...] *Determining* that the situation in Sudan continues to constitute a threat to international peace and security [...]'.

9 UN Security Council Resolution 1970 (2011): '*The Security Council*, [...] *Mindful* of its primary responsibility for the maintenance of international peace and security under the Charter of the United Nations [...]'.

10 UN General Assembly Resolution 71/248 (2016): '*The General Assembly*, [...] 2. *Stresses* the need for any political process aimed at resolving the crisis in the Syrian Arab Republic to ensure credible and comprehensive accountability for violations of international humanitarian law and human rights violations and abuses committed in the country in order to bring about reconciliation and sustainable peace [...]'.

11 See inter alia UN Security Council Resolution 1315 (2000), in relation to the SCSL ('[...] a credible system of justice and accountability for the very serious crimes committed there would end impunity and would contribute to the process of national reconciliation and to the restoration and maintenance of peace [...]'). See also UN General Assembly Resolution 71/248 (2016).

primarily pertains to the determination of culpability of an accused person, such judgments do nevertheless contribute to an account of history and provide a useful overview of the relevant facts.[12] This, in turn, helps victims, the affected communities and the international community as a whole to better understand what happened and move forward. The Rome Statute explicitly recognizes a truth-seeking function to the ICC.[13]

In sum, the establishment of international criminal jurisdictions clearly evidences a belief on the part of the international community that accountability is an integral part of conflict prevention as well as a means to help societies affected by mass crimes to reconcile and heal.

II THE DETERRENT EFFECT OF INTERNATIONAL CRIMINAL JUSTICE

The last paragraph of Section I begs the question: does international criminal justice really contribute to peace? Does it really help preventing mass atrocities?

The deterrent effect of international criminal justice on contexts of violence is empirically difficult to demonstrate. Furthermore, when looking at the countless outbreaks of violence in today's world, one may rightly wonder whether justice efforts of the last three decades, including the establishment of the ICC, has indeed contributed to prevent mass crimes. To cite but one example, crimes continued to be committed in the Balkans despite trials being ongoing and sentences being handed down by the ICTY.[14]

It may be premature to draw any definite conclusions with respect to the deterrent effect of international criminal justice. Indeed, as impressive as they may be, international criminal justice efforts of the last thirty years are far from having achieved a *consistent* pattern of accountability. The international criminal system has gaps where impunity regrettably continues to flourish. For as long as these impunity gaps exist, those capable of committing mass atrocities will not be discouraged to engage in such course of action. If one of the greatest achievements of the last thirty years has been to add the notion of accountability in the global agenda, in practice, accountability continues to be the exception rather than the rule.

[12] ICTY, Judgment of 29 May 2013 (TC), *Prlić et al.*, IT-04-74-T, Vol. 1 para. 2.

[13] ICC Statute, Art. 69(3) ('[. . .] The Court shall have the authority to request the submission of all evidence that it considers necessary for the determination of the truth.').

[14] For instance, the *Milan Milutinović et al.* case concerned crimes committed in Kosovo in early 1999. By that date, the ICTY had already convicted and sentenced a number of individuals, including its first accused Duško Tadić.

Impunity gaps result from two particular weaknesses in the current system of international criminal justice.

In the first place, the nature of the crimes itself curtails the reach of international justice.[15] International crimes will typically involve multiple perpetrators and thousands or hundreds of thousands of victims. It is unavoidable that justice for international crimes will need to be selective, regardless of whether it is applied at the international or national level. Prosecutorial discretion for this type of crime is typically very broad. At the international level in particular, prosecutorial efforts will normally focus on carefully selected events and perpetrators. Some international tribunals have been explicitly mandated to focus on those who bear the greatest responsibility. The statute for the SCSL, for example, limited the Special Court's jurisdiction to those who bore the greatest responsibility for the crimes committed on the territory of Sierra Leone.[16] As part of their downsizing, the ICTY and the ICTR were specifically requested by the UN Security Council to focus their efforts on leaders suspected to bear the greatest responsibility.[17] International cases only embrace a handful of the crimes committed in a given area during a given period. Certain crimes, which would also deserve prosecution, are inevitably left aside.

A second, more significant, weakness of the current international criminal justice system relates to the lack of universality of international criminal justice efforts.[18] Attention to situations of mass violence was initially, and remains today, essentially ad hoc.[19] The creation of the ICC as a permanent and general jurisdiction was intended to supplement ad hoc efforts by an institution that can address all situations equally or provide an incentive to national tribunals to do so. However, the ICC is not based on universal

[15] On this, see also the contribution by Frank Neubacher in Chapter 3.

[16] SCSL Statute, Art. 1(1) ('The Special Court shall [...] have the power to prosecute persons who bear the greatest responsibility for serious violations of international humanitarian law and Sierra Leonean law committed in the territory of Sierra Leone since 30 November 1996, including those leaders who, in committing such crimes, have threatened the establishment of and implementation of the peace process in Sierra Leone').

[17] UN Security Council Resolution 1534 (2004): '*The Security Council*, [...] 5. *Calls on* each Tribunal, in reviewing and confirming any new indictments, to ensure that any such indictments concentrate on the most senior leaders suspected of being most responsible for crimes within the jurisdiction of the relevant Tribunal as set out in resolution 1503 (2003); [...]'.

[18] On the jurisdictional limits of the ICC and the inherent selectivity in its practice, see also the contribution by Harman van der Wilt in Chapter 17.

[19] Even after the ICC had begun its activities in 2002, other ad hoc tribunals have been established: the Extraordinary Chambers in the Courts of Cambodia, the Special Tribunal for Lebanon, and the Kosovo Specialist Chambers.

jurisdiction. It is a global aspiration, but universal participation in the treaty is yet to be obtained.[20] As a result, entire situations fall outside the realm of international criminal justice. There is an expectation of accountability, which is not yet fully satisfied.

Deterrence can only be achieved if a consistent pattern of accountability can be established. However, we are not there yet: a consistent pattern of accountability can only materialize if it is managed to gradually reduce the impunity gaps by strengthening a global system of justice, where national, regional and international mechanisms play a role. In light of the nature of the crimes, only complementary efforts can achieve this result. No institution can do it on its own.

The international community has made significant progress in the strengthening of the international criminal system, leaning towards universality. The ICC was created as a complementary institution, whereby the primary responsibility to investigate and prosecute international crimes lies at the national level. As a positive result of this system, an increasing number of states have updated their national legislation to align it with the Rome Statute principles. Where possible, in the spirit of complementarity, the ICC Prosecutor first encourages genuine national proceedings for international crimes. The ICC is also making great efforts in reaching out to non-state parties, inviting them to consider joining the Rome Statute system. In parallel, some prosecutions by domestic or hybrid mechanisms[21] as well as the establishment of ad hoc regional mechanisms to address specific situations – such as Sierra Leone, Cambodia, Lebanon and, more recently, Kosovo – has also helped further tighten the impunity net. Yet, for as long as there is no universality, international criminal law will struggle to achieve full deterrence.

III PUNISHMENT AS A MEANS OF CONTRIBUTING TO RECONCILIATION AND HEALING OF VICTIMS

As discussed above, international criminal justice is also based on the assumption that justice can contribute to reconciliation and the healing of affected societies. However, reconciliation and healing through justice is particularly difficult for international tribunals, which are, by definition, detached from

[20] To date, 123 states are parties to the ICC Statute.

[21] The former president of Chad, Hissène Habré, was tried in Senegal before an ad hoc mechanism – the Extraordinary African Chambers in the Courts of Senegal – for crimes committed in Chad in the 1980s and early 1990s. The Extraordinary African Chambers were established pursuant to an agreement between Senegal and the African Union.

national systems and societies and need to proceed, most times, at a large distance from them. The delocalization of courtrooms as well as the length of international proceedings, which carry on for years, often creates a gap between victims and the administration of justice. International mechanisms need to struggle to reach out to victims and reduce the distance from affected societies.

The Rome Statute recognizes this problem and contains, for the first time, some elements of restorative justice intended to engage victims at all stages of the proceedings and increase their sense of ownership over proceedings, beyond their involvement as witnesses.[22] It acknowledges that the interests of victims are at stake during the whole criminal process, not only at the sentencing phase.

In particular, the Rome Statute allows victims to participate in the proceedings and express their views and concerns throughout the judicial cycle, from the pre-trial phase to the appeal phase.[23] This right to participate may take various forms: making submissions at the critical junctures, examining Prosecution and Defence witnesses and presenting evidence.[24] The possibility for victims to participate in proceedings can now be said to form an integral part of the international criminal justice system. Since the ICC was established, victims' participation has been incorporated in the legal framework of the Special Tribunal for Lebanon (STL)[25] as well as in that of the Kosovo Specialist Chambers.[26]

Yet, in practice, victims' participation has proven to be challenging. Given the usual high number of victims affected by crimes within the ICC jurisdiction – many thousands – there is often no alternative other than setting up a common legal representation scheme.[27] Such a system has undeniable financial and logistical benefits. The Court must ensure that common legal representation is organized in such a way that it is indeed representative and that it adequately voices the views and concerns of the victims. With its first cases being completed, the ICC is now reviewing its practices to improve and

[22] On this, see also contribution by Philipp Ambach in Chapter 20.

[23] ICC Statute, Art. 68(3).

[24] With respect to the possibility of making opening and closing statements, see ICC RPE, Rule 89(1). As regards the questioning of witnesses, see ICC RPE, Rule 91(3). In relation to presentation of evidence, see ICC Statute, Art. 69(3); ICC, Judgment of 16 July 2010 (AC), *Katanga and Ngudjolo Chui*, ICC-01/04-01/07-2288, para. 48.

[25] See STL Statute, Art. 17.

[26] See Rules of Procedure and Evidence before the Kosovo Specialist Chambers, Chapter 8; see also Law on Specialist Chambers and Specialist Prosecutor's Office, Art. 22.

[27] ICC Statute, Art. 68(3); ICC RPE, Rule 90.

strengthen victims' participation in its proceedings.[28] So far, 14,000 victims have participated in the proceedings, including more than 4,000 victims in the ongoing *Ongwen* case.

Participation is complemented by extensive outreach efforts on the ground, to bring proceedings closer to those who suffered. In the *Ongwen* case, for instance, in addition to web streaming, proceedings are broadcast regularly in the affected communities. Q&A sessions are also held to allow victims to better understand the way justice works in The Hague, to decipher what is often too cryptic for lay audiences.[29] The Court's legal framework also provides for the possibility to hold part of the proceedings on site.[30] In the *Ruto and Sang* case, as well as in the *Ntaganda* case, the respective Trial Chambers recommended that the commencement of trial be held in locations close to where crimes had allegedly been committed.[31] In the *Ongwen* case, a similar recommendation was made for the confirmation hearing.[32] The Presidency, which has the responsibility to decide on holding hearings elsewhere than in The Hague, declined to follow these recommendations, for reasons that pertained to costs and heightened security risks.[33] It is hoped that such a possibility will materialize in the near future.

That being said, retributive justice is simply not enough for mass atrocities, which shatter entire societies and exacerbate divisions. International criminal law has evolved towards including a component of restorative justice alongside punishment. The Rome Statute provides for the possibility of ordering reparations in case of conviction.[34] Reparations can be collective or

[28] See ICC press release of 31 October 2016, 'ICC judges hold second retreat to improve efficiency and effectiveness of judicial proceedings', available at www.icc-cpi.int/Pages/item.aspx?name=pr1249.

[29] ICC, 'Report on the Activities of the International Criminal Court', 2 November 2017, ICC-ASP/16/9, paras. 99–102.

[30] ICC RPE, Rule 100.

[31] ICC, Recommendation to the Presidency on where the Court shall sit for trial of 3 June 2013 (TC), *Ruto and Sang*, ICC-01/09-01/11-763; ICC, Recommendation to the Presidency on holding part of the trial in the State concerned of 19 March 2015 (TC), *Ntaganda*, ICC-01/04-02/06-526.

[32] ICC, Recommendation to the Presidency to hold the confirmation of charges hearing in the Republic of Uganda of 10 September 2015 (PTC), *Ongwen*, ICC-02/04-01/15-300.

[33] ICC Decision of the Plenary of Judges on the Joint Defence Application for a Change of Place where the Court Shall Sit for Trial in the case of *The Prosecutor* v. *William Samoei Ruto and Joshua Arap Sang* of 26 August 2013 (Plenary of Judges), *Ruto and Sang*, ICC-01/09-01/11-875-Anx; ICC, Public redacted version of Decision on the recommendation to the Presidency on holding part of the trial in the State concerned of 15 June 2015 (Presidency), *Ntaganda*, ICC-01/04-02/06-645-Red; ICC, Decision on the recommendation to the Presidency of 28 October 2015 (Presidency), *Ongwen*, ICC-02/04-01/15-330.

[34] ICC Statute, Art. 75.

individual, or a combination of both.[35] They are aimed at restoring, to the extent possible, victims in their previous situation.

Reparations are no longer a distant possibility. By way of example, in March 2017, a Trial Chamber granted to the victims of an attack in eastern Democratic Republic of the Congo individual reparations in the form of symbolic compensation of USD 250 per victim.[36] The Trial Chamber stressed that this symbolic amount, while not intended to compensate for the entirety of the harm, does provide some measure of relief to the victims for the harm they have suffered. The Trial Chamber also awarded specific collective reparations in the form of support for housing, support for income-generating activities, education aid and psychological support.[37] Reparations can also be ordered in respect of crimes against property. In August 2017, further to Ahmad Al Faqi Al Mahdi's conviction for the crimes of destruction of religious buildings in Timbuktu (Mali), the Trial Chamber ordered both individual and collective reparations – individual for those whose livelihoods depended upon the attacked buildings and those whose ancestors' burial sites were damaged; and collective for the rehabilitation of the sites and the financial loss and emotional distress suffered by the community in Timbuktu.[38]

Yet, as said, the factual scope of cases before international criminal courts is often narrower than the actual extent of the crimes. For instance, Thomas Lubanga was tried exclusively for crimes against child soldiers while there were allegations of other crimes having been committed against the civilian population in eastern Democratic Republic of the Congo. Another approach was followed in the recent *Ongwen* case. This case relates to alleged crimes committed by the Lord's Resistance Army in northern Uganda. The Prosecution opted to bring seventy charges against Dominic Ongwen in relation to a large array of crimes, including murder, torture, rape, sexual enslavement and pillage.[39]

Therefore, for reconciliation and healing to be significant, it is important that justice be complemented by extra judicial assistance to victims. For this

[35] ICC RPE, Rule 97.

[36] ICC, Order for Reparations of 24 March 2017 (TC), *Katanga*, ICC-01/04-01/07-3728-tENG, para. 300.

[37] ICC, Order for Reparations of 24 March 2017 (TC), *Katanga*, ICC-01/04-01/07-3728-tENG, para. 304.

[38] ICC, Reparations Order of 17 August 2017 (TC), *Al Mahdi*, ICC-01/12-01/15-236, para. 104.

[39] ICC, Decision of 23 March 2016 (PTC), *Ongwen*, ICC-02/04-01/15-422-Red.

purpose, states parties have established a Trust Fund for Victims,[40] funded by states and other private donors, which is a body distinct from the Court. The Trust Fund has a dual mandate. It may implement reparations ordered in case brought before the Court,[41] and also provide larger assistance to communities affected by crimes within the jurisdiction of the Court outside judicial proceedings.

IV PUNISHMENT AND THE CONVICTED INDIVIDUALS

Beyond deterrence of future crimes, beyond healing victims, international criminal law and punishment also concern the convicted perpetrators. The whole purpose of international criminal law is to hold *individuals* – and not states – accountable for the most serious crimes.[42]

International criminal law deals with inherently grave crimes. Sentences must reflect the gravity of such crimes, as revealed by the particular circumstances of each case.[43] Yet, punishment is not only about retribution. Sentences must also be aimed at favouring rehabilitation. As was the case before the ad hoc tribunals, the ICC's framework provides for the possibility of reducing a sentence.[44] It bears stressing that reduction of sentence is not a right, but a possibility. The ICC's practice in this regard balances rehabilitation against a number of factors, including genuine dissociation from the crimes, potential social instability and actions taken for the benefit of victims.[45]

The absence of genuine dissociation from his crimes as well as the absence of significant actions for the benefit of victims has been found decisive in the decision not to reduce Thomas Lubanga's sentence of 14 years of imprisonment.[46] The second review of Lubanga's sentence found there to be no significant change in circumstances since the first review that would merit a reduction of sentence.[47] In contrast, Germain Katanga benefitted from inter alia his cooperation with the Court's investigations and prosecutions and the genuine dissociation from his crimes while in detention in obtaining a

[40] ICC Statute, Art. 79.

[41] ICC Statute, Art. 75(2).

[42] Cf. *Trial of the Major War Criminals before the International Military Tribunal, Nuremberg 14 October 1945–1 October 1946*, Vol. I (Nuremberg: International Military Tribunal, 1947), 223.

[43] ICC Statute, Art. 78(1).

[44] ICC Statute, Art. 110.

[45] ICC RPE, Rule 223.

[46] ICC, Decision of 22 September 2015 (AC), *Lubanga Dyilo*, ICC-01/04-01/06-3173.

[47] ICC, Decision of 3 November 2017 (AC), *Lubanga Dyilo*, ICC-01/04-01/06-3375.

reduction of his sentence of 12 years. The review panel noted, in particular, Germain Katanga's testimony and his further decision to withdraw his appeal as indicative of an early and continuing willingness to cooperate with the Court's investigations and prosecutions. Katanga's withdrawal of his appeal and the expression of apologies to the victims through a video recording made available to the affected communities were found to reflect genuine dissociation from the crimes.[48]

V CONCLUSION

In an increasingly troubled world, international criminal jurisdictions are under close scrutiny. Trials generate high expectations from both the international community and victims. In addition, sentences are closely looked at. Punishment bears different dimensions at the international level, but serves no different purposes than domestic punishment: protecting the society by preventing further crimes, healing victims and rehabilitating individuals.

The international community has come a long way in the establishment of a system of global justice and embedding accountability for mass atrocities into international law. Yet, for the system to achieve its goals, we must continue to deploy all efforts to replace a pattern of impunity with a pattern of accountability.

[48] ICC, Decision of 13 November 2015 (AC), *Katanga*, ICC-01/04-01/07-3615.

PART I

Setting the Framework: Criminological, Historical and Domestic Perspectives

3

Criminology of International Crimes

FRANK NEUBACHER

I CRIMINOLOGY MEETS INTERNATIONAL CRIMINAL LAW

The criminology of international crimes is a neglected field, and even this is an understatement. Just a few years ago, distinguished scholars such as Alex Alvarez, John Hagan and Wenona Rymond-Richmond, Susanne Karstedt and Nicole Rafter started to contribute to this slowly emerging research area.[1] In different ways, they have searched for criminological explanations of international crimes. John Hagan and Wenona Rymond-Richmond were right when they stated in 2009: 'It took criminology a long time to address some

[1] See A. Alvarez, *Genocidal Crimes* (Abingdon/Oxon: Routledge, 2010); J. Hagan and W. Rymond-Richmond, *Darfur and the Crime of Genocide* (Cambridge: Cambridge University Press, 2009); S. Karstedt, 'Genozid (Völkermord)' in H.J. Schneider (ed.), *Internationales Handbuch der Kriminologie*, 2 vols. (Berlin: De Gruyter, 2009), Vol. II; N. Hahn Rafter, *The Crime of all Crimes: Towards a Criminology of Genocide* (New York/London: New York University Press, 2016) and, for German Criminology: S. Harrendorf, 'How Can Criminology Contribute to an Explanation of International Crimes?' (2014) 12 *Journal of International Criminal Justice* 231; J. Holling, *Internationaler Strafgerichtshof und Verbrechensprävention: Eine Analyse der Auswirkungen globaler Strafrechtspflege auf die Bekämpfung von Makrokriminalität* (Berlin/Münster: LIT Verlag, 2016); H. Jäger, *Makrokriminalität: Studien zur Kriminologie kollektiver Gewalt* (Frankfurt: Suhrkamp, 1989); D. Khakzad, *Kriminologische Aspekte völkerrechtlicher Verbrechen: Eine vergleichende Untersuchung der Situationsländer des Internationalen Strafgerichtshofs* (Mönchengladbach: Forum Verlag Godesberg, 2015); F. Neubacher, *Kriminologische Grundlagen einer internationalen Strafgerichtsbarkeit: Politische Ideen- und Dogmengeschichte, kriminalwissenschaftliche Legitimation, strafrechtliche Perspektiven* (Tübingen: Mohr Siebeck, 2005); F. Neubacher, 'How Can It Happen That Horrendous State Crimes Are Perpetrated? An Overview of Criminological Theories' (2006) 4 *Journal of International Criminal Justice* 787; F. Neubacher, 'Kriminologie und Völkerstrafrecht: Diskussionsstand, Forschungsperspektiven, Erklärungsansätze' (2015) 10 *Zeitschrift für Internationale Strafrechtsdogmatik* 485; S. Nimaga, *Grundlagen einer Wirkungsforschung des Völkerstrafrechts* (Berlin: Wissenschaftlicher Verlag Berlin, 2016); C. Reese, *Großverbrechen und kriminologische Konzepte: Versuch einer theoretischen Integration* (Münster: LIT, 2004).

of its most important topics, for example, white-collar crime. It took criminology even longer to confront its more deadly neglected topics, namely genocide, war crimes, and crimes against humanity.'[2] Since then, criminology has mainly focused on the crime of genocide while there is hardly anything specific on war crimes or crimes against humanity not to mention about other criminological aspects such as procedural, penological and victimological issues that still have been rarely addressed.

Before entering the field of international crimes, it seems appropriate to introduce criminology by raising the question of what criminology is about. According to Edwin Sutherland's (1883–1950) famous definition, criminology is the study of the making of laws, the breaking of laws and of society's reactions to the breaking of laws.[3] The development of criminology was vastly propelled by the preventive turn in criminal sciences at the end of the nineteenth century. In Germany, Franz von Liszt (1851–1919) challenged the retributive tradition of the classical school strongly influenced by Kant and Hegel by promoting prevention as the core concept in criminal law. According to him, prevention should be achieved through the deterrence of opportunistic offenders, the rehabilitation of those in need of it, and – if necessary – through the incapacitation of persistent offenders ('Marburger Programm').[4] In the following decades, the preventive approach changed the way of reasoning on criminal law, in particular on sentencing. Criminal law was in need of explanations for why people became offenders and how to rehabilitate them. Statistical data was supposed to help understand crime as a social phenomenon. Consequently, Franz von Liszt made the case for a strong criminology being an integral part of a 'whole' criminal science and ranking no longer below criminal law. Without the need to justify punishment in terms of prevention, without the interest in the consequences of different sanctions, there would not have been anything like criminology. Since then, criminology has embraced phenomenology, etiology, penology and victimology all under one umbrella.

This paper underlines the importance of criminology for the study of international crimes by addressing three key issues from a criminological point

[2] J. Hagan and W. Rymond-Richmond, 'Criminology Confronts Genocide: Whose Side Are You On?' (2009) 13 *Theoretical Criminology* 503.

[3] E.H. Sutherland and D.R. Cressey, *Principles of Criminology*, 7th ed. (Philadelphia: Lippincott, 1960), 3.

[4] F. von Liszt, 'Der Zweckgedanke im Strafrecht' (1883) 3 *Zeitschrift für die gesamte Strafrechtswissenschaft* 1, 3.

of view: First, what is the purpose of punishing perpetrators of mass atrocities; second, how do we explain international crimes; and third, the question of sentencing. The answers given aim at challenging some working routines of international criminal justice and at paving the way for more reflected reactions to international crimes.

II WHY PUNISH? – PREVENTING CRIME THROUGH INTERNATIONAL CRIMINAL LAW

When it comes to the purpose of punishment, criminal justice follows a unifying approach. This holds true at the national and international level. Retribution and deterrence are said to be 'equally important'. This has been underlined several times by the International Criminal Tribunal for the former Yugoslavia (ICTY) as well as the International Criminal Court (ICC).[5] Sometimes these short reflections are garnished with some expressivist thoughts on the importance to show that there is no impunity for international crimes or to strengthen faith in the rule of law. In general, however, we miss theories that are designed to specifically fit at the international level. What could they look like?

For a criminologist inclined to preventive theories of criminal law, justice cannot be a metaphysical endeavour. On the contrary, it must be rather concrete and serve human beings on earth. Criminology should then contribute to the knowledge and understanding whether the purposes of criminal law can be achieved in reality. As we all know, there are strong objections against the retributive philosophy of punishment. This is valid for international crimes in particular.[6] What could be an adequate punishment for multiple murder? What would be a proportional sanction for mass atrocities? In the end there is no 'just' punishment for genocide and, for many good reasons, international criminal law has abolished capital punishment. The Preamble of the Rome Statute is concerned about the 'peace, security and well-being of the world' and modestly declares the determination 'to put an end to impunity for the

[5] See M.A. Drumbl, *Atrocity, Punishment and International Law* (Cambridge: Cambridge University Press, 2007), 60; G. Werle and F. Jeßberger, *Völkerstrafrecht*, 4th ed. (Tübingen: Mohr Siebeck, 2016), 49 (referring to, inter alia, the ICTY Judgement in *Kupreškic et al.*, Trial Chamber, 14 January 2000, para 848). For statements on the aims of punishment by the main international and hybrid criminal courts, see the contribution by Sergey Vasiliev in Chapter 4. On the ICC in particular, see the contribution by Gerhard Werle and Aziz Epik in Chapter 18.

[6] But see the contributions by Mordechai Kremnitzer and Jens David Ohlin in Chapters 10 and 15.

perpetrators of these crimes and thus to contribute to the prevention of such crimes'.[7] This should be read as a commitment to prevention and is a rather mundane starting point in search for peace and security.

Generally, punishment is justified by prevention, and prevention in turn can be achieved through a combination of, first, deterrence (a classical purpose of punishment); second, strengthening faith in the rule of law (a purpose sometimes labelled as 'expressivist theory'); third, incapacitation of the culprits (whereas the length of the prison term is limited by the individual's degree of guilt); and fourth, offender rehabilitation.[8] It is reflecting a global consensus that according to Article 10(3) of the International Covenant on Civil and Political Rights of 16 December 1966 'the penitentiary system shall comprise treatment of prisoners the essential aim of which shall be their reformation and social rehabilitation'. Roughly speaking, these aims can be transferred to the international level if a few caveats are considered. On the international level, the situation might slightly differ from the national one (e.g. with regard to the community) and therefore require adaptations. Moreover, the state of empirical knowledge may even be weaker on the international level. Both are true for deterrence, for example; we will return to that point shortly.

The purpose of punishment in international criminal law still has to be something more, something that responds to the international nature of the crimes. Therefore, from a victimological perspective, the traditional aims of punishment should be complemented – for the victims' sake and for a more restorative justice – with two new aims, namely establishing the truth and acknowledging the victims' status (solidarity).[9] Favouring this broadening is due to the lack of trials on the national level where solidarity is painfully missed by the crime victims. There is substantial empirical evidence that crime victims are not expecting any kind of revenge from international courts but clarity and solidarity.[10] This holds true even if crime victims are very different in their individual needs and even if victim participation is a

[7] ICC Statute, Preamble, paras. 3 and 5. See also Nimaga, *Grundlagen einer Wirkungsforschung des Völkerstrafrechts*, 133.

[8] See A. Werkmeister, *Straftheorien im Völkerstrafrecht* (Baden-Baden: Nomos, 2015), 147 et seq.; Werle and Jeßberger, *Völkerstrafrecht*, 49 et seq.

[9] See Werkmeister, *Straftheorien im Völkerstrafrecht*, 316–328. For a similar argument, see the contribution by Daniela Demko in Chapter 11 (Section IV).

[10] Cf. E. Kiza, C. Rathgeber and H.-C. Rohne, *Victims of War: An Empirical Study on War-Victimization and Victims' Attitudes towards Addressing Atrocities* (Hamburg: Hamburg Edition online, 2006); see also E. Hoven, M. Feiler and S. Scheibel, *Victims in Trials of Mass Crimes: A Multi-perspective Study of Civil Party Participation at the Extraordinary Chambers in the Courts of Cambodia* (Köln: Institute for International Peace and Security Law, Universität

difficult field.[11] Criminal procedures can neither be satisfying for the victims in all cases nor should their satisfaction be the primary goal of international criminal justice. Victim participation may also be challenging for the legal professionals in international criminal trials.[12]

Obviously, there are some limitations to this concept of prevention, limitations that are more serious on the international level than on a national level. From a theoretical viewpoint, three major challenges arise:

(i) *Responsivity of the potential perpetrators*: Not every potential perpetrator is responsive to the messages sent out by the application of law. There are offenders who do not make a rational choice – in particular when it comes to politically motivated crimes or hate crimes. They just act out of the moment without prior planning or reasoning. Even if they did so, they might think that their risk of getting apprehended and sentenced is very low, at least for a considerable period of time.[13] And finally it is known that (instead of deterrence) moral standards are crucial for obeying the law and that perpetrators often care more about the reactions of their social environment (e.g. peers, fellows, soul-mates) than about the formal reaction of the law. In that regard, international criminal law is facing a serious problem because it is not the exemption but the rule that perpetrators feel encouraged by their social environment and act in full harmony with its expectations.

(ii) *Selectivity in the application of law*: Furthermore, deterrence completely depends on a regular and certain application of law. Compared to the national level, the limitations are even stronger on the international level because in general resources are limited, international police forces are inexistent and national prosecution has priority according to the principle of complementarity. As a natural and inevitable consequence, selectivity endangers both general deterrence and expressivist theories because, much too often, moral values and legal norms cannot be affirmed by court proceedings.

zu Köln, 2013), 25–30; Neubacher, *Kriminologische Grundlagen einer internationalen Strafgerichtsbarkeit*, 206–214.

[11] On victims' participation as a central aspect of modern international criminal justice and its challenges, see the contribution by Philipp Ambach in Chapter 20.

[12] Cf. E. Hoven, 'Civil Party Participation in Trials of Mass Crimes: A Qualitative Study at the Extraordinary Chambers in the Courts of Cambodia' (2014) 12 *Journal of International Criminal Justice* 81.

[13] Cf. J. Schense 'Conclusions: Findings and Recommendations', in J. Schense and L. Carter (eds.), *Two Steps Forward, One Step Back: The Deterrence Effect of International Criminal Tribunals* (Nürnberg: International Nuremberg Principles Academy, 2016), 333, 338.

(iii) *Legitimacy of international criminal justice*: In the end, the legitimacy of international criminal justice is in peril if the whole project can be dismissed as unjust or arbitrary. From criminology we know that perpetrators tend to minimize their responsibility and deny the injury and the victim. In this context, Gresham Sykes and David Matza have to be mentioned, who analysed the application of what they called 'techniques of neutralization'.[14] They encompass 'the denial of responsibility', 'the denial of injury', the 'denial of victim' and 'the appeal to higher loyalties'. One of the five techniques is the 'condemnation of the condemners'. Here, the perpetrator does not deny the wrongdoing – he or she claims that the adversary is even worse and not entitled to appeal to the law. We all know this kind of strategy from the Nuremberg Trial when the accused denounced the trial as 'victor's justice'. Obviously, these kinds of accusations are damaging for the mission of international criminal justice. They can undermine its legitimacy – rather in the eyes of the public than in the eyes of the culprits.[15]

When turning to the empirical evidence on punishment, first of all the issue of deterrence has to be addressed. It is surprising how much the discussion in international criminal law is detached from criminology. While international criminal law pretends that deterrent effects of punishment are a reality, criminological evidence referring to the effects of international criminal justice can in the best case be described as anecdotic or methodologically weak.[16] In fact, deterrence remains one of the most debated issues in general criminology.

Numerous scientific studies were conducted leading to inconsistent findings and pointing to the necessity of meta-studies and methodological rigour.[17] The lesson is clear: A potential deterrent effect may be moderate but depends on various variables and the applied methodology. One type of study considered the responsiveness of crime to various interventions of the criminal justice system (e.g. law-making, intensity of policing) using aggregate data

[14] G.M. Sykes and D. Matza, 'Techniques of Neutralization: A Theory of Delinquency' (1957) 22 *American Sociological Review* 664; A. Alvarez, 'Adjusting to Genocide: The Techniques of Neutralization and the Holocaust' (1997) 21 *Social Science History* 139; Neubacher, 'How Can It Happen That Horrendous State Crimes Are Perpetrated?', 787–799.

[15] Cf. Holling, *Internationaler Strafgerichtshof und Verbrechensprävention*, 182.

[16] See Schense and Carter, 'Introduction', in Schense and Carter (eds.), *The Deterrence Effect of International Criminal Tribunals*, 1, 4 et seq.

[17] Cf. D. Dölling, H. Entorf, D. Hermann and T. Rupp 'Is Deterrence Effective? Results of a Meta-Analysis of Punishment' (2009) 15 *European Journal on Criminal Policy and Research* 201.

from the macro-level, mostly crime statistics (or the number of casualties or dead[18]). These studies provide evidence in favour of a negative relationship between crime and the interventions applied. The finding, however, that a certain change in the criminal justice system results in reducing the number of crime remains debatable as crime statistics (reflecting the reporting behaviour and policing strategies) certainly are not a suitable measuring instrument, and this body of research fails to separate incapacitation effects from deterrent effects.[19] Another type of study (using experimental or interview data) chose individual-level risk perceptions as the key variable and found a 'weak, negative association that is usually interpreted as evidence of a slight deterrent effect on increased risk perceptions'.[20] It is commonly agreed, however, that the certainty of punishment has a much greater effect than the severity of punishment and that the deterrability of specific types of offenders may vary substantially.[21]

Altogether, the research area is too complex for simple answers as there are many other relevant variables. It makes no sense, for example, stating that lawful behaviour is an effect of deterrence if in fact the behaviour is resulting from a moral decision of the potential perpetrator[22] or from the anticipated reaction of the immediate environment. Still, the probability of informal sanctions via friends or family appears to have a greater deterrent potential than the probability of formal sanctions by the criminal justice system.[23] Dieter Dölling et al. conducted a statistical meta-analysis of 700 deterrence studies and found a relatively low general preventive effect. They summarise their findings as follows:

> The greatest effects are found in experimental studies which concern norms not intended to protect essential interests. The smallest effects are to be found in studies on the death penalty. In this area the relevant norms protect fundamental interests. Moreover, the deterrence hypothesis is more

[18] See Schense and Carter, 'Introduction', 4 et seq.

[19] See D.S. Nagin, 'Deterrence: A Review of the Evidence by a Criminologist for Economists' (2013) 5 *Annual Review of Economics* 83.

[20] T.A. Loughran, R. Paternoster, A. Chalfin and T. Wilson, 'Can Rational Choice Be Considered a General Theory of Crime? Evidence from Individual-Level Panel Data (2016) 54 *Criminology* 86, 89.

[21] Loughran, Paternoster, Chalfin and Wilson, 'Can Rational Choice Be Considered a General Theory of Crime?', 89; Nagin, 'Deterrence: A Review of the Evidence by a Criminologist for Economists', 87. On the selectivity in international criminal law as a problem for theories of punishment, see the contribution by Harmen van der Wilt in Chapter 18.

[22] P.-O.H. Wikström, A. Tseloni and D. Karlis, 'Do People Comply with the Law Because They Fear Getting Caught?' (2011) 8 *European Journal of Criminology* 401, 405.

[23] Dölling, Entorf, Hermann and Rupp, 'Is Deterrence Effective?', 217; Nagin, 'Deterrence: A Review of the Evidence by a Criminologist for Economists', 85.

> frequently confirmed when administrative offences are investigated as opposed to crimes. The relevance and acceptance of a norm appears therefore to be an important condition for the effectiveness of deterrence.[24]

Thus, there is substantial reason for doubting the deterrent effect of punishment. However, to make things worse for international criminal justice, what about the perception of sanction risk in the specific group of powerful leaders? Not only is their probability of being apprehended and sentenced lower than for ordinary criminals because international criminal justice is slow and highly selective both for legal and political reasons. What can they really know about the sanction regime and the sanction probably handed out in their case, if cases are rare and incomparable and if a general sentencing practice is lacking? Having started with the hope for deterrence, we have ended up with a tremendous relativization of the effects of punishment, in particular on the international level. That is why scholars and practitioners of international criminal justice badly need to know much more about perceptions of individuals and groups in order to link relevant deterrence to the work of international courts.[25] This is a major prerequisite for future attempts of achieving prevention through sending out messages to specified individuals or group of individuals ('targeted deterrence'[26]).

III ON THE EXPLANATION OF INTERNATIONAL CRIMES

While in criminal law the point of reference is the law, in criminology we have a behavioural point of reference. That makes a huge difference and explains why a certain behaviour may violate the law but at the same time remain in perfect consistence with the behavioural norms of the social environment. The behaviour may be illegal, but it is not deviant because in the given setting and for a certain period of time the behaviour is regarded as normal. Normativity and factuality can fall apart; and that is causing problems for international criminal justice, for the common practice on the national level may deviate from international law thus making it more difficult for national players to recognize the discrepancy.[27] Any criminological explanation of international crimes needs to bear in mind the societal and environmental norms – an individualistic approach would be misleading.

24 Dölling, Entorf, Hermann and Rupp, 'Is Deterrence Effective?', 223.

25 See Schense, 'Conclusion', 334.

26 Schense, 'Conclusion', 334.

27 On the possibility of norm-collisions between domestic and international criminal law, see the contribution by Klaus Günther in Chapter 13.

For heuristic reasons, three levels of explanations should be considered: A macro-, meso- and a micro-level.[28] They can be associated with the system (macro), groups or organizations (meso) and the individual (micro) respectively. Criminologists have already pointed out that some macro-level factors contribute to international crimes, particularly conflicts, social inequality, discrimination and a weak rule of law.[29] In a ground breaking book published by Nicole Rafter in 2016, genocidal organizations, the legal status of exemption and the expectation of impunity are listed as crucial causes for crimes of genocide.[30] In their case study on Darfur that is rich of empirical data collected from refugees who had fled Sudan, Hagan and Rymond-Richmond developed a theory of genocide based on a collective action theory. Not only did they differentiate between the macro-, meso- and micro-level; they furthermore attributed the relevant factors to the respective levels each. On the macro-level, the competition for land and a state-led, pro-Arab ideology shape collective action frames. As a reaction to the macro-level conflict, organized interest groups are formed on the meso level. On the micro-level, individual group members become active having internalized the state-led ideology. Altogether, 'such individual actions coalesce into collective action'.[31]

In his 2016 Sutherland Address to the American Society of Criminology Ross L. Matsueda continued tackling this 'micro-macro-problem' (also branded as 'the levels of explanation problem') advocating for an integrated approach that is mainly resting on the work of the sociologist James S. Coleman.[32] This approach aims at 'specifying causal mechanisms by which interactions among individuals produce social organizations outcomes'.[33]

[28] Neubacher, 'Kriminologie und Völkerstrafrecht', 489; see also Rafter, *The Crime of all Crimes*, 20. For further criminological insights, Karstedt, 'Genozid (Völkermord)'; S. Karstedt, 'Contextualizing Mass Attrocity Crimes: The Dynamics of "Extremely Violent Societies"' (2012) 9 *European Journal of Criminology* 499. Andreas Werkmeister has used these different levels to develop a meso-preventive theory of international punishment; see his contribution in Chapter 14 with references to his publication *Straftheorien im Völkerstrafrecht*.

[29] Holling, *Internationaler Strafgerichtshof und Verbrechensprävention*, 151.

[30] Rafter, *The Crime of all Crimes*, 204; see also S. Kühl, *Ganz normale Organisationen: Zur Soziologie des Holocaust* (Berlin: Suhrkamp, 2014).

[31] R.L. Matsueda, 'Toward a New Criminology of Genocide: Theory, Method, and Politics' (2009) 13 *Theoretical Criminology* 495, 496–497; J. Hagan and W. Rymond-Richmond, 'The Collective Dynamics of Racial Dehumanization and Genocidal Victimization in Darfur' (2008) 73 *American Sociological Review* 875, 878–882.

[32] J.S. Coleman, *Foundations of Social Theory* (Cambridge, Massachusetts: The Belknap Press of Harvard University Press, 1990), 6 seq.; see also Neubacher, 'Kriminologie und Völkerstrafrecht', 489.

[33] See R.L. Matsueda, 'Toward an Analytical Criminology: The Micro-Macro Problem, Causal Mechanisms, and Public Policy' (2017) 55 *Criminology* 493, 493.

It rejects the assumption that causality exclusively lies at the macro-level and that individuals can be ignored. On the other hand, methodological individualism argues that causality solely operates on the individual level and that groups and societies are simple aggregations of individual-level causal mechanisms. This view seems to be one-sided, too. Instead, the transitions between macro- and micro-level need to be studied carefully. What are the macro-level factors that affect the individual choice process? And what are, taking a look in the opposite direction, the 'rules by which individuals combine to produce a group outcome'?[34]

(i) *Macro-level:* The macro-level, that is the policy context, seems to be of utmost importance because in most cases there would hardly be an international crime without the involvement of state organizations or social organizations. The supra-individual level may be represented by the government, military, secret police or other state agencies, political parties, militias or armed groups. Mass media and the propaganda apparatus should be taken into account as well. In the context of international criminal justice, organizational or individual crime is usually resulting from a system triggering, legitimizing and/or tolerating violence. It is the political system that is appealing to a state of emergency (or at least to the perception of a security threat), it is the political system or a political party that is defining humans as enemies, that is setting up black lists, orchestrating the violence and justifying the attacks. How do they manage that? How do they involve organizations and individuals? The criminological answer is that above all they provide frames. In sociology, framing refers to processes through which relevant information is first separated from irrelevant information and is then placed in a certain field of meaning. In essence, it is about how information is presented and which meaning is attached to it. Not too long ago, for example, US soldiers were made to believe that waterboarding was not illegal torture but a legitimate and necessary instrument of gathering intelligence ('torture memos').[35] Of course, there are many more examples in history and in the world of today of how people are misled by political leaders. History has taught us that people feel authorized when adopting the justifications offered to them by the political

[34] Matsueda, 'Toward an Analytical Criminology', 497.

[35] H.C. Kelman, 'The Policy Context of Torture: A Social-Psychological Analysis' (2005) 87 *International Review of the Red Cross* 123; J. Hagan, J. Kaiser and A. Hanson, *Iraq and the Crimes of Aggressive War: The Legal Cynicism of Criminal Militarism* (Cambridge: Cambridge University Press, 2015), 64 et seq.; J. Hagan, *Who Are the Criminals? The Politics of Crime Policy from the Age of Roosevelt to the Age of Reagan* (Princeton/Oxford: Princeton University Press, 2012), 49.

system. In light of a mission, not only do 'they feel justified in overcoming their moral scruples; indeed they feel obliged to do so'.[36]

Here again, techniques of neutralization play a role. It should not go unnoticed that Sykes and Matza's theory contributed to the fundamental understanding that perpetrators are not so different from law-abiding people in that they usually do not reject the dominant social order and share the same values and norms. They have, however, learned to override norms in certain situations by applying 'techniques of neutralizations'. By this, they maintain a positive self-image despite committing the crime (or, as Sykes and Matza put it, 'they eat the cake and have it, too').[37] The conscience can be kept clean by denying the responsibility ('I did not mean it'), by denying the injury ('I did not really hurt anybody'), by denying the victim (who is dehumanized as aggressor or enemy), by condemning the condemners ('you are worse', 'you are a hypocrite') and by appealing to higher loyalties. In the last case perpetrators claim, for example, that they protected their family, defended national security or punished enemies. In any case, they have their reasons and in their eyes the end justifies the means. It is, then, normal people, not certain 'types of offenders' who gradually change sides by 'drifting' into delinquency. The techniques of neutralizations are perfectly applicable in the context of international criminal justice.[38] As Heinrich Himmler's infamous speech held in front of high-ranking SS-officers in Posen on 4 October 1943 demonstrated, even genocide can be presented as heroic if it is framed as a fight for purity and survival.[39]

On the macro-level, relevant political players are perceived as authorities by the people. Provided that the authority appears to be legitimate, most people are willing to follow. The Milgram experiment[40] has strikingly proven that it does not take much to make people obey given instructions. If authority just offers a 'good reason' (e.g. in Milgram's case, the sake of science), the majority of people are ready to inflict considerable harm to others – nota bene without being threatened by any kind of sanction in the case of disobedience. The lessons to be learnt from Milgram, whose findings were repeatedly replicated,

36 H.C. Kelman, 'Violence without Moral Restraint: Reflections on the Dehumanization of Victims and Victimizers' (1973) 29 *Journal of Social Sciences* 25, 44–45.

37 Sykes and Matza, 'Techniques of Neutralization', 664 et seq.

38 Neubacher, 'How Can It Happen That Horrendous State Crimes Are Perpetrated?', 762 et seq.; see also Alvarez, *Genocidal Crimes*, 115 et seq.

39 Neubacher, 'How Can It Happen That Horrendous State Crimes Are Perpetrated?', 796 et seq.

40 Cf. S. Milgram, 'Some Conditions of Obedience and Disobedience to Autority' (1965) 18 *Human Relations* 57.

are twofold: first, in certain circumstances it is not the kind of person but the kind of situation in which one is placed, that determines actions. In this sense, a situation can be shaped by authorization. And second, to a lesser extent, there are disobedient people too. What made them resist remains a bit obscure in the Milgram experiment, but the fact that some were obedient while others were not is confirming the assumption that macro- and micro-level factors collaborate.

(ii) *Meso-level:* Processes of authorization also have a large share in the functioning of groups and organizations as they are regularly structured in a hierarchical way. We only need to think of military units in which this is evident. Apart from authorization (what may be called the vertical dimension), soldiers let themselves equally be guided by the common practice of their comrades (the horizontal dimension). This exactly corresponds to the findings of military historians who analysed the wire-taped conversations of German military officers being held in prisoner camps at the end of World War II. It became clear that before they were captured they used to worry about what their comrades might have thought of them if they had stepped out of line.[41] Naturally they did not, as the group bonds were too strong. The same can be studied in the Milgram experiment where this phenomenon was labelled as 'group effects'.

In a collective, the burden of personal responsibility is lifted. Division of labour is effectively facilitating the process of distancing oneself from the outcome. Where many people get involved, nobody will really feel responsible for the whole. This effect, also known as bystander effect, is exacerbated by the fact that repeated joint action leads to routinization which is accompanied by 'numbing' as Herbert Kelman put it.[42] According to him,

> routinization fulfills two functions. First, it reduces the necessity of making decisions, thus minimizing occasions in which moral questions may arise. Second, it makes it easier to avoid the implications of the action since the actor focuses on the details of his job rather than on its meaning.[43]

By this, routinization helps stabilize the given frames as they are not questioned anymore. The way a situation is perceived hereby becomes a habit for those involved. Once again, Kelman: 'Routinization operates both at the level

[41] S. Neitzel and H. Welzer, *Soldaten: Protokolle vom Kämpfen, Töten und Sterben* (Frankfurt: S. Fischer, 2011), 16 et seq., 394.
[42] Kelman, 'Violence without Moral Restraint', 52.
[43] Kelman, 'Violence without Moral Restraint', 46.

of the individual actor and at the organizational level.' At the end, there is 'no expectation that the moral implications will be considered [...] nor is there any opportunity to do so'.[44] In this light, even mass killings have to be regarded as a 'job' which can be executed in a more or less efficient way and which requires refinements from time to time. One of the perpetrators of the Rwandan genocide, for example, stated: 'I would teach the people in the group how to kill, and how to kill people without too much noise. I taught them how to be clever in the killings.'[45] It is also telling how a former member of the Iraq security forces under Saddam Hussein described his sentiments and rationalizations when he was trained as a torturer.[46]

(iii) *Micro-level:* On the micro-level, there is a wide scope for potential individual motives. They range from political fanatism, 'fun' or greed to career interests (proving to be a reliable follower), thoughtlessness and even participation with disgust. In criminology, attempts have been undertaken to classify perpetrators by their motives. Alette Smeulers differentiated between 'the criminal mastermind', 'the fanatic', 'the criminal/the sadist', 'the profiteer', 'the careerist', 'the devoted warrior', 'followers and conformists', 'the compromised perpetrator' and 'the professional'.[47] That may well be true but it is doubtful whether criminology is hereby coming closer to the understanding of international crimes. It is their characteristic that they do not stem from the individual level. A distinction has to be made between an individual's motive and its social role. Motives can be different. It does not seem appropriate, however, to think of these motives as a primary cause of action. As already shown, social interaction is a paramount factor, and individuals are treated depending on their social roles (e.g. as soldiers). They get confronted with corresponding role expectations – no matter what their individual motives are. While individual motives may help in meeting the expectations of others, they do not override the social mechanisms. Even a reluctant individual will be drawn into the destructive dynamics of processes of authorization and routinization. Usually, this view does not result in exempting the individual from legal accountability. The individual is still responsible for accepting the

[44] Kelman, 'Violence without Moral Restraint', 47.

[45] A. Smeulers and L. Hoax, 'Studying the Microdynamics of Rwandan Genocide' (2010) 50 *British Journal of Criminology* 435, 450.

[46] See Hagan, Kaiser and Hanson, *Iraq and the Crimes of Aggressive War*, 29 et seq. ('Learning to Torture').

[47] A. Smeulers, 'Perpetrators of International Crimes: Towards a Typology' in A. Smeulers and R. Havemann (eds.), *Supranational Criminology: Towards a Criminology of International Crimes* (Antwerp: Intersentia Press, 2008), 244, 244 et seq.

frames and neutralizations offered, for his or her 'moral disengagement' and 'victim blaming' (Rafter) and, not least, for the consequential acts. Nevertheless, the criminological perspective sheds light upon those dynamics, minimizing the probability that individuals rebel or refuse cooperation.

In criminological literature, it has been worked out that genocide often is a top-down process. For the Rwandan genocide, Hollie Nyseth Brehm validated that 'state actors orchestrated and executed the violence' and that the government encouraged civilians to participate in the killings. Hutus were asked to form 'self-defense' groups and it was suggested that Tutsis would kill Hutus if they did not act first. Some participants in the genocide were forced to do so while many others were not.[48] Comparatively, more killings were executed in communities 'in close proximity to the extremist center of the violence' and in regions controlled by the reigning political party.[49] Even so, Nyseth Brehm advocated not viewing genocide exclusively as a top-down endeavour. By analysing the determinants of subnational levels of killings in 142 Rwandan communities, she found that fewer killings occurred in communities with higher marriage rates and higher formal employment rates, that she interpreted as an effect of social control and cohesion and described as 'meso-level factors'.[50] These findings are in line with the view presented here that a collaboration of macro- and meso-level factors mainly determine the actions.

In a previous study, Nyseth Brehm showed that the Rwandan genocide did not follow the age and gender distribution common to other crimes. The peak age of those tried in the Rwandan gacaca court system was 34 years (at the time of the genocide), which is older than the age for most other types of crime. Women were more likely to participate in crimes against property while they were less likely to commit genocidal murder. However, these results should be interpreted as chiefly reflecting different opportunity structures because both the division of labour (e.g. representation in the government) and the expectation to participate in the violence were highly gendered.[51] Having said that, women's participation in international crimes should not be underestimated

48 H. Nyseth Brehm, 'Subnational Determinants of Killing in Rwanda' (2017) 55 *Criminology* 5, 9.

49 Nyseth Brehm, 'Subnational Determinants of Killing in Rwanda', 25.

50 Nyseth Brehm, 'Subnational Determinants of Killing in Rwanda', 10.

51 H. Nyseth Brehm, C. Uggen and J.-D. Gasanabo, 'Age, Gender, and the Crime of Crimes: Toward a Life-Course Theory of Genocide Participation' (2016) 54 *Criminology* 713, 713, 720, 735.

in general. Those researchers are right who regard this topic a research field in its own right.[52]

However, it is not sufficient to have an idea about the interplay of the macro-, meso- and micro-level. We also need to understand that relevant situations are gradually emerging and can change over time. In this sense, collective violence certainly is a situational process. Situational means that this kind of violence is difficult to predict, that it can neither be explained by individual characteristics nor by motives only, and that it hardly makes sense to set up offender typologies. On the contrary, it is more realistic to assume that humans are capable of the most heinous acts while the same humans can heroically adhere to moral standards in another situation. Peer pressure may change, time for reflection may be lacking, role models may be present, personal mood or shape may vary as well. In the end, it might very well be that the situation, not the character, is the key.

In his study on violence, Randall Collins has argued that although confrontational situations are common, actual violence is quite rare because confrontational tension mixed with strong fears usually hinders people from resorting to violence. What is needed for the unleashing of violence is a state of imbalance, in which one side of the conflicting parties is gaining momentum, and emotional dominance, so that fears can break loose into a 'tunnel of violence'. Collins identified several pathways into this tunnel, the most dangerous of which is 'forward panic' when tension spills forward into atrocities. At the centre of Collins' study lies an interactional perspective explaining violence as a process between situationally placed individuals, not as something that can be studied as a personal trait. He is very clear on this point: 'First, put the interaction in the center of the analysis, not the individual, not the social background, the culture, or even the motivation: that is to say, look for the characteristics of violent situations.' In addition, on the same page: 'Not violent individuals, but violent situations – this is what a micro-sociological theory is about. We seek the contours of situations, which shape the emotions and acts of the individuals who step inside them. It is a false lead to look for types of violent individuals, constant across situations.'[53]

Even if that view may not be valid for all kind of conflict situations, it offers valuable insights that can contribute to the understanding of situations

[52] S. Linton 'Women Accused of International Crimes: A Trans-Disciplinary Inquiry and Methodology' (2016) 27 *Criminal Law Forum* 159.

[53] R. Collins, *Violence: A Micro-Sociological Theory* (Princeton: Princeton University Press, 2009), 1; see also S. Klusemann, 'Massacres as Process: A Micro-Sociological Theory of Internal Patterns of Mass Atrocities' (2012) 9 *European Journal of Criminology* 468, 468 et seq.

escalating into atrocities. Moreover, it perfectly fits with a theory that is widely accepted to reflect the current state of knowledge in criminology. The situational action theory combines a perception-choice process with a strong situational focus. According to it, crime is ultimately an outcome of a perception-choice process which is initiated and guided by relevant aspects of the person-environment interaction. A person's particular stability and change in exposure to criminogenic settings depends on processes of social and self-selection.[54] A person may find him- or herself placed in a moral environment (e.g. characterized by group members' attitudes) which is influencing the individual's perception and can even be stronger than the individual's morals. In this model, deterrence can only function as a control in the choice process if the person is deliberating at all (and not acting habitually) and if the impact of the moral environment is not too strong. This situational perspective is illustrating again, this time from a theoretical viewpoint, the limits of the concept of deterrence. Finally, another point deserves being mentioned: Per-Olof Wikström's concept of linking a situational model of crime to social contexts is perfectly compatible with the idea of macro-, meso- and micro-level factors because Wikström is drawing on Coleman's work.[55]

Another theory that should be mentioned in the context of international crimes is Charles Tittle's control balance theory.[56] It is based on the idea of control, which is, first, the degree to which others can limit an individual's behavioural options and, second, the extent to which an individual can exercise such control over others. According to this theory, deviance is the result of an imbalanced ratio of controls exercised to controls experienced. When mentioning 'repressive' types of deviance ('predation', 'defiance', 'submission') which result from control deficits, Tittle refers to behaviour similar to street crime, e.g. theft, rape, homicide, vandalism and political protest. In contrast, control surpluses are associated with 'autonomous' types of deviance ('exploitation', 'plunder', 'decadence') which – analogous to white-collar crime – are characterized by the abuse of power and the lack of control. As this also holds for political power and political organizations and as it is assumed that the greater the control surplus, the more serious the likely deviant conduct, this theory allows us to explain phenomena such as torture, genocide or extra-legal killings.

[54] P.-O.H. Wikström, 'Why Crime Happens: A Situational Action Theory' in G. Manzo (ed.), *Analytical Sociology: Actions and Networks* (Hoboken: John Wiley & Sons, 2014), 74, 74 et seq.

[55] Cf. Matsueda, 'Toward an Analytical Criminology', 496.

[56] C.R. Tittle, *Control Balance: Toward a General Theory of Deviance* (New York/London: Routledge, 1995); T. Newburn, *Criminology*, 3rd ed. (Abingdon/Oxon: Routledge, 2017), 256–261.

IV ON THE REACTION TO INTERNATIONAL CRIMES

International criminal courts are struggling with several problems. One of them is the long duration of the proceedings and that the judgement is handed out a long time after the crime, sometimes after decades. Another problem is the length of the sentences. Some of them can only be understood against the background of retributive theories of punishment. From the standpoint of preventive theories it is hard to understand why, for example, in *Krstić* the ICTY's Trial Chamber deemed it appropriate to impose a prison term of 46 years for aiding and abetting genocide that later was reduced to 35 years by the Appeals Chamber.

Mark A. Drumbl speaks of an 'erratic sentencing practice'.[57] To his mind, there is no 'cogent framework' or 'heuristic' on how to standardize the determination of a sentence. Judges are even said to be divided over the purpose of punishment. From a global perspective, there probably are very different ideas of what appropriate sentences look like and which duration of a sentence is appropriate. Article 78 of the ICC Statute is very short on the determination of the sentence.[58] According to it, the 'gravity of the crime' and 'the individual circumstances of the convicted person' are taken into account. Rule 145 of the Rules of Procedure and Evidence hardly bears a helping hand. Primarily, it names 'the culpability of the convicted person', then 'any mitigating and aggravating factors', and

> *inter alia* [. . .] the extent of the damage caused, in particular the harm caused to the victims and their families, the nature of the unlawful behaviour and the means employed to execute the crime; the degree of participation of the convicted person; the degree of intent; the circumstances of manner, time and location; and the age, education, social and economic condition of the convicted person.

It is common knowledge that the permanent ICC established in The Hague in 2002 has closed less than a dozen of cases so far. As of 1 December 2018, twenty-seven cases have been brought before the Court with verdicts in six cases: eight people have been convicted and two acquitted (with one case and five convictions for offences against the administration of justice). Most empirical studies have therefore dealt with the ICTY and the International Criminal Tribunal for Rwanda (ICTR). A recent analysis of all decisions issued by the ICTR found significant problems in its sentencing practice:

57 Drumbl, *Atrocity, Punishment and International Law*, 66.

58 Werle and Jeßberger, *Völkerstrafrecht*, 57.

most of them concerned omissions in the grounds for the judgement or were related to the violation of the ICTR Statute or fundamental procedural safeguards.[59] But things do not seem too bad, at least if we consider the results of a quantitative study conducted by a Dutch research team who applied a multiple regression analysis in order to study the extent to which selected factors predict sentence length in the sentencing practice of the ICTR and the ICTY.[60] As a result, the study suggested that similar patterns have emerged in the sentence practice. The conviction for genocide, the rank of the offender and the number of guilty counts appeared to be the strongest predictors.[61] Nonetheless, 'inconsistencies and disparities across cases' were identified (e.g. education or respected status were in some cases accepted as mitigating factors yet in others as aggravating factors) and, in general, the decisions seemed to be lacking 'transparency and clarity', for example by not indicating the weight assigned to individual sentencing factors and individual crimes in cases of multiple counts.[62]

A lack of transparency and clarity is harming international criminal justice. While it is crucial that justice is done, there cannot be justice without taking into account the individual culpability which has to be understood both as a limitation to punishment and as an indication of the degree of individual guilt. In this regard, international criminal justice needs to perform better by handing out persuasive judgements. Strangely enough, the ICC's Rules of Procedure and Evidence mainly mention 'the degree of participation' and 'the degree of intent' to distinguish different modes of participation and engagement. From a criminological point of view, it is not difficult to imagine many more factors, most of them mitigating: group pressure, the heat of the moment, alignment to frames, cognitive narrowing, group dynamics or group solidarity (particularly in combat). Some of them may represent situations of an inner conflict, situations to which the individual is drawn and from where there seems to be no way out, situations, however, that do not meet the legal requirements of a defence. It is striking how sometimes objective and subjective circumstances mismatch in international criminal law. The objective gravity of the crime may be very serious while the individual's culpability is

59 Cf. L. Babucke and K. Brettfeld, 'Probleme der Rechtsfolgengestaltung im Völkerstrafrecht: Eine kritische Analyse der Strafzumessungspraxis des ICTR in Ruanda' (2016) 99 *Monatsschrift für Kriminologie und Strafrechtsreform* 406.

60 Cf. B. Holá, C. Bijleveld and A. Smeulers, 'Consistency of International Sentencing: ICTY and ICTR Case Study' (2012) 9 *European Journal of Criminology* 539.

61 Cf. Holá, Bijleveld and Smeulers, 'Consistency of International Sentencing', 546–547.

62 B. Holá, 'Sentencing of International Crimes at the ICTY and ICTR: Consistency of Sentencing Case Law' (2012) 4 *Amsterdam Law Forum* 3, 14, 23.

diminished. That is why international criminal law provides such a broad range of sentencing. Yet it would be an asset to have a model of liability incorporated in the statutes or in the rules that systematically takes into consideration the degree of culpability.[63] On a vertical axis the individual's hierarchical position would be registered, for example as mayor or political leader, as superior, as chief in the chain of command, as a follower or bystander.[64] The horizontal axis would refer to the individual's discretional power: Has the individual acted voluntarily, on his or her own initiative, has he or she incited others or even exceeded given orders, and so on?

What the application of international criminal law needs is – roughly speaking – less selectivity and more well-founded judgements handing out shorter sentences where appropriate. The purpose of prevention would suffer no harm from that. In Chapter XXVII of his famous treatise 'On Crimes and Punishments', which is headed 'Of the Mildness of Punishments', Cesare Beccaria, the famous Italian philosopher and criminologist, stated in 1764:

> Crimes are more effectually prevented by the *certainty*, than the *severity* of punishment. Hence, in a magistrate the necessity of vigilance, and in a judge of implacability, which, that it may become an useful virtue, should be joined to a mild legislation. The certainty of a small punishment will make a stronger impression, than the fear of one more severe, if attended with the hopes of escaping [...].[65]

V CONCLUSION

Sure enough, from a criminological point of view, punishing the perpetrators of international crimes is an essential contribution to the prevention of future crimes. However, as formerly powerful political leaders normally do not display the deficits typical for the socialization of ordinary criminals, there are only a few starting points for offender rehabilitation programmes. They have to deal with the techniques of neutralization which helped the offender to suspend moral standards. The emphasis of punishment, however, will be put on incapacitation, by which the convicted is deprived of opportunities for

[63] On the culpability of the offender and its influence of the sentencing process, see the contribution by Gerhard Werle and Aziz Epik in Chapter 18.

[64] See Neubacher, *Kriminologische Grundlagen einer internationalen Strafgerichtsbarkeit*, 433; similarly, see Drumbl, *Atrocity, Punishment and International Law*, 25 who is differentiating 'conflict entrepreneurs' and 'leaders' from 'followers' and 'bystanders'.

[65] C. Beccaria, *On Crimes and Punishments* (A New Edition Corrected, Albany: W. C. Little & Co., 1872), 49 (emphasis in original).

offending.[66] If, beyond all this (offender treatment, incapacitation), the application of international law is supposed to deter potential perpetrators and to strengthen the faith of the legal community in the rule of law it will be necessary to enhance the risk of criminal prosecution substantially. Criminologically speaking, the deterrent effect of punishment will not be radiated from the type and severity of the (threatened) sanction but from the offender's estimation of how probable it is that he or she will be apprehended and sanctioned at all. From that, it is clear that for the sake of prevention extra-long sentences or life imprisonment are not required. International criminal justice needs to pay more attention to the problem of deterrence and its implications. Time is up for just claiming deterrence without bothering with authentic effects and scientific evidence. More efforts have to be made to increase the offenders' risk of being prosecuted and sentenced.

International criminal justice does not bear an overall responsibility. In fact, its competences (as well as resources!) are limited in terms of time and place. Furthermore, it is bound by the principle of complementarity and depends on state cooperation. Against this background, much has been achieved compared to the situation at the beginning of the 1990s when the ad hoc Tribunals were established. Yet, it has also been demonstrated that the administration of international criminal justice can be imperfect and agonisingly slow. The healing and restorative effects of justice in post-conflict situations take time, in some cases maybe a new generation. That is why it is even more important that scientists, judges and politicians alike recognize that justice and prevention cannot be achieved by criminal trials only. Causes of international crimes have to be tackled at all relevant levels. This includes, but is not limited to, outreach programmes that deliver the messages of international criminal justice to the communities affected.[67] It must not be overlooked that the perpetrator's socio-political environment was conducive to the crime. Without a change of attitudes in his or her community, the convicted will remain a 'hero' and the preventive effect is in danger. And finally, having in mind that international crimes typically originate from macro- and meso-level factors, justice also needs to be sought through conflict prevention, separation of powers, development[68] and capacity building; in other words, through a proactive peace politics.

[66] For a similar argument, see the contribution by Alex Whiting in Chapter 16.

[67] On the importance of outreach, see the contribution by Philipp Ambach in Chapter 20.

[68] On this, see Holling, *Internationaler Strafgerichtshof und Verbrechensprävention*, 160.

4

Punishment Rationales in International Criminal Jurisprudence

Two Readings of a Non-question

SERGEY VASILIEV*

The defendants who had been convicted were called after the recess to be sentenced. Standing there before us they behaved like men. I felt sick and miserable. We had seen them day-in day-out for a year. What right had I [. . .] I knew they deserved it.

Francis Biddle

'Why punish perpetrators of international crimes?' The answer to the question asked in the title of this volume may appear too self-evident for it to be seriously posed, unless the purpose is to provoke or polemicize. All the more so in the present times when policy debates and public rhetoric on accountability and redress for atrocities often short-circuit on international criminal justice institutions, which are typically presented as the ultimate machinery for enforcing international law against the gravest violations. An experimental and contingent enterprise in the early 1990s, international criminal justice derived its initial credit of moral authority from the stated ambition to improve on the Nuremberg and Tokyo precedents.[1] The project has since attained a substantial degree of acceptance and 'normalcy', if there is indeed such a thing when it comes to adjudication of crimes extraordinary in scope and gravity. Over the past two and a half decades, international criminal law has developed into a grandiose industry holding a considerable symbolic and political leverage and distinguished by a sophisticated institutional culture, normative and conceptual apparatus, and professional practices and routines. Although its track record and social impacts remain deeply contested, even increasingly so,

* The author is thankful to the editors for putting together this volume and for their encouragement, and to Immi Tallgren for her incisive feedback.

[1] Report of the International Tribunal for the Prosecution of Persons Responsible for Serious Violations of International Humanitarian Law Committed in the Territory of the Former Yugoslavia since 1991, UN Doc. A/49/342-S/1994/1007, 29 August 1994, paras. 3, 10, 54, 71, 190–198.

it has certainly got something – without implying enough – to show for all the financial and human capital investments. Scores of persons have been convicted by international and hybrid tribunals and sentenced to lengthy prison sentences for core crimes committed in the former Yugoslavia, Rwanda, Cambodia, Sierra Leone and some other African countries (yet, most problematically, not much anywhere else).

The mechanics of individual guilt and criminal punishment have become a default response to situations of humanitarian crisis and mass atrocity. Thus, whenever the question 'why punish?' is posed, the tables are quickly turned on those daring ask it: Why *not* punish? What else – let them go free? Yet, this answer does not truly engage with the question, and the tone of unassailable certainty hardly extinguishes it. The above quotation from the memoir of Justice Francis Biddle, the American judge at the Nuremberg International Military Tribunal (IMT), is paradigmatic.[2] It captures, in not so many words, the excruciating self-doubt, emotional discomfort, and moral anguish accompanying the act of punishment – the act which, one would expect, should be taken for granted, in particular in the case of someone found guilty of the most heinous crimes. Supposedly, today's international judge is struggling with the same cognitive dissonance of knowing that convicts must be punished while feeling uneasy about doing it to them. Like Justice Biddle, he or she will have qualms about his or her entitlement to punish and seek consolation in just deserts, deterrence and other justifications.

The debate on the goals of punishment is of respectable vintage in domestic criminal law philosophy and not new in international criminal law either. A short bibliographic survey also evinces that, if not entirely passé, it may well be past its heyday. Most of the key publications, with a few exceptions, date back to a decade or more ago.[3] The scholarly attention towards

[2] F. Biddle, *In Brief Authority* (New York: Doubleday, 1962) 476.

[3] W.A. Schabas, 'Sentencing by International Tribunals: A Human Rights Approach' (1997) 7 *Duke Journal of Comparative & International Law* 461; J.C. Nemitz, 'The Law of Sentencing in International Criminal Law: The Purposes of Sentencing and the Applicable Method for the Determination of the Sentence' (2001) 4 *Yearbook of International Humanitarian Law* 87; S. Beresford, 'Unshackling the Paper Tiger: The Sentencing Practices of the ad hoc International Criminal Tribunals for the Former Yugoslavia and Rwanda' (2001) 1 *International Criminal Law Review* 33; O.A. Olusanya, *Sentencing War Crimes and Crimes against Humanity under the International Criminal Tribunal for the Former Yugoslavia* (Groningen: Europa Law Publishing, 2005); M. Bagaric and J. Morss, 'International Sentencing Law: In Search of a Justification and Coherent Framework' (2006) 6 *International Criminal Law Review* 191; R.D. Sloane, 'Sentencing for the Crime of Crimes, The Evolving "Common Law" of Sentencing of the International Criminal Tribunal for Rwanda' (2007) 5 *Journal of International Criminal Justice* 713; M.B. Harmon and F. Gaynor, 'Ordinary Sentences for Extraordinary Crimes' (2007) 5 *Journal of International Criminal Justice* 683;

justifications of international criminal punishment has been scarce as of late. Prematurely so, it must be said, as international penology arguably has no coherent theory of punishment on offer that could help guide international courts or systematically critique their practice. The bulk of scholarship has been preoccupied with *how* convicts are to be punished, i.e. the determination of an appropriate sentence and weighing of different relevant factors in arriving at a just calculus. As the fundamental justifications of punishment in international criminal law have largely mirrored those in the domestic sphere, scholars have interrogated the analogy with domestic penal philosophy[4] and the applicability of the retributivist, deterrent and expressivist rationales to international criminal law.[5] While such critique is a stepping stone towards articulation of a punishment theory tailored to international criminal justice, a concerted rethink of the international penal philosophy is far from complete.

The present volume is a timely opportunity to reinvigorate this effort and take the debate to a new level, regardless of whether a coherent international punishment theory can be constructed, let alone made to bear upon the future sentencing practice. This chapter's contribution consists, firstly, in unveiling the functions of the punishment teleology in the jurisprudence of international and hybrid criminal courts; and, secondly, in analysing the tribunals' penological discourse on a meta-level. Why is it that those courts feel compelled to discuss punishment rationales over and over again in their judgments, and to say *why* they punish? The chapter posits that because the

M.A. Drumbl, *Atrocity, Punishment and International Law* (New York: Cambridge University Press, 2007); J.D. Ohlin, 'Towards a Unique Theory of International Criminal Sentencing' in G. Sluiter and S. Vasiliev (eds.), *International Criminal Procedure: Towards a Coherent Body of Law* (London: Cameron May, 2009); S. D'Ascoli, *Sentencing in International Criminal Law: The UN ad hoc Tribunals and Future Perspectives for the ICC* (Oxford: Hart, 2011).

4 On the domestic analogy (objection), see the contribution by Elies van Sliedregt in Chapter 5. See also, e.g., F. Harhoff, 'Sense and Sensibility in Sentencing – Taking Stock of International Criminal Punishment' in O. Engdahl and P. Wrange (eds.), *Laws at War – The Law as It Was and the Law as It Should Be* (Leiden: Brill, 2008) 123–134.

5 On validity of specific rationales, see, e.g., A.K.A. Greenawalt, 'International Criminal Law for Retributivists' (2014) 35 *University of Pennsylvania Journal of International Law* 969; J. Klabbers, 'Just Revenge? The Deterrence Argument in International Criminal Law' (2001) 12 *Finnish Yearbook of International Law* 249; J. Ku and J. Nzelibe, 'Do International Criminal Tribunals Deter or Exacerbate Humanitarian Atrocities?' (2006) 84 *Washington University Law Review* 777; H. Jo and B. Simmons, 'Can the International Criminal Court Deter Atrocity?' (2016) 70 *International Organization* 443; B. Wringe, 'Why Punish War Crimes? Victors Justice and Expressive Justifications of Punishment' (2006) 25 *Law and Philosophy* 159; R.D. Sloane, 'The Expressive Capacity of International Punishment: The Limits of the National Law Analogy and the Potential of International Criminal Law' (2007) 43 *Stanford Journal of International Law* 81.

criminal law framework imposes rigid constraints on the degree to which judges can engage with the 'why punish?' question, teleological ruminations in judgments represent speech acts by which courts preach international criminal law's founding articles of faith.

The chapter starts off by reflecting on the theoretical and practical relevance of the question 'why punish?' in international criminal justice. Section I sets forth the two readings of it, or two levels on which it can be answered. Section II presents statements on the aims of punishment by some international and hybrid courts as a way to trace the evolution of penal philosophy in judicial discourse. The ritualism, monotony and limited practical value of that discourse point to what courts actually do, as opposed to saying what they do, when meting out punishment. Section III puts this emphatic performativity in the judges' treatment of rationales in a methodological perspective, in particular the ongoing normative *v.* empirical tension in the discipline. For the courts, 'why punish?' can only be a non-question because treating it otherwise would have required them to overreach the belief system upon which the project is founded and which it is made to reinforce.

I WHAT'S IN THE QUESTION?

Before describing what different jurisdictions have said (or failed to say) about the goals of punishment, it is worth pausing on the meta-issue: the 'why' of 'why punish?' What is the importance of asking this question, and can doing so shed light on the ontology of the discipline? Is it consequential for the current configuration of international penal responses and the tribunals' *praxis*?

1 *Why Ask?*

The debate on justifications of international criminal punishment and the quest for the penal theory of international criminal law go back to the earliest instances of international prosecution. Before the notion of individual punishment for international crimes went mainstream through the institutionalization of international criminal justice, whether there is a point in punishing someone for the 'unimaginable atrocities' had been a genuine question. Can human punishment do justice to the extraordinary nature of such crimes and the ordinary set of penalties fit the bill? This query was famously articulated by Hannah Arendt in *The Origins of Totalitarianism*. The 'vastest, most improbable scale' on which Nazi crimes had been committed, she wrote, 'render[ed] all punishments provided by the legal system inadequate and absurd'. These were the 'crimes which men can neither punish nor forgive'.[6]

After the Nuremberg and Tokyo International Military Tribunals' trials concluded, reflection on punishment justifications continued as an academic exercise.[7] Paradoxically, not much changed with the advent of UN ad hoc Tribunals five decades later whose legal frameworks were conspicuously silent on the purposes of punishment.[8] With international criminal justice embedding itself firmly in the institutional landscape in the early 1990s, the fundamental debate on penal philosophy gained no traction in practice where it was treated in such a way as if it had long been settled. As Alexander K.A. Greenawalt observed, the international criminal law approach became over-determined (and simultaneously under-determined) by domestic penal theories.[9] Certainly, in this area of international criminal law, as in many others, practice shapes the agenda and theory is only secondary.[10] So here too, the limited demand for theory affected supply. The international criminal law scholarship has been more preoccupied with the question of 'how' rather than 'why'.[11]

Many writers have focused on consistency, proportionality and individualization in sentencing, using these principles to evaluate whether the punishments the tribunals meted out were appropriately harsh or otherwise.[12] Substantial research efforts – enriched by empirical approaches –, have been

[6] H. Arendt, *The Origins of Totalitarianism*, 3rd ed. (New York: Harcourt Brace & Company, 1973) 439 and 459 ('the unpunishable, unforgivable absolute evil which could no longer be understood and explained by the evil motives of self-interest, greed, covetousness, resentment, lust for power, and cowardice; and which therefore anger could not revenge, love could not endure, friendship could not forgive').

[7] E.g. F. Hassan, 'The Theoretical Basis of Punishment in International Criminal Law' (1983) 15 *Case Western Reserve Journal of International Law* 39, 48 et seq.

[8] ICTY Statute, Art. 24 and ICTR Statute, Art. 23.

[9] Greenawalt, 'International Criminal Law for Retributivists', 976–977.

[10] On the relationship between theory and practice, see also the contribution by Alex Whiting in Chapter 16.

[11] For notable exceptions, see I. Tallgren, 'The Sensibility and Sense of International Criminal Law' (2002) 13 *European Journal of International Law* 561; M.J. Osiel, 'Why Prosecute? Critics of Punishment for Mass Atrocity' (2000) 22 *Human Rights Quarterly* 118. The discipline of transitional justice arguably has a stronger track record of posing the 'why punish' question than the international criminal justice literature.

[12] A.M. Danner, 'Constructing a Hierarchy of Crimes in International Criminal Law Sentencing' (2001) 87 *Virginia Law Review* 415; M.M. DeGuzman, 'Harsh Justice for International Crimes?' (2014) 39 *Yale Journal of International Law* 1; J.D. Ohlin, 'Proportional Sentences at the ICTY' in B. Swart et al. (eds.), *The Legacy of the International Criminal Tribunal for the Former Yugoslavia* (Oxford: Oxford University Press, 2011); Harmon and Gaynor, 'Ordinary Sentences for Extraordinary Crimes', 711.

devoted to the putative inconsistency of sentencing across cases and across courts, with some scholars charging that it is irrational and unpredictable and others arguing that this problem is imaginary.[13] In face of this disagreement, scholars have advocated for greater transparency and clarity of sentencing determinations, in particular through developing guidelines.[14] Cross-tribunal – vertical as well as horizontal – inconsistency has mostly been regarded as problematic, although pluralism in sentencing also had its defenders.[15]

The sub-discipline of international sentencing still has a long way to go until 'a consistent and robust theory of international criminal punishment'[16] can be attained, despite notable efforts to that end.[17] Given the predominant emphasis on sentencing modalities, scholarship has fallen short of developing a normative theory of punishment uniquely suited to international criminal justice. Nor has it proffered a satisfactory conceptual framework that could help gauge and explain the importance of punishment teleology for the tribunals' sentencing practice.[18] In fact, key aspects of the international penal system have long gone presumed and under-theorized. Limited attention has been paid until most recently to the poorly designed regime for the

[13] Asserting that sentencing is inconsistent: e.g. Drumbl, *Atrocity, Punishment and International Law*, 6; U. Ewald, 'Predictably Irrational – International Sentencing and Its Discourse against the Backdrop of Preliminary Empirical Findings on ICTY Sentencing Practices' (2010) 10 *International Criminal Law Review* 365. Contesting this claim: e.g. J. Meernik and K.L. King, 'The Sentencing Determinants of the International Criminal Tribunal for the Former Yugoslavia: An Empirical and Doctrinal Analysis' (2003) 16 *Leiden Journal of International Law* 717; Harhoff, 'Sense and Sensibility in Sentencing', 134–135; J. Meernik, 'Sentencing Rationales and Judicial Decision Making at the International Tribunals' (2011) 92 *Social Science Quarterly* 588; B. Holá, A. Smeulers and C. Bijleveld, 'Is ICTY Sentencing Predictable? Empirical Analysis of ICTY Sentencing Practice' (2009) 22 *Leiden Journal of International Law* 79; B. Holá, C. Bijleveld and A. Smeulers, 'Consistency of International Sentencing: ICTY and ICTR Case Study' (2012) 9 *European Journal of Criminology* 539.

[14] E.g. B. Holá, 'Consistency and Pluralism of International Sentencing: An Empirical Assessment of the ICTY and ICTR Practice' in E. van Sliedregt and S. Vasiliev (eds.), *Pluralism in International Criminal Law* (Oxford: Oxford University Press, 2014); B. Holá, 'Sentencing of International Crimes at the ICTY and ICTR: Consistency of Sentencing Case Law' (2012) 4 *Amsterdam Law Forum* 3, 4. Cf. Harhoff, 'Sense and Sensibility in Sentencing', 139 (favouring more detailed explanations of sentencing outcomes but opposing the idea of binding guidelines).

[15] N. Combs, 'Seeking Inconsistency: Advancing Pluralism in International Criminal Sentencing' (2016) 41 *Yale Journal of International Law* 1; A.K.A. Greenawalt, 'Pluralism of International Criminal Law' (2012) 86 *Indiana Law Journal* 1063, 1125.

[16] See the Introduction by the editors.

[17] E.g. Ohlin, 'Towards a Unique Theory of International Sentencing'; Greenawalt, 'International Criminal Law for Retributivists'.

[18] For an outline of such a conceptual framework, see the contribution by Gerhard Werle and Aziz Epik in Chapter 18.

enforcement of sentences – an afterthought rather than an integral, carefully engineered part of the justice enterprise.[19] The same transpires from scholarly complacency with the unimaginative toolkit of penalties and continuous neglect in law and in practice of (additional) non-custodial sanctions such as fines and forfeitures.[20] The predominance of custodial punishment as a virtually exclusive penalty in international criminal law has not been seriously questioned, even though potential alternatives (for example, community service) may be more in sync with the objectives of international justice.[21]

These matters cannot be considered in isolation from the basic issue of rationales: 'how' is secondary to 'why'. What kinds of penalties are suited to the system, how they are to be determined in individual cases, where and how they are to be served, are but a few questions that cannot be answered without clarifying the reasons for imposing punishment and the objectives it is meant to achieve in the first place. Any reformist agenda to optimize the penal regime and perfect practice would lack conceptual grounding so long as the issue of penal objectives is circumvented. It is not this chapter's objective to provide such grounding, much less settle the teleological debates; instead, it is to examine the treatment this question has received in jurisprudence. Accordingly, the next paragraph highlights the two readings of 'why?' which will serve as analytical lenses in the following survey of judicial approaches. This binocular vision enhances the understanding of how judges have dealt with the query and the parameters of their discourse on the subject.

2 *Two Readings*

There are at least two layers to 'why punish?' and two ways of asking it, giving rise to different issues. It is instructive to see whether and how these have been

[19] On the normative and practical problems raised by the fragmented sentence enforcement regime, see R. Mulgrew, *Towards the Development of the International Penal System* (Cambridge: Cambridge University Press, 2013); D. Abels, *Prisoners of the International Community: The Legal Position of Persons Detained at International Criminal Tribunals* (The Hague: T.M.C. Asser Press, 2012).

[20] ICTY Statute, Art. 24(1) and ICTR Statute, Art. 23(1) ('The penalty imposed by the Trial Chamber shall be limited to imprisonment.'). But cf. ICC Statute, Art. 77(2) and ICC, Decision on Sentence pursuant to Article 76 of the Statute of 22 March 2017 (TC), *Bemba et al. (Bemba II)*, ICC-01/05-01/13-2123-Corr 22-03-2017, p. 99 (imposing fines on Kilolo and Bemba). M.G. Martínez, 'Forfeiture of Assets at the International Criminal Court: The Short Arm of International Criminal Justice' (2014) 12 *Journal of International Criminal Justice* 193.

[21] On the problematic 'quasi-monopoly' of incarceration, see M.A. Drumbl, 'International Punishment from "Other" Perspectives' in R. Mulgrew and D. Abels (eds.), *Research Handbook on International Penal System* (Cheltenham: Edward Elgar, 2016) 383–385.

taken up by the judges. One cannot presume that the tribunals would be equally prepared to attend to both aspects.

The accent on *why* in 'why punish?' prods one to look at theories justifying the act of punishment without questioning the presumed need for it. This reading has been influential in the mainstream literature, interrogating the validity of domestic analogies in respect of penological rationales. The debate on international penalties has been obsessed with the issue of importability into international criminal law of traditional retributivist and utilitarian considerations (deterrence, retribution, rehabilitation and incapacitation) and expressivism-based rationales (stigmatization, denunciation, engraining rule of law, etc.). Each of these theories has its defenders and critics. There are wide-ranging views on which of the penological justifications is more compelling for international criminal justice, considering the special nature of the crimes and of the offenders.

The intonational emphasis on *punish* ('why *punish?*') puts a dent in the very idea that punishment is an appropriate response. It is another way of asking whether a convict must indeed be punished through criminal law, rather than, say, summarily executed or have inflicted a type of harm Winston Churchill had in mind for the Nazi leaders.[22] This opens up yet other avenues: convicts could be forgiven, amnestied or pardoned, required to submit themselves to a truth and reconciliation process, traditional justice mechanism, etc. Insofar as this reading asks whether criminal guilt must have punishment as a consequence, it effectively displaces an assumption that it must – the orthodoxy that has seldom been questioned, in the past or nowadays.[23]

Unlike the first reading, the second is nothing short of a radical challenge to the international *criminal* justice enterprise as a whole. The institute of punishment is so central to the criminal law that the question 'why *punish*?' is equivalent to 'why *criminal law*?' The liberal criminal justice paradigm is inflexible. Whether it recognizes retributivist or utilitarian justifications, or both to an extent, it admits to no alternative ways of dealing with crime falling short of punishment. It is suspicious of penalties straying from the

[22] G.J. Simpson, *Law, War and Crime: War Crimes, Trials and the Reinvention of International Law* (Cambridge: Polity Press, 2007), 21 (Churchill's proposal was to have the captured Nazi leaders castrated).

[23] E.g. K. Jaspers, *The Question of German Guilt* (translation E.B. Ashton) (New York: Fordham University Press, 2000), 30 ('Crime meets with *punishment*.'); N. Bernaz, 'Sentencing and Penalties' in W.A. Schabas and N. Bernaz (eds.), *Routledge Handbook of International Criminal Law* (London: Routledge, 2011), 289 ('The imprisonment of these criminals seems to be an almost natural way of addressing the public's indignation towards their crimes and, arguably, it provides the surviving victims with some form of closure and a sense of justice.').

conventional forms. Serious crimes should entail custodial sentences, possibly combined with other sanctions while more lenient measures would be found wanting because they are neither proportionate to the gravity of the crime nor an adequate deterrent.

The mentality of suspicion towards non-punitive responses is built in international criminal law. One paradigmatic example is the ICC Prosecutor's misgivings about Colombia's Legal Framework for Peace as part of the draft Peace Accord. In 2013, the Office of the Prosecutor communicated to the Colombian government its considerations about the possibility of suspended, alternative or reduced sentences for the Fuerzas Armadas Revolucionarias de Columbia (FARC) members. In the Office's view, suspended sentences would fall short of effective penal sanctions[24] and fail the complementarity test of a genuine effort to bring perpetrators to justice.[25] More recently, the ICC Appeals Chamber ruled in the *Bemba II* case that a conditionally suspended sentence is not a penalty available under the ICC legislation and cannot be imposed by the Trial Chamber exercising an 'inherent power'.[26]

The out-of-box reading of 'why *punish?*' is more likely to provoke serious consideration in the formative stages such as in the lead up to Nuremberg. This is when the powers-that-be – parties prevailing in a conflict or members of a new regime emerging from a political transition – are facing the choice between submitting the vanquished or ousted opponents to a criminal law process, non-punitive transitional justice measures, and doing nothing of that kind. Sometimes the former option is favoured, other times not, and on occasions no choice can be made at all. In the recent years, international criminal justice finds itself at an existential crossroads. The project has been facing a legitimacy crisis and increasingly confronted with an array of fundamental critiques.[27] One complaint is the imposition of a historically,

[24] J. Stewart, 'Transitional Justice in Colombia and the Role of the International Criminal Court', 13 May 2015, Bogota, Colombia, p. 11: 'Suspending sentences for those most responsible for war crimes and crimes against humanity would amount to shielding the persons concerned from criminal responsibility. It could also suggest that proceedings were conducted in a manner that was inconsistent with an intent to bring the persons concerned to justice.'

[25] Statement of ICC Prosecutor, Fatou Bensouda, on the conclusion of the peace negotiations between the Government of Colombia and the Revolutionary Armed Forces of Colombia – People's Army, 1 September 2016: 'The paramount importance of genuine accountability – which by definition includes effective punishment – in nurturing a sustainable peace cannot be overstated.'

[26] ICC, Judgment of 8 March 2018 (AC), *Bemba et al. (Bemba II)*, ICC-01/05-01/13-2276-Red, paras. 3, 73–80 (striking down as *ultra vires* the suspended sentences for Mangenda and Kilolo).

[27] In more detail, S. Vasiliev, 'The Crises and Critiques of International Criminal Justice' in K.J. Heller et al. (eds.), *Oxford Handbook of International Criminal Law* (Oxford: Oxford University Press, 2020).

conceptually and culturally narrow notion of justice which is represented matter-of-factly as 'international' in the sense of 'global' or 'universal'.[28] Calls for loosening and transcending the limited punitive paradigm through pluralization of institutional and cultural responses to mass atrocity situations represent a pushback against the hegemonic construction of international criminal law as a liberal criminal justice system. The obnoxious rendition of 'why *punish?*' has therefore become ever more pressing.

At this juncture, it is time to turn to judicial statements on punishment rationales in international and hybrid criminal courts. Penological discourse in sentencing judgments reveals judges' adherence to specific penal philosophies, and how different chambers have made use of them. The next section inventories justifications of international punishment in jurisprudence and notes the features of judicial discourse going to the dual aspect of the 'why punish' question.

II WHAT COURTS SAY: RATIONALES IN CASE LAW

1 *Nuremberg and Tokyo International Military Tribunals*

The London and Tokyo Charters each endowed the respective Tribunal with a 'right' (IMT) and a 'power' (International Military Tribunal for the Far East (IMTFE)) to impose upon convicts 'death or such other punishment as shall be *determined by it to be just*'.[29] This may be taken as alluding to the retributivist rationale of 'just deserts' as the primary penal justification.[30] The IMT and IMTFE sentencing rulings were remarkably short and did no more than list individual sentences, without clarifying the goals pursued or the reasons for the specific penalties.[31] Out of nineteen Nuremberg convicts, twelve were sent to the gallows, three got life imprisonment, and four definite prison terms; in Tokyo, out of twenty-five defendants, seven were sentenced to death, sixteen to life imprisonment, and only two to definite terms in prison.

28 S.M.H. Nouwen and W.G. Werner, 'Monopolising Global Justice: International Criminal Law as Challenge to Human Diversity' (2015) 13 *Journal of International Criminal Justice* 157.

29 IMT Charter, Art. 27; IMTFE Charter, Art. 16.

30 See also N. Boister and R. Cryer, *The Tokyo International Military Tribunal: A Reappraisal* (Oxford: Oxford University Press, 2008), 247.

31 'Sentences' in *Trial of the Major War Criminals before the International Military Tribunal, Nuremberg 14 October 1945 – 1 October 1946*, Vol. I (Nuremberg: International Military Tribunal, 1947), 365–367; 'Majority Judgment' in N. Boister and R. Cryer (eds.), *Documents on the Tokyo International Military Tribunal: Charter, Indictment and Judgments* (Oxford: Oxford University Press, 2008), 626–628 [49, 854] (simply pronouncing the sentences for each of the twenty-five accused: either death by hanging or life imprisonment).

Three IMT accused (Hans Fritzsche, Franz von Papen and Hjalmar Schacht) were acquitted, but there were no acquittals in Tokyo.[32]

The IMT judges' penological views could in part be inferred from the inconclusive *obiter dictum* dismissing the *nullum crimen* challenge against the charge of the crimes against peace:[33]

> To assert that it is unjust to punish those who in defiance of treaties and assurances have attacked neighboring states without warning is obviously untrue, for in such circumstances the attacker must know that he is doing wrong, and so far from it being unjust to punish him, it would be unjust if his wrong were allowed to go unpunished.[34] [...] Crimes against international law are committed by men, not by abstract entities, – and only by punishing individuals who commit such crimes can the provisions of international law be enforced.[35]

These *dicta* hint to the penological approach informed by negative deontic retributivism that sees punishment as an inexorable and just consequence of the crime.[36] The convicted Nazi leaders *had* to be punished – not necessarily because of the intrinsic virtuousness of punishment as a response to criminal wrongdoing, but rather because *not* punishing them was not affordable. It would have been unjust and it would have frustrated the enforcement of international law.

The IMTFE judgment omitted to address punishment goals and to clarify how these impacted the sentences. In fact, the penalties were subject of heated debates during deliberations.[37] In acknowledging fundamental differences, individual judges elaborated on the matter in their separate opinions.[38]

[32] Concluding that the IMT and IMTFE sentencing policies were not at great variance, see Boister and Cryer, The Tokyo International Military Tribunal, 253; cf. R.H. Minear, *Victor's Justice: The Tokyo War Crimes Trial* (Princeton: Princeton UP, 1971), 31 fn. 24 (claiming that the Tokyo IMT sentencing was harsher).

[33] The discussion of the *nullum crimen* challenge to war crimes and crimes against humanity charges was even more curt and reticent on underlying penal philosophy. Referring to articles of the 1907 Hague Convention and the 1929 Geneva Convention as the bases for the criminalization of the respective conduct, the IMT held bluntly: 'that violation of these provisions constituted crimes for which the guilty individuals were punishable is too well settled to admit of argument': 'Judgment' in *Trial of the Major War Criminals before the IMT*, Vol. I, 253.

[34] 'Judgment' in *Trial of the Major War Criminals before the IMT*, Vol. I, 219.

[35] 'Judgment' in *Trial of the Major War Criminals before the IMT*, Vol. I, 223.

[36] A.A. Haque, 'Retributivism: The Right and the Good' (2013) 32 *Law and Philosophy* 59.

[37] Boister and Cryer, *The Tokyo International Military Tribunal*, 254.

[38] Separate dissenting opinions of Judges Bernard (France) and Pal (India) departed from the majority judgment in part of the verdicts and did not squarely address punishment and sentences. The dissent of Judge Röling (Netherlands), who would have acquitted Hata, Hirota,

Notably, the opinion of Sir Justice William Webb, the President of the Tribunal, contains pertinent observations. He regarded general deterrence as the principal justification – the view not fully in tune with convictions of his brothers in the majority – and he strongly opposed capital punishment.[39] The IMTFE President took the sentencing approach of the Nuremberg Tribunal as a point of reference and flagged what to him was a contradiction. Despite pronouncing the crime of aggression to be 'the supreme international crime', the IMT 'proceeded to impose life sentences and less on accused found guilty not merely of conspiring to wage, and planning and waging wars of aggression but also of war crimes and crimes against humanity; whereas an accused found guilty simply of crimes against humanity was sentenced to death by hanging.'[40]

Justice Webb suggested that the explanation for this incongruity was that in not imposing death sentences on the defendants found guilty on Count 1, the IMT 'took into account the fact that aggressive war was not universally regarded as a justiciable crime when they made war'.[41] Since the crimes of the Nuremberg defendants were 'far more heinous, varied and extensive than those of the Japanese accused', he posited, the latter were to be treated with no less consideration than the Germans. This led Justice Webb to conclude that 'none of the Japanese accused should be sentenced to death for conspiring to wage, or planning and preparing, or initiating, or waging aggressive war'. With respect to crimes against humanity and war crimes, his view was that deterrence to others was 'universally acknowledged [as] the main purpose of punishment', and that life imprisonment 'under sustained conditions of hardship in an isolated place or places outside of Japan' would have been a 'greater deterrent to men like the accused' than 'the speedy termination of existence on the scaffold or before a firing squad'.[42] Despite expressing his disagreement

Kido, Shigemitsu and Togo and convicted and sentenced some of the others differently than the majority did, gave no insight into his penal philosophy. See 'Opinion of Member for the Netherlands (Mr. Justice Röling)' in Boister and Cryer, *Documents on the Tokyo IMT*, 775 [178].

39 Boister and Cryer, *The Tokyo International Military Tribunal*, 255 (explaining this attitude by his concern about the validity of convictions and by his devout Catholic concern with mercy).

40 'U.S.A. and Others v. Araki and Others. Separate Opinion of the President' in Boister and Cryer, *Documents on the Tokyo IMT*, 637 [15], referring to Dönitz (10 years' imprisonment), Von Neurath (15 years' imprisonment) and Raeder (life imprisonment).

41 'Separate Opinion of the President' in Boister and Cryer, *Documents on the Tokyo IMT*, 638 [17] ('Many international lawyers of standing still take the view that in this regard the Pact of Paris made no difference.').

42 'Separate Opinion of the President' in Boister and Cryer, *Documents on the Tokyo IMT*, 638 [17] (also referring to the senior age of some of the accused: 'It may prove revolting to hang or shoot such old men.')

with some of the sentences handed down by the majority and doubt that they were 'most likely to achieve the main purpose of punishment', Justice Webb did not record dissent in this regard as he did not regard those penalties to be manifestly excessive or inadequate.[43] In the dissenting camp, Justice Röling pronounced in a similar vein on non-applicability of death penalty to those convicted of a crime against peace alone. But he was not as opposed to the supreme penalty as the President, and he considered it appropriate where the convicts had also been found guilty of conventional war crimes.[44]

In his separate concurring opinion, Justice Jaranilla of the Philippines regarded some of the penalties as 'too lenient, not exemplary and deterrent, and not commensurate with the gravity of the offense or offenses committed'.[45] He lamented that those sentences might be seen as 'weakness and failure', given that '[t]here can be and there is no comparison between national crimes and those monstrous international crimes against peace, war crimes and crimes against humanity which are against all mankind and which should [...] transcend national considerations if civilization is, as it should, survive.' That said, Justice Jaranilla did not rule out the entitlement of the defendants who were incurably ill, to 'such leniency as human conscience may permit'.[46] While he appeared to accept both retribution and deterrence as valid justifications, the particular gravity and even monstrosity of the crime against peace to him required harsher penalties regardless of any instrumentalist considerations. Judge Jaranilla's position therefore aligned more closely with retributivist philosophy tacitly espoused by the majority.

2 *UN ad hoc Tribunals*

The UN ad hoc Tribunals left behind a prolific legacy of sentencing jurisprudence. Unlike their predecessors, both the ICTY and ICTR almost invariably

43 'Separate Opinion of the President' in Boister and Cryer, *Documents on the Tokyo IMT*, 639 [21].

44 'Opinion of Member for the Netherlands (Mr. Justice Röling)', in Boister and Cryer, *Documents on the Tokyo IMT*, 775 [178] ('no one should be sentenced to death for having committed a crime against peace. Internment for life is, at this state, the appropriate punishment for this crime. [...] [Those who] should have been guilty of conventional war crimes, [...] should have been punished with the supreme penalty.').

45 'Concurring Opinion by the Honorable Mr. Justice Delfin Jaranilla, Member from the Republic of the Philippines' in Boister and Cryer, *Documents on the Tokyo IMT*, 659 [34].

46 'Concurring Opinion by the Honorable Mr. Justice Delfin Jaranilla' in Boister and Cryer, *Documents on the Tokyo IMT*, 659 [35].

included dedicated paragraphs on penal rationales in their sentencing rulings.[47] This discussion typically constituted one of the four layers of analysis that fed into sentencing determinations. The other three, from the general to the particular, were: (i) sentencing principles applicable across all cases (individualization, proportionality and consistency); (ii) general practice regarding prison sentences in the former Yugoslavia and Rwanda respectively; and (iii) case-specific factors of gravity and individual circumstances going to aggravation or mitigation. The latter two were mandatory for consideration as per statutes.[48] The penal teleology rests on the apex of this framework, being the most abstract of the sentencing determinants.

On average, the more frequently mentioned rationales were: (i) general and special deterrence; (ii) retribution; (iii) public reprobation, condemnation and stigmatization by the international community; and (iv) rehabilitation. The list was fluctuating over time and varied across chambers.[49] Some earlier judgments only mentioned retribution and deterrence,[50] or deterrence and reconciliation,[51] while others added rehabilitation and further aims.[52] Notably, the invocation of these goals was routinely justified with reference to the

47 Exceptions were rare: ICTY, Sentencing Judgment of 13 November 2001 (TC), *Sikirica et al.*, IT-95-8-S; ICTY, Judgment of 2 August 2001 (TC), *Krstić*, IT-98–33; ICTR, Judgment and Sentence of 25 February 2004 (TC), *Ntagerura et al.*, ICTR-99-46-T; ICTR, Judgment and Sentence of 28 April 2005 (TC), *Muhimana*, ICTR-95-1B-T, paras. 588–589; MICT, Judgment of 11 April 2018 (AC), *Šešelj*, MICT-16-99-A, para. 179.

48 ICTY Statute, Art. 24(1) and (2); ICTR Statute, Art. 23(1) and (2).

49 Noting the diversity of nomenclature, Holá, 'Sentencing of International Crimes at the ICTY and ICTR', 6.

50 ICTR, Judgment and Sentence of 4 September 1998 (TC), *Kambanda*, ICTR-97-23-S, para. 28; ICTR, Sentence of 2 October 1998 (TC), *Akayesu*, ICTR-96-4-T, para. 19; ICTR, Sentence of 5 February 1999 (TC), *Serushago*, ICTR-98-39-S, para. 20.

51 ICTR, Judgment and Sentence of 1 December 2003 (TC), *Kajelijeli*, ICTR-98-44A, para. 945; ICTR, Judgment of 17 June 2004 (TC), *Gacumbitsi*, ICTR-2001-64-T, paras. 335–336; ICTR, Judgment of 22 January 2004, *Kamuhanda*, ICTR-99-54A-T, paras. 753–755.

52 ICTR, Sentence of 21 May 1999 (TC), *Kayishema and Ruzindana*, ICTR-95-1-T, para. 2 (retribution, deterrence, rehabilitation, and the protection of society); ICTY, Sentencing Judgment of 10 December 2003 (AC), *Obrenović*, IT-02-60/2-S, para. 49 (retribution, deterrence and rehabilitation); ICTR, Sentencing Judgment of 16 November 2007, *Rugambarara*, ICTR-00-59-T, para. 11 (referring to deterrence, retribution and rehabilitation as 'relevant principles considered by the Chamber when imposing a sentence'). A string of appellate judgments specified 'individual and general affirmative prevention' separately from 'individual and general deterrence' as well as 'reprobation': ICTY, Judgment of 29 July 2004 (AC), *Blaškić*, IT-95-14-A, para. 678; ICTY, Judgment of 17 December 2004 (AC), *Kordić and Čerkez*, IT-95-14/2-A, para. 1073; ICTY, Judgment of 17 March 2009 (AC), *Krajišnik*, IT-00-39-A, para. 802.

object and purpose of establishing the ad hoc Tribunals.[53] The objectives of deterrence and combatting impunity were put on an equal footing with promoting reconciliation, discovery of truth, and the restoration and maintenance of peace.[54]

Chambers interpreted specific rationales in ways broadly corresponding to domestic theories, albeit with occasional deviations. In a number of cases, the ICTY contrasted retribution to vengeance and, falling back on the familiar notion of 'just deserts', underlined that retribution implies 'a just and appropriate punishment, and nothing more'.[55] The deterrent function of punishment, consisting of the discouragement from the commission of similar crimes in the future, was couched in the dual terms of general and special deterrence meant to deter unidentified potential offenders and turn the punished individual from reoffending, respectively.[56] The expressivist

[53] See judgments referenced in note 50; ICTY, Sentencing Judgment of 29 November 1996 (TC), *Erdemović*, IT-96-22-T ('*Erdemović* I Sentencing Judgment'), paras. 57–58 ('The International Tribunal's objectives as seen by the Security Council – i.e. general prevention (or deterrence), reprobation, retribution (or "just deserts"), as well as collective reconciliation – fit into the Security Council's broader aim of maintaining peace and security in the former Yugoslavia. These purposes and functions of the International Tribunal as set out by the Security Council may provide guidance in determining the punishment for a crime against humanity.'); ICTR, *Serushago* Sentence, para. 19; ICTY, Sentencing Judgment of 11 November 1999 (TC), *Tadić*, IT-94-1-Tbis-R117 ('*Tadić* II Sentencing Judgment'), para. 7.

[54] ICTY, Judgment of 10 December 1998 (TC), *Furundžija*, IT-95-17/1-T, para. 288; ICTY, *Tadić* II Sentencing Judgment, para. 7; ICTY, Sentencing Judgment of 5 March 1998 (TC), *Erdemović*, IT-96-22-T*bis* ('*Erdemović* II Sentencing Judgment'), para. 21 (referring to the duty 'to contribute to the settlement of the wider issues of accountability, reconciliation and establishing the truth behind the evils perpetrated in the former Yugoslavia. Discovering the truth is a cornerstone of the rule of law and a fundamental step on the way to reconciliation: for it is the truth that cleanses the ethnic and religious hatreds and begins the healing process.').

[55] ICTY, *Erdemović* I Sentencing Judgment, para. 65 ('The Trial Chamber also adopts retribution, or "just deserts", as legitimate grounds for pronouncing a sentence for crimes against humanity, the punishment having to be proportional to the gravity of the crime and the guilt of the accused.'); ICTY, *Kordić and Čerkez* Appeal Judgment, para. 1075 ('retribution should not be misunderstood as a way of expressing revenge or vengeance'); ICTY, *Krajišnik* Appeal Judgment, paras. 775 and 804; ICTY, Judgment of 24 March 2000 (AC), *Aleksovski*, IT-95-14/1-A, para. 185 ('not to be understood as fulfilling a desire for revenge but as duly expressing the outrage of the international community at these crimes'); ICTY, Judgment of 26 February 2009 (TC), *Šainović et al.*, IT-05-87-T, Vol. 3 para. 1145; ICTY, Judgment of 24 March 2016 (TC), *Karadžić*, IT-95-5/18-T, para. 6026.

[56] ICTY, Judgment of 10 December 1998 (TC), *Furundžija*, IT-95-17/1-T, para. 288 ('It is not only right that *punitur quia peccatur* (the individual must be punished because he broke the law) but also *punitur ne peccatur* (he must be punished so that he and others will no longer break the law). The Trial Chamber accepts that two important functions of the punishment are retribution and deterrence.'); ICTY, *Tadić* II Sentencing Judgment, para. 7; ICTY, *Blaškić* Appeal Judgment, para. 678 fn. 1420; ICTY, Sentencing Judgment of 18 March 2004 (TC), *Jokić*, IT-01-42/1-S, para. 33; ICTY, Sentencing Judgment of 11 March 2004 (TC), *Češić*, IT-95-

objectives of 'stigmatisation', 'reprobation' and promoting the culture of respect for the rule of law have also received recognition.[57] Oddly, however, some judgments failed to distinguish these objectives as autonomous, presenting them instead as mere aspects or corollaries of retribution.[58] Likewise, some chambers subsumed expressivism-based rationales within general deterrence.[59] From the domestic doctrinal angle, this is a peculiar

10/1-S, para. 25; ICTY, *Kordić and Čerkez* Appeal Judgment, paras. 1076–1078; ICTY, Sentencing Judgment of 29 June 2004 (TC), *Babić*, IT-03-72-S, para. 45; ICTY, *Krajišnik* Appeal Judgment, paras. 776 and 804; ICTY, *Šainović et al.* Trial Judgment, para. 1146; ICTY, *Karadžić* Trial Judgment, para. 6026.

57 ICTY, *Erdemović* I Sentencing Judgment, paras. 64 ('One of the purposes of punishment for a crime against humanity lies precisely in stigmatising criminal conduct which has infringed a value fundamental not merely to a given society, but to humanity as a whole.') and 65 ('the International Tribunal sees public reprobation and stigmatisation by the international community, which would thereby express its indignation over heinous crimes and denounce the perpetrators, as one of the essential functions of a prison sentence for a crime against humanity'.); ICTY, *Obrenović* Sentencing Judgment, para. 51 ('It is hoped that the Tribunal and other international courts are bringing about the development of a culture of respect for the rule of law and thereby deterring the commission of crimes.').

58 ICTY, *Aleksovski* Appeal Judgment, para. 185 ('a sentence … should make plain the condemnation of the international community of the behaviour in question and show "that the international community was not ready to tolerate serious violations of international humanitarian law and human rights"'. Footnotes omitted); ICTY, *Češić* Sentencing Judgment, para. 23 ('penalty thus conveys the indignation of humanity for the serious violations of international humanitarian law for which an accused was found guilty'); ICTY, *Obrenović* Sentencing Judgment, para. 50 ('retribution is understood as the expression of condemnation and outrage of the international community at such grave violations of, and disregard for, fundamental human rights at a time when people may be at their most vulnerable, namely during armed conflict'.); ICTY, *Jokić* Sentencing Judgment, para. 31 ('As a form of retribution, punishment expresses society's condemnation of the criminal act and of the person who committed it and should be proportional to the seriousness of the crimes. The Tribunal's punishment thus conveys the indignation of humanity for the serious violations of international humanitarian law for which an accused was found guilty.'); ICTY, *Blaškić* Appeal Judgment, para. 678 fn.1421 ('Retribution and public reprobation and stigmatisation by the international community are similar purposes in the context of punishing crimes.'); ICTY, *Šainović et al.* Trial Judgment, para. 1145 ('As a form of retribution, the sentence serves as condemnation by the international community of the crimes committed'); ICTY, *Karadžić* Trial Judgment, para. 6026 ('Retribution is not to be interpreted as desire for revenge or vengeance but as an expression of the outrage of the international community at the crimes committed').

59 ICTR, *Kayishema and Ruzindana* Trial Sentence, para. 2 ('As to deterrence, this Chamber seeks to dissuade for good those who will be tempted in the future to perpetrate such atrocities by showing them that the international community is no longer willing to tolerate serious violations of international humanitarian law and human rights.'); ICTY, *Babić* Sentencing Judgment, para. 45 ('With regard to general deterrence, imposing a punishment serves to strengthen the legal order in which the type of conduct involved is defined as criminal, and to reassure society of the effectiveness of its penal provisions.'); ICTY, *Blaškić* Appeal Judgment, para. 678 fn. 1420.

understanding of expressivism, and of retribution and deterrence for that matter, given the conflation of distinct rationales.

Furthermore, the unwieldy formula commingling prevention and didacticism was employed at times to refer to what was presented as a separate justification: 'individual and general affirmative prevention aimed at influencing the legal awareness of the accused, the victims, their relatives, the witnesses, and the general public in order to reassure them that the legal system is being implemented and enforced'.[60] As follows from the Appeals Chamber's reading, this 'affirmative prevention' rationale has a strong association with 'reprobation' or 'stigmatisation' and its content is as close as it gets to expressivism.[61] The *Kordić and Čerkez* appeal judgment pointed out the special importance of 'affirmative prevention' as the sentencing purpose in international criminal law in light of the 'the comparatively short history of international adjudication of serious violations of international humanitarian and human rights law':

> The unfortunate legacy of wars shows that until today many perpetrators believe that violations of binding international norms can be lawfully committed, because they are fighting for a 'just cause'. Those people have to understand that international law is applicable to everybody, in particular during times of war. Thus, the sentences rendered by the International Tribunal have to demonstrate the fallacy of the old Roman principle of *inter arma silent leges* (amid the arms of war the laws are silent) in relation to the crimes under the International Tribunal's jurisdiction.[62]

This rhetorical emphasis did not reverse the prominence of retributivism, with its focus on individualization and proportionality, in favour of

60 See appeal judgments referenced in fn. 52; ICTY, Judgment of 14 January 2000 (TC), *Kupreškić et al.*, IT-95-16-T, para. 848:

> another relevant sentencing purpose is to show the people of not only the former Yugoslavia, but of the world in general, that there is no impunity for these types of crimes. This should be done in order to strengthen the resolve of all involved not to allow crimes against international humanitarian law to be committed as well as to create trust in and respect for the developing system of international justice.

61 ICTY, *Krajišnik* Appeal Judgment, paras. 802 and 807 ('The educational function of a sentence imposed by the Tribunal aims at conveying the message that rules of humanitarian international law have to be obeyed under all circumstances, and in doing so, the sentence seeks to internalise these rules and the moral demands they are based on in the minds of the public.'); ICTY, *Kordić and Čerkez* Appeal Judgment, paras. 1081 ('stigmatising the offender's conduct and ending impunity serve the same goal pursued by affirmative general prevention: to reassure the public that the legal system has been upheld and to influence the public not to violate this legal system'.).

62 ICTY, *Kordić and Čerkez* Appeal Judgment, para. 1082.

instrumentalism, be it education in the rule of law or deterrence.[63] That said, expressivism emerged in segments of sentencing case law as a kind of ultimate, catch-all objective.[64]

The weight to be accorded to various punishment objectives became subject of judicial dialogue as judges attempted ranking amongst them. A plethora of cases recognized the primacy of two traditional rationales: retribution and deterrence.[65] Initially, some Trial Chambers – for instance, in the *Čelebići* case – posited that deterrence is the prevalent rationale.[66] The Appeals Chamber accepted the importance of general deterrence but took issue with such a categorical prioritization. It repeatedly stated that deterrence 'must not be accorded undue prominence in the overall assessment of the sentences to be imposed'.[67] All in all, the jurisprudence reaffirmed equal importance of retribution and deterrence without drawing a clear hierarchy.[68]

63 ICTY, *Obrenović* Sentencing Judgment, para. 52 ('One may ask whether the individuals who are called before this Tribunal as accused are simply an instrument through which to achieve the goal of the establishment of the rule of law. The answer is no.').

64 ICTY, *Obrenović* Sentencing Judgment, para. 54 ('In conclusion, the Trial Chamber endorses these principles of punishment that readily lend themselves to promoting the rule of law and the realisation that violations thereof will not be tolerated.').

65 ICTY, Judgment of 20 February 2001 (AC), *Delalić et al.*, IT-96-21-A, 20 February 2001, para. 806; ICTY, *Kordić and Čerkez* Appeal Judgment, para. 1074; ICTY, Judgment on Sentencing Appeal of 20 July 2005 (AC), *Deronjić*, IT-02-61-S, paras. 136–137; ICTY, Judgment of 22 March 2006 (AC), *Stakić*, IT-97-24-A, para. 402; ICTY, *Deronjić* Sentencing Appeal Judgment, para. 136; ICTY, *Krajišnik* Appeal Judgment, para. 775; ICTR, Judgment of 28 November 2007 (AC), *Nahimana et al.*, ICTR-99-52-A, para. 1057; ICTY, *Karadžić* Trial Judgment, para. 6025.

66 ICTY, Judgment of 16 November 1998 (TC), *Delalic et al.*, IT-96-21-T, paras. 1231 and 1234 ('Retributive punishment by itself does not bring justice'; 'Deterrence is probably the most important factor in the assessment of appropriate sentences for violations of international humanitarian law.'); ICTY, *Tadić* II Sentencing Judgment, para. 7.

67 ICTY, Judgment in Sentencing Appeals of 26 January 2000 (AC), *Tadić*, IT-94-1-A and IT-94-1-Abis, para. 48; ICTY, *Aleksovski* Appeal Judgment, para. 185; ICTY, Judgment on Sentencing Appeal of 4 February 2005 (AC), *Dragan Nikolić*, IT-94-02-A, para. 46; ICTY, *Kordić* and *Čerkez* Appeal Judgment, para. 1078; ICTY, *Delalić et al.* Appeal Judgment, para. 801. See also ICTY, *Babić* Sentencing Judgment, para. 45 ('it would be unfair, and it would ultimately weaken respect for the legal order as a whole, to increase the punishment imposed on a person merely for the purpose of deterring others. Therefore, in determining the appropriate sentence, the Trial Chamber does not accord undue prominence to deterrence.'); ICTY, *Obrenović* Sentencing Judgment, para. 52; ICTY, *Češić* Sentencing Judgment, para.26; ICTY, *Jokić* Sentencing Judgment, para. 34; ICTY, *Šainović et al.* Trial Judgment, para. 1146.

68 ICTY, *Furundžija* Trial Judgment, para. 288 ('The Trial Chamber accepts that two important functions of the punishment are retribution and deterrence.'); ICTY, *Erdemović* I Sentencing Judgment, para. 64; ICTY, *Tadić* II Sentencing Judgment, para. 9 ('The Trial Chamber shares the opinion expressed in the above-mentioned cases in respect of retribution and deterrence serving as the primary purposes of sentence.'); ICTY, *Aleksovski* Appeal Judgment, para. 185 ('An equally important factor is retribution.'); ICTY, *Krajišnik* Appeal Judgment para. 775;

The position was markedly different with regard to rehabilitation, which was also mentioned as the aim of punishment in numerous judgments. This rationale came to the fore especially in the guilty plea cases.[69] In some of these, the accused's affirmative steps towards rehabilitation as a punishment goal, were held to be a mitigating factor.[70] Overall, however, chambers considered rehabilitation, taken in the abstract, to be subordinate to retribution and deterrence. Due to the serious nature of crimes, it was not to be accorded a predominant role in the determination of an appropriate sentence.[71]

ICTR, *Kayishema and Ruzindana* Trial Sentence, para. 2; ICTY, *Deronjić* Sentencing Appeal Judgment, para. 136.

69 ICTY, *Babić* Sentencing Judgment, para. 46

> The loss of freedom, which is the form of punishment imposed by the Tribunal, provides the context for the convicted person's reflection on the wrongfulness of his acts and may give rise to an awareness of the harm and suffering these acts have caused to others. This process contributes to the reintegration of the convicted person into society. [...] [W]hen an accused pleads guilty, he takes an important step in this process.

ICTY, *Obrenović* Sentencing Judgment, para. 53 ('punishment must strive to attain a further goal: rehabilitation. [...] Criminal proceedings are only the starting point; the process continues upon the return of a convicted person to society and makes an active contribution towards reconciliation. [...] [R]ehabilitation may be particularly relevant in this case, given the particular circumstances of the accused.'); ICTY, *Češić* Sentencing Judgment, paras. 27 (rehabilitation is 'the need to take into account the rehabilitative potential of a convicted person; this will often go hands in hands with the process of reintegrating the convicted person into the society') and 28 ('when an accused pleads guilty, he or she takes an important step in the rehabilitation and reintegration processes'.); ICTY, *Jokić* Sentencing Judgment, paras. 35–36. Cf. ICTR, *Kambanda* Judgment and Sentence (no reference to rehabilitation despite guilty plea); ICTR, *Serushago* Sentence, para. 19 (rehabilitation mentioned as part of the discussion on mitigating circumstances but not as a punishment goal).

70 ICTY, *Obrenović* Sentencing Judgment, paras. 142–146. Cf. ICTY, Judgment on Sentencing Appeal of 8 March 2006 (AC), *Momir Nikolić*, IT-02-60/1-A, para. 46.

71 ICTY, *Erdemović* I sentencing judgment, para. 66 ('the concern for [rehabilitation] must be subordinate to that of an attempt to stigmatise the most serious violations of international humanitarian law, and in particular an attempt to preclude their reoccurrence'); ICTY, *Delalić et al.* Appeal Judgment, para. 806 ('although both national jurisdictions and certain international and regional human rights instruments provide that rehabilitation should be one of the primary concerns for a court in sentencing, this cannot play a *predominant* role in the decision-making process of a Trial Chamber of the Tribunal'); ICTY, *Stakić* Appeal Judgment, para. 402 ('Other factors, such as rehabilitation, should be considered but should not be given undue weight.'); ICTY, *Karadžić* Trial Judgment, para. 6025; ICTY, *Šainović et al.* Trial Judgment, para. 1146; ICTY, *Kordić and Čerkez* Appeal Judgment, para. 1079 ('In the light of the gravity of many of the crimes under the International Tribunal's jurisdiction, the weight of rehabilitative considerations may be limited in some cases.'); ICTY, *Deronjić* Sentencing Appeal Judgment, para. 136.

This survey brings to light a few standard, yet noteworthy, elements in the ad hoc Tribunals' treatment of punishment rationales. First, there is a noticeable variance of views and language on the normative content and significance of various justifications, and a certain sense of evolution in approach. This evolution, however, hardly fits in the neat pattern of linear development from the earlier to the later cases. There are no evident regularities, e.g. an ever-broadening recognition of punishment aims or the increasing detail, depth and precision of penological analyzes. The factors responsible for the variation appear to be each chamber's drafting preferences and 'path dependence' conditioned by the precedential authority of past rulings, especially those of the Appeals Chamber.[72] While said variations tend to confirm observations about the 'disarray' in the ad hoc Tribunals' sentencing case law,[73] the extent of that disarray should not be overstated considering the totality of sentencing jurisprudence. Given the sheer amount of judgments rendered over more than two decades by the ad hoc Tribunals, a glass-half-full view is warranted. The ICTY and ICTR penological ruminations are fairly consistent, or at least not as wildly inconsistent as one might be led to think.

Second, the Tribunals' penal philosophy rests on two pillars of uneven importance: domestic criminal law doctrine and the goals set for international criminal justice institutions. The Courts are indebted to the former for the classification, basic definitions and underlying principles of the punishment rationales while the latter coloured the content of those goals and ideas about their relative importance. As shown above, the Tribunals' exegesis of retributivism, deterrence and expressivism did not fall neatly along the lines of familiar domestic doctrines. Expressivism was occasionally 'massaged' into retribution or deterrence or both while its autonomy was recognized at different times under the labels of stigmatization, reprobation, affirmative deterrence and promotion of rule of law. There is little evidence of systemic thinking about the appropriateness of analogizing with domestic punishment rationales, or what their transposition to the international criminal law sphere might do to their relative weight. The interrogation of the domestic analogy did not go much further than vague allusions to the serious nature of crimes justifying the increased importance of retribution and deterrence and the reduced value of rehabilitation, and the imagery of legal order shattered by atrocities and a long history of violations of international humanitarian law.

72 ICTY, *Aleksovski* Appeal Judgment, paras. 107 and 113–114.

73 Holá, 'Consistency and Pluralism of International Sentencing', 195; Drumbl, *Atrocity, Punishment and International Law*, 65.

As part of the second, somewhat thinner, pillar of institutional goals, chambers bolstered their intuitive and unquestioning adoption of teleological *rationes* mimicking the domestic ones, by demonstrating their provenance in the broader mandates and socio-political objectives pursued by the establishment of the Tribunals. This led to a partial conflation of distinct sets of objectives associated with different tiers of the international criminal law teleology (e.g., deterrence as the objective of establishing courts *v.* deterrence as the punishment goal). This made it easy to assume a causal link between the two non-equivalent objectives, such as that punishment *per se* promotes peace-building and reconciliation – in itself a far-fetched and empirically dubious assertion.[74] More generally, one is left to wonder what the teleological considerations of the Tribunals' mandate-sponsors add to the validity of traditional punishment aims, and how institutional mandates inform the content of, and prioritization among, the different rationales.

Third, the practical import of penal objectives in sentencing determinations is another murky area. In the Tribunals' judgments, the discussion of the goals of punishment is placed at the top of the sections devoted to the determination of appropriate sentence (or the appeals therefrom). Judges occasionally proclaimed that punishment goals serve as a framework or 'matrix' when determining the appropriate sentence.[75] But except for a few guilty plea cases alluding to rehabilitation more than once, those rationales were typically *not* revisited again when reviewing sentencing factors and determining the penalty.[76] The individual or combined effect of penal rationales on the application of sentencing principles and on the weight accorded to various aggravating and mitigating circumstances are far from self-evident. It is uncertain what guidance, if any, judges draw from the aims of punishment in the exercise of their broad sentencing discretion, and how a greater, equal, or no emphasis on retribution, deterrence or reprobation ultimately informed the sentence *calculi*.[77]

74 See also Bagaric and Morss, 'International Sentencing Law', 208.

75 ICTY, *Tadić* II Sentencing Judgment, para. 9; ICTY, *Kordić and Čerkez* Appeal Judgment, paras. 1083 ('All the above mentioned sentencing purposes constitute the matrix in which the proportionate sentence is meted out, based on the sentencing factors as provided for in Article 24 of the Statute and Rule 101 of the Rules.').

76 Similarly, Holá, 'Consistency and Pluralism of International Sentencing', 195 (sentencing goals are often listed 'with no further discussion of what those objectives entail and how they should influence sentence determination in individual cases' and 'affect neither the structure of the further sentencing argumentation nor the factors the judges emphasize when meting out sentences.').

77 See also Holá, 'Sentencing of International Crimes at the ICTY and ICTR', 6 (unclear 'how exactly individual sentencing aims inform sentence determination').

Instead, the penalties were calculated primarily by weighing the gravity of the crimes and individual circumstances going to mitigation or aggravation. National sentencing practice was taken into account, and a horizontal comparison across cases could be made to prevent disparity in giving effect to the principle of consistency, commanding that comparable crimes be punished alike if relevant circumstances are substantially similar.[78] Although previous sentencing practice was not binding, it served as a guiding factor with its practical utility arguably being more tangible than that of abstract sentencing goals.[79] The sentence determination method was more casuistic and analogical than deductive. The little concrete value of abstract punishment rationales is amply demonstrated by the fact that the ICTY and ICTR were not handicapped in any way when sentencing convicts without prior consideration of the aims of punishment in some cases.[80]

3 *Hybrid Courts: Sierra Leone and Cambodia*

The sentencing practice of select internationalized tribunals – the Special Court for Sierra Leone (SCSL) and the Khmer Rouge Tribunal (ECCC) – warrants a brief review, if only to underscore that their penal approaches generally tracked that of the ad hoc Tribunals. The SCSL and ECCC sentencing judgments contain copious references to the ICTY and ICTR case law, which in the case of the SCSL has a statutory basis.[81]

The SCSL Trial Chambers recognized retribution, deterrence and rehabilitation as the main sentencing purposes,[82] with the former two assuming

[78] ICTY, *Delalić et al.* Appeal Judgment, paras. 756–759 (on consistency in punishment as '[o]ne of the fundamental elements of any rational and fair system of criminal justice' and 'an important reflection of the notion of equal justice' as the foundation of public confidence in courts).

[79] ICTY, *Furundžija* Appeal Judgment, para. 250 ('A previous decision on sentence may indeed provide guidance if it relates to the same offence and was committed in substantially similar circumstances; otherwise, a Trial Chamber is limited only by the provisions of the Statute and the Rules.'); ICTY, *Šainović et al.* Trial Judgment, para. 1143.

[80] See judgments referenced in fn. 47.

[81] Art. 20(3) of the SCSL Statute directed the SCSL appeal judges to seek guidance from the ICTY and ICTR Appeals Chamber's decisions. Moreover, the SCSL Trial Chambers were obliged to 'have recourse to the practice regarding prison sentences' in the ICTR and Sierra Leonean national courts when determining the terms of imprisonment: SCSL Statute, Art. 19 (1).

[82] SCSL, Sentencing Judgment of 19 July 2007 (TC), *Brima et al. (AFRC)*, SCSL-04-16-T, para. 14 (referring to the ICTY and ICTR case law); SCSL, Judgment on the Sentencing of Moinina Fofana and Allieu Kondewa of 9 October 2007 (TC), *Fofana and Kondewa (CDF)*,

primacy.[83] The goal of rehabilitation, despite being a 'relevant factor in sentencing', was deemed to have a more limited weight in the context of international criminality than in domestic jurisdictions.[84] The SCSL justices admitted that these rationales were derived directly from the national domain,[85] and frequent references to domestic penal doctrine are evidence of that.[86] The broader societal objectives pursued through the establishment of the SCSL mentioned in the UN Security Council Resolution 1315 (2000) – ending impunity and contributing to the process of national reconciliation and to the restoration and maintenance of peace – were also deemed relevant when meting out punishments.[87]

Like the ICTY and ICTR, the SCSL dissociated retribution from the desire for revenge and saw it as the way of 'expressing the outrage of the national and international community' at the crimes that must reflect a fair and balanced approach to punishment and translate in an individualized and proportionate penalty.[88] The SCSL Trial Chambers also emphasized that penalties must be such as to deter others from committing similar crimes in the future and to prevent criminal conduct by the convicted person, including by incapacitating or restraining him.[89] In endorsing some of the ad hoc Tribunals' statements, the expressivism-based goals of promoting legal awareness and ensuring the universal acceptance of international criminal law proscriptions, were at times presented as aspects of either retributivism or deterrence.[90] Following the lead of the Appeals Chamber in the *CDF* case, the autonomous objective of denunciating the crimes in question as unacceptable ('reflect[ing] revulsion of the international community') emerged as

SCSL-04-14-T, para. 26; SCSL, Sentencing Judgment of 8 April 2009 TC), *Sesay et al. (RUF)*, SCSL-04-15-T, paras. 13–14; SCSL, Sentencing Judgment of 30 May 2012 (TC), *Taylor*, SCSL-03-01-T, paras. 13–15.

[83] SCSL, *RUF* sentencing judgment, para. 13; SCSL, Judgment of 28 May 2008 (AC), *Fofana and Kondewa (CDF)*, SCSL-04-14-A, para. 532; *Taylor* sentencing judgment, para. 13.

[84] SCSL, *CDF* Sentencing Judgment, para. 28; SCSL, *RUF* Sentencing Judgment, para. 16; SCSL, *Taylor* Sentencing Judgment, para. 15.

[85] SCSL, *RUF* Sentencing Judgment, para. 12.

[86] SCSL, *CDF* Sentencing Judgment, para. 27 (adopting the definition of retribution as stated by Lamer J of the Supreme Court of Canada).

[87] SCSL, *CDF* Sentencing Judgment, para. 29; SCSL, *Taylor* Sentencing Judgment, para. 12.

[88] SCSL, *AFRC* Sentencing Judgment, para. 15; SCSL, *CDF* Sentencing Judgment, paras. 26 and 31; SCSL, *RUF* Sentencing Judgment, para. 13, SCSL, *Taylor* Sentencing Judgment, para. 13.

[89] SCSL, *AFRC* Sentencing Judgment, para. 16; SCSL, *CDF* Sentencing Judgment, para. 26; SCSL, *RUF* Sentencing Judgment, para. 13; SCSL, *Taylor* Sentencing Judgment, para. 14.

[90] SCSL, *CDF* Sentencing Judgment, para. 30.

paramount in later jurisprudence.[91] Like at the ad hoc Tribunals, the sentencing objectives did not make repeated appearance in judgments' sections determining individual sentences. Despite rhetorical assurances that sentence calculation takes into account 'all of the factors that are likely to contribute to achievement of these objectives',[92] the practical effects of penal teleology on sentence calculations were anything but clear cut.

Turning to the ECCC, its sentencing regime 'in the books' is highly indeterminate. The ECCC Agreement and Law merely provide for the minimum (5 years' imprisonment) and maximum penalty (life imprisonment) and are silent on the issues of sentencing objectives, principles and factors.[93] Accordingly, the ECCC chambers had to seek guidance in the international and Cambodian legal frameworks and in sentencing practice in comparable cases before international courts.[94] The ECCC penological analyzes have indeed relied heavily upon the sentencing jurisprudence of the ad hoc Tribunals.

Both of the ECCC trial judgments rendered to date in Cases 001 and 002/01, foreground expressivist and retributivist philosophy.[95] The *Duch* trial judgment did not specifically consider deterrence. In increasing Duch's

[91] SCSL, *CDF* Appeal Judgment, para. 565; see also paras. 561 ('In exercising its sentencing discretion, the Appeals Chamber re-emphasizes that it is an international court with responsibility to protect and promote the norms and values of the international community.') and 564 ('What should be one of the paramount considerations in the sentencing of an accused person convicted of crimes against humanity and war crimes is the revulsion of mankind, represented by the international community, to the crime and not the tolerance by a local community of the crime.'). See SCSL, *RUF* Sentencing Judgment, para. 15; SCSL, *Taylor* Sentencing Judgment, paras. 14 and 16.

[92] SCSL, *Taylor* Sentencing Judgment, para. 17.

[93] ECCC Agreement, Art. 10; ECCC Law, Art 38–39 new. See also ECCC, Judgment of 26 July 2010 (TC), *Kaing Guek Eav (Duch)*, 001/18-07-2007/ECCC/TC, para. 575 and 577 (noting that the legal instruments 'do not indicate whether sentencing before the ECCC is governed by international or Cambodian legal rules, or some combination of each' and ruling out 'the direct application of Cambodian sentencing provisions').

[94] ECCCC, *Duch* Trial Judgment, para 578; ECCC, Appeal Judgment of 3 February 2012 (SCC), *Kaing Guek Eav (Duch)*, 001/18-07-2007-ECCC/SC, para. 374; ECCC, Case 002/01 Judgment of 7 August 2014 (TC), *Nuon Chea and Khieu Samphan*, 002/19-09-2007/ECCC/TC, para. 1066.

[95] At the time of revising this chapter before publication, the ECCC is yet to issue the full written judgment in Case 002/02 whereby it sentenced Nuon Chea and Khieu Samphan to another term of life imprisonment. The available summary of the judgment does not mention the goals of punishment as part of the sentencing *desiderata*, over and above the considerations relating to 'the gravity of the crimes, including their scale and brutality as well as the number and vulnerability of victims [. . .] as well as relevant aggravating and mitigating circumstances'. ECCC, Summary of Judgment of 16 November 2018 (TC), *Nuon Chea and Khieu Samphan*, 002/19-09-2007/ECCC/TC, para. 71.

sentence from 35 years to life imprisonment, the Supreme Court Chamber underscored the importance of this rationale, next to retribution, considering the gravity of crimes.[96] Case 002/01 trial judgment mentioned deterrence, 'both to the accused and more generally'.[97] Rehabilitation was not mentioned as a punishment objective but as a mitigating circumstance of limited weight.[98]

With respect to expressivism-based justifications, the ECCC Trial Chamber reaffirmed that by 'reducing crimes of considerable enormity into individualised sentences', it sought to reassure the victims and broader public that 'the law is effectively implemented and enforced' and 'to convey the message that globally-accepted laws and rules have to be obeyed by all, irrespective of status or rank'.[99] Replicating the ICTY and ICTR discourse on retribution, the ECCC held that an 'obvious function' of a sentence is to punish, not to exact revenge. Hence, punishment must satisfy the requirements of equality before the law, proportionality and individualization in reflecting 'the culpability of the accused based on an objective, reasoned and measured analysis both of his or her conduct and its consequential harm' – the principles also reflected in Cambodian law.[100]

Overall, the ECCC sentencing discussions replicate the arguments and follow paths treaded by other courts. The Tribunal did not care to reflect on whether its unique circumstances, not least the passage of almost four decades since the crimes took place and the senior age and physical condition of the convicts, could or should affect the relative relevance of goals such as denunciation, rehabilitation and deterrence.

4 *International Criminal Court*

The ICC legal framework departs from the ad hoc Tribunals' legal regimes in several important respects. It limits the definite term of imprisonment to 30 years and allows for supplementary penalties (fines and forfeiture of ill-gotten gains).[101] It also provides for the far more detailed guidance for determination of sentences,[102] including specification of mitigating and aggravating circumstances and a non-exhaustive list of additional factors to be taken into

96 ECCC, *Duch* Appeal Judgment, paras. 380 and 382.
97 ECCC, Case 002/01 Trial Judgment, para. 1067.
98 ECCC, *Duch* Trial Judgment, para 611; ECCC, *Duch* Appeal Judgment, para. 370.
99 ECCC, *Duch* Trial Judgment, para 579; ECCC, Case 002/01 Trial Judgment, para. 1067.
100 ECCC, *Duch* Trial Judgment, paras. 780–781; ECCC, Case 002/01 Judgment, para. 1067.
101 ICC Statute, Art. 77.
102 ICC Statute, Art. 78(1) and ICC RPE, Rule 145.

account, over and above the gravity of the crime and individual circumstances of the convict.[103] Indeed, this amounts to a 'comprehensive scheme for the determination and imposition of a sentence',[104] particularly compared to the skeletal sentencing regimes elsewhere. The ICC's sentencing practice thus far spans five 'Article 76 decisions', four of which concern core crimes and one offences against administration of justice (Article 70). As a matter of design, all judgments include pronouncements on punishment rationales.

Since Articles 77–78 of the Statute are silent on the issue, the chambers have uniformly drawn penal objectives from the Preamble. It states that 'the most serious crimes of concern to the international community as a whole must not go unpunished', and that the states parties are '[d]etermined to put an end to impunity for the perpetrators of these crimes and thus to contribute to the prevention'.[105] Trial Chambers have construed this language as giving rise to the dual rationale, or the primary objectives, of retribution and deterrence.[106] The *Lubanga* Trial Chamber paid limited attention to the punishment rationales, whilst the *Katanga* and *Bemba* Chambers' analyzes went further. The *Katanga* Chamber held that the sentence must respond to 'the legitimate need for truth and justice voiced by the victims and their family members' and thus play a two-fold role: (i) punitive, as 'the expression of society's condemnation of the criminal act and of the person who committed it' and 'a way of acknowledging the harm and suffering caused to the victims' that would restrain any desire to exact vengeance; and (ii) deterrent, aiming to 'deflect those planning to commit similar crimes from their purpose'.[107] In the view of the *Katanga* Chamber, the severity of the sentence is less important than its inevitability. The subsequent sentencing decisions in

[103] ICC RPE, Rule 145(1)(c) and (2). For the sentencing procedure at the ICC, see also the contribution by Gerhard Werle and Aziz Epik in Chapter 18.

[104] ICC, Judgment on the appeals of the Prosecutor and Mr Thomas Lubanga Dyilo against the 'Decision on Sentence pursuant to Article 76 of the Statute' of 1 December 2014 (AC), *Lubanga*, ICC-01/04-01/06-3122, para. 32.

[105] ICC Statute, Preamble, paras 4 and 5.

[106] ICC, Decision on Sentence pursuant to Article 76 of the Statute of 10 July 2012 (TC), Lubanga, ICC-01/04-01/06-2901, para. 16; ICC, Decision on Sentence pursuant to article 76 of the Statute of 23 May 2014 (TC), Katanga, ICC-01/04-01/07-3484-tENG, para. 37 ('the sentence should act as a deterrent'); ICC, Decision on Sentence pursuant to Article 76 of the Statute of 21 June 2016 (TC), *Bemba*, ICC-01/05-01/08-3399, para. 10 ('the Preamble establishes retribution and deterrence as the primary objectives of punishment at the ICC.'); ICC, Judgment and Sentence of 27 September 2016 (TC), *Al Mahdi*, ICC-01/12-01/15-171, para. 66. See also *Bemba II* Article 76 decision, para. 19.

[107] ICC, *Katanga* Article 76 decision, para. 38.

Bemba, *Al Mahdi* and *Bemba II* defined retribution and deterrence in comparable terms.[108]

Characteristically, and in line with the ad hoc Tribunals' discourse, the *Katanga*, *Bemba* and *Al Mahdi* Chambers drew a connection between sentencing and desired socio-political effects of the ICC's operation. The sentence should reflect, they stated, 'the degree of culpability while contributing to the restoration of peace and reconciliation in the communities concerned'.[109] Chambers also held that the sentence may additionally facilitate the reintegration of the person into society, but that this cannot be regarded as a primordial goal because the sentence on its own cannot ensure social reintegration.[110] The latter point is indisputable but, following the same logic, the objectives such as contribution to peace and reconciliation and general deterrence should not enjoy emphasis either: an individual sentence alone cannot bring about said positive societal outcomes. Regardless, the *Katanga* Chamber ultimately did accord some weight to mitigating factors, namely Germain Katanga's young age at the time of the crime, and his family, which the judges regarded 'likely to make rehabilitation and reintegration easier'.[111] Similarly, the Trial Chamber took Ahmad Al Faqi Al Mahdi's admission of guilt and cooperation with the prosecution as an indication that he would 'likely successfully reintegrate into society', thus according a limited weight to this circumstance.[112]

One incongruity in the ICC sentencing jurisprudence to date relates to the treatment of punishment objectives in the context of sentencing for Article 70 offences. The *Bemba II* Chamber held the 'primary purpose' of retribution and deterrence to be applicable to sentencing under Article 70, as that provision 'seeks to protect the integrity of the proceedings before the Court by penalising the behaviour of persons that impedes the discovery of the truth,

[108] ICC, *Bemba* Article 76 decision, para. 11; ICC, *Al Mahdi* judgment and sentence, para. 67; ICC, *Bemba II* Article 76 decision, para. 19 (on deterrence: 'a sentence should be adequate to discourage a convicted person from recidivism (specific deterrence) as well as to ensure that those who would consider committing similar offences will be dissuaded from doing so (general deterrence).').

[109] ICC, *Katanga* Article 76 Decision, para. 38; ICC, *Bemba* Article 76 Decision, para. 11; ICC, *Al Mahdi* Judgment and Sentence, para. 67.

[110] ICC, *Katanga* Article 76 Decision, para. 38; ICC, *Bemba* Article 76 Decision, para. 11 ('Rehabilitation is also a relevant purpose [but it] should not be given undue weight.'); ICC, *Al Mahdi* Judgment and Sentence, para. 67. See also ICC, Decision on Sentence pursuant to Article 76 of the Statute of 22 March 2017 (TC), *Bemba et al. (Bemba II)*, ICC-01/05-01/13-2123-Corr 22-03-2017, para. 205.

[111] ICC, *Katanga* Article 76 Decision, paras. 38 and 144.

[112] ICC, *Al Mahdi* Judgment and Sentence, para. 97.

the victims' right to justice and, generally, the Court's ability to fulfil its mandate'.[113] The logic behind this transposition of sentencing rationales for Article 70 offences from the Preamble of the Statute, which only refers to the core crimes, is questionable, and so is the automatic equation of punishment justifications for both categories of offences. It is problematic that the Chamber did not care to properly consider other goals in this distinct legal policy context. The autonomous objective of expressing condemnation of the obstruction of ICC justice appears no less valid than deterrence or retribution. Nor is there an apparent reason to tacitly discard the objective of rehabilitation.[114] This objective tends – rightly or wrongly – to be attributed reduced weight in the sentencing for core crimes. If the nature of the crime is accepted as the ground for downgrading this rationale, one cannot assume its total irrelevance as a justification of punishment for criminal interference with the administration of justice. Unless the individual circumstances of the offender indicate otherwise, he or she should in principle be regarded as being susceptible to re-education, able to redeem him or herself, and capable of successful reintegration in the society.

5 *Contours of Judicial Discourse*

This broad-brush view of the tribunals' sentencing *acquis* provides insights into their punishment philosophy. The way teleological reflections are presented in the judgments, and their subsequent (non-)use in sentencing determinations, throws light on the motives for the courts to engage in this discussion. This helps distinguish the actual reasons for punishment from the reasons for which courts *say* they punish. But first, it is worthwhile noting some of the characteristic features of judicial treatment of punishment justifications in different jurisdictions.

First, all of the courts have uniformly and without reservation imported domestic rationales into their sentencing case law, as part of the criminal law doctrine, without ever seriously questioning their suitability in the international criminal law context. Not much has been made of the extraordinary nature of core crimes, other than their exceptional gravity underscoring the special importance of retribution and deterrence, and making rehabilitation

[113] ICC, *Bemba II* Article 76 Judgment, para. 19.

[114] The Appeals Chamber did not find, however, that the Trial Chamber entirely disregarded the rehabilitation goal as it did refer to the Main Case judgment and other cases in which reference was made to that objective: ICC, *Bemba II* Sentencing Appeal Judgment, para. 205. This is puzzling as the *Bemba II* TC did not mention rehabilitation, much less considered it in the context of the case.

the least weighty of the goals. The focus on the extreme gravity of the crimes, combined with intermittent enforcement of international law in the past, resulted in a rather subtle foregrounding of the objectives such as the expression of the international community's condemnation of the crimes and reinforcement of the culture of respect for the rule of law. However, such acknowledgments have not been particularly pronounced or systematic. Expressivism has often been presented as an aspect of either retribution or deterrence, thereby stretching and distorting the traditional understanding of those rationales without further argument.

Second, the tribunals sought to alleviate the conceptual discomfort arising from the direct transposition of domestic rationales into their penal realm. They attempted to bolster the validity of those rationales by grounding them in the intentions of their architects and by linking them to the socio-political objectives of international criminal justice. The judges often pointed to the alignment between the punishment goals and their own institutional mandates of fighting impunity, mass atrocity prevention, justice for the victims and reconciliation. However, it was never clear what substantive influence those objectives have on the scope and interpretation of traditional sentencing purposes, and how the former inform the balancing and prioritization amongst them. This linkage between the aims of setting up courts and the punishment rationales muddled together the analogous yet qualitatively distinct sets of objectives situated on the different planes of international criminal law teleology, leading to occasional attribution to criminal punishment of objectives it is neither meant nor necessarily suitable to serve directly, such as reconciliation and peace-making. The presumed causality between the institutional and the penal objectives, to the effect that punishment is meant to automatically promote atrocity prevention, reconciliation and peace, is an article of faith that is empirically impeachable.

Third, when it comes to the hierarchy of objectives, the sentencing jurisprudence has mostly placed the deterrent and the retributive rationales on an equal footing. Attempts to rank one higher than the other did not survive appeal. Rehabilitation was consistently rated as less important. However, in a handful of cases, which were disposed of consensually, this goal came to bear upon sentencing determinations; not directly but rather through a consideration of mitigating factors. Curiously, deterrence and retribution were invariably seen as concomitant and complementary justifications, rather than as competing objectives and philosophies.[115] Despite the existence of hybrid

[115] See also Bagaric and Morss, 'International Sentencing Law', 208 ('an unhappy mix of different theories of punishment (utilitarian and retributive) and [. . .] no attempt to rank the

theories in the domestic field, most accounts care to keep deterrent and retributive justifications apart. International sentencing jurisprudence, however, routinely views retributivism and consequentialism as two sides of the same coin and occasionally fuses them into a single master rationale. Thus, the *Katanga* Chamber referred to the twofold (retributive and deterrent) role of a sentence and the *Bemba II* Chamber labelled them as one 'purpose' in the singular.

Fourth, the practical value of punishment teleology is uncertain and difficult to gauge. The apparent effect that the goals of punishment, individually or in combination, have had on the sentencing *calculi* in specific cases is limited because they provide judges only with highly abstract and inconclusive guidance for meting out individual punishments. The punishment rationales indirectly inform the sentencing methodology through the imposition of general principles; in particular, the retributivist framework commands a mandatory focus on proportionality and individualization. Sentences are calculated based on gravity of the crime along with any aggravating or mitigating circumstances, possibly adjusted in light of the national sentencing practice and/or sentences meted out in similar cases by international tribunals. The sentencing approach is casuistic because chambers consult and compare cases from different tribunals to punish comparable crimes alike in avoidance of disparity. The judges are adamant that other courts' sentencing practice is not binding and its persuasive value is limited due to differences between sentencing provisions.[116] Even so, the actual effects of such practice are more tangible than that of penal teleology. Hence the more predominant sentencing method is analogy, not deduction from the abstract penal rationales.

The fifth observation goes to the form which the discussion of punishment purposes takes in sentencing judgments. The prevalent majority of rulings contain such a discussion, but the purposes of punishment are typically given short shrift. The analysis is mostly perfunctory and *pro forma*, as if the chambers felt compelled to include it only to comply with some drafting conventions, 'ticking the box' and moving on to the more important determinants, without the teleological reflections being truly material. More than any other, perhaps, this area of jurisprudence is a reign of unanimity, with little to no (appellate) litigation and debate among judges, chambers and tribunals. The degree of repetition and copy-paste is striking. Identical language

corresponding, often competing, goals stemming from the respective theories'). However, see also the contribution by Andreas Werkmeister in Chapter 14.

116 E.g. ICC, *Lubanga* Sentencing Appeal Judgment, paras. 76–77; ICC, *Al Mahdi* Judgment and Sentence, para. 107.

migrates from one judgment to another. The same mantras and tired formulas are used over and over again, possibly with just a few, if any, cosmetic modifications owed to each bench's stylistic preferences. It strains reality to contend that there has been an evolution of judicial philosophy of international punishment 'from Nuremberg to The Hague' and beyond. The only sign of progression from Nuremberg to modern courts is the now-established practice of stating rationales expressly. But otherwise the judges are comfortable rehashing the same language used by their predecessors and preaching the old dogmas in reaffirming the validity of the stated punishment goals through hypnotic repetition.

III WHAT COURTS DO: BENEATH THE SURFACE OF JUDICIAL PENOLOGY

What should be made of the courts' engagement with punishment teleology and its usage in sentencing? Do the persistent and formulaic assurances that perpetrators of international crimes are punished for the sake of retribution and deterrence constitute a meaningful answer to the 'why punish' question? One should be cautious of taking the judicial narrative at face value. The declared reasons for submitting perpetrators to punishment might not be the actual or all the reasons the courts have in mind when doing so. This Section looks at the judicial discourse through the binary lens of the two readings of the question highlighted above. As noted, the first reading (*why* punish?) enquires what theory or theories may account for the act of punishment the need for which is a given, while the second (why *punish*?) interrogates the very idea of punishment as a mandatory consequence of individual guilt.

1 *Sentencing Performativity: Expressivism as Meta-Justification*

To recap, on the first rendition of the question, the tribunals have consistently fallen back on an array of retributive and consequentialist justifications, treating them as complementary. Episodically, the judges construed the orthodox rationales broadly in a way that subsumed expressivist justifications, and cited further goals ('affirmative deterrence'), whose relationship with the former rationales was uncertain. While the abundance of penal objectives acknowledged in the jurisprudence could be taken as a solid foundation for international punishment, this is not necessarily the case. In their penal imaginations, the tribunals have been unwilling to arbitrate between potentially incompatible philosophies, preferring instead to have their cake and eat it too. Despite occasional flirtation with goals other than retribution and deterrence, jurisprudence contributes little by way of original thought to international penology and sentencing. Standard turns of speech are used by different chambers and tribunals in conveying unimpeachable truths about the meaning and importance of traditional objectives. This gives an impression that, in the courts' collective view, there is not much more to be said about philosophy of international punishment. Judges certainly do not treat '*why* punish?' as a question calling for genuine inquiry but rather as a mandatory occasion to press upon their audiences the messages of retribution and deterrence as the normative pillars of international criminal justice.

The rhetoric in sentencing rulings exposes the normative positions championed by the judges, but it hardly works as a credible descriptive account of what the tribunals actually do when meting out punishment. Deterrence and retribution are the main reasons the courts *say* they punish but are not necessarily the primary reasons for which they *do so* and which can explain fully the act of punishment. The penological discourse is illuminating in less evident ways. The standard restatements of retributive and deterrent purposes suggest that a certain performativity is at work. This impression is further strengthened if one considers the unabashed rehearsal of the same language from one judgment to another, especially in the apparent absence of any practical utility. Ceremonial and self-referential restatements of retributivism and deterrence accompanying each act of punishment, are speech acts whereby judges deliberately perform and perpetuate the criminal law dogmas – that punishment must be imposed because it is deserved by a guilty wrongdoing, and because this is the (only) way to deter the recurrence of such crimes in the future.

This performativity of judicial discourse accreting around the punishment ritual lends support to expressivism as the primary purpose and meta-justification of penalty.[117] Considering the form judicial discourse has taken, expressivism can best explain what international criminal jurisdictions are doing when they punish. By elaborating on the penal objectives in sentencing judgments, courts seek to reproduce and reinforce the normative belief system upon which the enterprise of international criminal prosecutions rests, and to propagate its commandments. Punishment is inflicted, first and foremost, for the sake of this effort to educate the convict, other potential offenders, their communities and the audiences at large about the unacceptability of violating

[117] For influential accounts in domestic criminal law theory, see J. Feinberg, 'The Expressive Function of Punishment' in J. Feinberg, *Doing and Deserving: Essays in the Theory of Responsibility* (Princeton: Princeton University Press, 1974); A. Duff, *Punishment, Communication, and Community* (Oxford: Oxford University Press, 2001).

the international criminal law norms. The act is motivated by the need to teach a lesson in retribution and deterrence, thereby reinstating faith in the rule of law and the authority and enforceability of the norms. In other words, the courts seek 'to demonstrate that the status and its claim of law are superior to the criminal who claims the power to do wrong'.[118] Judges in fact have limited means of knowing and showing whether the penalty fits the bill of gravity and 'just deserts', much less whether it would serve effectively as a specific or general deterrent. By way of describing what courts do, as opposed to what they proclaim normatively, the standard penal objectives are secondary to didacticism. Retribution and deterrence are the substance of the didactic message, but that message itself is the actual motive of punishment, or its meta-justification. That the very point of conveying the message is didactic explains the curious position expressivism holds in the jurisprudence, its simultaneous ubiquity and out-of-placeness. It makes sense then that this objective is a constant leitmotif in the judicial constructions and deployment of other, nominal 'primary' rationales.

2 *Disciplinary Identity and Discursive Constraints*

The second reading of the question ('why *punish*'?) is an upheaval in the idea of international criminal punishment. This issue is settled by default and irreversibly once a political decision is reached to unleash a *criminal* justice institution as a way to deal with a crisis in which crimes have been committed, as opposed to dispatching a truth and reconciliation commission or inquiry, grass-roots justice mechanism or a mass claims process. As it is beyond judicial purview to comment on the expediency of that decision, it is natural that international criminal jurisprudence has remained blind to non-penal alternatives. The tribunals have been able neither to acknowledge 'why *punish*?' as a genuine question, nor to attempt to answer it in earnest. Their identity as the creatures of the liberal criminal law would be compromised if this were any different.

The criminal law paradigm comes in a package with a fixed system of convictions about the relevance of punishment objectives and with curtailed imaginations and limited instrumentalities. The available penalties and penitentiary arrangements are interwoven with the disciplinary DNA of the criminal law. A challenge to the idea of punishment as an inescapable consequence of a criminal act is an attack on the basic idea of criminal law,

[118] G. Fletcher, *The Grammar of Criminal Law: American, Comparative, and International* (Oxford: Oxford University Press, 2007), 223.

which cannot be interrogated 'from within' the system. Therefore, demands for a more open-minded and creative or inquisitive approach on the part of the tribunals are bound to fall on deaf ears. The judges can only treat the second reading of 'why *punish*?' as a non-question; it is not answerable from within the punitive paradigm to which the courts are confined. Judges are there to preach, not to apostatize. The judicial function is to reassert the inflexible preference for punishment over alternatives as per the legalist script, and thus sentencing jurisprudence brings into sharper relief the rigid contours of international criminal law's identity. As an enterprise and a discipline, it operates under methodological constraints which curb its receptivity to counterarguments from 'outside the box', challenging the axioms at the heart of the belief system it embodies. The validity of retribution and deterrence is the unassailable truth, not a discussion point or a claim in need of defence. This remains so even in the face of hard data suggesting that criminal punishment falls short in delivering on the goals it is meant to pursue.

The fact-driven contestations of the tribunals' penal ideology are exemplary of the growing tension between the 'normative' and the more recent 'empirical' strands in the discipline vying for control over its methodological apparatus. The dynamics between the two strands are permeated by mutual neglect and irrelevance. The 'empirical turn' in international criminal law has the potential of generating evidence that can refute or confirm its normative certitudes, not least the adequacy of goal-setting or real-life effects in terms of prevention, reconciliation and peace. The tribunals' perfunctory and reiterative affirmations of sentencing rationales ring hollow to sceptics questioning whether punishment is the sole justified response. Such assurances can also be dismissed as self-serving: judges indulge in self-legitimization. While sceptics demand empirical proof for the deterrence claim or adduce countervailing evidence themselves, what they are railing against are quasi-religious beliefs immune to hard data. The degree to which the believers in the 'normative camp' are willing and able to engage with empirical arguments is negligible.

The point that criminal law is a normative enterprise is sometimes lost on the empiricists. In its ideological framework, punishment goals do not have to be empirically grounded and achievable to retain validity – and this often holds as a justification of international criminal justice more broadly. Whenever arguments are made and evidence is adduced that goals are ill-chosen and means to achieve them ill-suited (punishment does not deter, reconcile, promote peace or graft the rule-of-law culture), this is an attack at the article of faith that for 'normativists' is beyond question and beyond proof. They will resist or ignore findings going against the tide of their convictions. Even the opportunistic acceptance of empirical evidence in line with those convictions is but a form of ideological and cognitive resistance and does not displace the assumptions. Evidence confirming the deterrent effect would be taken as a concession that the faith in deterrence was correct all along, without making that faith itself dependent on any evidence.

As the adherents of both camps are likely to stick to their guns, it would greatly benefit the conversation if they were to be more aware of each other's ideological premises and methodological blind spots. Otherwise, they are bound to continue talking at cross purposes.

IV CONCLUSION

This chapter has explored how international criminal judges have engaged with the question of why those responsible for international crimes should be submitted to punishment. Without intending to produce a coherent normative theory of punishment for international criminal law – the project for another day – the objective was merely observational and analytical: first, drawing the contours of penological discourse the tribunals have conducted as part of their collective endeavour to justify the penalties and, second, making sense of the reasons why that discourse shaped up to be what it is. The examination of the jurisprudence proceeded with a keen eye to the two readings of the main question: the one attentive to the stated justifications for punishment and the other interrogating the choice of punishment over alternatives.

With regard to the former query, the courts have repeatedly reaffirmed the validity of traditional punishment rationales, while also emphasizing their harmony with the goals of fighting impunity, preventing international crimes, delivering justice for the victims, etc. More than anything, the judicial restatements of penal goals are performative utterances whereby the tribunals seek to re-enact the dogmas of criminal law: the inherent morality of punishment as a reaction to criminal wrongdoing and inexorable deterrent effects of penalties. The principal reasons articulated by the judges for punishing the perpetrators of international crimes, are not necessarily all there is to the act of punishment. Deliberate performativity of judicial affirmations of penal objectives, seen in light of their negligible practical import for the sentencing *calculi* in individual cases, suggests that for the courts expressivism is the primary *raison d'être* of penalties and a meta-justification of the act of punishment. Abstract penal goals provide highly inconclusive guidance for meting out individual punishments. Sentences are neither deduced from, nor informed by, those goals directly. Instead, sentencing determinations present exercises in casuistry, which is not to say they are arbitrary or incongruous considering the veritable undercover effort to harmonize the approach and keep penalties fairly consistent across comparable cases.

The second reading of the question presents a trickier challenge to international criminal justice mounted in the (hypothetical) presence of other avenues ranging wildly from summary executions to forgiveness. 'Why *punish?*' is not answerable from within the paradigm of criminal law, as it is tantamount to asking 'why *criminal law*?' Understandably, this is not a quandary that international tribunals could tackle head on, as that would have required them to inquire into the political expedience – rather than legality – of their own existence. Criminal justice is a take-it-or-leave-it deal. The centrality of punishment as a response to criminal wrongdoing cannot be meaningfully interrogated from within. The judicial rhetoric proclaiming unqualified preference for punishment over alternatives fully accords with the belief system of international criminal law, although it is bound to disappoint the critics, who insist on a more evidence-sensitive approach. This contention highlights the methodological constraints inherent in international criminal law as a normative project. For believers, any empirical proof refuting (or even supporting) the idea that by punishing individuals, international criminal tribunals *can* and *do* deter crimes, reconcile communities and pacify states, goes to the question they are not asking and do not regard as being of any consequence.

5

Punishment and the Domestic Analogy

Why It Can and Cannot Work

ELIES VAN SLIEDREGT

Punishment practice and theory in international criminal law is largely modelled on domestic criminal law. This is understandable: dealing with mass atrocities is done through the process of a criminal trial and, in doing so, judges rely heavily on domestic criminal law theory and practice.[1] International judges recruited from the criminal bench in their respective countries will bring with them domestic experience. More than any other branch of international law, international criminal law opened up to domestic law. Criminal law experience qualifies you for the international criminal law profession, be it as a judge, prosecutor or defence attorney. This is generally a good thing. After all, the core business of these international courts is running a criminal trial.

There are, however, a number of drawbacks with this import of national practice. First of all, it poses an obstacle to developing international criminal law into a coherent body of law with a common methodology and culture. It is difficult for domestic criminal law practitioners to lay off their national cloak and to 'forget' the system they have been educated and trained in. The amalgamation of different legal cultures in international criminal law makes it an inherently pluralist legal endeavour, which sometimes results in misunderstandings and even conflict.[2] The import of domestic legal practice has another disadvantage. It lumbers international criminal law with the domestic analogy of adopting criminal law paradigms drawn from domestic practice and

[1] On statements on rationales of international punishment in the jurisprudence of international and hybrid courts, see the contribution by Sergey Vasiliev in Chapter 4.

[2] See E. van Sliedregt, 'Joint Criminal Enterprise as a Pathway to Convicting Individuals for Genocide' (2007) 5 *Journal of International Criminal Justice* 184; E. van Sliedregt and S. Vasiliev, 'Pluralism: A New Framework for International Criminal Justice' in E. van Sliedregt and S. Vasiliev (eds.), *Pluralism in International Criminal Law* (Oxford: Oxford University Press, 2014), 3.

theory that insufficiently take account of the distinct legal, moral and constitutional context of international criminal law.

The question I aim to answer in this chapter is to what extent the domestic analogy 'works' when it comes to punishment theories in international criminal law. Does the use and reliance on domestic criminal law in international criminal law do justice to the specificities of international criminal law? This requires answering the question 'To what extent is international criminal law special?' To this end, I explore the special or sui generis nature of international crimes and international perpetrators (Section II). I start, however, by looking into the domestic analogy (Section I). I discuss the domestic analogy at two levels: first, at a meta-level, when discussing the international legal order and the authority to punish; and second, at a micro-level, when discussing sentencing purposes in international trials. The domestic analogy puts the legitimacy question on the table. In whose name do international courts punish? On behalf of the international community? On behalf of the affected region or local community? Questions of community and authority are particularly pertinent when we look into the restorative and reconciliation aspect of sentencing. In discussing punishment and sentencing purposes in international criminal law (Section IV), we see that retribution and deterrence lie at the heart of international criminal justice. At the same time, contemporary international courts and tribunals have been given a role to play in restoring peace, of bringing divided communities together, of 'peace through justice'.[3] In recent years, the debate around sentencing purposes has moved from community level to the individual level; from restoring peace between ethnic groups to reintegration of the individual into the community. After almost twenty-five years of international criminal practice, sentenced persons are being released having served their sentence. As a result, questions arise over their reintegration into society. Drawing on theories developed in national criminal justice systems, criminologists Barbora Holá and Joris van Wijk call for international courts to consider rehabilitation and reintegration when sentencing perpetrators of international crimes.[4] The sui generis argument can only go so far; it should not be an obstacle to taking on board rehabilitative considerations developed in domestic law. Moreover, it can be argued that rehabilitation contributes towards restoration of peace. While there is no evidence (yet) to back up the claim that individual rehabilitation

[3] See, e.g., the UN Security Council Resolutions establishing ad hoc Tribunals (ICTY: UN S/RES/827 (1993) of 25 May 1993; ICTR: UN S/RES/955 (1994) of 8 November 1994).

[4] B. Holá and J. van Wijk, 'Life after Conviction at International Criminal Tribunals – An Empirical Overview' (2014) 12 *Journal of International Criminal Justice* 109.

contributes positively to restoration and peace at group level, it is not hard to imagine that there is a mutual beneficial relationship between the two.

The most important outcome of the analysis in this chapter, is that there are fundamental flaws in the international criminal justice system that hamper restorative justice ambitions. International criminal justice is a criminal justice system that operates in a vacuum. It takes over from national justice systems in doing the retributive bit: prosecution and adjudication. In that sense, it is an imperfect, one-sided process. For the post-trial and restorative justice part, it reverts back to the sovereign state. The domestic analogy can and cannot work in international criminal law. It works to the extent that international courts can incorporate and apply theories of punishment in imposing sentences. It is, however, more difficult when it comes to restoration and enforcement of post-trial justice purposes such as reintegration and reconciliation.

I DOMESTIC ANALOGY

When discussing the domestic analogy in international criminal law, we can take two perspectives, the international law perspective and the criminal law perspective. Discussing the domestic analogy in the international law context requires us to discuss the theory as developed in international relations theory where it was relied upon to justify building a world order analogous to a domestic order. In the following, I will call this the 'domestic analogy proper' because it in this context that the domestic analogy-terminology was initially used. Taking a criminal law perspective, the domestic analogy concerns the (uncritical) international application of domestic criminal law concepts and theories.[5] This process of legal transplanting accounts for my terminology of the 'domestic analogy of transplant'. Domestic analogy proper discusses issues at a meta-level: the international legal order and the authority to punish. The domestic analogy of transplant discusses issues at micro- or criminal trial-level, for example punishment and sentencing in international criminal law.

1 *Domestic Analogy Proper*

The domestic analogy proper is the argument that the principles that apply to inter-individual relations apply to inter-state relations as well. Hedley Bull describes the domestic analogy as 'the argument from the experience of individual men in domestic society to the experience of states, according to

[5] See H. Suganami, 'Reflections on the Domestic Analogy: The Case of Bull, Beitz and Linklater' (1986) 12 *Review of International Studies* 145, 149.

which states, like individuals, are capable of orderly social life only if [. . .] they stand in awe of a common power'.[6] The domestic analogy proper has been instrumental in justifying the establishment of a supranational, world order. Such an order would lead to peace, or at least to an end of a Hobbesian state of nature, which is a state of war.[7]

The theory has had quite some traction in international law. It has been relied upon to advocate world government, going back to Grotius and Vitoria who argued in favour of a world community as a follow-up to the *Republica Christiana*.[8] Kant's work builds on the domestic analogy in proposing the concept of a global legal order[9] where international law is created through commonly accepted principles of international rights: *ius cosmopoliticum*.[10] This assumes an interstate system of international governance.[11]

> [N]ations [. . .] [and] peoples can be regarded as single individuals who injure one another through their close proximity while living in the state of nature (i.e., independently of external laws). For the sake of its own security, each nation can and should demand that the others enter into a contract resembling the civil one and guaranteeing the rights of each.[12]

6 H. Bull, *The Anarchical Society: A Study of Order in World Politics* (London: Macmillan, 1977), 46.

7 Suganami, 'Reflections on the Domestic Analogy', 145–146. See also C. Bottici, 'The Domestic Analogy and the Kantian Project of Perpetual Peace' (2003) 11 *The Journal of Political Philosophy* 392, 392.

8 See R. Lesaffer, 'The Grotian Tradition Revisited: Change and Continuity in the History of International Law' (2002) 73 *British Yearbook of International Law* 103.

9 Bottici, 'The Domestic Analogy and the Kantian Project of Perpetual Peace', 395. Patrick Capps and Julian Rivers in their paper 'Kant's Concept of International Law' (2010) 16 *Legal Theory* 229, argue that Kant's cosmopolitan world order is proposing a confederal rather than a federalist superstate type of governance.

10 I. Kant, *Die Metaphysik der Sitten* [1798] (Gesammelte Schriften VI, Berlin: Preussische Akademie der Wissenschaften, 1900ff.), 352 [§ 62: Das Weltbürgerrecht]: 'Dieses Recht, so fern es auf die mögliche Vereinigung aller Völker in Absicht auf gewisse allgemeine Gesetze ihres möglichen Verkehrs geht, kann weltbürgerliche (*ius cosmopoliticum*) genannt werden.' In English: *The Metaphysics of Morals* (translation M. Gregor) (Cambridge: Cambridge University Press, 1996), 6:352: 'This right, since it has to do with the possible union of all nations with a view to certain universal laws for their possible commerce, can be called *cosmopolitan right* (*ius cosmopoliticum*).' See also Capps and Rivers, 'Kant's Concept of International Law', 251.

11 See Capps and Rivers, 'Kant's Concept of International Law', 250–252, relying on Kant, *The Metaphysics of Morals*, 6: 351.

12 I. Kant, *Zum ewigen Frieden* [1795] (Gesammelte Schriften VIII, Berlin: Preussische Akademie der Wissenschaften, 1900ff.), 354: 'Völker als Staaten können wie einzelne Menschen beurtheilt werden, die sich in ihrem Naturzustande (d.i. in der Unabhängigkeit von äußern Gesetzen) schon durch ihr Nebeneinandersein lädiren, und deren jeder um seiner Sicherheit willen von dem andern fordern kann und soll, mit ihm in eine der bürgerlichen ähnliche

There are different interpretations of Kant's concept of cosmopolitan law. Daniele Archibugi argues that it comprises rights that are forerunners of human rights as comprised in the Universal Declaration of Human Rights.[13] Patrick Capps and Julian Rivers, however, adopt a more minimalist approach, where '[c]osmopolitan law is tied up with the conditions by which commerce between nations is possible'. An international legal order should only be built to the extent that mutual interests so require. In their view, Kant's world order is a federation of states based on mutual interests.[14] Such an order can be implemented and enforced by the state institutions themselves; it does not require institution building at the international level.[15] Kant's cosmopolitan world order is an inter-state, confederation of people, not a supranational world community.[16] We are reminded here of Georges Scelle's theory of 'dédoublement fonctionnel', which assumes that state agents or courts have a dual role: they act on behalf of the national or on behalf of the international legal order.[17] This, to use Antonio Cassese's words, 'role-splitting' makes a separate international institutional framework superfluous.[18] It aligns with Kant's view that international law can be an autonomous system of law properly institutionalized without implying the institutional forms that we associate with a unitary global state.[19]

Kant's work inspired international lawyers in the nineteenth and twentieth century and lead them to advocate the idea of world community and world government. Even after the horrors of the twentieth century, with wars, genocide and decolonization, there was support for the cosmopolitan world view.[20] After World War II, Hersch Lauterpacht stated faith in world

Verfassung zu treten, wo jedem sein Recht gesichert werden kann.' In English: *To Perpetual Peace – A Philosophical Sketch* (translation T. Humphrey) (Indianapolis: Hackett Publishing, 1983), 12 [8:354]; see also Capps and Rivers, 'Kant's Concept of International Law', 240.

13 D. Archibugi, 'Immanuel Kant, Cosmopolitan Law and Peace' (1995) 1 *European Journal of International Relations* 429, 429–430.

14 Capps and Rivers, 'Kant's Concept of International Law', 253.

15 Capps and Rivers, 'Kant's Concept of International Law', 253.

16 Bottici, 'The Domestic Analogy and the Kantian Project of Perpetual Peace', 397.

17 G. Scelle, *Précis de droit des gens. Principes et* systématique, Vol. I (Paris: Sirey, 1932), 43, 54–56, 217; Vol. II (Paris: Sirey, 1934), 10, 319, 450.

18 A. Cassese, 'Remarks on Scelle's Theory of "Role-Splitting" (*dédoublement fonctionnel*) in International Law' (1990) 1 *European Journal of International Law* 210, 212–213.

19 Capps and Rivers, 'Kant's Concept of International Law', 357.

20 M. Koskenniemi, 'The Subjective Dangers of Projects of World Community' in A. Cassese, *Realizing Utopia: The Future of International Law* (Oxford: Oxford University Press, 2012), 8.

government in his famous piece on the 'Grotian tradition'.[21] This optimism reached new heights with the establishment of international criminal tribunals and courts after the end of the Cold War. Antonio Cassese, one of international criminal law's main architects, can be seen to champion cosmopolitanism in his book *Realizing Utopia*.[22] Cosmopolitanism is the belief system that supports and pervades international criminal law and its supporters.

The domestic analogy has not been immune to critique.[23] With the argument that the international society is unique and different from any national legal order, Hedley Bull rejected the domestic analogy as a way to justify and explain the international legal order.[24] Martti Koskenniemi is equally critical of the idea of world government because, judging from the history of Western political thought, it presupposes imposition and hegemony.[25]

2 *Transplanting Domestic Theories*

In international criminal law, the domestic analogy plays a specific role. As Immi Tallgren points out, it is not about the relationship between the state and the international community.[26] International criminal law's main concern is the relationship between individuals, between perpetrators and victims. The domestic analogy in international criminal law is about mimicking the national criminal justice framework. The latter is the blueprint for any international criminal justice system, from the investigation and evidence-gathering phase through to the actual trial, its proceedings and attribution of criminal liability.

This mimicry has been criticized for a number of reasons and from different perspectives. Mark Drumbl was an early critic of transplanting domestic criminal justice to international criminal justice. In his work *Atrocity, Punishment and International Law*, he points to the paradox of international law-makers emphasizing the extraordinary nature of international crimes,

[21] Koskenniemi, 'The Subjective Dangers of Projects of World Community', in fn. 4 referring to H. Lauterpacht, 'The Grotian Tradition in International Law' (1946) 23 British Yearbook of International Law 1.

[22] A. Cassese, *Realizing Utopia: The Future of International Law* (Oxford: Oxford University Press, 2012).

[23] For an overview of some of this critique, see Suganami, 'Reflections on the Domestic Analogy', 145–158.

[24] Bull, *The Anarchical Society*, 46.

[25] Koskenniemi, 'The Subjective Dangers of Projects of World Community', 4.

[26] I. Tallgren, 'The Sensibility and Sense of International Criminal Law' (2002) 13 *European Journal of International Law* 561, 566.

demarcating the difference with ordinary common crimes, yet relying on the ordinary/domestic modality of punishment, theory of sentencing and process of determining guilt or innocence.[27] Moreover, he argues, international criminal justice insufficiently takes on board local, non-Western perspectives on justice, which, by embracing concepts such as collective guilt and punitive rituals that do not entail incarceration, deviate from key principles of Western-style justice.[28] This is especially problematic when victim communities themselves provide for such justice mechanisms; think of the gacaca system in Rwanda.[29] Western-style international criminal justice may feel distant for victims and undermine the efficiency of individualized criminal trials premised on incarceration.[30] Drumbl proposes what he calls a 'cosmopolitan pluralism' theory of punishment, based on universal values but diversified in its enforcement leaving room for grassroots and local justice mechanism that differ from and exist alongside Western-style criminal trials.[31]

Others have criticized the domestic analogy of transplant because it results in the uncritical application of national concepts and punishment theories to crimes that, in their view, differ fundamentally from 'garden variety' ordinary crimes.[32] International crimes have a unique, collective nature which does not square with individualized justice based on liberal values of autonomy and moral agency. Perpetrators of international crimes are different from perpetrators of 'ordinary' crimes. This is where we have to discuss the *sui generis* nature of international crimes and perpetrators of international crimes.

II *SUI GENERIS*

In Robert Sloane's view, international criminal law differs from domestic criminal law in at least three ways.[33] First, it serves multiple communities, ethnic and national, and the elusive international community, which itself

[27] M.A. Drumbl, *Atrocity, Punishment and International Law* (Cambridge: Cambridge University Press, 2007), 6.

[28] Drumbl, *Atrocity, Punishment and International Law*, 123–148.

[29] Drumbl, *Atrocity, Punishment and International Law*, 124.

[30] Drumbl, *Atrocity, Punishment and International Law*, 184.

[31] Drumbl, *Atrocity, Punishment and International Law*, 185–187.

[32] G.J. Bass, *Stay the Hand of Vengeance: The Politics of War Crimes Tribunals* (Princeton: Princeton University Press, 2000), 13–14; S.R. Ratner, 'The Schizophrenias of International Criminal Law' (1998) 33 *Texas International Law Journal* 237, 251; M.J. Osiel, 'Why Prosecute? Critics of Punishment for Mass Atrocity' (2000) 22 *Human Rights Quarterly* 118.

[33] R.D. Sloane, 'The Expressive Capacity of International Punishment: The Limits of the National Law Analogy and the Potential of International Criminal Law' (2007) 43 *Stanford Journal of International Law* 39, 41.

hosts multiple and competing constituencies and interests. Second, the collective nature of international crimes is *sui generis*. Third, international perpetrators act in an inverse universe where evil is the norm; they are not classic deviants. As a result, justifications for punishment common to national systems cannot be transplanted unreflectively to the distinct context of international criminal law. Two of the points, the *sui generis* nature of international crimes and of their perpetrators impact on the sentencing rationale. According to Sloane, the expressionist dimensions of punishment best capture both the nature of international sentencing and its unique institutional capacity.[34]

1 *Nature of International Crimes*

Each of Sloane's three points warrants reflection. The first point, on the community that international criminal law serves, will be discussed separately (in Section V). The second point concerns the serious nature of international crimes. Genocide sits on a different level of moral condemnation than (multiple) murder. The moral gravity stems from the fact that these are crimes that violate core values the international community aims to protect, and as a comity of nations was established to protect (right to life, humaneness, self-determination). The difference between domestic and international crimes becomes real when we look at the referral practice of international courts. In 2006, the International Criminal Tribunal for Rwanda (ICTR) prosecutor attempted to refer the *Bagaragaza* indictment, which included charges of genocide, to Norway. Because Norway's domestic law did not specifically include the crime of genocide, it proposed to prosecute the case as homicide under its national law. ICTR chambers rejected the referral to Norway because the crime of homicide, it noted, lacks the specific intent element required for genocide and, more importantly, homicide was not a crime of comparable gravity to genocide.[35] A conviction and punishment for murder would not have the same expressionist value.

The expressionist dimension of sentencing equally affects the broader question of criminal responsibility. The domestic criminal law framework

34 Sloane, 'The Expressive Capacity of International Punishment', 42. For a good overview on the argument of expressive justice in international criminal law and its limits, see B. Sander, 'The Expressive Limits of International Criminal Justice: Victim Trauma and Local Culture in the Iron Cage of the Law', (2016) iCourts Working Paper Series No. 38.

35 ICTR, Decision on Rule 11*bis* Appeal of 30 August 2006 (AC), *Bagaragaza*, ICTR-05-86-AR11*bis*, para.17.

may not have the capacity to sufficiently express moral repudiation. I use two examples from Dutch criminal law to illustrate my point. First the *Basebya* case, which concerns a Rwandan politician who was convicted for incitement to commit genocide by a Dutch court and sentenced to 6 years and 8 months.[36] The Court was apologetic in imposing the sentence; it felt that the sentence insufficiently expressed moral condemnation; especially bearing in mind that the defendant had not expressed any remorse.[37] Incitement in Dutch criminal law is criminalized in Section 131 of the Dutch Penal Code. It does not specifically refer to genocide, it concerns inciting any criminal offence that disturbs the public order. As such, it comes with a lenient sentence (5 years).[38] In 2003, the International Crimes Act came into effect, which criminalizes incitement to commit genocide separately and provides for a harsher sentence. Yet, because incitement is an inchoate form of liability – like attempt – a Penal Code provision still applies that reduces the sentence by a third.[39] This does not accord with international practice to impose serious sentences on those who mastermind mass criminality and instigate ethnic hatred by way of incitement. Because of the legality principle, prohibiting retroactive application of the law, the Court was bound by the law as it stood at the time of the offences. It imposed the sanction of Section 131 of the Penal Code (5 years) and increased it by a third because of multiple commission of incitement.[40]

The second example concerns an older case and is about the reliance on the defence of necessity. In the post-World War II case of *Fullriede*, the defendant raised the defence of necessity to deny liability for war crimes.[41] Jonas Nilsson Fullriede was a member of the German occupation forces in the Netherlands. As a reprisal measure for an assault on German officers, he

36 The Hague District Court, 1 March 2013, LJN: BZ4292. A summary in English is available at www.asser.nl.

37 The Hague District Court, 1 March 2013, LJN: BZ4292, paras 22.11 and 22.12.

38 A maximum of 5 years imprisonment applies: 'Hij die in het openbaar, mondeling of bij geschrift of afbeelding, tot enig strafbaar feit of tot gewelddadig optreden tegen het openbaar gezag opruit, wordt gestraft met gevangenisstraf van ten hoogste vijf jaren of geldboete van de vierde categorie.' When it concerns a terrorist offence the penality is increased with a third (Sec. 131(2) of the Dutch Penal Code).

39 In Sec. 3(2) the Dutch International Crimes Act provides that a person is punished for a third of the max penalty for genocide, which is 30 years imprisonment. Ergo for incitement to genocide it would be 10 years imprisonment. An English translation of the International Crimes Act is available at https://documents.law.yale.edu/sites/default/files/netherlands_-_international_crimes_act_english_.pdf.

40 Required by Sec. 57 of the Dutch Penal Code.

41 Dutch Special Court of Cassation, Judgment of 10 January 1949, (1948) *Nederlandse Jurisprudentie* 541.

was under the duty to inflict collective punishment on the population of the village of Putten. Ninety houses were burnt down and a few hundred men were arrested and deported to Germany. Fullriede claimed that he had executed the order in a mild way and that if it had been left to another, it would have been executed in full severity and 2,000 houses would have been burnt down. His resort to the defence of necessity/choice of evils ('noodtoestand') was declined. The Court held that necessity can never *justify* such a huge loss of life; never can 90 lives be balanced against 2,000 lives. In 'ordinary' Dutch criminal law, necessity can be a choice of evils-defence that fully exempts the defendant even when there is a loss of life.

The issue is even more pertinent when the defendant relies on the defence of duress to *excuse* him or her for succumbing to a pressure in taking human life to save his or her own. Duress in most civil law systems is a complete defence for murder. Most common law systems, however, do not accord duress the status of complete defence. In cases of murder, it can only mitigate the sentence. Interestingly, with regard to international crimes cases, there is no distinction between civil law and common law systems on this point. There is a reluctance across the board to accord duress the status of complete defence when it concerns international crimes. This was the position taken by the International Criminal Court for the former Yugoslavia (ICTY) Appeals Chamber in *Erdemović* when the defendant relied on the defence of duress for being forced – at gunpoint – to kill seventy Muslims.[42] This, in my view, is the appropriate position.[43] As in the case of *Fullriede*, Dražen Erdemović had killed a large number of people; such a crime cannot go unpunished. Even though he was forced to pull the trigger and anyone in his situation would have done the same, his conduct warrants punishment. That way, it serves the objective of justice for victims. More controversially, I would argue that it can serve the perpetrator himself. This is what Erdemović had come to accept.[44] The punishment, which was lenient – 5 years imprisonment – was an atonement that enabled him to start anew and return to his community, whose families had been affected by his acts. Both examples illustrate how ordinary domestic criminal law needs tweaking when international crimes are tried before domestic courts, mainly because of expressionist concerns of punishment.

42 ICTY, Judgment of 7 October 1997 (AC), *Erdemović*, IT-96-22-A.

43 For another – persuasive – view, see L.E. Chiesa, 'Duress, Demanding Heroism and Proportionality: The Erdemović Case and Beyond' (2008) 41 *Vanderbilt Journal of Transnational Law* 741. I sympathize with that view, see E. van Sliedregt, *Individual Criminal Responsibility in International Law* (Oxford: Oxford University Press, 2012), 259.

44 See statements by Erdemović at his trial: www.youtube.com/watch?v=rAQp27mSTAM.

2 Perpetrators of International Crimes

Sloane's third point concerns the nature of international perpetrators. Here we can draw on the work of criminologists. Herbert Kelman and V. Lee Hamilton have pointed out that international perpetrators may be perfectly law-abiding in ordinary circumstances.[45] A collapse of common values in a period of transition and disintegration, however, may turn them into criminals. In fact, as these crimes are often committed as part of a system, they may engender conduct that is criminal outside the system but actually comports with the system (Nazi Germany).[46] This resonates in Hannah Arendt's work on the *Eichmann* case where she describes evil as 'banal' for the sheer lack of moral reflection on the part of the defendant when performing his murderous task within the Nazi bureaucracy.[47] As Alette Smeulers argues in drawing up a typology of international perpetrators, rather than constituting *deviant* conduct, international crimes are 'crimes of obedience'.[48] In her typology, Smeulers distinguishes between perpetrators who would be perfectly law-abiding in normal circumstances and those who are 'genuinely' bad. Those such as Adolf Hitler, Saddam Hussein and Slobodan Milošević, who master-minded international crimes, are at the apex of Smeulers' typology and are considered inherently evil. This type of perpetrator will often be driven by hatred, sadism and have a narcissistic personality. They are referred to as 'enemies of mankind' or *hostis humanis*. Others who, one way or another, have found themselves forced to commit international crimes, such as Erdemović, do not qualify as such. Yet they are worthy of punishment. They are compromised by the situation or passive bystanders who fail to intervene and speak out against those who instigate and engender international crimes.

45 H.C. Kelman and V.L. Hamilton, *Crimes of Obedience: Toward a Social Psychology of Authority and Responsibility* (Boston: Harvard University Press, 1989).

46 See H.C. Kelman, 'The Policy Context of International Crimes' in A.P. Nollkaemper and H. van der Wilt (eds.), *System Criminality in International Law* (Cambridge: Cambridge University Press, 2009), 26. On this, see also the contribution by Frank Neubacher in Chapter 3.

47 Hannah Arendt's work has been criticized for giving rise to interpretations that portray Eichmann as a mere cog in the wheel, disguising his strong anti-Semitic views and support for the 'Endlösung'. See B. Stangneth, *Eichmann before Jerusalem: The Unexamined Life of a Mass Murderer* (New York: Knopf, 2014); D. Cesarani, *Becoming Eichmann: Rethinking the Life, Crimes, and Trial of a 'Desk Murderer'* (Cambridge: Da Capo Press, 2006).

48 A. Smeulers, 'Perpetrators of International Crimes' in A. Smeulers and R. Haveman (eds.), *Supranational Criminology: Towards a Criminology of International Crimes* (Antwerp: Intersentia, 2008), 233.

Not all perpetrators are brainwashed bureaucrats or compromised bystanders. One can think of Hassan Ngeze, the extremist editor-in-chief of the anti-Tutsi newspaper 'Kangura', who was convicted for genocide and incitement to commit genocide by the ICTR and who serves a 35-year sentence in Mali.[49] With regard to the situation in the former Yugoslavia, some perpetrators did what they always did and would have done: operate outside the law. They were thugs before, during and after the war. The war was just an opportunity to increase their criminal trade. Željko Ražnatović, also known as 'Arkan', headed a paramilitary group which in essence was a mafia-type mob, a criminal organization that made lots of money on the black market that flourished during the war. Theft, plunder and organized crime is intimately linked to armed conflict and mass atrocities. In his 2005 book *Hitler's Beneficiaries*, historian Götz Aly describes the Holocaust as 'the most single-mindedly pursued campaign of murderous larceny in modern history'.[50] Greed similarly drove the Hutus to kill and loot Tutsi households.[51]

The *sui generis* nature of international crimes and perpetrators should, therefore, not be exaggerated. There is an overlap between organized crime and international crimes, between 'ordinary perpetrators' and perpetrators of international crimes. When it comes to perpetrators, those who benefit from armed conflict by making money out of it, can be remarkably similar to the average gang leader or mafioso. Here, the *sui generis* argument against the domestic analogy does not work. When there are similarities between 'ordinary' and international crimes, there is no bar to the international application of domestically developed sentencing purposes.

III PUNISHMENT AND SENTENCING IN INTERNATIONAL CRIMINAL LAW

Punishment requires justification. Most criminal justice systems employ four main sentencing purposes: retribution, prevention, condemnation/denunciation and, to a greater or lesser degree, rehabilitation. In international criminal law, the first three play a prominent role. The ICTY, in one of its first

49 ICTR, Judgement of 28 November 2007 (AC), *Nahimana et al.*, ICTR-99-52-A.

50 G. Aly, *Hitler's Beneficiaries: Plunder, Racial War and the Nazi Welfare State* (New York: Holt Paperbacks, 2005), 285. See also M. Dean, *Robbing the Jews: The Confiscation of Jewish Property in the Holocaust, 1933–1945* (Cambridge: Cambridge University Press, 2008).

51 J. Hatzfeld, *Machete Season: The Killers in Rwanda Speak* (New York: Farrar, Straus & Giroux, 2005), 87, discussed in D. Jones, *Genocide – A Comprehensive Introduction*, 3rd ed. (London: Routledge, 2017), 531–532.

judgments reiterated the sentencing purposes, which it said were the Tribunal's objectives:

> [g]eneral prevention (or deterrence), reprobation, retribution (or 'just deserts'), as well as collective reconciliation – fit into the Security Council's broader aim of maintaining peace and security in the former Yugoslavia. These purposes and functions of the International Tribunal as set out by the Security Council may provide guidance in determining the punishment for a crime against humanity.[52]

Over the years, and certainly since Nuremberg, international legal practice has been more explicit in how it views sentencing purposes in relation to the wider objectives of international criminal justice. Nuremberg was still embracing a predominantly expressionist theory of punishment where the priority was moral condemnation. It was mainly backward-looking. In modern international criminal law, we witness a move to a communicative theory of punishment, which comes with the ambition of reconciliation and reparation, of peace through justice. A communicative theory of justice is backward-looking *and* forward-looking. In terms of sentencing purposes, this comes with an increased interest in the transitional justice functions of international trials, in recording history and post-conflict resolution. This tracks the success of restorative justice that became popular in national jurisdictions from the early 1990s onwards. Restorative justice is the justice process whereby parties with a stake in a specific offence resolve collectively how to deal with the aftermath of the offence and implications for the future.[53] It is increasingly popular in transitional settings because it holds a promise of conflict-solving. There are, however, serious obstacles to implementing it in situations of transition. I will discuss this further in Section IV.

[52] ICTY, Sentencing Judgment of 29 November 1996 (TC), *Erdemović*, IT-96-22-T, para. 58.

[53] T.F. Marshall, *Restorative Justice: An Overview* (Minneapolis: Center for Restorative Justice and Peacemaking, 1998), reprinted in G. Johnstone (ed.), *A Restorative Justice Reader* (Cullompton: Willan Publishing, 2003), 28. Albert Eglash, a psychologist, who worked in programmes for youthful offenders and adult prisoners, is credited with first using the term 'restorative justice'. He defined it as the technique of [creative] restitution, contrasting it to retributive and distributive justice, which he associated with techniques of punishment and therapeutic treatment, respectively, A. Eglash, 'Beyond Restitution: Creative Restitution' in J. Hudson and B. Galaway (eds.), *Restitution in Criminal Justice* (Lexington: D.C. Heath and Company, 1977), 91, referred to by K. Daly, 'The Punishment Debate in Restorative Justice', in J. Simon and R. Sparks (eds.), *The Handbook of Punishment and Society* (London: Sage Publications, 2013).

One of the sentencing purposes that plays an important role in domestic sentencing but hardly any in international criminal law, is rehabilitation.[54] In the *Erdemović* case rehabilitation was taken into account when sentencing the defendant. His young age and the fact that he had expressed genuine remorse played an important role in imposing a lenient sentence.[55] That way, the Court considered, he had the best chance to start again and return to his community. Rehabilitation does not play a role with the bigger fry, those who mastermind crimes. Neither is it taken into account with defendants who have orchestrated the commission of crimes or committed such crimes *con amore*, with conviction. Here the *hostis humanis* argument seems to hamper any post-conviction considerations. Having said that, just in general, even after an acquittal and when defendants have served their sentence, international courts and tribunals fail in paying attention to reintegration. For the post-trial justice part, international courts revert back to the sovereign state and the (former) defendant's domestic jurisdiction.

For years now, a number of former accused of the ICTR reside in a safe house in Arusha, Tanzania.[56] Some have been acquitted, and some have completed their sentences. They cannot leave Arusha and join their families, most of whom live in Western Europe and Canada. These states refuse to grant them asylum. States can lawfully do so on the basis of Article 1F(a) of the Refugee Convention, which stipulates that persons seeking refuge can be excluded from protection when there are 'serious reasons for considering' they committed war crimes, crimes against humanity or crimes against peace. The 'serious reason for considering'-threshold falls short of the criminal law standard of 'beyond reasonable doubt'. This means that even when acquitted, a person may remain undeserving for protection under the Refugee Convention. Sending acquitted and sentenced persons back to Rwanda is not an option as they will face prosecution for related charges and not necessarily receive a fair trial. Former ICTR President Judge Khan has deplored this problem of resettlement.[57] It is a fundamental expression of the rule of law to

[54] On the diminished role of rehabilitation as punishment rationale in the jurisprudence of international courts and tribunals, see also the contribution by Sergey Vasiliev in Chapter 4.

[55] ICTY, *Erdemović* Sentencing Judgment, para. 58.

[56] See the report on http://whenjusticeisdone.org/index.php/32-acquitted. See also the latest annual report of the Residual Mechanism for International Criminal Tribunals (MICT) of 1 August 2018, which suggests that there are still former defendants waiting to be resettled and residing in Arusha (para. 71), available at www.irmct.org/sites/default/files/documents/180801-sixth-annual-report-en.pdf.

[57] Letter dated 16 November 2011 from the President of the ICTR addressed to the President of the Security Council, S/2011/731.

guarantee acquitted and sentenced persons the right to live, including full enjoyment of education, employment and family. The registrar of the Rwanda Tribunal has tried to persuade countries to resettle those residing in the ICTR safe-house. He has not been very successful, so far very few states have come forward to volunteer and reintegrate former defendants. In this context, we can mention the rather uplifting ruling in the *Ruhumuliza* case where the UK Immigration Tribunal considered suitable for settlement, a Rwandese claimant who had been excluded from refugee protection while residing in the United Kingdom for over ten years.[58] After a character and conduct assessment, where his remorse and apologies regarding the genocide played an important role, the Tribunal held that these tests 'involve a consideration that goes beyond looking at the past'.[59] International criminal law is currently too one-dimensional, focused on prosecution and adjudication. Rehabilitation should be an integral part of international criminal justice, as it is in any sophisticated and human rights-compliant criminal justice system. Here the domestic analogy should guide international criminal justice in rebalancing the system and bolster the protective side of criminal justice.

When sentencing an individual who committed very serious but 'unusual' or extra-ordinary offences, in the sense that they are not part of the normal pattern of civil society, there are two conflicting forces. One is to say, offences are so serious that we must impose the most serious sentence available, which in international criminal law is life. The other is to say, normality needs to be brought back to a divided community and by having a sentence, which is measured and not overly harsh to one particular side, you are more likely to appease and bring about a process of reconciliation. Which way one goes, depends on the victim community. In Rwanda, imposing a lenient sentence is difficult to digest for victim communities as was the case for the Tutsi government and President Paul Kagame, who lead the civil war against the Hutu, which preceded the genocide. In the former Yugoslavia, the situation was different; ethnic divisions are more complex. ICTY defendants, especially those in senior positions, still enjoy support in parts of Serbia, Croatia and Bosnia. General Ante Gotovina, who was acquitted by the ICTY,[60] was greeted by 100,000 supporters upon his arrival in Croatia.[61] Croatians regarded his trial as an attack on the young state of Croatia. When he was acquitted, this

[58] [2016] UKUT 284 (IAC), section 5.

[59] [2016] UKUT 284 (IAC), section 11.

[60] ICTY, Judgment of 16 November 2012 (AC), *Gotovina and Markač*, IT-06-90-A.

[61] See J. van Wijk and B. Holá, 'Acquittals in International Criminal Justice: Pyrrhic Victories' (2016) 30 *Leiden Journal of International Law* 241, 243–244. See also B. Waterfield, 'Croatian Hero Ante Gotovina Acquitted of War Crimes', *The Telegraph*, 16 November 2012, available

felt like a collective vindication of the earlier felt stigma when he was charged and prosecuted.[62] Research by Holá and van Wijk, however, has shown that lower-level defendants have had a hard time returning to their communities in the former Yugoslavia.[63] The Serbian Zejnil Delalić lost his business during his 2-year pre-trial detention, was never compensated and lives in poverty as a result of it.[64] The Kupreškićs, former members of the Croatian Defence Council of the self-proclaimed state of Croatia in Bosnia, befell a similar fate.[65] They are still viewed by their neighbours as war criminals.

Post-trial rehabilitation and reintegration have been afterthoughts when setting up international courts. These sentencing purposes deserve more thought, especially when one of the goals of international criminal justice is reconciliation. Reintegration can accommodate and smooth reconciliation. More thought has to go into punishment theories that are tailored to a particular conflict situation or a particular defendant. Why should we not think about other sentences than incarceration? What about community sentences? Alongside a prison sentence, defendants could be required to contribute to a victim's trust fund or to participate in a community project. In that context, the Supreme Court Chamber of the Cambodia Tribunal's decision in the case of Kaing Guek Eav ('Duch') is interesting. It affirmed the Trial Chamber's sentencing decision to compile and post on the ECCC's official website all statements of apology and acknowledgements of responsibility made by Duch during the course of the trial, including the appeal stage.[66]

IV PUNISHMENT AND COMMUNITY

The biggest obstacle to having an international criminal justice system that provides for rehabilitation and reconciliation alongside reprobation and retribution, is the fact that it largely operates in a vacuum. International criminal justice is not embedded in a political community and relies heavily on state

online at www.telegraph.co.uk/news/worldnews/europe/croatia/9682855/Croatian-hero-Ante-Gotovina-acquitted-of-war-crimes.html.

62 van Wijk and Holá, 'Acquittals in International Criminal Justice', 243–244.

63 See van Wijk and Holá, 'Acquittals in International Criminal Justice'; B. Holá and J. van Wijk, 'Life after Conviction at International Criminal Tribunals', 109.

64 Van Wijk and Holá, 'Acquittals in International Criminal Justice', 257.

65 Van Wijk and Holá, 'Acquittals in International Criminal Justice', 257.

66 ECCC, Appeal Judgment of 3 February 2012 (Supreme Court Chamber), *Kaing Guek Eav ('Duch')*, 001/18-07-2007-ECCC/SC, para. 716.

cooperation to perform basic functions such as arresting accused persons, evidence-gathering and imprisonment. Having said that, the International Criminal Court (ICC) and the ad hoc Tribunals are said to represent the interests of the international community when prosecuting and punishing those who commit international crimes. What does that mean? The international community is a rather elusive and abstract notion. The best that can be said of this 'communitarianism' is that by setting up international justice, the UN and other multinational bodies such as the ICC side with victims who have no government or judicial authority to turn to when it comes to punishing their perpetrators. International courts temporarily replace and take over from a malfunctioning domestic justice system. This does not necessarily mean that the interests of an international court or tribunal align with those of the state or region whose justice system(s) is replaced. Milena Tripkovic convincingly argues that the ICTY will never be able to achieve reconciliation in the former Yugoslavia because of a lack of shared perception and consciousness that it acts in the name and for the sake of the ex-Yugoslav community. International prosecutions can only be a substitute for domestic processes if the aim of the international court to achieve justice is shared with the local community. Moreover, reconciliation via criminal justice is not possible when a common morality is affirmed for internally divided communities. In fact, international prosecutions may go against the interests of senior officials in those displaced jurisdictions; government ministers and presidents may be subject to investigations and prosecutions themselves. In such situations, international prosecutors work at cross-purposes with the interests of those in the higher echelons of a particular political community. The cases of the presidents of Kenya and the Ivory Coast, Uhuru Kenyatta and Laurent Gbagbo, at the ICC, and Radovan Karadžić at the ICTY, illustrate the point. The fact that international criminal justice operates in a vacuum hampers its ability to achieve reconciliation on the ground. At this point, we have to turn to Anthony Duff's work.

Duff in his work on punishment reconciles what for a long time was considered irreconcilable: the punishment paradigm and the restorative paradigm. He argues that restoration is not only compatible with retribution, it *requires* retribution in that the kind of restoration that crime makes necessary can 'be brought about only through retributive punishment'. Crime harms and wrongs a person, which requires a criminal response. Repair requires something that 'only an offender can provide', which 'involves the offender's punishment'. In his view, reparation must be burdensome if it is to serve its restorative purpose. It is not hard to see the parallel with the peace through justice maxim that underlies international criminal law.

Building on Duff's theory in reconciling punishment and restoration, we can engage with the other limb of his theory of punishment: communication. In *Punishment, Communication and Community*, Duff introduces his theory of punishment as a process of communication. This is different from an expressionist-communication theory of punishment, which is a one-sided exercise. Punishment in Duff's view is two-sided, it is an exercise of purposive communication, namely to educate the defendant and the victim community. Punishment is a retributive notion of censure which at the same time addresses the consequentialist concern of crime prevention. Punishment can be justified as a mode of moral education. It is owed to the community but it also benefits the offender. Here, an interesting parallel can be drawn with the Erdemović case in section III, where I argued that punishment enabled a return of the defendant to the community. One crucial question that Duff's theory throws up is: Who owes what to whom? This is not straightforward in transitional and civil war-like situations. Another important element of his two-sided communicative justice theory concerns the perpetrator's attitude. Whether punishment as communication works depends on the type of offender and whether he or she accepts punishment. Defiant offenders may not repent. As we saw earlier, in transitional situations the restorative justice aim, despite its appeal, may be very difficult to meet because divided communities do not feel represented by an international court. The same can be said about defiant offenders; they do not recognize the court as having punishing authority. Karadžić was regarded a hero by part of the Serbian community back home for rejecting the ICTY's authority to try him, by denying criminal responsibility and by glorifying his role and conduct during the Yugoslav war. His supporters belonged to another community than the (Bosnian) victim community with whom the ICTY sided. Karadžić completely placed himself outside the community that the ICTY represented. Here Duff's theory is doomed to fail. Erdemović was what Duff calls a shamed offender who 'owed up' to his crimes vis-à-vis the victim community. Here, restorative justice after punishment can work. This is a process left to the state. So far, there is no supranational restorative justice system. International criminal law only provides for the punitive part.

While it is impossible to do justice to Duff's theory of punishment in the context of this chapter, we can take away a few points, which may inspire us to rethink the claim of reconciliation as a sentencing purpose for international criminal law. First of all, punishment in a communicative theory as proposed by Duff aligns nicely with the maxim of peace through justice and the backword- and forward-looking purposes of modern international criminal justice. At face value, it is a good starting point for further developing and refining punishment theories in international criminal law. However, and this is my second point, in reality it will be difficult to accomplish reconciliation. Reconciliation cannot happen when communities feel unrepresented by an international justice system. To quote Duff, 'the court must speak in the voice of law on behalf of the political community'. Such a political community must consist of fellow citizens, citizens that feel wronged by the defendant and whom they allow to re-enter after punishment. Not representing a community is the biggest challenge to international criminal justice when it comes to reconciliation. Different reasons may account for this lack of representation, e.g. the fact that communities are divided or that there is no ownership over the justice process. The elusive international community does not necessarily speak for victim communities. In the words of a Srebrenica resident when asked about the impact of the ICTY on reconciliation: 'no reconciliation can come from a court than has so little relevance to our daily lives'. Martti Koskenniemi warns those who claim to speak in the name of humanity. Such claims are always 'infected' by the particularity of the speaker, his or her world view, knowledge, ignorance and experience. Drumbl is of a similar view and concludes that international courts have a limited potential when it comes to reconciliation. A third point that should make us rethink the claim of reconciliation is that there is no supranational infrastructure for restorative justice. This has to take place at the national level. International criminal law only provides for a punitive process. Reconciliation and restoration requires alignment and synchronization of international and domestic interests, which as we saw under the second point, is not easy to obtain. Only in cases of shamed and remorseful defendants is there a chance of success. Only then can the international punishment rationale be successfully linked to a national restorative process. Fourthly, there is a careful balance to be struck in how international criminal law approaches defendants. A communicative theory is about moral education by way of placing the defendant (temporarily) outside the (wronged) community yet allowing him or her to return after punishment. This seems to require moderation in treating defendants. After all, they must be able to re-enter. Branding war criminals as enemies of mankind who can be excluded from refugee protection, wholly placing them outside any community, is an obstacle to restoration and reconciliation. The defendant's attitude is important too. Undermining the legitimacy of the international criminal justice system and, more importantly, taking the court room as a podium for political speeches should be limited, naturally within the confines of fair trial-requirements. Criminal master minds and mass murderers may be regarded as 'beyond rehabilitation' but the majority of defendants are not and will eventually be released. International criminal law needs to own up to this reality.

V CONCLUSION

In discussing punishment theories and sentencing purposes in international criminal law, we see differences and similarities between domestic and international criminal justice. The domestic analogy (of transplant) pulls in different directions. We might not do justice to the specific nature of international crimes and perpetrators when we uncritically adopt and apply domestic theories of punishment. On the other hand, we should not overdo the focus on differences. Distinguishing international crimes from domestic crime is sometimes based on a caricature of domestic, 'garden variety' crime. This way, we fail to see the overlap and similarities between international crimes and certain forms of domestic (organized) crime. Also, we risk not grappling with the category of smaller fry; defendants who do not qualify as *hostis humanis*, enemy of mankind. In those cases, the domestic analogy can work. Adhering too much to the sui generis claim, might prevent us from benefitting from useful insights and research into alternative ways of punishment. There can be other or additional ways, other than imprisonment, to address international perpetrators. Such alternatives may be more effective in achieving restoration and reconciliation. In any event, there is a need to explore such avenues and adopt a broader approach to punishment. Domestic criminal justice is an important and rich source to draw on.

The domestic analogy ('proper') offers an insight into what is a fundamental flaw of international criminal justice: the fact that it operates in a vacuum and is a surrogate criminal justice system that for post-trial justice reverts to domestic criminal justice. Cosmopolitanism, which inspired the thinking about world community and world government, and that has had an important influence on international criminal justice, does not come with a fully fledged supranational criminal justice system. This in turn affects the domestic analogy of transplant. It cannot work. There is no international infrastructure to support restorative justice; it depends on State jurisdictions to provide for this part of the criminal process. International criminal justice reveals itself as an imperfect, one-sided exercise, solely interested in the punishment part of criminal justice.

What both the domestic analogy of transplant and the domestic analogy proper reveal when applied to international criminal law, is that the restorative potential of international criminal justice is limited because of 'community-concerns'. Peace through justice, reconciliation and restoration are drivers of international criminal law. They are a feature of modern-day international criminal justice. A prerequisite for restorative justice is that there is a community that not only has an interest in restoration but also a stake. This is not necessarily the case in transitional settings where different ethnic, religious and social-economic groups can be on conflicting sides. Indeed, in transitional situations, there can be a plethora of communities with different, sometimes opposing interests. This lack of a (homogeneous) community makes it difficult to reintegrate the offender and hampers the process of doing so. Doing justice in the name of the international community reduces this complex picture of interests and values. Justifying international criminal justice by capturing it in vague ambitions, such as ending impunity and protecting the interests of humanity, does not do much to achieve reconciliation. The lofty ambitions do not automatically align with the interests of the victim community. International courts risk alienating victim communities on whose behalf they claim to act when there is no further thought on why punishment is imposed and to what end. Duff's work on communicative punishment should make us think about the current process of punishing. We may need to rethink certain expressionist purposes of punishment. This could come about by embracing Drumbl's theory of cosmopolitan pluralism and allow, as part of the international criminal justice process, local, grass-roots justice.

Different defendants require different approaches. This is the case in any criminal justice system. This is multiplied in international criminal law because of the heterogeneity of the communities that defendants belong to or feel associated with. The reality of heterogeneity should always be in the forefront of our minds when we think about punishment theories in international criminal law. This may prompt us to work on creating conditions of punishment and reintegration that decrease a divisive effect. One way forward would be to rethink the function of Residual Mechanisms that have been set up after courts have closed down and that are tasked with prosecuting fugitives and with protecting the courts' legacy. Residual Mechanisms should prioritize post-trial, restorative justice support and focus solely on outreach activities with local authorities. This can take different forms, for instance telling the history of the conflict, preventing the rewriting history and glorifying battlefield myths. This should be the primary responsibility of any Residual Mechanism if peace through justice is to be taken seriously. I would go as far as to suggest that Residual Mechanisms should renounce prosecuting and trying remaining fugitives. When a tribunal or court closes, its judicial function closes. We move on. We have dealt with the conflict and its atrocities and need to focus on post-conflict justice.

A last observation concerns reintegration. As with the enforcement of sentences where states can agree to voluntarily imprison those convicted by the international courts, states should sign up to receive and resettle former defendants. The international community, presidents of international courts, NGOs and human rights organizations should get together and lobby for the setting up of a system of resettlement and reintegration. If states support the fight against impunity and the system of international prosecution and adjudication, they must accept this part of international criminal justice too.

6

Not Much, but Better than Nothing – Purposes of Punishment in International Criminal Law

A Comment on the Contributions by Frank Neubacher, Sergey Vasiliev and Elies van Sliedregt

KAI AMBOS

I A *IUS PUNIENDI* WITHOUT A STATE?

The overall topic of this volume – why punish perpetrators of mass atrocities? – is highly relevant for a solid theory of international criminal law. At its most profound level, the why-punish-question speaks to the highly contested issue of whether a right to punish *(ius puniendi)* can exist without a state. International criminal law practice does not seem to care much about this foundational issue given the amount and wealth of practical, nitty-gritty problems faced by international criminal law institutions, especially the International Criminal Court (ICC),[1] because, as rightly stated by Sergey Vasiliev, 'practice shapes the agenda and theory is only secondary' (in other words, in practice 'why' is secondary to 'how').[2] At any rate, international criminal law is clearly predicated on the assumption of such a *ius puniendi*. Most international criminal law theorists start from the classical position that there is no free floating *ius puniendi* without some institutional backing[3] and this position finds support in the classical view that the existence of a state encompasses its right to punish for the preservation of its existence.[4] If one favours such an

[1] To get a feeling of these problems, just skim through the ICC Commentary edited by Otto Triffterer and this author, 3rd ed. (München: Beck/Hart/Nomos, 2016).

[2] S. Vasiliev puts it at the inverse ('how is secondary to why'), but this is apparently an error (p. 51).

[3] G. Binder, 'Authority to Proscribe and Punish International Crimes' (2013) 63 *University of Toronto Law Journal* 278 (stressing the importance of an institutional 'punishing authority'); also A. Chehtman, 'The Extraterritorial Scope of the Right to Punish' (2010) 29 *Law and Philosophy* 127, 131 ('necessary link between a legal system being in force and a particular body holding the power to punish offenders').

[4] R. Dreier and S. Paulson (eds.), *Gustav Radbruch – Rechtsphilosophie. Studienausgabe* (Heidelberg: C.F. Müller, 1999), 151 et seq. (arguing, at 152, that the justification of criminal law alien to the state was overcome with the existence of the state, which entails that the doctrine of the reason of punishment is absorbed by the justification of the state itself).

'axiological linkage between punishment and State',[5] anything less than a state, even an existing, treaty-based international criminal court, does not seem to be able to do the job. However, as I have tried to show elsewhere, it is possible to take a human being- (instead of state) focused view and derive the *ius puniendi* from the human dignity of each and every person.[6] This is one – the normative – pillar of a supranational *ius puniendi*, which complements or compensates for the second pillar, i.e., the only incipient institutionality at the international level.[7] Clearly, any attempt to justify a *ius puniendi* without a state must take an individualistic or personalistic approach, i.e., it must construe criminal law accountability as answerability to the injured individuals, organized as a polity, society or mere community.[8]

II THE DOMESTIC ANALOGY

The 'why punish' question has a second, upper and more visible level with, albeit limited, practical implications. This level concerns the purposes of punishment and they have been treated by the three papers of Elies van Sliedregt, Sergey Vasiliev and Frank Neubacher. In this area, international criminal law does not need to reinvent the wheel but basically to transfer the well-known domestic (mainly retributivist and preventive) theories to the

The position is also well entrenched in case law. See, e.g., Judicial Committee of the Privy Council (JCPC), Proprietary Articles Trade Ass'n v A.-G. Can., (1931) 2 *Dominion Law Reports* 1, 1931 CanLII 385 (UK JCPC), 9 ('Criminal law connotes only the quality of such acts or omissions as are prohibited under appropriate penal provisions by authority of the State.').

5 S. Mir Puig, 'Die Funktion der Strafe und die Verbrechenslehre im sozialen und demokratischen Rechtsstaat' (1983) 95 *Zeitschrift für die gesamte Strafrechtswissenschaft* 413 ('axiologische Verknüpfung zwischen Straf- und Staatsfunktion').

6 K. Ambos, 'Punishment without a Sovereign? The *Ius Puniendi* Issue of International Criminal Law' (2013) 33 *Oxford Journal of Legal Studies* 293 ('derived from universal, indivisible and interculturally recognized human rights predicated upon a Kantian concept of human dignity'), 304 ('[. . .] normative international order, based on certain values worthy of being defended by international criminal law, can be traced back to the Kantian idea of human dignity as a source of fundamental human (civil) rights [. . .]') with multiple references.

7 Ambos, 'Punishment without a Sovereign?', 298 et seq.

8 In this vein, cf. R.A. Duff, 'Authority and Responsibility in International Criminal Law' in S. Besson and J. Tasioulas (eds.), *The Philosophy of International Law* (Oxford: Oxford University Press, 2010), 589, 595 (answerability to the community/polity of fellow citizens for 'public' wrongs, i.e., wrongs that concern the public). See also Sauvé v Canada (Chief Electoral Officer), [2002] 3 S.C.R. 519, para. 47 ('[. . .] right of the state to punish and the obligation of the criminal to accept punishment is tied to society's acceptance of the criminal as a person with rights and responsibilities [. . .]').

international level.[9] Van Sliedregt invokes the domestic analogy objection in this context – she even makes it part of the title of her chapter – but I think that she is overstretching the notion.

It is worthwhile remembering that this term, in the context of international criminal law,[10] was, as far as I can see, coined by the International Criminal Tribunal for the former Yugoslavia (ICTY) Appeals Chamber, Antonio Cassese presiding, in a very specific context, namely the issuing of a subpoena *(duces tecum)* by Judge McDonald to the Republic of Croatia and its Defence Minister in order to compel it to produce certain documents.[11] Trial Chamber II upheld McDonald's decision[12] but the Cassese Appeals Chamber reversed it as to the issuing of orders to a State official acting in official capacity,[13] invoking, inter alia, the domestic analogy objection:

> [...] the Prosecutor's reasoning, adopted by the Trial Chamber in its Subpoena Decision, is clearly based on what could be called 'the domestic analogy'. It is well known that in many national legal systems, where courts are part of the State apparatus and indeed constitute the judicial branch of the State apparatus, such courts are entitled to issue orders to other (say administrative, political, or even military) organs, including senior State officials and the Prime Minister or the Head of State. These organs, subject to a number of well-specified exceptions, can be summoned to give evidence, can be compelled to produce documents, can be requested to appear in court, etc. This is taken for granted in modern democracies, where nobody, not even the Head of State, is above the law (*legibus solutus*). The setting is totally different in the international community. [...][14]

9 Cf. K. Ambos, *Treatise on International Criminal Law*, 3 vols. (Oxford: Oxford University Press, 2013–2016), Vol. I (2016), 67 et seq.

10 Originally, the term was apparently introduced by H. Bull, 'Society and Anarchy in International Relations' in H. Butterfield and M. Wight (eds.), *Diplomatic Investigations. Essays in the Theory of International Politics* (London: Allen & Unwin, 1966), 35: '[...] the domestic analogy, the argument from the experience of individual men in domestic society to the experience of states, according to which the need of individual men to stand in awe of a common power in order to live in peace is a ground for holding that states must do the same'.

11 ICTY, Subpoena Duces Tecum of 15 January 1997 (TC), *Blaškić*, IT-95-14-T.

12 ICTY, Decision of 18 July 1997 (TC), *Blaškić*, IT-95-14-PT.

13 ICTY, Judgement of 29 October 1997 (AC), *Blaškić*, IT-95-14-AR, 108*bis*, III. Disposition: '(2) [...] the International Tribunal may not address binding orders under Article 29 to State officials acting in their official capacity'; '(5) Unanimously DECIDES to quash the *subpoena duces tecum* issued by Judge McDonald and reinstated by Trial Chamber II addressed to Croatia and the Croatian Defence Minister, Mr. Gojko Susak, it being understood that the Prosecutor is at liberty to submit to the appropriate Chamber, being Trial Chamber I, a request for a binding order addressed to Croatia alone.' (emphasis in the original). See, thereto, also ICTY Rule 54*bis*.

14 Bull, 'Society and Anarchy', 40.

While in this context – of state immunity vis-à-vis international tribunals – the domestic analogy objection fully operates, it does not in areas where a classical problem of criminal law – e.g., purposes of punishment – is dealt with at the international level. In these cases, international criminal law merely appears as criminal law at the international level/by the international community and it stands to reason that as such it borrows and imports concepts from national criminal law, benefitting from its centuries of theoretical development and practice. In other words, the domestic analogy concept should not be overstretched, one should be aware how far it really goes. In fact, van Sliedregt herself admits 'similarities' in two main areas where international criminal law may benefit from domestic criminal justice, namely in the areas of rehabilitation (as a punishment purpose) and the community sentence (as, what she calls, 'alternative ways of punishing'). Of course, 'similarities' is an understatement here as these concepts come from domestic sentencing theory and practice and thus are transferred to international criminal law as are the above-mentioned purposes of punishment.[15]

III TRANSFER OF PUNISHMENT PURPOSES, SENTENCING AND THE EMPIRICAL TURN

Vasiliev shows in his thorough analysis of the case law since Nuremberg that retribution and deterrence have always been the most prominent punishment purposes, their validity taken as 'unassailable truth, not a discussion point or claim in need of [empirical] defence'. However, apart from this traditional approach, international criminal justice always aspired to the higher goal of maintaining or restoring international peace and security by prosecuting and

[15] There are other affirmations by van Sliedregt I am struggling with. Why should the 'domestic criminal law' framework [. . .] not have the capacity to sufficiently express moral repudiation' as the international criminal law framework. In fact, domestic prosecutions of international crimes that on the whole exceed international prosecutions show otherwise. The truth is probably that, generally speaking, both kinds of prosecutions have this capacity but whether they actually express sufficient moral repudiation depends on many factors, independent of the international or domestic nature of the prosecution. Also, it is unclear why a sentencing reduction by one third for incitement to genocide, as apparently foreseen in Dutch law, should, in abstracto (sic!), 'not accord with international practice to impose serious sentences'. Does the sentence not depend on various factors of which the form of participation is only one? Does the very nature of incitement as an inchoate form of commission not logically call for a sentencing reduction (the amount of which is, of course, open to debate)? Last but not least, what would be a just and proportional sentence in a given case of incitement to genocide? Without even discussing all these (and other) questions, van Sliedregt's affirmation seems to be unfounded.

punishing international crimes. This started with Nuremberg and Tokyo,[16] made the International Law Commission call its several international criminal law draft codes 'Draft Codes of Crimes Against the Peace and Security of Mankind'[17] and the drafters of the ICC Statute's write in the preamble that 'such grave crimes threaten the peace, security and well-being of the world'.[18] In contrast, rehabilitation and expressivism – as 'ultimate, catch-all objective', 'meta-justification', covering public reprobation, condemnation, stigmatization by the international community, promoting/enhancing/reaffirming the rule of law, the sending of an anti-impunity message, etc. (i.e., what civil law jurisdictions normally call [negative and positive] general prevention)[19] – have only gained importance more recently. Of course, all depends here on the definition of these concepts and how explicitly tribunals speak to purposes of punishment. If the Nuremberg and Tokyo Tribunals stress the moral outrage and make general moral claims[20] this may well be seen, as van Sliedregt does,

[16] Thus, the General Assembly, three weeks after the Nuremberg Tribunal rendered its judgment on 1 October 1946, called the drafting of a code of 'offences against the peace and security of mankind' 'a matter of primary importance' (Resolution 95 (I) of 11 December 1946; Resolution 177 (II) of 21 November 1947).

[17] ILC, *Yearbook of the International Law Commission*, 2 vols. (New York/Genf: United Nations Publication, 1996), Vol. II (Part Two). See also Special Rapporteur's Alfaro reference to protection 'against violations of the international public order' and the provision of 'security through the organization of a permanent system of penal justice'. (ILC, Report on the Question of International Criminal Jurisdiction by Ricardo J. Alfaro, Special Rapporteur, A/CN.4/15 and Corr.1, (1950), 136–137).

[18] Thereto O. Triffterer, M. Bergsmo and K. Ambos, 'Preamble' in O. Triffterer and K. Ambos (eds.), 3rd ed., *The Rome Statute of the International Criminal Court* (München et al.: Beck/Hart/Nomos, 2016), 9 et seq.

[19] On the subsumtion of 'expressivism-based rationales within general deterrence', see also Vasiliev in Chapter 4; on the varying terminology with the same contents Ambos, Treatise Vol. I, 71–72 (positive general prevention as expressivism).

[20] E.g. International Military Tribunal Nuremberg, *Trial of the Major War Criminals*, 42 vols. (Nuremberg: International Military Tribunal Nuremberg, 1947), Vol. I, vii ('Recognizing the importance of establishing for history an authentic text of the Trial of major German war criminals [...]'); ibid. at 223 ('[...] only by punishing individuals who commit such crimes can the provisions of international law be enforced'); see also 'Trials of War Criminals before the Nuremberg Military Tribunals under Control Council' No 10 Vol. I, *US v Karl Brandt et al. ('The Medical Case')*, 1947, 27:

> The mere punishment of the defendants [...] can never redress the terrible injuries the Nazis visited on these unfortunate people. For them it is far more important that these incredible events be established by clear and public proof, so that no one can doubt that they were fact and not fable: and that this Court [...] stamp these acts, and the ideas which engendered them, as barbarous and criminal.

As to the Tokyo Tribunal, see J. Keenan, *Opening Statement for the Prosecution, International Military Tribunal for the Far East ('The Tokyo Trial')*, 1948, 3:

as 'embracing a predominant expressionist theory'. I would, however, not agree with her that '[i]n modern international criminal law, we witness a move to a communicative theory of punishment'. While expressive or communicative theories are particularly important in the context of international criminal law, especially with a view to the victims and the recognition of their victimhood, I am not sure that international criminal law, especially its case law, has reached this level of sophistication.[21]

From a principled perspective, there is nothing to say against a transfer of these purposes of punishment to international criminal law as long as this is not done too schematically (in the sense of 'legal transplants'[22]). Neubacher rightly accepts it – '[r]oughly speaking' – if only the international judges are conscious that they are sitting in an international criminal tribunal and that the punishment purposes may have to be adjusted to the specific aims of their tribunals. As rightly argued by Vasiliev, 'the tribunals sought to alleviate the conceptual discomfort arising from the direct transposition of domestic rationales [. . .] by linking them to the socio-political objectives of international criminal justice'. Of course, this adjustment has largely been a rhetorical exercise with tribunals alluding, inter alia, to international peace and security, the stigmatization of the adjudicated acts by the international community and the fight against impunity. In practical terms, international criminal law did not add anything substantial to the centuries-old purposes of punishment debate and, indeed, no realistic observer could expect that it would. 'The analysis is', as put by Vasiliev, 'mostly perfunctory and *pro forma*, as if the chambers felt compelled to include it only to comply with some drafting conventions [. . .]'.

> Our purpose is one of prevention or deterrence. It has nothing whatsoever to do with the small meaner purpose of vengeance or retaliation. But we do hope in these proceedings that it is neither impossible nor improbable that the branding of individuals who visit these scourges upon mankind as common felons, and punishing them accordingly, may have a deterring effect upon aggressive warlike activities of their prototypes of the future, should they arise.

[21] On punishment, desert and communication in modern penal theory cf. K. Ambos, 'Review Essay: Liberal Criminal Theory' (2017) 28 *Criminal Law Forum* 589, 597 et seq. (critically discussing the relevant contributions in A.P. Simester, A. Du Bois-Pedain and U. Neumann (eds.), *Liberal Criminal Theory. Essays for Andreas von Hirsch* (Oxford: Hart, 2014).

[22] For a fundamental (and affirmative) account of this phenomenon, cf. A. Watson, *Legal Transplants: An Approach to Comparative Law*, 1st ed. (Edinburgh: Scottish Academic Press, 1974), 21 and passim; comprehensively on *ratio*, effect, forms of appearance and traditional practice (from Roman law onwards) M. Siems, *Comparative Law*, 2nd ed. (Cambridge: Cambridge University Press, 2018), 231 et seq. (recognising its actual significance for the development of law, differentiating between positive and negative effects depending on context and identifying a more recent focus on policy).

At any rate, the transfer and the cursory treatment of the punishment purposes by the case law does not do any harm to the enterprise of international criminal justice as long as the sentences meted out appear to be just, fair and proportional. This, in turn, depends on the concrete sentencing factors[23] but not on the purposes of punishment alluded to in the respective judgments for these have practically no influence on the concrete sentence. Vasiliev rightly acknowledges that but does not go far enough if he, overly cautiously, considers it 'uncertain what guidance [. . .] judges draw from the aims of punishment [. . .]' and speaks of the 'little concrete value of abstract punishment rationales [. . .]'. At the same time, he rightly states, albeit somewhat inconsistently with a view to the previous statement, that 'the penalties were calculated primarily by weighing the gravity of the crimes and the individual circumstances going to mitigation or aggravation', that the penal objectives have a 'negligible practical import for the sentencing *calculi* in individual cases [. . .]'. At any rate, Vasiliev is right in stressing the importance of the concrete sentencing factors for the determination of the concrete sentence. It is for this reason that they should be the focus of any treatment of international criminal law sentencing law and practice,[24] separate from the treatment of the rather theoretical purposes of punishment.[25]

Neubacher, while accepting said transfer, convincingly takes issue with several questions. Neubacher is a representative of the 'empirical turn' (Vasiliev) of the international criminal law discourse and thus emphasizes, and rightly so, the empirical side of things. For an empirical approach, as nicely formulated by Vasiliev, 'has the potential of generating evidence that can refute or confirm its normative certitudes, not least the adequacy of goal-setting or real-life effects in terms of prevention, reconciliation and peace'. Of course, to accept the importance of empirical insight, does not mean, as insinuated by Vasiliev, to lose sight of the fact that (criminal) law is a 'normative enterprise'. It only means that we cannot ignore empirical evidence when taking our normative (value-based) decisions.

[23] On this, see M. Zeccola, *Die Strafzumessung im Völkerstrafrecht unter besonderer Berücksichtigung der Rechtssprechung der Ad-hoc-Tribunale der Vereinten Nationen* (Berlin: Duncker & Humblot, 2018), 52 et seq.

[24] K. Ambos, *Treatise on International Criminal Law*, Vol. II (Oxford: Oxford University Press, 2014), 283 et seq.

[25] I have therefore treated the sentencing factors in the context of sentencing (Ambos, Treatise Vol. II, 283 et seq.) and the punishment purposes as a foundational topic (Ambos, Treatise Vol. I, 67 et seq.). On punishment purposes and sentencing factors see, however, the contribution by Gerhard Werle and Aziz Epik in Chapter 18.

IV RETRIBUTION, DETERRENCE AND (RE-)AFFIRMATION

As to retribution, the well-known objections regarding its irrational, metaphysical nature, are reinforced by the fact that one can only retribute that much, e.g. life with life, but not multiple lives with one life (the one of the perpetrator). On a macro-level, this was articulated by Hannah Arendt (quoted by Vasiliev) writing that the sheer scale of Nazi crimes 'render all punishments [. . .] inadequate and absurd'.[26] While this mere numerical argument limits the explanatory force of retribution,[27] it does not mean that retribution plays no role at all.[28] Quite to the contrary, retribution is – with deterrence – the dominant punishment purpose explicitly alluded to in the case law (often under the more metaphysical term of 'just deserts')[29] and it is implicit in proportionality as a sentencing factor.[30] Neubacher himself acknowledges that the length of certain sentences 'can only be understood against the background of retributive theories'. Retribution is complemented by preventive purposes – negatively, by deterrence, and positively (affirmatively), by (contrafactual) reaffirmation of the values protected by criminal law (in Anglo-American and, for that matter, international criminal law parlance included in the above-mentioned expressivism) – but here the problem is empirical as we only have limited evidence as to these alleged effects of criminal law. Neubacher calls this evidence 'anecdotic or methodologically weak' and doubts 'the deterrent effect of punishment' in general and in particular with regard to international criminal law. In addition, there is the problem, as Neubacher correctly asserts, that we are targeting not just anybody but specific powerful individuals so that we need 'targeted deterrence'.

Perpetrators of international crimes are typically not as responsive as ordinary perpetrators to the threat of a criminal sanction. They may be driven by political or ideological motives and thus not act pursuant to rational choices. As Neubacher puts it: '[. . .] perpetrators feel encouraged by their *social environment* and act in full harmony with its expectations'.[31] As a

[26] H. Arendt, *The Origins of Totalitarianism* (New York: Harcourt Brace & Company, 1973), 439.

[27] Critically, also Ambos, *Treatise* Vol. I, 68–69.

[28] On retribution as purpose of punishment in international criminal law, see the contribution by Mordechai Kremnitzer in Chapter 10.

[29] Ambos, *Treatise* Vol. I, 69 with further references. For ICC case law, see e.g. ICC Decision of 23 May 2014 (TC), *Katanga*, ICC-01/04-01/07, para. 38: '[. . .] the role of the sentence is two-fold: on the one hand, punishment, [. . .] on the other hand, deterrence [. . .]'; ICC, Judgment of 27 September 2016, *Al Mahdi*, ICC-01/12-01/15 27, para. 66: '[. . .] the Preamble establishes retribution and deterrence as the primary objectives of punishment at the ICC'.

[30] Ambos, *Treatise* Vol. II, 285 et seq., 288.

[31] My emphasis.

consequence, punishment may even have a counterproductive effect because it is seen as unjust and as undermining the perpetrators' value system. The possible discrepancy between this value system and the value system underlying the (international) criminal law of the time speaks to the difference between deviance from the perpetrators' perspective and illegality/criminality from the mainstream (international criminal law) perspective. As Neubacher puts it: 'The behavior may be illegal, but it is not deviant because in the given setting and for a certain period of time the behavior is regarded as normal.' This discrepancy can only be explained using a behavioural approach that takes into account the societal context of the perpetrators' conduct and distinguishes between the macro-, meso- and micro-level. This is instructively set out by Neubacher.

Last but not least, the selectivity of international criminal justice[32] further weakens its deterrent and norm-reaffirming effect. We know that deterrence exists, if at all, not for the existence of the law in the books but for the high probability of being caught and thus being subjected to this law. Thus, arguably, the more selective a system is the less deterrence it produces. Concretely speaking, if a high-ranking (potential) perpetrator knows that he or she is out of the reach of the 'international criminal justice system'[33] he or she will not be deterred by this system's mere existence. The same applies, vice versa, to the positive preventive effect of norm reaffirmation: Such an effect can only exist if the criminal law is concretely applied and enforced. Thus, Neubacher is right if he calls for the enhancement of the risk of criminal prosecution. Of course, this begs the question of how such an enhancement should be brought about in an international criminal justice system which lacks the support of major powers.[34]

[32] K. Ambos, 'The International Criminal Justice System and Prosecutorial Selection Policy' in B. Ackerman, K. Ambos and H. Sikirić (eds.), *Visions of Justice. Liber Amicorum Mirjan Damaška* (Berlin: Duncker & Humblot, 2016), 23, 33 et seq.; also K. Ambos, *Treatise on International Criminal Law*, Vol. III (Oxford: Oxford University Press, 2016), 376 et seq. On selective enforcement as a problem for theories of punishment, see the contribution by Harmen van der Wilt in Chapter 17.

[33] On this concept, see Ambos, 'The International Criminal Justice System', 25 et seq.

[34] And is even attacked and actively undermined by them, see the recent threats against the ICC by John Bolton, former national security advisor of US-President Trump www.theguardian.com/us-news/2018/sep/10/john-bolton-castigate-icc-washington-speech. Bolton is, of course, well known to the ICC community as he has already lambasted the ICC being national security advisor of President Bush junior. For an analysis of the legality of threatening sanctions to the ICC, especially in light of the US-UN headquarters agreement, see D. Akande, 'The Bolton Speech: The Legality of US Retaliatory Action against Judges and Officials of the International Criminal Court?', EJIL: Talk!, 14 September 2018, www.ejiltalk.org/the-bolton-speech-the-legality-of-us-retaliatory-action-against-judges-and-officials-of-the-international-criminal-court.

V CONCLUSION

Given all these problems it is not surprising that international criminal law, somewhat eclectically, combines the existing theories adding some specific international criminal law ingredients, especially focusing on the victims' interests.[35] Criminologists such as Neubacher call this a victimological perspective and have no problem in calling for the acknowledgment of the victims' status, concrete (procedural) rights for victims and even the establishment of the truth by way of criminal proceedings. However, not all of them recognize, as Neubacher rightly does, the practical limits of such a pro-victims approach and its inherent risks, especially the creation of over-expectations and the ensuing frustration of victims that the system does not hold what it promises.[36]

At any rate, ultimately we have an international criminal justice system that highly selectively retributes international crimes and has a limited deterrent and norm-reaffirming effect. It incapacitates a very limited number of offenders, thereby acknowledging the status of victimhood and providing case-related truth. This is not much and far from enough, but it is better than nothing.

[35] On the increased importance of victims' interests in international criminal law, see the contribution by Philipp Ambach in Chapter 20.

[36] Cf. M. Damaška, 'The International Criminal Court between Aspiration and Achievement' (2009) 14 *University of California Los Angeles Journal of International Law and Foreign Affairs* 19, 20–21.

7

The *Why* Question in International Criminal Punishment – Framing the Landscapes of Asking

A Comment on the Contributions by Frank Neubacher, Sergey Vasiliev and Elies van Sliedregt

IMMI TALLGREN[*]

Setting the framework for the discussions 'with criminological, historical and domestic perspectives'[1] is the task in the first part of this volume *Why Punish Perpetrators of Mass Atrocities? Purposes of Punishment in International Criminal Law*. As the chapters and the symposium that preceded them demonstrate, however, there is no clear framework in which to ask such a question. In particular, it is difficult if not impossible to separate the question of *why punish* from other questions related to understanding and explaining mass atrocities: what mass atrocities are considered to consist of, who are to be understood as their perpetrators (in simplified terms: the boots on the ground or the Bembas and Gbagbos), how they are committed and why, for what causes and by which processes. What is even more challenging, as it became clear, is to treat the *why punish* question as a separate issue from describing one's disciplinary or personal preferences for dealing with mass atrocities in general. How should perpetrators of mass atrocities be punished and by whom? How should victims be dealt with? What kinds of institutions are needed (if any)?

The differences in approaching the *why* question could be discussed in terms of academic disciplines and expert knowledge. One could talk of 'epistemic communities' of international lawyers, international criminal lawyers, criminal lawyers, criminologists or international-relations scholars, to mention a few.[2] One could refer to the fragmentation of law and policies,

[*] I would like to thank warmly the organizers of the Hamburg symposium, Florian Jeßberger and Julia Geneuss, and its participants for stimulating discussions. Frédéric Mégret, Parvathi Menon, Sergey Vasiliev and Matthew Windsor provided astute comments on my draft, thank you again.

[1] See the table of contents of this volume.

[2] See e.g., P.M. Haas, 'Introduction: Epistemic Communities and International Policy Coordination' (1992) 46 *International Organization* 1; A. Bianchi, 'Epistemic Communities' in

or of professional expertise. Such talk does not go deep enough, however. The question *why punish?* evokes personal positions and convictions that fail to find an explanation merely with reference to one's academic education or belonging to a specific professional community.

Framing, frame and *framework* are code words used in social sciences and media studies, as well as in political science, psychology and economics, denoting a set of concepts and perspectives of inquiry into the processes of thought, interpersonal communication, and decision-making. Erving Goffman, the key reference here, suggests that framing reality takes place in order to 'negotiate it, manage it, comprehend it and choose appropriate repertories of cognition and action'.[3] Framing, as Robert Entman argues, certainly is a 'scattered conceptualization', a 'potential research paradigm that remains fractured', and it is 'often defined casually, with much left to an assumed tacit understanding of reader and researcher'.[4] I will not attempt an explicit definition here, either. Entman's description of what frames do is sufficiently helpful:

> Frames *define problems* – determine what a causal agent is doing with what costs and benefits, usually measured in terms of common cultural values; *diagnose causes* – identify the forces creating the problem; *make moral judgements* – evaluate the causal agents and their effects; and *suggest remedies* – offer and justify treatments for the problems and predict their likely effects.[5]

Framing has further meanings and dimensions beyond the disciplines mentioned above. Discussing the representation of atrocity, Susan Sontag points out that 'to photograph is to frame, and to frame is to exclude'.[6] The frame for a filmmaker, however, in contrast to a photographer or a painter, is not fixed but is rather a choice of movement, which at times results in the powerful inclusion of what is taking place outside the frame. It suffices to think of Michelangelo Antonioni or Michael Haneke, whose use of *hors-champ* underlines how what is shown in the frame is not what 'really happens': the spectator senses that what counts most is not visible.[7]

J. d'Aspremont and S. Singh (eds.), *Concepts for International Law* (Cheltenham: Edward Elgar, 2019).

3 E. Goffman, *Frame Analysis: An Essay on the Organization of Experience* (Boston: Northeastern University Press, 1986).

4 R.M. Entman, 'Framing: Toward Clarification of a Fractured Paradigm' (1993) 43 *Journal of Communication* 51, 51–52.

5 Entman, 'Framing', 52 (emphasis in the original).

6 S. Sontag, *Regarding the Pain of Others* (New York: Picador/Farrar, Straus and Giroux, 2003), 46.

7 See, e.g., Antonioni, *Blow-Up*, 1966; Haneke, *Funny Games*, 1997.

In the following, I set out the *why punish* question in a few frames that inform the question as it is raised in this volume. Some of them are explicitly evoked, others are implicitly present. I am not suggesting that these frames are the only ones, or that they are necessarily distinct from each other in all respects. The idea is simply to picture the landscape in which the *why* question is asked, and thereby to shed light on the contexts of that context of knowledge, its production, reproduction and subjectivities. By drawing attention to the plurality of perspectives that could be taken on punishment at the outset of this very welcome volume, I wish to challenge the discursive hegemonies on international criminal punishment. Whatever effort is undertaken to set the framework, be it in the contributions in this volume or elsewhere, it remains a contingent exercize that inevitably has an outside, whether or not we choose to make it visible.

I THE LANDSCAPES OF WHY

Criminal law and its institutional practice in international, hybrid and national tribunals became the main field of reference for naming and conceptualizing the phenomenon of mass atrocities and coping with it in a rapid turn that started in the early 1990s. The international criminal justice project[8] grew into what Sergey Vasiliev refers to as 'a grandiose industry holding a considerable symbolic and political leverage and distinguished by a sophisticated institutional culture [...] and practices and routines'.[9] The turn to criminal justice pushed into the background other discourses and policies such as democracy-building, international human rights with their supervisory mechanisms, international development and much of the discussion on humanitarian intervention with the legal and political analyzes of the use of force. To some extent, the absence of interventions in situations in which mass atrocities continued to be committed was perceived differently now that there was (criminal) justice to follow, sooner or later. The turn to criminal law was accompanied by efforts to explain mass atrocity as crime using language, models and structures commonly adopted to refer to deviance within a society. As a result of these efforts, the discipline of criminology entered the scene, as did various other genres of social sciences concerned with behaviour, either individual or collective: sociology, socio-psychology, psychology, psychiatry

8 The term as used here encompasses both international criminal law and the courts and tribunals involved in its institutional practice, as well as the political activity and advocacy related to international criminal responsibility in general.

9 See the contribution by Sergey Vasiliev in Chapter 4 (p. 45).

and anthropology, for example. The first frame I address is the one of approaching the *why* question with the expertise and vocabulary that emanates from law, followed by those emanating from criminology, morality, 'fantasmatic logic' (explained in Section I.4) and politics.

1 *The Frame of Law*

Why punish? Because the law says we must. This straightforward answer consists of steps in a sequence, from *why investigate*, *why prosecute* and *why convict* to *why punish*. The legal frame at its simplest reflects the domestic analogy of criminal justice, mirroring the (idealized) situation of a state in which there exists a comprehensive criminal code and adequate rules covering investigation, prosecution, trial and punishment in cases of mass atrocity, as well as competent authorities and independent courts with the resources to apply the law.[10] Within such a national legal system, mere information about the alleged commission of a criminal act should lead at least to a criminal investigation, with subsequent steps taken in accordance with the law and the decisions of judicial actors. Complementing domestic legal provisions is a broader net of systems in cases of certain types of mass atrocity (and other types of international crimes), including international agreements that oblige the state parties involved either to prosecute or to extradite. Finally, there are international jurisdictions with their own legal rules, most notably the International Criminal Court (ICC). In addition, parts of the material criminal law on mass atrocities could also be in force as customary international law, and *ius cogens*, as rich doctrinal discussions in the frame of law demonstrate.

Such an image of lawyers occupied with only their rules, safe in the confines of the legal system(s), distanced from the muddled social and political circumstances that, observed from the legal frame, belong to the past preceding the birth moments of the law, is of course a caricature. Yet with regard to mass atrocities, the legal frame nowadays appears to be over-invested. In stark contrast to the lack of criminological, sociological or political sciences research on international crimes until very recent times, research programmes and libraries have burst with legal analyzes of international criminal law and its institutional practice. Discussion on the legal *why* or *why not* in the context of current or recent international judicial institutions has focused on the dogmatic analysis of jurisdiction, complementarity or prosecutorial discretion, in light of the existing norms in force.

[10] On the domestic analogy, see the contribution by Elies van Sliedregt in Chapter 5.

2 The Frame of Criminology

Expressed in simplified terms, this frame approaches the problems relating to crimes and their control and suggests remedies based on beliefs about individual or collective human behaviour in communities and societies. The word *beliefs* carries no pejorative sense but refers to current knowledge in the social sciences, much of which is based on empirical research. As is known – and we are reminded of this by Frank Neubacher's reference to Cesare Beccaria[11] – such beliefs as well as the methodologies of empirical research have changed over time and will most likely continue evolving. The preoccupations of criminology as a field of study, typically in national contexts, include the causes of crime; the objectives, opportunities, costs and risks associated with crime control; and efforts to understand the conditions in which a person, an entity or a collective transgresses, as well as how systems of crime control and punishment affect individuals and entities.

As the editors of this volume and other commentators note, criminological analysis of mass atrocities is scarce.[12] Even if more interventions have been published recently, the key outcome remains a call for more research or more adequate research.[13] The analysis of mass atrocities as international crimes remains absent from textbooks of criminology, both in classics such as *Criminology*[14] and in more recent works such as the *Oxford Handbook of Criminology* – the fifth edition (2012) finally contains a chapter at least on *State Crime*.[15] Why would this be the case? The reluctance to deal with genocide and other mass atrocities is often attributed to the relationship between criminology and the state. The role of modern political states as pursuers of final solutions in their vastness and totality, with access to resources, administrative capacities and law-making competence, makes the

[11] See the contribution by Frank Neubacher in Chapter 3 referring to Beccaria's statement in 1764 (p. 43).

[12] See the Introduction by the editors; S. Parmentier, 'The Missing Link: Criminological Perspectives on Transnational Justice and International Crimes' in M. Bosworth and C. Hoyle (eds.), *What is Criminology?* (Oxford: Oxford University Press, 2011), 380; S. Harrendorf, 'How Can Criminology Contribute to an Explanation of International Crimes' (2014) 12 *Journal of International Criminal Justice* 231.

[13] See, e.g., C.W. Mullins and D.L. Rothe, 'The Ability of the International Criminal Court to Deter Violations of International Criminal Law' (2010) 10 *International Criminal Law Review* 771; A. Smeulers and R. Haveman (eds.), *Supranational Criminology: Towards a Criminology of International Crimes* (Antwerp: Intersentia Press, 2008).

[14] E.H. Sutherland and D.R. Cressey, *Criminology*, 10th ed. (Philadelphia: Lippincott, 1978).

[15] M. Maguire, R. Morgan and R. Reiner, *Oxford Handbook of Criminology* (Oxford: Oxford University Press, 2012).

basic criminological paradigm appear too reductive.[16] As Chris Cunneen writes: '[…] the positivist approaches in law and criminology [that] define "crime" as a breach of state criminal law, and count crimes from the data driven by state agencies. Within such state-centric discourses, it is difficult to conceptualize the incidence and nature of state crime.'[17] Criminologists and other social scientists in this frame may feel more at ease remaining within the confines of a state-enclosed paradigm because, as Andy Aitchison puts it, 'atrocity crimes take place in uncivilised or unpacified spaces'.[18] Katja Aas, as well, refers to the failure of 'territorial imagination' in a discipline limiting itself to 'pacified domestic spaces'.[19]

At the same time, criminologists and other social scientists 'had a decisive role in encouraging an internationalist view' of criminality, as Paul Knepper states. He studied how, at the turn of the twentieth century, the new discipline of criminology 'transformed criminal behavior into a universal problem about which scientists, doctors, judges, professors, politicians and anyone else engaged in social criticism had an opinion'.[20] Ever since, the criminologist has been involved in and contributed to analysing, explaining and at times preventing 'international crime' and thereby breathed life and meaning into the concept, often in collaboration with the national or international institutions manned with legal professionals with a mission to deal with 'international crime'.

How does the criminologist tackle the *why* question? The basic rationale behind the answers to *why?* in this frame is consequentialist and focused on perpetrators, the expectation being that punishment could shape the future behaviour of the criminal and others (potential perpetrators). This does not mean that every criminologist working in this frame necessarily adheres to such rationales or otherwise has the hubris to save the world from

[16] See W. Morrison, *Criminology, Civilisation and the New World Order* (Abington: Routledge, 2006); R. Gellately and B. Kiernan (eds.), *The Spectre of Genocide: Mass Murder in Historical Perspective* (Cambridge: Cambridge University Press, 2010).

[17] C. Cunneen, 'Postcolonial Perspectives for Criminology' in M. Bosworth and C. Hoyle (eds.), *What Is Criminology?* (Oxford: Oxford University Press, 2011), 249, 253.

[18] A. Aitchison, 'Criminological Theory and International Crimes' in I. Bantekas and E. Mylonaki (eds.), *Criminological Approaches to International Criminal Law* (Cambridge: Cambridge University Press, 2014), 22, 27.

[19] K. Aas, 'The Earth Is One but the World Is Not: Criminological Theory and Its Geopolitical Divisions' (2012) 16 *Theoretical Criminology* 5, 12.

[20] P. Knepper, *The Invention of International Crimes. A Global Issue in the Making, 1881–1914* (Basingtoke: Palgrave Macmillan, 2009), 10. See also, N. Rafter, 'Origins of Criminology' in M. Bosworth and C. Hoyle (eds.), *What Is Criminology?* (Oxford: Oxford University Press, 2011), 143, 145–146.

international crimes. Not everyone sets the goal as high as finding 'the keys to a future free of genocide', as Augustine Brannigan puts it in *Beyond the Banality of Evil: Criminology and Genocide*.[21] Alette Smeulers and Fred Grünfeld, authors of an interdisciplinary textbook, merely 'aim to contribute to a more humane future'.[22] Notably, however, critical or radical criminology, which questions the power and control exercised by criminal justice with its inequalities in domestic contexts, has remained marginal if not absent in discussions on international crime. This may relate to the openly punitive ideologies dominant in international criminal justice institutions and the broader political project. As Kelly Hannah-Moffat points out in a domestic context, criminologists typically cooperate with these institutions: '[i]nstitutional research practices can produce a context wherein some forms of intellectual inquiry are seen as "legitimate" and others as "threatening" or redundant'.[23] It cannot be excluded that with regard to international crime, the production of criminological knowledge is also subject to 'various forms of institutional protectionism and intellectual polarizations'.[24]

Criminological approaches adhering to the consequentialist rationale differ in terms of whether the focus is on the interaction between the individual perpetrator and his or her environment or, in contrast, on possible individual defects of the perpetrators. Importantly, there is a tendency to attach less importance to the social and economic context of the (potential) perpetrators of international crimes than in criminology in general. Perpetrators with the higher levels of hierarchical standing and responsibility, referred to as 'the bigger fry' by Elies van Sliedregt,[25] attract stigmas of evil, bestiality, moral devastation or duplicity, which were broadly debated in earlier scholarship on Nazi criminality. Criminological discussions that accompanied the turn to international criminal law in the early 1990s revisited the landmarks of that genre, including Hannah Arendt's account of Adolf Eichmann's trial giving birth to the trope of the obedient bureaucrat, supported by Stanley Milgram's controversial empirical studies.[26] Today's frame of criminology appears to be

[21] A. Brannigan, *Beyond the Banality of Evil: Criminology and Genocide* (Oxford: Oxford University Press, 2013).

[22] A. Smeulers and F. Grünfeld, *International Crimes and Other Gross Human Rights Violations: A Multi- and Interdisciplinary Textbook* (Leiden: Martinus Nijhoff Publishers, 2011), xiii.

[23] K. Hannah-Moffat, 'Criminological Cliques: Narrowing Dialogues, Institutional Protectionism, and the Next Generation' in M. Bosworth and C. Hoyle (eds.), *What Is Criminology?* (Oxford: Oxford University Press, 2011), 440, 445.

[24] Hannah-Moffat, 'Criminological Cliques', 445.

[25] See the contribution by Elies van Sliedregt in Chapter 5 (p. 94).

[26] H. Arendt, *Eichmann in Jerusalem: A Report on the Banality of Evil* (New York: Viking Press, 1963); S. Milgram, *Obedience to Authority* (New York: Harper and Row, 1974).

moving away from those emblematic discussions, however. As Frank Neubacher's chapter demonstrates, it tends to flag an acknowledgement of the overall complexity of criminological analyzes of mass atrocities. Branches of scholarship and expertise such as transnational criminology, international criminology and global criminology are surfacing, with new approaches such as a focus on extremely violent societies or a broader understanding of victimization by atrocity.[27]

A key aspect affecting the frame of criminology that the Hamburg symposium did not capture relates to the ongoing change of emphasis in the international criminal justice project. The question '*Why punish perpetrators of mass atrocities?*' acquires a new critical meaning in the current climate in the sense that the punitive aspect of international institutional practice is receding, giving space for a wider understanding of international criminal trials as contributing to social justice and community-building, presumably acting for and on behalf of victims in particular.[28] Criminal punishment, which is pivotal to the criminological paradigm in a domestic context, may appear an accessory if not redundant in the international sphere.[29] The international governance of penal power also assumes new tasks such as developing national legal systems to match the standard set by that governance, a policy that emerged in the ICC context and is known as 'positive complementarity'.[30] Criminological approaches will need to adjust to situations in which international legal discourse and institutional practice move towards a constellation that is increasingly detached from the national sovereign prerogative, acting in the name of a moral community of 'humanity',[31] as discussed in the following section.

[27] See, e.g., S. Karstedt, 'Contextualizing Mass Atrocity Crimes: The Dynamics of "Extremely Violent Societies"' (2012) 9 *European Journal of Criminology* 499; J. Hagan et al., 'Atrocity Victimization and the Costs of Economic Conflict Crimes in the Battle for Baghdad and Iraq' (2012) 9 *European Journal of Criminology* 481.

[28] For a discussion see, e.g., S. Kendall and S. Nouwen, 'Representational Practices at the International Criminal Court: The Gap between Juridified and Abstract Victimhood' (2014) 76 *Law and Contemporary Problems* 235.

[29] See, e.g., K. Lohne, 'Penal Humanitarianism Beyond the Nation State: An Analysis of International Criminal Justice' (2019) *Theoretical Criminology* forthcoming.

[30] J. Tillier, 'The ICC Prosecutor and Positive Complementarity: Strengthening the Rule of Law?' (2013) 13 *International Criminal Law Review* 507; C.K. Hall, 'Developing and Implementing an Effective Positive Complementarity Prosecution Strategy' in C. Stahn and G. Sluiter (eds.), *The Emerging Practice of the International Criminal Court* (Leiden: Brill, 2008) 219.

[31] See R. Teitel, *Humanity's Law* (Oxford: Oxford University Press, 2012); A.A. Cançado Trindade, *International Law for Humankind: Towards a New* Jus Gentium (Leiden: Martinus

3 The Moral Frame

In contrast to the preceding frames, here the *why* question is articulated neither in terms of 'Do these acts fall under the jurisdiction of the court?' nor 'Does punishment prevent crime?'. The moral frame is identifiable in two main senses. In the first, idioms that mark the frame connote retribution, just deserts, redemption, repentance and atonement. Underneath the current discourse of restorative justice, the Kantian retributive theory and the notion of radical evil, with its theological connotations, may have powerful purchase in explaining the emphasis on individual criminal responsibility in the international criminal justice project.[32]

In the second sense, the moral frame relates to the construction and representation of punishing power in the international criminal justice project: *why punish* is closely associated with the question *in whose name to punish*. Here, punishment is understood as emanating from a broadly shared moral outrage aroused by mass atrocities – the 'revulsion of the international community', to quote a judgment of the Special Court for Sierra Leone (SCSL)[33] – thereby building a (political) community of humanitarianism, united by the objective of protecting human life and the human species. To quote Anthony Duff: 'Some kinds of wrong should concern *us*, are properly *our* business, in virtue of our shared humanity with their victims (and perpetrators): for such wrongs the perpetrators must answer not just to their local communities, but to *humanity*.'[34] One of the intellectual resources of this frame is sociologist Emile Durkheim's interdisciplinary work on criminal law and punishment as a way of both establishing and safeguarding the moral core

Nijhoff, 2010). For a discussion, see I. Tallgren, 'The Voice of the International: Who Is Speaking?' (2015) 13 *Journal of International Criminal Justice* 135.

[32] For a traditionalist interpretation of Kant's theory of punishment, see, e.g., J.G. Murphy, *Kant: The Philosophy of Right* (Macon: Mercer University Press, 1970); J.G. Murphy, 'Kant's Theory of Criminal Punishment', in J.G. Murphy, *Retribution, Justice, and Therapy: Essays in the Philosophy of Law* (Dordrecht: D. Reidel, 1979) 82. For a reinterpretation towards deterrence, see B.S. Byrd, 'Kant's Theory of Punishment: Deterrence in Its Threat, Retribution in Its Execution' (1989) 8 *Law and Philosophy* 151. For recent discussion, see, e.g., F. Mégret, 'The Repentant Defendant and the Potential of International Criminal Justice' (2018) 21 *Contemporary Justice Review* 432.

[33] SCSL, Judgment of 28 May 2008 (AC), *Fofana and Kondewa (CDF)*, SCSL-04-14-A, para. 565.

[34] A. Duff, 'Authority and Responsibility in International Criminal Law' in S. Besson and J. Tasioulas (eds.), *The Philosophy of International Law* (Oxford University Press, 2010) 589, 601.

of a community by means of moral reaction to offences against a 'conscience collective'.[35] Although a sociological frame could be fully justified as a distinguishable frame to address the *why* question, the discourses advocating criminal punishment for mass atrocities in terms of expressivism or moral communication referred to in the Hamburg symposium and also in this volume typically treat the sociological frame as a mere tacitly 'helpful' extension of the moral frame.[36]

4 *The Frame of 'Fantasmatic Logic'*

Let us take a closer look at the question that constitutes the title of this volume: it is not an open question (such as 'Must perpetrators of mass atrocities be punished?') but a closed one ('Why punish them?').[37] This is a characteristic example of the dominant discourse in this specific social setting of international criminal justice that I have in mind when I term this frame that of 'fantasmatic logic', for lack of a better term. I would be tempted to call it the frame of *ideology*, were that word not as (in)famously used and understood in too many senses.[38] What is meant here is close to Jason Glynos's and David Howarth's idea of the 'fantasmatic logic' behind political projects that helps to 'maintain existing social structures by pre-emptively absorbing dislocations, preventing them from becoming [politicised and transformed]'.[39] Fantasmatic logic prevents positions or issues from becoming part of the political domain, in which these meanings, articulations and identities would be instituted and potentially challenged through hegemonic struggle, contestation and resistance.

35 See, I. Tallgren, 'The Durkheimian Spell of International Criminal Justice' (2013) 71 *Revue interdisciplinaire d'études juridiques – Droit en context, Dossier justice internationale pénale* 157; S. Nimage, 'An International Conscience Collective? Durkheimian Analysis of International Criminal Law' (2007) 7 *International Criminal Law Review* 561.

36 For discussion, see, e.g., R.D. Sloane, 'The Expressive Capacity of International Punishment: The Limits of the National Law Analogy and the Potential of International Criminal Law' (2007) 43 *Stanford Journal of International Law* 39; M. Drumbl, *Atrocity, Punishment, and International Law* (Cambridge: Cambridge University Press, 2007).

37 Sergey Vasiliev addressed this in the symposium; see also the contribution by Sergey Vasiliev in Chapter 4 (Section I.2).

38 See W. Rech, 'Ideology', in J. d'Aspremont and S. Singh (eds.), *Concepts for International Law* (Cheltenham: Edward Elgar, 2019), 393; S. Marks, *The Riddle of All Constitutions: International Law, Democracy and the Critique of Ideology* (Oxford: Oxford University Press, 2000), 8.

39 J. Glynos and D. Howarth, *Logics of Critical Explanation in Social and Political Theory* (London: Routledge, 2007), 146.

With regard to *why punish*, the depoliticizing appeal of a particular narrative is recognizable in dogmas such as of 'the fight against impunity' and 'no peace without justice'. As in the moral frame, of which this frame is a close neighbour, there is no opportunity to ask whether the international punishment, administered outside of, or in contradiction to, the political and social context of a nation-state, really leads to less crime and alleviates the suffering of victims, and whether it advances peace in this particular society. That the answers are positive is taken for granted, for that is the (ideological) premise: international criminal punishment, administered in the name of the international community/humanity, is always beneficial both to the individuals and to the societies concerned, as well as to humanity at large, regardless of the circumstances and, by extension, regardless of the objective quality of that justice, let alone its subjective quality from the perspective of those over whom it is exercised.[40] Questioning this is sacrilege. In that sense, this frame is reminiscent of religiousness.[41]

Even if frames of law and 'fantasmatic logic' are addressed separately here, this is not to suggest that law is separate from the latter. It is rather that the legal frame allows for articulations in which the power of the dominating narrative is disguised below the surface, as it is already embedded in the law. As Vasiliev puts it, the framework of international criminal law imposes such rigid constraints on the degree to which judges can engage with the question of *why punish* that 'teleological ruminations in judgements can be no more than speech acts by which courts preach international criminal law's founding articles of faith'.[42]

The frame of 'fantasmatic logic' is manifest throughout the international criminal justice project, from articulations of what is regarded as punishable mass atrocity to institutional architecture and communication policies adopted by the institutions. By way of an example, one can point to the sense of ownership of international criminal law and the lack of comprehension of non-adepts of the 'fantasmatic logic', visible as clashes across the disciplinary borders and the frames addressed here. Despite the frequent calls for more criminology, which we reiterated in Hamburg, those most vested in

[40] See M. Rauschenbach and D. Scalia, 'Les accusés du Tribunal pénal international pour l'ex-Yougoslavie: entre désenchantement et résistance' (2018) 42 *Déviance et Société* 535; M.-S. Devresse and D. Scalia, 'Hearing Tried People in International Criminal Justice: Sympathy for the Devil?' (2016) 16 *International Criminal Law Review* 796.

[41] For a discussion, see I. Tallgren, 'The Faith in Humanity and International Criminal Law', in P. Amorosa, M. Garcia-Salmones and M. Koskenniemi (eds.), *International Law and Religion* (Oxford: Oxford University Press, 2017), 334.

[42] See the contribution by Sergey Vasiliev in Chapter 4 (p. 48).

international criminal law appear less keen to engage in dialogue: '[c]riminologists and criminal lawyers who are uncomfortable with this *political dimension* would be advised to stick to domestic justice systems'.[43] The political dimension here means 'the selection of situations and of cases'.[44] In William Schabas's view, '[a]ll things considered, the one-sided prosecutions at Nuremberg, governed in their choice of defendants by political rather than judicial considerations, delivered a just result. They also contributed to an accurate portrait of the historical truth'.[45] Such confidence in 'just results' and 'historical truth' appears possible only when there is a strong identification with the particular politics and the actors, here the post-World War II dominant block in international relations. Similar confidence in and identification with today's institutions is demonstrated by Elies van Sliedregt's proposal to alleviate the 'reality of heterogeneity' that undermines the acceptance of sentences imposed by these international courts by means of limiting taking the court room as a podium for political speeches (within the limits of fair-trial rights); prioritize outreach activities by Residual Mechanisms, together with local authorities in telling the history of the conflict, prevent rewriting history and glorifying battlefield myths.[46] Inside the frame of 'fantasmatic logic', international criminal courts are granted the standing to 'authoritatively pronounce what and how history shall be remembered', making them not solely 'a potential source and site of memory, but a powerful arbiter thereof'.[47] The defensiveness of the status quo is at times expressed as rejection of the performance of those intruding into the frame, such as '[t]he rare appearances of criminologists at the international criminal tribunals'.[48]

5 *The Frame of Politics*

Why does the ICC punish perpetrators of mass atrocities committed in the Democratic Republic of the Congo, Libya and Uganda, but not in Syria? Even if this appears at first sight to be a question of the legal frame referred to as the first frame above, to which a pertinent reply could be swiftly produced by applying the Rome Statute, it is clear that the interpretation of the Statute

[43] W.A. Schabas, 'Criminology, Accountability and International Justice' in M. Bosworth and C. Hoyle (eds.), *What Is Criminology?* (Oxford: Oxford University Press, 2011), 346, 356 (emphasis added).
[44] Schabas, 'Criminology, Accountability and International Justice', 356.
[45] Schabas, 'Criminology, Accountability and International Justice', 356.
[46] See the contribution by Elies van Sliedregt in Chapter 5 (p. 99 et seq.).
[47] N. Henry, *War and Rape: Law, Memory and Justice* (London: Routledge, 2011), 130.
[48] Schabas, 'Criminology, Accountability and International Justice', 356.

or the UN Charter is not really the point here. The question falls in the frame of politics, recognizable in the vocabulary of power, feasibility, strategic considerations, risk analysis, diplomatic relations, collateral damage or conflict of interest, depending on the exact context. Here, responses to the *why* (often rather *why not*) question do not evoke liturgical statements on prevention or moral community; they rather point to the opportunity (or lack of) to punish in a particular situation given the cost, relevant alliances, armed conflict or risk of it and other comparable aspects. These considerations often fall under the meta-language of 'political realities', and they have a marked temporal and spatial aspect.

In this frame we can also identify underlying choices of political economy. Consider, for example, Frank Neubacher's suggestion that it is more important to fight the causes of international crimes and that 'justice also needs to be sought through [...] development' and that 'the perpetrator's socio-political environment' should be tackled as well.[49] The problem with such well-meant remarks is that, despite the oft-heard complaints about the costs and practical difficulties of international criminal trials, the alternative of structural reform is likely to be regarded as far more expensive and difficult, and thus as unrealistic. In that sense, criminal trials are a facile solution, a reaction of relative political expedience to outbursts of violence in conflicts that are structural and long term and would require comprehensive political, economic and social change to prevent mass atrocities.

The frame of politics is at times boldly explicit, but more often remains implicit, such as when choices are made about who gets access to forums in which the *why* question is addressed. Twenty years after the Rome conference on the establishment of the ICC, which has been strongly criticized for the gross inequality of participation,[50] 'we' in Hamburg still gathered to generate and share expertise on the *why* question in the complete absence of scholars and practitioners from the regions and societies that currently and most concretely face both mass atrocities and international efforts to punish them. Their only visible presence during the symposium was in a series of macro-photographs of the ICC accused projected onto a screen in the meeting room, labelled as 'big fish' or 'small fish'. The flashback to the notorious *Royal Museum for Central Africa* in Tervuren, close to Brussels, in which relics of

[49] See the contribution by Frank Neubacher in Chapter 3 (p. 44).

[50] See, e.g., C.M. Bassiouni, 'Preface' in O. Triffterer (ed.), *Commentary on the Rome Statute of the International Criminal Court* (Baden-Baden: Nomos, 1999) xix; A. Buchet and I. Tallgren, 'Sur la route de Rome – Les negotiations préalables à l'adoption du Statut de la Cour pénale international' in J. Fernandez and X. Pacreau (eds.), *Commentaire du Statut de Rome de la Cour Pénale Internationale* (Paris: Pedone, 2012), 171, 186–187.

Leopold II's regime in the Congo were, until recently, displayed in frames and vitrines, was no doubt unintentional.[51]

The framing out of individuals and research institutions from the relevant epistemic community to address the *why* question of international criminal punishment concretely demonstrates the continuity of a political hegemony over international (criminal) law and its institutions – the notorious historical lineage that undermines the current rhetoric of 'humanity's law'. It has cast a shadow over the institutional record of the ICC in recent years, and remains a subject of intense critique also among state parties to the Rome Statute. If the objective is, in the words of Judith Butler, to expose the 'orchestrating design of the authority who sought to control the frame',[52] these questions on the valued expertise and the interlocutors authorized to ask *why?* merit being posed.

II CONCLUSIONS

The frames sketched out above all have their particular histories, with their repetitions, continuities, false continuities and, at times, ruptures. Both the frames themselves and the dominant and subservient positions the frames have in the discourse on international criminal justice are not the same today as they were at the time of the often-pictured birth moments in Nuremberg and Tokyo, for example. Historicizing the frames in more detail and ranking their respective positions and influences fall, however, beyond the scope of my impressionist comments on the chapters in the first part of this volume. What the frames in any case have in common is how the dominant intellectual parameters of the social sciences and law originated in the context of Western societies, anchored in a certain tradition and form of life, and implicitly in a religion with its particular moral conceptions. Despite the collapse of the greatest empires of the past and decolonization, there is a risk that knowledge and expertise remain obscured by 'the imbalances of power and the dynamics of othering and social exclusion in the present world order'.[53]

[51] On the museum, see Morrison, *Criminology*, 177–205.

[52] J. Butler, *Frames of War* (London: Verso, 2010), 12.

[53] K. Aas, 'Visions of Global Control' in M. Bosworth and C. Hoyle (eds.), *What Is Criminology?* (Oxford: Oxford University Press, 2011) 406, 413, with reference to B. Agozino, *Counter-Colonial Criminology: A Critique of Imperialist Reason* (London: Pluto Press, 2003); C. Cunneen and J. Stubbs, 'Cultural Criminology and Engagement with Race, Gender and Post-colonial Identities' in J. Ferrell et al. (eds.), *Cultural Criminology Unleashed* (Portland: GlassHouse Press, 2004), 97; M. Bosworth and J. Flavin, *Race, Gender and Punishment: From Colonialism to the War on Terror* (Chapel Hill: Rutgers University Press, 2007).

All the frames discussed above are susceptible to this risk. Moral communication on values sounds reasonable and necessary, but whose values does one communicate, based on what, who talks and who listens? When assumed universal values are set aside, as repeatedly happens for a multitude of reasons, whose voice carries furthest? The fight against impunity is an unquestionable goal at first sight, but who fights whom with what means, and whose impunity is always tolerated or obscured in the end? Furthermore, 'othering' drastically affects political considerations, guided by presumably rational calculations of what is feasible, not always exclusively in terms of money but also in terms of human lives and their living spaces. In these cases, too, lives and spaces do not have the same price for the 'international community' that decides. The most striking differences in what counts in the frames are not, then, between the international and the imagined *domestic* model, but between states and regions with regard to their political, economic and military weight.

These differences are well known, yet they merit emphasis here because they directly affect how the question '*Why punish perpetrators of mass atrocities?*' is answered. In that sense, international criminal law and its current institutional practice represent one of the key mechanisms through which ideas about inferiority and subordination (political, social, economic, cultural and 'racial'[54]) are constructed and represented. Reflecting the filmmaker's techniques of framing and montage, international criminal justice as an intellectual and political project risks including the subordinated societies of the Global South solely on account of their criminality, leaving the societies themselves and their political agency definitively *hors-champ*.

The *why* word is out now, and that is a good thing. Outing the complex, defiant question '*why punish?*' is a key achievement of the Hamburg symposium and this volume. International criminal law should not remain a sanctuary to which criminologists, sociologists, political scientists and others less inclined to the repetitive credos in law and legal institutions are denied access. Empirical studies flourish today, and so they should. Theories are critically tested, and trusted articles of faith are interrogated. The tensions this creates in the normative groundings of international criminal law are healthy. These intellectual confrontations may end up contributing to the maturing of the enchanted vision of international punishment.[55] To be sure, one feels

[54] I am writing 'racial' to flag the lack of any scientific or legal consensus on a definition of the concept, see, e.g., C. Lingaas, *The Concept of Race in International Criminal Law* (Abingdon: Routledge, forthcoming 2019).

[55] On 'enchantment' as an intellectual position in international law, see I. Hurd, 'Enchanted and Disenchanted International Law' (2016) 7 *Global Policy* 96.

impotent reaching for frames that appear far too difficult to comprehend or act upon. Who could reform the UN Security Council or affect the global distribution of resources, in any case? Nevertheless, asking *why* beyond the obvious frames may affect the *how*, the *what*, and the *who*. Such frame breaks could – it is not prohibited to hope – engender change that ultimately contributes to the broadly shared and powerful objective of a world with less mass atrocity.

8

Is International Criminal Law Special?

A Comment on the Contributions by Frank Neubacher, Sergey Vasiliev and Elies van Sliedregt

JOCHEN BUNG

I THE NEED FOR EMPIRICAL EVIDENCE

In her contribution to this volume, Elies van Sliedregt correctly emphasizes that international criminal law features similarities and differences in comparison to the purely domestic criminal setting. This is true for both, the specific legal questions in the strict sense as well as for related perspectives that look into the subject of criminal law from a broader point of view, in particular criminological perspectives. Surely, we stick to our traditions and routines. They serve us as a basis on which we can operate, in the international area as well as in the national setting. However, as we should expect, there are some shortcomings in this approach. Van Sliedregt believes that international perpetrators differ significantly from the 'ordinary criminal' and that therefore there are problems in transferring purposes of punishment from domestic law to international criminal law.

Frank Neubacher shares this view. As a criminologist he makes the almost emphatic claim that we have to re-invent, or at least re-think, criminology for the area of international criminal law. He is convinced that the differences of international and domestic crimes are such that international criminal law has to be equipped with its own specific body of criminological research. In general, he argues, there is a lack of theories specifically designed to address the international level. In his chapter, he outlines the basic elements of such a theory – and a very promising project for future research.

In his contribution, Sergey Vasiliev goes beyond the conceptual framework of criminal legal or criminological doctrine by directly confronting international criminal law with the most fundamental question of all, which forms also the title of this volume: Why punish? Vasiliev reconstructs a debate between positions he calls 'empiricist' and 'normativist' and identifies, among other things, a paucity of reflection on the unquestioned and implicit theories carried along in the jurisprudence of the different international criminal tribunals. He calls them 'the belief systems on which criminal law rests' and diagnoses a kind of self-immunization especially against empirical evidence of the uselessness of certain punishing practices. I agree that there is a need to question the premises of punishment. We have to address the ambiguity in the question 'why punish'. As Nietzsche has put it, we must avoid sticking to the question of *reasons* (the purposes or aims of punishment), but also turn our interest to the *causes* and *effects* of punishment.[1] The act of punishment is such an inherent and deep-rooted matter that it cannot convincingly be traced back to reasons and purposes only. Empirical findings may help in getting a more informed view on the issue at stake. However, it seems to me that this is a shortcoming not specific to international criminal law, but, by no means less, of criminal law in general.

II ON THE ROLE AND SIGNIFICANCE OF PURPOSES OF PUNISHMENT

On closer examination, however, I doubt that it is the question of the aims and purposes of punishment or the question of the criminological dimension of international crime which bring shortcomings that are specific to international criminal law to the fore. In a similar vein, I would argue that the system of the classical purposes of punishment can very well serve as a basis for justification in international criminal law – for the simple reason that it can serve (or rather, it is often employed) as a basis to justify almost *everything* at any time. My (general) problem with the aims of punishment is that this debate is still regarded as being central to nearly all issues of criminal law. I do not believe that this is true. While Vasiliev correctly argues that the question of *why punish* is crucial, he also points out that the general debate on the aims of punishment, well beyond the context of international criminal law, has become self-referential and even ideological and sclerotic. I believe that the discourse on international criminal law can help us to recognize this. In fact, it provides further evidence that we should leave a self-referential and redundant debate behind us or at least avoid the mistake of overstating its significance. We should, in my view, understand that the aims of punishment must not be regarded as the holy grail of criminal legal wisdom. Rather, I believe, they are to be seen as tokens on the game board of academic discourse,

[1] This argument is developed in the second discourse of Nietzsche's 'Genealogy' [1887] *On the Genealogy of Morals* (translation M.A. Scarpitti) (London: Penguin Books, 2013), 62 et seq.

nothing more and nothing less. We know the moves, we foresee the series of moves, we know them sufficiently, there is no surprise.

Never have I received any kind of unexpected insight from pondering on the purposes of punishment. It is crystal clear that every form of sanctioning seeks to suffice the idea of equivalence, the idea of compensating something. A body of rules which lacks this reference could not be referred to as of legal nature. It is intrinsic, it is the definition, the core of the law. So how could we possibly proceed in this field without any notion of retribution? At the same time there is no doubt that this, the retributive claim, cannot be the whole story. In trying to determine the value of a crime, to weigh its gravity and assess the appropriate reaction, we do not seem to mean to increase the amount of pain and sorrow in the world but make the world a better place, make people behave better or at least try to make people feel better. There is an inevitable double-bind in the purposes of punishment, just as the idea of justice necessarily features two dimensions, a goal-oriented, distributive and technical one and a second that seeks its purpose in itself, formally in the performance of a kind of exchange.

Beyond that, it seems undeniable that every criminal trial constitutes a narrative in expressing 'something' and that an essential part of the story is the tale of victimization. Any criminal trial seeks to establish that what happened was a crime, not an accident or the fault of the victim, but the fault of the offender. This is why the victim deserves our solidarity. Every criminal proceeding tells this story. The difference, however, is that the audience in international cases is much bigger. This, however, follows directly from the notion of an international crime.

Finally, Vasiliev's observation, and van Sliedregt makes a similar point, that the aspect of offender rehabilitation is not of similar importance in international criminal law as it is in a domestic system has to be put into perspective. International custodial sentences are enforced in the domestic prison systems under the ordinary domestic regulations. This division of labour between an international jurisdiction on the one hand and the prison regimes on the other means that the well-known mix of sentencing purposes prevails in a more complex institutional setting. Nevertheless, it remains the same old mixture that is so familiar to us.

III THE CRIMINOLOGICAL DISCOURSE

A similarity of theories and arguments can also be detected regarding the criminological discourse on both international and domestic criminal law. Perhaps, to refer to the metaphor used above, the game of criminology offers a larger set of tokens and a more extended range of moves, but on the whole it resembles the game of aims and purposes of punishment in that it provides nothing more than a reiterative and foreseeable program. When I teach a course in 'macro-criminology', a concept that clearly covers the case of mass atrocities, I tend to disclaim the significance of Lombrosian-style arguments in order to make the subject easier to grasp. I think that is what van Sliedregt suggests when she argues that international perpetrators deviate in many ways from domestic ones. It seems as if we should really believe that in order to understand the unbelievable truth that the promoters and actors of the horrors paradoxically are to be conceptualized as average and everyday human beings. The perpetrator of mass atrocities is one of us. They are among us. No physical traits, no natural properties, no psychological trauma or social deprivation will lead us to them. Only an awareness of situational shifts and an understanding of the techniques of moral reframing, generally more knowledge of the psychology of social interaction, the social dynamics of groups and masses, could bring light into the mystery.

In his chapter, Neubacher convincingly outlines how we could proceed in this area. In my view, however, there is no need to reinvent criminology for the purposes of international criminal law. All relevant knowledge is already out there and well-established. The criminological theory of neutralization techniques, for example, presented by Gresham Sykes and David Matza in a famous article in 1957[2] and rediscovered and rightly recommended by Neubacher, is now over 60 years old; and the essential idea is even older. A fully developed theory of neutralization techniques can be found in Hegel's *Elements of the Philosophy of Right*. The theory of neutralization can serve as a strong explanation and help us understand why everyday people get actively involved in atrocities beyond imagination. Many of these cases can plausibly be described in the light of a shift in the moral system of these individuals. Some authority provides them with a narrative (they may have heard before or not), which immediately matches their fears and feelings and makes them believe that what they formerly regarded as evil – killing people, for example – is in fact a good thing, precisely because it is against the breed who threatens them, their families, their tribe. Two hundred years ago and long before the emergence of international criminal law, Hegel clearly described the moral shift in people setting aside their doubts about whether what they want is really

[2] G.M. Sykes and D. Matza, 'Techniques of Neutralization: A Theory of Delinquency' (1957) 22 *American Sociological Review* 664.

good and replacing the doubts with the certainty that what they want is really what is to be done – and what is morally right.[3]

This explanation, as compelling as it may be, however, does not seem to have the explanatory power to serve as a key concept in understanding international crimes. Then again, no single approach could do that. The matter is much more complex, and we certainly cannot renounce any help from traditional criminology. Of course, in addition, there are strange or bizarre people and psychopaths in the making out there; this holds true for conflict situations too. The staff in the concentration camps, for instance, was full of such figures, as we know, cruel and sadistic men (and a few women) who have tortured animals in their childhood. Criminology, as Michel Foucault has put it, is a 'labyrinth from which we have certainly not yet emerged'.[4] This is true for both, the domestic and the international context. As a result, we should be aware of oversimplification and overschematization and make use of all available arguments and theories.

IV THE DISTINCTIVENESS OF INTERNATIONAL CRIMINAL LAW: PIERCING THE SOVEREIGN VEIL

Despite the fact that the criminological discourse in our context is more complex than the discourse on the purposes of punishment, I see – from a methodological perspective – a strong similarity between the two: It is misguiding and moves away from the relevant phenomena if one assumes that the challenge is to identify a key concept or a leading theory. It is a mistake to think international crimes could be distinguished from domestic 'ordinary' crimes by way of different criminological or philosophical key concepts or theories. The differences between these two areas of criminal law do neither result from criminal legal nor from criminological reasoning. Instead, they arise from the historical fact that a specific area of criminal prosecution and proceeding has astonishingly evolved against the mighty rules and practices of classical international law, the axioms of territorial sovereignty and non-intervention. Against these sturdy and steely rules of international law, international criminal law pushed forward the idea of global responsibility for the integrity of fundamental rights and the principle of universal jurisdiction. In the history of human rights development, the emergence of international

3 This idea is expressed and set out in Hegel's 'Grundlinien' [1820], *Elements of the Philosophy of Right* (translation H.B. Nisbet) (Cambridge: Cambridge University Press, 1991), § 140.

4 M. Foucault, *Discipline and Punish – The Birth of the Prison* (translation A. Sheridan) (London: Penguin Books, 1991), 252.

criminal law was one of the most significant steps. Nuremberg, therefore, is nothing less than a cipher for a legal revolution.

The timeless discourse on the aims of punishment and the labyrinth of criminological theories and assumptions remain in an obvious detachment from this. That does not mean they are useless or dispensable. On the contrary, they are constitutive for international criminal law as a matter of institutionalized discourse, they create and verify international criminal law as a decent subject for academic exchange. They make possible to talk about them. What we should not expect, however, is that they help us in finding an answer on the most urgent questions of international criminal law. For instance, did international criminal law evolve as a stable trend in human history or was it a mere drift, an aberration, an exception? Will it vanish again? Are there any good reasons to hope it may vanish again? Has it helped to establish a collective memory that will prevent us from experiencing atrocities we have particularly seen in the course of the twentieth century? Is international criminal law a matter for everyone or rather a matter for experts and specialists? Is it sufficiently democratic or does it help us understand that the concept of democracy has to be developed and modified? Is international criminal law a sufficiently universal affair? Or is it a false promise, just another colonial strategy, as some suspect, another hegemonic narrative of Western self-understanding and Western superiority? Can international criminal proceedings get more effective and less selective, as Frank Neubacher hopes? Is international criminal law capable of self-criticism, as Sergey Vasiliev recommends, and does it have the ability to look beyond itself?

Purposes of punishment and issues of criminology, even if they do not relate to questions of such kind, nevertheless have an important function. They are not concerned with the history or the future of international criminal law, but they furnish it with a vocabulary and a grammar that we all understand and share. They ensure that all of us talk about the same thing. By using the metaphor of tokens on a game board, my intention was not to devaluate this practice but to underline its constitutive character. Without the board and without the tokens there is no game. What matters is that we do not forget that the real game does not end at the edge of the board but starts right there.

PART II

Rationales for Punishment in International Criminal Law: Theoretical Perspectives

9

'Can I Be Brought before the ICC?'

Deterrence of Mass Atrocities between Jus in Bello *and* Jus ad Bellum

JAKOB V.H. HOLTERMANN

'Can I be brought before the ICC?'[1] According to a recent book, former Prime Minister of Denmark Anders Fogh Rasmussen asked this question right at the eleventh hour only few days before he let the small Nordic country join the US-led war on Iraq in March 2003. The addressees of Rasmussen's question were the legal experts in the Danish Ministry of Foreign Affairs, several of whom have independently confirmed the incident in anonymous interviews. These same sources recount that, around the same time, the then Prime Minister of Great Britain Tony Blair had asked the same question to the legal advisors of his government.[2] Both incidents are further confirmed by the fact that shortly before the war Rasmussen and Blair each received from their respective legal advisors memos detailing the likely prospects of prosecution.[3]

For all its anecdotal flavour, the fact that there is thus tangible evidence of Rasmussen and Blair actually having felt compelled *in their respective positions at that particular point in time to ask this specific question* promises to throw interesting new light on ongoing debates about the philosophical justifiability of the International Criminal Court (ICC). This is especially the case if we see these events in light of recent developments in the ICC where the Assembly of States Parties in December 2017 decided to activate the crime of aggression amendments negotiated in Kampala in 2010.

[1] J. Tynell, *Mørkelygten, Embedsmænd Fortæller Om Politisk Tilskæring Af Tal, Jura Og Fakta*, 2nd ed. (Frederiksberg: Samfundslitteratur, 2016), 323 (my translation).

[2] Tynell, *Mørkelygten*, 323–324.

[3] Rasmussen's legal advice was provided on 17 March 2003 by the Ministry of Foreign Affairs' Office for Public International Law (cf. http://bo-elkjaer.dk/MT/irak/UDENRIGSPOLITISK%20NVN%20-%20BILAG%20FOLKETINGET/IRAK-udenrigspolitisk-naevn-9.pdf). Blair's legal advice was provided by the Attorney General, Lord Goldsmith on 7 March 2003 (www.theguardian.com/politics/2005/apr/28/election2005.uk1).

Combining these two events – Rasmussen's and Blair's questions to their legal advisors regarding the prospects of prosecution before the ICC, and the recent activation of the Court's jurisdiction over the crime of aggression – this chapter returns to this philosophical debate about the justifiability of the ICC and, more specifically, to the discussion about the potential for the Court of having a deterrent effect on the perpetration of mass atrocities.

In earlier work, I have argued that the widespread scepticism with regard to the existence of this potential for deterrence is exaggerated and that it rests on misunderstandings about the notion of deterrence. Against these critics, I have outlined the argument of why, other things being equal, we have stronger reasons to expect that the Court can work as a deterrent than we have for making the opposite claim.[4]

I believe that this argument remains fundamentally sound, and I shall use it as a framework for the present discussion also. However, the Danish and British prime ministers' questions to their legal advisors are interesting because they simultaneously both *lend support to*, *point to important lacunae in*, and *add nuance to* this argument – especially when seen in light of the activation of the crime of aggression. The prime ministers' questions lend support to the argument to the extent that they provide tangible evidence for the existence precisely of that which critics of deterrence either deny, or claim is so hypothetical as to reduce belief in it to wishful thinking. That is, they provide evidence for the presence in the minds of key actors of the kind of instrumental rationality relevant for any deterrence to work. At the same time, however, Rasmussen's and Blair's last-minute queries point to lacunae because of the replies which they subsequently received from their international law experts. Thus, both the Danish Public International Law Office and the British Attorney General could quickly reassure their respective superiors that as long as they intended to fight a clean war they could not be prosecuted because the ICC did not *at that time* have jurisdiction over the crime of aggression. This is where it is promising to see these events in light of the recent activation of the crime of aggression. In combination with the prime ministers' questions, this

4 Cf. J.v.H. Holtermann, '"A Slice of Cheese" – A Deterrence-Based Argument for the International Criminal Court' (2010) 11 *Human Rights Review* 289. Of course, nothing in that article (or in this one) goes to say that this promising potential is not fragile and cannot remain unrealized, e.g. for reasons of bad management or geopolitical contingencies. In this, I agree with the measured assessment made by former US President Bill Clinton when he signed the Rome Statute: 'I believe that *a properly constituted and structured* International Criminal Court would make a profound contribution in deterring egregious human rights abuses worldwide.' Bill Clinton, 'Statement by the President, December 31, 2000', http://clinton4.nara.gov/library/hot_releases/December_31_2000.html (emphasis added).

activation reminds us that the argument previously presented for the deterrent effect of the ICC has also been too coarse, and that it needs further nuance and should be more fine-grained. In particular, it seems that the argument could benefit from paying closer attention to the distinction between *jus ad bellum* and *jus in bello* crimes. While this distinction is well known in legal doctrine and in just war theory, its significance for a better assessment of the potential deterrent effect of the Court has so far not attracted attention.

The discussion proceeds as follows. In Section I, I provide a few remarks in order to situate the present contribution in a broader framework in the philosophy of punishment, in relation to other discussions about the ICC, and I add a few comments on the structure of the argument propounded in the following pages. In Section II, I outline the central elements in the general argument in favour of the principled justifiability of the establishment of an international criminal court on consequentialist deterrence-based grounds. In Section III, I take a closer look at Rasmussen's and Blair's questions, the context in which they were posed and the replies given by their respective legal advisors, and I relate these considerations to the recent activation of the crime of aggression in order to ascertain the lessons for deterrence theory in relation to the ICC. In Section IV, I briefly summarize my findings.

I FRAMING THE PHILOSOPHICAL DISCUSSION

Before entering the discussion on deterrence, a few remarks are necessary in order to situate the present contribution in a broader framework in the philosophy of punishment and in relation to other discussions about the ICC, and I clarify the structure of the argument propounded in the following pages. It is generally a sound principle of parsimony not always observed in discussions about the legitimacy of the ICC to approach this question as a special case of a more generic problematique, i.e., the overarching question of whether legal punishment *as such* can be justified, and if so on what grounds. For millennia, moral, political and legal philosophers have discussed this question, and it is only reasonable to expect that reflection on the justifiability of establishing punitive institutions *in the specific context of international criminal law* would benefit from this long-established generic theoretical framework.

This is of course not to say that international crime is not unique and, in many ways, different from domestic crime.[5] It is indeed, and we should pay

[5] From a criminological perspective, see the contribution by Frank Neubacher in Chapter 3.

close attention to these differences and the ways in which they affect general theoretical notions of punishment.[6] However, if we do not approach these differences from the more generic level, there is a risk of exaggerating the unicity of the field and subsequently of reinventing the wheel in the structuring of the discussion.[7] Also, a related risk stems from the tendency to tacitly presuppose faulty assumptions about the current state of affairs at the generic level, thus prejudicing specific discussion of the field of international criminal justice.

At the same time, there are obvious limits to this principle of parsimony. At its most fundamental level, the generic discussion in the philosophy of punishment has traditionally been staged as a more or less perpetual duel between the two great contenders in the philosophy of punishment: consequentialism (which justifies punishment on grounds of crime prevention) and retributivism (which justifies punishment on grounds of just desert). In addition, moving beyond the confines of punishment theory, this debate is, at a more fundamental level still, only a special case of the no less perpetual duel in moral philosophy between consequentialism and deontology. However, engaging in depth with this entire debate falls well outside the scope of one contribution to this volume and it would prevent us from approaching the specific question of the justifiability of punishment of international crimes.

Accordingly, this contribution narrows its focus only to one specific question, i.e., whether or not we have reason to believe that the establishment of a permanent international criminal court can deter enough potential perpetrators of mass atrocity to justify the cost of producing this effect. Admittedly, this is a fairly narrow focus. In particular, focusing thus on the possible deterrent effect means that the present discussion is of no relevance to those die-hard retributivists who categorically deny these kinds of consequences any role in justifying punishment.[8] Only philosophers who allow that deterrent effects could hypothetically play a role in the justification of punishment will find it relevant to discuss the prospects of such effects.[9]

6 Indeed, Sections II.2. and III contribute to doing exactly that.

7 For a similar argument, see the contribution by Jochen Bung in Chapter 8.

8 Retributivists have held such views on grounds that, e.g. deterrence-based justifications fail to guarantee the rights of the innocent or that they are instrumentalist and, in Hegel's famous words, treat 'man like a dog instead of with the freedom and respect due to him as a man'.

9 However, many modern retributivists (cf. e.g. A. von Hirsch and A. Ashworth, *Proportionate Sentencing: Exploring the Principles* (Oxford: Oxford University Press, 2005) and proponents of mixed theories (cf. e.g. H.L.A. Hart, *Punishment and Responsibility* (Oxford: Oxford University Press, 1968) actually do believe that consequences and in particular the possibility of deterrence should play some role in the justification of punishment.

Even consequentialist-minded punishment theorists may, however, find the present approach quite selective. Thus, in focusing only on deterrence, traditional criminological concerns about incapacitation or rehabilitation are left unaddressed.[10] Also, the chapter does not deal directly with other, essentially consequentialist questions about the Court's ability to produce truth or to contribute to peace through reconciliation. As will become clear, in spite of this close trim there is ample work in focusing solely on deterrence.

The contribution is narrow also in quite a different way. As will become obvious, it is clear that the discussion is premised on a general rationalistic assumption that it is not only possible and meaningful but indeed imperative to engage in this kind of philosophical discussion about the justifiability of an institution such as the ICC. The discussion takes for granted the assumption that this kind of arguments matters and that the reasons provided are important. This may all seem commonplace. However, certain kinds of scholarship, especially critical legal scholarship on the ICC, seem to challenge these assumptions quite fundamentally. Simplifying matters, they tend to propound the rather bleak view that the existence of the ICC is (like most legal matters) ultimately decided on other, more profane grounds such as, e.g., geopolitical power struggles or the vested interests of political and legal elites in creating lucrative future markets and venues.[11]

From this perspective, philosophical discussions along the lines presented in this chapter are reduced to an empty play of words. They are mere ex-post-rationalizations failing to cut the social realm at its seams. Or worse still, they are harmful (even when done in good faith) because they divert attention from the underlying power mechanisms that are the real drivers of development and ultimately responsible for the establishment of a court such as the ICC. A recent example at least partly along those lines was presented by Mark Drumbl in his contribution to a blog symposium[12] on an article by Hyeran Jo and Beth Simmons work on deterrence.[13] Already, the title of Drumbl's contribution

[10] Generally, such concerns seem to have attracted less attention in the context of international crime – although this tendency is not unambiguous as witnessed by a recent special issue on 'ICTY Celebrities: War Criminals Coming Home', B. Holá and O. Simic (eds.), (2018) 28 *International Criminal Justice Review* 285.

[11] For an overview of such approaches, cf. C. Schwöbel (ed.), *Critical Approaches to International Law – An Introduction* (London: Routledge, 2014).

[12] 'New Symposium: Can the International Criminal Court Deter?', 16 March to 7 April 2016 http://jamesgstewart.com/list-of-previous-symposia.

[13] H. Jo and B.A. Simmons 'Can the International Criminal Court Deter Atrocity?' (2016) 70 *International Organization* 443.

('Hey look at me: Deterreo, ergo sum'[14]) is telling of the perception of the problematic and ultimately distorting character of the discussion about the deterrent effect of the ICC. Furthermore, Drumbl 'suggest[s] that we talk a lot less about the ICC and deterrence',[15] and that we do so because, ultimately, this debate seductively closes our eyes to the opportunity costs of the ICC: 'We settle on the ICC as the icon of preventative justice at the expense of other options.'[16]

Dealing effectively with this kind of objection to the present kind of discussion is difficult. Ultimately, it requires stepping back from the making of first-order philosophical arguments and confronting the critique directly at a meta-level. This would fall outside the scope of the present study. Instead, I shall only flag here in the introduction that I believe that Drumbl's objection to the deterrence discussion rests on a false dilemma – in two ways. First, deterrence simply does not hold the kind of discursive hegemony asserted by Drumbl. Discursive pluralism and critiques are the order of the day (as amply illustrated by the variety of approaches to the issue in this volume and the limited discussion of deterrence). Second, proponents of deterrence are not inherently tied to 'the ICC as the icon of preventative justice at the expense of other options'. As I shall argue below in Section II.2, we shall conceive of our comprehensive atrocity preventive system as a 'broad-spectrum drug' in which the ICC constitutes one component.

II OUTLINING THE DETERRENCE-BASED ARGUMENT FOR THE INTERNATIONAL CRIMINAL COURT

1 *The Generic Argument for Deterrence*

The above-mentioned tendency to prejudice discussion in international criminal justice by making fallacious presuppositions about the state of affairs at the generic level of punishment theory is particularly pertinent in relation to deterrence. Thus, in discussions of the ICC, critics tend, tacitly but in general wrongly, to presuppose that a more or less conclusive case has already been made against deterrence on the generic level.[17] Thereby, an impression is

[14] M.A. Drumbl, 'Hey Look at Me: Deterreo, Ergo Sum', 17 March 2016, http://jamesgstewart.com/hey-look-at-me-deterreo-ergo-sum. For a reply to this criticism, see the contribution by Mark A. Drumbl in Chapter 12 (Section III).

[15] Drumbl, 'Hey Look at Me: Deterreo, Ergo Sum'.

[16] Drumbl, 'Hey Look at Me: Deterreo, Ergo Sum'.

[17] This first section of the present contribution restates and refines the argument originally outlined in Holtermann, '"A Slice of Cheese" – A Deterrence-Based Argument for the ICC'. For congenial approaches, cf. notably A. Ellis, 'War Crimes, Punishment and the Burden of

further created that the specific attempt to justify international criminal tribunals on deterrent grounds is already dubious business from the outset, and that any discussion thereof proceeds only on account of charity. In order to counter this problematic tendency, it is therefore necessary in this section to address explicitly, and reject such implicit doubts about, the deterrent effect of punishment at the generic level before moving on in Section II.2 to the specific discussion about the prospects of deterrence in international criminal justice.

First, this scepticism generally tends to exaggerate the burden of proof that reasonably befalls the deterrence-based argument. Critics write for instance that 'social science cannot *prove* that deterrence works' or that 'nobody knows whether punishment deters enough to justify the cost of producing this effect'.[18] However, it is generally unreasonable to expect proponents of deterrence to be able to deliver conclusive evidence of deterrence beyond a certain absolute level of probability. Determining the exact effect of the threat of punishment is notoriously difficult, involving countless variables not to mention the practical and ethical challenges in testing hypotheses on these matters systematically. From the point of view of consequentialism, the situation in philosophy of punishment is one of determining rational behavior under uncertainty when forced to choose between two mutually exclusive alternatives, i.e., between creating punitive institutions and refraining from so doing. And in this situation, it is rational to act on the balance of probabilities thus simply asking whether we have *more* reason to expect that punitive institutions can reduce crime through deterrence than vice versa.

Second, many seem to misrepresent the specific character of those empirically well-founded doubts that actually do remain, even on this lower threshold of proof regarding the deterrent effect of punishment. The disheartening conclusion that 'nothing works' is often cited in support of the claim that we have no reason to expect a significant crime reductive effect of the threat of punishment. However, we should remember that this specific conclusion was

Proof' (2010) 16 *Res Publica* 181, but also P. Akhavan, 'Beyond Impunity: Can International Criminal Justice Prevent Future Atrocities?'(2001) 95 *American Journal of International Law* 7 and A. von Hirsch and V.C. Schorscher, 'A System of International Criminal Justice for Human Rights Violations: What Is the General Justification for Its Existence?' in J.V. Roberts and L. Zedner (eds.), *Principles and Values in Criminal Law and Criminal Justice* (Oxford: Oxford University Press, 2012), 209.

18 Cf. e.g. M. Davis, 'Punishment Theory's Golden Half Century: A Survey of Developments from (about) 1957 to 2007' (2009) 13 *Journal of Ethics* 73.

originally drawn in relation to *rehabilitation* programs as crime preventive strategies and not to deterrence as such.[19] Furthermore, to the degree that criminologists have in fact emphasized lacunae in our knowledge about deterrence, these doubts relate only to the effect of incremental changes in the severity and swiftness of punishment, *not* to the effect of the threat of punishment as such. On the contrary, regarding this latter question, most serious criminologists seem to agree in all fundamentals with Hume's age-old sobering assessment:

> 'Tis indeed certain, that as all human laws are founded on rewards and punishments,'tis suppos'd as a fundamental principle, that these motives have an influence on the mind, and both produce the good and prevent the evil actions.[20]

In other words, it seems that, on balance, we are more justified in believing that the threat of punishment has a significant deterrent effect, than we are in believing the opposite.[21]

Third, there is a distinct tendency among critics to exaggerate the preventive effect required to justify punishment on deterrent grounds. I shall return to this shortly, but here it should just be emphasized that the claim that legal punishment can be justified on deterrent grounds is not a claim that *all* potential perpetrators will be deterred *all* the time. It is only a claim that *some* potential perpetrators will be deterred *some* of the time, and that *a sufficient number* of potential perpetrators will be deterred to outweigh the cost of producing this effect.

[19] The catchword 'nothing works' stems from D. Lipton, R. Martinson and J. Wilks, *Effectiveness of Correctional Treatment: A Survey of Treatment Evaluation Studies* (Springfield: Praeger, 1975).

[20] L.A. Selby-Bigge and P.H. Nidditch (eds.), *David Hume: A Treatise of Human Nature*, 2nd ed. (Oxford: Oxford University Press, 1978), 410.

[21] Cf. e.g. D.S. Nagin, 'Deterrence and Incapacitation' in M. Tonry (ed.), *The Handbook of Crime and Punishment* (Oxford: Oxford University Press, 1998), 345, 359: '[T]he accumulated evidence on deterrence leads me to conclude that the criminal justice system exerts a substantial deterrent effect.' Such assessments are further supported – anecdotally diehard sceptics might claim – by reports on the extreme criminogenic effect of the detention of the entire Danish police force by the German occupying forces in 1944 during World War II (J. Trolle, *Syv Maaneder uden Politi* (Copenhagen: Nyt Nordisk Forlag, 1945), and also – less anecdotally – by the fact that there are no recorded instances of long-term viable human societies that do not have some kind of punitive institution, cf. D.E. Brown, *Human Universals* (New York/London: McGraw-Hill, 1991), 138.

2 *The Specific Argument for Deterrence in International Criminal Law*

Summing up discussion thus far, the implication seems to be that debate on deterrence-based justifications of the ICC (or similar institutions) should proceed not, as is so often the case, on account of charity of a rather dubious hypothesis. On the contrary, the more reasonable starting point is surely that the fundamental assumptions on the basis of which deterrence theory rests are sound, and that the existence of a system of criminal justice does have a significant deterrent effect on the perpetration of crime. It is *this* firm assumption that should be the baseline for discussion. Consequently, the way forward in the specific context of international criminal justice should be to ask whether we have any reason to believe that this default assumption breaks down when the crimes we are dealing with are mass atrocities, and when the threat of punishment is issued by an international criminal court. In the literature, this is often phrased as the question of whether the *domestic analogy* breaks down in international criminal justice, and I shall adopt the same terminology.[22]

There are of course many ways in which the perpetration of mass atrocities and prosecution thereof differ substantially from the well-known context of domestic crime. Many of these differences give reason to reconsider the solidity of the domestic analogy, and ideally a comprehensive theory of deterrence in international criminal law should examine all these differences carefully. Based on an overview of the literature, it seems useful for present purposes to group the alleged differences into three areas where criticism has been particularly persistent. These three areas are (a) the multi-causality and multi-agency of mass atrocity; (b) the critique of the rational actor assumption in the context of mass atrocity; and (c) the peace versus justice dilemma.

a) The Multi-causality and Multi-agency of Mass Atrocity

Critics of deterrence routinely emphasize the social complexity of the situations in which mass atrocities are committed. In a characteristic passage, Drumbl reminds us that more than 'a handful of people are responsible for endemic levels of violence' and further stresses 'the myriad political, economic, historical and colonial factors that create conditions precedent for violence'.[23] His claim is that the focus of criminal law on the responsibility

[22] For the domestic analogy (objection), see the contribution by Elies van Sliedregt in Chapter 5.

[23] M.A. Drumbl, *Atrocity, Punishment, and International Law* (Cambridge: Cambridge University Press, 2007), 172.

and guilt of individual perpetrators distorts this fundamental fact about mass atrocity.

In assessing this argument in relation to the deterrence-based justifications of the ICC, we should be careful not to confound things that ought to be kept apart. On the one hand, Drumbl is surely right that mass atrocities are usually committed in exceptional and highly complex contexts and only through the participation of a large number of people. This is all well documented in genocide studies and related disciplines. Thus, e.g., Ervin Staub has convincingly argued that we should understand genocide as the result of a complex historical process that he calls the 'continuum of destruction', and that is constituted by a set of conditions in the absence of which genocide simply does not seem to take place.[24] Analogous points have been made experimentally by social psychologists[25] and by historians.[26]

On the other hand, however, it is mistaken to assume that these well-established empirical findings should somehow be in contradiction with the assumptions of deterrence theory. Unlike what Drumbl seems to assume, deterrence theory does not imply any commitment to an assumption about *sole responsibility* or *all-guilt* of the individual actor or actors prosecuted in court. On the contrary, unlike, e.g., retributivist punishment theories, deterrence theory is perfectly compatible with an analysis of mass atrocities as the end result of a complex large set of individually necessary and only jointly sufficient conditions along the lines that Staub describes. Deterrence theory only requires that among these conditions we *also* count the (perceived) existence of de facto impunity for the particular kinds of actions by the particular kinds of actors whom the ICC targets with its threat of punishment.

In fact, from the point of view of deterrence *theory*, it is unnecessary and a cause for conceptual confusion to speak thus vaguely of *guilt* of and *responsibility* for mass atrocities. Instead, I have suggested using the concept of a NESS-test as this term was originally introduced by Richard W. Wright[27]

[24] Staub mentions (i) difficult life conditions (e.g., economic problems, widespread violence, and social disorganization leading to an experience of threat to physical safety, etc.); (ii) cultural and personal preconditions (e.g., ingroup-outgroup differentiation, orientation to authority, etc.); and (iii) societal-political organization (e.g., totalitarian system, discriminating social institutions, etc.) E. Staub, *The Roots of Evil: The Origins of Genocide and Other Group Violence* (Cambridge: Cambridge University Press, 1989), cf. Chapter 2.

[25] Cf. e.g. S. Milgram, *Obedience to Authority: An Experimental View* (London: Pinter & Martin, 1997, first published 1974).

[26] Cf. e.g. C.R. Browning, *Ordinary Men: Reserve Police Battalion 101 and the Final Solution in Poland* (New York: Aaron Asher Books, 1992).

[27] R.W. Wright, 'Once More into the Bramble Bush: Duty, Causal Contribution, and the Extent of Legal Responsibility' (2001) 54 *Vanderbilt Law Review* 1.

(building on H.L.A. Hart and Anthony Maurice Honore's groundbreaking work on causality in law[28]). NESS is acronym for **n**ecessary **e**lement of a **s**ufficient **s**et, and this concept is particularly useful for improving our understanding of the multi-causal character of mass atrocities with all its myriad f/actors involved. One main advantage is that the NESS-test allows us to conceive our crime preventive strategy in accordance with the so-called Swiss cheese model originally developed by James T. Reason in the field of risk analysis and risk management in complex human security systems such as nuclear plants, aviation control, etc.[29]

Reason invites us to conceive preventive systems as successive layers of Swiss cheese that each aim to remove one particular condition known to be a NESS-condition for a particular adverse effect to take place (nuclear melt down, aviation disaster, etc. as the case may be). The holes in each slice of cheese allude to the fact that no preventive measure is perfect. Figuratively speaking, the challenge is therefore to add as many 'slices' as possible and to line them up in such a way that the successive layers do not 'permit a trajectory of accident opportunity'.[30]

In the context of atrocity prevention, then, the Swiss cheese model reminds us, first, that we do not have to put all our eggs in one basket. [31] We can, indeed should, use 'broad-spectrum drug' and design different layers of Swiss cheese so that each individually target different factors known to be NESS-conditions for mass atrocity. Second, the Swiss cheese model invites us to conceive the deterrence-based argument for the ICC as the claim that a 'properly constituted and structured' (see footnote 4) international criminal tribunal can work as a distinct new slice of cheese added to the ones already at work in international geopolitics and which target one or more of the different NESS-conditions that jointly constitute the 'continuum of destruction' (e.g. economic problems, ingroup-outgroup differentiation, totalitarianism, etc.). (See Figure 1.)

The holes in the cheese further remind us of the relevance of the above-mentioned modesty of ambition of a deterrence-based argument, also, or especially, in the case of the ICC. There is indeed no claim that *all* potential

[28] H.L.A. Hart and A.M. Honore, *Causation in the Law* (Oxford: Clarendon Press, 1959), xxxii, 454.

[29] J.T. Reason, 'Human Error: Models and Management' (2000) 320 *British Medical Journal* 768.

[30] Reason, 'Human Error', 769.

[31] A parallel model can be used in the familiar context of domestic crime prevention where the threat of punishment is not considered the only crime preventive measure. Social security, stable job opportunities, etc. are routinely invoked as measures that contribute to the prevention of crime.

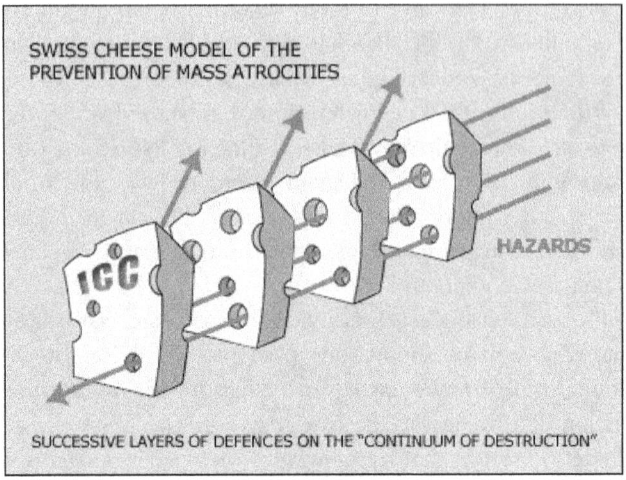

FIG. 1 The ICC added to the Swiss cheese model applied to the prevention of mass atrocities.

perpetrators of mass atrocity will be deterred *all* the time (and certainly no claim about bringing an end to impunity). As already emphasized, there is only a claim that *some* potential perpetrators will be deterred *some* of the time, and that *a sufficient number* of potential perpetrators will be deterred to outweigh the cost of producing this effect.

This more modest phrasing of the ICC's ambition may seem to fall victim to what Fréderic Mégrét somewhat polemically describes as recent attempts to 'soft-land the project' and to 'fudge the issue of success',[32] thereby insinuating a somewhat spurious meddling with the premises of discussion by the Court's proponents. However, one might also claim – equally polemically – that critics have repeatedly failed to adopt the principle of charity in discussions about the Court preferring always to latch on to the first and best wildly exaggerated and atheoretical claim about its promising potential made by policymakers or legal practitioners. The counterclaim would be that we should consider the more modest version of the ambition of the Court (and related attempts at 'managing expectations', as it has aptly been called)[33] as a much needed précis of the best case for the ICC. As always, failure is a

[32] F. Mégret, 'The Anxieties of International Criminal Justice' (2016) 29 *Leiden Journal of International Law* 197, 217.

[33] K. Cronin-Furman, 'Managing Expectations: International Criminal Trials and the Prospects for Deterrence of Mass Atrocity' (2013) 7 *International Journal of Transitional Justice* 434.

function of ambition, and the more utopian the depiction of the project the easier it is to establish a negative conclusion.

b) The Critique of the Rational Actor Assumption in the Context of Mass Atrocity

A second line of critique is related but makes a distinct claim about why the domestic analogy breaks down in the context of mass atrocity. On this approach, the problem is that the assumption of perpetrator rationality on which deterrence relies is undermined in the particular circumstances in which mass violence is carried out.[34] One central reason referred to is the extreme situational pressures to which perpetrators are often exposed when they commit mass atrocity.[35]

Again, we should be careful to keep things apart in the assessment of this argument. In particular, we should observe that there is no empirical support for a categorical claim that perpetrators of mass atrocity are strictly speaking *irrational*. On the contrary, perpetrator studies overwhelmingly document how perpetrators are indeed rational in the relevant sense of that word. Most often, they have had their beliefs distorted so that, e.g., members of a particular ethnic group are perceived as existential threats, and/or they have had their values perverted so as to consider, e.g., the suffering inflicted on the victim group to be just punishment. As a result, behaviour that is ordinarily seen as inhuman and wildly irrational, can nevertheless seem rational for the actors engaged in that behaviour. Or, put differently, perpetrator studies do not contradict the rational actor assumption; they confirm it.

Of course, this does not change the fact that even if perpetrator studies do not undermine the rationality assumptions of deterrence theory, they nevertheless illustrate how, in certain exceptional circumstances, the deterrent effect of a hypothetical threat of punishment may be too weak to have a decisive influence on perpetrator behaviour. Perpetrator studies tend to tell us that in such circumstances being deterred may not be the rational thing to do. However, there are a number of reasons why this conclusion should be taken

[34] Cf. e.g., M. Minow, *Between Vengeance and Forgiveness: Facing History after Genocide and Mass Violence* (Boston: Beacon Press, 1998), 50; Drumbl, *Atrocity, Punishment, and International Law*, 171; F. Mégret, 'Three Dangers for the International Criminal Court: A Critical Look at a Consensual Project' in M. Koskenniemi and J. Petman (eds.), *Finnish Yearbook of International Law* (Leiden: Martinus Nijhoff Publishers, 2001), Vol. XII, 195, 203; I. Tallgren, 'The Sensibility and Sense of International Criminal Law' (2002) 13 *European Journal of International Law* 561, 584.

[35] On situational pressure, see the contribution by Frank Neubacher in Chapter 3.

with some caution because metaphorically speaking even if these studies leave holes in the distinct ICC slice of Swiss cheese, they do not have the effect of turning the entire slice into one big hole.

First, it is well documented that at least some perpetrators engage in concealment efforts during perpetration of mass atrocity.[36] This behaviour only makes sense on the assumption that the actors are not completely succumbed to situational pressures but at least to some degree do take into account possible future costs of their behaviour. Second, situational pressures and wildly erratic beliefs about imminent danger arguably seem more widespread among foot soldiers. However, the ICC is predominantly a big-fish court going after political and military leaders. It is not unreasonable to presume that such political and military leaders will generally be acting under less situational pressure than foot soldiers, and also that they will generally be able to act strategically, taking the prospects of prosecution into account before engaging in problematic behaviour. As we shall see, this is precisely what the example of Rasmussen's and Blair's questions to their legal advisors indicate, and also why the crime of aggression seems particularly interesting from the point of view of deterrence.

c) The Peace versus Justice Dilemma

A third line of attack on the domestic analogy takes a quite different tack. This is at the same time a stronger attack than the other two in the sense that it does not merely claim that the Court is impotent and may thus lead to an unfortunate use of scarce resources. Instead, this argument claims that the Court is in fact actively working *against* peace and in that sense has a *criminogenic, not a crime preventive effect*. In a nutshell, this argument makes the claim that the threat of punishment can accelerate violence because issuance of arrest warrants gives perpetrators who are still under arms a strong incentive to remain at large, if necessary through continued violence and armed conflict.

As a preliminary, it should be emphasized how critics often overlook that this argument is internally inconsistent with the argument against the domestic analogy considered immediately above.[37] It is simply not possible without contradiction to maintain, on the one hand, that perpetrators of mass atrocities

[36] D. Wippman, 'Atrocities, Deterrence, and the Limits of International Justice' (1999) 23 *Fordham International Law Journal* 473, 480.

[37] Holtermann, '"A Slice of Cheese" – A Deterrence-Based Argument for the ICC', 308. A recent article makes the same point, cf. Jo and Simmons 'Can the International Criminal Court Deter Atrocity?', 445–446.

are not rational actors who can be affected by the threat of punishment, while simultaneously holding, on the other, that that very threat of punishment is perfectly capable of influencing those same perpetrators in the opposite direction, i.e., inciting them to accelerate violence.

Of course, this does not change the fact that there is a risk that the threat of punishment may in fact have adverse effects and lead to an acceleration of atrocity. However, we should observe first that in and of itself, this peace versus justice dilemma does not imply a *breakdown* of the domestic analogy for the simple reason that the same phenomenon is very well known from domestic criminal justice. To illustrate, no one would expect the threat of punishment to have *any* deterrent effect on, say, a bank robber who has taken hostages and who is now trying to escape the police. On the contrary, upholding the threat of punishment in this scenario gives the bank robber a strong incentive to remain at large, if necessary through continued perpetration. In this sense, the peace versus justice dilemma in fact *consolidates* the domestic analogy, i.e., by merely presenting a familiar domestic criminal justice dilemma writ large.

If anything, we are therefore dealing with a generic challenge to deterrence theory as such: Why is it that the criminal justice system insists that its threat of punishment should be activated and not withdrawn against perpetrators who have already perpetrated, even when we have reason to believe that this will incentivize them to further perpetration? This is a challenge that reminds us of one of the core assumptions of deterrence theory. It is simply a mistake, often entertained by proponents of deterrence, to expect the threat of punishment to prevent people who have already perpetrated but remain at large.

More specifically, this expectation signals a confusion of the distinction between *deterrence* and *compellence* helpfully introduced by Thomas C. Schelling.[38] Both deterrence and compellence are preventive measures operating through threats of force. However, deterrence aims to prevent actions from taking place in the first place. Compellence aims to stop or turn back actions already undertaken. Accordingly, people who have already engaged in perpetration cannot be *deterred* by the threat of punishment; they can only be *compelled* to stop – which is a job for law enforcement (or, in the case of international crime, for the military). In terms of crime prevention, the job of the criminal justice system, on the other hand, is not to compel actual perpetrators but to deter potential perpetrators, i.e., all those people *who have not yet* perpetrated in the first place, and who, therefore, are not yet due

[38] T.C. Schelling, *Arms and Influence* (New Haven: Yale University Press, 1995), 69–76.

punishment.[39] And for the credibility of this threat, it is particularly important that it cannot be stopped once it has started. In this sense, the criminal justice system is analogous to the famous doomsday machine from the film Dr. Strangelove:

> This is the whole idea of this machine [the doomsday machine], you know: Deterrence is the art of producing in the mind of the enemy [. . .] the FEAR to attack, and so, because of the automated and irrevocable decision-making process which rules out human meddling, the doomsday machine is terrifying and simple to understand [. . .] and completely credible and convincing.[40]

The possible adverse effects of not stopping the threat of punishment in such cases are therefore viewed as necessary costs for achieving credibility vis-à-vis all the potential perpetrators who have not yet perpetrated and thus for harvesting the general crime preventive effect through deterrence.

III DETERRENCE AND THE DISTINCTION BETWEEN *JUS IN BELLO* AND *JUS AD BELLUM*

On the basis of the considerations hitherto presented, it seems that the most influential critiques against the ICC have failed to prove their case. The most reasonable default assumption is that in general the threat of punishment does have a deterrent effect. Furthermore, it seems that (notwithstanding a long list of fairly obvious but less important differences between the context of ordinary crime and mass atrocity) the domestic analogy between these two contexts remains fundamentally sound. However, while claims about a virtual *breakdown* of the domestic analogy may therefore be unjustified, the investigation

[39] The tendency to confuse this distinction is widespread. For instance, one might argue that the Prosecutor's eagerness to speed up the arrest warrants against Muamar Gaddafi and his sons in 2011 in the middle of the ongoing conflict in Libya betrays a confusion of this distinction between deterrence and compellence, cf. e.g.: 'Arresting those who ordered the commission of crimes will contribute to the protection of civilians in Libya because it will deter ongoing crimes. It will deter crimes by removing those who ordered the crimes, and by sending a serious message to other potential perpetrators, in Libya and in other situations, that the international community will not condone such crimes.' (ICC Office of the Prosecutor, 'Statement to the United Nations Security Council on the Situation in the Libyan Arab Jamahiriya, Pursuant to UNSCR 1970 (2011)', 4 May 2011, para. 25. Also, a comprehensive research report by the Nuremberg Academy nominally dealing with deterrence seems in fact to be dealing with the compellent effect of the court in a number of specific situations – which, as one might expect, they conclude is weak (www.nurembergacademy.org/fileadmin/media/pdf/publications/DETERRENCEPUBLICATION.pdf).

[40] Cf. www.imdb.com/title/tt0057012/quotes/?tab=qt&ref_=tt_trv_qu.

has also shown that the analogy looks at least somewhat strained on a couple of issues. In particular, the strength of the situational pressures active during perpetration of mass atrocity seems to magnify considerably certain challenges already found in domestic criminal law. Furthermore, the absence of anything remotely resembling the monopoly of force of sovereign nation states makes the credibility of the threat of punishment considerably lower in international than in domestic criminal law.[41]

These considerations remind us that the holes in the particular slice of Swiss cheese constituted by the ICC are bigger than the ones in the analogous slice in the domestic criminal justice system. However, the question is whether there is reason to expect that these comparative deficiencies in the preventive system of international criminal justice can be ameliorated to some degree and, if so, how. In addition, this is where the combination previously alluded to of, first, the questions of the Danish and British prime ministers to their legal advisors, and, second, the recent activation of the Court's jurisdiction over the crime of aggression enters the picture. As mentioned in the introduction, the claim made in this part of the chapter is that the combined attention to these two facts allows the discussion of deterrence in international criminal justice to become more nuanced and fine-grained. In particular, it allows us to reflect on the specific significance from the point of view of deterrence theory of differentiating between different kinds of international crimes, especially crimes *ad bellum* and crimes *in bello*, and relatedly between different kinds of perpetrators.

Going back to March 2003 when Rasmussen and Blair asked their respective legal advisors about the prospects of being brought to The Hague, the respective government offices had already been unusually busy for at least half a year. Thus, it had long been clear that both the Danish and the British prime minister were adamant that in the event of war it would not only be in their respective countries' best interest but even their moral duty to follow the US. Therefore, as a crucial part of the planning for this imminent event, the legal experts in the public international law offices of both countries had been asked to continually assess and stand ready to deliver the best case available for the legality of an invasion of Iraq.

As things developed, this proved to be quite a daunting task for the Danish and British legal experts, even with the help of their American colleagues. Unfolding events in the UN Security Council, in government offices, diplomatic circles and on the ground in Iraq had the effect of turning the legal case

[41] For a similar argument, see the contribution by Jochen Bung in Chapter 8.

for the war into a moving target. In the case of the UK, this process is particularly well described. The Chilcot Report recounts how during these hectic months the argument for the legality of the war gradually became more strained, in the end almost to the level of sophistry, as the initial more open-ended request for an expert legal opinion gradually turned into an explicit order of the 'right' conclusion.[42] The Danish case appears not to have been much different in this regard.[43]

This particular story is no doubt worth telling (and retelling), not least in countless legal philosophy courses and courses on professional ethics offered at law faculties around the world. However, Rasmussen's and Blair's last-minute questions are distinct in character from their other communications with the international law experts and they raise different and, for present purposes, even more interesting issues, which to my knowledge have not attracted scholarly attention so far.

Rasmussen's and Blair's last-minute concerns about the risk of being brought to The Hague are interesting because they provide rare testimony of the occurrence at the highest political level of a particular change of fundamental perspective on (international) law. Until this moment in time, the work of the legal advisors in both countries seems to have been focused on producing lines of argumentation that could serve, in the abstract, to build the legal case in support of the claim that the war was not illegal. This legal case was never intended for a courtroom. It was intended to win over public opinion and political support both domestically and on the world stage of international politics – and perhaps, on a charitable reading, it was also intended to convince the decision makers' own conscience by placating earnestly held doubts about acting outside the law. However, this ultimately rather abstract play of words is

[42] The Chilcot Report is available at www.iraqinquiry.org.uk/the-report, especially Volume 5.

[43] Cf. Tynell, Mørkelygten, 283–328. However, the Danish civil servants do seem to have been a tat more obliging and 'dutiful' than their British counterparts. Not only is there no account of any of them acting like Deputy Legal Advisor Elizabeth Wilmshurst, who took the consequence of the clash between the answer which her professional juristic conscience told her was the right one and that which her superiors demanded of her, and resigned her post as Deputy Legal Advisor (http://news.bbc.co.uk/2/hi/uk_news/politics/4377605.stm). It also seems that the Danish legal experts never explicitly took a stance on the actual legality or not of a war but restricted their role instead to outlining the best arguments available in different scenarios and emphasizing the different rhetorical strengths and weaknesses of these arguments. Tynell's account leaves the impression that this somewhat more cynical approach may also be due to a more general perception that there really is no right answer, and that the available sources inevitably underdetermines the conclusions to *any* question of valid international law. It is an interesting question, although well beyond the scope of this contribution, whether this difference can be ascribed to the prominent role of Scandinavian legal realism on the Danish legal profession.

all put to one side when suddenly, right at the eleventh hour, Rasmussen and Blair both ask their lawyers '*Can **I** be brought before the ICC?*'. With this question, concern for the abstract legal argument is replaced by the pure self-interest of someone who wants to avoid being adversely affected by his own actions. As such, the new perspective embroiled in the prime ministers' questions expresses almost too perfectly a turn to that which Oliver Wendell Holmes, Jr. has famously called 'the view of the bad man':[44]

> But if we take the view of our friend the bad man we shall find that he does not care two straws for the axioms or deductions, but that he does want to know what the Massachusetts or English courts are likely to do in fact. I am much of this mind. The prophecies of what the courts will do in fact, and nothing more pretentious, are what I mean by the law.[45]

This is particularly interesting in the present context because the point of view of the bad man precisely encapsulates the point of view of that kind of potentially malevolent actor whose actions deterrence theory in general and the ICC in particular wish to influence with the threat of punishment. Rasmussen's and Blair's questions to their legal advisors thereby connect the case of the Iraq War directly to the discussion about the deterrent effect of the Court. And, as already mentioned, in so doing they simultaneously lend support to, point to lacunae in and add nuance to this discussion.

The prime ministers' questions *lend support* to the deterrence-based argument in so far that they provide tangible evidence for the existence precisely of that which critics of deterrence either deny, or claim is so hypothetical as to reduce belief in it to wishful thinking. That is, Rasmussen's and Blair's questions testify to the manifest existence of instrumental rationality in the mind of key actors about to engage in the kind of behaviour that the ICC wishes to prevent. This incident shows therefore that the situational pressures are not all-encompassing but that the Court, remote as it may be, is in fact capable of entering the deliberations of key actors. Thereby, it testifies to the actual empirical effect of the ICC. Rasmussen and Blair would not have asked the particular question they did in the particular situation they were in unless they feared that, however independently attractive going to war with the Americans might seem to them at the time, there could be a risk that this decision could adversely affect each of them personally in the future.

[44] 'A man who cares nothing for an ethical rule which is believed and practiced by his neighbors is likely nevertheless to care a good deal to avoid being made to pay money, and will want to keep out of jail if he can.' O.W. Holmes, 'The Path of the Law' (1897) 10 *Harvard Law Review* 457, 459.

[45] Holmes, 'The Path of the Law', 460–461.

These considerations do not come without cautions. In particular, they do not warrant blanket assertions that if either Rasmussen or Blair had received a different and less reassuring answer from their advisors, they would have been deterred and chosen not to join the US-led Iraq War. Considering the strong political signals sent by both prime ministers to the Americans since at least the summer of 2002 and considering the political capital which both Rasmussen and Blair had already invested in the heated debate leading up to the war, withdrawing from the war at the last moment was an option open to both of them only at considerable cost. However, had they been given a different answer to their question about prosecution, this would at least have made it clear that following the Americans would also come with a(n additional) considerable cost, and the threat of prosecution could in that sense have entered into and possibly influenced their deliberations. And this is all deterrence theory hopes for.

I mentioned that Rasmussen's and Blair's questions also *point to lacunae* in the deterrence-based case for the ICC. This follows straightforwardly from the answer that they each received from their respective advisors. Most independent experts in public international law agree that the Iraq War was an unlawful war. Indirectly, this assessment is further supported by the exceeding difficulty (as described earlier in this section) with which even the Danish and British legal advisors struggled to deliver the 'right' verdict at their superiors' urgent request. However, when asked specifically about the prospects of individual prosecution those same advisors appear to have found no comparable difficulty. Thus, the legal advisors of both countries could quickly inform their respective prime ministers in no uncertain terms that the Court did not have jurisdiction over the crime of aggression and that a de facto state of impunity therefore existed for this crime at that time. In other words, Rasmussen's and Blair's questions and particularly the replies they received serve to remind us of the, after all, quite banal fact that even if on a theoretical and empirical level the possibility conditions for effective deterrence are perfectly satisfied, and the generic doubts of sceptics are therefore put to shame, deterrence simply cannot work on behaviour that is not criminalized at the relevant time. As long as the Court does not have jurisdiction over the crime of aggression, a big corner will therefore be missing in the metaphorical slice of cheese that constitutes the ICC's contribution to the – alas, too imperfect – comprehensive international system of atrocity prevention.[46] And this is of course the lacuna which is immediately closed by the recent activation of the crime of aggression.

However, the activation does not merely close a lacuna to which Rasmussen's and Blair's questions have helped draw our attention. Combining the

[46] A similar argument is made by Silvia Fernández de Gurmendi in Chapter 2 regarding the lack of universality of the ICC as an obstacle to a deterrent effect.

two simultaneously reminds us that the argument previously presented has in certain regards been too coarse, and it gives us an opportunity to *further nuance or fine-grain* our understanding and discussion about deterrence. In particular, the prime ministers' questions and the specific character of the crime of aggression indicate that the argument for deterrence could benefit from paying closer attention to the distinction between *jus in bello* and *jus ad bellum* crimes.[47] From the point of view of deterrence, the Court's lack of jurisdiction over the crime of aggression should not merely be thought of as a quantitative limitation; metaphorically speaking, as a missing quarter of a slice of cheese in the Swiss cheese model. In terms of deterrence, it seems that there is a crucial qualitative difference between the criminalizing of the crime of aggression and the criminalization of the other three international crimes.

First of all, the crime of aggression is different because it is a kind of meta-crime in international armed conflict, encompassing within it, so to speak, war crimes, crimes against humanity and genocide. In philosophical terms, the crime of aggression constitutes the possibility condition of the other crimes: without war – broadly defined – there are no (or hardly any) war crimes, crimes against humanity, or genocide. In fact, this is not entirely true because history reminds us that it is only too possible to commit war crimes, crimes against humanity and genocide also when fighting a just war. However, as history also reminds us, a considerable share of these crimes are committed in unjust wars. As there is an asymmetric dependency between at least *these* particular *in bello* crimes and the *ad bellum* crimes (the former depending on the latter but not vice versa), successfully deterring (some of) the latter would necessarily imply preventing those of the former that would otherwise have been committed had this deterrence not taken place.

However, the crime of aggression is different from the other three kinds of crime not merely in virtue of *logically* preceding the latter in the way cause will always precede effect. The crime of aggression is different also in a *temporal* and in an *actor-related* way. Both these aspects are related to the

[47] In a recent article, Jo and Simmons make a related point emphasizing the need 'to [avoid] generalized claims and instead [advance] conditional arguments about ICC deterrence [...]. We are careful to craft arguments conditional on who is expected to be deterred.' Jo and Simmons, '"A Slice of Cheese" – Can the International Criminal Court Deter Atrocity?', 446. However, thus stated the point is too strong. Scientific discourse always involves a tradeoff between generality and specificity. Specificity comes with the promise of greater accuracy but at the cost of reducing scope, and vice versa with generality. It is therefore never wise (nor strictly speaking possible) to pursue one entirely to the exclusion of the other but pragmatic factors including resources, stage and overall purpose of discourse generally determine when it is convenient to pursue one over the other.

possibility condition aspect just mentioned but they are analytically different in ways that are relevant from the point of view of deterrence. Temporally, the crime of aggression is different because it is well known that there is huge inertia in mass violence. Payam Akhavan has made this point succinctly in relation to the war in the former Yugoslavia and the prospects of achieving substantive deterrence through the International Criminal Tribunal for the formere Yugoslavia (ICTY), which was established long after the hostilities had been initiated:

> [It is] unrealistic to suppose that the ICTY could have instantaneously deterred crimes in the midst of a particularly cruel interethnic was in the former Yugoslavia. Hastily erected bulwarks cannot be expected to save lives when the deluge has already begun. The threat of punishment – let alone an empty threat – has a limited impact on human behavior in a culture already intoxicated with hatred and violence.[48]

As Akhavan indicates, the social dynamics at play when conflict evolves substantively change the situational pressures under which people act. One significant effect of ongoing widespread violence is the distortion of our sense of proportion in relation to human suffering and misery. With a view to deterrence, this has the effect of making the perceived severity of a threat of punishment crumple. However, the crime of aggression is less vulnerable to this deflationary mechanism because by definition, and unlike with the other three *in bello* crimes, the crime of aggression takes place before 'the deluge has already begun'. It takes place before any such distortion of our sense of proportion on human suffering and misery really starts to kick in.[49]

This connects to the actor-related aspect of the crime of aggression. Only the top political and military leaders have the power to initiate inter-state wars, and they are therefore the only immediate addressees of the Court's activation of the crime of aggression. As argued above, political and military leaders typically act under less immediate pressure from the surroundings than do foot soldiers, who are under orders and at gunpoint.[50] In general, this fact makes it

[48] Akhavan, 'Beyond Impunity', 10.

[49] Conversely, this implies that unlike with the other three crimes any deterrent effect of the crime of aggression is also fleeting and fragile; a one-off and all-or-nothing effect. Ultimately, this connects discussion of the crime of aggression with discussion about the peace versus justice dilemma; cf. Holtermann, '"A Slice of Cheese" – A Deterrence-Based Argument for the ICC', 307–311.

[50] For extended discussion, cf. Holtermann, '"A Slice of Cheese" –A Deterrence-Based Argument for the ICC', 306–307.

more likely that top-level leaders are capable of taking the threat of punishment into account in their deliberations before possible perpetration. Other things being equal, we would expect any such mechanisms to be even more outspoken when *ab initio* such political and military leaders stand at the fork in the road and are deliberating whether to take their country to war or not. At least, this contention is supported by the records of Rasmussen's and Blair's questions to their legal advisors about the prospects of personal prosecution in The Hague.

Linked to this, finally, is another actor-related aspect, which makes the prospects of a deterrent effect particularly likely in relation to the crime of aggression. Jo and Simmons helpfully distinguish between what they call *prosecutorial deterrence* and *social deterrence*, which they define in the following way:

> *Prosecutorial deterrence* is a direct consequence of legal punishment: it holds when potential perpetrators reduce or avoid law-breaking for fear of being tried and officially punished. *Social deterrence* is a consequence of the broader social milieu in which actors operate: it occurs when potential perpetrators calculate the informal consequences of lawbreaking.[51]

As already observed, only top-level political and military leaders have the power to wage war and therefore to commit the crime of aggression. In general, we have good reason to expect that such leaders would feel greater vulnerability towards both kinds of possible consequences stemming from the ICC. Even if they may feel fairly confident that they will ultimately evade actual punishment and prosecutorial deterrence will therefore fail, it is not unlikely that social deterrence will still work as they may avoid lawbreaking for fear of the informal social costs of lawbreaking. Again, such considerations may appear speculative but they are consistent not only with the conspicuous behavior of Rasmussen and Blair prior to the Iraq War but also with Jo and Simmons, who on the basis of comprehensive empirical studies conclude that the ICC can have a deterrent effect primarily with governments and with those rebel groups that seek legitimacy.[52]

[51] Jo and Simmons, 'Can the International Criminal Court Deter Atrocity?', 444.

[52] Jo and Simmons, 'Can the International Criminal Court Deter Atrocity?', 468–470. To be sure, Jo and Simmons' study was carried out well before the activation of the crime of aggression but it is relevant to the degree that it shows the particular vulnerabilities of political and military leaders to deterrent threats of the ICC.

IV CONCLUSION

In this contribution, I have outlined the fundamental argument for the claim that the ICC could have a deterrent effect and hence that the institution can be (partly) justified on consequentialist grounds. Furthermore, I have discussed and further developed this argument in light of two separate but related incidents. First was the fact that both former Danish Prime Minister Anders Fogh Rasmussen and former British Prime Minister Tony Blair prior to leading their countries into the US-led Iraq War asked their legal advisors whether so doing could bring them personally before the ICC. Second was the fact that in December 2017 the Assembly of States Parties decided to activate the crime of aggression. I have argued that, viewed in combination, these two facts have the effects of:

First, lending further support to deterrence-based arguments for the ICC by providing evidence of the existence of that which critics of the Court notoriously deny or claim is so speculative as to reduce believe in it to wishful thinking, i.e., they provide evidence of the existence in the minds of key actors of the kind of instrumental rationality necessary for deterrence to work.

Second, pointing to lacunae in the previous argument by demonstrating the particular significance of the previous lack of activation of the crime of aggression even or particularly when, on a theoretical and empirical level, the possibility conditions for effective deterrence are perfectly satisfied, and the doubts of sceptics are thereby put to shame.

And third, adding nuance to our understanding by showing the significance for the theory of deterrence of distinguishing between the *ad bellum* and *in bello* crimes over which the ICC has jurisdiction. More specifically, the crime of aggression is categorically different from war crimes, crimes against humanity and genocide in virtue of logical, temporal and actor-related features.

10

An Argument for Retributivism in International Criminal Law

MORDECHAI KREMNITZER*

International criminal law norms and rulings, similarly to domestic criminal proceedings, are usually based on two main purposes or rationales of punishment – prevention and retribution.[1] In this contribution, an argument is laid down in favour of retribution as a rationale of punishment, opposing a claim that it should be dismissed or marginalized.[2] However, support of retribution should not be mistaken for rejection of deterrence. Deterrence is a valid purpose for punishment, but only when adjoined by retribution based on guilt. To put it simply, it is not an either/or situation.

Before the argument on the importance of the retributive rationale is laid out, it will be defined and its reciprocal relations with other central purposes will be described. At its core, retribution is based on the notion that those who acted wrongfully deserve a proportionate punishment. It contains a dominant element of condemnation, which has, deliberately or not, a deterrent effect.[3]

* I wish to thank Yael Sara Wiesel for her superb research assistance and contribution to the paper. The responsibility for any failures and misgivings is exclusively mine.

1 M.A. Drumbl, *Atrocity, Punishment, and International Law* (Cambridge: Cambridge University Press, 2007), 60–61; M.R. Damaska, 'What Is the Point of International Criminal Justice' (2008) 83 *Chicago-Kent Law Review* 329, 331; ICTY, Judgment of 15 July 1999 (AC), *Tadić*, IT-94-1-A, paras. 7–9. On the role of prevention and retribution as rationales of international punishment in the jurisprudence of main international and hybrid courts, see also the contribution by Sergey Vasiliev in Chapter 4.

2 M.A. Niggli, 'Security as a Goal of Criminal Justice', Asian Society's 4th Annual Conference, 20–22 August 2012, 1, 4–5, available at www.unifr.ch/ius/assets/files/chaires/CH_Straf_und_Rechtsphilo/files/PDFs/NiggliSeoulSecurity.pdf; K. Günther, 'The Criminal Law of "Guilt" as Subject of a Politics of Remembrance in Democracies' in E. Christodoulidis and S. Veitch (eds.), *Lethe's Law: Justice, Law and Ethics in Reconciliation* (Oxford: Hart, 2001), 3, 4–5.

3 Much of the effectiveness of the deterrent effect can be attributed to its influence on legal advisors and enforcement forces. Their internalization of the norm is translated into actions and helps shape the legal regime in a way that is better compatible with the norm, and thus ensures greater compliance with it ex-ante.

This effect is similar in nature to both deterrence and expressivism. The former is composed of individual and general prevention. Individual prevention is meant to discourage the doer him- or herself from recidivating. Retribution supports this goal by conveying a condemning message in regards to the criminals' deeds. General deterrence is aimed at the general public and is intended to decrease the crime rate by the threat of punishment.[4] A firm condemnation of an offence may increase the threat of punishment – in terms of severity and of certainty – and thus strengthen the deterrent effect. Retribution is also deterrent-like in that it reflects the emotional rejection of the crime by the society, sublimating it into a reasoned and calculated punishment. Channeling societal frustration and anger to a legal response, rather than a violent and revengeful one, is effective in both preventing crimes and reinforcing the rule of law and the public's commitment to it. This latter function of retribution also overlaps with expressivism.

Expressivism, also known as positive prevention, emphasizes the communicative function of the law. Its central claim is that the criminal law projects and reinforces norms, so that the general public internalizes them and voluntarily complies.[5] The imposition of a just punishment supports this psycho-social process by validating the violated norm.[6] One deduces the wrongfulness of the action from the punishment imposed for it. The offences dealt with by international criminal law are in general neither condemned nor punished on state involved in perpetration level, so that they are perceived as de facto permissible. International criminal law intervenes to fill this void, and by doing so it expresses the importance of the values it seeks to protect. As international offences are all *mala in se*, the re-established threat of punishment actually serves as a reminder and an affirmation of the moral disapproval.

The argument is that the retributivist rationale for punishment is important for three main reasons: Firstly, according to several theories of punishment, only a punishment based on retributivist grounds is morally justified and legitimate. It is thus especially important to adhere to retribution in a system that suffers from a legitimacy deficit, such as the international criminal law system. The second reason is an instrumental one: Strengthening the retributivist purpose will help reestablish the role that retribution plays in determining the specific penalty. This re-establishment is critical in view of the potential erosion of the proportionality principle in international criminal

4 J. Andenaes, 'The General Preventive Effects of Punishment' (1966) 114 *University of Pennsylvania Law Review* 949, 949.

5 Drumbl, *Atrocity, Punishment, and International Law*, 173–174.

6 Andenaes, 'The General Preventive Effects of Punishment', 963.

law. The third reason is the positive relation between retribution and proper prevention, as shown earlier in this introduction.

I THE THEORETICAL REASON: RETRIBUTION AS LEGITIMACY

The strong link between retribution and justice is deeply embedded in our civilization from time immemorial, to the extent that it is difficult to envisage our civilization without it.[7] If for a moment we do envisage it, we see that general deterrence by itself endows punishment with meaning in the sphere of necessity and utility, but at the same time creates distress in the area of justice, due to its instrumental character and the making use of the offender as a tool for societal purposes. It is of paramount importance to ground punishment on both justice and utility, and retribution is therefore considered a necessary condition for just punishment. This argument is made even more valid in the context of international criminal law, as it is still struggling for its legitimacy and acceptance and should therefore rely on firm moral foundations such as retribution.[8]

In Kantian terms, the only legitimate use of coercive state measures is based on guilt and desert. Using state power for any other purpose is a use of the convicted criminal as a mere means to an external end, and is therefore forbidden.[9] This perception requires strict adherence to the proportionality principle, according to which every punishment should reflect the culpability of the criminal it is imposed on. Therefore, relying solely or mainly on

7 See for example: Aristotle, *The Nicomachean Ethics* (L. Brown (ed.), *Aristotle – The Nicomachean Ethics* (translation D. Ross) (Oxford: Oxford University Press, 2009), 1132b; *Genesis* 3:14–24; *Epistle to the Colossians* 3:23–25.

8 There are various explanations for the legitimacy deficit that the international criminal law faces, among which one prominent explanation is its dependency on the member states' cooperation; see H.-P. Kaul, 'The International Criminal Court: Current Challenges and Perspectives', Keynote Speech delivered at Salzburg Law School on International Criminal Law on 8 August 2011:

> It has become more known in the last years that the ICC is absolutely, one hundred percent, dependent on effective cooperation with States Parties in preparing criminal cases, in particular when it comes to the key issue of arrest and surrender of the accused; this lack of any form of executive power is another weakness of the Court, its Achilles' heel, so to speak. The matter is simple: no arrests, no trials.

On the ICC Prosecution's dependency on state cooperation, see also the contribution by Alex Whiting in Chapter 16. In addition, due to the alleged anti-African bias of the ICC, this challenge is not merely procedural, but also political; see *Is Africa on Trial?* BBC News, 27 March 2012, www.bbc.com/news/world-africa-17513065. That is, African states that do not trust the Court might stop cooperating with it and thus effectively tie its hands.

9 I. Kant, *Gesammelte Schriften*, Vol. VI (Berlin: De Gruyter, 1973), 331.

deterrence or expressivism is problematic and causes serious infringement of human dignity.[10]

The connection between retribution and legitimacy can also be explained from a social contract point of view. The social contract is based on the state's commitment to prevent crimes, but because prevention is not always possible a derivative duty to punish arises. A crime is an attack on the norm protected by the criminal prohibition. The state ought to respond to such attacks in order to restore the factual validity of the norm and ensure that it is binding.[11] The punishment serves as a reason for law abiding citizens to continue to obey the rules. It assures them that freedom will be taken away from whoever takes for him- or herself more freedom than the equal share of freedom that is endowed to all citizens.[12] This reason is crucial in order to keep the social contract intact. The same is applicable to the international level, where the international system is charged with the responsibility to prevent international crimes or at least to punish their perpetrators.[13]

A similar obligation to punish can be derived from the rights of the victims. It has been suggested that in international criminal law, under certain conditions, showing mercy to an offender is a violation of the victims' human rights.[14] Adil Ahmad Haque based this argument on the relational theory. He described a triangular relationship between the wrongdoer, the victim and the punisher, in which a violation of a victim's right by the wrongdoer imposes a duty to punish him or her on the punisher.[15] Unlike the obligation to punish presented by Kant and the social contract theorists, here it is an obligation

[10] However, see the contribution by Andreas Werkmeister in Chapter 14, who also places human dignity at the core of his meso-preventive theory of international punishment.

[11] Andenaes, 'The General Preventive Effects of Punishment', 963; K. Günther, 'Criminal Law, Crime and Punishment as Communication', Normative Orders: Cluster of Excellence at Goethe University Frankfurt/Main Working Paper (February 2014), 2, 8–9, available online at http://publikationen.ub.uni-frankfurt.de/files/34663/Guenther_Criminal_Law_Crime_and_Punishment.pdf.

[12] C.W. Morris, 'Punishment and the Loss of Moral Standing' (1991) 21 *Canada Journal of Philosophy* 53.

[13] Indeed, Thomas Hobbes' political theory was adapted to the international level by many scholars and theorists, mainly based on a side note from his formative book *Leviathan*: 'Concerning the offices of one sovereign to another, which are comprehended in that law, which is commonly called the *Law of Nations*, I need not say anything in this place; because the Law of Nations, and the Law of Nature, is the same thing' (R. Tuck (ed.), *Hobbes, Leviathan – Revised Student Edition* (Cambridge: Cambridge University Press, 1992), 244 et seq.).

[14] On the victims' right to punishment for international crimes, see the contribution by Jens David Ohlin in Chapter 15.

[15] A.A. Haque, 'Group Violence and Group Vengeance: Toward a Retributivist Theory of International Criminal Law' (2005) 9 *Buffalo Criminal Law Review* 273, 278.

owed to the victims, rather than to an impersonal goal.[16] It is different from the traditional retributive justice as it focuses on the victim's harm rather than the offender's guilt.[17]

In most cases dealt by international criminal law, punishment can be justified on both deterrent and retributivist grounds. However, there may be cases where retribution appears to be the sole or main justification to punishment, whereas deterrence is less relevant. These cases further clarify how important and necessary the retributivist justification is, both in domestic and in international criminal law. In such circumstances, criminals who are undoubtedly blameworthy will not be punished. This result is unreasonable because one cannot tolerate avoidance of punishment of the horrific crimes international criminal law deals with.[18]

For example, if we assume a state of affairs in which penology is exclusively deterrence-centered, we will find it difficult to justify punishment of hate crimes, because those are typically committed out of irrational motives and thus are unlikely to be deterred.[19] Similarly, assume a situation of systematic and organized extermination of a certain population, in which the perpetrators are sympathetic to other populations and therefore no other population is under risk. According to a strict deterrence approach,[20] there is no justification to punish in such case. Moreover, if we exempt the criminals who committed the severest crimes ever recognized, the legitimacy of punishments imposed on 'regular' crimes is put to question. This questioning might jeopardize public confidence in both international and domestic criminal law.

These results are unacceptable as they harshly conflict with the retributive intuition, and with the Kantian imperative to punish guilty criminals, according to which those who avoid punishing become implicated in the

16 Haque, 'Toward a Retributivist Theory of International Criminal Law', 279, 288.

17 Haque, 'Toward a Retributivist Theory of International Criminal Law', 280. It should be noted that Haque's article is confined to international criminal law only. This is important because his use of the relational theory as a justification to punishment is only applicable to crimes that are aimed at individuals; otherwise there are no victims whose suffering establishes a duty to punish. In international criminal law context there appears to be no problem, as the international crimes specified in the ICC's Rome Statute involve victims.

18 ICC Statute, Art. 5: The crime of genocide, crimes against humanity, war crimes and the crime of aggression.

19 In general, deterrence is largely ineffective in regard to crimes committed without any rational thinking process. In cases of crime committed without rational consideration, it cannot be expected that there will be effective deterrence at the time of the act.

20 According to a more expansive approach of deterrence, which emphasizes general prevention, there can be a justification for punishment in this case, in order to prevent the annihilation of other populations by other perpetrators.

crime.[21] Pardoning or imposing disproportional light sentences – especially in a systematic manner – is a violation of this imperative.

II THE INSTRUMENTAL REASON: SUPPORTING THE PROPORTIONALITY PRINCIPLE

In the theory of punishment, the two issues of justifications to punishment in general and of determining the specific punishment for a concrete crime are separate issues.[22] Nonetheless, the distinction between the two is analytical and useful mainly for a philosophical discourse; it is much less salient in the reality of criminal law and international criminal law as practices.[23] It is widely accepted that the determination of a specific punishment should be guided by retributive justice, implemented via the proportionality principle.[24] This is, inter alia, dictated by constitutional law requiring proportionality when infringing upon human rights. Nonetheless, international criminal courts might be tempted to deviate from this principle, due to the various challenges they face. This temptation is most prominent in two complementary and contradicting troubling tendencies – over-punishing the 'small fish' and giving up on punishing 'the big fish' properly and deservedly.[25] For this reason, we think that it is useful to emphasize retribution as a justification to punishment, in order to ensure the commitment to it and its application in determining the specific punishment.

The first worrying tendency is to impose liability on 'victimizers-victims', whom we referred to as 'small fish'. Victimizers-victims are people who suffered from the domination or coercion of powerful others. There are two types of coercion – a type that prevents any practical ability to make free moral choices, and a type that significantly reduces this ability. In the extreme

[21] Kant, *Gesammelte Schriften*, Vol. VI, 331; N.T. Potter Jr., 'The Principle of Punishment Is a Categorical Imperative' in J. Kneller and S. Axinn (eds.), *Autonomy and Community: Readings in Contemporary Kantian Social Philosophy* (Albany: State University of New York Press, 1998), 169.

[22] H.L.A. Hart, *Punishment and Responsibility Essays in the Philosophy of Law* (Oxford: Clarendon Press, 1978).

[23] M.S. Moore, 'Justifying Retributivism' (1993) 27 *Israel Law Review* 15, 17. On theories of punishment and the ICC's sentencing decisions, see the contribution by Gerhard Werle and Aziz Epik in Chapter 18.

[24] Drumbl, *Atrocity, Punishment, and International Law*, 63.

[25] The trends are complementary in the sense that the danger of over-punishing the 'small fish' may evolve as an attempt to compensate for the under-punishing of the 'big fish' and the loss of hope in regard to bringing them to justice. On the other hand, the trends are also contradicting in that one of them leads to excessive punishments and the other leads to lenient punishments.

circumstances of the first type, the 'small fish' are not blameworthy and are not criminally accountable, even though they have committed international crimes. The second type does not justify full exemption, but rather a significant mitigation of punishment.[26]

According to the principle of proportionality, there should be an exemption from criminal liability, when acting under circumstances of duress.[27] While it is tempting to exclude severe crimes from this rule and ignore the duress under which they may have been performed, it is important to adhere steadfastly to the proportionality principle. The punishment imposed on crimes large or small should be commensurate with the culpability of the actor, not discounting duress. The outcome of the deed should be considered in the examination of culpability, because the greater the atrocity the greater resistance is expected.[28] Still, at the end of the day what can be demanded must suit normal human beings in extreme exceptional circumstances and not heroes or saints.[29] In other words, where guilt cannot be established, punishment does not serve justice and should be avoided even if the defendant caused a great evil.

The enforcement and punishment challenges of the international criminal system might worsen this tendency, if international courts would impose disproportionate punishments as compensation or a substitute for the systemic deficiencies. For this reason too, deterrence should be limited by retribution based on guilt.

The 'Kapos' are a paradigmatic case of victims who victimized others. Kapos were Jewish prisoners in Nazi concentration camps who were ordered to supervise and manage other prisoners. In doing so, they enabled serious crimes, or even committed some themselves. Several Kapos were brought to

[26] In order to distinguish between the two types, two indications can be useful: (i) Do the perpetrator's actions reflect his or her personality? (ii) Is he or she dangerous? If the answers are clearly negative, it is most probably the first type, and the doer should be exempted from responsibility. When the negative answers are less explicit, it is the second type, which may justify a significant relief of punishment. M. Gur-Ariye, 'Conflict of Laws in Criminal Law: Duress under International Criminal Law as a Test Case' in C. Wasserstein Fassberg, B. Medina and J. Weisman (eds.), *Essays on Law in Honor of Avigdor Levontin* (2013), 477, 484 (in Hebrew).

[27] Gur-Ariye, 'Duress under International Criminal Law as a Test Case', 477, 484; R. Ehrenreich Brooks, 'Law in the Heart of Darkness: Atrocity & Duress' (2003) 43 *Virginia Journal of International Law* 861.

[28] On the idea of civic courage in international criminal law, see the contribution by Klaus Günther in Chapter 13.

[29] Here the difference between deterrence and retribution is clearly manifested, because in a deterrence-based theory the more severe the urge or temptation are, the more severe is the punishment required.

trial in Israel years later under Nazis and Nazi Collaborators (Punishment) Law.[30] At the time of the trials, the knowledge of the Holocaust in Israel was rather limited, and so was the understanding of the survivors' experiences. Accordingly, the Israeli court in the Kapo trials used very strict rhetoric to describe and denounce their actions during the war, but imposed very light penalties.[31] This duality reflects the alienating and condescending attitude toward Holocaust survivors in Israel of those days, alongside the compassion toward the victims of the Kapos.[32]

Punishing these Jews, who acted under duress, is a blatant disregard of the unique circumstances that were forced on them. Kapos and Judenrats were indeed part of the Nazi annihilation system, which systematically exploited local community members to facilitate its terrible deeds; but should their forced contribution to the system be criminalized? We think that if we take the historical context into account, the answer must be negative. Criminal law should not demand courageous resistance, but rather reasonable behaviour in the circumstances. Judge Landau articulated this idea in the case of Hirsch Berenblat:

> It is a bitter truth that in the extraordinary atmosphere of pressure of those days, morality was different. But it would be arrogance and sanctimoniousness on our part [...] to make this truth a ground for criticizing those 'little people' who did not rise to a supreme level of morality, while they were subject to rampant persecution by a government whose first purpose was to dehumanize them. We must not interpret the law [...] according to a measure of moral behavior that only few were capable of.[33]

By ignoring the circumstances, one can easily attribute the Holocaust to Jews who actively participated in its facilitation, and thus portray the victims as perpetrators. Indeed, Holocaust deniers often express such positions.[34] This is a distortion of the truth and an additional injustice to the victims. Therefore, although the Israeli legislature chose to exclude Nazis and Nazi collaborators from the protection of the duress defence, we think that it should have been applied to the victims of the Nazis.[35] Jews during the Holocaust, including

30 Nazis and Nazi Collaborators (Punishment) Law, 5710–1950, 4 LSI 154 (Isr.).

31 M.A. Drumbl, 'Victims Who Victimise' (2016) 4 *London Review of International Law* 217, 232–234.

32 I. Levin, *Kapo on Allenby Street* (Jerusalem: Yad Ben Tzvi & Moreshet Publications, 2015).

33 CrimaA 77/64, Hirsch Berenblat v. Attorney General 18(2) PD 70, 101 [1964] (Isr.).

34 Hirsch Berenblat v. Attorney General, 95; see also Drumbl, 'Victims Who Victimise', at 230–231.

35 Nazis and Nazi Collaborators (Punishment) Law §8. Alongside the aforementioned exception, the law does grant several defenses and acknowledges several extenuating circumstances.

Kapos and Judenrats, acted under a general-duress defence. The intensity of the threat, its immediacy and its near to certain feasibility were equal to the usual conditions of duress. As in concrete duress, the Jews' ability to make moral decisions was robbed from them. Therefore, Kapos who did not 'make love to their employment'[36] should not bear criminal responsibility. Criminal responsibility in these cases should only be imposed on those who did more than required out of lust for power and control or out of cruelty and sadism as such.

A contemporary case of victimizers-victims is the case of child soldiers, who are children 'associated with armed forces or armed groups'.[37] The question of their justiciability under international criminal law has arisen in recent years following the cases of Omar Khadr and Dominic Ongwen, and is very much debated. Khadr's case[38] is an exception to the trend of international courts to refrain from prosecuting children.[39] The UN Special Representative for Children in Armed Conflict expressed her opposition to the trial, stating that: 'Since World War Two, no child has been prosecuted for a war crime. Child soldiers must be treated primarily as victims and alternative procedures should be in place aimed at rehabilitation or restorative justice.'[40] The dilemma gets even more complex in the case of Ongwen, a senior commander who is currently being tried in the International Criminal Court (ICC) for the same crimes committed against him as a child soldier.[41] The Court will have to

According to Art. 10, a persecuted person who committed an offence specified in the law will be released from criminal responsibility if – (a) acted in order to save himself from an immediate death, while doing his best to avert the consequences of the act; or (b) if acted with intent to avert consequences more serious than those which resulted from the act, and actually averted them. In addition, according to Art. 11, the court can mitigate the punishment of a persecuted person who (a) committed the offense under circumstances that would exempt him from responsibility if it were not for Art. 8, while doing his best to avert the consequences of the act; or (b) if he acted with intent to avert severest consequences, and there was indeed a chance to avert them. However, these provisions only apply to some of the offenses.

36 William Shakespeare, *Hamlet*, Act 5 Scene 2.

37 M.A. Drumbl, *Reimagining Child Soldiers in International Law and Policy* (Oxford: Oxford University Press, 2012), 4.

38 Omar Khadr, who was 15 years old when arrested, was convicted of war crimes by a US Military Commission through a plea bargain, the legality of which was later questioned. He was sentenced to 40 years of imprisonment, and 2 years later, due to Canadian diplomatic efforts, he was repatriated in Canada. See Drumbl, Reimagining Child Soldiers, 21, 147, 212.

39 Drumbl, Reimagining Child Soldiers, 21–22.

40 Canadian Guantanamo inmate's trial bad precedent-UN, Reuters, 10 August 2010, www.reuters.com/article/idUSN09274807.

41 M. Kersten, 'The Dominic Ongwen Trial and Prosecution of Child Soldiers – A JiC Symposium', Justice in Conflict, 11 April 2016), https://justiceinconflict.org/2016/04/11/the-dominic-ongwen-trial-and-the-prosecution-of-child-soldiers-a-jic-symposium.

decide what influence his background as a child soldier has on his responsibility and punishment, if any. These cases induce mixed intuitions, and thus illustrate how probable is the tendency presented here to over-punish the 'small fish'.

The problem is that protecting the innocence of such perpetrators may come at the expense of their victims. The victims expect the court to stand by them and to enforce their right that justice will be fully served, and with a firm hand. This understandable demand must be borne in mind when constructing the penology operated by international criminal courts. Thus, the chosen judicial policy must match the interests of the victims to the maximum extent possible. However, it is a criterion that enters into action only when deciding between reasonable alternatives, and in our case, the alternative of punishing those who are not culpable is unreasonable. The principle we shall present below is intended to respect the victims' demand for justice, without violating the conflicting demand for justice on the part of the 'victimizers-victims'.

International criminal justice should consider the interests of the victims without violating the defendants' rights, by implementing restorative remedies such as compensation for the damage and suffering (based on wrong-doing and not necessarily on proven guilt), truth discovery, apology, reconciliation or preventing recurrence.[42] This toolkit should apply also in situations where guilt is reduced or does not exist, in addition to the doctrine we later suggest.

The second problematic tendency concerns the 'big fish', those who conducted the international crimes as puppeteers, and usually those who coerced the 'small fish' to act on their behalf. When it comes to them, the international criminal system can be rather limited, due to two structural constrains: First, no punishment can fully match the severity of the acts, and second, international criminal law depends on collaboration of the states concerned, and cannot gain jurisdiction or execute its judgment without it.[43] Therefore, some think that international criminal law should give up retributive justice altogether as it is unachievable, even in cases where it is most needed.[44] The logic of this conclusion is not only questionable, but

[42] See UN General Assembly Resolution 60/147, UN GAOR, 60th Session, Supp. No. 49, UN Doc. A/60/509/Add.1, 24 March 2006.

[43] See the text and references in fn. 8; H. Arendt, *Eichmann in Jerusalem: A Report on the Banality of Evil* (New York: Viking Press, 1963), 250

[44] Arendt, Eichmann in Jerusalem, 250: 'the most common argument was that Eichmann's deeds defied the possibility of human punishment, and that it was pointless to impose the death sentence for crimes of such magnitude – which, of course, was true, in a sense, except that it could not conceivably mean that he who had murdered millions should for this very reason escape punishment'.

fundamentally flawed. If a life-sentence is not commensurate to the severity of a crime, does it make any sense to impose lighter punishments, such as 10 years in prison, or to refrain from punishment altogether? By all accounts, partial justice is preferable to complete injustice. Accordingly, if retribution cannot be achieved to the full extent, it should at least be approached to do so as much as possible.[45]

The limited range of punishments is not a unique problem of international law. Domestic criminal law is also limited in its ability to match the severity of murder, especially in cases of mass murders and repeated or serial murders. In both cases, the fact that it is always possible to imagine worse crimes does not imply that the heaviest penalties should be kept in reserve for them. Otherwise there will be no limit, and this approach will always lead to mitigation in favour of the worst criminals. The necessary result of such approach is a devaluation of human life. Moreover, stressing the severity of the crimes on one hand and casting a punishment that shows the opposite on the other hand, turns the rhetoric into a mockery and calls for cynicism and lack of credibility towards it. The public expects to see a correlation between words and actions, especially as the former are easy to produce while the latter are considered more reliable. Therefore, it is important to try to obtain the just result within the boundaries of the usual punishments.

The second objection to the retributive approach in international criminal law is that it was doomed to be theoretical and is not practically possible. The ICC does not try individuals unless they are present in the courtroom.[46]

[45] An approach that gives up on punishing the 'big fish' may spread from academia to courts, and express itself in the imposition of too lenient penalties. One may fear that such influence has already taken place, in cases such as Naser Orić's, a commander in the Srebrenica enclave during the Bosnian war. Orić was found guilty of 'failure to discharge his duty as a superior to take necessary and reasonable measures to prevent the occurrence of murder' and of cruel treatment. He was sentenced to 2 years including his period of custody, and was released immediately after the judgment. Even after taking the mitigating circumstances into account, the punishment seems exceptionally light, and may perhaps be understood in the light of intellectual atmosphere described above. See ICTY, Judgment of 30 June 2006 (TC), *Orić*, IT-03-68-T. The ICTY provides some further examples, such as the cases of Enver Hadžihasanović case and Rasim Delić. Both were senior commanders of the army of Bosnia and Herzegovina. Both were found guilty of failure to prevent or punish cruel treatment, and were sentenced to 3.5 and 3 years (respectively). See ICTY, Judgment of 22 April 2008 (AC), *Hadžihasanović and Kubura*, IT-01-47-A and ICTY, Judgment of 15 September 2008 (TC), *Delić*, IT-04-83-T. Similarly, Tihomir Blaškić, a commander of the Croatian Defence Council, was charged with inhumane treatment and cruel treatment and was only sentenced to 9 years imprisonment. ICTY, Judgment of 3 March 2000 (TC), *Blaškić*, IT-95-14-T.

[46] ICC Statute, Art. 63.

This rule allows defendants to gain de facto immunity, as in the notorious case of Omar Al Bashir.[47] There are pending charges against Al-Bashir, the former president of Sudan, for alleged crimes against humanity, war crimes and genocide. The first warrant for his arrest was issued in 2009, but Al Bashir never attended The Hague and his proceedings remained at the pre-trial stage ever since. Al Bashir's case is not unique; there are currently no less than eight defendants who refrain from appearing in front of the ICC, ignoring a summons or an arrest warrant.[48] As the 'big fish' are usually heads of states, high-ranked generals or senior government officials, they can easily evade international criminal law, as is evident from the cases described. This option is clearly problematic from the perspective of retributive justice, as it allows the biggest criminals to easily and systematically get away with punishment.

However, this inadequacy is by no means a reason to abandon the principle of retribution. The strong assumption that partial justice is preferable to injustice applies here too. Thus, practical challenges should not hinder justice being done whenever it can be done.[49] The same logic applies with regard to the problem of selectivity in international criminal law.[50] The fact that leaders from powerful states enjoy a de facto immunity is indeed bad and wrong, but even that does not justify a total concession of justice. Justice should be pursued in the given reality of power relations.

III THE PRINCIPLE OF CONSERVATION OF CRIMINAL ENERGY

Thus far we have argued that punishments in the international criminal law should have a retributivist justification. The intrinsic reason for this claim is that retribution is strongly connected to legitimacy, both essentially and in the eyes of the general public. The instrumental reason is that the principle of proportionality in international criminal law faces two major threats – over-punishing the 'small fish' and despair from the ability to punish the big ones. In order to resist those tendencies, it is useful to re-establish retribution as a

47 ICC, Warrant of Arrest of 4 March 2009 (PTC), *Al Bashir*, ICC-02/05-01/09.

48 Based on a review of the ICC's defendants' database, available at www.icc-cpi.int/Pages/cases.aspx.

49 Having said that, the procedural obstacle is indeed a problem and it should be taken care of. At the end of this contribution, we propose a possible solution that does not involve a deviation from retributive justice.

50 Drumbl, *Atrocity, Punishment, and International Law*, 151. On selectivity in international criminal law, see also the contribution by Harmen van der Wilt in Chapter 17.

strong justification to punishment. We shall now take one step further and clarify how exactly retributive justice should be implemented.

Our suggestion is to embrace what we call the principle of conservation of criminal energy – the responsibility that was reduced from the 'small fish' should not be lost, but attributed to the 'big fish'. It is a theoretical move, justified in terms of retributive justice. The subordinates' reduced guilt, either actual or hypothetical, serves as an aggravating circumstance to the deeds of the 'big fish'.

The idea is based on three assumptions. First, the 'small fish' are in the extreme cases mere screws and in the less extreme cases close to screws in the mechanism of evil and should not be held responsible for the full scope of atrocities. Second, those who established these mechanisms and administered them are responsible for both what they have done themselves and what they have done using others. The lesser the guilt of the direct perpetrators is, the greater the guilt of those who created the conditions for its formation. And last, victims deserve full legal relief for their suffering so long as it is not violating the obligation to do justice to the perpetrator.

Focusing on the 'big fish' in court requires a similar focus in enforcement and persecution – no effort should be saved in the attempt to convict them, including the willingness to make concessions to obtain implicating evidence against them.

The suggested principle is also justified from the point of view of deterrence and prevention, which are effectively the same in the absence of an international police force. The aggravated condemnation is in fact part of the response as well as of the prevention and deterrence efforts. If high-ranking officials know that they are exposed to severe international criminal liability not just for their own deeds but also for those of their subordinates, it provides them with an additional reason not to act. This argument assumes the rationality of the perpetrators but this seems to be true when it comes to those who reached the top of the pyramid.[51]

Deterrence and prevention are more complex with regards to the 'small fish'. Legal deterrence seems to be insignificant in light of the threat they are under, even in cases of mere mitigation and not of full exemption. Although the inability to deter in such situations is the price to be paid for a just punishment system, efforts should be made to promote at least some preventive effect. First, the full excuse shall apply in appropriate cases; not every

[51] J.v.H. Holtermann, 'A "Slice of Cheese" – a Deterrence-Based Argument for the International Criminal Court' (2010) 11 *Human Rights Review* 289. Specifically regarding the crime of aggression, see also the contribution by Jakob v.H. Holtermann in Chapter 9.

soldier who acted under orders automatically deserves an exemption or mitigation. Our suggestion applies only to people who went through brainwashing or acted under extreme circumstances that are close to duress, either particular or general duress. The second course of action is to spread messages that promote awareness of both the severity and consequences of crimes against humanity, genocide, war crimes and the crime of aggression. These messages should be spread in real time and through all the media types, old and new. The idea is to supply counterweight to the local propaganda, which provides racist and 'patriotic' messages, demonizing the victims in order to justify the criminal acts committed against them.

One may argue that our suggestion worsens the problems the system faces due to its dependency on the participating states. Indeed, the principle will reduce international crime trials to defendants from the senior and middle echelons only, and those – especially the senior ones, are very hard to prosecute. It can therefore be argued that our proposal may lead to a problematic and unfortunate situation of no international criminal enforcement of international crimes. In our opinion, this difficulty does not legitimize a deviation from the principle of proportionality or turning against 'small fish', but it does require examining ways of coping with the problem.

Due process is always important, and even more so in a legal system that still lacks legitimacy. However, it is unreasonable to entrust the defendant with the power to decide whether to prosecute him or her, or not. The defendant is given an invaluable opportunity to thwart the legal process, and the system thus suffers from helplessness and weakness. Ways have to be considered in order to give the defendant his or her day in court without being present, such as full virtual participation via video or participation through a legal representative, etc. However, in case of total refusal to participate, the proceedings should be allowed without his or her participation. We are aware that this sort of conviction and punishment is far from guaranteeing their execution; and yet, a verdict is more significant than a summons because there is a profound difference between an accused, which enjoys the presumption of innocence, and a person, refusing to participate, found guilty. The latter situation is a significant step towards the execution of justice, as the chances of cooperation of states for this purpose will increase.

IV CONCLUSION

We have shown that giving up on retribution is intrinsically and consequentially wrong. The consequential reason is that the retributivist justification may be useful in making the proportionality principle more resistant to the threats it faces in the international context. In view of the two major threats – over-punishing the 'small fish' and despair from punishing the 'big fish' – we suggested a retributive principle that attributes the reduced culpability of the former, which was caused by the latter, to the latter.

11

An Expressive Theory of International Punishment for International Crimes

DANIELA DEMKO

In respect of its criminal law-based justification, international criminal law – similar to national criminal law – has to answer to the question as to its purpose of punishment.[1] In the current academic debate on the purpose of punishment, expressive theories of punishment are becoming increasingly important for both national criminal law and international criminal law.[2]

1 See, e.g., G. Werle and F. Jeßberger, *Principles of International Criminal Law*, 3rd ed. (Oxford: Oxford University Press, 2014), 36–39; K. Ambos, *Treatise on International Criminal Law* Vol. I (Oxford: Oxford University Press, 2013), 67–73; A. Epik, *Die Strafzumessung bei Taten nach dem Völkerstrafgesetzbuch* (Tübingen: Mohr Siebeck, 2017), 78–165; K.F. Gärditz, *Weltrechtspflege* (Berlin: Duncker & Humblot, 2006), 316–349; K. Günther and V. Reuss, 'Legitimation des Völkerstrafrechts in Deutschland – Völkerstrafrecht als Bürgerstrafrecht' in C. Safferling and S. Kirsch (eds.), *Völkerstrafrechtspolitik. Praxis des Völkerstrafrechts* (Berlin/ Heidelberg: Springer, 2014), 127, 145; J.C. Nemitz, *Strafzumessung im Völkerstrafrecht* (Freiburg: edition iuscrim, 2002), 9–63, 146–175; F. Melloh, *Einheitliche Strafzumessung in den Rechtsquellen des ICC-Statuts* (Berlin: Duncker & Humblot, 2010), 92–157; C. Möller, *Völkerstrafrecht und Internationaler Strafgerichtshof – kriminologische, straftheoretische und rechtspolitische Aspekte* (Münster: LIT, 2003), 423–612; A. Werkmeister, *Straftheorien im Völkerstrafrecht* (Baden-Baden: Nomos, 2015), 118–381.

2 See, e.g., D.M. Amann, 'Group Mentality, Expressivism, and Genocide' (2002) 2 *International Criminal Law Review* 93, 123; R. Cryer et al., *An Introduction to International Criminal Law and Procedure* (Cambridge: Cambridge University Press, 2014), 36–37; A.M. Danner, 'Constructing a Hierarchy of Crimes in International Criminal Law Sentencing' (2001) 87 *Virginia Law Review* 415, 490–491; M.M. DeGuzman, 'Harsh Justice for International Crimes?' (2014) 39 *Yale Journal of International Law* 1, 33; M.A. Drumbl, *Atrocity, Punishment, and International Law* (Cambridge: Cambridge University Press, 2007), 61, 173–175; K.J. Fisher, *Moral Accountability and International Criminal Law* (London, New York: Routledge, 2012), 49–56; J.D. Ohlin, 'Towards a Unique Theory of International Criminal Sentencing' (2009) *Cornell Law Faculty Publications* 373, 387; W.A. Schabas, 'Sentencing by International Tribunals: A Human Rights Approach' (1997) 7 *Duke Journal of Comparative & International Law* 461, 502; D. Demko, 'Hegels Straftheorie im Lichte gegenwärtiger expressiver Straftheorien' in M. Kubiciel, M. Pawlik and K. Seelmann (eds.), *Hegels Erben? Strafrechtliche Hegelianer vom 19. bis zum 21. Jahrhundert* (Tübingen: Mohr Siebeck, 2017), 277; Epik, *Strafzumessung*, 46–50, 73–74, 149–152; T. Hörnle, *Straftheorien* (Tübingen: Mohr

The aim of this chapter is to develop the basic features of an expressive theory of international punishment for international crimes within which the symbolic and communicative factor and various communicative content and relationship aspects of the international punishing act are of crucial significance. The range of communicative aspects of international punishment is discussed below in greater depth. The chapter also examines whether and how the absolute and relative theories of punishment – retributive and preventive theories – and whether and how the specific purposes of international criminal law can be classified in an expressive theory of international punishment. Furthermore, the present chapter examines the communicative significance of two important functions of international punishment, namely to strengthen trust in norm validity (Section II) and to assign responsibility (Section III).

I COMMUNICATIVE CLASSIFICATION OF INTERNATIONAL PUNISHMENT IN THE STATEMENT OF CONTENT OF INTERNATIONAL LAW AND INTERNATIONAL CRIMINAL LAW

The law is an expression of a how a human community wishes to live. That means that the human community, through its law, expresses an *affirmative* statement of content and clarifies the values it wishes to protect on behalf of its members and their interpersonal coexistence. Law, particularly criminal law, also expresses what the human community does *not* want, namely, the commission of crimes.[3] However, law is not limited to this *negative* statement of content (committing offences as being 'what one does *not* want'). Rather, the negative statement of content forms part of the primary and supreme affirmative statement of content of the law (the protection of values and legal interests for interpersonal coexistence as 'what one *wants*').[4] The normative reference point for these affirmative and negative statements of content in the law is in the context of international criminal law and international punishment, the *universal* level with a connection to 'the international community as

Siebeck, 2011), 29–43; Melloh, *Einheitliche Strafzumessung*, 110–120; Werkmeister, *Straftheorien im Völkerstrafrecht*, 272–347.

3 The consequence of the negating statement of content of criminal law is the statement of criminal law – in case of a contravention of the prohibition of committing a criminal act – that it will lead to prosecution and punishment of the perpetrated criminal act.

4 See, e.g., A. Cassese et al., *Cassese's International Criminal Law* (Oxford: University Press, 2013), 9; Cryer et al., *Introduction*, 8–10; W.A. Schabas, *An Introduction to the International Criminal Court* (Cambridge: University Press, 2011), 207; Werle and Jeßberger, *Principles*, 33–34; Melloh, *Einheitliche Strafzumessung*, 55–74, 81–92; D. Nitsche, *Der Internationale Strafgerichtshof ICC und der Frieden* (Baden-Baden: Nomos, 2007), 43–46, 69.

a whole'.[5] International criminal law thus forms part of the statement that the international community – in the form of its international legal order including universal human rights – addresses to all people internationally and enables the international community to convey to all people that they are protected by the international legal order in their peaceful coexistence with the concomitant preservation of human rights.[6]

International criminal law serves to preserve and enforce the legal interests of the international community and makes an important contribution to the protection of the international legal order.[7] The current international legal order – consider, for example, the UN Charter, the multitude of human rights treaties and the jurisdiction of international courts – is no longer just a symbol of inter-state law, but rather a symbol of a *universal* community of nations.[8] This universal community of nations is bound by a minimum level of universal basic values and universal human rights and can be characterized as a universal, objective system of values, as a human rights order and as an order of peace.[9] With the explicit emphasis on the protection of world peace and international security in the UN Charter, the international community communicates two of its key international legal interests.[10] International criminal law also explicitly declares world peace and security and, in addition, the well-being of the world as legal interests to be protected by international criminal law.[11] International criminal law thus participates in the protection of

[5] ICC Statute, Preamble paragraphs 4 and 9 and Art. 5 sentence 1; Werle and Jeßberger, *Principles*, 33–36; K. Gierhake, *Begründung des Völkerstrafrechts auf der Grundlage der Kantischen Rechtslehre* (Berlin: Duncker & Humblot, 2005), 168–287; Günther and Reuss, 'Legitimation des Völkerstrafrechts', 152; G. Manske, *Verbrechen gegen die Menschlichkeit als Verbrechen an der Menschheit* (Berlin: Duncker & Humblot, 2003), 333–338, 356–358; Melloh, *Einheitliche Strafzumessung*, 95, 130; Werkmeister, *Straftheorien im Völkerstrafrecht*, 277–279, 291, 360.

[6] See, e.g., M. Herdegen, *Völkerrecht* (München: C.H.Beck, 2015), 48–61; D. Kühne, *Materielle Konstitutionalisierung im Völkerrecht* (Zürich: Schulthess, 2014), 49–241; Melloh, *Einheitliche Strafzumessung*, 83–92; Möller, *Völkerstrafrecht und Internationaler Strafgerichtshof*, 416–417, 419–423.

[7] See, e.g., Werle and Jeßberger, *Principles*, 33–36; Melloh, *Einheitliche Strafzumessung*, 83–92; Möller, *Völkerstrafrecht und Internationaler Strafgerichtshof*, 416–417, 419–423.

[8] See, e.g., A. Emmerich-Fritsche, *Vom Völkerrecht zum Weltrecht* (Berlin: Duncker & Humblot, 2007), 110–111, 338–362; Herdegen, *Völkerrecht*, 48–61; F. Kastner, *Transitional Justice in der Weltgesellschaft* (Hamburg: Hamburger Edition, 2015), 123–125.

[9] See, e.g., Ambos, *Treatise* Vol. I, 60–67; Emmerich-Fritsche, *Vom Völkerrecht zum Weltrecht*, 110–111, 338–362, 1062, 1064–1065; Herdegen, *Völkerrecht*, 48–61.

[10] UN Charter, Preamble as well as Arts. 1, 2, 11, 12, 15, 18, 23, 24, 33, 34, 37, 39, 42, 43, 47, 48, 51, 52, 54, 73, 76, 84, 99, 106.

[11] ICC Statute, Preamble paragraph 3; see, e.g., Melloh, *Einheitliche Strafzumessung*, 86, 88–92.

international legal interests of the international community,[12] but the use of international criminal law is a last resort *(ultima ratio)* and is limited to grave violations of these basic values of the international community.[13] On the basis of the protection of specific (combined supra-individual – individual) legal interests,[14] international criminal law is employed to prosecute and punish the core crimes that the international community considers 'the most serious crimes of concern to the international community as a whole'[15] and 'the most serious crimes of international concern'[16] that 'deeply shock the conscience of humanity'.[17]

For the expressive theory of international punishment, it is important to determine which communicative content should be conveyed to which addressees by international law and international criminal law and by international punishment on a normative level. The function of strengthening trust in norm-validity communicated by international punishment is linked to the *affirmative* statement of content of international criminal law. The function of assigning responsibility – also communicated through international punishment – is connected to the negative statement of content of international criminal law. In the affirmation, confirmation and support of international law and international criminal law and its affirmative statement of content, international punishment expresses, first, the validity of international criminal law, including the legal interests protected by it, and, second – and this is decisive – the fact that all persons worldwide can *trust* in the validity and protective force of international criminal law.[18] Likewise, international punishment conveys in the affirmation, confirmation and support of international law and international criminal law and its *negative* statement of content that breaches of legal norms – i.e, violations of international law and international criminal law in the form of the perpetration of international crimes – will be prosecuted

[12] See, e.g., Werle and Jeßberger, *Principles*, 33–36.

[13] See, e.g., Werle and Jeßberger, *Principles*, 53; Melloh, Einheitliche Strafzumessung, 85, 89.

[14] See, e.g., Ambos, *Treatise* Vol. I, 66; Gierhake, *Begründung des Völkerstrafrechts*, 24–25, 252–263; Melloh, *Einheitliche Strafzumessung*, 89–92.

[15] ICC Statute, Preamble paragraphs 4 and 9 and Art. 5, see in addition ICC Statute, Art. 1 sentence 2; see, e.g., Werle and Jeßberger, *Principles*, 34.

[16] ICC Statute, Art. 1 sentence 2.

[17] ICC Statute, Preamble, paragraph 2; see, e.g., Werle and Jeßberger, *Principles*, 34; O. Höffe, *Gibt es ein interkulturelles Strafrecht?* (Frankfurt: Suhrkamp, 1999), 109–110; A. Goppel, 'Globales Strafrecht' in A. Niederberger and P. Schink (eds.), *Globalisierung. Ein interdisziplinäres Handbuch* (Stuttgart: J.B.Metzler, 2011), 291.

[18] See, e.g., Ambos, *Treatise* Vol. I, 71–73; Werle and Jeßberger, *Principles*, 34–35, 37–38; Günther and Reuss, 'Legitimation des Völkerstrafrechts', 149; Melloh, *Einheitliche Strafzumessung*, 89–90, 128; Möller, *Völkerstrafrecht und Internationaler Strafgerichtshof*, 509, 522–528.

and punished.[19] With this substantive communicative content, international punishment directs itself internationally at every human being, that is at all persons of the world community. That means that the global target group of international punishment includes not only the current and potential perpetrators of international crimes and the current and potential victims of international crimes, but any other person in the world community.[20]

It is not only a confirmation of norm validity that international punishment expresses with reference to a *norm* level.[21] The *norm*-oriented expressive theories of punishment are rightly criticized because of their excessive one-sided focus on reference to norms.[22] Rather, it is important and necessary for the expressive theory of international punishment to include – in addition to the norm reference level – the central and crucial *human-interpersonal* reference level.[23] At the heart of the expressive theory of international punishment lie the human being and the community of humanity in their existence as a global communication community and as a global community of trust.[24] International punishment is directed not only to the reference level of norms, but rather primarily to all persons of the community of humanity and expresses to all human beings worldwide that human beings as trusting beings and their trust in the norm validity as such are of decisive relevance for international punishment.[25]

II THE FUNCTION OF STRENGTHENING TRUST IN NORM VALIDITY COMMUNICATED BY INTERNATIONAL PUNISHMENT

What is apparent is, first, the close connection between the significance of international punishment in its function of confirming and strengthening trust

19 See, e.g., Höffe, *Gibt es ein interkulturelles Strafrecht?*, 109–110; Kastner, *Transitional Justice in der Weltgesellschaft*, 125–128.

20 See, e.g., Gierhake, *Begründung des Völkerstrafrechts*, 168–172, 208–209, 246; Günther and Reuss, 'Legitimation des Völkerstrafrechts', 152; Hörnle, *Straftheorien*, 29–41; Melloh, *Einheitliche Strafzumessung*, 95, 130.

21 See, e.g., W. Bottke, *Assoziationsprävention. Zur heutigen Diskussion der Strafzwecke* (Berlin: Duncker & Humblot, 1995), 61–69; Demko, 'Hegels Straftheorie', 286–287; Hörnle, *Straftheorien*, 30–32.

22 See, e.g., Demko, 'Hegels Straftheorie', 286; Hörnle, *Straftheorien*, 31–32.

23 See, e.g., Demko, 'Hegels Straftheorie', 286–290; Bottke, *Assoziationsprävention*, 61–69; Hörnle, *Straftheorien*, 32.

24 See further references in fn. 27; see, in addition, e.g., Demko, 'Hegels Straftheorie', 286–290; Emmerich-Fritsche, *Vom Völkerrecht zum Weltrecht*, 81; Günther and Reuss, 'Legitimation des Völkerstrafrechts', 149; Nitsche, *Der Internationale Strafgerichtshof*, 177; Werkmeister, *Straftheorien im Völkerstrafrecht*, 277–279.

25 See, e.g., Demko, 'Hegels Straftheorie', 286–290.

in norm validity on the one hand and the meta-communicative understanding of international law and international criminal law on the other hand.[26] Taking the global connection between all human beings as a normative basis, international law, international criminal law and international punishment demonstrate the importance of humanity operating as a global community of trust and concomitantly the importance of humanity as a global community of values, solidarity and responsibility.[27]

Second, the function of strengthening trust in norm validity can be assigned to the purposes of punishment of positive individual and general prevention and individual and general deterrence. For the inclusion of positive individual and general prevention and individual and general deterrence in the statement of contents of international punishment, however, the need for a communicative shift in emphasis and the need for a communicative prioritization on the one hand,[28] as well as the hierarchical relationship that exists between the purposes of punishment of positive individual and general prevention and individual and general deterrence on the other hand, are to be considered.[29] Positive general prevention, which is communicatively integrated by international punishment, is the central and most important aspect of the statement of content of international punishment. It is by referring to and expressing the purpose of positive general prevention that international punishment conveys to all people across the globe that they can trust in the validity of international law and international criminal law.[30] This purpose of

[26] See, e.g., D. Demko, 'Universalisierung, Relativierung, Pluralisierung und Interkulturalisierung bei den Menschenrechten, im Völkerstrafrecht und im Europäischen Strafrecht' in D. Demko, G. Brudermüller and K. Seelmann (eds.), *Menschenrechte. Begründung-Bedeutung-Durchsetzung* (Würzburg: Königshausen & Neumann, 2015), 71, 85–88; Günther and Reuss, 'Legitimation des Völkerstrafrechts', 152–153; W. Hassemer, 'Vielfalt und Wandel' in O. Höffe, *Gibt es ein interkulturelles Strafrecht?* (Frankfurt: Suhrkamp, 1999), 157, 159–160, 170, 178–179.

[27] See, e.g., V. Beck, *Eine Theorie der globalen Verantwortung* (Berlin: Suhrkamp, 2016), 76–82, 128–176, 185–238, 255–288; F. Dübgen, *Was ist gerecht? Kennzeichen einer transnationalen solidarischen Politik* (Frankfurt: Campus, 2014), 142–239, 240–254; Epik, *Strafzumessung*, 48, 151–152; Günther and Reuss, 'Legitimation des Völkerstrafrechts', 152; Melloh, *Einheitliche Strafzumessung*, 61; Möller, *Völkerstrafrecht und Internationaler Strafgerichtshof*, 420–423; Werkmeister, *Straftheorien im Völkerstrafrecht*, 321.

[28] See, e.g., Epik, *Strafzumessung*, 46, 50, 152.

[29] See, e.g., Nemitz, *Strafzumessung im Völkerstrafrecht*, 114–117, 160–175, 274–276.

[30] See, e.g., P. Akhavan, 'Beyond Impunity: Can International Criminal Justice Prevent Future Atrocities?' (2001) 95 *American Journal of International Law* 7, 30; J.C. Nemitz, 'Sentencing in the Jurisprudence of the International Criminal Tribunals for the Former Yugoslavia and Rwanda' in H. Fischer, C. Kreß and S. R. Lüder (eds.), *International and National Prosecution of Crimes under International Law* (Berlin: Berliner Wissenschafts-Verlag, 2004), 605, 613; R. Sloane, 'The Expressive Capacity of International Punishment: The Limits of the National

positive general prevention can in turn be used to classify and integrate certain sub-statements, each of which expresses specific individual aspects of trust in norm validity. These specific individual aspects include elements of re-socializing special prevention (rehabilitation) and of securing special prevention (protection of society) as well as elements of individual and general deterrence.[31]

1 *The Symbolic and Communicative Element as the Decisive Foundation of the Normative Justification of International Punishment*

For the expressive theory of international punishment, the symbolic and communicative element, including the communicative aspects of content and relationship, is the decisive foundation for the normative justification of international punishment.[32] The symbolic and communicative element (as one of its aspects) includes addressing all people globally. In doing so, each person as rational subject and as communicative contact person is recognized and taken seriously with respect to his or her human dignity.[33] For this very reason, the target audience includes all people to whom international punishment conveys that they can trust in the continuing validity of international law and international criminal law (i.e., that the law will be valid before, after and despite the commission of the international crime).[34] What is apparent here is the communicative inclusion of the elements of positive general prevention in international punishment.[35] At the same time, the present and future reference to the expression and communication of trust that international

Law Analogy and the Potential of International Criminal Law' (2007) 43 *Stanford Journal of International Law* 39, 75–77; Epik, *Strafzumessung*, 48, 50, 73, 144–149, 152; C. Kamardi, *Die Ausformung einer Prozessordnung sui generis durch das ICTY unter Berücksichtigung des Fair-Trial-Prinzips* (Berlin: Springer, 2009), 20–21; Nemitz, *Strafzumessung im Völkerstrafrecht*, 18, 164–170, 276; C. Reichert, *Intersubjektivität durch Strafzumessungsrichtlinien* (Berlin: Duncker & Humblot, 1999), 255–257; Werkmeister, *Straftheorien im Völkerstrafrecht*, 273–274, 304.

31 See Section II.2.

32 See, e.g., Sloane, 'The Expressive Capacity', 70–71; Werle and Jeßberger, *Principles*, 38; Bottke, Assoziationsprävention, 45, 61–69; Demko, 'Hegels Straftheorie', 279; Epik, *Strafzumessung*, 46; Hörnle, *Straftheorien*, 29; G. Jakobs, *System der strafrechtlichen Zurechnung* (Frankfurt: Klostermann, 2012), 13–14; Werkmeister, *Straftheorien im Völkerstrafrecht*, 272–273.

33 See, e.g., Demko, 'Hegels Straftheorie', 289–290, 295–296; A. von Hirsch, 'Begründung und Bestimmung tatproportionaler Strafen' in W. Frisch, A. von Hirsch and H.-J. Albrecht (eds.), *Tatproportionalität* (Heidelberg: Verlag, 2003), 47, 54; Melloh, *Einheitliche Strafzumessung*, 110; Reichert, Intersubjektivität durch Strafzumessungsrichtlinien, 256; Werkmeister, *Straftheorien im Völkerstrafrecht*, 273, 300, 312–313.

34 See, e.g., Demko, 'Hegels Straftheorie', 288–290.

35 See, e.g., Epik, *Strafzumessung*, 48, 50, 71, 73, 152; Günther and Reuss, 'Legitimation des Völkerstrafrechts', 149.

punishment addresses to all people is evident.[36] For the expressive theory of international punishment, therefore, the communicative conveyance of trust in the continuing validity of international law and international criminal law – which is important and necessary for the present and future development, confirmation and strengthening[37] of trust – is of great significance.[38] However, the expressive theory of international punishment does not regard empirical evidence of a future formation (i.e., empirical evidence for a successful realization of affirmative individual or general prevention or individual or general deterrence) as a decisive element of justification of international punishment.[39]

The fact that an empirically proven future is not regarded as a decisive element of justification of international punishment does not mean that the expressive theory of international punishment overlooks or ignores the issues and criticisms that are levelled against affirmative individual and general prevention and individual and general deterrence. Rather, the expressive theory of international punishment pays particular attention to these issues and points of criticism, but places emphasis on other priorities and places emphasis on their central symbolic and communicative significance. Without making the normative justification of international punishment dependent on successful communication (i.e., on the successful realization of affirmative individual and general prevention and individual and general deterrence), the expressive theory of international punishment focuses more on the significance of the symbolic and communicative factor as such, as well as on the communicative content and relationship aspects of international punishment and on those aspects that can be influenced by the communicating international community (in the form of international law and international criminal law and international punishment) and which are therefore assigned to the international community as a task to be performed responsibly. Included in the communication content of international punishment are various aspects on the basis of which certain elements of affirmative individual

[36] See, e.g., Bottke, *Assoziationsprävention*, 46, 65; Demko, 'Hegels Straftheorie', 292–295; Werkmeister, *Straftheorien im Völkerstrafrecht*, 273.

[37] See, e.g., Epik, *Strafzumessung*, 145–146; Günther and Reuss, 'Legitimation des Völkerstrafrechts', 149; Melloh, *Einheitliche Strafzumessung*, 118, 129; Möller, *Völkerstrafrecht und Internationaler Strafgerichtshof*, 517–522; Nemitz, *Strafzumessung im Völkerstrafrecht*, 3, 18, 168–169.

[38] See, e.g., Bottke, *Assoziationsprävention*, 61–69.

[39] See, e.g., Bottke, *Assoziationsprävention*, 63; Hörnle, *Straftheorien*, 29, 31; Melloh, *Einheitliche Strafzumessung*, 105–106; Reichert, *Intersubjektivität durch Strafzumessungsrichtlinien*, 60, 141–142, 145, 256; Werkmeister, *Straftheorien im Völkerstrafrecht*, 273.

and general prevention and individual and general deterrence – as well as certain elements of the absolute theory of punishment (retribution)[40] – are conveyed in a communicative form and in a communicative transformation.

2 *Positive Affirmative General Prevention as the Central Aspect of the Statement of Content of International Punishment*

Alongside recognizing each person as rational subject and as communicative contact person with respect to his or her human dignity, international punishment appeals to all people in their communicative responsiveness as well as in their associated ability and responsibility to uphold universally recognized human rights and international law and international criminal law.[41] This also includes the fact that international punishment makes an appeal to all people in their ability and responsibility with a view to refusing normative orders that are in conflict with human rights, international law and international criminal law.[42] The international community, with the help of international punishment, conveys to all people the message that the international crime is regarded as a criminal offence,[43] and that every person – regardless of whether his or her involvement was at the command, implementation or execution level – who committed the international crime, will be punished in accordance with the requirement of individual reproachability (i.e., the requirement of personal culpability).[44] International punishment expresses with great symbolism and emphasis, and with the communicative

[40] See Section III.2.

[41] See, e.g., Günther and Reuss, 'Legitimation des Völkerstrafrechts', 151–152, 154–155; von Hirsch, 'Begründung und Bestimmung tatproportionaler Strafen', 53–54; Melloh, *Einheitliche Strafzumessung*, 105–106, 110–114; Werkmeister, *Straftheorien im Völkerstrafrecht*, 312–313.

[42] See, e.g., Epik, *Strafzumessung*, 127, 147–148; Günther and Reuss, 'Legitimation des Völkerstrafrechts', 150–151, 154–159; Nemitz, *Strafzumessung im Völkerstrafrecht*, 123.

[43] See, e.g., Drumbl, *Atrocity, Punishment, and International Law*, 174–175; J. Malamud-Goti, 'Transitional Governments in the Breach: Why Punish State Criminals?' (1990) 12 *Human Rights Quarterly* 1, 13; Schabas, 'Sentencing by International Tribunals', 502; Epik, *Strafzumessung*, 145, 151; Möller, *Völkerstrafrecht und Internationaler Strafgerichtshof*, 522–528.

[44] See, e.g., Ambos, Treatise Vol. I, 93–95; Cryer et al., *Introduction*, 503–504; Danner, 'Constructing a Hierarchy of Crimes', 453; S. D'Ascoli, *Sentencing in International Criminal Law: The UN ad hoc Tribunals and Future Perspectives for the ICC* (Oxford: Hart, 2011), 29, 297–298; Fisher, *Moral Accountability*, 53–55; Ohlin, 'Unique Theory of International Criminal Sentencing', 384; J. Peglau, 'Penalties and the Determination of the Sentence in the Rules of Procedure and Evidence' in H. Fischer, C. Kreß and S. R. Lüder (eds.), *International and National Prosecution of Crimes under International Law* (Berlin: Berliner Wissenschafts-Verlag, 2004), 141, 147–148; Werle and Jeßberger, *Principles*, 41–42; Epik, *Strafzumessung*, 81–83, 145, 151, 304–306, 309; Melloh, *Einheitliche Strafzumessung*, 309; Nemitz, *Strafzumessung im Völkerstrafrecht*, 152; ICC RPE, Rule 145(1)(a): 'Bear in mind that the

inclusion of the elements of positive affirmative general prevention, that no human being is above the law[45] and that no one can hide behind collective, systemic and macro-criminal structures.[46] Thus, the international community makes an important contribution to the development, confirmation and strengthening of humanity's trust in the continuing validity of international law and international criminal law.[47]

By explaining to humanity as a whole (and in this context also specifically to the current and potential perpetrators of the international crime), first, the legal interests of international law and international criminal law and their great importance for the universal protection of human rights and for living together peacefully, and, second, the protection of these legal interests by international law and international criminal law, international punishment (with due communicative integration of positive general prevention) makes an important contribution to the fact that all people worldwide acknowledge the legal interests of international law and international criminal law and comply therewith.[48] In addition, international punishment (with the communicative inclusion of elements of the re-socializing individual prevention (rehabilitation)) thereby increases the chance that the offender also, having committed the international crime, acknowledges the legal interests of international law and international criminal law and will comply with international criminal law in future.[49] In relation to offenders unwilling to comply with international criminal law in the future and continuing to pose a threat of further violations of international criminal law, international punishment also conveys elements of protection of society: International punishment (in the form of a conviction and prison sentence) conveys to humanity the acknowledgement of its need for safeguarding humanity against

totality of any sentence of imprisonment and fine, as the case may be, imposed under article 77 must reflect the culpability of the convicted person.'

45 See, e.g., Epik, *Strafzumessung*, 151.

46 See, e.g., Epik, *Strafzumessung*, 151.

47 See, e.g., Reichert, *Intersubjektivität durch Strafzumessungsrichtlinien*, 62–63.

48 See, e.g., Werle and Jeßberger, *Principles*, 37–38; Kamardi, *Ausformung einer Prozessordnung sui generis*, 20–21; Möller, *Völkerstrafrecht und Internationaler Strafgerichtshof*, 522–528; Nemitz, *Strafzumessung im Völkerstrafrecht*, 164–170.

49 See, e.g., Melloh, *Einheitliche Strafzumessung*, 105–106; D'Ascoli, *Sentencing*, 138–139, 273; M.B. Harmon and F. Gaynor, 'Ordinary Sentences for Extraordinary Crimes' (2007) 5 *Journal of International Criminal Justice* 683, 693; Ohlin, 'Unique Theory of International Criminal Sentencing', 384.

such an offender from whom the danger of future international crimes emanates.[50]

By conveying these elements of re-socializing special prevention (rehabilitation) and of securing special prevention (protection of society) not only to the offender who has committed an international crime, but also to every human being worldwide, and thereby in communicating these specific singular aspects of trust in norm validity to all people all over the world – in addition to positive general prevention communicated by international punishment as the central aspect of the statement of content of international punishment – international punishment also in this manner conveys to all people all over the world (and in this case again with the communicative integration of positive general prevention) that they can trust that international law and international criminal law will protect them.

Elements of individual and general deterrence can also be communicatively integrated into the statement of content of international punishment. However, the correct communicative focus and the correct communicative emphasis are particularly important here too. The viewpoint that the discovery, prosecution and punishment of international crimes is important for the functioning of individual and general deterrence[51] is addressed in a communicative manner by international punishment and emphasized by way of 'communicative reversal and communicative subsequent conclusion'. In so doing, it is important to observe that the normatively decisive content of the communication of international punishment must be clarified and emphasized. This normatively decisive communication content of international punishment is the confirmation of trust in the validity of the norm with the integration of positive affirmative general prevention. Part of this normatively decisive communication content of international punishment (as an aspect of content along with several other aspects) is the message communicated by international punishment that in the event of the perpetration of an international

[50] See, e.g., S. Beresford, 'Unshackling the Paper Tiger – The Sentencing Practises of the Ad Hoc International Criminal Tribunals for the Former Yugoslavia and Rwanda' (2001) 1 *International Criminal Law Review* 33, 44; Drumbl, *Atrocity, Punishment, and International Law*, 72; Epik, *Strafzumessung*, 118; Melloh, *Einheitliche Strafzumessung*, 147–148; Möller, *Völkerstrafrecht und Internationaler Strafgerichtshof*, 478–485.

[51] See, e.g., Amann, 'Group Mentality, Expressivism, and Genocide', 115–117; Beresford, 'The Sentencing Practises of the Ad Hoc International Criminal Tribunals', 40–42; Cryer et al., *Introduction*, 503; Danner, 'Constructing a Hierarchy of Crimes', 444–445; D'Ascoli, *Sentencing*, 135; Drumbl, *Atrocity, Punishment, and International Law*, 151–153, 170; Fisher, *Moral Accountability*, 51–52; DeGuzman, 'Harsh Justice for International Crimes?', 16; Schabas, 'Sentencing by International Tribunals', 498; Epik, *Strafzumessung*, 134–136; Melloh, *Einheitliche Strafzumessung*, 137–140.

crime, the prosecution and punishment of this international crime will occur. It is therefore through international punishment to communicate (not the deterrence thereof as such, but rather) the prosecution and punishment of the international crime and with it the confirmation of trust in the validity of the norm.[52] That the current or potential offender might be deterred from committing a future international crime is communicated only as a mere (language) reflex, but it is not the direct communicative message of international punishment.[53]

It is also the function of confirming trust in norm validity that is decisive for international punishment, and on the basis of which it must be answered whether a judicial punitive decision alone can be justified or whether, in addition, a subsequent actual punishment (hard treatment) can be justified.[54] The judicial punitive decision already communicates in words those statement contents that are connected with the function of confirming trust in norm validity and with the function of assigning responsibility. The requirement of an additional 'tangible' confirmation and strengthening of the verbal communication of these statements by subsequent actual punishment can only be justified if and for so long as a human community (in the context of international criminal law, humanity), with respect to their trust in the norm validity, rates a purely verbal communication of the statement content by the judicial punitive decision as insufficient and considers an additional 'tangible' confirmation and strengthening by actual punishment as necessary.[55] Both the judicial punitive decision and the point of view of whether there is an additional need for actual punishment,[56] therefore, depend on the assessment of a human community at a specific time – and could, therefore, also change over time – i.e., they depend on whether the human community for its trust in

[52] See, e.g., Melloh, *Einheitliche Strafzumessung*, 120; Reichert, *Intersubjektivität durch Strafzumessungsrichtlinien*, 52.

[53] See, e.g., Melloh, *Einheitliche Strafzumessung*, 120; Möller, *Völkerstrafrecht und Internationaler Strafgerichtshof*, 506–507; Nemitz, *Strafzumessung im Völkerstrafrecht*, 170–173, 274–275.

[54] See, e.g., Epik, *Strafzumessung*, 46–50; Hörnle, *Straftheorien*, 41–43; Melloh, *Einheitliche Strafzumessung*, 110–114; Reichert, *Intersubjektivität durch Strafzumessungsrichtlinien*, 143; Werkmeister, *Straftheorien im Völkerstrafrecht*, 300–303, 330–342, 351–352.

[55] See, e.g., Epik, *Strafzumessung*, 49–50; Günther and Reuss, 'Legitimation des Völkerstrafrechts', 139–140, 147–148; Reichert, *Intersubjektivität durch Strafzumessungsrichtlinien*, 143 f.

[56] See, e.g., Epik, *Strafzumessung*, 49–50, 73–74; Günther and Reuss, 'Legitimation des Völkerstrafrechts', 139–140.

the norm validity determines a judicial punitive decision (without a subsequent actual punishment) to be sufficient or insufficient.[57]

III THE FUNCTION OF ASSIGNING RESPONSIBILITY COMMUNICATED BY INTERNATIONAL PUNISHMENT

1 *The Disapproval Function as Part of the Function of Assigning Responsibility*

The function of international punishment of assigning responsibility builds on a disapproval function that precedes it. The disapproval function is an intermediate step for assigning responsibility to the offender as communicated by international punishment. In recognizing the perpetrator of the international crime as rational subject and as communicative contact person with respect to his or her human dignity, international punishment normatively conveys to the offender of the international crime committed in the past – and to the victims of the international crime and to all other human beings – first, that the commission of international crimes is strictly rejected and disapproved of as a breach of legal norms[58] and, second, and this is decisive, that the offender is assigned the responsibility for the breach of legal norms in accordance with the requirement of individual reproachability (the requirement of personal culpability).[59]

[57] See, e.g., D'Ascoli, *Sentencing*, 50; Drumbl, *Atrocity, Punishment, and International Law*, 161; A.K.A. Greenawalt, 'International Criminal Law for Retributivists' (2014) 35 *University of Pennsylvania Journal of International Law* 969, 984; Demko, 'Hegels Straftheorie', 293–294; Epik, *Strafzumessung*, 50, 101–102; Günther and Reuss, 'Legitimation des Völkerstrafrechts', 139–140; Hörnle, *Straftheorien*, 42–43; Reichert, *Intersubjektivität durch Strafzumessungsrichtlinien*, 124, 254.

[58] See, e.g., Amann, 'Group Mentality, Expressivism, and Genocide', 123; Danner, 'Constructing a Hierarchy of Crimes', 490–491; Drumbl, *Atrocity, Punishment, and International Law*, 61; Sloane, 'The Expressive Capacity', 70–71, 83; M.D. Dubber, 'Positive Generalprävention und Rechtsgutstheorie: Zwei zentrale Errungenschaften der deutschen Strafrechtswissenschaft aus amerikanischer Sicht' (2005) 117 *Zeitschrift für die gesamte Strafrechtswissenschaft* 485, 494–495; Epik, *Strafzumessung*, 46–47, 150–151; von Hirsch, 'Begründung und Bestimmung tatproportionaler Strafen', 50–51; Reichert, *Intersubjektivität durch Strafzumessungsrichtlinien*, 144–145.

[59] See, e.g., Ambos, *Treatise* Vol. I, 93–95; Malamud-Goti, 'Why Punish State Criminals?', 12–13; Schabas, 'Sentencing by International Tribunals', 502; Werle and Jeßberger, *Principles*, 41–42; Epik, *Strafzumessung*, 81–83, 145, 151, 304–306, 309; Melloh, *Einheitliche Strafzumessung*, 309; Nemitz, *Strafzumessung im Völkerstrafrecht*, 152; Reichert, *Intersubjektivität durch Strafzumessungsrichtlinien*, 57–64, 145; ICC RPE, Rule 145(1)(a): '[…] must reflect the culpability of the convicted person'.

The disapproval function of international punishment addresses a negation-of-the-negation relation, i.e., it points to a relationship of reciprocal negation between international law and international criminal law (as the first statement), the international crime (as the second statement in the form of a negation statement) and international punishment (as the third statement in the form of a negation-of-the-negation statement).[60] The negation statement expressed by international crime – with which the offender contradicts valid international law and international criminal law – is contradicted by international punishment (as a negation-of-the-negation statement) and in this manner the confirmation and strengthening of the continuing validity of international law and international criminal law is symbolized and communicated.[61] The disapproval function of international punishment is to be separated from being an element of censure[62] that expresses certain emotions (such as outrage, anger, feelings of revenge, feelings of retaliation or retribution).[63] It is important and necessary that a legal community (and in the context of international criminal law, this is the international legal community) takes the people living in it and their emotions that arise in connection with (international) crimes seriously.[64] However, the (international) legal community *itself* must not make such emotions its own and must not adopt such emotions when executing the claim for criminal punishment that has been transferred to it.[65] The consideration of an element of censure based on emotions as an independent element of an expressive theory of international punishment is therefore to be rejected.[66]

60 See, e.g., Bottke, *Assoziationsprävention*, 62–63, 65–66; Demko, 'Hegels Straftheorie', 285–286, 290–292.

61 See, e.g., Bottke, *Assoziationsprävention*, 62–63, 65–66; Epik, *Strafzumessung*, 145, 148; Günther and Reuss, 'Legitimation des Völkerstrafrechts', 158–159; Hörnle, *Straftheorien*, 31–32; Reichert, *Intersubjektivität durch Strafzumessungsrichtlinien*, 28, 53, 58.

62 See, e.g., Demko, 'Hegels Straftheorie', 296–300; Epik, *Strafzumessung*, 46–47; von Hirsch, 'Begründung und Bestimmung tatproportionaler Strafen', 50–51; Hörnle, *Straftheorien*, 32–36; Werkmeister, *Straftheorien im Völkerstrafrecht*, 298–300.

63 See, e.g., Demko, 'Hegels Straftheorie', 296–299; Epik, *Strafzumessung*, 24–25, 27, 47; Günther and Reuss, 'Legitimation des Völkerstrafrechts', 146–147; Nemitz, *Strafzumessung im Völkerstrafrecht*, 163; Reichert, *Intersubjektivität durch Strafzumessungsrichtlinien*, 59–60, 145.

64 See, e.g., Demko, 'Hegels Straftheorie', 296–299; Epik, *Strafzumessung*, 47; Hörnle, *Straftheorien*, 35.

65 See, e.g., Demko, 'Hegels Straftheorie', 298; Reichert, *Intersubjektivität durch Strafzumessungsrichtlinien*, 59–60, 145.

66 See, e.g., Epik, *Strafzumessung*, 46–47; Reichert, *Intersubjektivität durch Strafzumessungsrichtlinien*, 59–60, 145.

2 *Selected Content Aspects of International Punishment with Respect to Its Function of Assigning Responsibility*

The visible connection with regard to the negation-of-the-negation relationship that exists between the function of confirming and strengthening trust in norm validity and the disapproval function of international punishment continues and is deepened in the function of assigning responsibility.

The fact that, on the level of evaluation, punishment is regarded as compensation for the criminal offence for which the offender is individually criminally responsible[67] can also be transferred to international criminal law. Of course, punishment, including international punishment, cannot undo, on an objective-real level, the infringement of (international) criminal law (i.e., breach of legal norms) and the infringement of the victims' legal interests caused by an (international) criminal offence.[68] First of all, however, the evaluation and assessment and the meta-communicative significance of international punishment are connected with international punishment according to which international punishment must be regarded as compensation for the international crime perpetrated.[69] Second, in order to assess the punishability of the offender and to determine the extent of punishment, international punishment must first examine whether and to what extent the offender is individually criminally responsible for commission of the international crime (principle of personal culpability).[70]

Although, in view of the tremendous injustice and gravity of international crimes, it is difficult to imagine that international punishment can be considered as compensation for their perpetration,[71] it is important to emphasize that the requirement of individual reproachability – in relation to the

[67] See, e.g., H.-H. Jescheck, *Lehrbuch des Strafrechts. Allgemeiner Teil* (Berlin: Duncker & Humblot, 1978), 3–4, 51–52, 59; Melloh, *Einheitliche Strafzumessung*, 119; Nemitz, *Strafzumessung im Völkerstrafrecht*, 113.

[68] See, e.g., Epik, *Strafzumessung*, 97; Jescheck, *Lehrbuch des Strafrechts*, 3.

[69] See, e.g., Epik, *Strafzumessung*, 101 f.; Jescheck, *Lehrbuch des Strafrechts*, 3–4, 51–52, 59; Melloh, *Einheitliche Strafzumessung*, 119.

[70] See, e.g., Ambos, *Treatise* Vol. I, 93–95; Epik, *Strafzumessung*, 24, 81–98, 193–248, 304–306, 309–312, 466–467, 472–481, 489–504; Melloh, *Einheitliche Strafzumessung*, 309; Reichert, *Intersubjektivität durch Strafzumessungsrichtlinien*, 141; ICC RPE, Rule 145(1)(a).

[71] See, e.g., Drumbl, *Atrocity, Punishment, and International Law*, 155–157; DeGuzman, 'Harsh Justice for International Crimes?', 17–19; Harmon and Gaynor, 'Ordinary Sentences for Extraordinary Crimes', 692; Epik, *Strafzumessung*, 91–92; Melloh, *Einheitliche Strafzumessung*, 118–119; Möller, *Völkerstrafrecht und Internationaler Strafgerichtshof*, 451.

assignment of responsibility to the offender – is to be considered.[72] This shows that international punishment – in its function of assigning responsibility – integrates elements of the absolute theories of punishment (retribution) communicatively. However, international punishment must free itself of ideas of retribution and atonement and of metaphysical ideas of justice.[73] The only decisive point of reference of international punishment for the assignment of responsibility to the offender as communicated by it is individual reproachability for the commission of the international crime (principle of personal culpability).[74] This assignment of responsibility to the offender communicated through international punishment constitutes one of the conditions (and, indeed, the minimum condition) for international punishment to be regarded – on a level of evaluation – as compensation for the international crime perpetrated by the offender.[75] Simultaneously, this assignment of responsibility to the offender communicated through international punishment constitutes one of the conditions (and, again, the minimum condition) for the trust of people worldwide in the continuing validity of international law and international criminal law. This trust in the norm validity also includes the trust that the offender – who has violated international law and international criminal law – will be assigned responsibility for the international crime for which the offender is individually criminally responsible and within the framework of the individual reproachability of the offender.[76] The close connection is demonstrated here, but also the ranking order (the relation of priority and subordination) which both exist between (on the one hand) the confirmation of trust in the validity of the norm – as all-embracing and superordinate main statement and overall statement of international punishment – communicated by international punishment, and (on the

[72] See, e.g., Ambos, *Treatise* Vol. I, 93–95; Werle and Jeßberger, *Principles*, 41–42; Epik, *Strafzumessung*, 81–83, 92–98, 145, 151, 304–306, 309; Melloh, *Einheitliche Strafzumessung*, 309; Nemitz, *Strafzumessung im Völkerstrafrecht*, 152; ICC RPE, Rule 145(1)(a).

[73] See, e.g., Werle and Jeßberger, *Principles*, 37; Epik, *Strafzumessung*, 24–26; Möller, *Völkerstrafrecht und Internationaler Strafgerichtshof*, 456–459.

[74] See, e.g., Epik, *Strafzumessung*, 24, 81–98, 309–312, 466–467, 472–481, 489–504.

[75] See, e.g., Cryer et al., *Introduction*, 40–41; D'Ascoli, *Sentencing*, 139–140; Werle and Jeßberger, *Principles*, 37, 41–42; Epik, *Strafzumessung*, 24, 81–98, 309–312, 466–467, 472–481, 489–504; Jescheck, *Lehrbuch des Strafrechts*, 51–52, 59; Nemitz, *Strafzumessung im Völkerstrafrecht*, 113, 276–277; Reichert, *Intersubjektivität durch Strafzumessungsrichtlinien*, 254.

[76] See, e.g., Ambos, *Treatise* Vol. I, 93–95; Cryer et al., *Introduction*, 40–41; D'Ascoli, *Sentencing*, 139–140; Werle and Jeßberger, *Principles*, 41–42; Epik, *Strafzumessung*, 28, 81–83, 145, 151, 304–306, 309; Melloh, *Einheitliche Strafzumessung*, 309; Nemitz, *Strafzumessung im Völkerstrafrecht*, 20, 113, 152; Reichert, *Intersubjektivität durch Strafzumessungsrichtlinien*, 57–65, 145, 255–257; ICC RPE, Rule 145(1)(a): '[...] must reflect the culpability of the convicted person'.

other hand) the assignment of responsibility communicated by international punishment.[77]

With a view to determining whether and the extent to which the offender is to be assigned individual reproachability for committing an international crime, the function of assigning responsibility requires a retrospective view. That means that the function of assigning responsibility necessarily requires a look into the past in which the international crime was perpetrated.[78] However – due to the classification of the function of assigning responsibility under the overarching and superordinate function of confirming trust in norm validity – this does not change the important and decisive meaning of the present and future reference to the expression and communication of trust that international punishment addresses to all people worldwide.[79] In that the expressive theory of international punishment, first, classifies the function of assigning responsibility under the overarching and superordinate function of confirming trust in norm validity and, second, assigns absolute and relative theories of punishment to these two functions of international punishment,[80] the expressive theory of international punishment developed here shows itself to be a normative theory of international punishment that removes the separation between absolute and relative theories of punishment.[81]

IV SPECIFIC PURPOSES OF INTERNATIONAL CRIMINAL LAW AND THEIR COMMUNICATIVE INTEGRATION INTO INTERNATIONAL PUNISHMENT

The protection of the truth, the protection of victims and the rejection of a collective guilt thesis are currently being discussed as criminal purposes

[77] See, e.g., Epik, *Strafzumessung*, 50–56, 73, 164–165; Nemitz, *Strafzumessung im Völkerstrafrecht*, 113, 164, 169–170, 276–277; Reichert, *Intersubjektivität durch Strafzumessungsrichtlinien*, 255–257; Werkmeister, *Straftheorien im Völkerstrafrecht*, 304.

[78] See, e.g., Melloh, *Einheitliche Strafzumessung*, 48, 100–102; Reichert, *Intersubjektivität durch Strafzumessungsrichtlinien*, 141, 254–255.

[79] See Section II.1.; see, e.g., Melloh, *Einheitliche Strafzumessung*, 100–102, 117; Nemitz, *Strafzumessung im Völkerstrafrecht*, 113, 120–121, 164, 169–170; Reichert, *Intersubjektivität durch Strafzumessungsrichtlinien*, 255–257.

[80] See Sections II.1. and 2. and Section III.2.

[81] See, e.g., D'Ascoli, *Sentencing*, 294–296; Drumbl, *Atrocity, Punishment, and International Law*, 149–150; L. May, *Aggression and Crimes against Peace* (Cambridge: University Press, 2008), 319–321; Demko, 'Hegels Straftheorie', 294–295, 300; Reichert, *Intersubjektivität durch Strafzumessungsrichtlinien*, 57–60; Werkmeister, *Straftheorien im Völkerstrafrecht*, 353–354, 379–380.

specific to international criminal law coping with the past.[82] These specific purposes of international criminal law can be integrated into the statement of content of international punishment (and its two communicative functions). This demonstrates that, and to what extent, these specific purposes of international criminal law are not independent criminal purposes.[83]

With regard to the purpose of protecting the truth, a differentiation must be drawn between the international criminal law-related determination of the truth (which is connected with criminal proceedings against the accused offender) on the one hand and the determination of the truth (beyond the criminal proceedings) in order to clarify the entire historical event on the other hand.[84] The international criminal law-related determination of the truth – which concerns the truthful determination of the facts relating to the individual criminal responsibility of the offender, and to which the criminal proceedings are to refer[85] – is a necessary pre-requisite for the subsequent determination of the existence or non-existence of individual criminal responsibility of the accused offender. This international criminal law-related determination of truth is therefore integrated communicatively as an indispensable and immanent part of international punishment (and its two communicative functions).

With regard to the determination of the truth (beyond the criminal proceedings) in order to clarify the entire historical event, criminal proceedings and international punishment express that criminal proceedings and international punishment indeed do not provide a comprehensive clarification of the entire historical event, but guarantee the clarification of at least a part thereof (namely, the international criminal law-related part referring to the international crime of the accused offender). Criminal proceedings and international punishment as such are therefore not sufficient for a comprehensive clarification of the entire historical event, but criminal proceedings

82 See, e.g., Werle and Jeßberger, *Principles*, 38–9; Epik, *Strafzumessung*, 154–161; Günther and Reuss, 'Legitimation des Völkerstrafrechts', 135–144; Möller, *Völkerstrafrecht und Internationaler Strafgerichtshof*, 426–438, 528–611.

83 See, e.g., Epik, *Strafzumessung*, 157, 159–160.

84 See, e.g., May, *Aggression and Crimes against Peace*, 323–324; C. Stahn, 'Between "Faith" and "Facts": By What Standards Should We Assess International Criminal Justice' (2012) 25 *Leiden Journal of International Law* 251, 272; Werkmeister, Straftheorien im Völkerstrafrecht, 286–290.

85 See, e.g., May, Aggression and Crimes against Peace, 323–324; Stahn, 'Between "Faith" and "Facts"', 272; Epik, *Strafzumessung*, 155–156.

and international punishment make an important and necessary contribution to a subsequent comprehensive clarification and review of the entire historical event, including associated reconciliation processes for the peaceful coexistence of humanity.[86]

The specific criminal purposes of victim protection and the rejection of a collective guilt thesis are also integrated by international punishment (and its two communicative functions). By assigning to the offender the responsibility for the international crime the offender has committed, international punishment communicates not only to the convicted offender, but also to the victims of international crime and to all other human beings in a clear and unambiguous manner to whom – namely, to the convicted offender – individual reproachability (individual criminal responsibility) for the international crime is to be assigned.[87] At the same time, international punishment communicates (first) that the suffering and the injuries of the victims are not the result of an accident or a misfortune,[88] but rather a direct result of the international crime for which the offender is individually criminally responsible.[89] International punishment thereby expresses the recognition of the victims of the international crime and their suffering and conveys to the victims of the international crime that they can trust in the international law and international criminal law that protect them.[90] In addition, by assigning responsibility to the offender, international punishment at the same time expresses (second) that the guilt for the international crime is not borne by a collective, but rather by the offender who is individually criminally responsible for the international

[86] See, e.g., Akhavan, 'Beyond Impunity', 7; D'Ascoli, *Sentencing*, 38; Drumbl, *Atrocity, Punishment, and International Law*, 174–175; Epik, *Strafzumessung*, 155–157; Kamardi, *Ausformung einer Prozessordnung sui generis*, 21–22; Nitsche, *Der Internationale Strafgerichtshof*, 175–177; Werkmeister, *Straftheorien im Völkerstrafrecht*, 286–293.

[87] See, e.g., Werle and Jeßberger, *Principles*, 39; Bottke, *Assoziationsprävention*, 67–68; Epik, *Strafzumessung*, 47–48, 151–152; Günther and Reuss, 'Legitimation des Völkerstrafrechts', 139; Kamardi, *Ausformung einer Prozessordnung sui generis*, 21.

[88] See, e.g., Bottke, *Assoziationsprävention*, 67–68; Hörnle, *Straftheorien*, 39; Werkmeister, *Straftheorien im Völkerstrafrecht*, 328–329, 338.

[89] See, e.g., Drumbl, *Atrocity, Punishment, and International Law*, 174–175; Malamud-Goti, 'Why Punish State Criminals?', 13; Epik, *Strafzumessung*, 146; von Hirsch, 'Begründung und Bestimmung tatproportionaler Strafen', 52–53; Melloh, *Einheitliche Strafzumessung*, 111.

[90] See, e.g., Cryer et al., *Introduction*, 40–41; D'Ascoli, Sentencing, 38; Drumbl, Atrocity, Punishment, and International Law, 150, 174–175; Epik, *Strafzumessung*, 155; Günther and Reuss, 'Legitimation des Völkerstrafrechts', 135–140; von Hirsch, 'Begründung und Bestimmung tatproportionaler Strafen', 52–53; Möller, *Völkerstrafrecht und Internationaler Strafgerichtshof*, 552–562, 601–607; Nitsche, *Der Internationale Strafgerichtshof*, 172–174; Werkmeister, *Straftheorien im Völkerstrafrecht*, 321, 324–329.

crime the offender has committed.[91] In other words, international punishment contradicts a collective guilt thesis.[92] Thus, international punishment makes an important contribution to the reconciliation of the 'offender' and 'victim' groups and at the same time conveys to all people worldwide that they can trust in the international law and international criminal law that protect them.[93]

V CONCLUSION

The intention of this chapter was to develop the basic features of a normative expressive theory of international punishment. It has been shown that, and in which manner, international punishment expresses two important communicative functions: the function of confirming and strengthening trust in norm validity and the function of assigning responsibility. It has been explained how the combination and interaction between these two communicative functions of international punishment and their ranking order are shaped. At the same time, it has been explained how the traditionally prevailing absolute and relative criminal theories and the specific purposes attached to international criminal law are to be accomodated within the framework of these two communicative functions of international punishment. In doing so, the positive general prevention that is communicatively integrated by international punishment has proved to be the main aspect of the statement of content of international punishment.

91 See, e.g., Malamud-Goti, 'Why Punish State Criminals?', 13; D'Ascoli, *Sentencing*, 38; Drumbl, *Atrocity, Punishment, and International Law*, 174–175; E. van Sliedregt, *The Criminal Responsibility of Individuals for Violations of International Humanitarian Law* (The Hague: T.M.C. Asser Press, 2003), 5–6, 347–362; Epik, *Strafzumessung*, 158–159; Kamardi, *Ausformung einer Prozessordnung sui generis*, 19; Möller, *Völkerstrafrecht und Internationaler Strafgerichtshof*, 529–535; Nitsche, *Der Internationale Strafgerichtshof*, 168–172; Werkmeister, *Straftheorien im Völkerstrafrecht*, 294–295.

92 See, e.g., Werle and Jeßberger, *Principles*, 39; Werkmeister, *Straftheorien im Völkerstrafrecht*, 294–295.

93 See, e.g., Epik, *Strafzumessung*, 158–159; Möller, *Völkerstrafrecht und Internationaler Strafgerichtshof*, 606–607; Nitsche, *Der Internationale Strafgerichtshof*, 168–172.

12

We're Exhausting Ourselves, Let's Get Busy Instead

A Comment on the Contributions by Jakob v.H. Holtermann, Mordechai Kremnitzer and Daniela Demko

MARK A. DRUMBL

Matthew the Levite: 'I spoke, hegemon, of how the temple of the old beliefs would fall down and the new temple of truth would be built up.'

Procurator Pilate: 'Why should a tramp like you upset the crowd in the bazaar by talking about truth, something of which you have no conception? What is truth?'

At this the Procurator thought: 'Ye gods! This is a court of law and I am asking him an irrelevant question [. . .].'

Mikhail Bulgakov, *The Master and Margarita* (1938), Book I, Chapter 2 'Pontius Pilate'

Courts and truth(s), the trueness of the outputs that courts manufacture, their verities, as well as the correlations among questions and relevance and trials and life generally – all of these threads weave through three contributions in this part of this volume. These contributions – authored by Jakob v.H. Holtermann, Mordechai Kremnitzer and Daniela Demko – unspool the aims of punishment in international criminal law.

These chapters begin by parsing the objectives of prosecuting and sentencing perpetrators of atrocity crimes. Each author questions whether these objectives derive from, or ought to transcend, what operates at the national level for ordinary common crimes. The inquiries then continue. How should these objectives be quantified in sentencing? Should it be germane, from the perspective of the victim, if the accused is powerful and (formerly) in command; or subject to the authority of others while exercising command over many; or meek and weak, recalling of course that in the cataclysm of atrocity the meek and the weak may situationally lord absolute power over the life and death of others. Might the prosecutors of today pause, like Pilate, and acknowledge the possibility that courts may not know what truths are? What is the connection between trials and Matthew the Levite's temples? What role can trials play to drain the invidiousness of old *beliefs* and build up the modernity and hipness of new *truths*? At what point does what one *believes* give way to what just *is*?

While these three contributions lock arms in terms of discussing punishment in international criminal law, they stand independently in that each explores a different justification for the punitive function: Demko considers expressivism, Kremnitzer unpacks retribution and Holtermann picks up deterrence. Whereas Demko and Kremnitzer examine these objectives within the system of law as a whole, toggling between the national and the international, Holtermann plays with the deterrence function of the International Criminal Court (ICC) specifically.

Retribution and general deterrence are the two most prominently cited punishment goals in international criminal law, in particular in the outputs of international courts and tribunals.[1] Expressivism, which underscores the communicative function of law, has generated considerable academic writing and, it is fair to say, implicitly colours much of the work of both national and international courts when sentencing perpetrators of *jus cogens* crimes.[2] On occasion, international judges also refer to other penological rationales including rehabilitation, incapacitation and reconciliation. These rationales, however, are not salient. Rehabilitation in particular is a lonely afterthought. The international community has little patience for thinking of how a convicted war criminal may be retooled or repurposed, salvaged or saved.

I RETRIBUTION

Although there are many divergent schools of retributivism, what retributivists generally share is an understanding that the infliction of punishment rectifies the moral balance, in particular, through condemnation of the criminal conduct.[3] Simply put, punishment is what the perpetrator deserves. Punishment, therefore, is to be proportionate to the extent of the harm caused by the

1 Situation in the Central African Republic in ICC, Decision of 21 June 2016 (TC), *Bemba Gombo*, ICC-01/05-01/08-3399, para. 10 (citing also the ICC *Katanga* Sentencing Decision, ICTY *Popović et al.* Appeal Judgement, and ECCC *Kaing* Appeal Judgment); ICTY, Judgement of 22 March 2006 (AC), *Stakić*, IT-97-24-A, para. 402 (stating that 'the Appeals Chamber notes that the jurisprudence of the Tribunal and the ICTR consistently points out that the two main purposes of sentencing are deterrence and retribution'). On retribution and (general) deterrence as rationales of international punishment in the jurisprudence of international and hybrid courts, see also the contribution by Sergey Vasiliev in Chapter 4.

2 M.A. Drumbl, *Atrocity, Punishment, and International Law* (Cambridge: Cambridge University Press, 2007).

3 See generally H.L.A. Hart, *Punishment and Responsibility* (Oxford: Clarendon Press, 1968), 234–235.

crime and also to the offender's degree of intentionality. In terms of retribution, the severity of a prison sentence for a senior-level perpetrator of extraordinary international crimes (genocide, crimes against humanity, systematic war crimes, the crime of aggression), however, may never be able to reciprocate the gravity of the harm. Meting out tangible 'just deserts' in such cases ominously suggests the abandonment of core principles of international human rights law (whether in terms of the length of sentence, form of sanction or conditions of confinement). Quizzically, many international convicts receive sentences that are not any longer than those that national justice systems routinely mete out to ordinary common criminals. The ICC's three sentences thus far are 14, 12 and 9 years (a fourth sentence of 18 years was overturned on appeal in June 2018 owing to the acquittal of the accused, Jean-Pierre Bemba; a fifth sentence, against Bosco Ntaganda, is under deliberation by ICC judges at the time of writing). Barbora Holá, who has conducted extensive empirical analysis of the ad hoc Tribunals' sentencing practices, determines that the International Criminal Tribunal for the former Yugoslavia (ICTY) has issued a modest number of life sentences (approximately 6 per cent of the total): its fixed-terms sentences range from 2 years to 40 years (as of the time of writing) with a median sentence of 15 years and a mean sentence of a touch over 15 years.[4] The International Criminal Tribunal for Rwanda (ICTR) has finalized fifty-nine sentences, seventeen of which are life sentences. Among the ICTR's determinate sentences, according to Holá, the median is 25 years and the mean is 24.67 years. The range among determinate sentences at the ICTR is 6 to 47 years.

Knotty tensions arise for the pursuit of retributive aims when it comes to the lower ranks of offenders insofar as crimes of terrible gravity may in fact be committed by persons with low intent and limited agency. Mark Osiel couches this as the phenomenon of administrative massacre within a totalitarian apparatus.[5] How to proceed in such instances?

This is the tricky angle that Kremnitzer explores in his compelling and thoughtful contribution. Kremnitzer writes about the 'small fish'. He focuses not on those who thoughtlessly or unknowingly commit harm, but rather on the closely concentric circle of those who may know but have neither choice nor capacity – whose 'choiceless choices', so to speak, result in the infliction of terrible wrongs upon others. Kremnitzer unpacks what to do with victims,

4 Data extracted from M.A. Drumbl, '"And Where the Offence Is, Let the Great Axe Fall": Sentencing Under International Criminal Law' in P. Kastner (ed.), *International Criminal Law In Context* (Abingdon: Routledge, 2018), 309 (citing the research of Barbora Holá, with permission, and available from the author).

5 M.J. Osiel, 'Ever Again: Legal Remembrance of Administrative Massacre' (1995) 144 *University of Pennsylvania Law Review* 463.

bereft of agency, who victimize others. Kremnitzer draws from the iniquity of Auschwitz, in which Jewish inmates functionalized the Nazi policy of 'prisoner self-administration'. These inmates were compelled and coaxed by Nazis into 'leadership' roles, but at times came forward on their own to serve in these capacities – notably that of Kapo (heads of barracks and forced labour groups) and, in the different context of the ghetto, into positions of authority in police forces. Kremnitzer also places child soldiers, an historical as well as contemporary phenomenon, in this liminal category.[6]

These are tough questions indeed: should the persecuted, when they persecute other group members, be held criminally responsible for the harm they cause? To be harmed, after all, by an individual determined to be a victim is among the loneliest places to inhabit. It is just so hard for such an individual to speak of his or her pain or achieve justice for the harm he or she endured because the harm-doer him- or herself is taken to be a victim and thereby attracts the empathy of any interlocutor. So how to properly speak of these harms? Where, if anywhere, to address them? And if so, how?

In the 1950s the state of Israel had an answer. It criminally prosecuted, as Kremnitzer sets out, roughly forty Kapos in Israeli courts of general jurisdiction. Prosecutions were held under the 1950 Nazi and Nazi Collaborators (Punishment Act). I have elsewhere written that these proceedings accomplished little.[7] They accomplished little because subjecting as compromised a character as a Kapo to the hydraulics of the criminal trial and the pneumatics of sentencing leads to frustrating results and a general sense of futility. The Kapo trials oozed with gnarly language, many acquittals and evidentiary challenges. In the Kapo trials, what is more, the prosecution narratively exaggerated the agency available to the Kapo whereas the defense responsively contracted it – as both sides should, after all, as these are the roles placed upon them by the machinery of adversarial criminal proceedings. The result, however, was tense jurisprudence and vacillating outcomes. Israeli judges often condemned the defendants in coarse language but also 'trembled' when having to sentence them, meaning that there were frequent acquittals and a mean sentence of a meagre 17 months. Judges offered no sentencing theory to speak of, though the sadism of the violence did appear to factor into longer sentences. Duress was raised, often successfully.

6 I have done the same: M.A. Drumbl, 'Victims Who Victimise' (2016) 4 *London Journal of International Law* 217.

7 Drumbl, 'Victims Who Victimise'. See also M.A. Drumbl, 'Histories of the Jewish "Collaborator": Exile, Not Guilt' (2017), available at https://papers.ssrn.com/sol3/papers.cfm?abstract_id=3009231.

Can it be said that punishing a Kapo serves retributive purposes, i.e., to channel the outrage of the international, national or local community? Does this deliver 'just deserts'? What kind of proportionality is at play here? Perhaps prosecuting victims who victimize ironically diverts outrage away from the powerful actors who mastermind genocide in the first place. As to deterrence, what are the effects here? Is the goal to prioritize resistance and sacrifice over negotiation and survivalism? Is the goal to induce the persecuted not to persecute others? Holocaust survivor Primo Levi painfully wrote that the law of the *Lager* (the concentration camp) was 'eat your own bread, and if you can, that of your neighbor'?[8] By prosecuting Kapos criminally, is the goal to unsettle what Levi perceived as the *Lager*'s informal 'law'? Is it to encourage what Viktor Frankl, another Holocaust survivor, framed as every person's duty to exercise his or her agency in ways that lessen the pain experienced by others?[9] Is it to condemn those who survive by grifting or hurting others and thereby dissuade such conduct? To dignify those who elected not to pursue such strategies and ultimately died?

Kremnitzer agrees that the Kapo trials – although reflecting the *Zeitgeist* of a historical moment for the newly created state of Israel – ultimately proved pointless. He underscores, however, that a small space should be left open. According to Kremnitzer, '[c]riminal responsibility in these cases should only be imposed on those who did more than required out of lust for power and control or out of cruelty and sadism as such'.[10] This same thinking, then, can vault into the context of child soldiers – whether current or former. Dominic Ongwen, formerly a child soldier, faces criminal prosecution at the ICC.[11] Abducted into Joseph Kony's Lord's Resistance Army at the age of nine or ten, abused and battered, soldiering when he turned fourteen, Ongwen came of age within this violent group. He grew into its youngest Brigadier Commander ever, in his late twenties. While in his forties he escaped, after being tortured by Kony, and sought shelter with US Special Ops forces who turned him over to the ICC. His whole life, really, has been the Lord's Resistance Army.

Ongwen is unique among persons prosecuted in the solemnity of The Hague: He has suffered certain of the crimes he is subsequently alleged to have committed. He is also singular in that he faces the largest number of charges

8 P. Levi, *Survival in Auschwitz: The Nazi Assault on Humanity* (translation S. Woolf) (New York: Simon & Schuster, 1993), 160.

9 V.E. Frankl, *Man's Search for Meaning* (Boston: Beacon Press, 2006; first published 1956).

10 See the contribution by Mordechai Kremnitzer in Chapter 10 (p. 169).

11 See C. Ramos, 'Dominic Ongwen on Trial: Problematizing Definitional Boundaries and Exploring the Possibilities of Socialization' in M.A. Drumbl and J. Barrett (eds.), *Research Handbook on Child Soldiers* (Cheltenham: Edward Elgar, forthcoming 2019).

(seventy) ever brought against anyone facing international prosecution.[12] Perhaps Ongwen might fit into the residual space that Kremnitzer leaves open for the kinds of victims who cede their victim status to the point of meriting criminal prosecution as perpetrators. Certainly, the ICC Chief Prosecutor feels that way. I would nonetheless encourage greater reticence in such instances for the criminal law. Any such circumspection, however, runs against the current *Zeitgeist*. The increasing emergence of the right *to* criminal punishment further pushes courts as the primary place in which to host such conversations[13] – this is a move that I find somewhat disconcerting.

Although Kremnitzer makes a bold case for retributivism in the punishment of senior perpetrators of atrocity crimes, for the most part international lawyers are timid in this regard. International lawyers tend to see retributive impulses as unappealing, visceral and primeval. The ICTY Appeals Chamber has therefore carefully emphasized that 'retribution should not be misunderstood as a way of expressing revenge or vengeance'.[14] Rather, it conceives of retribution as the 'expression of condemnation and outrage of the international community'.[15] In this regard, retributive motivations meander in the direction of expressivism. The expressivist punishes to strengthen faith in rule of law among the general public, as opposed to punishing simply because the perpetrator deserves it or will be deterred by it. From an expressivist perspective, punishment proactively embeds the normative value of law within the community. This in theory leads to positive general prevention.

On this note, might one purpose of prosecuting victims who victimize be to expose the etiology of atrocity, i.e., the reality that ordinary people who face 'choiceless choices' might inflict terrible harms on others, and those others who survive those harms may feel a need to speak of those harms, and that when speaking of harms inflicted by the hands of another victim it may be very difficult for that speaker to be properly listened to? If so, then, are criminal trials a suitable venue to host these conversations? Are criminal trials a congenial place to narrate the historical realities that atrocity becomes massive because large numbers of compromised and desperate individuals become perpetrators? The Israeli Kapo trials would suggest caution in this regard. So,

[12] Ramos, 'Dominic Ongwen on Trial'.

[13] On the victims' right to punishment for international crimes, see, e.g., the contribution by Jens David Ohlin in Chapter 15. For a critique, see S. Mohamed, 'Criminal Punishment as a Human Right?' (working draft paper on file with the author, 2018).

[14] ICTY, Judgement of 17 December 2004 (AC), *Kordić and Čerkez*, IT-95-14/2-A, para. 1075. The ICC proceeds similarly: ICC, Decision of 23 May 2014 (TC), *Katanga*, ICC-01/04-01/07, para. 38.

[15] ICTY, Judgment of 2 December 2003 (TC), *Nikolić*, IT-02-60/1-S, para. 86.

too, would the ongoing Ongwen proceedings. Perhaps other venues, for example, non-judicial ones, might be more suitable.

II EXPRESSIVISM AND TRUTH

Daniela Demko's treatment of expressivism, while at times cryptic, remains comprehensive. Her chapter returns me, or I return her chapter back to, Bulgakov's marvelous surrealistic journey that toggles between memory and fantasy; to mistress Margarita's bouncy broom-ride, during which she bumps joyfully into things in the dark night; and then also to the devil who does not grant light but instead grants rest, thereby preferring peace to truth. Throughout Demko's work – as with Bulgakov's, and as with expressivists generally – the notion of truth looms large, notably Pontius Pilate's agony over what is the truth and whether a court of law can deliver truths at all, and – if so – what sorts of truths. If communication is central to the expressive function, then how good are courts at communicating?

Demko's chapter is a *bouillabaisse* that stews many references: her effort is not on emphasis but more diffusely on emphases. Her treatment of expressivism is sprawling. She connects expressivism to other justifications for punishment, though consistently the communicative aspect surfaces. Unlike Kremnitzer and Holtermann, who ground their words in the lives of people (Kapos and child soldiers in Kremnitzer's case, the Iraq War and the leaders of the UK and Denmark in Holtermann's case), Demko operates at a disembodied level. There are no actual people – neither protagonists nor antagonists (nor bystanders or side-standers) in her chapter. There is only law – considerable law, law personified – which Demko unfurls with sophistication.

Demko's *bouillabaisse* has many ingredients. I focus on two: the ordinal superiority of law's 'truths' vis-à-vis other truths and, paradoxically, the internal fragility of law's 'truths' vis-à-vis themselves. As far as communicators go, I feel that courts talk over others while at times delivering a fragmented and fragile message. Although I remain attracted to expressivist theory as among the most realistic ambitions of international punishment, as I have elaborated upon in earlier work,[16] as time passes I worry a bit more about the externalities that may arise when, paraphrasing Marshall McLuhan, the medium (the court) becomes the message.[17]

[16] Drumbl, *Atrocity, Punishment, and International Law*, Chapter 6.

[17] M. McLuhan, *Understanding Media: The Extensions of Man* (Massachusetts; Massachusetts Institute of Technology Press, 1964).

As to truth(s), Demko makes the following differentiation:

> With regard to the purpose of protecting the truth, a differentiation must be drawn between the international criminal law-related determination of the truth (which is connected with criminal proceedings against the accused offender) on the one hand and the determination of the truth (beyond the criminal proceedings) in order to clarify the entire historical event on the other hand.[18]

Demko perseveres. She notes that the 'international criminal law-related determination of the truth' is a 'necessary pre-requisite for the subsequent determination of the existence or non-existence of individual criminal responsibility of the accused offender'. When it comes to the broader

> determination of the truth (beyond the criminal proceedings) in order to clarify the entire historical event, criminal proceedings and international punishment [. . .] do not provide a comprehensive clarification of the entire historical event, but guarantee the clarification of at least a part thereof (namely, the international criminal law-related part referring to the international crime of the accused offender).

According to Demko:

> Criminal proceedings and international punishment as such are therefore not sufficient for a comprehensive clarification of the entire historical event, but criminal proceedings and international punishment make an important and necessary contribution to a subsequent comprehensive clarification and review of the entire historical event [. . .]

Fair enough. But from where do the remaining contributions emerge? Criminal trials, as South African Justice Albie Sachs has beautifully posited, convey those microscopic truths indulged by the formal (and often exclusionary) rules of procedure and evidence; criminal trials do not foster dialogic or experiential truths.[19] In fact, as Demko herself notes, the truths of individual criminal punishment depend on the denial and abnegation of collective responsibility.[20] Yet atrocity fundamentally is a story of the collective. Atrocity

[18] Quotations in this discussion are from the contribution by Daniela Demko in Chapter 11 (Section IV).

[19] A. Sachs, Lecture at Columbia University School of Law of 13 April 1999, discussed in Drumbl, *Atrocity, Punishment, and International Law*, 275 fn. 126.

[20] See Demko's contribution in Chapter 20 (p. 194): '[B]y assigning responsibility to the offender, international punishment at the same time expresses, (second), that the guilt for the international crime is not borne by a collective, but rather by the offender who is individually criminally responsible for the international crime committed the offender has committed.'

is sourced by many factors that collude and collide; these factors connive and conflate and conspire. Mass violence necessarily entails a myriad of actions and reactions that in the minds of many individuals fall short of genocidal intent, or tangible *mens rea*, but without which the hate could never metastasize into something normal (or, *pace* Arendt, banal). The condition precedent of atrocity is the participation of the many. For the most part this participation, especially of benefitting bystanders and complicit side-standers, is not caught (or seen) by the criminal law nor captured by its vocabulary or vernacular. The criminal law thereby offers a rather distorted photograph of what happened and why and because of whom. And it is a convenient 'truthiness', after all, because it absolves the many of their responsibility by individualizing everything onto the shoulders of the (a) few. The guilt of a handful triggers the innocence of the multitudes.

The truth(s) of the law will not really bear contestations from the other truth(s) that Sachs identifies. Other sources may supplement and complement law's truths but they may not contradict them. Hence, the official narrative of 1994 Rwanda is that generated by the ICTR, which only prosecuted horrific Hutu power genocide. So, too, in Sierra Leone, where the work of the Sierra Leone Truth and Reconciliation Commission was operationally rendered subordinate to that of the Special Court for Sierra Leone.[21] Demko's 'necessary' but 'not sufficient' presence of criminal proceedings in the communicative process belies the reality of criminal proceedings as *controlling* the narrative and as authenticating the historical record. Hence when criminal proceedings assign responsibility they do so in a rather ideological manner. They construct the past in a way that in fact is rather assuaging for many members of aggressor collectives. While soothing for aggressor societies because these 'truths' may ease political and social transition and thereby promote peace through a combination of dignity and denialism, this is a calculated utilitarian move. It is not a deracination of what actually happened. It is the pursuit of rest, not light.

On the other hand, from within law, contradictions may emerge. Here, the role of dissenting judges looms large. What is the official narrative of the Tokyo Tribunal? It is, putatively, that the guilt of the Japanese Class 'A' war criminals (on charges of crimes against the peace and crimes against humanity) narrated a 'truthy' story of Japan's pursuit of imperialist ambitions at a time when aggressive imperialism no longer could be pursued as a strategy. Yet,

[21] M. Sirleaf, 'Regional Approach to Transitional Justice? Examining the Special Court for Sierra Leone and the Truth and Reconciliation Commission for Liberia' (2009) 21 *Florida Journal of International Law* 209, 234.

other counter-'truths' emerged, notably in the stinging (and long-winded) dissent of Judge Pal, the Indian judge, who saw things differently. Pal saw Japan as mimicking the West and losing in a war but that loss did not equate to finding Japan guilty of international crimes as those crimes had not yet been defined in international law and, moreover, could only become defined once structural racism and economic inequities were overcome in a truly egalitarian world-order. Hence, while law may not permit contradictions from outside – e.g., contestations in the kinds of expressive narratives Sachs writes about (namely, from truth commissions) – law may tolerate contradictions from within, e.g., the fracturing power of the dissent.[22] Another source of fragmentation can be chalked up to the realities of appeals judges overturning certain narratives that may have led to convictions at trial, or vice versa. The June 2018 ICC Appeals Chamber judgment in *Bemba*, for example, took a very different view on command responsibility than the Trial Chamber, leading to a highly controversial acquittal. Following *Bemba*, what *is* command responsibility? How to be sure that one might or might not be liable? These questions bear upon the deterrence function, to be discussed next in this commentary.

For expressivism, to recap, all this is to say that law's truths may dominate others but, in turn, may be less clear, singular and coherent than the expressivist may fancy. The fact remains: when the truth of 'what happened' and 'why' hinges upon the convictions of a few – the 'international criminal law-related' truth in Demko's words – the result is an authenticated history that bends and distorts, that excludes and constrains, and is riddled with partiality and incompleteness. If communication matters so much, then, is the courtroom necessarily the best communicator? Procurator Pilate himself knows it is not, and knows better than to ask too much of it.

Within the law-speaking function, moreover, unison may be lacking. The dissent may shatter. And silences emerge as well: e.g., the cases of those perpetrators deliberately not accused for a whole host of tactical reasons. Returning to 1946 Tokyo, General MacArthur omitted the self-evidently most responsible offender, the Emperor, because of MacArthur's professed wish to preserve His (the Emperor's) dignity and thereby ease peace, not full light, in the aftermath of the Allied victory, once again like the devil's work in Bulgakov's *The Master and Margarita*.

Expressivism, moreover, connects criminal punishment to the voicing of outrage and also to the consolidation of law and, thereby, towards positive

[22] At Tokyo, General MacArthur made a firm yet ultimately unsuccessful push not to have any dissents at all.

general prevention.[23] On this latter note, expressivism, as Demko observes, moves into the direction of deterrence.

III DETERRENCE

General deterrence considers that the purpose of prosecuting and punishing individuals who commit mass atrocity is utilitarian in nature, i.e., there to dissuade others from offending in the future. Specific deterrence implies that punishing the offender will deter that one offender from re-offending. When the activity of international criminal justice institutions is taken as a whole, however, the focus of deterrence remains oriented towards general deterrence. From a deterrence perspective, punishment is inflicted because of the consequentialist effect of reducing the incidence of crime: 'The generality of men are naturally apt to be swayed by fear rather than reverence, and to refrain from evil rather because of the punishment that it brings than because of its own foulness.'[24]

Whether the sentencing practices of international institutions attains their avowed deterrent goals remains a thoroughly unsettled question. I remain unconvinced.[25] So do others,[26] including Kremnitzer who posits that the specificity of extraordinary international criminality, in particular when fuelled by hate and socialization and propaganda, atrophies the power of deterrence.[27]

Holtermann disagrees. Holtermann is committed to making a case for deterrence as a penological aspiration, specifically within the context of the

[23] See Demko's contribution in Chapter 11, Section II.2: 'Positive affirmative general prevention as the central aspect of the statement of content of international punishment.'

[24] Aristotle, *The Nicomachean Ethics*, Book 10, Chapter 9 (L. Brown (ed.), *Aristotle – The Nicomachean Ethics* (translation D. Ross) (Oxford: Oxford University Press, 2009).

[25] Drumbl, *Atrocity, Punishment, and International Law*.

[26] P. McAuliffe, 'Suspended Disbelief? The Curious Endurance of the Deterrence Rationale in International Criminal Law' (2012) 10 *New Zealand Journal of Public and International Law* 227.

[27] See Kremnitzer's contribution to this volume in Chapter 10 (p. 165):

> [I]f we assume a state of affairs in which penology is exclusively deterrence-centered, we will find it difficult to justify punishment of hate crimes, since those are typically committed out of irrational motives and thus are unlikely to be deterred. Similarly, assume a situation of systematic and organized extermination of a certain population, in which the perpetrators are sympathetic to other populations and no other population is under risk. According to a strict deterrence approach, there is no justification to punish in such case.

See also fn. 19): 'In general, deterrence is largely ineffective in regards to crimes committed without any rational thinking process.'

ICC. He is adamant in this regard, and I greatly admire his tenacity. In his current project, Holtermann begins anecdotally with former Danish Prime Minister Rasmussen and former British Prime Minister Blair. Holtermann returns the reader to the sad hurly-burly around the US-led 'coalition' invasion of Iraq in 2003. Holtermann recounts how, in their respective eleventh hour(s) of deciding whether to join this invasion or not, Rasmussen and Blair both were concerned with the prospect that they might 'be brought before the ICC'.[28] While it is true that aggression was not then a crime over which the ICC had jurisdiction, so neither leader actually could have been brought to the ICC, both leaders commissioned lawyers to advise them about the conceptual legality of the invasion. The advice, as legal advice often is, was splintered and fragmented, chalk-full of caveats, and triggered resignations and replacements. No surprise, after all, for such is often the case in many contexts – Enron, a spectacular corporate implosion, had officials who also decided based upon advice by retained legal counsel. The fact remains, however, that the Iraqi invasion happened. And both the Danes and the British indeed joined in. The Danish and British leaders asked about lawfulness, got answers, and *still did it anyway*.

For Holtermann, the fact that these two leaders felt compelled to ask this question 'throw[s] interesting new light on ongoing debates about the philosophical justifiability of the International Criminal Court', all the more so now because, unlike at the time of the Iraqi invasion, the crime of aggression has moved forward in terms of concretizing within the ICC's jurisdiction. After all, as of July 17, 2018, the ICC will be able to exercise jurisdiction regarding the crime of aggression.

Holtermann develops a model he calls the 'Swiss cheese' model. Deterrence is a stack of Swiss cheese layered upon criminal conduct. Swiss cheese, of course, has holes. So while some criminal conduct is deterred, so to speak, other conduct slips through the holes in the cheese. The more layers of cheese that are placed on top of each other, according to Holtermann, the more conduct is deterred because there are fewer holes. As the ICC is another layer of Swiss cheese placed upon other layers of cheese (those ostensibly provided inter alia by national justice systems), the simple fact that another layer of cheese exists helps deter atrocity because this layering shrinks the holes. This only works, of course, if the different slices of cheese have holes in different places. Holtermann assumes that the slice of 'deterrence' provided by the ICC has holes that do not correspond to the holes already existent in the other slices.

[28] See the contribution by Jakob v.H. Holtermann in Chapter 9.

In the end, the core of Holtermann's dogged argument is actually rather anemic, and heavily qualified, namely – the italics being his own – that by virtue of the ICC:

> *Some* potential perpetrators will be deterred *some* of the time, and that a *sufficient number* of potential perpetrators will be deterred to outweigh the cost of producing this effect[29].

As for the cost, the operating budget to date of the ICC has been over USD 1 billion.[30] It has over 900 staff members working in a swanky new building.[31] In seventeen years of operation the ICC has convicted a total of four individuals, each associated with rebel groups: three in the DRC and one in Mali (the latter on a guilty plea). One of these convictions is under appeal; a fifth conviction, that of Bemba, was overturned on appeal.

One gap with the deterrence value of international criminal law, even in cases where some rationality can be assumed (i.e., outside of the case of Kremnitzer's example of mass hate crimes), is that as the content of the law drifts away from massive hate crimes the actual question of whether something is legal or illegal becomes more and more nebulous. Iraq is a case in point. There was no clear advice. The law itself is gauzy. One can always see oneself as acting within the law in such instances, so the deterrent value of the law fades.

Holtermann dismisses 'critics' (including me), namely, scholars who question the ICC's deterrent effect. For Holtermann, doubters 'propound' a 'bleak view' which has become 'widespread'. Critics, according to Holtermann, are simply uncharitable. For Holtermann, *critics* become *cynics*.

As I read Holtermann, I recall the Gospel of John (John 20:24–29), to wit, John's account of Thomas, the Doubting Apostle. Thomas was not initially present following Jesus's resurrection when Jesus came to visit the eleven others. When the others told Thomas what they had seen, Thomas did not believe them. Thomas doubted. Jesus then appears to Thomas. Jesus chides Thomas, Jesus really guts him, for his lack of faith:

> Now Thomas, one of the Twelve, was not with the disciples when Jesus came. So the other disciples told him, 'We have seen the Lord!'
>
> But he said to them, 'Unless I see the nail marks in his hands and put my finger where the nails were, and put my hand into his side, I will not believe.'

[29] See Holtermann's contribution in Chapter 9 (p. 144).

[30] See www.theguardian.com/global-development-professionals-network/2017/apr/05/international-criminal-court-fit-purpose.

[31] See www.icc-cpi.int/about.

> A week later his disciples were in the house again, and Thomas was with them. Though the doors were locked, Jesus came and stood among them and said, 'Peace be with you!' Then he said to Thomas, 'Put your finger here; see my hands. Reach out your hand and put it into my side. Stop doubting and believe.'
>
> Thomas said to him, 'My Lord and my God!'
>
> Then Jesus told him, 'Because you have seen me, you have believed; blessed are those who have not seen and yet have believed.'

Deterrence cannot be seen. Nor heard. At best it can be believed though a combination of anecdote, superimposition to The Hague of what is supposed to happen in national legal systems for ordinary crimes, and faith. Yet for every anecdote marshalled in favour of an erstwhile perpetrator who 'turned the other cheek', there is an anecdote of a perpetrator who did not, or of perpetrators who still remain in power. The likelihood of getting caught is more influential than any other factor in discouraging criminal conduct. Yet the likelihood of getting caught and prosecuted by an international institution in cases of atrocity crimes remains low, unless of course one is a rebel targeted by a state party who outsources the judicialization of the conflict to the ICC.

In the end, Pádraig McAuliffe captures it well when he suggests that support of the deterrence value of international criminal law roots in 'theological terms', like much of human rights discourse that promotes an 'eschatological will to extricate society from the tragedy of history'.[32] So, indeed, 'blessed are those who have not seen and yet have believed'. Blessed are those who see deterrence where others see emptiness or false exuberance; blessed are those who believe without seeing nail marks and wounds, compelling facts or figures. At the end of the day, then, the question boils down to who discharges the burden of proof? Is it the believer or the doubter? Is the assumption that the ICC deters just because it exists? Is this a *res ipsa loquitur* argument? In light of great difficulty in locating nail marks, and facts and figures, the theological move is easy to make, that is, to cast the non-believer as failing, as cynical, as petulant, as part of the problem, as a selfish obstacle to the self-evidently linear path of the arc of justice. And when the ICC staggers and falls, like Jesus along the fourteen Stations of the Cross – then it behooves the believers to believe even more. True belief grows in the face of adversity. Such is the beauty of faith.

[32] McAuliffe, 'Suspended Disbelief?', 243.

The content of international criminal law spans a gamut. At its core, international criminal law seeks to prohibit massive collectively fuelled discrimination- and hate-based violence (genocide, core crimes against humanity). This is the kind of violence that I (along with many others, including Kremnitzer) posit is the least likely to involve the rational cost-benefit analysis upon which the effectiveness of deterrence hinges. Yet to date the ICC has prosecuted very little of this violence. It has instead largely convicted for war crimes, including ones relatively lacking in gravity (pillage, child soldiering and intentional attacks on cultural property) and only in cases involving rebel forces (no state actors). Yet perhaps these are the sorts of crimes that can best be deterred by an international institution. Perhaps they can be best deterred because national armies can adopt rules that prohibit the enlistment of minors (though, once again the ICC has not convicted any national actor); can develop specific rules that protect cultural buildings in armed conflict; can devise oversight over the commander who pillages. Perhaps these kinds of crimes are more deterrable than the massive core crimes. And perhaps, then, this is where the Swiss cheese of the ICC adds something. Perhaps by clarifying the law regarding these distant crimes some detectable deterrence function can be found.

But such a vision of the ICC conflicts with how Holtermann sees it. For Holtermann, the ICC's cheese contribution is that it is 'predominantly a big fish court going after political and military leaders' who would act 'under less situational pressure than foot soldiers' and, hence, are putatively more deterrable.[33] The point remains, however, that the ICC has been utterly unsuccessful in bringing political and military leaders within its remit, let alone convicting them – the three final convicts to date have been a middling Koranic teacher in Timbuktu who affiliated with Al Qaeda in the Maghreb and two rebel leaders in the Democratic Republic of the Congo. No big fish here. As for the inchoate crime of aggression, as a matter of black-letter law only the most senior political and military leadership of a state can be prosecuted. Aggression is the only ICC crime with a leadership requirement. In light of the middling fish the ICC has been able to catch, it seems that the net of the crime of aggression will catch very little. But once again we can hope. But this leads to another question. What if there is in fact a deterrent value to the crime of aggression. Let us believe. What sorts of aggressive acts shall be deterred? Acts undertaken in a sense of self-defence? These are unlikely to be deterred, as such acts might be justifiable under the colour of

[33] See Holtermann's contribution in Chapter 9 (Section II.2b).

law and, besides, which leader wishes to abandon state sovereignty on the altar of legalisms? As for Iraqi-style invasions and Ukraine-style interventions, well, it is quite easy to agree that deterring these sorts of acts might be desirable, but what about humanitarian duties to protect? What leader will take a risk to pursue a humanitarian armed entanglement elsewhere if that could mean being prosecuted for initiating an aggressive war? Perhaps in the end we are better off with fewer such 'intercessions' meaning that more current 'human rights abusers' remain in power.

As for the ongoing ICC proceedings against Ongwen, which involve graver crimes than the three of the ICC's other convictions to date, who exactly are these proceedings intended to deter? Are they to deter a child abducted into an armed group and tormented for many years from rising in the ranks of that group and ultimately becoming an adult who refuses to command? That is a tall order and, to be frank, applies to a very limited set of individuals.

Holtermann becomes impatient with scholars, such as myself, who no longer wish to talk too much about the ICC's role in deterrence because of the endless unprovabilities and incommensurabilities of the conversation. I worry, in addition, that these circular conversations focus our collective gazes on the ICC which, in the grand scheme of things, is under tremendous strain – so many ambitions and altitudinous goals are placed on its sloping shoulders such that its gait is becoming shuffling. The cross of these hopes and dreams might simply be too much for the ICC to bear. Perhaps it might be more interesting to shy way from adding more judicial Swiss cheese to the conversation and instead experiment with different food products – ham, lettuce, tomatoes – something else, just to spruce and spice things up, perhaps something whose holes are not so evident; hence, to nudge a move towards pluralism and diversity and away from monoculture. But this would mean looking beyond and around the ICC, and criminal law generally. Perhaps more productive conversations could involve different questions. What sorts of initiatives could deter better, or more innovatively, and at far less cost? Every time we talk about the deterrent effect of the ICC, opportunity costs arise – these are the opportunity costs of the conversations not had, the paths not taken, roads not followed, trails not pursued. Kremnitzer mentions the principle of the conservation of energy in his contribution. This is a neat idea. I would like to apply it here. I would like to apply it to trying to move beyond the well-worn debates of whether (hopefully, keeping fingers – and toes – crossed) deterring 'some' perpetrators 'some of the time' at the ICC's massive cost and meagre results is worth it. Robert Frost is inspirational here, with his 1916 poem *The Road Not Taken*, which was published in a collection entitled

'Mountain Interval'. Beginning with two roads that 'diverged in a yellow wood', Frost wonders where to wander:

> I shall be telling this with a sigh
> Somewhere ages and ages hence:
> Two roads diverged in a wood, and I –
> I took the one less traveled by,
> And that has made all the difference.

IV CONCLUSION

Perhaps what emerges most from the triptych of these three impressive contributions is that, when it comes to punishing perpetrators of massive hate crimes, as international criminal lawyers we do not really know what we are doing or why we do what we do. We guess and shadowbox with each other's best guesses. And perhaps that is alright. Punishment is a window into the soul, in a sense, and our souls are rich and textured, hopeful and fearful, optimistic and pessimistic alike. Perhaps none of retribution, deterrence or expressivism is capable of scientism, certitude or causation. And that is fine too. But there is one part, or consequence, that is less fine to me. And that involves the triumph of the courtroom and jailhouse, iconically, as the 'best' way to deliver justice in the aftermath of atrocity. On this note, if we are muddling through doing what we do when it comes to punishing, then perhaps we should be less sanguine about the self-evident righteousness (or appositeness) of courtrooms, legalism and sequestered incarceration as the best way forward, in a progressive sense, to spark the arc that bends towards justice in the aftermath of mass atrocity. Perhaps justice should be about much more than law. If so, law should recede, not regale. Rather than *exhausting* ourselves justifying what it is that we (international criminal lawyers) do, through all these claims and theories, perhaps we should *busy* ourselves by looking beyond our capacities.

13

Positive General Prevention and the Idea of Civic Courage in International Criminal Law

KLAUS GÜNTHER

Among the many different purposes and functions of international criminal justice and punishment that have been suggested, expressive or communicative functions seem to be very prominent. Whereas preventive functions with regard to future crimes and atrocities committed by governments are at least contestable for empirical reasons, and retributive functions can be doubted for moral reasons already on the level of national criminal law, a communicative function seems to be obvious. One can hardly deny that proceedings, as well as convictions, before an international criminal court are always gaining great public attention on a global scale. The observation that criminal processes and convictions as well as punishments communicate certain messages to the public, primarily on a national level, is one of the main reasons for the suggestion that the communicative aspect of criminal justice is at least as important as its other preventive, retributive and restorative functions.[1]

But, of course, everything depends on the answer to the question, Which kinds of messages are expressed or communicated by criminal justice?[2] The empirical observation that there are certain messages does not tell anything about their propositional content and purpose. Additionally, it does not tell anything about its normative meaning and justification. Prima facie, one could say that the message sent by criminal conviction and punishment under

[1] J. Feinberg, 'The Expressive Function of Punishment', and A. von Hirsch, 'Censure and Proportionality', both reprinted in R.A. Duff and D. Garland (eds.), *A Reader on Punishment* (Oxford: Oxford University Press, 1995). For an analysis of the expressive function of law in general see C. Sunstein, 'On the Expressive Function of Law' (1996) 144 *University of Pennsylvania Law Review* 2021. On communicative theories of punishment see T. Hörnle, *Straftheorien*, 2nd ed. (Tübingen: Mohr Siebeck, 2017).

[2] See, e.g., the definition of an expressive theory of punishment in international criminal law developed by Daniela Demko in Chapter 11.

an authoritarian, fascist regime violating the human rights of minorities will differ from the message sent in a constitutional, democratic state taking human rights seriously. It is also obvious that international criminal law and in particular the judgments of the International Criminal Court (ICC) as well as its predecessors such as the International Criminal Tribunal for the former Yugoslavia (ICTY) or the International Criminal Tribunal for Rwanda (ICTR) gain much public attention in the mass media on a global scale. The spectre of possible messages ranges here from satisfying the victim, declaring the wrongfulness of the atrocities, making the defendant responsible, etc.

In the following, I shall give a short sketch of the communicative structure of criminal law in general and of international criminal law in particular. In the next step, I shall suggest a justifiable interpretation of the message. In the last step, I shall draw some consequences, also for national criminal law.

I THE COMMUNICATIVE STRUCTURE OF CRIMINAL LAW

With regard to the formal structure of criminal law, two aspects are relevant. First, one has to distinguish the different parts or stages of criminal law that are sending messages, and second, one has to identify the addressees of the messages.

With regard to the first aspect, the different parts or stages of criminal law, many expressivist theories and justifications focus on punishment only. Joel Feinberg, who was one of the first legal scholars to elaborate on the expressivist meaning, began with the question, What distinguishes punishment from other sanctions like taxes or administrative penalties?[3] He argued that it is the expressivist meaning that makes the difference. Penalties and punishment both turn out to be a kind of hard treatment – they make someone suffer, either by losing her[4] freedom, by paying money or by other measures that cause suffering. Only punishment has an additional symbolic dimension by which disapproval of the unlawful behaviour is expressed, its wrongfulness rejected and the perpetrator censured. But punishment is only the final stage of a whole process of reaction on crime. It is a communicative sequence, which begins with criminal law legislation, goes to the crime itself and then

3 Feinberg, 'The Expressive Function of Punishment' and von Hirsch, 'Censure and Proportionality'.

4 Although 'he or she' is used generally in this book, the generic feminine is used in this chapter, due to the large number of instances.

leads to the criminal procedure of imputation and attribution of responsibility, the judgment and, finally, to punishment.[5]

With regard to the second aspect of the addressees of communication, one has to distinguish between three different directions. The criminal justice system sends its message to different addressees with a different emphasis, taking into account the specific situation of each of them. The first is related to the offender, the second to the victim and the third to society, the general public. In the following, I shall briefly consider the different stages of the communicative sequence and elaborate on the three different directions.

Criminal legislation and the criminal law itself publicly declare a certain behaviour as criminal by announcing that it will be punished. This means that the behaviour is rejected by legislator, and that it is not tolerated or accepted. Additionally, when legislation is democratic and constitutional, criminal law is considered as justified by public reasons which are and could be shared by the members of the community. Under a democratic or republican legislation, these reasons emerge from a deliberative and inclusive public process of opinion and will formation. 'In claiming authority over the citizens, it claims that there are good reasons, grounded in the community's values for them to eschew such wrongs. [...] It speaks to the citizens as members of the normative community.'[6] It is also important to see that in a democratic republic, citizens recognize each other as co-legislators, that is, they share the normative authority, which they exercise over themselves as the law's addressees. Having the political right (not the obligation) to participate in the legislative process by raising one's voice in the public sphere is also a procedural reason that justifies the claim to obey the law. Recognition as a co-legislator also implies the mutual attribution of responsibility as a precondition for participation in the public sphere and the deliberative political process of opinion and will formation. One's actions and assertions can be accounted to one's communicative authority as a person who takes responsibility.

The next step in the communicative sequence is the crime itself. The crime is the event that activates the communicative content of the law in a particular case. Crimes violate the legal norm that prohibits the act that was committed by the perpetrator. Many crimes also violate another person, the victim, who is hurt and humiliated, sometimes even traumatized by the criminal act. In

5 K. Günther, 'Crime and Punishment as Communication' in A.P. Simester, A. Du Bois-Pedain and U. Neumann (eds.), *Liberal Criminal Theory, Essays for Andrew von Hirsch* (Oxford: Hart, 2014), 123.

6 R.A. Duff, *Punishment, Communication, and Community* (Oxford: Oxford University Press, 2003), 80 seq.

addition, the crime conveys a communicative message too. To the extent that the perpetrator can be recognized as a responsible person, her action has a meaning, includes a communicative assertion. On the one hand, the meaning of the act consists in the perpetrator's individual intention, what she wants to get by the crime as a means (e.g., committing a robbery to get money). However, in addition, the act has an objective meaning too. The action communicates the assertion, that the relevant norm of criminal law (e.g., prohibition of robbery) shall not be valid, and that instead of the valid criminal law another norm, the perpetrator's norm, shall be considered as valid. A perpetrator who commits a robbery publicly declares that theft is permitted and that there shall be no legal property as well as that the psycho-physical integrity of another person may be damaged in favour of the money she wants to have. The perpetrator usurps the normative authority of a legislator for herself and declares that a new law shall be valid. In a democratic republic where citizens recognize each other as co-legislators, the perpetrator's assertion of a new norm has an additional meaning. The perpetrator abuses her status as a co-legislator in order usurp normative authority for her alone, excluding all other citizens of the normative community. The usurpation of normative authority by the perpetrator conveys also a message to the victim, namely, that she has no voice, no say against the normative authority of the perpetrator, that her 'no' can be ignored. By this the perpetrator dominates the victim. In an authoritarian state, a crime lacks this additional meaning, it is nothing more than a fight between two normative authorities, the perpetrator openly challenges and provokes the legislator, and the crime causes suffering to the victim.

The third stage is the criminal trial itself. The trial is the public scene where the law's communicative message is performed with regard to a particular case of its violation and an individual offender. For this purpose, the offender may legally be forced to appear on stage, in order to confront her with the valid norms she has (probably) violated. To confront the offender means that she will be brought to a public forum where she has a status as a defendant who has a voice. She is 'called to account' and she may 'render account', i.e., the offender 'is bound to answer to his fellow citizens for his alleged public wrongs, and the trial is the formal process through which he is to answer'.[7] Trials also have the purpose of finding the truth about the crime, because truth is a necessary prerequisite for calling a defendant to account, and

7 R.A. Duff, 'Process, not Punishment: The Importance of Criminal Trials for Transitional and Transnational Justice' (2014) *University of Minnesota Law School Legal Studies Research Paper Series*, Research Paper No. 14–03, 5.

therefore also for a justified performance of the law's communicative message.[8] If the facts about the case have been proven sufficiently according to fair procedural rules to the defendant's detriment, the communicative act of a legal conviction of the offender has to be performed. The violated norm will be re-stated, its validity demonstrated or, as Anthony Duff says, the trial and the conviction are 'an assertion or demonstration of the law's authority' over the offender, but also with regard to the community and the victim.[9] It reassures the community's belief in the shared reasons for its law and, in a democratic republic, it restores its own normative authority by rejecting the defendant's usurpation. The victim is recognized as a fellow-citizen whose trust in the validity of the law was correct. She is reassured that the harm she had to suffer was not fate, nature or her own fault, but a wrong, which is not shared by her fellow-citizens.[10] An essential part of the message is also that the defendant is taken seriously as a person who is recognized as responsible person in a fair trial, and therefore as a fellow-citizen too, and not as a dangerous individual or an enemy against whom the community wages a war.[11] This part of the message also relates to the victim, and the community. The message that is sent by the legal procedure of a fair attribution of criminal responsibility is the confirmation and reproduction of the principle of individual responsibility as a fundamental principle of the normative community. It is a public performance where everybody can see (and learn) what it means to live together under a system of shared legal rules, where each citizen is responsible for her conduct und its consequences under the law, and where – in a democratic republic – each citizen has her share as a co-legislator in the collective responsibility for legislation.

Only the fourth and final stage of the criminal justice system and the communicative sequence of its operation leads to punishment with hard treatment. Most of the messages usually attributed to and communicated by punishment have already been sent by the trial before. Therefore, Duff is correct with his statement: 'Process, not punishment!'[12]

[8] On the communicative integration of truth into international punishment, see also the contribution by Danela Demko in Chapter 11 (Section IV).

[9] Duff, 'Process, not Punishment', 5.

[10] On this message to the victims, see also the contribution by Frank Neubacher in Chapter 3.

[11] However, according to Günther Jakobs, punishment according to international criminal law is punishment of enemies, not of citizens, see G. Jakobs, 'Bürgerstrafrecht und Feindstrafrecht' (2004) 5 *Höchstrichterliche Rechtsprechung im Strafrecht* 88.

[12] Duff, 'Process, not Punishment', 5.

II THE CONTENTS OF THE MESSAGE COMMUNICATED BY INTERNATIONAL PUNISHMENT

1 *Community and Dual Membership*

So far, we have dealt with national criminal law only or, in a more general fashion, with the communicative function of the whole criminal justice sequence within a particular normative community, such as a nation state. As one can see, important addressees of the communicative messages are the members of the community. This relates to the theories of positive general prevention. The core idea of the theories of positive general prevention is that punishment, as well as the legal procedure with a fair attribution of norm violation to the defendant and the treatment of the defendant as a responsible person as well as a member of the community, shall altogether contribute to the restoration of the people's trust in the validity of criminal law. In addition, the people's trust in the validity of the legal rules of procedure, imputation and attribution of responsibility is activated and confirmed – in some cases against a widespread belief that a brief process with a harsh judgment were a better choice. Different to the conception of negative prevention by deterrence, which causes fear of punishment in the minds of the members of a community, the positive meaning of prevention stems from the fact that it re-builds and restores trust or overcomes possible irritations among the citizens about the validity of their criminal law.

With regard to international criminal law, the central question will be whether these messages could be easily transferred from the national to the international level. As Duff has demonstrated, this is possible with some modifications, in particular with regard to the normative community as its addressee.[13] If one focuses mainly on the general public order the normative community as the addressee of international criminal law, one usually takes the citizens of a nation state into account. But on the international level, we cannot find an analogy for this. As Duff has pointed out, in international criminal law the community of addressees is often defined as humankind, the international community or the community of nation states.[14] These definitions are obviously not wrong, but they are missing an important aspect. As long as people live in a global community that consists of nation states, international criminal law always points into two different directions. Apart from the international community (or its analogies), it always points at the

[13] Duff, 'Process, not Punishment', 5.

[14] Duff, 'Process, not Punishment', 5.

same time into the direction of the citizens of a nation state; not only to the citizenry as a whole, but also to each citizen individually. This leads to an essential change of the position of each citizen of a nation state. With the emergence of international criminal law, each citizen is now in a position where she is legally obliged to obey two different legal systems. The first one is the national legal system. Here, the law claims to have legitimate authority over its citizens – they have a corresponding duty to obey to the law. With the system of international criminal law, a second legal duty comes in. Each citizen has an additional duty to obey the norms of international criminal law. This means that each citizen has a legal duty to refrain from massive violations of elementary human rights on a grand scale.

2 *Norm Collisions and the Duty to Disobey*

Under normal circumstances, i.e., circumstances of a well-functioning national legal system with a democratic legislation, an independent judiciary and effective respect of human rights, it does not matter whether apart from the national legal system there is a second system of international criminal law. In this case, there is no collision between the two legal systems, because a well-functioning national legal system will hinder any attempt to transform it into a normative order that permits or commands actions as they are prohibited by international criminal law. One could say that the national or domestic legal system and international criminal law more or less coincide. Each citizen's legal duty to obey the norms of international criminal law remains silent as long as the fulfilment of the first duty to obey to the national legal norms does not violate international criminal law.[15]

The other case is completely different. When a well-functioning legal system changes and is transformed into an authoritarian state with a new legal order that commands, encourages or does not prohibit massive violations of elementary human rights, the sleeping duty to obey the norms of international criminal law wakes up and asks for obedience. In this case, a citizen could be confronted with two demands: first, to obey the norm of the national legal system; and second, to obey the norms of international criminal law. If obeying the norm of the national legal system means to violate international criminal law, a case of norm collision arises. Legal obedience to international

[15] Obviously, even in a well-functioning legal system as described above, there will be cases of violation of the constitution or of fundamental individual rights by the state. But as long as they do not happen on a grand scale and as long as there are effective legal remedies, one can still speak of a well-functioning legal system.

criminal law can only be exercised if the norms of the national legal order are not obeyed. Most collision cases are even more difficult. It is quite rare that a state transforms its legal order into an order that violates human rights openly and directly. In many cases, there is at least a dual state with a functioning order of private and administrative law, even with criminal law. Theft and murder are prosecuted and punished as in any other well-functioning legal system. There are only some norms, e.g., apartheid norms or other discriminatory norms against minorities of different kinds that violate human rights and lead to disadvantages and repression – sad enough – but not necessarily to the extent of a massive violation of human rights on the level of crimes according to international criminal law. Often, there are also norms that look fine on the surface in the law book, but are used for repressive measures and human rights violations in practice. Today, the 'fight against terrorism' is often justified by legal norms of criminal law that look quite innocent on the surface, but can be or are in fact instrumentalized to prosecute all political dissenters and oppositions. Nevertheless, one can find norms of empowerment that allow the executive branch to commit crimes that reach the stage of crimes against humanity or even genocide.

If one of the communicative messages of international criminal law is directed to each citizen of a nation state, its meaning in a case of norm collision can only be that each citizen has a duty to disobey the demands of the national legal system insofar as obedience means violating international criminal law. What it requires, then, is civic courage and the willingness to engage in non-conformist behaviour with regard to the repressive state and those parts of its legal order that directly or indirectly (through secondary rules or permissions) constitute massive human rights violations.[16]

3 *Critical Reflective Attitude with Regard to Human Rights Violations*

If the duty to disobey is the communicative message that is sent by international criminal law to each citizen of a nation state, who is in a position where she has to obey to two different systems of legal norms, then one should also take into account the consequences for the 'ordinary', the standard case.

[16] V. Reuss, *Zivilcourage als Strafzweck des Völkerstrafrechts. Was bedeutet positive Generalprävention in der globalen Zivilgesellschaft?*, (Münster: LIT Verlag, 2012); V. Reuss and K. Günther, 'Legitimation des Völkerstrafrechts in Deutschland – Völkerstrafrecht als Bürgerstrafrecht' in C. Safferling and S. Kirsch (eds.), *Völkerstrafrechtspolitik – Praxis des Völkerstrafrechts* (Berlin/Heidelberg: Springer, 2014), 127.

The observation that in the standard scenario, where both systems more or less coincide, the duty to obey international criminal law is dormant does not mean that nobody should care about it. The emergence of international criminal law goes hand in hand with a fundamental change in the position of each citizen. From this moment on, each citizen is not only a member of her national community under a national law, but also a member of a greater community based on truly human rights, as they are protected by international criminal law. In the role of a member of the community of human rights, each citizen has to take care and to pay attention for her national legal system.

The corresponding attitude of each citizen, which is required by this fundamental change and the dual status that each member has, could be characterized by H.L.A. Hart's notion of a *critical reflective attitude*. Hart introduces this concept in his analysis of the of *Concept of Law* in order to clarify the difference between two different types of obedience to the law.[17] The first type of attitude does not derive from an obligation to follow the law, but from mere habit or from the anticipation of negative consequences for deviant behaviour, e.g., the fear of punishment. In these cases, the addressee follows the law from an *external* or observer's point of view. Only the second type explains what it means to have an obligation to follow the law. This type of attitude consists of a certain practice of the addressees with regard to rules. It is made explicit by a certain conduct: criticism and self-criticism with regard to deviant behaviour, demands for conformity to a rule and the acknowledgement that such criticisms and demands are justified with regard to rule deviant behaviour. All this is articulated by a normative terminology. What is also important is – and this is constitutive for every social practice – that it is considered as 'a common standard' of behaviour, an attitude shared by all the members of a normative community:

> What is necessary is that there should be a *critical reflective attitude* to certain patterns of behaviour as a common standard, and that this should display itself in criticism (including self-criticism), demands for conformity, and in acknowledgements that such criticism and demands are justified, all of which find their characteristic expression in the *normative terminology* of 'ought', 'must', and 'should', 'right' and 'wrong'.[18]

[17] H.L.A. Hart, *The Concept of Law* (Oxford: Oxford University Press, 2012).

[18] Hart, *The Concept of Law*, 57 (emphasis added).

This description of the practice of a critical reflective attitude can be transferred to our analysis of the position a citizen has with regard to her domestic legal system. Here, the critical reflective attitude becomes a common standard among the citizens with regard to fundamental human rights and refers to the domestic legal system and its practice, and to the orders given or the measures taken with a justificatory relationship to the legal system. Human rights violations that are justified, permitted or not sanctioned by the domestic legal system and its officials are the relevant behaviour to which the critical reflective attitude refers. It is criticized by the citizens of a nation state as a deviant behaviour with regard to human rights (and the citizens should also criticize themselves if they tolerate such a practice without giving the priority to human rights). Citizens have to make use of a corresponding normative language of human rights by which they perform the criticism of their own domestic legal order.

Now we can explain what the communicative message of international criminal law is about. It demands and expects a critical reflective attitude of citizens with regard to the human rights legitimacy of their domestic law. Citizens have to examine their domestic law critically from the point of view of human rights, and they have to protest and resist against any transformation of their domestic law and its practice into a system of massive human rights violations. International criminal law states nothing less than a legal right and obligation of each citizen to acknowledge that she is also a member of the normative community of human rights, and, consequently, has a right and an obligation to examine and to evaluate her domestic law from the point of view of human rights. In a case of collision, it demands that she not obey the domestic law or the commands and orders that were proposed by officials of the state.

This is a central part of the justification of international criminal law. Each trial, each conviction, and each punishment communicate this message to each citizen of a nation state. The fact is often overlooked that, with international criminal law, the first step is taken to give the global normative community of human rights a more robust legal form. Although there is and should be no world-government with a monopoly of power to execute human rights for various reasons, it is important to notice that with the emergence of international criminal law and the institutionalization of the ICC, a huge step is taken towards the formation of a global normative community of human rights. In a more pathetic and probably utopian language, one could say that this is an important step towards a *cosmopolis of human rights*. From this moment on, we are all citizens of two worlds: of the nation state with its particular legal system and of the cosmopolis of human rights.

4 *The Punishment of High-Ranking Officials*

There seems to be an easy objection to this outline of the – probably utopian – message of international criminal law. The usual suspects of violations of international criminal law are not average citizens, but, mostly, high-ranking members of a government and of the military forces, or, in cases of civil wars, the leaders of armed groups and their officers. Until now, the majority of those who were convicted by the ICTY and other international ad hoc criminal Tribunals, and by the ICC were high-ranking officials, not to mention the defendants convicted in the Nuremberg Trial in 1946. Nobody denies that one of the major achievements of the ICC's Rome Statute consists of the rejection of the former doctrine of government members' immunity from criminal law. The interpretation of the communicative message does not deny that a message is *also* sent to the perpetrators, and I will sketch the meaning of this part of the message immediately below. But nevertheless, with the conviction (and hard treatment) of high-ranking officials, there is also a message sent to all of us, reminding us of our dual status as a citizen of a nation state and as a member of the normative community of human rights.

If this is one part of the communicative message, one could now also ask the opposite. Why punish the officials, the persons who have public power, members of government and of the army? Should they only be punished to send a message to ordinary citizens, who more or less remained silent and passive when the transformation of their well-functioning legal order into a repressive system began? There is one point in putting officials on trial under international criminal law that is intrinsically related to the general message sent to the citizens, which has not been mentioned yet. If the citizens in a case of norm collision are required to disobey their domestic legal system in order to obey the norms of human rights and international criminal law, they need something like an assurance that the obligation to obey the domestic order is invalid and unjustified. This is not only because human rights and international criminal law consider the domestic legal order as invalid. There are also general legal reasons for such an assurance. The communicative message of the conviction and punishment of officials entails the important aspect that it invalidates anti-human rights legislation as a legitimate *source of law*. It denies the legislative authority's claim to be legitimate.[19] The legislative authority was legally unable to enact valid law and was not justified in demanding legal obedience. This message assures the citizens that they

[19] For the concept of legitimate authority, see J. Raz, *The Authority of Law*, 2nd ed. (Oxford: Oxford University Press, 2009).

should not trust in the validity of their domestic law, while it restores trust in the validity of human rights and its protection by international criminal law. Again, we see the demanding message – the citizens shall trust in the validity of human rights and distrust their own domestic legal order.

In addition, there are also messages communicated directly to the perpetrators, elaborated by theories of positive general prevention and expressivist or communicative theories of punishment. There are in the main two messages that do not differ very much from the messages sent by national criminal law. The first one is the rejection of the perpetrators' unlawful act, i.e., the public declaration that she committed a wrong, which is not accepted by the members of the normative community. This rejection gets an additional meaning with regard to international criminal law. In most cases of crime, it is a necessary, but not always a difficult, task to deny the implicit rule that is expressed with the unlawful act. Theft, murder and rape are crimes that obviously cannot become a general rule of social relations. But sometimes, perpetrators present a justificatory narrative or a narrative of excuses for their unlawful act. Then it is important to look for the justificatory reasons and to decide whether they can be defended or not – in most cases, not. But in many cases of international criminal law, the government members and the high-ranking officers often tell long and comprehensive stories in order to justify or excuse the atrocities they had ordered, endorsed or benevolently tolerated. These stories are often more complicated and challenging than the simple or naive ones of a thief or a murderer. Because of their prominent position, many people who listen to these stories are therefore also tempted to believe in them. Often, these stories became a central part of the founding narrative of the state and of the ideology of the regime. If they stay undenied or undoubted, these narratives can dominate and structure the community's collective memory of the past, now and in the future. Therefore, it is even more important to dismantle and to reject them, and to deny the status of the perpetrator as an authentic and trustworthy narrator to whom one should listen and who should become a founder of the community's collective memory. The criminal procedure also has to take care that the perpetrator, even when convicted, may not leave the courtroom with his justificatory narrative being still intact and undoubted. For this reason, it is more important in an international than in a national criminal procedure to deny publicly the truth and correctness of these justificatory ideologies – in particular with regard to the victims, whose suffering is often justified by these ideologies.

Another essential part of the communicative message directed to the perpetrator was already mentioned in the beginning of this chapter. The perpetrator has to be taken seriously as a responsible person. This means that she should be recognized as a person who is responsive to reason, who may be called to account in order to confront her with the shared reasons of the normative community. Here, the normative reasons are the human rights with their claim to have priority over the domestic legal order. This also means that she has to be treated on trial as a member of the normative community of human rights – and not as an enemy against whom the normative community wages a war.

Finally, another consequence is the *de-authorization* of the members of government (or of those who had legislative power) as a legislator, as a source of valid law. This corresponds to the first communicative message, the denial of the validity of the legal system that permitted or commanded massive human rights violations.

5 *A Message to the Victims*

International criminal law does not only communicate the messages mentioned above to the citizens of the nation state and, at the same time, to the members of the normative community of human rights, and to the perpetrator, but also, perhaps most importantly, to the victim.[20] What is most important with regard to the victim is the public declaration that there is no justification or excuse for her suffering, but that it was a wrong which violated her human rights. This declaration is important, because it explains to the victim as well as to the perpetrator and to the members of the community that what happened to the victim was not bad luck, fate or the effect of a natural event such as an earthquake. As already mentioned earlier in this section, perpetrators often like to present justification narratives for their atrocities and ideologies that suggest they were necessary for the survival of the normative community against certain enemies, or that they were unavoidable because of other reasons, like, e.g., a battle between Good and Bad. If those justification narratives were believed by other citizens, they also determine the view they have of the victim, and consequently, the view the victim has on herself, i.e., that she was on the 'wrong side' of the fictious battle. In addition, with the declaration that what happened was a wrong the victim is recognized and re-integrated into the normative community as an equal citizen. Furthermore, mirroring the attribution of responsibility to the perpetrator, the victim receives the message that the wrong she suffered was the perpetrator's fault and not her own. This part of the message is necessary in order to overcome

[20] On victims as addressees of the message communicated by international punishment, see the contribution by Philipp Ambach in Chapter 20.

the experience of helplessness by the victim that, if it became a habit, could cause depression, passivity and a serious lack of self-confidence. These psychological deficits could also damage her status as an equal citizen and her ability to make use of her political rights.

Again, there are some additional features of the message that come from the specific properties of international criminal law. First of all, the victim's critical reflective attitude towards her domestic legal system is confirmed and re-affirmed, so that she can continue to believe in the validity of human rights and international criminal law. Hand in hand with this goes a public recognition and confirmation of her dual status, i.e., the status of a citizen of her nation and the status of a member of the normative community of human rights. She will be encouraged to regain and to defend her dual role – an encouragement to civic courage.

III CONCLUSION: A DEVELOPING SYSTEM OF INTERNATIONAL CRIMINAL JUSTICE

To summarize, we have now four addressees of the communicative message of international criminal law: the national citizenry, the perpetrator, the victim and the community of nations as a whole. The community of nations consists of all nation states but in addition forms, as a community of its own, a normative community of human rights, at least to the extent that human rights are protected by international criminal law. This also means that the law of nation states stands in a justificatory and critical relationship to human rights with the consequence that, in a case of collision, human rights gain priority over domestic law.

Nevertheless, there is a huge difference between the normative community of a nation state's legal order, and the normative community of human rights. Unlike the nation state, the cosmopolis of human rights has no centralized legislation, no sovereignty and, correspondingly, there is no monopoly of power. Membership in the cosmopolis as a human rights subject is not like citizenship in a nation state. However, insofar as human rights are protected by the international community under international criminal law, it is a first step towards a cosmopolis becoming an institutional fact, as small and weak as it is. It is a normative community in transition between a legal and a moral order. This has consequences for the kind of obligation citizens have with regard to their membership in the cosmopolis. As a critical reflective attitude, it has to be practised from an *internal point of view*. According to Hart, the legal system of a nation state can be observed also from an observer's point of view, when the addressee obeys only because she wants to avoid bad consequences that will happen to her if she violates a legal rule. With regards to the norms of the cosmopolis, it is difficult to imagine that its norms could be observed only form an observer's point of view. The norms of international criminal law and the underlying human rights have to be accepted by the members of the normative community, and only then can they develop a critical reflective attitude as a habit. Nevertheless, the existence of an international court of criminal justice and the exercise of justified punishment also allows for a transition into the usual habit of citizens of a nation state. Then, international criminal law can be observed from an internal as well as from an observer's point of view.

In the end, one could ask whether this outline only fantasizes about a utopian dream which will never come true, which has no hold in reality. This is not the case. In the ICTY *Kupreškić et al.* judgment, one can find the following paragraph in the context of justifications for sentencing crimes according to international criminal law. Between elaborations about the justifications of retribution, deterrence and rehabilitation, the Tribunal makes a statement about its general policy of sentencing:

> The Trial Chamber is further of the view that another relevant sentencing purpose is to show the people of not only the former Yugoslavia, but of the world in general, that there is no impunity for these types of crimes. This should be done in order to strengthen the resolve of all involved not to allow crimes against international humanitarian law to be committed as well as to create trust in and respect for the developing system of international criminal justice.[21]

The last sentence, in particular, of this statement points to the direction that has been elaborated here – 'creating trust in and respect for the developing system of international criminal justice'. The final stage of this development could (and should) be the self-understanding of each citizen of a nation state as a member of the cosmopolis of human rights under international criminal law. It is the trust in the recognition as a human rights subject who has a legal duty to exercise her critical reflective attitude with regard to her domestic legal system from the point of view of human rights.

[21] ICTY, Judgment of 14 January 2000 (TC), *Kupreškić et al.*, IT-95-16-T, para. 848.

14

The Individual and the International Community

An Outline for a Combined Meso Preventive Theory of International Punishment

ANDREAS WERKMEISTER*

Theories of punishment are of fundamental relevance to any society. It is therefore not surprising that we can resort to a centuries-old discussion on theories of punishment in domestic law. By contrast, theories of *international* punishment are still in their infancy. Punishment beyond the nation state, as a tool of the international community, needs further reflection. However, this does not necessarily mean that international criminal law demands a 'specific' theory of punishment or that to legitimize it one would have to rely on grounds outside the ordinary criminal law paradigm. On the contrary, this chapter proposes that international punishment should be based on a general theory of criminal law that places human dignity at its core and is founded on the idea that punishment requires limits to be legitimate (Section II). Within this general framework, however, the international context makes it necessary to rethink and rearticulate the purposes of punishment. Against this backdrop, I will argue that neither retributive theories nor offender-oriented expressive theories are able to justify international punishment. The inherent problems of these concepts grow even larger in the international context (Sections III, IV.1). Instead, I contend that combined preventive theories provide a comprehensive structure to justify international punishment. However, I argue that this theory of punishment needs to be more individualistic in order for it to be non-instrumentalizing. It has to include a victim-related (Section IV), a special preventive (Section V.2) and, most importantly, a 'meso preventive' aspect that is located between general and special prevention (Section V.4). Before discussing these modifications, the underlying

* The main arguments leading to the combined theory of punishment for international criminal law presented in this contribution, are part of my monograph published in German, see A. Werkmeister, *Straftheorien im Völkerstrafrecht* (Baden-Baden: Nomos, 2015).

perspective of this theory, the legitimation vis-à-vis the individual, needs to be explained (Section I).

I PERSPECTIVE: LEGITIMATION VIS-À-VIS THE INDIVIDUAL

1 *The Methodological Framework*

In standard liberal criminal law theory, rationales of punishment are developed not only in a legitimation discourse vis-à-vis the society but also vis-à-vis the individual who is most directly affected by the sanction: the perpetrator.[1] At the core of the liberal perspective lies the idea that an appropriate rationale of punishment has to at least be in line with the human dignity of that person.[2] This is based on the assumption that punishment entails a restriction of individual rights of fundamental severity. Punishment ultimately reduces freedom and, by doing so, also communicates social disapproval.[3]

In the following, I apply this standard liberal (or individualistic) approach to international criminal law.[4] This is not only for substantive but primarily for methodological reasons. Just as in the domestic context 'the individual is the unit of punishment';[5] just like domestic punishment, international punishment entails a severe restriction of the individual rights of the offender. If we want to punish violations of human dignity and human rights, we have to

1 See, e.g., M.S. Moore, *Placing Blame: A Theory of the Criminal Law* (Oxford: Clarendon Press, 1997) 30; A. von Hirsch, *Fairness, Verbrechen und Strafe*, (Berlin: Berliner Wissenschafts-Verlag, 2005), 50; G. Ellscheid, 'Zur Straftheorie von Anthony Duff' in H. Radtke et al. (eds), *Muss Strafe sein?* (Baden-Baden: Nomos, 2004), 25, 30; B. Schünemann, 'Zum Stellenwert der positiven Generalprävention in einer dualistischen Straftheorie' in B. Schünemann et. al. (eds.), *Positive Generalprävention* (Heidelberg: Cf. Müller, 1998), 109, 114; from a constitutional law perspective: J. Kaspar, *Verhältnismäßigkeit und Grundrechtsschutz im Präventionsstrafrecht* (Baden-Baden: Nomos, 2014), 619.

2 Werkmeister, *Straftheorien im Völkerstrafrecht*, 96 et. seq.; D. Robinson, 'A Cosmopolitan Liberal Account of International Criminal Law' (2013) 26 *Leiden Journal of International Law* 127, 132.

3 The notion of punishment has been discussed extensively, see, e.g., L. Greco, *Lebendiges und Totes in Feuerbachs Straftheorie* (Berlin: Duncker & Humblot, 2009), 302; von Hirsch, *Fairness, Verbrechen und Strafe*, 24.

4 See also K. Günther and V. Reuss, 'Legitimation des Völkerstrafrechts in Deutschland – Völkerstrafrecht als Bürgerstrafrecht' in C. Safferling and S. Kirsch (eds.), *Völkerstrafrechtspolitik* (Heidelberg: Springer, 2014), 127, 145–146; L. May, *Crimes Against Humanity* (Cambridge: Cambridge University Press, 2005), 80.

5 Robinson, 'A Cosmopolitan Liberal Account of International Criminal Law', 140.

show that punishment itself is not an infringement of those rights.[6] Admittedly, I leave aside other important questions, such as the 'concept of law' in international criminal law and the legitimation of international criminal law vis-à-vis the sovereign (democratic)[7] state.[8] Nevertheless, narrowing the focus of the analysis in this manner does not reduce its importance because the legitimation vis-à-vis the individual is a necessary condition of a legitimate practice of international punishment.

2 *The Notion of Human Dignity*

The justification of punishment and the debate about the 'correct' understanding of human dignity share an intricate relationship. Thus, a meaningful discussion of the rationales of punishment demands a clear and explicit description of the notion of human dignity that underlies the analysis. Consent only exists regarding the core, i.e., the idea that the human being has an intrinsic or absolute value, that persons are 'subjects' not 'objects'.[9] The state and any other public authority 'exist for the sake of the individual human being, and not vice versa'.[10] The exact theoretical concept of human dignity, however, is very contentious.[11] Obviously, the details of this discussion would

6 On the discussion about a human right not to be punished in the context of criminalization, see D. Husak, *Overcriminalization: The Limits of the Criminal Law* (New York: Oxford University Press, 2008), 92 et seq. See also J.D. Shepard, 'A Human Right not to Be Punished? Punishment as a Derogation of Rights?' (2012) 6 *Criminal Law and Philosophy* 31, who discusses the ICCPR in this context.

7 In the context of European criminal law, it is argued that restrictions of democratic self-determination in the field of criminal law are 'particularly sensitive': see German Constitutional Court *(Bundesverfassungsgericht)* BVerfG, Judgment of the Second Senate of 30 June 2009, 2 BvE 2/08, paras. 252 et seq. = BVerfGE Vol. 123, 267, 359 et seq.

8 See, e.g., B. Broomhall, *International Justice and the International Criminal Court. Between Sovereignty and the Rule of Law* (New York: Oxford University Press, 2003).

9 J.C. Joerden, 'Menschenwürde bei Margalit und Kant' in E. Hilgendorf (ed.), *Menschenwürde und Demütigung* (Baden-Baden: Nomos, 2013), 37, 41; K. Seelmann and D. Demko, *Rechtsphilosophie*, 6th ed. (München: C.H. Beck, 2014), § 12 paras. 5–6; Robinson, 'A Cosmopolitan Liberal Account of International Criminal Law', 132; N. Petersen, 'Human Dignity, International Protection', in Max Planck Encyclopedia of Public International Law, October 2012, para. 5.

10 C. McCrudden, 'Human Dignity and Jurdicial Interpretation of Human Rights' (2008) 19 *European Journal of International Law* 655, 679; see also G. Dürig, 'Der Grundsatz von der Menschenwürde' (1956) 81 *Archiv für öffentliches Recht* 117, 123; Greco, *Feuerbachs Straftheorie*, 166.

11 Cf. Petersen, 'Human Dignity, International Protection', para. 3 et seq.; McCrudden 'Human Dignity', 655; M. Düwell, 'Human Dignity: Concepts, Discussions, Philosophical Perspectives' in M. Düwell et al. (eds), *The Cambridge Handbook of Human Dignity* (Cambridge: Cambridge University Press, 2014), 23. On central relevance of the offender's human dignity for

be beyond the scope of this chapter. It is sufficient to outline two different approaches concerning human dignity as a theoretical concept.

In the most influential idealistic line of thought – going back to Immanuel Kant – human dignity is understood as an objective concept based on human reason; the core of this concept is the principle of non-instrumentalization.[12] Kant's principle of non-instrumentalization forbids all acts that treat the individual only as a means to an end.[13] Although it does not forbid acts that treat the individual *also* as a means to an end,[14] it is the most important constraint against utilitarian or consequentialistic treatment of human beings. However, what about constraining behaviour that is 'intrinsically' wrong – irrespective of a consequentialistic structure? For example, torture or the death penalty (which, by the way, was supported by Kant) today are sometimes seen as a violation of human dignity even if such treatment was not a means to an end.[15] This, indeed, suggests that the principle of human dignity entails more than the principle of non-instrumentalization.[16]

Another line of argument, therefore, supports the idea that human dignity cannot only be regarded as an objective concept, but must also be understood subjectively.[17] Dignity protects the integrity of the personal identity, the autonomy of 'empirical man' – and not an abstract person with the gift of reason. In Avishai Margalit's important study 'The Decent Society', for example, we find human dignity itself conceptualized in a forward-looking way based on the capacity 'of reevaluating one's life at any given moment, as

substantive criminal law, cf., e.g., M. Gur-Arye, 'Human Dignity of Offenders: A Limitation on Substantive Criminal Law' (2012) 6 *Journal of Criminal Law and Philosophy* 187; cf. S. Beck, 'Human Dignity, Human Rights and Criminal Law – The German Perspective' in E. Hilgendorf and M. Kremnitzer (eds.), *Human Dignity and Criminal Law* (Berlin: Duncker & Humblot, 2018), 171, 178 et seq.

12 I. Kant, *Grundlegung zur Metaphysik der Sitten* [1784] (Berlin: Suhrkamp, 1968), 66.

13 Fundamentally: Kant, *Grundlegung zur Metaphysik der Sitten*, 66.

14 See e.g. N. Hoerster, 'Zur Bedeutung des Prinzips der Menschenwürde' (1983) *Juristische Schulung* 94.

15 See e.g. M. Herdegen, in T. Maunz and G. Dürig (eds.), *Grundgesetzkommentar*, 82nd ed. (München: C.H. Beck, 2018) Art. 1 para. 1 fn. 36; see also E. Hilgendorf, 'Instrumentalisierungsverbot und Ensembletheorie der Menschenwürde' in H.U. Paeffgen et al. (eds.), *Strafrechtswissenschaft als Analyse und Konstruktion. Festschrift für Ingeborg Puppe* (Berlin: Duncker & Humblot, 2011), 1658.

16 See E. Hilgendorf, 'The Abuse of Human Dignity – Difficulties in Using the Human Dignity Topos Taking the Bio-Ethics Debate as an Example' in E. Hilgendorf and M. Kremnitzer (eds), *Human Dignity and Criminal Law* (Berlin: Duncker & Humblot, 2018), 39, 45 et seq.

17 See P. Häberle, 'Die Menschenwürde als Grundlage der staatlichen Gemeinschaft', in J. Isensee and P. Kirchhof (eds.), *Handbuch des Staatsrechts der Bundesrepublik Deutschland* (Heidelberg: C.F. Müller, 1987), 840; K. Lüderssen, 'Resozialisierung und Menschenwürde' (1997) *Kritische Justiz* 179, 181.

well as the ability to change one's life from this moment on'.[18] Human dignity is not primarily a quality; it is also a relational and communicative concept[19] and humiliation is 'any sort of behavior or condition that constitutes a sound reason for a person to consider his or her self-respect injured'.[20] The implications of these different and demanding notions of human dignity on the theories of international punishment will be one focus of this chapter.

II THE PRECONDITIONS OF LEGITIMATE PUNISHMENT BEYOND THE STATE

1 *Punishment beyond the Nation State and the Individual*

Before delving into further detail, some more general thoughts on how the international context affects the legitimation vis-à-vis the individual are essential. The international context intensifies the legitimatory problem of punishment. The (nation) state is 'the historically grown and globally recognized form of organization of a viable political community'.[21] Obviously, such a state does not exist (and should not exist) at the global level. The 'international community' of states and world citizens,[22] which is the public authority behind international punishment, is not a 'world state' and has not yet fully 'constitutionalized' into a stably functioning legal community.[23] Within a scenario of disaggregated and shared public authority, international criminal law represents the idea of enforceable cosmopolitan rights without a global

[18] A. Margalit, *The Decent Society* (Cambridge/London: Harvard University Press, 1996), 75.

[19] H. Hofmann, 'Die versprochene Menschenwürde' (1993) *Archiv des öffentlichen* Rechts 353, 364; T. Hörnle, 'Menschenwürde als Freiheit von Demütigungen' (2008) Zeitschrift für Rechtsphilosophie 41, 58; similarily K. Günther, 'Die symbolisch-expressive Bedeutung der Strafe – Eine neue Straftheorie jenseits von Vergeltung und Prävention?' in C. Prittwitz, M. Baurmann and K. Günther (eds.), Festschrift für Klaus Lüderssen (Baden-Baden: Nomos, 2002), 205, 211.

[20] Margalit, *The Decent Society*, 9.

[21] That is the way the German Constritutional Court puts it, BVerfG, Judgment of the Second Senate of 30 June 2009, 2 BeV 2/08, para. 224 = BVerfGE Vol. 123, 267, 346.

[22] See from a philsophical perspective, e.g., J. Habermas, *Philosophische Texte* (Frankfurt: Suhrkamp, 2009), 335; from a legal perspective, e.g., H. Mosler, *The International Society as a Legal Community* (Alphen aan den Rijn and Germantown: Sijthoff & Noordhoff, 1980); A.L. Paulus, *Die internationale Gemeinschaft im Völkerrecht: Eine Untersuchung zur Entwicklung des Völkerrechts im Zeitalter der Globalisierung* (München: C.H. Beck, 2001).

[23] For further references, see, e.g., C. Walter, 'Constitutionalizing (Inter)national Governance – Possibilities for and Limits to the Development of an International Constitutional Law' (2001) 44 *German Yearbook of International Law* 170; S. Kadelbach and T. Kleinlein, 'Überstaatliches Verfassungsrecht' (2006) *Archiv des Völkerrechts* 235; C. Mattheis, *Die Konstitutionalisierung des Völkerrechts aus systemtheoretischer Sicht* (Berlin: Springer, 2018).

monopoly of power.[24] International criminal law has never been a one-time legislative act of an imaginary legislator but can evolve gradually in response to individual events.[25] Based on a narrow but sustainable basis of judgment anchored in common cultural dispositions, the diverse world society integrates 'on a case by case basis',[26] as Jürgen Habermas put it, 'whenever there is consonance of moral indignation over massive human rights violations'.[27] The enforcement of the validity of human rights does not only rest with nation states[28] 'but with the individually responsible world citizens as subjects of international law'[29] who have to show a cosmopolitan commitment to the project of international human rights protection or even *disobey state law* that violates human rights.[30]

But what does all this mean regarding the focus of this chapter, i.e., the legitimation of punishment vis-à-vis the individual? If human dignity is seen as the 'overall purpose' of the state, the state itself is not an end in itself but only a means to protect human dignity.[31] From this point of view, the state – whose development into a guarantor of dignity was itself partly dependent on contingencies[32] – does at least not seem to be an *a priori* imperative for any legitimate punishment. But, indeed, in the case of international punishment the problem of human dignity is particularly pronounced: being punished by the nation state the perpetrator lives in and being punished by the

24 On this, see the contribution by Kai Ambos in Chapter 6 (Section I). See also K. Ambos, 'Punishment without a Sovereign? The *Ius Puniendi* Issue of International Criminal Law: A First Contribution towards a Consistent Theory of International Criminal Law' (2013) 33 *Oxford Journal of Legal Studies* 293, 298 et. seq.

25 H. Satzger, 'Die internationalisierung des Strafrechts als Herausforderung für den Strafrechtlichen Bestimmtheitsgrundsatz' (2004) *Juristische Schulung* 943, 944 et seq.

26 Habermas, *Philosophische Texte*, 313, 344.

27 J. Habermas, 'Eine politische Verfassung für die pluralistische Weltgesellschaft?' (2005) *Kritische Justiz* 222, 242 '[a]us dem Gleichklang der moralischen Entrüstung über massive Menschenrechtsverletzungen' (translated by the author).

28 The role of states in international criminal law is described in greater detail by F. Jeßberger and J. Geneuss, 'A Success? Reflections on the First Ten Years of the International Criminal Court' in T. Eger, S. Oeter and S. Voigt (eds.), *The Economic Analysis of International Law* (Tübingen: Mohr Siebeck, 2014), 217, 224.

29 Günther and Reuss, 'Völkerstrafrecht als Bürgerstrafrecht', 139; see also V. Reuss, *Zivilcourage als Strafzweck des Völkerstrafrechts* (Berlin: LIT.-Verlag, 2012), 19.

30 On this argument, see the contribution by Klaus Günther in Chapter 13 (Section II.2).

31 McCrudden, 'Human Dignity', 679; see also Dürig, 'Der Grundsatz von der Menschenwürde', 123; Greco, *Feuerbachs Straftheorie*, 166.

32 Generally, S. Kadelbach and K. Günther, 'Recht ohne Staat?' in S. Kadelbach and K. Günther (eds.), *Recht ohne Staat: Zur Normativität nichtstaatlicher Rechtsetzung* (Frankfurt: Campus, 2011), 9, 16 et seq.

international community are different things.[33] On the one hand, there is the danger of being instrumentalized for the interest of the 'world society' with which the offender is just very loosely connected. From the perspective of the individual, metaphorically speaking, there is a risk that he or she will not only be used for 'visible' other members of his concrete community but also sacrificed for an 'invisible' world community. On the other hand, there is the danger of a violation of a culturally determined personal identity by the 'world community', which is intervening from 'abroad' into the personal sphere of the individual.

2 *Forfeiture of Dignity?*

In my view, this problem cannot be 'solved' by relying on grounds outside the ordinary liberal criminal law paradigm, by suggesting that the perpetrator of core crimes be viewed as an 'outlaw', an enemy,[34] a *hostis humani generis*, the enemy of all mankind, who has at least partly forfeited his or her dignity.[35] An outlaw is necessarily placed 'outside' constituted legal conditions, he or she is excluded (or, in fact, excludes him- or herself) from the punishing community. They reduce themselves to the state of nature[36] and therefore do not have an intrinsic value *within* the punishing international community; in fact, they

33 Werkmeister, *Straftheorien im Völkerstrafrecht*, 212.

34 Some German scholars directly (or indirectly) link international criminal law to the legal theoretical concept of enemy criminal law *(Feindstrafrecht)*; see G. Jakobs, 'Das Selbstverständnis der Strafrechtswissenschaft vor den Herausforderungen der Gegenwart (Kommentar)' in A. Eser et al. (eds.), *Die deutsche Strafrechtswissenschaft vor der Jahrtausendwende: Rückbesinnung und Ausblick* (München: C.H. Beck, 2000), 47, 54; G. Jakobs, 'Bürgerstrafrecht und Feindstrafrecht' (2004) *Höchstrichterliche Rechtsprechung im Strafrecht* 88, 94; G. Jakobs, *Staatliche Strafe: Bedeutung und Zweck* (Paderborn: Verlag Ferdinand Schöningh, 2004), 43 et seq.; M. Pawlik, 'Strafe oder Gefahrenbekämpfung?' (2006) *Zeitschrift für internationale Strafrechtsdogmatik* 274, 289. This concept of enemy criminal law is not only used to describe and criticize international criminal law but also to legitimate international criminal as enemy criminal law; e.g., L. Greco, *Feindstrafrecht* (Baden-Baden: Nomos, 2010) and T. Hörnle, 'Deskriptive und normative Deminesionen des Begriffs "Feindstrafrecht"' (2006) *Goltdammer's Archiv* 80, 80–82, 89–95 rightly criticize the different aspects of enemy criminal law.

35 For an in-depth discussion, A. Werkmeister, 'International Criminal Law as a Means to Fight the 'Hostes Humani Generis'? On the Dangers of the Concept of Enemy Criminal Law' in M. Fenwick and S. Wrbka (eds.), *Legal Certainty in a Contemporary Context – Private and Criminal Law Perspectives* (Singapore: Springer, 2016), 180, 186.

36 Jakobs, *Staatliche Strafe*, 44, for example, argues that international criminal law must be regarded as a criminal law in the natural state *(Naturzustand)*.

are not part of that community at all.[37] It is, however, at the core of human dignity that it is an inclusive conception and an absolute constraint that cannot be forfeited.[38] Just consider the subjective dignity conception, which is based on the ability to change one's life in the future; a forward-looking right to dignity is necessarily guaranteed irrespective of the individual quality of the 'identity formation' in the past.[39] Raimond Gaita, therefore, rightly argues that '[e]ven the most terrible evil doers are owed this respect as human beings and that we owe it to them because we are human beings'.[40]

3 *The Limitation Principles of Punishment*

Instead of resorting to the semantics of an 'outlaw' or an 'enemy criminal law', it is necessary to minimize the danger of instrumentalization and subjectivity within the international community. In this regard, it is essential to keep in mind that human dignity forms the origin of certain fundamental principles that *limit* punishment. Darryl Robinson rightly highlights that the 'basic commitment' to human dignity, 'translates into certain fundamental principles' of constraint.[41] He argues that the principle of guilt (as a deontic constraint of criminal law) refers to 'the commitment to treat persons as moral agents, [...] capable of directing their behaviour by reason'.[42] Robinson applies the objective dignity conception, which is based on the gift of human reason. The subjective understanding of human dignity, which, inter alia, safeguards self-respect within the extreme conditions of imprisonment, can be associated with the right of the offender to be granted the *opportunity* to regain freedom and to be reintegrated into the liberal community.[43] In my view,

37 Greco, *Feindstrafrecht*, 47; D. Luban, 'A Theory of Crimes against Humanity' (2004) 29 *Yale Journal of International Law* 85, 140 discusses that not only the outrage about the crime but also 'the withdrawal of social protection is universal'.

38 See e.g. Petersen, 'Human Dignity, International Protection', para. 3; U. Neumann, 'Die Tyrannei der Würde. Argumentationstheoretische Erwägungen zum Menschenwürdeprinzip. Arthur Kaufmann zum 75. Geburtstag' (1998) *Archiv für Rechts- und Sozialphilosophie* 153, 154.

39 See Werkmeister, *Straftheorien im Völkerstrafrecht*, 108 et seq.

40 R. Gaita, *Good and Evil – an Absolute Conception*, 2nd ed. (London/New York: Routledge, 2004), 2.

41 Robinson, 'A Cosmopolitan Liberal Account of International Criminal Law', 132.

42 Robinson, 'A Cosmopolitan Liberal Account of International Criminal Law', 131; see also M. Kremnitzer and T. Hörnle, 'Human Dignity as a Protected Interest in International Criminal Law' (2011) 44 *Israel Law Review* 115 with a different perspective.

43 This right is accepted inter alia by the German Constitutional Court, see BVerfG, Judgment of the First Senate of 21 June 1977, 1 BvL 14/76 = BVerfGE Vol. 45, 187, 229; BVerfG, Decision of

these limiting principles, which are usually discussed as parts of the purposes of punishment – the principle of guilt is associated with retribution and the right to reintegration is identified with a rehabilitative purpose of punishment – should be guaranteed irrespective of the concrete (retributive, expressive or preventive) purpose of punishment. They form part of the constitutional 'preconditions' of any legitimate punishment.

What these limitation principles exactly mean in the context of core crimes is, of course, a very difficult question.[44] However, the claim that they would not apply at all is, in my view, inadequate.[45] Only if the international community recognizes limitation principles and makes them the basis of its criminal practice can it be understood as a *partially constituted* community. Only as such can it claim legitimacy with regard to punishment in a culture of human rights.[46] Even though the international community is not a fully constitutionalized community, one 'constitutional function' must be preexisting: the function of limiting the exercise of *supranational* power.[47] As the sovereign powers of nation states are intrinsically limited by human dignity (and human rights), this should also be the case for the *supranational powers of international organizations*. Therefore, the offender's right to human dignity and the limiting principles of punishment, which are intertwined, should be regarded as the minimal basis of an 'international constitutional law'.[48]

the Second Senate of 24 April 1986, 2 BvR 1146/8 = BVerfGE Vol. 72, 105, 113 and the ECtHR Judgment of 9 July 2013, *Vinter and Others v. the UK*, Application No. 66069/09, 130/10, 3896/10.

44 Regarding the problem of collectivity and culpability, K. Ambos, *Internationales Strafrecht*, 5th ed. (München: C.H. Beck, 2018), § 7 para. 9 et seq.; from a theoretical perspective, Robinson, 'A Cosmopolitan Liberal Account of International Criminal Law', 140 et seq.

45 Robinson, 'A Cosmopolitan Liberal Account of International Criminal Law', 138 highlights that we must 'be willing to contemplate such questions not only in the familiar compartment of a state [...] but under other possible configurations' such as the international community. See also W.A. Schabas, 'Sentencing by International Tribunals: A Human Rights Approach' (1997) 7 *Duke Journal of Comparative & International Law* 461, 503.

46 In more detail, Werkmeister, *Straftheorien im Völkerstrafrecht*, 98 et seq.

47 See Walter, 'Constitutionalizing (Inter)national Governance', 192; Mattheis, *Die Konstitutionalisierung des Völkerrechts*, 195 et seq.

48 Art. 21(3) of the ICC Statute could be understood as the link to incorporate a minimal constitution into the framework of the positive international criminal law. Some authors argue that Art. 21(3) of the ICC Statute creates a hierarchy. For further discussion and references, see, e.g., A. Cassese, *International Criminal Law*, 3rd ed. (Oxford: Oxford University Press, 2013), 11.

III THE RETRIBUTIVE THEORIES AND THE WORLD SOCIETY

1 *The Concept of Retribution*

In the next step, I analyze which theory can provide a comprehensive legitimation within the outlined framework. The first theory to be discussed is the retributive theory. In this theory, punishment is considered as 'intrinsically' justified; it compensates for past wrongful acts as a demand of justice. The offender's guilt does not only limit his or her punishment but also justifies it. Punishment should not go beyond but it should also not fall short of his or her guilt. But in fact, as I indicated in Section II.3., the principle of guilt as a limitation of punishment does not necessarily require the recognition of retribution.[49] Instead – and I quote John Rawls – 'it is acknowledged for the sake of liberty itself'.[50]

A problem faced by any concept that views retribution as the (single) *justifying* principle of punishment is overcoming the allegation that it is the same as vengeance (as its primitive ancestor). As the Chief Prosecutor of the Nuremberg Military Tribunal Justice Robert H. Jackson put it:

> The former high station of these defendants, the notoriety of their acts, and the adaptability of their conduct to provoke retaliation, make it hard to distinguish between the demand for a just and measured retribution, and the unthinking cry for vengeance which arises from the anguish of war. It is our task, so far as it is humanly possible, to draw the line between the two.[51]

Modern retributive positions in academia furthermore accept that 'justice' as such is not a tangible goal for a human institution and that, therefore, the traditional retributive theory of punishment has to be relativized.[52]

[49] For example, the prevention theory developed by German criminal law scholar Claus Roxin is based on the combination of preventive aims of punishment and its limitation by the guilt of the offender, C. Roxin and L. Greco, *Strafrecht Allgemeiner Teil I*, 5th ed. (München: C.H. Beck, 2019), § 3 para. 51–52.

[50] J. Rawls, *A Theory of Justice*, revised ed. (Cambridge: Harvard University Press, 1999), 212.

[51] 'Opening Speeches' in *Trial of the Major War Criminals before the International Military Tribunal, Nuremberg, 14 October 1945 – 1 October 1946*, Vol. I (Nuremberg: International Military Tribunal, 1947), 5.

[52] See T. Weigend, in H.W. Laufhütte et al. (eds), *Leipziger Kommentar Strafgesetzbuch* (Berlin: De Gruyter, Berlin, 2007), 12th ed., Einleitung para. 65. In this line of thought, it is not sufficient to directly rationalize international punishment as a 'universal command of justice'

Justice should not be *a priori* the recreation of an abstract idea of a legally perfect reality, but is necessary to re-establish liberal (or fair) conditions (as a prerequisite for peace) in society.[53] Antje Du Bois-Pedain, however, puts forward the idea that international criminal law has not developed to the stage of a just retribution. As it is not about an internal matter of a stabilized global community, but rather about a legal intervention from outside, international punishment can only be (partly) legitimized as 'institutionalized vengeance'.[54] Michael Pawlik's considerations, which interpret the offence as disloyalty to a common civil rights project of freedom, point in the same direction.[55] Pawlik supports a legitimation of international punishment on grounds outside the ordinary criminal law paradigm. In his view, the 'international community' at the present stage of development does not have the power to function as a real (subsidiary) guarantor of freedom.[56] However, his terminology of a 'project' – the common civil rights project of freedom – seems to highlight an important aspect of international criminal law. It combines the idea that a liberal international legal order or world citizen rights are at least available as a legal project[57] and that any such project does not only require the power of community-created institutions, but also the 'common effort of all citizens'.[58] As I mentioned in Section II.1, the enforcement of the validity of human rights does not only rest with the international community of states but also with the individually responsible world citizens. But it is indeed doubtful whether the future-oriented evolutionary dynamics of the international community can be adequately grasped from the perspective of a backward-looking retributive punishment theory.

to compensate the wrongfulness of the core crimes. Comprehensivly from a Kantian perspective, K. Gierhake, *Begründung des Völkerstrafrechts auf der Grundlage der Kantischen Rechtslehre* (Berlin: Duncker & Humblot, 2005), 170.

53 See, e.g., M. Pawlik, *Person, Subjekt, Bürger – Zur Legitimation von Strafe* (Berlin: Duncker & Humblot, 2004), 90; J. Finnis, *Natural Law and Natural Rights* (Oxford: Oxford University Press, 1980), 263 et seq.; G. Sher, *Approximate Justice* (Lanham: Rowman & Littlefield, 1997), 166.

54 See A. du Bois-Pedain, 'Von der "moralischen Wollust des Strafens" oder: Strafgewalt ohne Staatsgewalt aus hegelianischer Sicht' in A. v. Hirsch et al. (eds), *Strafe – Warum?: Gegenwärtige Strafbegründungen im Lichte von Hegels Straftheorie* (Baden-Baden: Nomos, 2011), 205, 230 et seq.

55 Pawlik, 'Strafe oder Gefahrenbekämpfung?', 283.

56 Pawlik, 'Strafe oder Gefahrenbekämpfung?', 290.

57 Werkmeister, *Straftheorien im Völkerstrafrecht*, 123 et seq.

58 Pawlik, *Person, Subjekt, Bürger*, 90.

2 *The Problem of 'Self-Punishment'*

The main problem of retributive theories is the justification vis-à-vis the individual. I need to emphasize that the retributive theory places the principle of non-instrumentalization at the core of its conception. Retributive concepts do not treat the offender as a means to an end. My concerns are based on the idea that human dignity itself entails more than the principle of non-instrumentalization (see Section I.2). Human dignity is not only objective and backward looking; it is also a subjective and future-oriented concept.

This perspective casts doubt on the retributive idea of an intrinsic justification of punishment. It is linked with an idea of 'self-punishment'.[59] Hegel famously said that the 'criminal is honoured as reasonable, because the punishment is regarded as containing his own right' and that the 'honour would not be shared by him, if the conception and measure of his punishment were not deduced from his very act'.[60] Similarly, in Kant's view punishment is something that the offender as *homo noumenon* would do to himself.[61] Under such a conception, the dignity of the abstract person demands the punishment of the real offender.

Neither do modern conceptions, such as Pawlik's, overcome the idea of self-punishment.[62] Pawlik uses the citizen status *against* the perpetrator. Because the perpetrator remains a citizen, he or she must be punished.[63] He argues that the perpetrator who violates his or her loyalty obligation has to put up with 'demonstrating at his own expense the indissolubility of the connection between freedom and loyalty commitment' and accept the interference with his or her rights of freedom. His or her primary obligation turns into a secondary obligation to participate in the project 'peace through law'.[64] But being punished is not a civic duty such as, for example, paying taxes. It is a restriction of freedom of a different quality.

In my view, the idea of self-punishment that uses the concept of human dignity or citizen status to *justify* and not to *limit* punishment runs the risk of ignoring the needs and deficits of the empirical man.[65] It means that if a

[59] Explicitly in this sense, H. Morris, 'Persons and Punishment' in S.E. Grupp (ed.), *Theories of Punishment* (London: Bloomington, 1971), 76 (77): 'the criminal's right to be punished'.

[60] G.W.F. Hegel, *Grundlinien der Philosophie des Rechts* [1821] (Berlin: Suhrkamp-Ausgabe, 1986), § 100, in English: *Philosophy of Right* [1821], translation by S.W. Dyde (London: George Bell, 1986).

[61] I. Kant, *Metaphysik der Sitten* [1798] (Berlin: Suhrkamp, 1968), 453–454.

[62] Werkmeister, *Straftheorien im Völkerstrafrecht*, 123 et seq.

[63] Pawlik, *Person, Subjekt, Bürger*, 90.

[64] Pawlik, *Person, Subjekt, Bürger*, 90, 91, 95.

[65] In this line of thought, e.g., W. Hassemer, 'Variationen der positive Generalprävention' in Schünemann et al. (eds.), *Positive Generalprävention* (Heidelberg: C.F. Müller, 1998), 29, 30.

person were to commit a crime, his or her dignity or his or her citizen status (which is based on human dignity) would turn against him or her instead of functioning as a safeguard of his or her rights and interests. This counter-argument claims even more relevance within the diverse and fragmented world society. Taking into account that there are fewer social bonds between the citizens of the world than between those of a single nation, punishment cannot simply be seen as the *demand* of the 'world citizen' status of the perpetrator.

IV EXPRESSIVE THEORIES

1 *The Concept of Expressivism*

Over the past few years, expressive (or communicative) theories of punishment have received much attention.[66] They trace back to an influential article by Joel Feinberg.[67] He argued that 'punishment is a conventional device for the expression of attitudes of resentment and indignation [...] on the part of either the punishing authority himself or of those in whose name the punishment is inflicted'.[68] One has to distinguish between theories that focus on the message towards the victim and theories that focus on the message towards the perpetrator.

Regarding the victim, it is argued that one can distinguish between ultimately unjustifiable desires (such as revenge) and acceptable communicative interests of the victim.[69] Peter F. Strawson quite influentially showed that 'personal reactive attitudes' and 'generalized reactive attitudes' are 'connected not merely logically' but 'humanely'; 'they rest on, or reflect [...] the [same] expectation of [...] regard on the part of others, not simply towards oneself, but towards all those on whose behalf moral indignation may be felt, i.e. [...] towards all men'.[70] In this regard, punishment could be seen as an act of

For the recent discussion about the individualization of retributive theories, H. Dancig-Rosenberg and N. Dagan, 'Retributarianism: A new Individualization of Punishment' (2019) 13 *Criminal Law and Philosophy* 129.

66 For an expressive theory of punishment, see the contribution by Daniela Demko in Chapter 11.

67 J. Feinberg, *Doing & Deserving – Essays in the Theory of Responsibility* (Princeton: Princeton University Press, 1970), 98

68 Feinberg, *Doing and Deserving*, 98.

69 T. Hörnle, *Straftheorien*, 2nd ed. (Tübingen: Mohr Siebeck, 2017), 36 et seq.; Günther, 'Die symbolisch-expressive Bedeutung der Strafe' 205.

70 P.F. Strawson, 'Freedom and Resentment' in J.M. Fischer and M. Ravizza, *Perspectives on Moral Responsibility* (Ittaca/London: Cornell University Press, 1993), 45, 57.

expressing those reactive attitudes – which are most directly felt by the victims.[71] Thereby the community shows solidarity with the victims and declares that the violation is not the victim's fault but a wrong that is not accepted by the community.[72]

In international criminal law, victim-oriented expressivism, at first sight, seems to be particularly important.[73] The victims' interests do not depend on the existence of a fully constitutionalized world order or even a world state.[74] Even without such an order these interests call for a symbol that recognizes and acknowledges how seriously victims were wronged. Because the (nation) state appointed to protect the victims tends to pursue the transcoding of victims' rights, they are particularly dependent on the solidary communication of the evolving 'world public'.[75] The victims' interests lie in the 'world-public declaration that the violation is wrong and that this is not accepted by the world public'.[76]

Offender-oriented expressive theories focus on the message delivered to the offender. Strawson, for example, argues that besides 'personal' and 'genener-alized reactive attitudes' there are 'self-reactive attitudes associated with demands on oneself for others'; he mentions 'such phenomena as feeling bound [. . .]; feeling guilty, or remorseful or at least responsible'.[77] Following

71 The claim to give the victims a place within a theory of punishment, however, does not necessarily entail an individual right to punishment vis-à-vis the state (or the international community); see also Kaspar, *Verhältnismäßigkeit und Grundrechtsschutz*, 84–85. On the victims' right to punish perpetrators of international core crimes, see the contribution by Jens David Ohlin in Chapter 15. See also ECtHR, Judgement of 26 March 1985, X and Y vs. Netherlands, Application No. 8978/80; IACHR, Judgment of 29 July 1988, Velásquez Rodríguez vs. Honduras, (Ser. C) No. 4 (1988); and in Germany, e.g., BVerfG, Decision of the Second Senate of 6 October 2014, 2 BvR 1568/12, published in (2015) Neue Juristische Wochenschrift 150; BVerfG, Decision of the Second Senate of 19 May 2015, 2 BvR 987/11, published in (2015) Juristenzeitung 890.

72 See K. Günther, 'Falscher Friede durch repressives Völkerstrafrecht?' in W. Beulke et al. (eds.), *Das Dilemma des rechtsstaatlichen Strafrechts* (Berlin: Berliner Wissenschaftsverlag, 2009), 79, 90; Günther and Reuss, 'Völkerstrafrecht als Bürgerstrafrecht', 139. See also the contribution by Klaus Günther in Chapter 13.

73 See R. Merkel, 'Universale Jursidiktion bei völkerrechtlichen Verbrechen. Zugleich ein Beitrag zur Kritik des § 6 StGB', in K. Lüderssen (ed.), *Aufgeklärte Kriminalpolitik oder Kampf gegen das Böse?* (Baden-Baden: Nomos, 1998), 237, 261; C. Möller, *Völkerstrafrecht und Internationaler Strafgerichtshof – kriminologische, straftheoretische und rechtspolitische Aspekte* (Münster: Literatur-Verlag, 2003), 604.

74 Werkmeister, *Straftheorien im Völkerstrafrecht*, 320 et seq.; Günther and Reuss, 'Völkerstrafrecht als Bürgerstrafrecht', 137 et seq.

75 Werkmeister, *Straftheorien im Völkerstrafrecht*, 318.

76 See Günther, 'Falscher Friede durch repressives Völkerstrafrecht?', 90; Günther and Reuss, 'Völkerstrafrecht als Bürgerstrafrecht', 139.

77 Strawson, 'Freedom and Resentment', 57.

this line of thought, Anthony Duff regards punishment as a form of secular penance. He argues that punishment should communicate blame to the perpetrator and thereby provide him or her with the opportunity to repent the crime.[78] Duff's approach is based on a moderate communitarian state and understanding in the society.[79] In his words: '[P]unishment [...] should be inclusionary, as something that we can do, not to a "them" who are implicitly excluded from the (law-abiding) community of citizens, but to *ourselves* as full, if imperfect, members of that community.'[80] For Duff, the authoritative community, within which the offender is to be blamed and within which he or she should repent, is 'the whole of humanity'.[81] However, while this community has not (yet) formed a legal-political community, it is already present as a 'moral' community.[82] This moral community – humanity – in dialogue censures the perpetrator and prompts him or her to respond by doing penance.[83] According to Duff's view, the perpetrator is responsible 'as a human being who is answerable to us, as her fellow human beings, for wrongs that concern all human beings'.[84]

2 *Legitimation of 'Hard Treatment' vis-à-vis the Individual*

The main problem of the expressive theories is how they can justify hard treatment (prison!). Hard treatment is not purely communicative but an actual restriction of freedom (most evidently a restriction on the freedom of movement).[85] One might argue that a purely symbolic response, such as a public confession of guilt or something similar, is sufficient to express resentment towards the perpetrator and solidarity towards the victim.[86]

78 R.A. Duff, *Punishment, Communication and Community* (Oxford: Oxford University Press, 2001), 79–80.

79 R.A. Duff, 'Prävention oder Überredung?', in B. Schünemann et al. (eds.), *Positive Generalprävention* (Heidelberg: C.F. Müller, 1998), 181, 193.

80 Duff, *Punishment, Communication and Community*, 77.

81 R.A. Duff, 'Authority and Responsibility in International Criminal Law' in S. Besson and J. Tasioulas (eds.), *The Philosophy of International Law* (Oxford: Oxford University Press, 2010), 589, 600.

82 Duff, 'Authority and Responsibility in International Criminal Law', 600.

83 R.A. Duff, 'Can We Punish the Perpetrators of Mass Atrocities?' in T. Brudholm et al. (eds.), *The Religious in Responses to Mass Atrocity* (Cambridge: Cambridge University Press, 2009), 79, 88.

84 Duff, 'Can We Punish the Perpetrators of Mass Atrocities', 88.

85 See, e.g., Hörnle, *Straftheorien*, 43; Kaspar, *Verhältnismäßigkeit und Grundrechtsschutz*, 655–656.

86 Duff, *Punishment, Communication and Community*, 29.

Consider offender-oriented expressivism. Its attempt to overcome this obstacle only reinforces the self-punishment problem. Duff's theory, for example, is centred around its claim to treat the perpetrator as a moral, self-responsible person who is able to respond in the communicative process of punishment.[87] 'To take crimes seriously [. . .] as the wrongdoings of responsible agents is to be committed to censuring those who commit them.'[88] Compared to the traditional retributive theories, Duff rightly views punishment itself as a communicative process and thereby highlights a more individualized (communicative) conception of the person. He views perpetrators as 'fallible moral agents' who 'need [. . .] penances to assist and deepen repentance'.[89] Nevertheless, Duff derives the necessity of punishment as repentance (including hard treatment) from the ontological status of the perpetrator as a person.[90] This remains problematic because the status of the perpetrator turns against him or her. It is used to justify his or her punishment instead of functioning as a limit and a safeguard of the perpetrator's rights.[91]

Authors who propose a victim-oriented approach consider hard treatment a necessary annex to the communication of disapproval.[92] They introduce an argument proposed by John Kleinig. He said that hard treatment is required as an 'empathetic appreciation of what our conduct constituted for someone else' and it 'may register where words fail'.[93] In my view, however, this argument is partly misleading, too.[94] It is doubtful whether one can consider the hard treatment element (which is the severest part of punishment) as a mere annex to the communication of disapproval. Effects beyond communication, that is deprivation of freedom, need a justification that goes beyond the

[87] Duff, *Punishment, Communication and Community*, 80; Duff, 'Can We Punish the Perpetrators of Mass Atrocities', 82.

[88] Duff, *Punishment, Communication and Community*, 28.

[89] Duff, *Punishment, Communication and Community*, 108.

[90] The idea behind this approach is that the 'speech act' of punishment that is shaped by a participative attitude and directed towards the offender, respects the offender in his or her status as a person (see von Hirsch, *Fairness, Verbrechen und Strafe*, 50).

[91] Werkmeister, *Straftheorien im Völkerstrafrecht*, 312.

[92] R. Hamel, *Strafen als Sprechakt – Die Bedeutung der Strafe für das Opfer* (Berlin: Duncker & Humblot, 2009), 159; T. Hörnle, 'Die Rolle des Opfers in der Straftheorie und im materiellen Strafrecht' (2006) *Juristenzeitung* 950, 956.

[93] J. Kleinig, 'Punishment and Moral Seriousness' (1991) 25 *Israel Law Review* 401, 417.

[94] This is why I tend to reject specifically *international* forms of expressivsm. M.A. Drumbl, *Atrocity, Punishment and International Law* (Cambridge: Cambridge University Press, 2007), 174, for example, quite impressingly puts together expressivsm and historical truth. However, in my view, hard treatment cannot be justified by telling the individual that one has to create a historical record. See Werkmeister, Straftheorien im Völkerstrafrecht, 284.

communicative process itself.[95] The victims only have a reason to believe the message of punishment if they can assume that the penalty is capable of reaffirming and stabilising the infringed norm[96] and thereby capable of *preventing* the offender or other potential offenders from future violations of this norm.[97] As a consequence, the victim-oriented expressive theories are partly dependent on prevention. The communication towards the victim can only be part of a preventive legitimation of punishment.[98] The victim-related aspect itself can only be viewed as a single justifying purpose of punishment if this punishment does not entail hard treatment. That is the case if the perpetrators (e.g., as a result of their old age) are too ill to be imprisoned at all. For the victims, it is also relevant in such a case that the judgment determines the responsibility of the offender and characterizes the conduct of the perpetrator towards the victim, his victimization, as a wrong.

V PREVENTIVE THEORIES OF INTERNATIONAL PUNISHMENT

1 *Prevention and Instrumentalization*

The central objection against preventive theories is the aforementioned instrumentalization of the perpetrator. As I have highlighted (Section II.2), this is particularly pronounced in international criminal law: the perpetrator is not only used for the prevention of criminal offences in his or her domestic society, but also within a diverse and loosely connected world society.[99] The objection can only be overcome if two requirements are satisfied.

First, essential *limiting* principles need to be guaranteed 'externally' (as principles of international constitutional law, see Section II.2). This implies that only a theory combining (consequentalistic) preventive reasoning and limiting (deontic) principles can provide a justification of punishment in the international context.

95 I. Puppe, 'Strafrecht als Kommunikation – Leistungen und Gefahren eines neuen Paradigmas in der Strafrechtsdogmatik' in E. Samson (ed.), *Festschrift für Grünwald* (Baden-Baden: Nomos, 1999), 469, 475.

96 Hamel, *Strafen als Sprechakt*, 184.

97 See Puppe, 'Strafrecht als Kommunikation', 477.

98 Within the preventive design of punishment, the victim typically only perceives the verdict as credible if the severity of the sentence reflects the disapproval at least to some degree (similarly, Hörnle, 'Die Rolle des Opfers', 956).

99 Werkmeister, *Straftheorien im Völkerstrafrecht*, 212. The notion of 'Gemeinschaftsgebundenheit' of the individual, which is used in domestic criminal law to legitimize preventive punishment (see C. Roxin, *Strafrechtliche Grundlagenprobleme* (Berlin: De Gruyter, 1973), 19), must be rethought.

Second, we have to show that the consequentialistic *justification* itself is in line with human dignity. To that end, it is necessary to distinguish a variety of preventive theories of punishment and deal with them separately. While special prevention aims at deterring the perpetrator from repeating an offence, general prevention focuses on the dangerous imitation effect, i.e., the risk of infection emanating from the individual act, and wants to discourage others from committing crimes.[100]

2 *Special Prevention*

a) The Conception of Special Prevention

As a first step, the role of special prevention has to be discussed. I focus on rehabilitation, which is the most important special preventive aspect from a human rights perspective.[101] First, recall (see Section II.3) that rehabilitation is not only a justification but also a limitation of punishment. The right to the 'opportunity for freedom' forms part of the general constitutional principles of punishment. Rehabilitation as a justification of punishment means communicating to the offender the necessity of reform and aims to enable the perpetrator to live a crime-free life in the future.[102] This theory of punishment indeed focuses on the specific deficits and needs of the individual that might have caused his or her criminal behaviour and thereby embraces a subjective and forward-looking conception of human dignity. Rehabilitation presumes the ability to change one's life. Quite similar to Duff's offender-oriented expressivism, the perpetrators are seen as 'fallible moral agents' who 'need' punishment to live a life in freedom (Section IV.2). However, in contrast to Duff's view, reform does not necessarily entail repentance and is not intrinsically justified but is only a tool for crime prevention.

Rehabilitation, however, faces the objection that reform via punishment is very difficult to attain ('nothing works').[103] Even though more recent studies at least suggest that 'something works', meaning that certain rehabilitative

[100] See Greco, *Feuerbachs Straftheorie*, 392.

[101] Claus Roxin, for example, argues that rehabilitation precedes general prevention as long as the sanction does not go below the so-called 'general preventive minimum', see Roxin and Greco, *Strafrecht AT I*, § 3 para. 41.

[102] T. Weigend, 'Resozialisierung – die gute Seite der Strafe?' in H. Radtke et al. (eds.), *Muss Strafe sein?* (Baden-Baden: Nomos, 2004), 181, 184; Kaspar, *Verhältnismäßigkeit und Grundrechtsschutz*, 685–686.

[103] Martinson, *The Public Interest* 1974, 22.

measures within the practice of punishment have proved to be effective,[104] we have to ask: what works in international criminal law? Some scholars argue that, e.g., genocidal acts are committed in isolated and socially exceptional situations and that the perpetrators are well integrated into society as members of the government apparatus or the military.[105] But are the perpetrators also integrated into the world society based on the primacy of human rights? International crimes are made possible by, inter alia, the perpetrators taking advantage of the 'flexibility of the normative system' of the world society and by revaluing it for their own purposes.[106] A goal of rehabilitation in international criminal law, therefore, may be to disclose the neutralization techniques and to deconstruct the legitimation narrative of the respective core crime.[107] Punishment should bring to the consciousness of the perpetrator that the values built around human dignity cannot be neutralized but are enforceable law.[108]

b) Legitimation vis-à-vis the Individual

The main normative problem faced by special prevention is the legitimation vis-à-vis the individual. In order to overcome the instrumentalization objection, it could be argued that punishment is 'beneficial' for the perpetrator.[109] However, portraying punishment *primarily* as an advantage for the offender

[104] See Weigend, 'Resozialisierung', 184; for details, K. Drenkhahn, *Sozialtherapeutischer Strafvollzug in Deutschland* (Mönchengladbach: Forum Verlag Godesberg, 2007), 60–64.

[105] Comprehensively, Möller, *Völkerstrafrecht und Internationaler Strafgerichtshof*, 465–466, 475.

[106] See, generally, G.M. Sykes and D. Matza, 'Techniken der Neutralisierung: Eine Theorie der Delinquenz' in F. Sack and R. König (eds.), *Kriminalsoziologie* (Frankfurt: Suhrkamp, 1968), 360, 365–371; see, in the context of international criminal law, F. Neubacher, 'Strafzweck und Völkerstrafrecht' (2006) Neue Juristische Wochenschrift 966, 968; S. Harrendorf, 'How Can Criminology Contribute to an Explanation of International Crimes' (2014) 12 *Journal of International Criminal Justice* 231, 249–251.

[107] A special preventive purpose of punishment is also highlighted by G. Werle and F. Jeßberger, *Principles of International Criminal Law*, 3rd ed. (Oxford: Oxford University Press, 2014), para. 108 et seq. and F. Melloh, *Einheitliche Strafzumessung in den Rechtsquellen des ICC-Statuts* (Berlin: Duncker & Humblot, 2010), 148. For a similar argument, see the contribution by Elies van Sliedregt in Chapter 5 (Section III).

[108] In this regard, F. Streng, 'Die Wirksamkeit strafrechtlicher Sanktion – Zur Tragfähigkeit der Austauschbarkeitsthese' in F. Lösel (ed.), *Kriminologie und wissensbasierte Kriminalpolitik* (Mönchengladbach: Forum Verlag Godesberg, 2007), 65, 74 emphasizes: '[...] when the offender is identified, the reaction of society [...] must reflect the weight of the offense. If this does not happen, then expectations of the offender are disappointed, which can lead to norm irritation.'

[109] See, e.g., W. Hassemer, *Einführung in die Grundlagen des Strafrechts*, 2nd ed. (München: C.H. Beck, 1990), 310.

would not be adequate.[110] 'Inner' conversion (which might be necessary for rehabilitative reasons) is not per se an advantage but can take more time than 'just deserts'; it might involve an intervention into the sphere of personal integrity. To be legitimate, rehabilitation presupposes a voluntary behaviour of the offender.[111] These doubts, in my opinion, do not delegitimate any rehabilitative measure within a practice of punishment. To the contrary, such measures (which take into account the specific needs of the concrete offender) at least have to be *offered*. However, it is clear that the practice of punishment needs further grounds to be justified vis-à-vis the perpetrator who is unwilling to reform.

3 *General Prevention and Meso Prevention*

a) The Concept of Negative General Prevention

According to the negative general prevention theory, the purpose of punishment is deterrence. In the tradition of Paul Johann Anselm von Feuerbach, theorists usually emphasize that negative general prevention does not relate to the 'immediate deterrence of others by the pain of the evil inflicted on the wrongdoer',[112] but that the law, in particular the threat of criminal punishment, leads to the deterrent effect.[113] In this regard, the enforcement of sentences imposed on individual offenders is necessary to avoid empty threats. Others, i.e., potential perpetrators, are deterred because they see that the threat of punishment is real. This idea is usually based on the model of the rationally calculating *homo oeconomicus*, who puts his or her own interests first (rational choice model).[114] The 'ideal' *homo oeconomicus* of course does not exist in reality.[115] Modern deterrence theorists, therefore, take the view of a

[110] See also Roxin and Greco, *Strafrecht AT I*, § 3 para. 17.

[111] Roxin and Greco, *Strafrecht AT I*, § 3 para. 16.

[112] P.J.A. v. Feuerbach, *Lehrbuch des gemeinen in Deutschland gültigen peinlichen Rechts*, 14th ed. (Giessen: Georg Friedrich Heyer's Verlag, 1847), 40.

[113] See v. Feuerbach, *Lehrbuch*, 38, 42.

[114] E.g., G. Becker, 'Crime and Punishment: An Economic Approach' in G. Becker and W. Landes (eds.), *Essays in Economics of Crime and Punishment* (New York/London: National Bureau of Economic Research, 1974), 1 et seq.; R.A. Posner, 'An Economic Theory of International Law' (1985) 85 *Columbia Law Review*, 1193.

[115] For further references, see, e.g., P. Wittig, *Der rationale Verbrecher* (Berlin: Duncker & Humblot, 1993); P. Wittig, 'Der ökonomische Ansatz zur Erklärung kriminellen Verhaltens' (1993) *Monatsschrift für Kriminologie und Strafrechtsreform* 328; M. Englerth, *Der beschränkt rationale Verbrecher. Behavioral Economics in der Kriminologie* (Berlin: Duncker & Humblot, 2010).

bounded rational individual or a 'minimal anthropology', according to which it is at least possible that people are guided by 'prudential reasons'.[116]

But what about the deterrent effect of international punishment? Many international crimes continue to go unpunished after the establishment of the ICC, even if they become known.[117] To compensate for these deficits, a deterrent effect might only be achieved by the exemplary introduction of draconian punishments: 'The international community would [...] act as the keeper of the international "Panopticon".'[118] This, of course, cannot be the solution. Core crimes can only be sanctioned within the limits of individual guilt and a stronger deterrent effect must be based on a reduction of selectivity.

b) The Conception of Positive General Prevention

A second, more recent strand of general prevention relies on norm internalization or positive general prevention.[119] By punishing individuals, the fundamental norms of criminal law are reaffirmed and thereby internalized by the public.[120] Just like the expressive theory of punishment, the theory

[116] Especially Greco, *Feuerbachs Straftheorie*, 369; von Hirsch, *Fairness, Verbrechen und Strafe*, 53.

[117] On the ICC's jurisdictional contraints and selectivity, see the contribution by Harmen van der Wilt in Chapter 17. See also, e.g., S. Nimaga, 'An International Conscience Collective? A Durkheimian Analysis of International Criminal Law' (2007) 7 *International Criminal Law Review*, 561, 616; C.W. Mullins and D.L. Rothe, 'The Ability of the International Criminal Court to Deter Violations of International Criminal Law: A Theoretical Assessment' (2010) 10 *International Criminal Law Review* 771, 778; R.D. Sloane, 'The Expressive Capacity of International Punishment: The Limits of the National Law Analogy and the Potential of International Criminal Law' (2007) 43 *Stanford Journal of International Law* 39, 72.

[118] See, for a comprehensive discussion, I. Tallgren, 'The Sensibility and Sense of International Criminal Law' (2002) 13 *European Journal of International Law* 561, 576.

[119] A different catecory of positive general prevention understands the concept mainly as a way of channelling (and taming) the punitive needs existing in the society (in the context of international criminal law: C. Safferling, *Internationales Strafrecht* (Berlin: Springer, 2011), § 4 para. 69; Sloane, 'The Expresive Capacity', 78. However, in my opinion, these approaches are problematic. Within the society, there do not only exist rational needs for protection but also ultimately unjustifiable needs of retribution or even vengeance. Sometimes it is argued that these retributive feelings justify punishment without any preventive framework (see, e.g., K.M. Carlsmith, J.M. Darley and P.H. Robinson, 'Why Do We Punish? Deterrence and Just Deserts as Motives for Punishment' (2002) 83 *Journal of Personality and Social Psychology* 284; T. Walter, 'Vergeltung als Strafzweck: Prävention und Resozialisierung als Pflichten der Kriminalpolitik' (2011) *Zeitschrift für Internationale Strafrechtsdogmatik* 636).

[120] W. Hassemer and U. Neumann, in U. Kindhäuser et al. (eds.), *Nomos Kommentar Strafgesetzbuch*, 5th ed. (Baden-Baden: Nomos, 2017), Vor § 1 para. 293; Hassemer, Einführung in die Grundlagen des Strafrechts, 326.

of norm internalization quite rightly views punishment as a form of communication. However, the focus is slightly different: It is about communication on the macro- level of the society and communication is seen as a tool for crime prevention.[121] In its most interesting version, this theory creates a link to the legal goods that stand behind the criminal norms and provide for their legitimacy.[122] These goods should be confirmed and strengthened by the punishment; punishment is a strong symbol that demonstrates to the public that the legitimacy of the criminal norms is irrefutable.[123] By reaffirming the norms and values, the punishment restores the 'loss of trust' and repairs the 'intellectual' or 'normative' damage the crime has caused in society.[124]

But is any such communication about criminal norms and its legitimacy possible in the context of international criminal law? Sometimes it is suggested that international punishment is not about the reaffirmation of an existing legal order, but about the coercive creation of a new one.[125] Where core crimes are committed, Günther Jakobs writes, effective norms do not exist or are perverted.[126] However, it is necessary to differentiate between the macro-level of the world society and the macro-level of the affected society. In my view, Jakobs mainly refers to the macro-level of the *affected society* where the normative order is indeed destroyed or perverted. International punishment could still aim to reinforce the international legal order on the macro-level of the world society. On this level a global awareness of human dignity and its legitimacy pre-exists at least in a rudimentary form.[127] Its reinforcement marks 'the vindication of the most blatant violations of the values resulting

[121] G. Jakobs, *Strafrecht Allgemeiner Teil. Die Grundlagen und die Zurechnungslehre. Lehrbuch, Studienausgabe*, 2nd ed. (Berlin: De Gruyter), para. 9 et seq., para. 15.

[122] Hassemer, *Einführung in die Grundlagen des Strafrechts*, 323; M. Baurmann, 'Vorüberlegungen zu einer empirischen Theorie der positiven Generalprävention' in B. Schünemann et al. (eds.), *Positive Generalprävention* (Heidelberg: C.F. Müller, 1998), 1. Prevention should not only be realized via a threat but via the persuasive power of the legally protected goods.

[123] Kaspar, *Verhältnismäßigkeit und Grundrechtsschutz*, 649.

[124] See, e.g., H. Müller-Dietz, 'Vom intellektuellen Verbrechensschaden' (1983) *Goltdammers's Archiv* 481, 484; see also Jakobs, *Staatliche Strafe*, 32.

[125] Jakobs, 'Bürgerstrafrecht und Feindstrafrecht', 94.

[126] Jakobs, *Staatliche Strafe*, 54; Jakobs, 'Bürgerstrafrecht und Feindstrafrecht', 94.

[127] See R. Merkel, '"Lauter leidige Tröster" – Kants Friedensschrift und die Idee eines Völkerstrafgerichtshofs' in R. Merkel and R. Wittmann (eds.), *Zum ewigen Frieden – Grundlagen, Aktualität und Aussichten einer Idee von Immanuel Kant* (Frankfurt: Suhrkamp, 1996), 309, 345; H. Jäger, 'Ist Politik kriminalisierbar?' in K. Lüderssen (ed.), *Aufgeklärte Kriminalpolitik oder Kampf gegen das Böse?* (Baden-Baden: Nomos, 1998), 121, 136.

from the religion built around human dignity in order to prevent a dwindling belief in these values'.[128]

c) Meso Prevention

However, the differentiation between the macro-level of the world society and the macro-level of the affected society reveals a deeper problem of general prevention. The macro-levels as such can hardly be addressed by the punishment of a single perpetrator. Punishment as a communicative endeavour needs to specify its addressees. In my view, a target group-specific argumentation is required.[129] The message of punishment, for example, has to be different depending on whether one addresses (potential) followers or leaders.[130] Regarding (potential) followers, it is important to note that the affected norm addressees must not only be motivated to comply with international law, but also to resist the pressure to conform to their domestic norm system.[131] In that sense, Vasco Reuss and Klaus Günther correctly highlight the 'necessity of civic courage' as a purpose of international punishment.[132] The leaders, however, are held responsible because they created the perverted domestic norm system (and not because they did not show disobedience to a perverted domestic norm system). It is necessary to deconstruct their legitimation narratives (see Section V.2.a) and communicate to the other potential leaders that any such legitimation narrative is not accepted by the international community and thereby reinforce the values developed around human dignity. In this regard, we also have to take into account that the group of high-level potential perpetrators is relatively small. There are only a few people who potentially are in the position of heads of state or government, or militia leaders, etc.

Therefore, I suggest adding what are known as meso-levels.[133] The term meso-level is also used in criminology; in the context of the core crimes it is, for instance, highlighted by Dawn L. Rothe in her integrated theory of

[128] Nimaga, 'A Durkheimian Analysis of International Criminal Law', 610–611, 617.

[129] Similarly, K. Lüderssen, *Abschaffen des Strafens?* (Frankfurt: Suhrkamp 1995), 112 et seq.

[130] A. Hoyer, 'Internationaler Strafgerichtshof und nationalstaatliche Souveränität' (2004) *Goltdammer's Archiv* 321 even rejects the legitimacy of the punishment of followers.

[131] Reuss, *Zivilcourage als Strafzweck des Völkerstrafrechts*, 16.

[132] On the idea of civic courage in international criminal law, see the contribution by Klaus Günther in Chapter 13. See also Günther and Reuss, 'Völkerstrafrecht als Bürgerstrafrecht', 139; Reuss, *Zivilcourage als Strafzweck des Völkerstrafrechts*, 70 fn. 265.

[133] Werkmeister, *Straftheorien im Völkerstrafrecht*, 223, 268, 363 et seq. On the differentiation between macro-, meso- and micro-levels in the explanation of international crimes, see the contribution by Frank Neubacher in Chapter 3.

international law violations.[134] The meso-level is located between the micro- and the macro- level. Whereas the micro-level is concerned with the individual perpetrator or victim and the macro-level focuses on society as such, the meso-level comprises organizational units and subunits of the macro-level such as the *transnational* groups of potential future high-level (leaders) or mid- and low-level perpetrators (followers). In my view, the macro-level of the society as such can only be addressed via these meso groups. By integrating the meso-level into the theory of punishment, a new form of prevention between special and general prevention emerges.

d) The Legitimation vis-à-vis the Individual

The main normative problem of any theory that relies on a preventive effect of punishment *on people other than the perpetrator him- or herself* is to overcome the instrumentalization objection. I mentioned before (see Section I.2) that it is not *per se* illegitimate to use the individual *also* as a means to an end. Nevertheless, it is necessary to give reasons to the perpetrator as part of legitimatory dialogue as to why he or she is punished 'for the sake of others'.[135]

As part of general preventive theories, 'the others' is the society as such. Consequently, the reasons provided by these theories need to refer to the macro- level of the society as such. The theory of *negative* general prevention usually uses a certain version of the social contract theory.[136] In a social contract, the *homo oeconomicus* or an individual guided by prudential reasons would consent to a society's practice of punishment out of self-interest, even if this restricts his or her freedom to commit such crimes, because his or her expected benefit of not being a victim of crime outweighs this loss.[137] The positive general preventive theories inter alia refer to the discursive, democratic participation: the person, who was part of the democratic procedure that led to the creation of the norm he or she violated, can be addressed by punishment because he or she is one of the authors of this norm.[138] Neither the social contract model nor the democratic model use a self-punishment argument; it is not the status of the perpetrator as a *homo oeconomicus* or as a

[134] D. Rothe, *State Criminality: The Crime of All Crimes* (Lanham: Lexington Books, 2009), 102.

[135] See, e.g., Hörnle, *Straftheorien*, 49.

[136] See the critique developed by P. Wittig, 'Eine "neue ökonomische Welt": Rettet der dispositionelle Nutzenmaximierer den ökonomischen Ansatz?' (1998) *Rechtstheorie* 73, 100.

[137] N. Hoerster, *Muss Strafe sein? Positionen der Philosophie* (München: C.H. Beck, 2012), 89.

[138] See, e.g., K. Günther, *Schuld und kommunikative Freiheit* (Frankfurt: Klostermann, 2005), 253 et seq.

deliberative person but his or her prior consent in the social contract or his or her democratic participation that is used as an argument against him or her.

In international criminal law, however, the social contract model and the democratic model face problems. There is neither a democratic world legislature[139] nor a union of people that establishes a sovereign power of punishment by means of a (hypothetical) mutual promise regarding a certain territory.[140] These concepts could only apply in a modified way,[141] based on a (provisional) horizontal contract of all world citizens[142] who mutually promise human rights to each other and thereby safeguard the preconditions of any form of 'collective autonomy'.[143] This need for modification, however, reveals a deeper problem. The arguments (stemming from the macro-level) are too abstract to form a part of a legitimatory dialogue that leads to practical consequences.[144] Just consider the social contract model again. The person affected is punished because, as a *homo oeconomicus* (or an individual guided by prudential reasons), he or she agreed to this punishment in the social contract. But punishment needs to be justified vis-à-vis the empirical man, not vis-à-vis a *homo oeconomicus* or an individual guided by prudential reasons.

Indeed, another argument seems necessary. I suggest that the idea of meso prevention can help to shape that argument. As part of meso prevention, 'the others' – for the sake of which the offender is punished – is not the society as such but the affected meso groups. Therefore, the justification of punishment vis-à-vis the individual can be derived from the meso-level. The perpetrator is not addressed as a single individual within an evolving world society. Instead, he or she is addressed as a member of case-specific transnational groups with whom he or she shares certain features. The perpetrator is connected much more closely with these rather small groups than with the world society as such. Via his or her acts, the perpetrator has the power and the discursive 'standing' to influence the (future) behaviour of this group and thereby has 'world events' in his or her hands. Just like the international community is discursively developed within transnational forums and circles, i.e., groups, the perpetrators are addressed as members of certain transnational groups.

139 From a Kantian perspective, see Gierhake, *Begründung des Völkerstrafrechts*, 239 et seq.
140 See Günther, 'Falscher Friede durch repressives Völkerstrafrecht?', 98.
141 M.C. Bassiouni, 'Global Criminal Justice: An Idea Whose Time Has Passed' in M. Bohlander (ed.), *Globalization of Criminal Justice* (Farnham/Burlington: Routledge, 2010), 193, 226.
142 See Neubacher, *Strafzweck und Völkerstrafrecht*, 967.
143 Werle and Jeßberger, *Principles*, para. 97 et seq.; Günther and Reuss, 'Völkerstrafrecht als Bürgerstrafrecht', 152 et seq.; see also A, Werkmeister, 'Eine Bestandsaufnahme der Legitimationsprobleme des Völkerstrafrechts' (2016) *Anwaltsblatt* 459, 462.
144 See also Hörnle, *Straftheorien*, 54 et seq.

Against this backdrop, international punishment can be justified as part of an *individualized* discursive process (which integrates the rehabilitative and victim-related elements). Victor Tadros rightly highlights the relevance of duties 'incurred as a result of wrongdoing'.[145] The result of wrongdoing, the 'intellectual crime damage', that is the loss of trust in the law's promise to protect human dignity, cannot only be located on the micro-level of the directly affected victims but also on the meso-level of 'indirectly' affected groups. The case-specific group of potential perpetrators corresponds with another case-specific group of 'indirect' victims.[146] In this regard, Tadros rightly argues that the perpetrator does not only owe something to the victim of the wrongdoing but also to those who the victim wishes to protect, who are intimately related to the victim[147] and who potentially suffer a 'wrongdoing of a similar kind'.[148] As a part of meso prevention,[149] I generally agree with this account[150] and propose rationalizing international punishment as a form of intellectual (communicative) compensation[151] to the direct and indirect victims of the crime.

Just as the purpose of punishment defined by meso prevention lies in between general (macro) and special (micro) prevention, the conception of human dignity reflected by this theory lies in between the objective and the subjective model of dignity. Even though the international community authoritatively communicates to the perpetrator the need to compensate for the 'intellectual crime damage' he or she caused, the perpetrator remains *an author of the concrete design of the compensation he or she has to provide*. As such, the perpetrator is viewed as someone who is able to respond within the communicative process of punishment. He or she compensates the

[145] V.Tadros, 'Doing without Desert' (2017) 11 *Criminal Law and Philosophy* 229, 229; see in detail V. Tadros, *The Ends of Harm* (Oxford: Oxford University Press, 2011), 273 et seq.; V. Tadros, *Wrongs and Crimes* (Oxford: Oxford University Press, 2017), 47 et seq.

[146] Werkmeister, *Straftheorien im Völkerstrafrecht*, 369 et seq, 375 et seq.

[147] Tadros, 'Doing without Desert', 244.

[148] Tadros, 'Doing without Desert', 247.

[149] Admittedly, such an account has deficits to justify general prevention; it does not show that offenders can be punished for the sake of the society as a whole, see, e.g., Hörnle, *Straftheorien*, 53 et seq. But meso prevention is based on the idea that offenders are punished for the sake of the affected meso groups.

[150] I am not sure, however, that this necessarily involves the idea that 'this is an end that, were he [the perpetrator] well-motivated, he would also intend to pursue', see Tadros, 'Doing without Desert', 248). Instead, I assume that this only presumes that the perpetrator is able to understand that aim and is capable of responding to it in the discursive process of punishment.

[151] See U. Neumann, 'Normative Kritik der Theorie der positiven Generalpräventionen – 10 Thesen' in B. Schünemann et al. (eds.), *Positive Generalprävention* (Heidelberg: C.F. Müller, 1998), 147, 151.

intellectual crime damage either by using the punishment for his or her rehabilitation or, if he or she refuses rehabilitation, by passively 'enduring' the imprisonment. In the first case, the perpetrator provides the others (the affected meso group) with an example of the persuasiveness of the norm he or she has violated. In the second case, the punishment demonstrates to the others (the affected meso group) the 'force' of the norm. Either way, the punishment is communicating solidarity with the victims.

VI CONCLUSION

1 *Preconditions of Legitimate Punishment*

I have focused on the legitimation vis-à-vis the individual affected and thereby applied the standard liberal (or individualistic) approach to international criminal law. The central concern of this approach, the human dignity of the affected person, is particularly pronounced in international criminal law. As a tool of the international community that has not yet fully constitutionalized, international punishment cannot be legitimized as an 'exceptional' measure against the enemies of mankind who partly forfeit their dignity. Instead, it forms part of the process of constitutionalization of the international community. Therefore, it necessarily has to adhere to the (deontic) limiting principles of criminal law. Only if the international community recognizes limitation principles and makes them the basis of its criminal practice can it be understood as a *partially constituted* community. In this sense, the limitation principles of punishment, such as the principle of guilt and the right to reintegration, transform the international community into a partly constituted community.

2 *Prevention and Communication: Micro- and Meso-Level*

Retributive theories have problems with the justification of punishment in international criminal law. However, the alleged 'insolvability' of the criminal-theoretical problem in international criminal law is, in my view, not a consequence of (the nature or structure of) international criminal law, but of the merely backward-looking retributive theories of punishment themselves. In my view, the central category of any theory of punishment, the human dignity of the offender, cannot serve as a principle to limit punishment and, at the same time, justify punishment. Human dignity itself cannot be considered exclusively as an objective concept, but must also be understood subjectively; in a forward-looking way, it is based on the capacity 'of reevaluating one's life at any given moment, as well as the ability to change one's life from this moment on'.[152]

Just as the evolutionary dynamic of the international community is future oriented, the purpose of international punishment is future oriented as well. In my view, the combined preventive theories provide, in principle, a suitable model for the justification of international punishment. These theories combine consequentialist *grounds* of punishment and deontological *limitations* to punishment in a sustainable way.

Regarding the exact purposes of punishment, I rejected theories that directly focus on the macro-level of the society as such, like the general preventive theories. They rely on grounds that are too abstract to form part of a legitimatory dialogue that leads to severe practical consequences. Instead, I argued that punishment – as a communicative endeavour – primarily has to address the meso- and the micro-level.

By integrating the meso-level into the theory of punishment, a new form of prevention between special and general prevention emerges. On this meso-level, those who are 'indirectly' affected by a core crime are considered addressees of criminal communication. The meso prevention fits the insight that the message of punishment has to be different depending on whether one addresses (potential) followers or leaders. When we address (potential) leaders, the message of punishment is actually directed only at a relatively small group of people because only a few people will ever reach the position of power of state presidents, militia leaders, etc.

Furthermore, the micro-level of the individual perpetrator and the individual victims has to be addressed. Regarding the perpetrator, special prevention – rehabilitation – aims to deconstruct the legitimation narrative of the perpetrator. Regarding the victims, the punishment communicates that the international community acknowledges the violation of their rights and declares that violation is unacceptable, and thereby renews the law's promise of protection. The victim-related aspect, and the special preventive, rehabilitative purpose, however, cannot justify the hard treatment on their own, but can only contribute to its concrete design.

3 *Punishment and Human Dignity*

According to this concept, the offender will continue to be punished 'for the others'. Nevertheless, this theory does not violate the principle of

[152] Margalit, *The Decent Society*, 75.

non-instrumentalization. The perpetrator is not addressed as a single individual within the evolving world society. Instead, he or she is addressed as a member of a case-specific transnational group. The perpetrator is connected much more closely with this rather small meso group than with the world society as such.

I proposed rationalizing international punishment as a form of compensation for the 'intellectual crime damage' the offender has caused. I thereby relied on duties 'incurred as a result of wrongdoing'.[153] The intellectual crime damage cannot only be located on the micro-level of the directly affected victims but also on the meso-level of 'indirectly' affected groups. The case-specific group of potential perpetrators corresponds with another case-specific group of 'indirect' victims. It is to these addressees that the perpetrator owes the compensation.

The perpetrator remains *an author of the concrete design of the compensation.* He or she is viewed as someone who is able to respond within the communicative process of punishment and therefore compensates the 'intellectual crime damage' he or she has caused either by using the punishment for his or her rehabilitation or, if he or she refuses rehabilitation, by passively 'enduring' the imprisonment. Either way, the punishment is communicating solidarity with the victims.

[153] Tadros, 'Doing without Desert', 229; see, in detail, Tadros, *The Ends of Harm*, 273 et. seq.; Tadros, *Wrongs and Crimes*, 47 et seq.

15

The Right to Punishment for International Crimes

JENS DAVID OHLIN

On 1 October 2002, Magnus Gäfgen was taken into custody by the Frankfurt police in connection with the kidnapping of a young boy held for ransom.[1] What happened next is well known both to the German public and to international lawyers interested in criminal law. The police threatened Gäfgen with various forms of torture (including a reference to sexual assault) unless he divulged the location of the boy. Gäfgen quickly relented and led the police to the boy, who was already dead. Gäfgen was convicted of murder and the police were convicted of coercion.[2] However, the District Court *(Landgericht)* in Frankfurt concluded that the police, though culpable, were not appropriate subjects of punishment, and therefore sentenced them to small monetary fines, which were then suspended.[3] Essentially, the police escaped serious consequences for their behaviour.

This is where the story gets interesting. Gäfgen, unhappy that his torturers were not punished, filed a case against Germany at the European Court of Human Rights (ECtHR).[4] Gäfgen argued that Germany's failure to punish his torturers violated his human rights as protected by the European Convention on Human Rights (ECHR).[5] The European Court concluded that Gäfgen was right – the German government was obligated to punish perpetrators of torture, and by failing to do so adequately, Germany violated Gäfgen's human rights.

[1] ECtHR, Judgement of 1 June 2010 (Grand Chamber), *Gäfgen v. Germany*, Application No. 22978/05, para. 14.

[2] German Criminal Code, Sec. 240(1), (4)(2) Nr. 2 (Nötigung im Amt).

[3] See Landgericht Frankfurt a.M., Judgment of 20 December 2004, 5/27 Kls - 7570 Js 203814/03, published in *Neue Juristische Wochenschrift* 2005, 692–696.

[4] See ECtHR, *Gäfgen v. Germany*, para. 2.

[5] ECtHR, *Gäfgen v. Germany*, para. 75.

Although the ECtHR's *Gäfgen v. Germany* decision received widespread attention, I do not believe that international criminal lawyers fully digested its implications.[6] In this chapter, I hope to demonstrate the significance of *Gäfgen*, as well as the prior ECtHR cases it relied upon, and show that it points the way towards a general theory of a state's responsibility to punish. This human rights approach is significant for several reasons. First, theorists of punishment are usually in the business of constructing *justifications* for punishment, that is, an argument in favour of coercive state action if the state elects to exercise that power. But the *Gäfgen* approach focuses almost exclusively on the state's *duty* to punish. Second, and relatedly, if the state forgoes its option to punish, theorists have often viewed such exercises of 'mercy' as normatively desirable events.[7] However, the *Gäfgen* approach suggests that such moments of mercy may, in some circumstances, be problematic from the perspective of international human rights law. Third, the legal foundation for the obligation stems not from an obligation owed to the entire community but rather an obligation owed to the victims. Fourth, and finally, human rights activists and lawyers are more used to discussing human rights in the context of *constraints* on punishment.[8] In this case, however, the notion of human rights is being deployed in *favour* of punishment as an absolute requirement of a system of law that respects human rights. Instead of the Defence appealing to human rights in arguing for the forbearance of punishment; we now have the

[6] A notable exception is the excellent article by F. Jeßberger, 'Bad Torture – Good Torture? What International Criminal Lawyers May Learn from the Recent Trial of Police Officers in Germany' (2005) 3 *Journal of International Criminal Justice* 1059.

[7] See, for example, J.G. Murphy, 'Forgiveness, Mercy, and the Retributive Emotions' (1988) 7 *Criminal Justice Ethics* 3; C.A.H. Hage Johnson, 'Entitled to Clemency: Mercy in the Criminal Law' (1991) 10 *Law and Philosophy* 109. However, see S.P. Garvey, 'Is It Wrong to Commute Death Row? Retribution, Atonement, and Mercy' (2004) 82 *North Carolina Law Review* 1319, 1334 ('Keep in mind that the imperfect obligation to show mercy always competes with the perfect obligation to achieve retributive justice. As such, with every act of mercy comes a corresponding denial of justice. At some point, so it would seem, the demands of justice must prevail against those of mercy.'); R.A. Duff, 'The Intrusion of Mercy' (2007) 4 *Ohio State Journal of Criminal Law* 361, 381:

> I have argued so far that mercy does have a proper, although limited, role in the context of criminal law and punishment, but that that role cannot be captured or explained within the perspective of criminal or penal justice: seen from within that perspective, mercy must appear as something arbitrary or unreasonable (since it is not grounded in what can count as relevant reasons from that perspective). Mercy marks, not an application of penal justice, but rather an intrusion into the sphere of penal justice by moral values and concerns that are not matters of justice.

[8] See, e.g., W.A. Schabas, *The Abolition of the Death Penalty in International Law*, 3rd ed. (Cambridge: Cambridge University Press, 2002).

prospect of the Prosecution appealing to human rights in arguing for the *necessity* of punishment.

It would be useful, therefore, to connect these nascent developments in human rights theory to the literature on human rights in international criminal law. There is already a rich literature on punishment written by international criminal lawyers, often canvassing the important debates between retributivism, deterrence and expressivism.[9] There is also a growing literature on the role that human rights law can and should play in international criminal law, especially in the context of international criminal procedure.[10] Finally, there also is a foundational enterprise of appealing to the anti-impunity norm as a basic *grundnorm* of international criminal law.[11] These various strands should be pulled together to create a human rights-centric theory of punishment. At its heart, the theory will do nothing less than demonstrate that mercy is, in fact, not morally undesirable, but and in fact legally unconscionable – a human rights violation. If this argument is true, it has wide implications for both the theory and practice of international criminal law, as well as domestic law. For indeed, there are a wide variety of places where the state exercises mercy: suspended sentences, pardons, commutations, supervized released programs, etc. In each of these cases, however, the sovereign 'grace' expressed by acts of mercy may violate the human rights of the victims. Or, at the very least, grants of *excessive* mercy may violate this right.

The goal of this chapter is to show that the argument in *Gäfgen* is generalizable to other contexts. Although the case arose from a particular procedural posture – a violation, by police officers, of the prohibition against torture – there is little reason to suspect that the arguments in *Gäfgen* will not hold for other crimes as well. At the very least, these arguments can be extended, without logical disruption, to other international crimes that states are under a legal obligation to criminalize, such as war crimes, crimes against humanity and genocide. Moreover, if the structure of these arguments is conceptually

9 For a good discussion, see M.A. Drumbl, *Atrocity, Punishment, and International Law* (Cambridge: Cambridge University Press, 2007).

10 See G. Sluiter et al. (eds.), *International Criminal Procedure: Principles and Rules* (Oxford: Oxford University Press, 2013), 81 ('There is no reason to doubt that customary norms on human rights apply to international organizations.').

11 Compare J. Mayerfeld, 'Ruthlessness, Impunity, and the Effacement of International Human Rights Law' (2010) 8 *Santa Clara Journal of International Law* 289, 293 with K. Engle, 'Anti-Impunity and the Turn to Criminal Law in Human Rights' (2015) 100 *Cornell Law Review* 1069, 1119 ('Yet, the fight against the culture of impunity – with impunity narrowly defined as foreclosing the option of criminal punishment – has not only taken up a significant amount of the human rights movement's space; it has helped shape the direction of human rights advocacy as well as both international human rights and international criminal law.').

sound, in theory they should apply outside of the European context, unless the argument is based on a particular right that is only protected by the ECHR and not by international law. Also, if these arguments are sound, they should also apply when international tribunals are prosecuting these crimes, even though international tribunals are not directly bound by international human rights obligations, although almost every international tribunal recognizes that its decisions should remain faithful to international human rights law.[12] Finally, it should make no difference whether the object of prosecution is a state agent, as it was in *Gäfgen*, or whether it is a private actor found guilty of committing another international crime. What matters is the status of the victim, not the status of the perpetrator.

The conclusion may be hard to swallow and may sound counter-intuitive. The idea that mercy is a human rights violation goes against the rich tradition of human rights advocacy. One might argue that the *Gäfgen* case got it wrong, or that the European Court long ago took a wrong turn in overseeing punishments handed down in domestic criminal cases. But I hope to demonstrate that *Gäfgen* is not wrongly decided. Moreover, I hope to demonstrate that if we take the reasoning in *Gäfgen* seriously, it requires that we recognize that victims of international crimes have a legal right to see their perpetrators punished. Moreover, not only cases of zero punishment but also cases of *inadequate* punishment constitute a violation of that human right. It is in this sense that we may legitimately talk of a 'right to punishment' under human rights law.[13]

I THE FACTS OF THE CASE

Although the facts of Gäfgen's case are well known, it is important to revisit them to determine whether the reasoning in the ECtHR's decision is *sui generis* – that is, intimately and inextricably tied to the facts of the case – or whether it is generalizable to other international crimes.

[12] For example, see ICTY, Decision of 22 September 2004 (TC), *Milošević*, IT-02-54-T, para. 29 (citing and applying procedural protections recognized in human rights treaties).

[13] My use of the phrase 'right to punishment' should be distinguished from the Kantian use of that phrase, which suggests that offenders have a right to punishment because all offenders have a 'right' to be treated as a moral agent. See H. Morris, *On Guilt and Innocence: Essays in Legal Philosophy and Moral Psychology* (Oakland: University of California Press, 1976), 41; R.L. Christopher, 'The Prosecutor's Dilemma: Bargains and Punishments' (2003) 72 *Fordham Law Review* 93, 128. This is not the sense in which I use the phrase. When I refer to the 'right to punishment', I refer to the remedial right of victims to see their victimizers punished.

When Gäfgen was brought into police custody for questioning, his victim was already dead. According to the police and the prosecutors, Gäfgen killed the boy first and only then attempted to extract a ransom from the boy's family by pretending that the boy was still alive.[14] However, when the police started their interrogation, they were ignorant of this fact. The police lieutenant in charge of the detective unit, Lieutenant Wolfgang Daschner, ordered detectives under his command to threaten Gäfgen to get him to divulge the location of the kidnapped boy.[15] On Daschner's orders, the detectives told Gäfgen that he would be placed in a cell with several individuals who would anally rape him. The detectives also told him that a police specialist was arriving who had instruments capable of producing intolerable levels of pain without causing permanent injury.[16] The point of this last threat seemed to suggest that the police were unafraid of the consequences of torturing Gäfgen because they could do so with impunity; the lack of physical injuries would entail that no one would believe Gäfgen. Finally, the police detectives also planned to administer a truth serum that would force Gäfgen to divulge the information.[17]

Gäfgen quickly divulged the location of the boy and the police took him to the field where he walked – apparently barefoot – to the general location of the body.[18] Gäfgen was then charged with murder. Toward the end of his trial, Gäfgen gave a statement to the Court where he conceded that he murdered the boy, saying that his confession was 'the only way to accept his deep guilt' and express 'the greatest possible apology for the murder of the child'.[19]

Gäfgen argued that because his treatment was improper, and violated his basic dignity under Article 1 of Germany's Basic Law *(Grundgesetz)*, he was owed an extraordinary remedy: the dismissal of all charges and his eventual release.[20] The German courts decided on a more limited remedy: Gäfgen's statement regarding the boy's location was excluded from the trial because it was the product of his mistreatment, but the Court allowed the introduction of downstream evidence that the police gathered (the fruit of the poisonous tree),

[14] See ECtHR, *Gäfgen v. Germany*, paras. 11–12.

[15] ECtHR, *Gäfgen v. Germany*, para. 15.

[16] ECtHR, *Gäfgen v. Germany*, para. 15.

[17] ECtHR, *Gäfgen v. Germany*, para. 20. It is unclear if this latter plan was communicated to Gäfgen as a threat; if yes, the threat to Gäfgen would suggest to him that there was no reason to endure the torture, as they would get the information anyway, thus encouraging him to divulge the information.

[18] ECtHR, *Gäfgen v. Germany*, para 20.

[19] ECtHR, *Gäfgen v. Germany*, para. 32.

[20] ECtHR, *Gäfgen v. Germany*, para. 24.

including the forensics evidence from the boy's body.[21] Moreover, Gäfgen's testimony at trial provided an alternative confession that established his guilt even though the original statement was not admissible. The European Court confirmed this finding and refused to agree with Gäfgen that his mistreatment required dismissal of the charges against him.[22]

However, Gäfgen was successful in convincing the ECtHR that the German courts had erred in their treatment of Daschner and the police detectives who carried out the torture scheme. Daschner made no attempt to hide his involvement and drafted a memo to the official file the day after the interrogation that explained and justified his actions.[23] Following an investigation, Daschner and the other detectives were criminally charged and found guilty of criminal coercion or incitement to coercion for their mistreatment of Gäfgen.[24] The Court concluded that Daschner was not entitled to the defence of justified necessity, nor the defence of excused necessity, for a variety of reasons.[25] First, the boy he sought to save was not a close family relation. Second, the use of torture was not an 'appropriate' means to resolve the emergency because it violated Gäfgen's inviolable human dignity protected by Article 1 of the Basic Law.[26]

However, despite the Frankfurt District Court's refusal to exonerate Daschner and the other police detectives, finding that their actions were legally culpable, at the same time the Court refused to punish Daschner. The Court concluded that imprisonment was not appropriate in the case and instead 'assessed' a monetary fine for the offence. However, the Court then exercised its discretion to defer the fine and transform it into a warning. In so doing, the Court applied Section 59 of the German Penal Code, which allows for deferment of fines when the court concludes that the defendant is not expected to commit additional offences, an evaluation of the offence and the offender reveals special circumstances that negate the need to impose the punishment, and the requirements of general deterrence do not require the imposition of the punishment. This left a curious result: The Court concluded that Daschner had violated an important provision of the German Penal Code but nonetheless was not an appropriate subject of state punishment. This finding walked a fine line; the decision maintained the sanctity of

21 ECtHR, *Gäfgen v. Germany*, para. 27.
22 ECtHR, *Gäfgen v. Germany*, para. 179.
23 ECtHR, *Gäfgen v. Germany*, para. 20.
24 ECtHR, *Gäfgen v. Germany*, para. 49.
25 ECtHR, *Gäfgen v. Germany*, para. 48. The trial court's application of the necessity defence is analyzed in Jeßberger, 'Bad Torture – Good Torture?', 1064.
26 Jeßberger, 'Bad Torture – Good Torture?', 1065.

the criminal law prohibition on torture by refusing to apply any affirmative defences (not even an excuse), yet in the refusal to apply a punishment it also expressed sympathy with the defendants and their predicament.

Gäfgen was not as impressed with the judges' subtlety as (most) legal commentators were. Gäfgen argued before the ECtHR that the Frankfurt Court's failure to punish Daschner had violated Gäfgen's human rights. Indeed, Germany's position was somewhat precarious. If its domestic courts had concluded that Daschner was not guilty because he was protected by either excused or justified necessity under the German criminal code, then that would have been a different matter. However, the District Court explicitly conceded that Daschner was guilty enough to be convicted, just not guilty enough to be punished. It was precisely this conceptual move that allegedly violated Gäfgen's human rights. His human rights having been violated, it was imperative that the state punish the perpetrators; their failure to do so violated human rights law.[27]

II THE GRAND CHAMBER OPINION

As noted above, the European Court's Grand Chamber concluded that Gäfgen's human rights were violated when Germany declined to punish his torturers. The opinion includes several moving parts. The goal of this section is to break down the essential parts and then, in the following section, to see whether the legal argument can be generalized and extended beyond the torture context.

Germany violated Gäfgen's rights under Article 3 of the ECHR, which states that '[n]o one shall be subjected to torture or to inhuman or degrading treatment or punishment', a requirement that is also codified in the Convention Against Torture.[28] According to the European Court's existing jurisprudence, implicit in this prohibition is the requirement that a victim have adequate access to avenues of redress. This is both a procedural norm and an outcome requirement – including government compensation and punishment of offenders. This view of Convention rights is created by reading Article 3 in conjunction with Article 1, the jurisdictional provision of the Convention, which requires that states 'shall secure to everyone within their jurisdiction the rights and freedoms defined in Section I of this Convention'.[29] So the duty to

[27] See ECtHR, *Gäfgen v. Germany*, para. 124.
[28] Convention for the Protection of Human Rights and Fundamental Freedoms (European Convention on Human Rights), Art. 3, opened for signature 1950, entered into force 1953.
[29] ECHR, Art. 1.

punish comes from the interplay between the prohibition against torture and the positive obligation to secure the rights of the Convention to all who are protected to it. As the ECtHR has observed, 'under Article 19 of the Convention and in accordance with the principle that the Convention is intended to guarantee rights that are not theoretical or illusory, but practical and effective, the Court has to ensure that a State's obligation to protect the rights of those under its jurisdiction is adequately discharged'.[30]

The European Court therefore scrutinized, as it has in many cases before, whether Germany's investigation of the complainant's mistreatment by state officials was adequate and effective – ultimately finding that it was adequate.[31] However, the state's failure to adequately punish Daschner and his colleagues was not acceptable. According to the ECtHR, the Court felt a legal obligation to review the domestic application of criminal penalties in this case:

> Nevertheless, imposing almost token fines of 60 and 90 daily payments of EUR 60 and EUR 120 respectively, and, furthermore, opting to suspend them, cannot be considered an adequate response to a breach of Article 3, even seen in the context of the sentencing practice in the respondent State. Such punishment, which is manifestly disproportionate to a breach of one of the core rights of the Convention, does not have the necessary deterrent effect in order to prevent further violations of the prohibition of ill-treatment in future difficult situations.[32]

What is interesting about this conclusion is that it appears to combine both retributive and deterrent rationales for concluding that the punishment was inappropriately lenient. The token fines, which were not even imposed, were 'manifestly disproportionate', a point that the Grand Chamber later elaborated on when it referred to the 'manifest disproportion between the gravity of the act and the punishment imposed'.[33] This suggests a retributive calculation because the punishment must be proportional to the 'gravity' of the act, rather than proportional to a particular consequence. At the same time, however, the Court also articulated a deterrence rationale, suggesting that the failure to punish would fail to deter future offenders or prevent further violations.

The structure of these two normative duties is quite different. The first, the retributive consideration, is tied directly to the victim's interest – the interest in seeing his perpetrators adequately punished. The second, the deterrence rationale, is by logic not tied directly to the interest of the victim in the case,

[30] See ECtHR, *Gäfgen v. Germany*, para. 123.
[31] ECtHR, *Gäfgen v. Germany*, para. 4.
[32] ECtHR, *Gäfgen v. Germany*, para. 124.
[33] ECtHR, *Gäfgen v. Germany*, para. 123.

as whether future offenders are deterred impacts not the past victim but *future* unspecific victims. It is unclear why failure to deter acts against future victims violates the human rights of the prior victim. For that reason, the retributive rationale seems to be the strongest of the two arguments. Applying the facts of the case to this legal standard, the ECtHR also concluded that Germany's failure to hand down appropriate administrative consequences – transferring Daschner to an equivalent post rather than demoting or firing him – was also impermissible.[34]

In scrutinizing the sufficiency (or lack thereof) of Daschner's sentence, the ECtHR committed itself to a 'supervisory function' of domestic penal sanctions, a role that it wholeheartedly embraced rather than shied away from.[35] According to the Grand Chamber, '[i]t follows that while the Court acknowledges the role of the national courts in the choice of appropriate sanctions for ill-treatment by State agents, it must retain its supervisory function and intervene in cases of manifest disproportion between the gravity of the act and the punishment imposed'.[36] In other words, while trial courts are especially well-suited to determining the appropriateness of specific penal sanctions (having heard the relevant evidence during a trial), trial court decisions are not to be accepted without judicial scrutiny. In cases of 'manifest disproportion', it is appropriate for a regional or international tribunal to declare that the inadequate sentence violated the state's obligations under European human rights law. It should be noted, of course, that a finding of 'manifest disproportion', as in Gäfgen's case, simply entailed a legal finding and an order of compensation from Germany to the victim; it did not result (because it could not) in a judicial nullification of Daschner's sentence or in a judicial order to the German courts requiring them to re-sentence Daschner consistent with human rights law. Such a result, though theoretically possible, would presumably have violated the requirements of domestic criminal procedure and the rights of the defendant.

It remains to be seen how much of the Court's analysis is specific to the crime of torture. Although the decision is, by its terms, tethered to the Article 3 prohibition against torture, the real conceptual work is done by Article 1 of the ECHR. It would be illogical to suggest that torture is the only human rights prohibition that requires punishment. Indeed, Article 1 requires that the state 'secure' convention rights to all individuals, and this positive obligation could be logically combined with other convention rights. The most

[34] ECtHR, *Gäfgen v. Germany*, para. 125.

[35] ECtHR, *Gäfgen v. Germany*, para. 123.

[36] ECtHR, *Gäfgen v. Germany*, para. 123.

important examples are the Article 2 obligation to protect the right to life, the Article 4 prohibition on slavery and forced labour, and the Article 5 protection of security and liberty. There are others. Each of these legal protections, when combined with Article 1, could and should generate the same duty to punish as found in the context of torture.

Indeed, other ECtHR cases have articulated a duty to punish in other contexts. For example, in *Ali and Ayşe Duran v. Turkey*, the European Court concluded that there was a human rights violation wherein the government failed to enforce the sentences of police officers who were convicted of ill-treatment of the complainant.[37] In that case, the government's failure to punish the officers, who were convicted, 'demonstrated a clear disproportion between the gravity of the offence in question and the punishment imposed'.[38] Incidentally, this conclusion goes even further than *Gäfgen*, because it suggests that even where punishment is imposed at law (by the judiciary), there might be a human rights violation if the punishment is never brought to fruition by the executive branch.

Similarly, in *Özcan and Others v. Turkey*, the ECtHR concluded that Turkey was responsible for its failure to punish police officers involved in an unlawful killing. In *Özcan*, however, the alleged mistreatment was not a violation of the Article 3 of the ECHR prohibition against torture, but rather a violation of the Article 2 right to life:

> Concerning the Government's objection to the applicants' victim status based on the issue of compensation the Court reiterates that, in cases concerning deprivations of life, Contracting States have an obligation under Article 2 of the Convention to conduct an effective investigation capable of leading to the identification and punishment of those responsible. That obligation would be rendered illusory if, in respect of complaints under Article 2 of the Convention, an applicant's victim status were to be remedied by merely awarding damages [...] Confining the authorities' reaction to incidents of deprivations of life to the mere payment of compensation would also make it possible in some cases for agents of the State to abuse the rights of those within their control with virtual impunity, and the general legal prohibitions on killing, despite their fundamental importance, would be ineffective in practice [...][39]

[37] ECtHR, Judgement of 8 April 2008 (Third Section), *Duran v. Turkey*, Application No. 42942/02.

[38] ECtHR, *Duran v. Turkey*, para. 71.

[39] See ECtHR, Judgement of 20 April 2010 (Second Section), *Özcan and Others v. Turkey*, Application No. 18893/05, para. 54.

So it is clear that the obligation to punish extends beyond cases of torture to all cases involving unlawful killings in violation of the right to life. Because most cases of serious violations of domestic and international criminal law involve an unlawful and arbitrary deprivation of life, one can already see the seeds of a generalized theory of a duty to punish offenders in order to vindicate the rights of victims. The ECtHR issued a virtually identical holding in *Nikolova and Velichkova*.[40]

Moreover, there is no reason to limit the state's obligation to punish to misconduct by public actors. In the famous *M.C. v. Bulgaria* case, Bulgaria was held responsible for its failure to apply its rape jurisprudence in a way that would provide an adequate remedy for victims of sexual violence.[41] Specifically, the Bulgarian system had retained allegedly obsolete force and resistance requirements that made it difficult for the police or prosecutor to hold perpetrators responsible for acts that the ECtHR concluded constituted rape. In making this determination, the Court stated that:

> The Court reiterates that the obligation of the High Contracting Parties under Article 1 of the Convention to secure to everyone within their jurisdiction the rights and freedoms defined in the Convention, taken together with Article 3, requires States to take measures designed to ensure that individuals within their jurisdiction are not subjected to ill-treatment, including ill-treatment administered by private individuals.[42]

In this regard, the Court's holding in *M.C. v. Bulgaria* was a reaffirmation of its prior holding in *A. v. United Kingdom* that the duty to punish applies to 'ill-treatment administered by private individuals' and that '[c]hildren and other vulnerable individuals, in particular, are entitled to State protection, in the form of effective deterrence, against such serious breaches of personal integrity'.[43]

Taken together, these precedents make it unsurprising that the ECtHR in *Gäfgen* would conclude that Germany had violated the complainant's human rights. The obligation to ensure an effective remedy is a combination of an

[40] See ECtHR, Judgement of 20 December 2007 (Fifth Section), *Nikolova and Velichkova v. Bulgaria*, Application No. 7888/03, para. 55.

[41] ECtHR, Judgement of 4 December 2003 (First Section), *M.C. v. Bulgaria*, Application No. 39272/98.

[42] ECtHR, *M.C. v. Bulgaria*, para. 149.

[43] See ECtHR, Judgement of 23 September 1998, *A. v. United Kingdom*, Application No. 25599/94, para. 22. See also ECtHR, Judgement of 26 March 1985, *X and Y v. The Netherlands*, Application No. 8978/80 paras. 21–27 (concluding that civil law remedies were an insufficient remedy for rape and that only a criminal law remedy, with effective penalties, would secure the victim's rights under the Convention).

Article 1 of the ECHR 'securing' obligation with another human rights protection, including the right to life. Civil compensation by itself is inadequate if the perpetrators do not receive a criminal punishment. More importantly, even the application of a criminal punishment may be inadequate if there is a 'manifest disproportion' between the gravity of the crime and the punishment. This requirement is both backward looking in the sense that it must satisfy retributive concerns with regard to that particular victim and forward looking in the sense that it must respond to the interests of future victims. If this process requires international human rights law – as a body of law – to look over the shoulder of the criminal process, then so be it.

III THE GENERAL THEORY

In the following section, I hope to articulate in conceptual terms a general theory that expresses the state's duty to punish offenders as a requirement of the individual human rights of victims – hence the expression 'the right to punishment'. Unlike the prior section, which articulated this account within the context of existing ECtHR jurisprudence, this section will offer an *a priori* account appealing to first principles. By drawing on shared intuitions of human rights, I hope to demonstrate that even outside of the context of the European Court's jurisprudence, victims have a human right to adequate recourse that includes the punishment of their victimizers, and the law should recognize this right. The ultimate goal of this normative account is to show that excessive forms of mercy are not just undesirable in a broad sense but also infringe the rights of individuals. It is not just society that loses something when excessive or inappropriate mercy is conferred on perpetrators; specific individuals are harmed by this process. Criminal lawyers are trained to view punishment as an institutional relationship between the state and the offender who is punished. This section will redraw that portrait as a triangle that connects the state, the perpetrator and the victim.

The right not to be deprived of life arbitrarily is one of the most fundamental human rights. All individuals, simply by virtue of their human dignity, have a right to life. Closely akin to this right is the right to be secure in their persons and the right to be free from torture and other forms of mistreatment. Taken together and broadly construed, these rights articulate a general prohibition against brutality and the right not to be subject to criminal violence. When an individual is victimized by illegal violence, the crime constitutes both a public and private wrong – a wrong perpetrated against the legal order (the community) and the individual victim.

For the moment, the exact conceptual ground for these rights is irrelevant to the argument, because everyone is in agreement that these rights are universal. One might appeal to the human dignity of all individuals as expressed in Kantian terms, i.e., the fact that each individual is entitled, by virtue of their status as moral agents, to be treated in accordance with universal human legislation.[44] Or, one might appeal to a neo-Kantian social contract framework, wherein these rights are guaranteed because they would have been selected by bargainers negotiated in the original position behind a veil of ignorance.[45] Alternatively, the rights are implied by a republican conception of freedom as non-denomination.[46] In other words, all human beings have an inherent right to freedom, and their subjection to violence against their bodily integrity puts them in a state of domination between the perpetrator and the victim – a status of subordination that offends the very essence of human freedom.

Both public and private violence offend this basic right to be free from mistreatment, although the structure of each violation is slightly different. When state officials engage in the violence, the state is in the direct position of violating the rights of its own citizens. In the case of private violence, both the aggressor and the victim are private individuals, and the state is responsible, if at all, insofar as it owes positive obligations to the victim to prevent and punish the violations. In the first scenario, the state is responsible for its commission; in the second scenario, the state is responsible for its omission, i.e., its failure to take adequate steps in response to the victimization.

The more contested issue is how to draw the line from the original rights violation to a rights-claim regarding an adequate remedy in the criminal law – the requirement to punish. It is in this area where the ECtHR precedents are at their thinnest – all they say is that without a criminal consequence, perpetrators will continue to commit crimes with impunity, and by extension, the rights of the Convention will be merely hypothetical instead of actual. Is there anything more that could be said on this score?

The answer lies not just in the original victimization by the perpetrator but also in a second-order right to live in a community where rights-violations are taken seriously. When a state refuses to punish offenders, it expresses its de facto approval of their conduct in the form of tacit endorsement. At the very

44 See Universal Declaration of Human Rights, U.N. GAOR, 2d Special Sess., Supp. No. 2, pmbl., at 72, U.N. Doc. A/810 (1948); I. Kant, *Grounding for the Metaphysics of Morals* (translation J.W. Ellington), 3rd ed. (Indianapolis: Hackett Publishing Company, 1993), 36–37.

45 See J. Rawls, *A Theory of Justice*, revised ed. (Harvard: Harvard University Press, 1999), 123.

46 See P. Pettit, *Republicanism: A Theory of Freedom and Government* (Oxford: Oxford University Press, 1999).

least, the failure to punish suggests a form of moral equivocation, i.e., it is uncertain how 'wrong' the conduct really was. This notion is certainly true in the *Gäfgen* case; the German courts refused to punish Daschner and his officers because they were sympathetic to their plight. The reason for this sympathy was precisely one example of this moral equivocation – a suggestion that their actions were not fully blameworthy, under the circumstances, despite their commission of the criminal offence.

In this vein, the state responsibility towards victims of private wrongs is a communicative obligation – an obligation to adequately express not just the nature of society's disapproval of the human rights violation but also the *intensity* of that disapproval relative to the gravity of the human rights violation. Failure to express disapproval constitutes tacit endorsement of the rights violation – an endorsement that runs smack into the state's obligations under international human rights law. The obligation is not just to refrain from committing human rights violations, it is also an obligation to express their unconditional disapproval when private actors engage in acts of mistreatment. This theoretical obligation is codified in legalistic provisions requiring that states 'secure' the rights of the convention in practice.

There is a remaining question, which is why this communicative conception of punishment requires the imposition of harm upon the offender. What is to be gained by making the victim suffer and how exactly does that communicate anything to the victim, to the perpetrator and to society at large? Indeed, the difference between a token punishment and a non-token punishment is that the former imposes no suffering on the offender while the latter imposes substantial suffering on him or her. Retributive theorists have proposed numerous answers to this question. Some have argued, for instance, that suffering allows the offender to engage in penance – a process that promises to return the offender into the moral community as a member in good standing.[47] The result in that situation is a form of 'redemption' in the eyes of the community, a result that is only possible when the offender takes seriously – through his or her acceptance of their suffering – the moral wrongs they have inflicted on innocent parties.[48] But a firmer conceptual ground is

47 See C. Bennett, *The Apology Ritual: A Philosophical Theory of Punishment* (Cambridge: Cambridge University Press, 2010), 118–119.

48 See J. Forman Jr., 'A Prison Sentence Ends. But the Stigma Doesn't', *New York Times*, 15 September 2017 ('Harvard's [denial of admission to convicted murderer] reveals the truth about why mass punishment persists and the lie we are telling ourselves about the possibility of redemption.').

provided by teasing out the implications of an expressive theory of punishment.[49] The punishment of the offender expresses not only society's condemnation of the behaviour but also its solidarity with the victim, at least as regards to the particular criminal transaction in question (rather than blanket or wholesale solidarity). Although some form of expression is possible using other mechanisms – such as a legal declaration – only the perpetrator's suffering adequately communicates the profound moral devastation caused by the perpetrator's actions. Consider, for a moment, a community that refuses to punish a perpetrator but instead publishes a statement declaring that the perpetrator violated someone's rights in the most horrendous way possible. The perpetrator's impunity in that case communicates the community's lack of solidarity with the victim. It says, in other words, we care about your rights but we do not care about them enough to impose coercive measures on the individuals who violated your rights. If they do it again, we will issue another statement, and they might do it again, and on and on. This result communicates society's commitment to impunity more than solidarity with the victim.

The obligation to express society's disapproval of the criminal offence, and to stand in solidarity with the victim, entails not just the exercise of punishment but also the correct amount of punishment. At this point, one might object that any amount of punishment, even a token punishment, could in theory express society's disapproval of the actions involved. Indeed, why should the amount of punishment matter at all? If the point is to communicate something, the 'gesture' could be completed by any ministerial act without significant consequence for the perpetrator. A monetary fine would certainly be permissible. Or, to borrow a line from contract law theory, perhaps depriving a perpetrator of a mere peppercorn would be enough to express social disapproval.[50]

But even a cursory inspection of actual cases shows why this is not possible in reality. Punishment via a token sentence almost always reveals a form of tacit encouragement, or at the very least moral equivocation. For example, why was Daschner given the token sentence? Yes, of course, the token punishment expressed society's disproval of the action, but the whole reason the Frankfurt District Court imposed the token fines was because it wished to communicate that Daschner's actions were not a typical case of torture. Indeed, the punishments in his case communicated tacit encouragement

[49] See Drumbl, *Atrocity, Punishment, and International Law*, 174 ('The fact that consequences follow a guilty verdict makes law all the more real to the community.').

[50] See E.A. Farnsworth, *Contracts* (Boston: Little, Brown & Company, 1982) § 2.11 at 66 n. 2, quoting E. Coke on Littleton 222 (1628).

because that is precisely what motivated the District Court's decision: They were not fully convinced that Daschner's behaviour was truly as blameworthy as other cases of torture or police coercion. Consequently, disproportionately lenient punishment violates the same conceptual prohibition as not punishing a perpetrator at all because it fails to express society's disapproval of the action in question.[51]

Surely, though, a state should be permitted to dispense mercy, even in tough cases where the defendant has committed a grievous wrong. Some states refuse to punish offenders when the offender, though culpable, is severely old or ill. Sometimes parole boards release offenders after evidence of good conduct, expressions or remorse, or rehabilitation. Presidents, governors, or heads of state issue pardons that exempt individuals from criminal responsibility – and punishment – for their crimes. In some circumstances, offenders are released on compassionate grounds – 'compassion' for the offender, not the victims, incidentally. For example, Scottish officials released Abdelbaset al-Megrahi on compassionate grounds in 2009, despite his conviction in 2001 for participation in the bombing of Pan Am Flight 103, which was destroyed over Scottish airspace in 1988, littering the bodies (and body parts) from the 243 passengers and 17 crew over miles of farmland. Although al-Megrahi had not yet completed his full sentence, he was released when it became apparent that he was suffering from prostate cancer and allegedly only had months to live. He returned to Libya where he was met with a hero's welcome as a figure of national significance – hardly a situation where the audience recognized his culpability for the harm that he caused.[52] Despite the original diagnosis, he eventually survived for another 3 years, ultimately dying in 2012. He lived his last 3 years in freedom.[53]

What these and other examples demonstrate is that 'mercy' has a shadow side. It communicates the state's sympathy towards the plight of the defendant

[51] See M. Penrose, 'Lest We Fail: The Importance of Enforcement in International Criminal Law' (1999) 15 *American University International Law Review* 321, 383–386; S. Beresford, 'Unshackling the Paper Tiger: The Sentencing Practices of the Ad Hoc International Criminal Tribunals for the Former Yugoslavia and Rwanda' (2001) 1 *International Criminal Law Review* 33, 90; M.M. DeGuzman, 'Harsh Justice for International Crimes?' (2014) 39 *Yale Journal of International Law* 1, 33 ('An especially troubling critique may come not from retributivists but from expressivists. Proponents of the expressive function of international punishment may argue that mild or moderate punishment fails to express sufficient condemnation to promote the norms prohibiting international crimes.'). It should be noted that DeGuzman goes on to criticize that position.

[52] J.F. Burns, 'New Questions in Lockerbie Bomber's Release', *New York Times*, 21 August 2009.

[53] R. McFadden, 'Megrahi, Convicted in 1988 Lockerbie Bombing, Dies at 60', *New York Times*, 20 May 2012.

in the face of the coercive machinery of state punishment. The sympathy might be generated by a medical predicament, by the offender's virtuous conduct while incarcerated, or by a sense that the law was unkind to the offender by insisting on the strict application of criminal law provisions. But these expressions of sympathy are often a zero-sum game. By concluding that the offender should be exempt from punishment, the state is also, inevitably, saying something profound about the nature of the victimization of the case. Why? Because the state always has the option of forgoing mercy in some cases – cases of horrendous brutality where mercy is off the table. By agreeing that in some cases mercy remains *on* the table, the state is communicating something about its assessment of the conduct in the case. The only way around this conclusion is to think that the decision to dispense mercy is always solely based on considerations of the offender's predicament. But it rarely is. More typically, mercy decisions weigh considerations of the offender's predicament against the offender's blameworthiness for the criminal behaviour. And that balancing process inevitably involves the state expressing a particular judgment on the significance of the original harm in the case.

Along the same lines, one might wonder whether the duty to punish is subject to balancing along with other state interests. In other words, should the state obligation to punish be absolute, or should it give way when the state has other interests that counsel in favour of mercy? Indeed, exercising mercy, or foregoing punishment entirely, may be necessary to advance a particular utilitarian goal. A state might have limited resources that it wishes to devote to policing and incarceration. Or the state might have empirical evidence that punishment will increase the likelihood of recidivism, rather than reduce it, at least with regards to certain situations or certain pockets of the population.[54] Finally, to be cynical, state exercises of mercy may communicate a government's grace; the population may reward the government's exercise of mercy with renewed gratitude, loyalty and fidelity to the government's rule. The push and pull of these competing interests may require the state to balance away the duty of punishment. Is this acceptable?

This question need not be answered here. Some rights, such as the right to human dignity, are inviolable and are recognized as such in many legal cultures. But let us assume that the right to punishment is one among many rights to which the state is a guardian. Even if ultimately balanced away, in favour of some exercise of mercy, it is important to recognize the moral

[54] See *United States v. Luna-Jasso*, No. CR 14-3523 JB, 2015 WL 1006390, 15 (D.N.M. Feb. 19, 2015) ('The Court has previously noted that the certainty of being caught is a greater deterrence than the severity of the punishment and that incarceration increases recidivism rates.').

interests of the victim and to express those interests in the language of human rights. Then, and only then, can the balancing proceed faithfully. In balancing, by definition, something is lost when something is gained, and it is important to articulate what is lost in the most forceful terms possible before it can be determined that society can and should live with the loss.

Some philosophers and legal theorists argue that mercy is normatively desirable and that the criminal justice system should be designed in such a way as to promote mercy wherever possible. For example, consider Martha Nussbaum's argument in favour of mercy:

> In a sense, the merciful judge looks backward. But at the same time, while acknowledging the fact of wrongdoing, and thus expressing society's commitment to core values, the judge also looks forward to a world of reintegration. The general spirit is that of Transition-Anger: there is outrage at the wrong done, but a generous spirit takes the place of the punitive spirit. In addition to the usual concern about specific and general deterrence, and sometimes incapacitation, this judge also asks about how, in a world of human frailty, we may all be able to live together as well as possible. This concern may sometimes take the form of specific mercy to a specific defendant.[55]

Although Nussbaum goes on to concede that mercy should not lead to mitigation in every case, the overall tenor of her argument is in favour of mercy because she views punishment as a last resort.[56] If society can protect the welfare of its citizens, in a forward-looking way, with non-penal sanctions, then criminal punishment is neither desirable not justifiable.

Nussbaum's pro-mercy view runs the risk of focusing more on the offender than the victim. Later, she concludes that the system should communicate that 'the crime is outrageous, but we can see the offender, with sympathy, as someone who is more and better than the crime, capable of good in future, and we can adjust our sentencing in light of that thought'.[57] Then, Nussbaum suggests 'we redouble our dedication to creating more propitious conditions for all'.[58] The problem with this view is that the victim recedes into the background and the state's merciful response to the victimization seems calibrated to preventing *future* victims rather than responding to the past victimization, by the offender, of this particular human being whose rights and humanity were disrespected in some profound way.

55 M. Nussbaum, *Anger and Forgiveness: Resentment, Generosity, Justice* (Oxford: Oxford University Press, 2016), 207.

56 Nussbaum, *Anger and Forgiveness*, 207.

57 Nussbaum, *Anger and Forgiveness*, 207–208.

58 Nussbaum, *Anger and Forgiveness*, 208.

For Nussbaum, mercy is the perfect antidote to anger, a negative emotion that she considers intimately and inevitably wrapped up with retributivism. For her, anger is best viewed as a negative emotion without redeeming qualities. The concepts of righteous indignation or noble anger are, at best, foolhardy notions; at worst, they are inherently contradictory, because anger is fatally corrosive rather than noble. However, the field of international criminal law is an entire field built on noble anger – anger at the evil that men and women do and the fields that were littered with human beings who were treated like inanimate objects, disrespected and casually disposed like pieces of rotten flesh. That anger has spurred a generation of international lawyers, and civil society organizations, to insist that no one should be above the law or immune from criminal consequences. That was how the anti-impunity norm achieved its prominent place in our present global consciousness. International criminal law is the house that rage built.

The anti-punishment 'consensus' that dominated South Africa's Truth and Reconciliation process is the exception that proves the rule, not a framework for future justice in all places.[59] The perpetrators who went unpunished in that process earned (or had bestowed on them) a form of impunity that certainly ran afoul of the basic normative prescription underlying the *Gäfgen* decision. While horrendous crimes of state were left unpunished, quotidian crimes committed by ordinary citizens in their daily lives yielded imprisonment, and continue to do so to this day. One wonders what message this result sent to the perpetrators, to the victims and to the world. It is almost never the case that mercy and forbearance are handed out universally or evenly. Decisions about which cases deserve mercy and which ones do not invariably camouflage implicit judgments about which crimes are taken more seriously than others.

The view that we have sketched out in this section might best be described as a form of expressive retributivism, in keeping with a line of quasi-retributivist accounts of punishment articulated by, among others, Anthony Duff.[60] I have defended a particular version of expressive retributivism that requires coercive punishment imposed against offenders.[61] In the absence of

[59] Nussbaum, *Anger and Forgiveness*, 211 et seq.

[60] See R.A. Duff, *Trials and Punishments* (Cambridge: Cambridge University Press, 1986), 233–266; J. Feinberg, 'The Expressive Function of Punishment' (1965) 49 *Monist* 397. For a critique of expressivism, see M.D. Adler, 'Expressive Theories of Law: A Skeptical Overview' (2000) 148 *University of Pennsylvania Law Review* 1363, 1369.

[61] See also D. Markel, 'Are Shaming Punishments Beautifully Retributive? Retributivism and the Implications for the Alternative Sanctions Debate' (2001) 54 *Vanderbilt Law Review* 2157, 2189 (discussing theory of 'confrontational retributivism'); D. Markel, 'What Might Retributive

that punishment, society expresses the sentiment that the perpetrator enjoys impunity for his or her actions.[62] Conversely, when the offender is punished, the community expresses its conviction that impunity is intolerable and expresses its solidarity with the victims. This anti-impunity version of expressive retributivism owes much to the anti-impunity discourse at the heart of international criminal law.[63] In this sense, international criminal law has much to teach domestic criminal law, in the sense that theorists of domestic criminal punishment should bring the anti-impunity norm 'home' to justify punishment in their municipal systems. It is somewhat odd that the anti-impunity rhetoric has mostly been limited to the international context.

IV IMPLICATIONS FOR INTERNATIONAL CRIMINAL LAW

The first question for the international criminal lawyer is whether the right to punishment outlined above is a creature of European human rights law or whether it is embodied in international human rights law as well. Although there are no international decisions articulating the right in the same language at the international level, this is only because there are fewer fora for adjudicating international human rights when compared with their European analogs. Consequently, one must scrutinize the underlying rights to see whether they are uniquely European or whether they are both European and international at the same time (as many rights are).

First, the right to be free from torture and other forms of mistreatment is codified in international instruments, notably the Convention Against Torture but also Article 7 of the International Covenant on Civil and Political Rights (ICCPR), which prohibits both torture and cruel and degrading treatment. Second, the right to life is also protected not just by European law but also

Justice Be? An Argument for the Confrontational Conception of Retributivism' in M.D. White (ed.), *Retributivism: Essays on Theory and Policy* (Oxford: Oxford University Press, 2011), 49, 58–59.

62 If forced to describe my theory of punishment, I would describe it as the 'anti-impunity conception of expressive retributivism'. Although theorists of punishment have never explicitly identified and defended such a variant of expressive retributivism, I think it articulates a widely shared intuition among international criminal lawyers and human rights activists. However, differences emerge when you ask lawyers why expressing anti-impunity is important. A few will argue that expressing anti-impunity is important to deter future crime, whereas I (and others) would assert that expressing anti-impunity has intrinsic rather than instrumental moral value.

63 See, e.g., R. Bergman, 'Why Did Israel Let Mengele Go?', *New York Times*, 6 September 2017 ('The capture and trial of Eichmann – and his execution – were enough to teach the world about the Holocaust and to convey to the message that Jewish blood cannot be spilled with impunity'.).

Article 6 of the ICCPR, which states that: 'Every human being has the inherent right to life. This right shall be protected by law. No one shall be arbitrarily deprived of his life.' Third, even in cases where death does not occur, victims have a right to 'liberty and security of person' under Article 9 of the ICCPR and a right to respectful treatment consistent with their 'inherent dignity' according to Article 10.

Fourth, and finally, the state obligation to provide a remedy is not a European-only right. It is clearly international and codified in the ICCPR in at least two places. As noted above, Article 6 of the ICCPR requires that the right to life be protected by law, which arguably, although implicitly, might refer to the need for an adequate remedy. But more importantly, Article 2 of the ICCPR requires that states '*ensure* to all individuals within its territory and subject to its jurisdiction the rights recognized in the present Covenant [...]'. This provision is controversial because its interpretation implicates the question of the extra-territorial scope of the Convention. But putting aside that controversy, which is not relevant here, it is undeniable that Article 2 of the ICCPR imposes not only a negative duty that a state refrain from violating human rights, but also imposes a positive obligation to take actions necessary to 'ensure' the rights in the Convention. Just as the European Convention requires that states take action to 'secure' the convention's rights, so too the ICCPR requires that states take actions to 'ensure' the rights in the international convention. In both cases, there is a strong argument that the positive duty entails the imposition of appropriate and proportionate criminal penalties on perpetrators who violate the rights of human beings whose inherent dignity is protected by the law. The structural argument is the same in both contexts.

Consequently, international criminal lawyers should recognize that the right to punishment is a human right enjoyed by victims of particularly grave international crimes. Doing so would dovetail with the existing anti-impunity foundation for international criminal law, adding content to its otherwise indeterminate edges, and would also have practical consequences for the practice of international institutions.

The anti-impunity norm is recognized in the Preamble of the Rome Statute of the International Criminal Court (ICC), which articulates, inter alia, the following normative commitments:

> *Affirming* that the most serious crimes of concern to the international community as a whole must not go unpunished and that their effective prosecution must be ensured by taking measures at the national level and by enhancing international cooperation [...] *Determined* to put an end to impunity for the perpetrators of these crimes and thus to contribute to the

> prevention of such crimes [. . .] *Recalling* that it is the duty of every State to exercise its criminal jurisdiction over those responsible for international crimes [. . .][64]

Each of these clauses reaffirms that a core purpose of international criminal law is to prosecute and punish individuals who would otherwise escape punishment for international crimes.

The logic of the anti-impunity norm is brought to fruition with the principle of complementarity. The ICC only has jurisdiction over situations and crimes that are not adequately investigated and prosecuted by domestic jurisdictions. Where there is no sincere or credible domestic prosecution, the ICC gains the jurisdiction necessary to close that impunity gap. But if a domestic jurisdiction is able and willing to prosecute the offenders, there is no impunity gap to be filled and the ICC's putative jurisdiction evaporates.[65]

For these reasons, the human right to punishment should be of particular concern for international institutions working to fulfil this anti-impunity goal. Indeed, in the first clause of the preamble quoted above, the existence of a judicial process is itself insufficient to satisfy the anti-impunity goal; international cooperation is required to ensure that 'serious crimes of concern [. . .] must not go *unpunished*'. Indeed, if a state prosecutes an offender or offenders but then grants a blanket pardon to all involved, or even introduces a token punishment *a la Daschner*, then the anti-impunity norm is not fulfilled.

Some scholars have already cashed out the complementarity principle in punishment terms. For example, Kevin Jon Heller has argued that a state prosecution satisfies the complementarity principle if the defendant is subject to criminal punishment that equates with the punishment that the defendant would receive in an international forum, that is at the ICC.[66] If the defendant faces a lesser punishment at home then he would at The Hague, the complementarity principle is not satisfied and the ICC should retain jurisdiction. Or so says Heller.[67] Without taking a stand on Heller's interpretation of the complementarity principle, it is sufficient to note that some scholars have already explicitly linked the duty to punish with the Court's jurisdiction. The duty to punish, whether in a state's system of criminal justice or at an international institution, is already codified in the Rome Statute. What I have tried to show in this chapter is that the Rome Statute's recognition of

64 ICC Statute, Preamble paragraphs 4, 5 and 6.
65 ICC Statute, Art. 17.
66 K.J. Heller, 'A Sentence-Based Theory of Complementarity' (2012), 53 *Harvard International Law Journal* 85, 131.
67 Heller, 'A Sentence-Based Theory of Complementarity', 87.

the duty to punish did not materialize out of thin air. Many observers have assumed that states constructed the ICC out of a sense of beneficence – a simple desire to make the world a better place. However, the account sketched out in the present essay suggests that the creation of the ICC (and other international institutions) was legally obligatory. If indeed victims have a fundamental right to see their tormenters punished, and this right is embodied in international human rights law, then creating a system of justice based on the anti-impunity norm was required by international law, not simply permitted by it. In other words, states constructed the Rome Statute and the ICC as a way of fulfilling their obligations to punish under international human rights law.

The question arises of what consequences, if any, the human right to punishment might have for the actual operation of international criminal justice. For starters, both the International Criminal Tribunal for the former Yugoslavia (ICTY) and the ICC include provisions allowing for early release before the completion of a sentence. These procedures should be pursued delicately because their implementation might infringe the human right to punishment. If a defendant is convicted of a crime against humanity but is released after only serving, say, 5 years of a 30-year sentence, there is a strong argument that the commutation is an impermissible example of tokenism. For example, Article 110 of the ICC Statute contemplates that the Court may reduce, at any time, the sentence of a convicted person. Furthermore, Article 110(3) of the ICC Statute stipulates that all defendants shall be entitled to a hearing regarding reduction in sentence once they have served 25 years in prison or two-thirds of their sentence, whichever comes first. The criteria that the court is directed to consider include: (i) the defendant's willingness to cooperate; (ii) the defendant's assistance with forfeiture and reparations; and (iii) a change in circumstances that would justify the sentence reduction. Presumably, a change in circumstances regarding the defendant's acceptance of blame, rehabilitation, or mental or physical health might satisfy the 'change in circumstance' criteria.

Noticeably absent from the Article 110 criteria is any mention of the gravity of the offence or the impact on the right of the victims to see their perpetrators adequately punished and whether releasing the defendant will compromise that right. In this regard, the ICTY Rules of Procedure and Evidence are far superior, because Rule 125 offers the following guidelines for the President's consideration of pardons and commutations:

> In determining whether pardon or commutation is appropriate, the President shall take into account, inter alia, the *gravity of the crime or crimes for which*

> *the prisoner was convicted*, the treatment of similarly-situated prisoners, the prisoner's demonstration of rehabilitation, as well as any substantial cooperation of the prisoner with the Prosecutor.[68]

The ICC Statute provision should be amended to require it to take into account the same criteria. However, despite the inclusion of this rigorous standard in the ICTY Rules of Procedure and Evidence, the Rule is deficient in that it allows the Tribunal's President, rather than the full court, to make this determination. This provision allows the President to effectively unwind a sentencing determination made by a full panel of judges who sat through a trial or appellate proceeding, with information that the President may not have fully absorbed or appreciated. The ideal scenario would be a provision that combines the correct standard from the ICTY Rules of Procedure and Evidence with the ICC Statute's procedural requirement that the sentence reduction come from the full court rather than one individual alone.

This raises a last question: Are international tribunals bound by international human rights law? Under a restrictive and highly formalist reading of human rights law, only states are bound to follow its requirements. An international tribunal is not a state, and even though individual judges come from particular states, their judicial decisions are not acts of state but are, rather, actions of an international tribunal. If this view is correct, it suggests that international tribunals are not bound by the human rights conception I have outlined here, either in their initial sentencing decision or in a petition for a pardon or sentence reduction. Are international tribunals unconstrained in this manner?

There are two important answers to this objection. The first is that international tribunals make frequent references to international human rights law, both in terms of provisions violated by perpetrators but also in terms of procedural protections for defendants. It is widely assumed by judges that defendants are owed a fair process, not just by virtue of the provisions in the rules of procedure and evidence, but also by virtue of their human rights, which codify that all individuals have a right to a fair judicial process.[69] Of course, the human right to a fair process goes to the benefit of the defendant, while the human right to punishment runs to the detriment of the defendant because it counsels in favour of punishing the guilty. But these two aspects of human rights law are conceptually linked; international tribunals are bound to apply the law and that law extends beyond the four corners of the Rome

68 Emphasis added.

69 See, e.g., ICTY, Decision of 22 September 2004 (TC), *Milošević*, IT-02-54-T, para. 29.

Statute or whatever constitutive document governs the creation of the tribunal.

Furthermore, even if we were to concede that states are the ones bound by international human rights law, states have created these tribunals, either directly through treaty in the case of the ICC or indirectly through international institutions such as the UN Security Council (in the context of the ad hoc Tribunals). In that case, states may bear an indirect responsibility under international human rights law to create international institutions that respect the human right to punishment. In *Gäfgen*, the right in question required that the state conduct its criminal process in a manner consistent with this human right. In the international context, the right entails that states have an obligation to create international institutions with procedures and standards in place that will respect the rights of victims to an adequate criminal remedy. If states create international institutions that flagrantly violate that right because of a structural problem in the standards articulated in their statutes, then indirectly states may be responsible under human rights law for violating the right to punishment. Admittedly, this argument cuts against the current trend regarding the responsibility of international organizations, though perhaps international law is evolving in a direction where it can appreciate that states may be responsible, in some derivative way, for the acts of the international institutions that they create. Someday, international law may 'pierce the veil' of international institutions. Even before then, though, international tribunals already consider international human rights law as a valid source of law for them to apply in their decisions.

V CONCLUSION

This chapter has defended a particular conception of punishment grounded in the human rights of victims; specifically, the right of victims that generates a corresponding duty on the part of the state to punish wrongdoers responsible for the original victimization. The chapter started with an analysis of the European Court's *Gäfgen* case, which articulated the existence of this right in cases of torture and other forms of mistreatment. Then, following that logic to its ultimate conclusion, this chapter suggests that the same arguments apply, *mutatis mutandis*, to all international crimes.[70] In cases of aggression,

[70] The argument in this chapter could also, in theory, be extended to domestic penal offences as well. Although this is beyond the scope of this contribution, one could argue that victims have a right to see their perpetrators punished for all crimes that rise in seriousness above a certain threshold – say offences that implicate the security of the person at a fundamental level. This

genocide, crimes against humanity and war crimes – the punishment of the perpetrators is not just legally permitted; it is legally required. This subtle change in emphasis – moving from punishment as a licence to punishment as a legal requirement – has profound consequences for the operation of international criminal justice. States and international tribunals are required to punish perpetrators as a matter of human rights law, and their failure to follow through on this obligation violates not just some vague or inchoate *ergo omnes* obligation, it also violates an obligation owed directly to the victims of that particular atrocity.

Recognizing this fact will augment the role and significance of victims in international criminal procedure. Regardless of whether victims are formal participants of the criminal process as *partie civile*, victims are legal stakeholders in the outcome of the criminal process, i.e., the punishments that are handed down to vindicate their human rights. Finally, acts of mercy or compassion, such as sentence reductions in the form of pardons, commutations and compassionate release for health reasons, potentially infringe the right to punishment. Although acts of mercy are not necessarily illegal, at the very least, acts of mercy must take into consideration the interests of the victims in the execution of the criminal sanction to prevent cases of excessive mercy from opening a back-door to impunity.

would capture cases of domestic murder and rape that are illegal under domestic law but which states are not under an obligation to penalize in the sense in which they are obligated to punish genocide and torture by virtue of international agreements. However, if the argument in this chapter is correct, the human right to punishment is larger than international crimes, because the relevant provisions in the ICCPR and the ECHR make no mention of war crimes, crimes against humanity and genocide. A victim's right to punishment – with the corollary obligation not to bestow excessive mercy – would apply to state actors engaged in the quotidian work of the domestic criminal lawyer. Although this application of the thesis was not defended in this chapter, the logic of its argument is strongly suggestive of an affirmative conclusion. At the very least, this presents an intriguing avenue of future research for domestic criminal law theory.

PART III

Consequences for the Practice of the International Criminal Court

16

Prosecution Strategy at the International Criminal Court in Search of a Theory

ALEX WHITING*

The theories of punishment embraced by the Office of the Prosecutor of the International Criminal Court (ICC) have been shaped by the realities of its limited powers. Rather than theory dictating practice, it has been the other way around: Institutional constraints on the Court's investigative and prosecutorial tools have largely determined the Prosecutor's justifications for opening situations and identifying cases. The strategy of the Prosecutor's Office has evolved over the years, but it has consistently been reactive to, and constrained by, the limits on the Court's authority. The story of the evolution of the Prosecutor's theoretical positions both illuminates the workings of the Court – its promises but particularly its shortcomings – and provides insight into the relationship between theory and practice within international criminal justice institutions.

At the core of the analysis is a central fact about the Court. While the Office of the Prosecutor is *independent* when it comes to initiating investigations and prosecutions, it is almost entirely *dependent* on state cooperation to conduct its work. The Office lacks independent authority and tools to gather evidence of crimes. In some instances, it can turn to compulsory legal process to obtain evidence – such as search warrants, subpoenas and wiretaps – but only with the acquiescence and assistance of state authorities. In the absence of cooperation from state actors, the Office's investigators are entirely reliant on evidence voluntarily provided to the Court, and even these avenues of investigation can be limited by state action.

The Prosecutor's strategy at the ICC has represented an effort to succeed, the definition of which is itself a contested and evolving notion, in light of

* My thanks to Florian Jeßberger and Julia Geneuss and all of the participants in the October 2017 Hamburg symposium for their useful comments, edits and feedback, and to Marissa Brodney for invaluable research assistance.

these limitations. In the early years of the ICC, many hoped that the Court could build on the successes of the ad hoc international criminal Tribunals that preceded it – such as the International Criminal Tribunal for the former Yugoslavia (ICTY) and the International Criminal Tribunal for Rwanda (ICTR) – and that, as a permanent court, it could even achieve gains in speed, efficiency and expertise. As it turned out, however, scaling up the ad hoc Tribunal model to a single, permanent court led not to greater successes but instead exposed the fragility of the project and its essential and continual dependence on political will. Accordingly, the first Prosecutor moved towards a strategy of acting quickly and decisively to take advantage of existing political will before the world's attention turned to the next crisis. This approach pushed the Prosecutor towards embracing a theory of disruption and specific deterrence, seeking to intervene in real time to stop ongoing crimes.

This approach succeeded in making the Court 'relevant', but it resulted in narrowly charged cases that proved to be vulnerable at the confirmation and trial stages. When a number of these cases failed, the new Prosecutor moved to a strategy that acknowledged the limitations on the Court in a different way. She committed the Office of the Prosecutor to bringing cases that would essentially be 'trial ready' when charged, which has meant that the Office has conducted longer investigations and has brought fewer cases. This approach has resulted in the ICC becoming more of a court of 'opportunity' and has pushed the Prosecutor away from specific deterrence towards an expressivist theory of punishment. Success for the first Prosecutor was relevance; for the second Prosecutor, the priority has become cases that will succeed in court.

These two strategies show how much the Court is shaped by its limitations, and the dilemma faced by the Prosecutor. Relevance and effectiveness require speed and efficiency, but successful prosecutions demand time in light of the investigative and resource limitations on the Court. A central challenge for the Prosecutor is fashioning a strategy and theory of prosecution that threads the needle and accounts for the Court's constraints.

I THE PROSECUTOR'S CONTEXT

Commentary about the ICC frequently begins by acknowledging that it is a court dependent on state cooperation. However, the implications of this point are not always fully appreciated when it comes to the Prosecution's investigations. On paper, the Prosecutor's powers to collect evidence appear formidable. Part IX of the ICC Statute sets forth extensive legal obligations for states parties to cooperate with ICC investigations. Article 86 says that 'States Parties shall [...] cooperate with the Court in its investigation and prosecution of crimes within the jurisdiction of the Court'.[1] Article 93 catalogues a variety of forms of cooperation that state parties are legally required to provide, including identifying and locating persons or items, taking evidence, questioning of suspects, examination of sites, execution of searches and seizures, provision of records and all other types of investigative assistance not prohibited by the law of the requested state.[2] Other provisions of Part IX of the Statute require states parties to cooperate in the arrest and surrender of accused persons.[3]

The Statute seems to provide the Prosecutor, therefore, with all of the tools he or she needs to investigate crimes within the Statute, including, critically, various forms of compulsory legal process. Creation of the institutional infrastructure to deploy these tools was the focus of the early years of the Court, and in short order the core pieces of the Court were in place: investigators, prosecutors, judges, registrar, courtrooms, etc. But although the Court has all the elements of an independent, fully functioning criminal court, the reality is very different. While the ICC quacks like a duck and walks like a duck, it is in fact not a duck.[4]

Four elements impede the work of the Prosecution in its investigations, and these are found in the structure of the Court, its constituent rules, the nature of the crimes being investigated and the Court's budget. First, as an international court, the institution operates across borders and legal cultures. Investigators and prosecutors operating in a domestic system have immediate recourse to evidence and to the legal mechanisms to collect it. ICC investigators must always traverse borders to do their work, and that introduces enormous friction in the process. The Office of the Prosecutor has even established a division that operates alongside the investigation and prosecution divisions, called the Jurisdiction Complementarity and Cooperation Division, whose principal function is to facilitate the work of investigators across borders. The ad hoc Tribunals benefitted from being able to operate in the same environment over a long period of time, allowing them to develop institutional (and staff) relationships and evidence collection practices. By contrast, each time the ICC commences a new investigation it has to start from scratch to put into place the mechanisms to gather evidence. Moreover, most ICC investigations span multiple countries. When the ICC began investigating in Libya at the end of February 2011, after the Security Council

1 ICC Statute, Art. 86.
2 ICC Statute, Art. 93.
3 ICC Statute, Arts. 89–92.
4 Sentinel, John 'Communist Expose The Case of the Duck'. *Milwaukee (WI) Sentinel*, 29 September 1946.

referral of the situation to the ICC, investigative opportunities arose in Libya, Tunisia, Egypt, Malta, Italy, the United Kingdom and the United States, among other countries.

Each time the ICC wishes to gather evidence within a particular country, it must make a request through diplomatic channels (though when there are repeated requests to a country, such as to the one where the crimes occurred, the procedures will be routinized by agreement).[5] Each country has its own requirements with respect to cooperation requests and some require that investigators at the Office of the Prosecutor work with and through domestic ones. When permission is granted, investigators must to travel to the requested state to obtain the evidence and ordinarily must navigate language and cultural barriers in the process. Evidence collection is an iterative process – each act of collection generates additional leads, often including follow-up questions or requests – and at the ICC each step must go through a similar process. Because the ICC is international and operates in many different investigative environments at once, evidence collection becomes extremely belaboured and cumbersome.

Second, although the Rome Statute mandates cooperation with ICC requests, including requests for compulsory legal process, the enforcement mechanisms are virtually non-existent. As a result, states can 'slow roll' or even resist cooperation requests without any consequence. Article 87(7) of the ICC Statute allows the Prosecution to complain to the Court's judges when states parties fail to comply with a cooperation request.[6] If the judges find a failure to cooperate, they then decide whether to refer the matter to the Assembly of States Parties, or to the UN Security Council if it pertains to a situation referred to the ICC by the Security Council.[7] That is where the matter is likely to end.

In the Kenya situation, the Prosecution filed a motion for a finding and referral of non-compliance by the Government of Kenya on 29 November 2013.[8] After extensive litigation, that included an appeal to the Appeals Chamber, the Trial Chamber referred Kenya's failure to cooperate to the Assembly

5 ICC Statute, Art. 87 ('The Court shall have the authority to make requests to States Parties for cooperation. The requests shall be transmitted through the diplomatic channel or any other appropriate channel as may be designated by each State Party upon ratification, acceptance, approval or accession.').

6 ICC Statute, Art. 87(7).

7 ICC Statute, Art. 87(7).

8 ICC, Prosecution's application for a finding of non-compliance under Article 87(7) of the Statute against the Government of Kenya of 29 November 2013, *Kenyatta*, ICC-01/09-02/11-866-Conf-Exp.

of States Parties nearly three years later, on 19 September 2016.[9] But this led to no consequences; neither the Assembly nor any of the states parties took any apparent steps to compel Kenya's cooperation. Similarly, the Prosecutor has complained twice a year to the Security Council since 2007 about the failure of Sudan to cooperate with the ICC regarding evidence and the surrender of fugitives, and numerous states have been referred to the Security Council for failing to arrest Omar Al-Bashir when he visited. In response, the Security Council has taken no action against those states that failed to cooperate with the Court and has adopted no measures to entice Sudan's cooperation.

The ad hoc Tribunals succeeded because of sustained political support from influential states, including the United States (US) and European countries (through the European Union (EU)). With respect to the ICTY, for example, both the US and the EU pressured Serbia and Croatia to cooperate with that Court by conditioning aid (the US) or ascension to the EU (the EU) on concrete steps to provide evidence or arrest fugitives. However, the multiplicity of crises addressed by the ICC has made it difficult for the Court to receive sustained political and diplomatic support for its range of situations and cases. For this reason, states that have openly defied the Court have generally suffered no diplomatic or political consequences.

In fact, most of the defiance occurs under the radar. Open defiance, such as that by Sudan and Kenya, and which at least results in a public finding by the Court of non-cooperation, is relatively rare. More common is false or incomplete cooperation: states that *act* as if they are cooperating but delay requests for weeks and months, ultimately providing little or no assistance of value.[10] Carla del Ponte, the former Prosecutor of the ICTY, termed this 'the *muro di gomma*, the wall of rubber, the rejection disguised so it won't appear as a rejection'.[11] When this happens, there is not enough explicit defiance to warrant litigation under Article 87(7) of the ICC Statute, but not enough cooperation to advance the work of the Prosecution. This kind of subterranean failure to cooperate with the Court results in tremendous drag on the work of the Prosecution.

[9] ICC, Second decision on Prosecution's application for a finding of non-compliance under Article 87(7) of the Statute of 19 September 2016 (TC), *Kenyatta*, ICC-01/09-02/11.

[10] ICC, Second decision on the Prosecution's application for a finding of non-compliance under Article 87(7) of the Statute of 19 September 2016 (TC), *Kenyatta*, ICC-01/09-02/11, paras. 16–22.

[11] C. del Ponte and C. Sudetić, *Madame Prosecutor: Confrontations with Humanity's Worst Criminals and the Culture of Impunity* (New York: Other Press, 2008), 3.

Third, the nature of the cases being investigated by the ICC is such that time often is required for evidence to emerge.[12] Domestic, that is 'ordinary' crime is usually aberrational and societal processes and norms are oriented towards identifying and condemning criminal activity. By contrast, mass atrocity crimes often occur in a context that flips the script: criminality is no longer aberrational but rather becomes much more the norm.[13] The result can be that significant evidence will not emerge until time passes. Ongoing conflict can obstruct access to evidence – including to crime sites, witnesses and documents – and in the polarized moment of conflict and atrocity, witnesses will often be highly partisan and may not perceive criminal acts as 'criminal'. As a result, they may not be willing to cooperate with investigators until they have some distance, and perspective, on events. The ad hoc Tribunals benefitted from being able to focus on one conflict for a sustained period, and at the ICTY in particular some of the most significant evidence uncovered by that Court emerged only many years after the events. Because the ICC must investigate multiple situations and always be ready to turn its attention to the next crisis, it may feel more pressure to produce results quickly.

Fourth, the ICC's budget narrows the possibilities for the Court. The approved budget for the ICC for 2018 is just under 150 million euros.[14] That is not much more than the annual budget of the ICTY or the ICTR at the peak of their operations.[15] The ICC's budget was also not fixed at an ideal number to allow it to perform its essential functions. The Office of the Prosecutor calculated that in order for the ICC to reach its 'basic size', meaning a level of staffing that would allow it to conduct essential investigations into new situations without sacrificing quality or efficiency, the budget would need to be increased by at least 33 per cent.[16] One could debate these numbers – and argue that either more or less resources are in fact required – but few would dispute that the ICC lacks the resources required to conduct thorough and in-depth investigations across multiple situations. Each year, the

[12] See generally, A. Whiting, 'In International Criminal Prosecutions, Justice Delayed Can Be Justice Delivered' (2009) 50 *Harvard International Law Journal* 323.

[13] On the difference between domestic crime and crimes under international law, see the contribution by Elies van Sliedregt in Chapter 5.

[14] See Resolution ICC-ASP/16/Res.1, available at https://asp.icc-cpi.int/iccdocs/asp_docs/Resolutions/ASP16/ICC-ASP-16-Res1-ENG.pdf.

[15] D. Wippman, 'The Costs of International Justice' (2006) 100 *American Journal of International Law* 861.

[16] ICC, Report of the Court on the Basic Size of the Office of the Prosecutor, ICC-ASP/14/21, 17 September 2015, available at www.legal-tools.org/doc/b27d2a/pdf.

Prosecutor is required to prioritize certain investigations while delaying others. Despite repeated requests for additional funds from the Prosecutor and the other parts of the Court, the Assembly of States Parties has held the budget generally constant, approving extremely modest increases in some years. It appears that the states parties have a conception of the Court, its size and its level of activity that will not significantly vary in the near future and that will necessarily constrain the work of the Prosecution.

Together, these factors shape the work of the Prosecutor and the strategy options for the Office. The theories of punishment embraced by the Prosecution in its selection of situations and cases have largely sought to justify the choices that the Prosecutor has made in light of these constraints.

II PROSECUTION STRATEGY AND THEORIES OF PUNISHMENT

1 *Theories of Punishment at Sentencing*

The Office of the Prosecutor at the ICC has relied on various theories of punishment at different stages of the proceedings. In their sentencing submissions for convicted defendants, the Prosecution has deployed a range of arguments to justify severe sentences.[17] Working within the framework of Rule 145 of the ICC Rules of Procedure and Evidence, which provides the structure for the determination of sentence, the Prosecution has focused primarily on ensuring that the Court would recognize the gravity of all cases and avoid trying to create an internal scale of ICC crimes.[18] To this end, the Prosecution has emphasized the particular gravity of each case and has cited the full range of justifications for severe punishment. During the sentencing of Jean-Pierre Bemba, the Prosecution set forth its view on the rationale of punishment:

> For sentencing purposes, having regard to the Preamble to the Statute, consideration should be given to the heinous nature of the crimes prosecuted by the Court and to the objectives of ensuring deterrence and ending impunity for these crimes that threaten the peace, security and well-being of the world, in the interests of present and future generations.[19]

[17] On rationales of punishment in the ICC's sentencing decisions, see the contribution by Sergey Vasiliev in Chapter 4.

[18] In favour of a hierarchy of crimes under the jurisdiction of the ICC in order to determine the gravity *in abstracto* of the crime as a factor in the sentencing process, see the contribution by Gerhard Werle and Aziz Epik in Chapter 18.

[19] ICC, public redacted version of the Prosecution's Sentencing Submissions of 11 April 2016, *Bemba Gombo*, ICC-01/05-01/08-3363-Conf, para. 14.

In the later sentencing of Ahmad Al Faqi Al Mahdi, the Prosecutor identified the two principal purposes of sentencing to be 'retribution and deterrence', but also recognized the purposes of reconciliation and in some cases even rehabilitation.[20] Given the nature of the cases prosecuted by the ICC, arguments grounded in either retribution or deterrence can be relied upon to justify a high sentence recommendation, particularly when the ICC crimes are compared to domestic ones.

However, because the Office of the Prosecutor has to date charged cases relatively narrowly, the principal challenge for the Prosecution has been to counter arguments that the crimes proven were not 'as grave' as other crimes that might come before the Court (i.e., the problem of the internal ICC sentencing scale). The aim of the Office has been to sacrifice significant differentiation among ICC crimes in favour of high sentences across the board. So, at the sentencing of Thomas Lubanga, convicted of enlisting and conscripting child soldiers, the Prosecution sought a severe penalty – emphasizing the direct role of Lubanga, the vulnerability of the victims, the harsh treatment of the children and the impact on the community – and then appealed the 14-year sentence, arguing that it was 'manifestly inadequate and disproportionate to the gravity of the crime'.[21] In *Al Mahdi*, who pled guilty to the destruction of cultural monuments, the prosecution argued that 'the nature of the crime, the long history of the prohibition on cultural destruction, the extent of the damage caused by the crime, and the circumstances of manner, time and location' warranted a significant sentence.[22] Ultimately, Al Mahdi was sentenced to 3 years of imprisonment.[23]

In sum, because of the nature of the cases at the ICC and the purposes of sentencing, the Prosecution is able to rely on an array of arguments and theories in support of its sentencing recommendations. At the situation and case selection stages, however, the Office of the Prosecutor is pressed to make choices that require it to advance more specific theoretical rationales. The Prosecutor can move quickly or deliberately, can focus on few cases or many, can charge narrowly or broadly, etc. The Prosecutor's strategy has

[20] ICC, public redacted version of 'Prosecution's submissions on sentencing' of 22 July 2016, *Al Mahdi*, ICC-01/12-01/05-139-Red, paras. 11–14.

[21] ICC, Prosecution's Sentence Request of 14 May 2012, *Lubanga Dyilo*, ICC-01/04-01/06-2881, paras. 3–6, 30–40; ICC, Prosecution's Document in Support of Appeal against the 'Decision on Sentence Pursuant to Article 76 of the Statute' of 3 December 2012, *Lubanga Dyilo*, ICC-01/04-01/06-2901, para. 2.

[22] ICC, *Al Mahdi* Prosecution's Submissions on Sentencing, para. 16.

[23] ICC, Judgment and Sentence of 27 September 2016 (TC), *Al Mahdi*, ICC-01/12-01/15-171.

evolved, but it has consistently been reactive to the circumstances limiting the Office's powers.

2 The First Prosecutor's Strategy

The starting point of the first Prosecutor's strategy was to focus on gravity, which made sense given the perception that the Court could have many potential situations and cases to choose from. Gravity is an element to be established to open a situation and to commence a case.[24] However, Luis Moreno-Ocampo also turned to gravity to determine which situations to prioritize.[25] Accordingly, he moved in his first year to persuade both Uganda (January 2004) and the Democratic Republic of the Congo (April 2004) to refer themselves to the ICC. The following year, he said at a conference in Washington that '[t]he Congo is the gravest situation under our treaty jurisdiction, and Northern Uganda is the second gravest'.[26]

Regarding timing, in both situations the Office of the Prosecutor brought cases within about 18 months of the referrals. In July 2005, the Prosecutor sought and obtained arrest warrants for Joseph Kony and four other members of the Lord's Resistance Army for war crimes and crimes against humanity allegedly committed in Uganda. In February 2006, the Office sought and obtained an arrest warrant for war crimes for Thomas Lubanga in the Democratic Republic of the Congo and he was surrendered to the Court 1 month later, marking him as the first accused to appear in The Hague. There was hope that Kony and his co-accused would also be arrested in short order, but as it turned out, the first of the group to be arrested was Dominic Ongwen, who was captured 10 years later in 2015. Of the remaining accused, two have died and two are still fugitives, including Kony himself.

In the 2005–2006 period, particularly with the arrest of Lubanga, it was reasonable to assume that state cooperation would lead to the arrests of fugitives, that the commitment that created the ICC would carry over to

[24] See ICC Statute, Arts. 17, 53.

[25] M.M. deGuzman, 'Choosing to Prosecute: Expressive Selection at the International Criminal Court' (2012) 33 *Michigan Journal of International Law* 265, 286 ('The ICC prosecutor, mindful of the expectation that he selected the most serious situations and cases for investigation and prosecution, has made gravity central to his selection policies.').

[26] L. Moreno-Ocampo, 'Keynote Address: Integrating the Work of the ICC into Local Justice Initiatives' (2006) 21 *American University International Law Review* 497, 498. See also, Statement by L. Moreno-Ocampo, Fourth Session of the Assembly of States Parties, 28 November 2005, available at www.icc-cpi.int/NR/rdonlyres/0CBFF4AC-1238-4DA1-9F4A-70D763F90F91/278514/LMO_20051128_English.pdf.

support for its work. That view would change, however, with the Sudan case. In March 2005, the UN Security Council unexpectedly referred the Darfur situation to the ICC.[27] Because three of the permanent members of the Security Council are not states parties to the ICC, and the United States had in the early years of the ICC adopted a position of overt hostility to the Court, nobody imagined that situations would arrive at the ICC through Security Council referrals. However, allegations of genocide and crimes against humanity in Darfur resonated in the United States, particularly in the evangelical community with influence in the George W. Bush administration, and Washington came to see that the ICC was the only institution with the potential to influence events in the region. Accordingly, the United States ultimately acceded to a Security Council resolution sending the Darfur case to the ICC.

From the perspective of the Office of the Prosecutor, this referral appeared to further underscore the continued and even growing support for the ICC. In many ways, the Court had already exceeded expectations. Few thought that the Rome Statute would receive the sixty ratifications required to make the Court operational in just 4 years, and the self-referrals of Uganda and the Democratic Republic of the Congo, while encouraged and prompted by the Prosecutor, also seemed to signal commitment to the institution. The Darfur case proved to be complex because Sudan, not a state party, provided virtually no cooperation – despite the obligation to do so pursuant to the UN Security Council referral Resolution 1593 – and therefore the Office of the Prosecutor had to conduct its investigation almost entirely from outside the country, largely on the basis of witnesses who had fled Sudan. Approximately two years later, the Prosecutor sought and obtained arrest warrants for Ahmad Muhammad Harun, the Minister of State for the Interior of the Government of Sudan, and Ali Muhammad Ali Abd-Al-Rahman (Ali Kushayb), a senior leader in the tribal hierarchy and member of the Popular Defence Forces.[28]

What happened next appears to have significantly shaped both the Prosecutor's strategy at the ICC and the theory of punishment deployed to justify it. And what happened next is, nothing. Sudan continued its posture of noncooperation and refused to surrender the two accused, which was to be expected. After all, there were already indications that the President of Sudan, Omar Al-Bashir, was complicit in the genocide and crimes against humanity.

[27] UN Security Council Resolution 1593, 31 March 2005, UN Doc. S/RES/1593 (2005).

[28] ICC, Prosecutor's Application under Article 58(7) of 27 February 2007, *Situation in Darfur*, ICC-02/05-56; ICC, Decision of 27 April 2007 (PTC), Harun and Kushayb, ICC-02/05-01/07-1-Corr.

However, it was the failure of the Security Council (or the Assembly of States Parties for that matter) to act that was striking. One lesson of the ad hoc Tribunals might have been that international criminal prosecution efforts established by the UN Security Council would succeed precisely *because* they were endorsed by the Security Council. But it quickly became clear in the Darfur situation that the Security Council would take no steps to enforce the arrest warrants. In 2007, the Prosecutor complained that:

> [T]he issue of the arrest warrants [in Darfur] has been removed from the agenda of the international community. Justice was not formally on the agenda of the U.N. Security Council's [2006] trip to Khartoum. The terms of reference called on the Sudanese government to cooperate on humanitarian aid, security, and economic reforms, but not justice. Justice was not mentioned in the U.S. Secretary-General's subsequent reports on Darfur, which instead developed a three-prong approach where humanitarian, political, and security components, but not justice, were considered.[29]

And there was no support for the ICC's cases in Darfur outside the Security Council either. In fact, the ad hoc Tribunals did not succeed because of sustained Security Council support, but because states with influence prioritized the success of those courts in their political, economic and diplomatic policies. But in the Darfur situation, after the arrest warrants were issued for Harun and Kushayb, no significant political support for the warrants was forthcoming from any state or group of states with influence over Sudan. Two years later, the ICC Prosecutor upped the stakes by bringing an arrest warrant against Bashir himself for genocide (a charge that was eventually issued by the judges only after an appeal) and crimes against humanity.[30] The attention (and controversy) that this new arrest warrant brought did not, however, translate into political support for the cases. More than ten years later, the (second) Prosecutor is still complaining to the Security Council about any lack of support for the cases in Darfur.

The lesson that the Prosecutor appeared to draw from this episode is that time is of the essence, that the Court must act quickly while there is maximum attention on a particular crisis. At moments, particular conflicts capture the attention of states, international organizations, NGOs, journalists and even the public. Yugoslavia. Rwanda. Sierra Leone. Darfur. Libya. Syria. One can

[29] L. Moreno-Ocampo, 'The International Criminal Court: Seeking Global Justice' (2008) 40 *Case Western Reserve Journal of International Law* 215, 222 (publishing a speech originally given on 16 October 2007).

[30] ICC, Decision of 4 March 2009 (PTC), *Al Bashir*, ICC-02/05-01/09-3, and ICC, Decision of 12 July 2010 (PTC), *Al Bashir*, ICC-02/05-01/09-95.

certainly debate what crises are on the list and which are not, and how it occurs that some conflicts suddenly receive global attention, but the point is that the attention that conflicts receive is often fleeting and before long the attention of significant actors moves on to the next crisis. That is certainly the case with Darfur; at the time of the ICC referral in 2005, there was significant discussion around the world of the crisis, which helps explain the referral itself. But that focus has long be supplanted by other crises around the world. By the time the Prosecutor brought charges in 2007, and again in 2009, it was clear that the world's attention had moved on.

The Prosecutor shifted then to a strategy of bringing arrest warrants (or summonses) as quickly as possible.[31] In Kenya, the Office of the Prosecutor commenced its investigation in March 2010, after a protracted period during which the Kenyan government considered whether to prosecute the cases itself, and sought summonses to appear against six suspects just 9 months later in December 2010.[32] In Libya, the UN Security Council referred the situation at the end of February 2011, and the Prosecutor commenced an investigation days later at the beginning of March 2011 and filed an application for arrest warrants just 2 months later in May 2011.[33] In Côte d'Ivoire, the Prosecutor received permission from the Pre-Trial Chamber to commence an investigation in October 2011 and sought an arrest warrant just weeks later.[34]

This strategy allowed the Office of the Prosecutor to try to strike while the iron was hot, to try to take advantage of the attention of important actors engaged in the crisis in question to engender support for arrests and additional supporting evidence. In addition, it aligned with a vision that the Prosecutor had for the role of the Court in conflict. In Ocampo's view, by de-legitimizing certain forms of violence, the Court had the potential to disrupt violence generally and be a force for diplomacy and peace. In an interview in 2012, he said that 'we have turned the Court into an institution that is part of the international landscape'.[35] He further explained that 'the Court's intervention

[31] See D. Bosco, 'Luis Moreno-Ocampo: Chief Prosecutor, International Criminal Court', *The Atlantic*, November 2011 ('This year, determined to respond to conflicts in real time, Moreno-Ocampo steered the ICC toward the center of events in Libya.').

[32] ICC, Decision of 31 March 2010 (PTC), *Situation in the Republic of Kenya*, ICC-01/09-01/11-19; ICC, Decision of 8 March 2011 (PTC), *Muthaura, Kenyatta and Ali*, ICC-01/09-02/11-01; ICC, Decision of 8 March 2011 (PTC), *Ruto, Kosgey and Sang*, ICC-01/09-01/11-01.

[33] UN Security Council Resolution 1970, 26 February 2011, UN Doc. S/RES/1970 (2011); ICC, Decision of 27 June 2011 (PTC), *Gaddafi, Gaddafi and Al-Senussi*, ICC-01/11-01/11-1.

[34] ICC, Decision of 3 October 2011 (PTC), *Situation in the Republic of Côte d'Ivoire*, ICC-02/11-14; ICC, Decision of 30 November 2011 (PTC), *L. Gbagbo*, ICC-02/11-01/11-9-Red.

[35] T. Papenfuss, 'Interview with Luis Moreno-Ocampo, Chief Prosecutor of the International Criminal Court', *IPI Global Observatory*, 25 January 2010.

stops intentions to ignore victims and appease the criminals. When people are committing massive atrocities to stay in power, Hitler, or Gaddafi, or whoever, it's difficult to let them [stay] in power without committing crimes, because they will fall'.[36] Elsewhere he wrote, 'Leaders will not be allowed to use massive atrocities to retain or to gain power; protecting their communities will not be accepted as an alibi for committing crimes'.[37]

These two strands – the perceived practical need to move quickly in order to maximize cooperation and a vision of the Court as a counter to conflict and violence – coalesced in the embrace of a theory of specific deterrence. The first Prosecutor argued that the primary objective of the Court, from which it would derive its relevance, was to act quickly to stop those most responsible from committing further crimes. By acting quickly, the Court could both create a path for the arrest of atrocity perpetrators and marginalize the use of such tactics in conflict. In 2007 Ocampo wrote that:

> The International Criminal Court is part of the transitional justice project because it aims to confront centuries-old methods of behavior – those of conflict and war, the abuse of civilians, women and children – and to reshape the norms of conduct while violence is still ongoing, thus aiming, as stated in the Rome Statute, to contribute to the prevention of future crimes.[38]

Prevention was the watchword. 'The goal of the Rome Statute is to end the impunity for the most serious crimes of international concern – genocide, crimes against humanity, and war crimes – and to contribute to the prevention of such crimes.'[39] Repeatedly, the Prosecutor emphasized the importance of acting quickly, while the crimes were still being committed. With regard to Libya, he said that, 'When I received the referral, we started the investigation immediately, and in the middle of the conflict we had the evidence and we indicted Gaddafi, Saif, and Sanoussi.'[40] The Prosecutor hoped to influence unfolding events on the ground and said, 'That is the most important reason to

36 Papenfuss, 'Interview with Luis Moreno-Ocampo'.

37 L. Moreno-Ocampo, 'The Prosecutor's Use of Legal Policies', in M. Minow, C. True-Frost and A. Whiting (eds.), *The First Global Prosecutor, Promises and Constraints* (Ann Arbor: University of Michigan Press, 2015), 16.

38 L. Moreno-Ocampo, 'Transitional Justice in Ongoing Conflicts' (2007) 1 *International Journal of Transitional Justice* 8, 8–9.

39 Moreno-Ocampo, 'Seeking Global Justice', 216 (publishing a speech originally given on 16 October 2007).

40 'A World in Need of a Grand Strategy, Interview with Luis Moreno-Ocampo', *Yale Law Journal*, 2 June 2014. Available at http://yalejournal.org/interview_post/a-world-in-need-of-a-grand-strategy

move fast. We have to stop the crimes.'[41] Once the arrest warrants were issued in Libya, Ocampo told the Security Council that arrest was essential to stop ongoing crimes:

> Arresting those who ordered the commission of crimes will contribute to the protection of civilians in Libya because it will deter ongoing crimes. It will deter crimes by removing those who ordered the crimes, and by sending a serious message to other potential perpetrators, in Libya and in other situations, that the international community will not condone such crimes.[42]

Later, even though the suspects were not arrested, the Prosecutor insisted that the rapid issuance of arrest warrants had in fact helped to prevent crimes, declaring that 'Libya was a successful story in terms of stopping the crimes'.[43]

3 *The Second Prosecutor's Strategy*

Many assessed that the first Prosecutor's strategy established the relevance of the ICC, precisely because the Court was seen to act quickly while attention was still focused on the crisis at hand, but ultimately the approach came at a cost. Cases brought rapidly after short investigations proved to be not very resilient when subjected to the confirmation and trial processes. The Rome Statute imposes an increasingly onerous burden of proof for each stage of the proceedings – reasonable basis to believe for arrest, substantial grounds to believe for confirmation and beyond a reasonable doubt for trial[44] – and in some cases it appeared that the Prosecutor proceeded with arrest as soon as the first standard was met, with the hope that additional evidence could later be collected to satisfy the subsequent stages. While this approach has been criticized at the ICC, prosecutors at the ad hoc Tribunals, particularly in the early years, often followed a similar approach, but with better results; the difference was that at the ad hoc Tribunals, political support for the cases and a flexible approach by the judges allowed for the Prosecution to shore up cases evidentially after arrests.[45] At the ICC, however, many of the cases brought quickly faltered. The six Kenya cases broke down either at confirmation,

[41] F. Biedermann, 'Experts say Libya war crimes indictments may harm peace effort', *The National*, 18 May 2011.

[42] L. Moreno-Ocampo, Statement to the United Nations Security Council on the situation in the Libyan Arab Jamahiriya, pursuant to UNSCR 1970 (2011), 4 May 2011.

[43] Papenfuss, 'Interview with Luis Moreno-Ocampo'.

[44] ICC Statute, Arts. 58, 61 and 66.

[45] A. Whiting, 'Investigations and Institutional Imperatives at the International Criminal Court', in M. Minow, C. True-Frost and A. Whiting (eds.), *The First Global Prosecutor, Promises and Constraints* (Ann Arbour: University of Michigan Press 2015), 128.

before trial or during trial. The prosecutions of two of the accused from the Democratic Republic of the Congo failed either at the confirmation stage (Callixte Mbarushimana) or at trial (Mathieu Ngudjolo Chui). One conviction, of Jean-Pierre Bemba from the Central African Republic, was reversed on appeal. Some prosecutions succeeded to be sure (Thomas Lubanga, Germain Katanga), but enough cases failed to warrant a new approach.

Early in her tenure, the new Prosecutor, Fatou Bensouda, issued a strategic plan for 2012–2015 that changed the Office of the Prosecutor's approach investigations, prosecutions, and situation and case selection. The document was candid about the Office's prior approach:

> During the first 9 years of existence the Office was able to create a functioning organization and to respond to high demand by using a strategy of focused investigations and prosecutions combined with rotating staff to cases with the greatest needs. This strategy made the Office relevant in the international arena and resulted in the first signs of its impact: the monitoring of situations under preliminary examination has impacted positively on national proceedings; the Office has been able to conduct multiple investigations in 7 situations; two referrals have been made by the UN Security Council; the importance of the justice component in peace negotiations is more and more apparent; and there are signs that the intervention of the Office might have resulted in (at least temporary) decreases in some of the types of crime committed. Such results have to be seen as positive in light of the start-up phase and the complex environment in which the Office had to operate.[46]

While noting the positive benefits of the Office of the Prosecutor's initial approach, the strategic document also recognized its shortcomings. By moving quickly on cases in multiple situations, the Office was stretching its resources. Further, it was encountering more complex cases, requiring more prolonged investigation. But the biggest problem with the approach of the Office until that time was in the results:

> While the jurisprudence is still developing, judges are indicating through their decisions that they are expecting the OTP to be (more) trial-ready at an earlier stage in the proceedings and that they are expecting the OTP to submit more and different kinds of evidence than what the Office considered would suffice in its focused investigations and prosecutions.[47]

[46] ICC, Office of the Prosecutor, Strategic Plan June 2012–2015, 11 October 2013, 5, available at www.icc-cpi.int/iccdocs/otp/OTP-Strategic-Plan-2013.pdf.

[47] ICC, Office of the Prosecutor, Strategic Plan June 2012–2015, 5.

Accordingly, the plan announced that the Office of the Prosecutor would move away from 'focused' (that is: quick) investigations towards more in-depth ones, and that it would seek to bring cases that were 'trial-ready' at an earlier stage:

> Due to the higher evidentiary standards and the expectation to be trial-ready earlier, the notion of focused investigations is replaced by the principle of in-depth, open-ended investigations while maintaining focus. The Office will expand and diversify its collection of evidence so as to meet the higher evidentiary threshold. It will apply multiple case hypotheses throughout the investigation which will further strengthen decision-making in relation to actual prosecutions.
>
> It will aim at presenting cases at confirmation hearing that are as trial ready as possible. If meeting such a threshold would not be possible at the moment of applying for an arrest warrant or a summons to appear, the Office intends to only proceed with the application if there are sufficient prospects to further collect evidence to be trial-ready within a reasonable timeframe.[48]

Fatou Bensouda, who had been Deputy Prosecutor under Luis Moreno-Ocampo, thus looked at the very same practical challenges facing the Court that Ocampo saw but ended up devising a very different strategy. For Ocampo, the Court's dependence on political will and cooperation required quick action in order to stay relevant and to seize the moment when cooperation might be most forthcoming. For Bensouda, the Court's dependence on cooperation represents an institutional fragility that requires the Office of the Prosecutor to proceed slowly and carefully to build strong cases.

In keeping with this perspective, Bensouda also introduced greater pragmatism in the Office's approach to situation and case selection. Ocampo's vision put the Court at the centre of international responses to conflict and atrocity; he believed that the Court should lead and that states would follow, supporting the Court in its work. He later described this as a new 'global strategy, a grand strategy, for the world' that would focus on law and diplomacy, rather than force, to counter violence and atrocity.[49] Bensouda saw, however, that state support for the Court was episodic and inconsistent and that they would support the Court only when they decided that it was in their interest to do so. Accordingly, she developed what might be seen as a humbler, or more realistic, vision of a Court that would focus its work on its judicial tasks.

48 ICC, Office of the Prosecutor, Strategic Plan June 2012–2015, 6.

49 'A World in Need of a Grand Strategy, Interview with Luis Moreno-Ocampo'.

This vision found expression in Bensouda's *Case Selection and Prioritisation Policy* issued in September 2016.[50] The policy reiterates the Office of the Prosecutor's focus on gravity and on those most responsible, though it also embraces pragmatic concerns, particularly in the case prioritization section:

> The Office will also take into consideration the following operational case prioritisation criteria, to ensure that the Office focuses on cases in which it appears that it can conduct an effective and successful investigation leading to a prosecution with a reasonable prospect of conviction.[51]

As factors to consider, the policy lists the quantity of evidence in the Office's possession, the availability of additional evidence, the degree of international cooperation and judicial assistance regarding the case, the security situation on the ground and with respect to witnesses, and the potential to secure the appearance of accused persons in The Hague.[52] While these factors are listed for case prioritization, it seems likely that they will also shape situation and investigation prioritization as well.

The acknowledgement of pragmatic considerations in the *Case Selection and Prioritisation Policy* is striking. While it is likely that the first Prosecutor took account of these factors as well in making decisions about situations and cases, Bensouda's decision to make them explicit signals a greater willingness to embrace them. Putting together the different parts of Bensouda's policies concerning investigations and the selection of situations and cases, what emerges is a strategy that is focused on achieving success, meaning strong cases that will succeed in court.

The different strategic approaches of the two Prosecutors have produced very different results in the Court. During Ocampo's term, the Court opened investigations into seven different situations and publicly brought charges against twenty-nine individuals. Under Bensouda, the pace has slowed considerably. Some of the accused charged during the Ocampo years have been arrested or surrendered during Bensouda's term, which has consumed Office of the Prosecutor's resources, but it is still striking that in the first 6 years of Bensouda's mandate, she has publicly brought charges against just thirteen individuals, eight of whom were charged with offences against the administration of justice charges under Article 70 of the ICC Statute. Thus, only five have been charged with the core crimes under the ICC's jurisdiction, and of

[50] ICC, Office of the Prosecutor, Policy Paper on Case Selection and Prioritisation, 15 September 2016, available at www.icc-cpi.int/itemsDocuments/20160915_OTP-Policy_Case-Selection_Eng.pdf.

[51] ICC, Office of the Prosecutor, Policy Paper on Case Selection and Prioritisation, para. 51.

[52] ICC, Office of the Prosecutor, Policy Paper on Case Selection and Prioritisation, para. 51.

that group, only three have appeared in The Hague (the two Mali accused, one of whom pled guilty, and an accused from Central Africa Republic). The Office of the Prosecutor under Bensouda has opened investigations in more challenging situations, including Georgia[53] and Burundi,[54] but the numbers show that the Prosecutor's new policy of conducting more thorough investigations has completely changed the orientation of the Office away from quick arrest warrants towards more long-term investigations.

With respect to case selection, it appears that the Prosecutor has gravitated towards extremely strong cases with a high likelihood of success in court. In this respect, the ICC has become a Court of opportunity, jumping on cases that present with strong evidence and a high likelihood of obtaining the suspected perpetrator. While the first Prosecutor also at times pursued suspects that he knew he could likely get to The Hague (Lubanga, Bemba, Mbarushimana), for Bensouda, both the strength of the case and prospects for arrest appear to have been central motivating factors. Under Bensouda's leadership, Al Mahdi (Mali) was charged after he confessed to the alleged crimes, which he committed on video, and after he expressed a willingness to plead guilty and cooperate, which he subsequently did. Al Hassan (Mali) was charged while he was already detained in Mali, and therefore could be immediately surrendered, for alleged crimes that he directly committed. Al-Werfali (Libya) was charged with crimes that he committed on video. Khaled (Libya) was charged with crimes that in some cases he directly committed.

In all of the cases for core ICC crimes charged during Bensouda's mandate, therefore, the suspect is alleged to have committed at least some of the crimes himself. In two cases, the crimes were committed on video. Although only two of the four suspects have appeared in The Hague, there was in all cases a strong likelihood that the accused could be arrested or surrendered (though this factor appears to have been secondary to the strength of the case). Thus while the first Prosecutor believed that the ICC could contribute to a change in the conversation, could help drive a new approach to responding to violence and atrocities, the second Prosecutor has overall accepted a more circumscribed and humble role for the Court, and has adopted a more reactive stance that focuses on opportunities to pursue strong cases.

Necessarily, the theories of punishment underlying the Office of the Prosecutor's new approach to investigations and situation and case selection have evolved. The new approach no longer supports a theory of disruption of violence, ending ongoing crimes, or specific deterrence, the rationales most

[53] ICC, Decision of 27 January 2016 (PTC), *Situation in Georgia*, ICC-01/15-12.

[54] ICC, Decision of 25 October 2017 (PTC), *Situation in the Republic of Burundi*, ICC-01/17-X.

often invoked by the first Prosecutor. Instead, Bensouda has pushed towards a theory that might best be described as expressivism, finding opportunities to affirm the force of the law. This theoretical justification for punishment sees the criminal enforcement of the law as a way of expressing, shaping and enforcing norms.[55] At times, even Ocampo offered expressivist rationales for his strategy, contending that his office would bring only a small number of 'representative' cases in each situation.[56] For Bensouda, an expressivist rationale is at the core of the theoretical justifications for her strategy. Successful prosecutions affirm the force of the law in the face of atrocity, and even bringing a small number of cases can serve to affirm norms, particularly if the cases touch on novel areas of the law.[57]

Bensouda evoked expressivist themes in her opening statement of the *Al Mahdi* trial (which was in fact an extended guilty plea). Although the case was 'small' in comparison to other cases brought at the ICC and other international tribunals – Al Mahdi was a mid-level figure charged with the destruction of religious and cultural monuments over a ten-day period in 2012 – Bensouda contended that the trial had enormous normative significance:

> Today's trial is indeed historic. And it is all the more historic in view of the destructive rage that marks our times, in which humanity's common heritage is subject to repeated and planned ravages by individuals and groups whose goal is to eradicate any representation of a world that differs from theirs by eliminating the physical manifestations that are at the heart of communities. The differences and values of these communities are thus simply denied and annihilated.[58]

Bensouda traced the significance of the monuments that were attacked in Timbuktu and explained how 'deliberate attacks on cultural property are often the precursor to the worst outrages against a population', that 'deliberate attacks on cultural property have become actual weapons of war', and that 'the protection of cultural heritage is an essential part of the post-conflict social

[55] DeGuzman, 'Expressive Selection at the ICC', 312–313; M.A. Drumbl, 'Collective Violence and Individual Punishment: The Criminality of Mass Atrocity' (2005) 99 *Northwestern Law Review* 539, 592; R.D. Sloane, 'The Expressive Capacity of International Punishment: The Limits of the National Law Analogy and the Potential of International Criminal Law' (2007) 43 *Stanford Journal of International Law* 39.

[56] DeGuzman, 'Expressive Selection at the ICC', 314.

[57] But see Drumbl, 'Collective Violence and Individual Punishment', 593 (arguing that expressivism is weakened by selectivity).

[58] Statement of the Prosecutor of the International Criminal Court, Fatou Bensouda, at the opening of Trial in the case against Mr. Ahmad Al-Faqi Al Mahdi, 22 August 2016, available online at www.icc-cpi.int/Pages/item.aspx?name=otp-stat-al-mahdi-160822.

reconstruction and reconciliation process'.[59] In other words, she posited that a single, successful prosecution could have important expressivist ramifications by affirming the relevance of legal prohibitions and putting a spotlight on the broader consequences of cultural and religious attacks. In Bensouda's vision, therefore, the Court may not be a player in real time, acting quickly to interrupt violence as it happens, but rather acts as a beacon for the law and a reminder of important societal norms.

III CONCLUSION

A central challenge facing each of the first Prosecutors of the ICC has been to find a path forward given the challenges faced by the Court. In this process, theory has largely followed practice rather than the other way around. Ocampo, the first Prosecutor, embraced a strategy of moving quickly to seize the moment of international attention and cooperation, and defined success for the office in the disruption of ongoing crimes. Faced with the failure of some of the cases in the courtroom, Bensouda has changed course, pursuing long-term investigations and focusing on a small number of strong cases, justified by a rationale of expressivism.

The relationship between theory and practice within the Office of the Prosecutor at the ICC reveals something about the Court, and perhaps something about theory as well. As the Office seeks to define its strategy, one thing should be clear: there are imperatives for the Prosecution both to act quickly and to conduct thorough and careful investigations. The fact that the Prosecution has had to choose between the two underscores the mismatch between the mission that has been given to the Prosecution and its resources and tools. Going forward, the Prosecutor will continually need to adjust and navigate between these different imperatives.

Further, the ICC Prosecutor's struggle to devise a theory to buttress the practice of the office suggests that theories of punishment are a handmaiden to 'the possible' or, to put it another way, that robust theories of prosecution are a luxury of actors with power. The absence of tools and enforcement mechanisms at the ICC means that the Court is in many circumstances not in control of its direction and destiny. It is necessarily reactive to events and opportunities, and it finds success more often than it creates it. In this space, theory often becomes an ex-post justification of what the Court can do rather than a guiding principle for future action.

59 Statement of the Prosecutor of the International Criminal Court, Fatou Bensouda, at the opening of Trial in the case against Mr Ahmad Al-Faqi Al Mahdi.

17

Selectivity in International Criminal Law

Asymmetrical Enforcement as a Problem for Theories of Punishment

HARMEN VAN DER WILT

The Preamble of the Rome Statute proclaims that the states parties to the Statute are determined to put an end to impunity for the perpetrators of 'the most serious crimes of concern to the international community as a whole' and thus 'to contribute to the prevention of such crimes'.[1] The linkage to a well-known theory of punishment – general and special prevention – is intriguing, because it reflects the assumption that punishment is instrumental in dissuading people from engaging in criminal conduct. The laudable aspiration to end impunity for the most heinous crimes begs the question as to the scope of the venture. Does it imply that indeed all very serious crimes under international law must be investigated and that all perpetrators, if found guilty, must be punished? That would be compatible with – if not demanded by – the most rigid interpretation of retributive criminal justice, as propounded by Immanuel Kant.[2] For sure, such a Herculean task could never be accomplished by the International Criminal Court (ICC) alone, but that was never the intention of the states parties. The complementarity principle entails that the Court would serve as an instance of last resort, whenever states would take no initiative at all or would prove to be unable or unwilling to genuinely investigate and prosecute international crimes. Even the latter situation would not automatically imply that the ICC would intervene, if other states would be willing and capable to exercise criminal jurisdiction on

[1] ICC Statute, Preamble, paras. 4 and 5.

[2] For a Kant-inspired defence of criminal law enforcement as a categorical imperative in case of international crimes, see C.K. Hall, 'The Danger of Selective Justice: All Cases Involving Crimes under International Law Should Be Investigated and the Suspects, When There Is Sufficient Admissible Evidence, Prosecuted' in M. Bergsmo (ed.), *Criteria for Prioritizing and Selecting Core International Crimes Cases*, 2nd ed. (Oslo: Torkel Opsahl Academic EPublisher, 2010), 171.

the basis of the universality principle.[3] In that way, at least on the drawing table, a watertight system of criminal law enforcement had been conceived.

However, the clause in the Preamble of the Rome Statute does not compel us to the conclusion that prosecution and punishment must categorically be undertaken. One could, reversely, argue that any criminal trial, once in a while, would communicate the symbolic message that the international community condemns international crimes and that perpetrators should not be confident that they can always get away with it. While such an interpretation is not very attractive for those who advocate (general) deterrence, it would possibly appeal to the proponents of expressivism as the major objective of (international) criminal law.

Whatever the normative merits of these extreme positions, legal practice has corroborated neither of them. Ever since the establishment of the ICC, the Court, in tandem with national jurisdictions, has by no means addressed all international crimes but its accomplishments have at least surpassed the level of mere ritual. Still, it is fair to contend that, compared to domestic jurisdictions that are confronted with similar crimes, the ICC has been very parsimonious in the selection of cases that qualify for investigation and prosecution.[4] Due to limited resources, the ICC's Office of the Prosecutor has been compelled to make tough choices. The selection occurs at the level of 'situations' – armed conflicts or patterns of gross human rights violations, amounting to crimes against humanity or genocide – and again in the identification of specific 'cases' within these broader contexts. The conceptual demarcation and overlap between situations and cases have been elucidated elsewhere and need not detain us here.[5] Suffice to mention that a 'situation' can be referred to the Court by a state party, by the UN Security Council or

[3] This is disputed by some authors who argue that the ICC takes precedence over states exercising universal jurisdiction, see K. Ambos, *Treatise on International Criminal Law*, Vol. III (Oxford: Oxford University Press, 2016), 269.

[4] Compare W.A. Schabas, 'Selecting Situations and Cases' in C. Stahn (ed.), *The Law and Practice of the International Criminal Court* (Oxford: Oxford University Press, 2015), 365: 'In domestic legal systems, there is the presumption that all serious crimes against the person will be investigated and prosecuted, subject to limited exceptions and special rules. [...] The international system of criminal prosecution distinguishes itself from national justice mechanisms by its extreme selectivity.'

[5] See Schabas, 'Selecting Situations and Cases'. For exquisite legal analyses of these concepts, see R. Rastan, 'What is a "Case" for the Purpose of the Rome Statute?' (2008) 19 *Criminal Law Forum* 435; R. Rastan, 'Situation and Case: Defining the Parameters' in C. Stahn and M. El Zeidy (eds.), *The International Criminal Court and Complementarity: From Theory to Practice* (Cambridge: Cambridge University Press, 2011), 421; and R. Rastan, 'The Jurisdictional Scope of Situations before the International Criminal Court' (2012) 23 *Criminal Law Forum* 1.

the Prosecutor may *proprio motu* initiate investigations.[6] The Prosecutor can subsequently decide to open an investigation into a specific case after he or she has assessed whether the Court has jurisdiction, the case is admissible and the investigation serves the interests of justice. The admissibility essentially boils down to an evaluation of the 'ability and willingness' of a state to carry out investigations or prosecutions and the gravity of the case.[7]

Although some decisions of the Prosecutor are subject to review by the Pre-Trial Chamber, he or she has – at least at first blush – considerable powers of discretion. In the exercise of this discretion, theories of punishment are obviously of major importance. After all, prosecutorial decisions to focus on specific situations, crimes and perpetrators are guided by general opinions on what one seeks to achieve with the application of criminal law. The prosecutorial policy at the ICC has been the subject of extensive scholarly debate.[8] Some of the commentators have explicitly censured the Court for its one-sided attention on Africa or for being biased in the selection of cases.[9] Although I share some of the misgivings, in this contribution I do not intend to join the chorus of guardians of the Court. Rather, I would like to focus on the – legal, structural and political – constraints that actually limit the room for manoeuvre of the ICC in general and the Office of the Prosecutor in particular. These very constraints may govern the process of selection and be at odds with the main objectives of (international) criminal law enforcement. To that purpose, I will first present a survey of the parameters that delimit the selection of 'situations' and 'cases', indicating to what extent they may be conducive of a 'skewed' prosecution of certain categories of perpetrators (while letting others off the hook) and whether such outcomes were intentional (Section I). Section II will reflect on the repercussions of such inherent selectivity for

[6] ICC Statute, Arts. 13–15.

[7] ICC Statute, Arts. 17 and 53.

[8] See, for instance, R. Cryer, *Prosecuting International Crimes: Selectivity and the International Criminal Law Regime* (Cambridge: Cambridge University Press, 2014); M.M. DeGuzman, 'Choosing to Prosecute: Expressive Selection at the International Criminal Court' (2012) 33 *Michigan Journal of International Law* 265; A.K.A. Greenawalt, 'Justice without Politics: Prosecutorial Discretion and the International Criminal Court' (2007) 39 *NYU Journal of International Law and Politics* 583; M.H. Zakerhossein, *Situation Selection Regime at the International Criminal Court – Law, Policy, Practice* (Cambridge/Antwerp/Portland: Intersentia, 2017).

[9] See W.A. Schabas, 'Victor's Justice: Selecting Situations at the International Criminal Court' (2010) *Marshall Law Review* 535 (although Schabas acknowledges that the ICC is not the only one to be blamed); W.A. Schabas, 'Complementary in Practice: Some Uncomplimentary Thoughts' (2008) 19 *Criminal Law Forum* 5 and, more recently, A. Kiyani, 'Group-Based Differentiation and Local Repression: The Custom and Curse of Selectivity' (2016) 14 *Journal of International Criminal Justice* 939.

distinct theories of punishment. And Section III rounds up with some final conclusions.

I CONSTRAINTS ON THE SELECTION OF SITUATIONS AND CASES

As briefly indicated above, selectivity is usually associated with prosecutorial discretion. The ICC has limited financial and human resources at its disposal, but within these margins the Office of the Prosecutor has considerable leeway to select situations and cases for examination and prosecution. Such choices may be subject to criticism when tested against time-honoured theories of punishment.[10]

This contribution seeks to partially challenge the assumption that the Prosecutor enjoys considerable prosecutorial discretion by demonstrating that her hands are more tied than often is suggested.[11] I will argue that the constraints, extraneous to the ICC, in particular put the objectives of international criminal law enforcement at peril.

In selecting a situation, the Court is bound by its own limited jurisdiction. The Appeals Chamber in the *Lubanga* case has helpfully elucidated the components of that concept:

> [t]he notion of jurisdiction has four different facets: subject-matter jurisdiction also identified by the Latin maxim jurisdiction *ratione materiae*, jurisdiction over persons, symbolized by the Latin maxim jurisdiction *ratione personae*, territorial jurisdiction - jurisdiction *ratione loci* - and lastly jurisdiction *ratione temporis*. These facets find expression in the Statute. The jurisdiction of the Court is laid down in the Statute: Article 5 specifies the subject-matter of the jurisdiction of the Court, namely the crimes over which the Court has jurisdiction, sequentially defined in articles 6, 7, and 8. Jurisdiction over persons is dealt with in articles 12 and 26, while territorial jurisdiction is specified by articles 12 and 13 (b), depending on the origin of the proceedings. Lastly, jurisdiction *ratione temporis* is defined by article 11.[12]

In his typology of selectivity, Asad Kiyani has dubbed these constraints examples of design selectivity.[13] Some of them are more problematic or controversial than others. The subject matter jurisdiction of the Court is

[10] Margret M. DeGuzman reproaches the Court for failing to articulate clear goals and priorities, DeGuzman, 'Expressive Selection at the ICC', 295–298.

[11] For a similar argument regarding political constraints limiting the ICC Prosecutor's discretion, see the contribution by Alex Whiting in Chapter 16.

[12] ICC, Judgment of 14 December 2006 (AC), *Lubanga*, ICC-01/04-01/06-772, paras. 21, 22.

[13] Kiyani, 'Group-Based Differentiation and Local Repression', 942.

confined to the 'core' crimes that are defined in Articles 6–8 of the ICC Statute. These crimes incur individual criminal responsibility under customary international law.[14] One may perhaps deplore that the jurisdiction is not more expansive and does not cover for instance 'slow violence', like the effects of international sanction regimes,[15] but the structure of criminal law sets limitations to the attempts to tailor all man-made human misery to criminal offences. Moreover, it makes sense to restrict the jurisdiction of a supranational court to those crimes in respect of which states have a notoriously bad record in criminal law enforcement and, finally, their precise circumscription serves the *lex certa* principle.

Similar concerns for (aspects of) the *nullum crimen* principle sustain the regulation of temporal jurisdiction. Article 11 of the ICC Statute stipulates that the Court has jurisdiction only with respect to crimes committed after the entry into force of this Statute, which in fact implies 'since 1 July 2002'. The provision is obviously intended to preclude retroactive application of the Statute. Limitations of temporal jurisdiction have been conducive of accusations of bias in the context of the operations of the ad hoc Tribunals and different hybrid tribunals. The controversies surrounding the restriction of the temporal jurisdiction of the Rwanda Tribunal to crimes committed in the year 1994, effectively ousting both alleged French involvement in the planning of the genocide and crimes committed by the Tutsi-dominated government after that year, are well-known.[16] However, the rather arbitrary choice of 30 November 1996 as the starting point for the jurisdiction of the Sierra Leone Special Court encountered similar opposition, especially from Sierra Leone itself, and excluded members of the United Nations Mission in Sierra Leone (UNAMSIL) and other foreign peacekeepers from prosecution.[17] Because Article 11 only sets in the most general terms the starting date of the operation of the Court, similar apprehensions are less likely to arise in the assessment of the temporal jurisdiction of the ICC, although the temporal boundaries of a 'situation' may elicit some knotty legal issues.[18]

[14] See W.A. Schabas, *The International Criminal Court – A Commentary on the Rome Statute* (Oxford: Oxford University Press, 2010), 405, in his discussion of the drafting of Art. 22 of the ICC Statute on *nullum crimen sine lege*.

[15] In that sense, Kiyani, 'Group-Based Differentiation and Local Repression', 943.

[16] For an in-depth discussion, see L. van den Herik, *The Contribution of the Rwanda Tribunal to the Development of International Law* (Leiden: Brill, 2005), 80–84.

[17] N.B. Novogrodsky, 'After the Horror: Child Soldiers and the Special Court for Sierra Leone' in C. Jalloh (ed.), *The Sierra Leone Special Court and Its Legacy; The Impact for Africa and International Criminal Law* (Cambridge: Cambridge University Press, 2014), 369.

[18] See Rastan, 'The Jurisdictional Scope of Situations before the ICC', 21–23 and 28–33.

The consequences of the Court's limited territorial and personal jurisdiction are more drastic. The Court's exercise of jurisdiction is dependent on the territorial state and/or the state of which the accused person is a national having accepted the jurisdiction of the Court.[19] The provision connotes the consensual nature of the arrangement and underscores the relevance of territoriality and nationality as bases for criminal jurisdiction. To date, 123 countries are party to the Rome Statute. That seems a lot, but together they only represent about 50 per cent of the world population, as some of the most populous – and powerful! – nations have kept aloof. Moreover, ratification of the Rome Statute is geographically unevenly spread, with nearly all Latin American and European countries and the majority of African states having endorsed the Statute, while most Asian states having refrained from becoming a party. Of course, the consensual system can be circumvented by a referral of a situation by the Security Council acting under Chapter VII of the UN Charter.[20] However, the permanent members of the Security Council have been reluctant to initiate such a referral – the United States in the case of Iraq – or have outright vetoed a resolution to that effect – China and Russia in the case of Syria – whenever a referral would thwart their interests or affect one of their allies.

Nationals of non-states parties are not shielded against prosecution and trial by the Court, whenever they commit core crimes on the territory of a state party. Again, however, the superpowers have succeeded in protecting their nationals by claiming exclusive jurisdiction. UN Security Council Resolution 1593, referring the situation in Darfur to the Court, alludes to Article 98(2) on bilateral agreements and stipulates in paragraph 6:

> Decides that nationals, current or former officials or personnel from a contributing State outside Sudan which is not a party to the Rome Statute of the International Criminal Court shall be subject to the exclusive jurisdiction of that contributing State for all alleged acts or omissions arising out of or related to operations in Sudan established or authorized by the Council or African Union, unless such exclusive jurisdiction has been expressly waved by that contributing State.[21]

[19] ICC Statute, Art. 12(2).

[20] ICC Statute, Art. 13(2).

[21] UN Security Council Resolution 1593, 31 March 2005, UN Doc. S/RES/1593 (2005).

While the Resolution appears to confound the cooperation regime with the concept of jurisdiction, the net result is that the Court is powerless vis à vis (for instance) American soldiers who engage in war crimes on Sudan territory.[22]

In an excellent empirical study, Alette Smeulers, Maartje Weerdesteijn and Barbora Holá have assessed the ICC Prosecutor's selection of situations.[23] They have composed an 'aggregate seriousness index' of countries, on the basis of several databases that offer yardsticks of political violence and large-scale human rights violations, and have compared this with the selection of situations by the ICC Prosecutor. Contrary to mainstream opinion, the authors conclude that the Prosecutor indeed has focused on the gravest situations.[24] For the purpose of this chapter, the observation that 'the main reason why the ICC has not started investigations into other situations of similar gravity is that it lacks jurisdiction' is of paramount importance.[25] The combined effects of Myanmar, Nepal and Pakistan having not ratified the Rome Statute and the Security Council's lukewarm attitude towards highly alarming situations of humanitarian crisis have enabled these states to steer clear of the ICC's clutch.[26] Such findings put the alleged unfair bias of the ICC on African countries in an entirely different perspective. The reason why the ICC has focused on the African continent is that some situations in these countries indeed rank among the most egregious, combined with its jurisdictional capacity to address these situations. Reversely, the fact that other grave situations have remained outside the purview of the ICC can be attributed to the successful attempts of states or their powerful allies to deprive the ICC of jurisdiction.

After the selection of a situation, the Office of the Prosecutor must zoom in on specific crimes and perpetrators in order to build a 'case'. The ICC Statute itself supplies an important factor for the selection of cases by emphasizing the (lack of) gravity of the case as a ground for (in)admissibility (Article 17(1)(d)). While all the crimes within the jurisdiction of the Court are inherently

22 Compare Rastan, 'Situation and Case: Defining the Parameters', 431, who correctly observes that '[w]hile an Article 98 agreement may modify the cooperation obligations of a state, it does not deprive the court of jurisdiction per se'.

23 A. Smeulers, M. Weerdesteijn and B. Holá, 'The Selection of Situations by the ICC: An Empirically Based Evaluation of the OTP's Performance' (2015) 15 *International Criminal Law Review* 1.

24 Smeulers, Weerdesteijn and Holá, 'The Selection of Situations by the ICC', 38.

25 Smeulers, Weerdesteijn and Holá, 'The Selection of Situations by the ICC', 35–36.

26 Smeulers, Weerdesteijn and Holá, 'The Selection of Situations by the ICC', 28: 'Despite the fact that we can clearly conclude that the situation in all three of these countries [Myanmar, Nepal, Pakistan, addition by HvdW] is or was grave these countries do not, according to the UNSC, pose a threat to international peace and security.'

serious, cases can still be weighed (and prioritized) on the basis of quantitative and qualitative criteria. In the Kenya decision, the Pre-Trial Chamber borrowed from the factors for the determination of sentence, incorporated in Rule 145 of the Rules of Procedure and Evidence of the ICC, arguing that these factors could provide useful guidance in the examination of (qualitative) gravity.[27] The Chamber summarized these factors as

i) The scale of the alleged crimes (including assessment of geographical and temporal intensity);
ii) The nature of the unlawful behaviour or of the crimes allegedly committed;
iii) The employed means for the execution of the crimes (i.e., the manner of their commission); and
iv) The impact of the crimes and the harm caused to victims and their families.[28]

Within the realm of the ICC, there is apparently a broad consensus on the appropriateness of these factors as indications for 'gravity'. The Office of the Prosecutor has copied them verbatim in its latest *Policy Paper on Case Selection and Prioritisation*.[29] Focusing on the perpetrators, rather than on the crime, the policy paper qualifies the 'degree of responsibility of alleged perpetrators' as the second criterion for selection. According to Helen Brady and Fabricio Guariglia, this is a more nuanced standard than the previous criterion of 'most responsible', as it includes mid-level and even lower-level perpetrators who indulge in particularly heinous crimes.[30] It certainly meets the often pronounced objection that a fixation on the 'highest in command' neglects the interests of victims who prefer to see their direct tormentors in the dock. Moreover, the Policy Paper announces that 'the charges will constitute, whenever possible, a representative sample of the main types of victimization and of the communities which have been affected by the crimes in the

[27] ICC, Decision of 31 March 2010, *Situation in the Republic of Kenya* (PTC), ICC-01/09, para. 62. On these sentencing factors, see also the contribution by Gerhard Werle and Aziz Epik in Chapter 18.

[28] ICC, Decision of 31 March 2010, Situation in the Republic of Kenya, ICC-01/09, para. 62.

[29] ICC Office of the Prosecutor, Policy Paper on Case Selection and Prioritisation, 15 September 2016, available at www.icc-cpi.int/itemsDocuments/20160915_OTP-Policy_Case-Selection_Eng.pdf. This policy paper is the latest edition of similar papers that addressed the problem of selection of cases in 2006 and 2013. For a discussion, see H. Brady and F. Guariglia, 'Arguendo: An Insider's View: Consistency and Transparency While Preserving Prosecutorial Discretion', available at www.international-criminal-justice-today.org/arguendo/an-insiders-view.

[30] Brady and Guariglia, 'Consistency and Transparency While Preserving Prosecutorial Discretion'.

situation', simultaneously indicating that it will pay special attention to those crimes that have traditionally been neglected. As examples of the latter category, the paper mentions crimes against children, rape and other sexual or gender-related crimes, attacks against cultural, religious, historical and other protected objects and attacks against humanitarian and peacekeeping personnel.[31]

The Office of the Prosecutor must certainly be commended for elucidating and refining the criteria for case selection and prioritization. The key question is whether these laudable aspirations can be accomplished. Of course, the Office is not blind to 'practical obstacles' that emerge from (awkward) political realities.[32] As one of the strategic case prioritization criteria, the Office identifies 'the impact and the ability of the Office to pursue cases involving opposing parties to a conflict in parallel or on a sequential basis'.[33] However, it realistically balances these lofty intentions against the practical feasibility of investigations and prosecutions. The criteria to assess the 'operational viability' of a case include:

(a) the quantity and quality of the incriminating and exonerating evidence already in the possession of the Office and the availability of additional evidence;
(b) international cooperation and judicial assistance to support the Office's activities;
(c) the Office's capacity to effectively conduct the necessary investigations within a reasonable time; and
(d) the potential to secure the appearance of suspects before the Court, by arrest and surrender or pursuant to a summons.[34]

It is remarkable that the Policy Paper is silent on the tension between the strategic aim of investigating both sides to the conflict and the conditions for effectively and successfully completing investigations and prosecutions. After all, it is unlikely that public authorities will generously cooperate with the Prosecutor, whenever such assistance may be conducive of their own criminal conviction. It is a well-known structural flaw of the international criminal justice system that immediately came to the fore in the first (auto) referral by Uganda. Obviously, President Museveni intended to cajole the ICC Prosecutor to focus his attention on the prosecution of Museveni's foes, the Lord

[31] ICC, Office of the Prosecutor, Policy Paper on Case Selection and Prioritisation, paras. 45, 46.
[32] On this, see the contribution by Alex Whiting in Chapter 16.
[33] ICC, Office of the Prosecutor, Policy Paper on Case Selection and Prioritisation, para. 50.
[34] ICC, Office of the Prosecutor, Policy Paper on Case Selection and Prioritisation, para. 51.

Resistance Army (LRA), while simultaneously distracting him from the crimes committed by the Ugandan Armed Forces. He cleverly used the Prosecutor's dependence on Ugandan cooperation for the purpose of the prosecution of LRA suspects as bargaining chip.[35] The ICC Prosecutor at least formally thwarted Museveni's attempt to unilaterally direct the prosecution of the Lord's Resistance Army by pointing out that he would investigate crimes committed by both sides. He submitted that 'the scope of the referral encompasses *all* crimes committed in Northern Uganda in the context of the ongoing conflict involving the Lord's Resistance Army'.[36] Nonetheless, the Prosecutor has not investigated any of the Ugandan Army's attacks on the civilian population, nor have the perpetrators of such crimes been held accountable by Ugandan courts.[37]

Although the practice of self-referrals may be especially vulnerable to such machinations to steer the ICC Prosecutor's policy, other triggering mechanisms have not remained immune from them either.[38] The situation in Kenya that was initiated by a *proprio motu* investigation of the Prosecutor, collapsed spectacularly after the government had refused to transfer evidence vital to the case that could have implicated current president Kenyatta and his close ally, Deputy President William Ruto.[39] In the situation in Ivory Coast that also emanated from post-election violence, the Prosecutor only investigated and pressed charges against the vanquished party, to wit former president Gbagbo

35 Compare S. Nouwen and W. Werner, 'Doing Justice to the Political: The International Criminal Court in Uganda and Sudan' (2011) 21 *European Journal of International Law* 941, 950: '[...] a referral of the situation concerning the LRA would make the ICC's Prosecutor dependent on the cooperation of the Ugandan government; and he might hesitate to jeopardize such cooperation by charging his cooperative friends with crimes committed in neighbouring DRC'.

36 ICC, Decision of 2 December 2005 to Convene a Status Conference on the Investigation in the Situation in Uganda in Relation to the Application of Article 53 (PTC), *Situation in Uganda*, ICC-02/04-01/15-44, para. 4 (emphasis added).

37 Nouwen and Werner, 'Doing Justice to the Political', 951: 'To date, he [the ICC Prosecutor, added by HvdW] has not opened an investigation into alleged crimes by state actors, officially on the basis of (a dubious application of) gravity as selection criterion.'

38 In a previous article, I have rendered a moderately positive assessment of self-referrals against the backdrop of the establishment of a fair and effective system of international criminal justice. However, I acknowledge the danger of 'victor's justice'. See H. van der Wilt, 'Self-Referrals as an Indication of the Inability of States to Cope with Non-state Actors' in C. Stahn and M. El Zeidy (eds.), *Law and Practice of the International Criminal Court* (Oxford: Oxford University Press, 2015).

39 ICC, Decision of 31 March 2015 on the withdrawal of charges against Mr. Kenyatta (TC), *Kenyatta*, ICC-01/09-02/11-1005.

and his wife Simone, while leaving the winner, President Ouattara, virtually untouched.[40] In addition, it is common knowledge that Sudan's incumbent president, Omar Al Bashir, is still at large, although he has been accused of war crimes and crimes against humanity, after the Security Council had referred the situation to the ICC, more than ten years ago. No state party to the Rome Statute has had the nerve to surrender him to the Court.

The rather disenchanting conclusion can only be that certain 'situations', crimes and perpetrators are outside the purview of the ICC and perhaps even of all (international) criminal justice. Whether this is a matter of grave concern from the perspective of theories of criminal punishment is the topic of the next section.

II SKEWED PROSECUTORIAL POLICY AND THE THEORIES OF PUNISHMENT

The aim of this section is to test the skewed prosecutorial policy at the ICC, caused by structural and political factors, against the dominant theories of punishment. To that purpose, we must briefly revisit those theories and discuss how they have been interpreted in the context of international criminal justice.

Trial Chambers of the ad hoc Tribunals have paved the way in outlining the determining factors in sentencing and, by doing so, have shed light on the broader objectives and justifications of international criminal law. In general, Trial Chambers are inclined to refer to the all too familiar goals of retribution and deterrence. In the *Erdemović* case, the International Criminal Tribunal for the former Yugoslavia (ICTY) Trial Chamber addressed, under the heading of sentencing, the wider mission of the Yugoslavia Tribunal, as interpreted by the UN Security Council:

> The International Tribunals' objectives as seen by the Security Council – id est general prevention (or deterrence), reprobation, retribution (or 'just deserts'), as well as collective reconciliation – fit into the Security Council's broader aim of maintaining peace and security in the former Yugoslavia.[41]

40 Mark Kersten observed 10 years ago that '[...] five years on, not a single member of the Ouattara camp has been prosecuted for international crimes – domestically or at the ICC. Some insiders believe that the days of victor's justice in Côte d'Ivoire are numbered and that the ICC is on the verge of issuing warrants for alleged perpetrators close to Ouattara', available at https://justiceinconflict.org/2016/05/13/as-battle-over-victors-justice-looms-maybe-the-icc-should-let-cote-divoire-prosecute-simone-gbagbo. The 'insiders' have proved to be wrong.

41 ICTY, Sentencing Judgment of 29 November 1996 (TC), *Erdemović*, IT-96-22-T, para. 58. In a similar vein, ICTR, Sentence of 5 February 1999 (TC), *Serushago*, ICTR-98-39-S, para. 20.

Courts have often taken the trouble to elaborate on their specific understanding of these theories. In the *Kordić* case, the ICTY Appeals Chamber sought to emphasize the distinction between mere vengeance and retribution by pointing at the latter's demand for proportionality: '[...] unlike vengeance, retribution incorporates a principle of restraint: retribution requires the imposition of a just and appropriate punishment, *and nothing more*'.[42]

Alluding to general deterrence in particular, the Trial Chamber in the *Furundžija* case quoted Cesare Beccaria's famous observation that 'punishment should not be harsh, but must be inevitable', adding that 'it is the infallibility of punishment, rather than the severity of the sanction, which is the tool for retribution, stigmatization and deterrence'.[43] And the Trial Chamber in *Erdemović* presaged the increasingly popular theory of normative expression when it remarked that

> The International Tribunal sees public reprobation and stigmatisation by the international community, which would thereby express its indignation over heinous crimes and denounce the perpetrators, as one of the essential functions of a prison sentence for a crime against humanity.[44]

The easy conflation of theories of criminal punishment at a domestic and at an international level has been criticized for ignoring essential structural, political and moral differences between these contexts. The domestic analogy is a fallacy, so the argument goes, because the international community whom the ICC is intended to serve and represent is pluralistic.[45] Unlike a nation, it is not a moral community, whose members share certain values and have consented in endowing an entity with the power to enforce those values by punishing trespassers.[46]

None of the theories of punishment is quite successful in accounting for the justification of criminal law enforcement by international criminal tribunals

[42] ICTY, Judgment of 17 December 2004 (AC), *Kordić and Čerkez*, IT-95-14/2-A, para. 1075 (emphasis in original).

[43] ICTY, Judgment of 10 December 1998 (TC), *Furundžija*, IT-95-17/1-T, para. 290. On this, see also the contribution by Frank Neubacher in Chapter 3.

[44] ICTY, Sentencing Judgment of 29 November 1996 (TC), *Erdemović*, IT-96-22-T, para. 65. The TC in the Furundžija case (ICTY, Judgment of 10 December 1998 (TC), *Furundžija*, IT-95-17/1-T, para. 289) coined this opinion in respect of war crimes and other serious violations of international humanitarian law.

[45] On the domestic analogy (objection), see also the contribution by Elies van Sliedregt in Chapter 5.

[46] R.D. Sloane, 'The Expressive Capacity of International Punishment: The Limits of the National Analogy and the Potential of International Criminal Law' (2007) 43 *Stanford Journal of International Law* 39, 41; I. Tallgren, 'The Sensibility and Sense of International Criminal Law' (2002) 13 *European Journal of International Law* 561, 566.

in respect of perpetrators of international crimes. The problem is compounded if we include the structural selectivity of prosecution in our analysis.

1 *Retribution*

The embarrassment of retributive theories – with its emphasis on just desert and proportionality between crime and punishment – to explain penalties that are woefully incommensurate to the enormity of the crimes has been famously captured by Hannah Arendt. In her correspondence with Karl Jaspers, she notes that

> The Nazi crimes, it seems to me, explode the limits of law; and that is precisely what constitutes their monstrousness. For these crimes, no punishment is severe enough. It may well be essential to hang Göring, but it is totally inadequate. That is, this guilt, in contrast to all criminal guilt, oversteps and shatters any and all legal systems.[47]

Retribution demands that at least those bearing the greatest culpability for the most heinous crimes are to be punished. Mark Drumbl correctly observes that selectivity is hence retributive theory's greatest challenge and enemy. While *any* selectivity sits uncomfortably with the aims and principles of retribution, Drumbl has acutely anticipated the political constraints that we have addressed in the previous section and that have haunted the ICC Prosecutor: 'Cases may be turned away because of politics and initiated because of politics, instead of cases initiated or turned away solely because of the gravity of the alleged violations of international law that they actually present.'[48]

Whereas Drumbl suggests that the Prosecutor would at least have a certain leeway to navigate between the political hurdles, the reality has appeared to be even bleaker. As we discussed in the previous section, the Prosecutor's room for manoeuvre is effectively curtailed by structural and political constraints.[49]

[47] L. Kohler and H. Saner (eds.), *Hannah Arendt/Karl Jaspers: Correspondence* (translation R. and R. Kimber) (Philadelphia: Saunders College Publishing, 1992), 54.

[48] M.A. Drumbl, *Atrocity, Punishment and International Law* (Cambridge: Cambridge University Press, 2007), 152. See also, for a discussion of the 'trials and tribulations' of retributive theory to come to terms with international criminal law enforcement, DeGuzman, 'Expressive Selection at the ICC', 301–306 and Sloane, 'The Expressive Capacity', 77–81.

[49] Compare M. Osiel, 'The Banality of Good: Aligning Incentives against Mass Atrocity' (2005) 105 *Columbia Law Review* 1751, 1821 who avows that the inability of international courts to indict leaders of major world powers creates legitimacy problems.

2 *Prevention*

Deterrence as justification for criminal law enforcement and punishment does not fare well either, when confronted with international crimes. General prevention theory assumes that potential offenders are dissuaded from committing crimes by the threat of punishment. Moreover, it postulates that persons are likely to obey the (criminal) law because they internalize its values. The theory has suffered attacks at different epistemological levels. The most principled objection from a Kantian perspective is that each human being is an end in itself and no one should be 'abused' as an instrument to influence the behaviour of others. From a practical perspective, general deterrence proponents are challenged – also in the domestic context – to present empirical evidence that sustains their contentions. They are accused of harbouring a simplified vision of crime and lumping different manifestations together. Deterrence may 'work' in case of tax evasion or traffic offences, but the threat of punishment is less likely to be effective in case of crimes of passion.

In the case of international crimes, the criticism becomes more acute. The 'internalization-thesis' is questioned in the narratives on 'inversed moral universes' where the commission of atrocities is considered normal or even laudable and abstention is considered socially deviating behaviour.[50] Furthermore, the effectiveness of general deterrence is predicated on two factors: the severity of punishment and the likelihood of being caught and brought to trial.[51] Obviously, our assessment of the structural and political constraints on the prosecutorial versatility ties in with the latter aspect. When perpetrators of international crimes are confident that they can remain off the hook, there is no incentive that makes them abstain from committing those crimes.

Whereas general prevention is concerned with the weakness of human beings inclined to yield to temptations and engage in evil, special prevention focuses its attention on the concrete perpetrator, who must be kept from lapsing into the same behaviour. This can be achieved through rehabilitation or incapacitation. The former solution has not received much attention in international criminal law, which can be mainly attributed to the nature of the crimes.[52] From the perspective of the prevention of recurrence, incapacitation

[50] Tallgren, 'The Sensibility and Sense of International Criminal Law', 575; and, in a similar vein, Sloane, 'The Expressive Capacity of International Punishment', 76.

[51] Tallgren, 'The Sensibility and Sense of International Criminal Law', 575–576.

[52] See also Drumbl, *Atrocity, Punishment and International Law*, who makes an exception for child soldiers.

may often not be necessary, because international crimes are typically crimes of opportunity that are not likely to be repeated when the circumstances have drastically changed. David Luban points at the exceptions to the rule, observing that 'incapacitating toxic political leaders – a Goering, a Milosevic, a Charles Taylor – can be absolutely crucial'.[53] It is telling, however, that he refers to persons who have been prosecuted by tribunals with abundant powers that cannot be compared to the ICC. It is far less likely that incumbent or even former political leaders will stand trial before the ICC, unless they have suffered humiliating defeat, in which case the need for incapacitation is questionable.[54]

3 *Norm Expression*

The last criminal law theory that deserves a brief discussion is norm expression or 'expressivism'. According to its proponents, (international) criminal law's main purpose is to communicate to the general public the moral and social values that sustain the legal framework. This educative function serves to strengthen the people's faith in the rule of law and reinforce communal bonds. Indebted to the pioneering work of Émile Durkheim, the concept had first taken root in general criminal law theory, before being embraced by international criminal law scholars.[55] Moreover, the theory has resonated in the case law of the ICC and international criminal tribunals. The Trial Chamber of the Special Court for Sierra Leone (SCSL) in the *RUF* case held that 'punishment in international criminal law must also reflect the

[53] D. Luban, 'Fairness to Rightness: Jurisdiction, Legality, and the Legitimacy of International Criminal Law' in S. Besson and J. Tasioulas (eds.), *The Philosophy of International Law* (Oxford: Oxford University Press, 2010), 575.

[54] See also Tallgren, 'The Sensibility and Sense of International Criminal Law', 579: 'The way the "international criminal justice system" works currently, however, there are very limited possibilities to formulate such a policy of granting the ICC jurisdiction in the most serious cases. This would seem to be possible only in cases of a change of government or of occupation, perhaps in the form of a notorious "victor's justice"'.

[55] In domestic criminal law theory: J. Feinberg, 'The Expressive Function of Punishment', in J. Feinberg, *Doing and Deserving: Essays in the Theory of Responsibility* (Princeton: Princeton University Press, 1970), 95. Among the advocates of norm expression in international criminal law: E.M. Wise, 'The International Criminal Court: A Budget of Paradoxes' (2000) 8 *Tulane Journal of International and Criminal Law* 261, 267; M. Damaška, 'What is the Point of International Criminal Justice?' (2008) 83 *Chicago-Kent Law Review* 329; DeGuzman, 'Expressive Selection at the ICC', 312–319; Sloane, 'The Expressive Capacity', 81–84; Luban, 'Fairness to Rightness', 576: 'In my view, the most promising justification for international tribunals is their role in norm projection: trials are expressive acts broadcasting the news that mass atrocities are, in fact, heinous crimes and not merely politics by other means.'

revulsion of the international community to such conduct and denounce it as unacceptable'.[56] In a similar vein, the Trial Chamber in *Katanga* held that 'punishment was the expression of society's condemnation of the criminal act and of the person who committed it, which is also a way of acknowledging the harm and suffering caused to the victims'.[57]

Presumably, the theory owes its popularity to two factors. First, it embodies international criminal law's shift in emphasis from punishment to the trial.[58] It is precisely during the trial that the normative message can best be dispersed. Second, the theory of norm expression accommodates international criminal law's inherent selectivity and is therefore better suited to the system than retribution and general prevention that both lose much of their appeal if prosecution is 'haphazard'.[59] Exemplary justice is the hallmark of normative expression and the theory would at first blush fit the ICC's mission like a glove. However, the theory's merits simultaneously connote its vulnerabilities. Immi Tallgren has observed that the role of international criminal law 'as the loudspeaker echoing the values of the international community' invites similar reproaches as utilitarianism from Kantians, for using a person as a tool, rather than an end.[60] The criticism is arguably too harsh and not entirely accurate, because the theory of normative expression hovers between deontology and utilitarianism. After all, with deontological theory it shares the conviction that the offender really deserves his or her punishment and that the moral message will only hit home if the punishment is proportionate to the crime. Normative expression is on the same page as the advocates of general prevention to the extent that they both consider the increase of human happiness and the decrease of crime and violence as a necessary and desirable offshoot of criminal law enforcement.[61]

[56] SCSL, Sentencing Judgment of 8 April 2009 (TC), *Sesay, Kallon and Gbao (RUF trial)*, SCSL-04-15-T, para. 15.

[57] ICC, Decision of 23 March 2014 on Sentence pursuant to Article 76 of the Statute (TC), *Katanga*, ICC-01/04-01/07, para. 38.

[58] Luban, 'Fairness to Rightness', 575.

[59] Compare DeGuzman, 'Expressive Selection at the ICC', 315: 'The ICC's selectivity is significantly less problematic if one adopts a primarily expressive theory of the institution's work rather than one focused on deterrence or retribution', adding that '[b]oth deterrence and retribution are undermined by the ICC's inability to prosecute the vast majority of international crimes'.

[60] Tallgren, 'The Sensibility and Sense of International Criminal Law', 592.

[61] See, for a probing discussion of what he dubs as 'positive general prevention', G.P. Fletcher, *The Grammar of Criminal Law, Volume One: Foundations* (Oxford: Oxford University Press, 2007), 253–254. Fletcher attributes this approach, which is according to him an 'intriguing compromise between the two schools that dominate the Anglo-American discussion (to wit:

More to the point is Tallgren's second – pragmatic – objection, where she holds that 'the negotiations on the ICC demonstrated clearly the lack of will to genuinely realize the jurisdictional basis for the functioning of (the) symbolism'.[62] As she does not elaborate on this point, it is a bit arcane what she intends to covey. Her reference to 'crippled jurisdiction', however, makes me surmise that the argument strikes at the heart of our topic. Exemplary justice immediately begs the question: What example? What message? Which justice? Whereas I agree with Meg DeGuzman that norm expression allows for a system that grants the Prosecutor a free hand to pick and choose on the basis of a set of standards, it cannot be reconciled with preordained selectivity that systematically absolves entire categories of perpetrators from accountability. This issues the perverse message that criminal responsibility depends on the party/nation one belongs to and the side on which one fights.

In other words, as little as retribution and deterrence, the theory of normative expression cannot provide a satisfying answer to the question of why a system of international criminal law that is only capable of targeting some culprits, while others are systematically exempted can be justified or even tolerated.

III CONCLUSION

The previous section ended in a minor key. Our investigations demonstrate that none of the theories of punishment can sustain or warrant a system of criminal law enforcement in which selectivity is imposed by the structural and political constraints that we have identified in Section I. How should we move forward? In my view, there are three options.

First, the *fatalistic* position: we could suggest that the ICC close its doors and abandon the entire venture. One may concede that international criminal law and politics are intertwined, but if political power prevails to the extent that it can dictate who can be prosecuted and who should be excluded, international criminal justice should gracefully retreat on pain of becoming a travesty of itself.

The second – *opportunistic* – position proposes to slightly downplay the importance of theories of punishment. Our intuition tells us to continue the quest for international criminal justice, because it feels the right thing to do

retribution and deterrence)' to the German criminal law theorists Claus Roxin and Günther Jakobs.

62 Tallgren, 'The Sensibility and Sense of International Criminal Law', 592.

and we have no other option.[63] We are living in an imperfect world and our theories of punishments, as products of the human mind, are necessarily imperfect as well. If these theories cannot sustain the current system that represents a marriage of convenience between law and politics, so much the worse for those theories. In the meantime, we may count our blessings, whenever the ICC or other international criminal tribunals manage to successfully complete a trial, especially if they succeed in bringing one of those 'bearing the greatest responsibility' to the dock.

The third approach, that I would like to call the position of *dauntless perseverance* and that has my personal preference, is a qualification and refinement of the previous one. Although, obviously, one may disagree with the Prosecutor's choices, the ICC would be well advised to hold a steady course. Normative expression may be the overarching goal, but it is a hollow phrase if the objectives are not further substantiated or fleshed out. The aim 'to end impunity' is too vague, general and arguably unrealistic. In two aspects, the ICC has made progress over the last years. First, it has broadened its horizon beyond Africa by starting preliminary examinations in Afghanistan, Colombia, Iraq/United Kingdom, Palestine, the Philippines, Ukraine and Venezuela.[64] Second, the Office of the Prosecutor has succeeded in fine-tuning its criteria for the selection of cases and situations. From a communicative and educational perspective, these are important developments. One aspect is glaringly absent in the messages to the general public: an explanation why the ICC is structurally precluded from addressing certain highly urgent situations. The ICC is exposed to heavy criticism; sometimes rightly so, more often not. In the latter case, it should dispassionately elucidate that it is unable to proceed, because a state has opted to keep aloof, the UN Security Council has no interest or the ICC is taken hostage by a government that threatens to halt all cooperation if the Prosecutor gets serious in targeting its representatives. One of the components of normative expression is that the public should be informed on who is to blame for disrupting international criminal justice.

[63] See Tallgren, 'The Sensibility and Sense of International Criminal Law', 564, toying with the idea.

[64] The situation in Georgia is 'under investigation' – one step further down the road – but it has lingered on for 10 years now.

18

Theories of Punishment in Sentencing Decisions of the International Criminal Court

GERHARD WERLE AND AZIZ EPIK*

Why punish perpetrators of mass atrocities?[1] This question primarily concerns the fundamental discourse on the justification of punishment in international criminal law. Finding a persuasive and coherent answer is indispensable with a view to the legitimacy of international criminal law as such; only if the international community can provide a rational justification for the infliction of criminal sanctions, can international criminal law be legitimized as an adequate legal response to mass atrocities.[2]

The question has, however, at least one additional dimension. Judges applying international criminal law in practice also need to conclusively determine why they are punishing an individual perpetrator for the crime he or she has been convicted for in order to arrive at a fair, coherent and proportionate sentence. This is because the definition of the objectives that are pursued in the context of sentencing in a particular criminal justice system predetermine the sentencing process and its outcome:[3] First, the sentencing objectives affect the sentencing method that judges follow in allocating a specific sentence in a particular case; second, they determine the criteria that can be taken into account in sentencing; and third, they impinge on the

* The authors would like to thank Professor Florian Jeßberger, Professor Volker Nerlich and Dr Leonie Steinl, LL.M. (Columbia) for their helpful comments on earlier drafts of this chapter. Lisa von Mansberg was most helpful in editing this chapter.

1 See G. Werle, 'Menschenrechtsschutz durch Völkerstrafrecht' (1997) 109 *Zeitschrift für die gesamte Strafrechtswissenschaft* 808, 821 et seq.

2 M.M. DeGuzman, 'Proportionate Sentencing at the ICC' in C. Stahn (ed.), *The Law and Practice of the International Criminal Court* (Oxford: Oxford University Press, 2015), 932 et seq.; A. Werkmeister, *Straftheorien im Völkerstrafrecht* (Nomos: Baden-Baden, 2015), 42 et seq.

3 But see the contribution by Kai Ambos in Chapter 6.

extent and type of punishment, including the prospect of suspended sentences and parole.[4] Thus, before even further considering an appropriate sentence for an accused, the Trial Chamber has to establish a proper foundation for its sentencing decision by determining the sentencing objectives guiding the sentencing process.

Following an analysis of the statutory framework provided by the Statute and the Rules of Procedure and Evidence of the International Criminal Court (ICC), this chapter will assess the sentencing decisions pronounced by the ICC to date with a view to the sentencing objectives identified and applied by the Chambers. We will analyze whether it is already possible to identify a fairly consistent concept in the case law of the ICC and, if so, whether such a concept is also reflected in the sentencing practice of the Court. Implementing such a concept is of crucial importance for the development of a consistent, fair and proportionate sentencing practice at the ICC and also to prevent allegations of inconsistency and unpredictability in sentencing that have often been raised in the context of international criminal justice in the past.[5]

I THE STATUTORY FRAMEWORK

Neither the ICC Statute nor the Rules of Procedure and Evidence contain provisions explicitly outlining the sentencing objectives.[6] An analysis of the relevant provisions of the Statute and Rules reveals, however, that the

4 A. Epik, *Die Strafzumessung bei Taten nach dem Völkerstrafgesetzbuch* (Tübingen: Mohr Siebeck, 2017), 19; F. Melloh, *Einheitliche Strafzumessung in den Rechtsquellen des IStGH-Statuts* (Berlin: Duncker & Humblot, 2010), 39. In a similar vein J. Book, *Appeal and Sentence in International Criminal Law* (Berlin: Berliner Wissenschafts-Verlag, 2011), 28 et seq.: 'Yet, sentencing law is able to derive some guidance from these principles, although the influence that a particular concept exerts on the length of a sentence is often impossible to determine. The rationales outlined above rather serve as general factors directing the overall structure of sentencing law.'

5 K. Ambos, *Treatise on International Criminal Law*, Vol. II (Oxford: Oxford University Press, 2014), 269 et seq.; Book, *Appeal and Sentence*, 14; B. Holá, A. Smeulers and C. Bijleveld, 'Is ICTY Sentencing Predictable? An Empirical Analysis of ICTY Sentencing Practice' (2009) 22 *Leiden Journal of International Law* 79, 80; J. Meernik and K. King, 'The Sentencing Determinants of the International Criminal Tribunal for the Former Yugoslavia: An Empirical and Doctrinal Analysis' (2003) 16 *Leiden Journal of International Law* 717, 718.

6 ICC, Decision of 23 May 2014 (TC), *Katanga*, ICC-01/04-01/07-3484, para. 37; ICC, Judgment of 27 September 2016 (TC), *Al Mahdi*, ICC-01/12-01/15-171, para. 66.

traditional purposes of punishment, on which most domestic criminal justice systems rely, apply – with some adjustments – regardless of the macro-criminal character of international crimes and the inherent shortcomings of each purpose.[7] As in the domestic context, it is therefore not a single objective – a single theory of punishment – that justifies and defines international punishment, but a combination of retributive and preventive considerations,[8] which we will briefly demonstrate in the following. We will, however, not go into detail regarding each of the sentencing objectives, their philosophical background, their shortcomings, or the academic discussion on whether a particular objective is actually compatible with the specific features of international criminal law.[9] Instead and in line with the topic of this chapter, our discussion will be limited to the law *de lege lata* and its interpretation by the ICC.

7 On the domestic analogy (objection), see the contribution by Elies van Sliedregt in Chapter 5; G. Werle and F. Jeßberger, *Principles of International Criminal Law*, 3rd ed. (Oxford: Oxford University Press, 2014), para. 106; see also S. D'Ascoli, *Sentencing in International Criminal Law* (Oxford: Hart, 2011), 295; Epik, *Strafzumessung*, 80 et seq. However, as the ICTY outlined in its first sentencing decision, caution is warranted when transferring the purposes of punishment from the domestic to the international level, see ICTY, Judgment of 29 November 1996 (AC), *Erdemović*, IT-96-22-T, para. 62: 'Although, in determining the purpose of a term of imprisonment for crimes against humanity the Chamber may have recourse to the functions of penalties identified within national criminal systems, it needs to do so cautiously; the *ratione materiae* jurisdiction of the International Tribunal differs fundamentally from that of a national court which punishes all sorts of offences, usually ordinary crimes.' Critical with a view to the applicability of traditional purposes of punishment, R.D. Sloane, 'The Expressive Capacity of International Punishment: The Limits of the National Law Analogy and the Potential of International Criminal Law' (2007) 43 *Stanford Journal of International Law* 39, 40 et seq., 45 et seq.; I. Tallgren, 'The Sensibility and Sense of International Criminal Law' (2002) 13 *European Journal of International Law* 561 et seq.

8 D'Ascoli, *Sentencing*, 295; Epik, *Strafzumessung*, 152 et seq.; L. May, 'Defending International Criminal Trials' in L. May and J. Brown (eds.), *Philosophy of Law* (Chichester: Wiley-Blackwell, 2010), 423 et seq.; Werle and Jeßberger, *Principles*, paras. 106 et seq.

9 We have outlined elsewhere that in our view the traditional purposes of punishment can, in general, also justify punishment in international criminal law, see Epik, *Strafzumessung*, 80 et seq.; Werle, 'Menschenrechtsschutz durch Völkerstrafrecht', 821; Werle and Jeßberger, *Principles*, paras. 106 et seq. For a detailed discussion, see, among others, K. Ambos, *Treatise on International Criminal Law*, Vol. I (Oxford: Oxford University Press, 2013), 67 et seq.; R. Cryer et al., *An Introduction to International Criminal Law and Procedure*, 3rd ed. (Cambridge: Cambridge University Press, 2014), 29 et seq.; M.A. Drumbl, *Atrocity, Punishment, and International Law* (Cambridge: Cambridge University Press, 2007), 149 et seq.; May, 'Defending International Criminal Trials', 423 et seq.; Werkmeister, *Straftheorien im Völkerstrafrecht*, 118 et seq.

1 *Retribution*

While nowadays retributive theories of punishment exist in a wide variety with different philosophical foundations,[10] in the practice of international criminal law, in particular in the case law of the ad hoc Tribunals, retribution has been understood as a principle demanding the compensation of the offender's guilt through a proportionate punishment that is reflective of the harm done by and the culpability of the offender.[11] In this sense, retribution provides a measurement tool for the sentencing process and restrains the extent of punishment permissible in a particular case by demanding proportionality.[12] Based on this understanding, retribution can clearly be deduced as an important – if not the primary – sentencing objective from the ICC Statute and the Rules of Procedure and Evidence:

A first indication that the drafters of the Statute envisaged retribution as a relevant theory of punishment can already be found in the ICC Statute's Preamble. Its fourth paragraph affirms 'that the most serious crimes of concern to the international community as a whole must not go unpunished'. Read together with the fifth preambular paragraph ('determined to put an end to impunity for the perpetrators of these crimes [...]'), it indicates that perpetrators of international crimes must be punished because they have committed a crime against international law and thus, on principle, regardless of any other considerations. This is typical for a retributive approach that focuses on the crime committed and not on possible future delinquency in order to justify the punishment of a perpetrator.[13]

The importance of the retributive theory in the context of sentencing at the ICC is further confirmed by an analysis of the sentencing provisions in the ICC Statute and the Rules of Procedure and Evidence. First, the principle of

[10] For an overview, see A. Ashworth, *Sentencing and Criminal Justice*, 6th ed. (Cambridge: Cambridge University Press, 2015), 93 et seq.; T. Hörnle, *Straftheorien*, 2nd ed. (Tübingen: Mohr Siebeck, 2017), 17 et seq.; Melloh, *Einheitliche Strafzumessung*, 103 et seq.

[11] ICTY, Judgment of 17 December 2004 (AC), *Kordić and Čerkez*, IT-95-14/2-A, para. 1075; ICTY, Judgment of 17 March 2009 (AC), *Krajišnik*, IT-00-39-A, paras. 775, 804; see also Epik, *Strafzumessung*, 85 et seq. with further references in fn. 37.

[12] ICTY, Judgment of 17 December 2004 (AC), *Kordić and Čerkez*, IT-95-14/2-A, para. 1075.

[13] D'Ascoli, *Sentencing*, 271 et seq.; Drumbl, *Atrocity, Punishment, and International Law*, 150; Epik, *Strafzumessung*, 81 et seq.; K.J. Heller, 'A Sentence-Based Theory of Complementarity' (2012) 53 *Harvard International Law Journal* 85, 127 n. 220; Melloh, *Einheitliche Strafzumessung*, 103; B. Schmitt, 'Schuld im Römischen Statut' in T. Fischer and E. Hoven (eds.), *Schuld* (Baden-Baden: Nomos, 2017), 251, 261; O. Triffterer, M. Bergsmo and K. Ambos, 'Preamble', in O. Triffterer and K. Ambos (eds.), *The Rome Statute of the International Criminal Court: A Commentary*, 3rd ed. (München: C.H. Beck 2016), Preamble para. 15.

personal culpability, which demands proportionality between the harm done by and the culpability of the offender and his or her punishment, is embedded in Article 78(1) of the ICC Statute ('gravity of the crime') as well as in Rule 145 (1)(a) of the ICC Rules of Procedure and Evidence ('culpability').[14] This principle does not only include the core idea of the retributive theory, demanding proportionality between individual responsibility and punishment, but also prevents an overemphasis on preventive purposes of punishment in the determination of a sentence.[15] A sentence that falls short of or exceeds the offender's individual responsibility for the harm done would not be compatible with the principle of personal culpability and, thus, the applicable law. Second, the inclusion of sentencing criteria such as the 'gravity of the crime' in Article 78(1) of the ICC Statute, 'the extent of the damage caused, in particular the harm caused to the victims and their families', 'the nature of the unlawful behaviour' or 'the degree of participation of the convicted person' in Rule 145(1)(c) of the ICC Rules of Procedure and Evidence can best be explained with a view to retributive considerations.[16] These criteria define the harm done by and the culpability of the offender, they lie in the past and do not play any role in determining a sentence that follows primarily preventive purposes for which the risk of recidivism, the need for public reassurance or the dangerousness of a perpetrator would be decisive.[17] Finally, the relevance of retribution in sentencing is confirmed by the applicable standard for the review of sentences laid down in Article 83(3) of the ICC Statute. According to that provision, the Appeals Chamber can 'vary the sentence' if it finds 'that the sentence is disproportionate to the crime'. Whether such a disproportion is given has to be determined with a view to the 'degree of harm caused by the crime and the culpability of the perpetrator'.[18] Thus, the standard against which a sentence has to be measured on appeal is reflective of the core concept of retribution.[19]

[14] D'Ascoli, *Sentencing*, 29; J. Peglau, 'Penalties and the Determination of the Sentence in the Rules of Procedure and Evidence' in H. Fischer, C. Kreß and S. Lüder (eds.), *International and National Prosecution of Crimes Under International Law* (Berlin: Berliner Wissenschafts-Verlag, 2001), 141, 147; Werle and Jeßberger, *Principles*, para. 120.

[15] For similar, see A.M. Danner, 'Constructing a Hierarchy of Crimes in International Criminal Law Sentencing' (2001) 87 *Virginia Law Review* 415, 453.

[16] Cryer et al., Introduction, 503 et seq.; Danner, 'Constructing a Hierarchy of Crimes', 452 et seq.

[17] Epik, *Strafzumessung*, 83.

[18] ICC, Judgment of 1 December 2014 (AC), *Lubanga*, ICC-01/04-01/06-3122, para. 40.

[19] See on the connection between proportionality and retribution D'Ascoli, *Sentencing*, 25 et seq., 64 et seq.; R. Henham, 'Developing Contextualized Rationales for Sentencing in International Criminal Trials' (2007) 5 *Journal of International Criminal Justice* 757, 758; for a critical view, DeGuzman, 'Proportionate Sentencing', 936 et seq.

2 *Deterrence*

The term deterrence refers to two distinct sentencing objectives: general and special deterrence. While general deterrence, i.e., negative general prevention, focuses on discouraging the general public from committing similar crimes by demonstrating that the commission of such crimes results in negative consequences (punishment), special deterrence aims to influence an individual perpetrator by showing him or her the consequences of criminal behaviour in order to prevent recidivism.[20] The applicable law indicates that both general and special deterrence are important sentencing objectives in the context of the Rome Statute. This is already clear from the fifth paragraph of the Preamble, which states the determination of the states parties 'to put an end to impunity for the perpetrators of these crimes and thus to contribute to the prevention of such crimes'.[21] Here, the ICC Statute, while not expressly referring to deterrence, recognizes that the Court's function includes contributing to the prevention of future crimes by punishing those responsible for crimes already committed.[22] This link has sensibly been interpreted as a reference to (general) deterrence.[23] The inclusion of special deterrence into the ambit of the relevant sentencing objectives can further be inferred from Article 78(1) of the ICC Statute. This provision mentions the 'individual circumstances of the convicted person' as a central sentencing criterion. Such individual circumstances can be relevant in deciding which punishment is necessary in order to effectively deter an individual and to prevent recidivism.[24]

[20] Cryer et al., *Introduction*, 32.

[21] Cryer et al., *Introduction*, 33; D'Ascoli, *Sentencing*, 272; Epik, *Strafzumessung*, 106; J.C. Nemitz, *Strafzumessung im Völkerstrafrecht* (Freiburg: edition iuscrim, 2002), 18; W.A. Schabas, *The International Criminal Court: A Commentary on the Rome Statute*, 2nd ed. (Oxford: Oxford University Press, 2016), 1163; Schmitt, 'Schuld im Römischen Statut', 261; Triffterer, Bergsmo and Ambos, 'Preamble', para. 15; Werle and Jeßberger, *Principles*, para. 108.

[22] On deterrence with regard to the crime of aggression, see the contribution by Jakob v.H. Holtermann in Chapter 9.

[23] D'Ascoli, *Sentencing*, 272; Triffterer, Bergsmo and Ambos, 'Preamble', para. 15; Schabas, *The International Criminal Court*, 1163; G. Werle and F. Jeßberger, *Völkerstrafrecht*, 4th ed. (Tübingen: Mohr Siebeck, 2016), para. 119.

[24] Epik, *Strafzumessung*, 106. In favour of including special deterrence, see also ICC, Decision of 21 June 2016 (TC), *Bemba*, ICC-01/05-01/08-3399, para. 11; ICC, Judgment of 27 September 2016 (TC), *Al Mahdi*, ICC-01/12-01/15-171, para. 67.

3 *Positive General Prevention*

In the context of international criminal law, positive general prevention plays a crucial role in the creation and reinforcement of an international awareness of law as well as the promotion of peace and reconciliation.[25] By punishing those responsible for the most serious crimes under international law, the international community should 'make humankind conscious of the fact that international law is law and will be implemented against lawbreakers'[26] and thereby express that it will not tolerate the commission of such crimes.[27] Furthermore, the punishment of those responsible for international crimes demonstrates to the victims that the international community acknowledges them as such and contributes to the individualization of responsibility for the harm done. Thereby, international criminal law ideally promotes sustainable peace by preventing the establishment of competing narratives as well as the attribution of collective guilt to a particular group, which could serve as a trigger for further violence in the future.[28]

As with other sentencing objectives, positive general prevention is not expressly mentioned in the Rome Statute. However, the fifth preambular paragraph of the Rome Statute that refers to the determination of the states parties to 'put an end to impunity for perpetrators of these crimes and thus contribute to the prevention of such crimes' and even more the Statute's eleventh preambular paragraph that reads '[r]esolved to guarantee lasting respect for and the enforcement of international justice' indicate that the rationales underlying the theory of positive general prevention are also relevant for the application of the ICC Statute. In particular, the eleventh paragraph can be read as a reference to the aim of creating and strengthening

[25] Ambos, *Treatise* Vol. I, 71 et seq.; DeGuzman, 'Proportionate Sentencing', 957; V. Reuss, *Zivilcourage als Strafzweck des Völkerstrafrechts* (Berlin: LIT Verlag, 2012), 14; Werkmeister, *Straftheorien im Völkerstrafrecht*, 253 et seq.; Werle, 'Menschenrechtsschutz durch Völkerstrafrecht', 821.

[26] H. Jescheck, *Die Verantwortlichkeit der Staatsorgane nach Völkerstrafrecht* (Bonn: Roehrscheid, 1952), 195 (translated from German).

[27] D. Golash, 'The Justification of Punishment in the International Context' in L. May and Z. Hoskins (eds.), *International Criminal Law and Philosophy* (Cambridge: Cambridge University Press, 2010), 201, 217 et seq.; Werle and Jeßberger, *Principles*, para. 108. It is clear, however, that international criminal law can only be one element in this regard and that it needs to be combined with other mechanisms in order to sustainably contribute towards the goal of creating and enforcing an international awareness of law.

[28] Epik, *Strafzumessung*, 146 et seq.; Golash, 'Justification of Punishment', 218; Werle, 'Menschenrechtsschutz durch Völkerstrafrecht', 821 et seq.; Werle and Jeßberger, *Principles*, para. 112. For a critical perspective, Drumbl, *Atrocity, Punishment, and International Law*, 150.

an international awareness for the inviolability of the norms of international criminal law.[29]

4 *Rehabilitation*

Of major importance in domestic jurisdictions, the objective of rehabilitation refers to the reintegration of the convicted offender into the relevant society by means of pronouncing and enforcing a just punishment.[30] Besides being guaranteed by international human rights law,[31] the sentencing law of the ICC leaves room for rehabilitative considerations in determining an appropriate sentence. Article 78(1) of the ICC Statute and Rule 145 of the ICC Rules of Procedure and Evidence refer to the individual circumstances of the convicted person, in particular his or her age, education, as well as social and economic condition. Such criteria are relevant in individualizing the sentence in order to further the reintegration of the individual offender.[32] Conversely, including such sentencing factors would not have been necessary if sentencing at the ICC was to follow retributive or general preventative objectives only, as they are of little relevance in this context. Rehabilitation is therefore a relevant sentencing objective under the applicable law. This conclusion is further supported by Article 110(4)(c) of the ICC Statute read together with Rule 223(b) of the ICC Rules of Procedure and Evidence, which explicitly refer to the resocialization of the offender as a relevant consideration in the Court's decision of whether a sentence should be reduced after a convicted person has served two thirds (or 25 years in the case of life imprisonment) of his or her sentence. Even though these provisions only apply in the enforcement stage of the process, read together with the sentencing provisions and taking into account the aim of the states parties to prevent future crimes,[33] they support the conclusion that rehabilitative considerations have to be taken into account already at the sentencing stage.[34]

[29] K. Ambos and J. C. Nemitz, 'Judgement, Sentence and Plea of Guilty' in A. Klip and G. Sluiter (eds.), *Annotated Leading Cases of International Criminal Tribunals*, Vol. II (Antwerp: Intersentia, 2001), 835 et seq.; Epik, *Strafzumessung*, 140; Melloh, *Einheitliche Strafzumessung*, 306 et seq.; Nemitz, *Strafzumessung im Völkerstrafrecht*, 14 et seq., 17 et seq.

[30] For a detailed discussion, see Werkmeister, *Straftheorien im Völkerstrafrecht*, 162 et seq.

[31] See ICCPR, Art. 10(3).

[32] See Epik, *Strafzumessung*, 119.

[33] ICC Statute, Preamble, para. 5.

[34] In this vein, D'Ascoli, *Sentencing*, 273; Melloh, *Einheitliche Strafzumessung*, 307; Nemitz, *Strafzumessung im Völkerstrafrecht*, 17 et seq.

5 *Further Objectives?*

Further sentencing objectives – such as incapacitation, which concentrates on the protection of society from dangerous offenders – or expressivist considerations, which primarily focus on the communicative function of punishment,[35] cannot be clearly deduced from specific provisions of the ICC Statute or the Rules of Procedure and Evidence. This does not mean, however, that the Court is barred from taking them into account. As the applicable law does not conclusively define the relevant sentencing objectives, the judges are generally free to apply any objectives that are compatible with the applicable law. Furthermore, in the literature, incapacitation and expressivist theories of punishment have even been considered to be general principles of law under Article 21(1)(c) of the ICC Statute.[36]

6 *Interim Conclusion*

In conclusion, the ICC cannot focus on a single purpose of punishment but has to take into account different objectives when determining an appropriate sentence. However, not all sentencing objectives are of equal weight. Instead, the primary objective that has to be taken into account in the determination of a just sentence – again, not the primary theory of punishment justifying international criminal law as such – is retribution, understood as a principle demanding proportionality between individual responsibility for the harm done and punishment. This is clear from the predominant role that the Statute and the Rules attribute to the principle of proportionality between the culpability of the offender and the sentence.[37]

In addition, preventive purposes, in particular deterrence, but also rehabilitation and positive general prevention need to be taken into account. The exact weight attached to the respective preventive purposes cannot be determined in the abstract but will depend on the circumstances of the individual case; their consideration must not, however, lead to sentences that are no

[35] On these objectives, see Cryer et al., *Introduction*, 35; Drumbl, *Atrocity, Punishment, and International Law*, 173 et seq.; Werkmeister, *Straftheorien im Völkerstrafrecht*, 189 et seq., 242 et seq.

[36] Melloh, *Einheitliche Strafzumessung*, 492, 495 et seq., 510.

[37] For a detailed discussion, see Epik, *Strafzumessung*, 152 et seq. This conclusion is in line with the sentencing jurisprudence of the ad hoc Tribunals, see only ICTY, Judgment of 17 December 2004 (AC), *Kordić and Čerkez*, IT-95-14/2-A, para. 1087: 'The individual guilt of each Accused limits the range of the sentence. Other goals and functions of a sentence can only influence the range within the limits that are defined by the individual guilt.'

longer proportionate to the gravity of the crime and the culpability of the offender.[38]

II THE SENTENCING DECISIONS OF THE INTERNATIONAL CRIMINAL COURT

To date, the ICC has passed five sentencing decisions,[39] two of which have been reviewed by the Appeals Chamber.[40] In all of its sentencing decisions, the Court considers the purposes of punishment, albeit briefly. However, the sentencing decision in the *Bemba et al.* case[41] and the respective Appeals Chamber judgment[42] concerned offences against the administration of justice under Article 70 of the ICC Statute so that only such considerations that equally apply to sentencing for the core crimes are relevant in the context of this chapter.[43]

In the Court's first sentencing decision in the *Lubanga* case, Trial Chamber I did not commit itself explicitly to specific sentencing objectives. The decision does not engage with the discussion on the purposes of punishment and instead merely highlights paragraphs 4, 5 and 9 of the Preamble:

> In considering the purposes of punishment at the ICC, the Chamber has taken into account the Preamble of the Statute, which provides that 'the most serious crimes of concern to the international community as a whole must not go unpunished'. The Preamble further provides that the States Parties are '[d]etermined to put an end to impunity for the perpetrators of these crimes and thus to contribute to the prevention of such crimes'. The ICC was established 'to these ends and for the sake of present and future generations'.[44]

While we have pointed out that it is possible to deduce certain objectives from these preambular paragraphs, reiterating them without any further analysis does not contribute to clarification.[45] It is therefore difficult to determine

38 Epik, *Strafzumessung*, 153 et seq.

39 ICC, Decision of 10 July 2012 (TC), *Lubanga*, ICC-01/04-01/06-2901; ICC, Decision of 23 May 2014 (TC), *Katanga*, ICC-01/04-01/07-3484; ICC, Decision of 21 June 2016 (TC), *Bemba*, ICC-01/05-01/08-3399; ICC, Judgment of 27 September 2016 (TC), *Al Mahdi*, ICC-01/12-01/15-171; ICC, Decision of 22 March 2017 (TC), *Bemba et al.*, ICC 01/05-01/13-2123-Corr.

40 ICC, Judgment of 1 December 2014 (AC), *Lubanga*, ICC-01/04-01/06-3122; ICC, Judgment of 8 March 2018 (AC), *Bemba et al.*, ICC 01/05-01/13-2275.

41 ICC, Decision of 22 March 2017 (TC), *Bemba et al.*, ICC 01/05-01/13-2123-Corr.

42 ICC, Judgment of 8 March 2018 (AC), *Bemba et al.*, ICC 01/05-01/13-2275.

43 On the sentencing considerations in *Bemba et al.*, see the contribution by Sergey Vasiliev in Chapter 4 (Section II.4).

44 ICC, Decision of 10 July 2012 (TC), *Lubanga*, ICC-01/04-01/06-2901, para. 16.

45 DeGuzman, 'Proportionate Sentencing', 933 et seq.

which sentencing objectives Trial Chamber I applied in sentencing the accused to 14 years imprisonment.

In its *Katanga* sentencing decision, Trial Chamber II took a different approach and outlined the sentencing objectives it considered to be relevant in more detail.[46] Referring to paragraphs 4 and 5 of the Preamble, the judges identified 'punishment' and 'deterrence' as the main sentencing objectives.[47] In this context, the vague term 'punishment' seems to refer to retributive considerations and, more importantly, to the expressive capacity of international punishment:

> When determining the sentence, the Chamber must also respond to the legitimate need for truth and justice voiced by the victims and their family members. It therefore considers that the role of the sentence is two-fold: on the one hand, punishment, or the expression of society's condemnation of the criminal act and of the person who committed it, which is also a way of acknowledging the harm and suffering caused to the victims; and, on the other hand, deterrence, the aim of which is to deflect those planning to commit similar crimes from their purpose.[48]

In line with the development of the modern discourse on theories of punishment,[49] the Chamber thus clarified that its understanding of retribution has nothing to do with revenge and harsh punishment but focuses primarily on acknowledging the harm done to the victims and the need to communicate to perpetrators, victims and their relatives as well as to the public that the international community is not willing to accept the commission of international crimes. At the same time, the Chamber recognized that, according to Rule 145(1)(a) of the ICC Rules of Procedure and Evidence, the sentence has to reflect the perpetrator's culpability and, thereby, acknowledged the principle of proportionality between the perpetrator's responsibility for the harm done and the sentence.[50]

46 ICC, Decision of 23 May 2014 (TC), *Katanga*, ICC-01/04-01/07-3484, paras. 36 et seq.

47 ICC, Decision of 23 May 2014 (TC), *Katanga*, ICC-01/04-01/07-3484, paras. 37 et seq.

48 ICC, Decision of 23 May 2014 (TC), *Katanga*, ICC-01/04-01/07-3484, para. 38.

49 Originally closely linked to the *lex talionis* (expressed through the maxim 'an eye for an eye, a tooth for a tooth'), retributive theories have since developed and modern retributive theories have evolved, see Ambos, *Treatise* Vol. I, 67 et seq., focusing *inter alia* on removing an unfair advantage the offender has acquired by committing his or her crime or on conveying the society's condemnation of the crime committed, see for a discussion with a view to international criminal law, with further references, Melloh, *Einheitliche Strafzumessung*, 105 et seq. See also, with a critique of retributive proportionality in the context of international criminal law, DeGuzman, 'Proportionate Sentencing', 936 et seq.

50 ICC, Decision of 23 May 2014 (TC), *Katanga*, ICC-01/04-01/07-3484, para. 38.

With regard to deterrence, the Chamber pointed out that the aim of the sentence has to be to 'deflect those planning to commit similar crimes from their purpose'[51] and thus referred primarily to general deterrence. At the same time, the judges clarified that it is 'not so much the severity of the sentence that should prevail as its inevitability'.[52] While it is commendable that the Chamber addressed one of the primary criticisms voiced against deterrence as a theory of punishment, namely that it tends to promote ever higher sentences, the current state of enforcement of international criminal law does not even come close to an 'inevitability' of punishment.[53] It is therefore questionable whether such reasoning can justify deterrence vis-à-vis the individual offender.[54]

Besides retribution and deterrence, the Chamber also took into account 'the restoration of peace and reconciliation in the communities concerned'[55] and considered the reintegration of the convicted person into the society to be of relevance, even though it stressed that 'in particular in the case of international criminal law, this goal cannot be considered to be primordial as the sentence of its own cannot ensure the social reintegration of the convicted person'.[56]

In its *Bemba* sentencing decision, Trial Chamber III adopted this reasoning for the most part. The Chamber determined 'that the Preamble establishes retribution and deterrence as the primary objectives of punishment at the ICC'[57] and thus not only confirmed the *Katanga* sentencing decision but also stressed the prominent position both sentencing objectives have vis-à-vis other purposes of punishment. The Chamber also elaborated further on the Court's concept of retribution:

> Retribution is not to be understood as fulfilling a desire for revenge, but as an expression of the international community's condemnation of the crimes. In this way, a proportionate sentence also acknowledges the harm to the victims and promotes the restoration of peace and reconciliation.[58]

[51] ICC, Decision of 23 May 2014 (TC), *Katanga*, ICC-01/04-01/07-3484, para. 38.

[52] ICC, Decision of 23 May 2014 (TC), *Katanga*, ICC-01/04-01/07-3484, para. 38.

[53] On the selective enforcement of international criminal law and theories of punishment, see the contribution by Harmen van der Wilt in Chapter 17.

[54] See, for a discussion, Epik, *Strafzumessung*, 134 et seq., with further references.

[55] ICC, Decision of 23 May 2014 (TC), *Katanga*, ICC-01/04-01/07-3484, para. 38. On this, see also the contribution by Sergey Vasiliev in Chapter 4.

[56] ICC, Decision of 23 May 2014 (TC), *Katanga*, ICC-01/04-01/07-3484, para. 38.

[57] ICC, Decision of 21 June 2016 (TC), *Bemba*, ICC-01/05-01/08-3399, para. 10.

[58] ICC, Decision of 21 June 2016 (TC), *Bemba*, ICC-01/05-01/08-3399, para. 11.

This statement demonstrates quite clearly what has been said before: The Trial Chambers view retribution as closely linked to the expressive capacity of punishment on the one hand and as demanding proportionate sentences on the other.

Trial Chamber III further clarified that the term 'deterrence' does not only refer to general deterrence but also includes specific deterrence.[59] With regard to rehabilitation, the Chamber followed the reasoning in *Katanga* and held that rehabilitation, although a relevant purpose of punishment, 'should not be given undue weight'.[60]

In its judgment in the *Al Mahdi* case, Trial Chamber VIII confirmed not only that retribution and deterrence are the 'primary objectives of punishment at the ICC'[61] but also endorsed the interpretation of these objectives by Trial Chambers II and III. The Chamber highlighted once more that 'the sentence must be proportionate to the crime and the culpability of the convicted person'.[62] In line with the *Bemba* sentencing decision, the Chamber further confirmed the relevance of special deterrence as a sentencing objective and also affirmed the stance that rehabilitation is of limited relevance in the context of international criminal law.[63]

Finally, while the Appeals Chamber has so far not gone into detail regarding the purposes of punishment, it has stressed the importance of the principle of proportionality between the sentence and the crime and culpability of the convicted person.[64]

III A CONSISTENT APPROACH?

Read together, the sentencing decisions passed so far reveal a fairly consistent approach with regard to the sentencing objectives. After initial hesitation in *Lubanga*, the Chambers have determined a set of relevant sentencing objectives that have been referred to in all the following sentencing decisions. The primary sentencing objectives identified by the Chambers are retribution as well as general and specific deterrence, while the promotion of peace and reconciliation, and – to a lesser extent – rehabilitation are also relevant purposes of punishment. The sentencing objectives applied by the Chambers have their basis in the ICC Statute, in particular in the Preamble, in

[59] ICC, Decision of 21 June 2016 (TC), *Bemba*, ICC-01/05-01/08-3399, para. 11.
[60] ICC, Decision of 21 June 2016 (TC), *Bemba*, ICC-01/05-01/08-3399, para. 11.
[61] ICC, Judgment of 27 September 2016 (TC), *Al Mahdi*, ICC-01/12-01/15-171, para. 66.
[62] ICC, Judgment of 27 September 2016 (TC), *Al Mahdi*, ICC-01/12-01/15-171, para. 67.
[63] ICC, Judgment of 27 September 2016 (TC), *Al Mahdi*, ICC-01/12-01/15-171, para. 67.
[64] ICC, Judgment of 1 December 2014 (AC), *Lubanga*, ICC-01/04-01/06-3122, paras. 40, 43.

Article 78 of the ICC Statute, and the Rules of Procedure and Evidence as is clear from our analysis in Section II.

It is noticeable, however, that the Chambers generally do not elaborate in greater detail on each sentencing objective, nor do the judges explain which impact each sentencing objective has on the specific sentencing decision. Rather, the sentencing objectives are listed in two paragraphs at the beginning of each sentencing decision and not referred to again in the respective decision. While this is in line with the practice of the ad hoc Tribunals,[65] such an approach renders it impossible to assess whether and how exactly the sentencing objectives guide and influence the sentencing decision.

In addition, by refraining from further discussion on the exact relevance of and weight attached to each sentencing objective, the ICC has thus far also passed up on the opportunity to explicitly develop a coherent sentencing model based on the sentencing objectives pursued. This is not to say that the sentences passed by the Court to date are unconvincing in approach or outcome. However, as the sentencing practice of the ICC develops, a clearly structured and transparent sentencing model based on the relevant sentencing objectives would serve the Court in avoiding allegations of inconsistency or arbitrariness.[66] In Section IV, we will therefore outline elements of coherent sentencing that draw on the sentencing objectives applicable under the statutory framework of the ICC, taking into account the ICC's early sentencing decisions.

IV ELEMENTS OF COHERENT SENTENCING

A coherent sentencing model undoubtedly has to be based on the relevant sentencing provisions, in particular Articles 77 and 78 of the ICC Statute and Rule 145 of the ICC Rules of Procedure and Evidence. However, as outlined above, it also needs to provide a framework for pursuing, to the greatest extent possible, the relevant sentencing objectives. In this section, we will outline elements of coherent sentencing that can be deduced from the sentencing objectives that we have identified above.

65 As B. Holá, 'Sentencing of International Crimes at the ICTY and ICTR' (2012) 4 *Amsterdam Law Forum* 3, 7, points out for the ICTY and the ICTR:

> The role the sentencing purposes play in meting out individual sentences is also not very clear. [...] It is not possible to assess how the sentencing objectives guide determination of a particular sentence. In the majority of cases it seems that the purposes are only pro forma listed at the beginning of the sentencing part of the judgment with no explanation what they entail and no clear link to the rest of the sentencing argumentation.

66 See DeGuzman, 'Proportionate Sentencing', 933.

1 *Ensuring Proportionality*

In accordance with the applicable law, the ICC has acknowledged retribution and deterrence as the primary sentencing objectives. Among them, retribution takes primacy over deterrence to the extent that it demands proportionality between the sentence and the crime as well as the culpability of the offender.[67] Taking this determination as a starting point, the most important requirement to be met by any sentencing model is to ensure proportionate sentencing outcomes that adequately reflect the gravity of the crime and the culpability of the offender.[68] This is clearly laid down in the sentencing provisions of the ICC Statute: Article 78(1) of the ICC Statute refers to the 'gravity of the crime' as the primary sentencing factor, Articles 81(2)(a) and 83(3) of the ICC Statute clarify that a sentence may only be successfully appealed if it is disproportionate to the crime,[69] and Rule 145(1)(a) of the ICC Rules of Procedure and Evidence provides that the totality of any sentence must reflect the culpability of the convicted person. Sentences that are not reflective of the gravity of the crime and the culpability of the perpetrator would therefore be considered to be legally erroneous and consequently not stand up to appellate scrutiny.

From this it follows that the crucial point in any sentencing process, after establishing the applicable penalties,[70] has to be the determination of the gravity of the crime and the culpability of the offender, which provides the basis for deciding on the length of the sentence.[71] Or, in the words of the Appeals Chamber in *Lubanga*: 'Proportionality is generally measured by the degree of

[67] See above Section I.6. The ICC has implicitly recognized this, see ICC, Judgment of 1 December 2014 (AC), *Lubanga*, ICC-01/04-01/06-3122, para. 40; ICC, Judgment of 27 September 2016 (TC), *Al Mahdi*, ICC-01/12-01/15-171, para. 67.

[68] ICC, Decision of 21 June 2016 (TC), *Bemba*, ICC-01/05-01/08-3399, para. 11: 'The objectives underlying sentencing are fulfilled with "the imposition of a just and appropriate sentence, and nothing more". As reflected in Art. 81(2)(a) and Rule 145(1), and as emphasized by the Appeals Chamber, the sentence must be proportionate to the crime and the culpability of the convicted person.' See also D'Ascoli, *Sentencing*, 292.

[69] ICC, Judgment of 1 December 2014 (AC), *Lubanga*, ICC-01/04-01/06-3122, para. 40; ICC, Decision of 21 June 2016 (TC), *Bemba*, ICC-01/05-01/08-3399, para. 11.

[70] In the context of the ICC Statute, this is a rather straightforward task: As the Statute does not provide specific sentencing ranges for each crime, Art. 77 of the ICC Statute applies to all core crimes. According to Art. 77(1), the Court may impose imprisonment for a specified number of years, which may not exceed a maximum of 30 years or a term of life imprisonment when justified by the extreme gravity of the crime and the individual circumstances of the convicted person. In addition, but not in lieu of imprisonment, Art. 77(2) allows the Court to order a fine or a forfeiture of proceeds, property and assets derived directly or indirectly from the crime.

[71] K.A.A. Khan, 'Article 78: Determination of the Sentence' in Triffterer and Ambos (eds.), *The Rome Statute of the International Criminal Court*, Art. 78 para. 15.

harm caused by the crime and the culpability of the perpetrator and, in this regard, relates to the determination of the length of the sentence.'[72] Other sentencing considerations, in particular such that are not related to the gravity of the crime or the culpability of the perpetrator, can only be taken into account within the limits defined by the proportionality principle and should therefore only be considered once the judges have determined a range of sentences that they deem to be proportionate in the particular case.[73] But which factors should be considered in determining the gravity of the crime and the offender's culpability?

Neither the Statute nor the Rules of Procedure and Evidence provide a definition of the gravity concept.[74] Following the case law of the ad hoc Tribunals,[75] the Trial Chamber in *Katanga* has held that '[i]n order to determine the gravity, the particular circumstances as well as the nature and degree of participation of the convicted person in the commission of the crime must be taken into account'.[76] Thus, the gravity of the crime is a 'twofold concept'[77] referring to elements related to the offence, namely its seriousness and the harm caused by it, *and* the offender, namely his or her individual responsibility for the harm caused.[78] Consequently, the gravity of the crime already includes considerations related to the culpability of the offender so

[72] ICC, Judgment of 1 December 2014 (AC), *Lubanga*, ICC-01/04-01/06-3122, para. 40.

[73] This concept is known as 'Spielraumtheorie' in German sentencing doctrine, see BGHSt Vol. 7, 28, 32, Vol. 20, 264, 266 et seq.; G. Schäfer, M. Sander and G. van Gemmeren, *Praxis der Strafzumessung*, 6th ed. (München: C.H. Beck, 2017) paras. 828 et seq. For a critical view see T. Hörnle, *Tatproportionale Strafzumessung* (Berlin: Duncker & Humblot, 1999), 27 et seq.

[74] Ambos, *Treatise* Vol. II, 291.

[75] See, e.g., ICTY, Judgment of 30 June 2016 (AC), *Stanišić and Župljanin*, IT-08-91-A, para. 1106: 'The determination of the gravity of the crime requires a consideration of the particular circumstances of the case, as well as the form and degree of the accused's participation in the crime.', and ICTR, Judgment of 14 December 2015 (AC), *Nyiramasuhuko et al.*, ICTR-98-42-A, para. 3431: 'The determination of the gravity of the offence requires a consideration of the particular circumstances of the case, as well as the form and degree of the participation of the convicted person in the crime.', respectively with further references.

[76] ICC, Decision of 23 May 2014 (TC), *Katanga*, ICC-01/04-01/07-3484, para. 43. In a similar vein, ICC, Judgment of 27 September 2016 (TC), *Al Mahdi*, ICC-01/12-01/15-171, para. 71.

[77] Ambos, *Treatise* Vol. II, 293.

[78] Ambos, *Treatise* Vol. II, 293; D'Ascoli, *Sentencing*, 145 et seq.; Epik, *Strafzumessung*, 304. At the same time, the inclusion of offender-related elements into the gravity of the crime creates problems regarding the delimitation of the gravity criterion from other sentencing factors, in particular the individual circumstances of the convicted person, see Ambos, *Treatise* Vol. II, 295.

that it is not possible to disentangle these factors. Rather, it seems sensible to consider factors related to the culpability of the offender in determining the gravity of the crime.[79]

a) Gravity *in abstracto*

In its sentencing decisions to date, the ICC has not conclusively determined whether the reference to the 'gravity of the crime' in Article 78(1) of the ICC Statute is limited to the gravity *in concreto*, as determined by the specific circumstances of the case, or also includes the gravity *in abstracto*.[80] In our view, it is possible and necessary to consider not only the concrete gravity of a case, but also take into account abstract considerations drawing on the already existing normative framework of the Rome Statute.[81] This is because focusing exclusively on the individual circumstances of each case tends to prioritize the – particularly in the context of international crimes undoubtedly essential[82] – individualization of sentences at the expense of predictability,

79 We will nevertheless consider the culpability of the offender additionally under a separate heading in order to clarify the importance of this factor.

80 While some sentencing decisions include considerations related to the gravity *in abstracto* (see ICC, Decision of 10 July 2012 (TC), *Lubanga*, ICC-01/04-01/06-2901, paras. 37 et seq.; ICC, Decision of 23 May 2014 (TC), *Katanga*, ICC-01/04-01/07-3484, para. 43), other Chambers have explicitly held that 'the gravity of the acts committed by the convicted person has to be assessed *in concreto*' (ICC, Judgment of 27 September 2016 (TC), *Al Mahdi*, ICC-01/12-01/15-171, para. 71); see also ICC, Judgment of 8 March 2018 (AC), *Bemba et al.*, ICC 01/05-01/13-2275, paras. 59 et seq.; Schabas, The International Criminal Court, 1169 et seq.

81 Other authors have likewise pointed out the importance of a more structured approach to sentencing. D'Ascoli, Sentencing, 305, argues that:

> the legal characterisation of the offence (*gravity in abstracto*) should never have priority over the actual seriousness of the offence in hand, that is the circumstances in which the crime is committed, the specific harm caused by the offence and the suffering inflicted on victims (*gravity in concreto*); nevertheless, the normative aspect of international crimes is an important element for a proper assessment of the gravity of crimes in certain cases and can help the actual commensuration of punishment.

Ambos, *Treatise* Vol. II, 302 et seq., has pointed out that 'a more structured approach to sentencing is required. A more formalized approach would accord international sentencing the importance and attention it deserves'. He argues that '"soft" sentencing guidelines' should be adopted, leaving a range of discretion to the judges while at the same time providing guidance through sentencing ranges based on abstract criteria.

82 See Holá, Smeulers and Bijleveld, 'Is ICTY Sentencing Predictable?', 96. As international crimes are regularly committed by a collective of perpetrators, individualization of sentences is also of particular importance in order to reflect the offender's individual responsibility.

consistency and proportionality,[83] principles adherence to which is indispensable in promoting a fair sentencing system.[84]

Therefore, instead of immediately taking into account the particular circumstances of the case and assessing the gravity *in concreto*, judges should first consider the abstract gravity of the crime in question as defined by the contextual element of the crime as well as the individual act committed. This would allow them, as a first step, to identify a narrower range within the universal sentencing range of Article 77(1) of the ICC Statute that reflects the abstract wrongfulness of a particular crime. In a second step, this narrower sentencing range could then be concretized by taking into account the particular circumstances of the case at hand. As a result, cases of similar abstract seriousness would generally be placed in the same tier of the universal sentencing range and vice versa, thus adhering to the principle that like cases should be treated alike[85] while leaving considerable discretion to the judges to individualize the sentence. Such an approach ensures that the process of sentencing follows clear guidelines that are consistently applied in each case.[86] It is, at the same time, flexible enough to allow for deviations where necessary.

83 As D'Ascoli, *Sentencing*, 65, puts it: 'The application of this principle requires the establishment of a range of penalties providing a sort of scale (from the most serious sentence reserved to the most serious offences to a more lenient one for lesser crimes) based on a progressive graduation of punishment according to gravity of offence.'

84 See Ambos, *Treatise* Vol. II, 269 et seq.; Book, *Appeal and Sentence*, 14; Holá, Smeulers and Bijleveld, 'Is ICTY Sentencing Predictable?', 80; Meernik and King, 'The Sentencing Determinants', 718; see also ICTY, Judgement of 20 February 2001 (AC), *Delalić et al.*, IT-96-21-A, para. 756.

85 ICTY, Judgement of 20 February 2001 (AC), *Delalić et al.*, IT-96-21-A, para. 756; Council of Europe, 'Consistency in Sentencing: Recommendation to Member States and Explanatory Memorandum' (1993) 4 *Criminal Law Forum* 355; D'Ascoli, *Sentencing*, 199; Henham, 'Developing Contextualized Rationales', 769; Holá, 'Sentencing of International Crimes at the ICTY and ICTR', 3; Hörnle, *Tatproportionale Strafzumessung*, 70; Melloh, *Einheitliche Strafzumessung*, 159 et seq.; C. Tata and N. Hutton, 'What "Rules" in Sentencing? Consistency and Disparity in the Absence of "Rules"' (1998) 26 *International Journal of the Sociology of Law* 339.

86 This refers to the concept of consistency in approach, which requires that the process of determining a sentence follows a specific and predetermined structure that applies to each case equally, see Holá, 'Sentencing of International Crimes at the ICTY and ICTR', 3 et seq.; S. Krasnostein and A. Freiberg, 'Pursuing Consistency in an Individualistic Sentencing Framework: If you Know Where You're Going, How do You Know When You've Got There?' (2013) 76 *Law and Contemporary Problems* 265, 270 et seq.; Melloh, *Einheitliche Strafzumessung*, 168. Such an approach guarantees that each case is treated formally the same and reduces the susceptibility for arbitrary decisions while simultaneously leaving intact the discretion of sentencing judges to tailor the sentence to fit the individual circumstances of the case.

In determining the abstract gravity of the crime, the Court should in particular take into account (i) the gradation in seriousness between the core crimes, or, to put it differently, the hierarchy of crimes as well as the gradation in seriousness between the various individual acts within each core crime; (ii) the modes of participation under Article 25(3)(a)–(d) and Article 28 of the ICC Statute, which reflect the degree of responsibility for the commission of the crime; and (iii) whether the crime was completed or only attempted.[87]

(I) HIERARCHY OF CRIMES The judges of the ICC have so far not clarified the issue of whether there is a 'hierarchy' of crimes under the Rome Statute. The Trial Chambers in *Katanga* and *Al Mahdi* have, however, recognized that 'not all crimes forming the grounds for a criminal conviction are necessarily of equivalent gravity and the Chamber has the duty to weigh each by distinguishing, for example, between those against persons and those targeting property'[88] and thus accepted that different tiers of gravity exist at least with regard to the individual acts of the core crimes.[89]

This approach is convincing as it is indeed possible to establish a scale of seriousness on which, as a general rule, individual acts resulting in death would be placed at the top while individual acts exclusively directed against property would generally be placed at the lower end. It is further possible to distinguish between individual acts that cause a specific result and acts that only create an abstract or specific risk that such a result may occur.[90] The main criteria for positioning an individual act on the scale are the legal interests that the individual act aims to protect and the wrongfulness resulting from its commission, which can be assessed by taking into account the objective and subjective elements of the offence.[91]

[87] Similarly, B. Holá, 'Consistency and Pluralism of International Sentencing' in E. van Sliedregt and S. Vasiliev (eds.), *Pluralism in International Criminal Law* (Oxford: Oxford University Press, 2014), 187, 205.

[88] ICC, Judgment of 27 September 2016 (TC), *Al Mahdi*, ICC-01/12-01/15-171, para. 72; see also ICC, Decision of 23 May 2014 (TC), *Katanga*, ICC-01/04-01/07, paras. 43, 145.

[89] However, the sentencing decision in *Bemba* raises some doubts in this regard: The sentences (16 years of imprisonment for murder as a war crime and as a crime against humanity, 18 years of imprisonment for rape as a war crime and a crime against humanity and 16 years of imprisonment for pillaging as a war crime) do not indicate that the Trial Chamber considered any gradation *in abstracto*. See ICC, Decision of 21 June 2016 (TC), *Bemba*, ICC-01/05-01/08-3399, para. 94.

[90] For an example of such a gradation, see §§ 6–13 of the German Code of Crimes against International Law [VStGB]; see also Epik, *Strafzumessung*, 444 et seq.

[91] In a similar vein, Ambos, *Treatise* Vol. II, 294 et seq., stressing that additional criteria need to be taken into account; D'Ascoli, *Sentencing*, 307 et seq.

It remains to be seen whether the ICC will extend this approach to the relationship between the core crimes. The legal framework of the Rome Statute certainly provides a sound basis to do so. In fact, and even though all core crimes can be described as 'most serious crimes of concern to the international community as a whole',[92] a gradation of the core crimes of genocide, crimes against humanity and war crimes,[93] based on the wrongfulness of these crimes, can be established by analyzing the objective and subjective elements of each crime and by taking into account their respective contextual elements.[94] Articles 31(1)(c), 33(2), and 124 of the ICC Statute[95] as well as Article 25(3)(e) of the ICC Statute[96] also indicate such a gradation. On this basis, the crime encompassing the highest degree of

[92] ICC Statute, Preamble paragraph 5.

[93] The crime of aggression will not be considered in this context as (i) its structure is not comparable with those of genocide, crimes against humanity and war crimes and (ii) it does not aim to protect individual interests and can therefore not be compared to the other core crimes. Seen in the abstract, the commission of a crime of aggression is however likely to trigger high sentences, not least because it can only be committed by state leaders and threatens the peace of the world as a whole.

[94] See Ambos, *Treatise* Vol. II, 252 et seq.; Epik, *Strafzumessung*, 461 et seq.; M. Vesper-Gräske, *Zur Hierarchie der Völkerrechtsverbrechen nach dem Statut des Internationalen Strafgerichtshofs* (Baden-Baden: Nomos, 2016), 61 et seq.

[95] Art. 31(1)(c) of the ICC Statute excludes the criminal responsibility of a person that acts reasonably to defend property that is essential for the survival of the person or another person or property that is essential for accomplishing a military mission only in cases of war crimes while in cases of genocide and crimes against humanity criminal responsibility will not be excluded if the person acted to protect property. Art. 33(2) of the ICC Statute clarifies that 'orders to commit genocide or crimes against humanity are manifestly unlawful' so that a superior order to commit genocide or crimes against humanity can never relieve a person of criminal responsibility according to Art. 33(1) of the ICC Statute. Finally, Art. 124 of the ICC Statute determines that a state, 'on becoming a party to this Statute, may declare that, for a period of seven years after the entry into force of this Statute for the State concerned, it does not accept the jurisdiction of the Court with respect to the category of crimes referred to in article 8 when a crime is alleged to have been committed by its nationals or on its territory'. From this it can be deduced that, under the ICC Statute, war crimes entail a lesser degree of gravity than genocide and crimes against humanity, see Ambos, *Treatise* Vol. II, 252 et seq.; Epik, *Strafzumessung*, 464; for a detailed discussion, see Vesper-Gräske, *Zur Hierarchie der Völkerrechtsverbrechen*, 200 et seq.

[96] Art. 25(3)(e) of the ICC Statute provides a separate ground for criminalizing a separate form of complicity, namely incitement to commit genocide. Such a separate offence does not exist with regard to crimes against humanity or war crimes. This indicates that the drafters of the Statute have recognized the elevated abstract gravity of the crime of genocide, which justifies the criminalization of acts that take place before a genocide is even attempted. In this vein, see Vesper-Gräske, *Zur Hierarchie der Völkerrechtsverbrechen*, 231 et seq.

wrongfulness in this regard is genocide, followed by crimes against humanity and war crimes, all else being equal.[97] The qualification, all else being equal, is important as it clarifies that, first, a clear degree of overlap between the core crimes exists and, second, each core crime encompasses various individual acts that are not equally serious. Accordingly, a war crime of wilful killing can, of course, constitute greater harm and thus be qualified as more serious than a crime against humanity of imprisonment. However, if the underlying acts are comparable (e.g., the crime against humanity of murder and the war crime of wilful killing), the hierarchy between the core crimes comes to bear.[98] The opposite view, rejecting such a hierarchy of crimes, that has – among others – been adopted by the ad hoc Tribunals,[99] fails to convince. It narrowly focuses on the absence of sentencing ranges and fails to analyze the actual elements of the crimes and their relevance in expressing different degrees of wrongfulness.[100] Sentencing judges are thus tasked to consider, first, the underlying acts that have been committed and, second, the core crime that is fulfilled in order to determine the abstract gravity of the crime in question.

(II) MODE OF PARTICIPATION In addition to the wrongfulness inherent to the crime in question, the Court should also consider the relevant mode of participation, which, as such, reflects the abstract blameworthiness of the offender and therefore can be utilized to determine the abstract gravity of

97 See, in further detail, P. Akhavan, *Reducing Genocide to Law* (Cambridge: Cambridge University Press, 2014), 56 et seq.; Ambos, *Treatise* Vol. II, 252 et seq.; Danner, 'Constructing a Hierarchy of Crimes', 472 et seq.; D'Ascoli, *Sentencing*, 303 et seq.; Epik, *Strafzumessung*, 461 et seq. (with further references); Vesper-Gräske, *Zur Hierarchie der Völkerrechtsverbrechen*, 323 et seq., based on a thorough analysis of the contextual elements and the respective *mens rea* requirements as well as a systematic interpretation of the ICC Statute and a comparative analysis of domestic legal systems.

98 Ambos, *Treatise* Vol. II, 252 et seq.; D'Ascoli, *Sentencing*, 307; Epik, *Strafzumessung*, 464 et seq.

99 ICTY, Judgment of 26 January 2000 (AC), *Tadić*, IT-94-1-A and IT-94-1-A*bis*, para. 69; ICTY, Judgment of 21 July 2000 (AC), *Furundžija*, IT-95-17/1-A, para. 243; ICTY, Judgment of 12 June 2002 (AC), *Kunarac et al.*, IT-96-23 and IT-96-23/1-A, para. 171; ICTR, Judgment of 1 June 2001 (AC), *Kayishema and Ruzindana*, ICTR-95-1-A, para. 367; see also the references in Epik, *Strafzumessung*, 340 n. 160, 383 n. 303.

100 Ambos, *Treatise* Vol. II, 252.

the crime.[101] This view is not undisputed[102] and accordingly the Trial Chamber in *Katanga* held:

> [...] article 25 merely identifies and lists various forms of illegal conduct and, in that respect, the proposed distinction between the liability as a perpetrator of a crime and that of an accessory to a crime does not in any way amount to a hierarchy of blameworthiness, let alone prescribe, even by implication, a scale of punishments. The convicted person's degree of participation and intent must therefore be assessed *in concreto*, on the basis of the Chamber's factual and legal findings in its judgment.[103]

A literal, contextual and teleological interpretation of Article 25(3)(a)–(d) of the ICC Statute reveals, however, that the ICC Statute provides for a differentiation model and thereby a hierarchy of the modes of participation and does not merely enumerate the various modes of individual criminal responsibility.[104] Indeed, if we accept, in accordance with the prevailing view in the Court's case law,[105] that the delimitation between principal[106] and accessorial[107] liability is determined on the basis of the control over the crime theory, it is only logical to assign a higher degree of blameworthiness to those who are controlling the commission of the crime as opposed to those who are only contributing to its commission, without having the power to actually initiate its commission, influence its course or stop its progress.[108] The Appeals Chamber in *Lubanga* has made this very clear when it held:

[101] Ambos, 'Article 25: Individual Criminal Responsibility' in Triffterer and Ambos (eds.), *The Rome Statute of the International Criminal Court*, Art. 25 para. 2; Ambos, *Treatise* Vol. I, 145 et seq.; G. Werle and B. Burghardt, 'Establishing Degrees of Responsibility: Modes of Participation in Article 25 of the ICC Statute' in E. van Sliedregt and S. Vasiliev (eds.), *Pluralism in International Criminal Law* (Oxford: Oxford University Press, 2014), 301, 311 et seq., 315 et seq.; Werle and Jeßberger, *Principles*, paras. 517 et seq.; see also Schabas, *The International Criminal Court*, 567 et seq.

[102] See the Separate Opinion of Judge Fulford and Judge Van den Wyngaert, ICC, Judgment of 14 March 2012 (TC), *Lubanga*, ICC-01/04-01/06-2842, Separate Opinion of Judge Adrian Fulford, paras. 8 et seq.; ICC, Judgment of 18 December 2012 (TC), *Ngudjolo Chui*, ICC-01/04-02/12-4, Concurring Opinion of Judge Christine Van den Wyngaert, paras. 22 et seq.

[103] ICC, Decision of 23 May 2014 (TC), *Katanga*, ICC-01/04-01/07-3484, para. 61. See also the conviction judgment, ICC, Judgment of 7 March 2014 (TC), *Katanga*, ICC-01/04-01/07-3436, paras. 1386 et seq.

[104] Werle and Burghardt, 'Establishing Degrees of Responsibility', 306 et seq., 311 et seq., 315 et seq.; Werle and Jeßberger, *Principles*, paras. 517 et seq.; see also Ambos, *Treatise* Vol. I, 145 et seq.

[105] ICC, Judgment of 1 December 2014 (AC), *Lubanga*, ICC-01/04-01/06-3121-Red, paras. 469 et seq.; ICC, Judgment of 7 March 2014 (TC), *Katanga*, ICC-01/04-01/07-3436, paras. 1394 et seq.

[106] ICC Statute, Art. 25(3)(a).

[107] ICC Statute, Art. 25(3)(b)–(d).

[108] ICC, Judgment of 14 March 2012 (TC), *Lubanga*, ICC-01/04-01/06-2842, paras. 998 et seq.

> This indicates that the Statute differentiates between two principal forms of liability, namely liability as a perpetrator and liability as an accessory. In the view of the Appeals Chamber, this distinction is not merely terminological; making this distinction is important because, generally speaking and all other things being equal, a person who is found to commit a crime him- or herself bears more blameworthiness than a person who contributes to the crime of another person or persons. Accordingly, it contributes to a proper labelling of the accused person's criminal responsibility.[109]

The same principle can also be applied to the relationship between the three forms of accessorial liability. The more a person can influence the actual commission of a crime, the higher his or her responsibility. Accordingly, ordering, soliciting or inducing is a more serious mode of participation than aiding, abetting or otherwise assisting, while the latter is more serious than the contribution to a group crime 'in any other way'.[110] Another relevant argument in favour of taking into account these differences in sentencing is that, in the interest of furthering the predictability, consistency and proportionality of sentences, the normative categories provided by the statutory framework should be used to structure the sentencing decision.[111]

Whether the future practice of the ICC will consider such an approach remains open. The Appeals Chamber judgment in *Lubanga* certainly provided a basis to do so. However, the Appeals Chamber in *Bemba et al.* was quite critical in this regard and stressed the importance of the individual circumstances of each case.[112] Furthermore, the Appeals Chamber pointed out that the 'Court's legal framework does not indicate an automatic correlation between the person's form of responsibility for the crime/offence for which he or she has been convicted and the sentence, nor does it provide any form of mandatory mitigation in case of conviction as an accessory to a crime/offence'.[113] Even though the judgment did not concern crimes under Article 5 of the ICC Statute, the Appeals Chamber's position seems to have shifted since *Lubanga*.

[109] ICC, Judgment of 1 December 2014 (AC), *Lubanga*, ICC-01/04-01/06-3121-Red, para. 462. But see ICC, Judgment of 8 March 2018 (AC), *Bemba et al.*, ICC 01/05-01/13-2275, para. 59.

[110] Werle and Burghardt, 'Establishing Degrees of Responsibility', 315 et seq.; Werle and Jeßberger, *Principles*, para. 520.

[111] Werle and Burghardt, 'Establishing Degrees of Responsibility', 311 et seq.

[112] ICC, Judgment of 8 March 2018 (AC), *Bemba et al.*, ICC 01/05-01/13-2275, paras. 59 et seq.

[113] ICC, Judgment of 8 March 2018 (AC), *Bemba et al.*, ICC 01/05-01/13-2275, para. 60.

(III) COMPLETION OR ATTEMPT In determining the gravity *in abstracto*, the Court finally has to take into account whether a crime was completed or attempted.[114] In general, an attempted crime will be of a lesser abstract gravity as 'the crime does not occur'[115] so that the wrongfulness resulting from the crime is limited to the perpetrator's intent to violate protected legal interests. Even though this intent needs to have been manifested by an action that commences the execution of the crime by means of a substantial step, it is not necessary that any objective element of the crime has been completed.[116] The presence of the subjective elements of a crime and a substantial step towards the execution of its objective elements does, however, not result in the same degree of wrongfulness as the completion of the crime.[117] Thus, the abstract gravity of the crime will differ depending on whether it was completed or merely attempted.

b) Gravity *in concreto*

Taking into account the hierarchy of crimes, the modes of participation and the question of completion or attempt, the Court can narrow down the general sentencing range of Article 77(1) of the ICC Statute for the purposes of sentencing in the case at hand. It is important to note, however, that the narrower sentencing range resulting from such a determination is not rigid, but can and should be adjusted with a view to the gravity *in concreto*.[118] In this regard, the Court has considered various factors in its early sentencing decisions, namely: the extent of the damage caused;[119] the large-scale and widespread nature of the crimes involving a high number of victims;[120] the suffering and harm caused to the victims and their

[114] See ICC Statute, Art. 25(3)(f).

[115] ICC Statute, Art. 25(3)(f).

[116] See Ambos, *Treatise* Vol. I, 252 et seq.; Ambos, 'Article 25', para. 41; Werle and Jeßberger, *Principles*, para. 704.

[117] In this vein, Werle and Jeßberger, *Principles*, para. 706.

[118] Nevertheless, it assists the trial judges in structuring their sentencing decision and rendering the steps taken to arrive at a certain sentence more transparent and revisable by the Appeals Chamber.

[119] ICC, Decision of 10 July 2012 (TC), *Lubanga*, ICC-01/04-01/06-2901, para. 44.; ICC, Decision of 21 June 2016 (TC), *Bemba*, ICC-01/05-01/08-3399, paras. 23 et seq., 32, 40, 51; ICC, Judgment of 27 September 2016 (TC), *Al Mahdi*, ICC-01/12-01/15-171, paras. 76, 78.

[120] ICC, Decision of 10 July 2012 (TC), *Lubanga*, ICC-01/04-01/06-2901, paras. 45 et seq., 50; ICC, Decision of 23 May 2014 (TC), *Katanga*, ICC-01/04-01/07-3484, paras. 44, 47; ICC, Decision of 21 June 2016 (TC), *Bemba*, ICC-01/05-01/08-3399, paras. 24, 40, 49, 51.

relatives;[121] the *actual* – but not the abstract[122] – degree of participation, including the offender's hierarchical position;[123] the degree of intent of the convicted person;[124] the discriminatory dimension of the crimes[125] and the (religious) motives of the offender;[126] as well as the long-term effects of the crimes on the affected communities.[127] Furthermore, the Court has taken into account the time, manner and location of the commission[128] as well as the means employed to execute the crimes.[129] In its *Al Mahdi* decision, the Trial Chamber also referred to the religious, symbolic and emotional value of the buildings that were destroyed for the inhabitants of Timbuktu and their protection as UNESCO World Heritage sites.[130] It is evident that some of these factors are already explicitly listed as separate sentencing factors in Rule 145(1)(c) of the ICC Rules of Procedure and Evidence.[131]

[121] ICC, Decision of 23 May 2014 (TC), *Katanga*, ICC-01/04-01/07-3484, paras. 49 et seq., 57 et seq.; ICC, Decision of 21 June 2016 (TC), *Bemba*, ICC-01/05-01/08-3399, paras. 29 et seq., 38 et seq., 49 et seq.

[122] The TC in *Katanga* has rejected the view that Art. 25(3) of the ICC Statute establishes a 'hierarchy of blameworthiness, let alone prescribe, even by implication, a scale of punishments', ICC, Decision of 23 May 2014 (TC), *Katanga*, ICC-01/04-01/07-3484, para. 61.

[123] ICC, Decision of 10 July 2012 (TC), *Lubanga*, ICC-01/04-01/06-2901, para. 52; ICC, Decision of 23 May 2014 (TC), *Katanga*, ICC-01/04-01/07-3484, paras. 45, 61 et seq., 67 et seq.; ICC, Decision of 21 June 2016 (TC), *Bemba*, ICC-01/05-01/08-3399, para. 17; ICC, Judgment of 27 September 2016 (TC), *Al Mahdi*, ICC-01/12-01/15-171, para. 84.

[124] ICC, Decision of 10 July 2012 (TC), *Lubanga*, ICC-01/04-01/06-2901, para. 52; ICC, Decision of 21 June 2016 (TC), *Bemba*, ICC-01/05-01/08-3399, paras. 59 et seq.; ICC, Judgment of 27 September 2016 (TC), *Al Mahdi*, ICC-01/12-01/15-171, para. 85.

[125] ICC, Decision of 23 May 2014 (TC), *Katanga*, ICC-01/04-01/07-3484, paras. 44, 53 et seq.

[126] ICC, Judgment of 27 September 2016 (TC), *Al Mahdi*, ICC-01/12-01/15-171, para. 81.

[127] ICC, Decision of 23 May 2014 (TC), *Katanga*, ICC-01/04-01/07-3484, paras. 44, 52, 55 et seq.; ICC, Decision of 21 June 2016 (TC), *Bemba*, ICC-01/05-01/08-3399, para. 23; ICC, Judgment of 27 September 2016 (TC), *Al Mahdi*, ICC-01/12-01/15-171, paras. 78, 80.

[128] ICC, Decision of 23 May 2014 (TC), *Katanga*, ICC-01/04-01/07-3484, para. 46; ICC, Decision of 21 June 2016 (TC), *Bemba*, ICC-01/05-01/08-3399, paras. 24, 32, 40, 51; ICC, Judgment of 27 September 2016 (TC), *Al Mahdi*, ICC-01/12-01/15-171, para. 76.

[129] ICC, Decision of 23 May 2014 (TC), *Katanga*, ICC-01/04-01/07-3484, para. 49; ICC, Decision of 21 June 2016 (TC), *Bemba*, ICC-01/05-01/08-3399, paras. 24, 32.

[130] ICC, Judgment of 27 September 2016 (TC), *Al Mahdi*, ICC-01/12-01/15-171, paras. 79 et seq.

[131] Rule 145(1)(c) of the ICC Rules of Procedure and Evidence provides a non-exhaustive list of sentencing factors that have to be considered 'in addition' to the factors already mentioned in Article 78(1) of the ICC Statute. As all factors mentioned in Rule 145(1)(c) of the ICC Rules of Procedure and Evidence are worded neutral, the Court has to determine their impact on the sentence in every case individually. Thus, every factor can have an aggravating or a mitigating effect, dependent on the circumstances of the particular case. The relationship between these sentencing factors and those already included in Art. 78(1) of the ICC Statute is subject to a controversy that has not yet been resolved by the Court: A plain reading of the two provisions seems to suggest that the factors listed in Rule 145(1)(c) of the ICC Rules of Procedure and Evidence are separate sentencing factors that have to be taken into account *in addition* to the

c) Culpability of the Offender

With regard to the culpability of the offender, judges have to ensure that the sentence reflects the individual responsibility of the offender for the harm resulting from his or her culpable conduct. This can be achieved by taking into account the actual crime(s) committed by the offender, the overall context of his or her criminal conduct and his or her individual criminal responsibility, in particular the form and degree of his or her participation, the degree of his or her intent, whether there were any circumstances falling short of constituting grounds for exclusion of criminal responsibility (see Rule 145(2)(a)(ii) of the ICC Rules of Procedure and Evidence), as well as considering individual circumstances of the offender that could have influenced his or her decision to commit the crime, among others his or her indoctrination by a macro-criminal system, peer pressure and superior orders,[132] where these circumstances have not been considered in assessing the gravity of the crime. A failure to take them into account would not only infringe Rule 145(1)(a) of the ICC Rules of Procedure and Evidence but also violate the overarching principle of personal culpability. At the same time, it should be noted that other individual circumstances, such as the education or social and economic condition of the offender, cannot be considered at this stage as the offender's culpability is solely defined by his or her culpable conduct and factors bearing an influence on it but not by other personal factors that can still be considered with a view to preventive sentencing objectives.

gravity of the crime and the circumstances of the convicted person (ICC, Judgment of 1 December 2014 (AC), *Lubanga*, ICC-01/04-01/06-3122, para. 62). In contrast, the Trial Chamber in *Lubanga* held that these factors actually determine the gravity of the crime, thus utilizing them as mere defining features of the gravity criterion (ICC, Decision of 10 July 2012 (TC), *Lubanga*, ICC-01/04-01/06-2901, para. 44). The Appeals Chamber in *Lubanga* has outlined possible different interpretations of the two provisions without conclusively deciding on the matter (ICC, Judgment of 1 December 2014 (AC), *Lubanga*, ICC-01/04-01/06-3122, paras. 62 et seq). The recent Appeals Chamber judgment in *Bemba et al.* has held that the factors mentioned in Rule 145(1)(c) of the ICC Rules of Procedure and Evidence:

> are not neatly distinguishable and mutually exclusive categories. Rather, certain facts may reasonably be considered under more than one of the categories. What is of importance, therefore, is not so much in which category a given factor is placed, but that the Trial Chamber identifies all relevant factors and attaches reasonable weight to them in its determination of the sentence, carefully avoiding that the same factor is relied upon more than once (see ICC, Judgment of 8 March 2018 (AC), *Bemba et al.*, ICC 01/05-01/13-2275, para. 4).

[132] On the relevance of these factors see Epik, *Strafzumessung*, 500 et seq.

d) Interim Conclusion

In conclusion, it is for the sentencing judges to ensure proportionality by considering the gravity of the crime – not only *in concreto* but also *in abstracto* – as well as the culpability of the perpetrator before they take into account sentencing factors not related to the harm done or the individual responsibility of the offender. By doing so, judges can identify a range of sentences that they consider to be reflective of the offender's guilt, within which they can then – in a second step – determine a concrete sentence that reflects the individual factors of the case that deserve consideration. This approach ensures individualization to the extent possible without risking disproportionate sentencing outcomes.

2 *Individualizing the Sentence*

Special deterrence and rehabilitation both require that sentencing judges take the individual circumstances of the offender into account. In this context, it should be noted that Article 78(1) of the ICC Statute refers to the individual circumstances of the convicted person as the second main factor to be considered in the determination of the sentence. This reference allows the Court to take into account circumstances that relate to the personal situation of the offender, such as his or her age and socio-economic background, as well as his or her (general) conduct where such circumstances have not been considered in the determination of the gravity of the crime.[133] In addition, circumstances relating to the preventive objectives of sentencing can be considered in this context, such as the risk of recidivism or the prospect of his or her reintegration into society.[134] Thus, the individual circumstances should cover those sentencing factors that do not bear relevance for determining the seriousness of the offence or the culpability of the offender, but are nevertheless germane in the individualization of the sentence.[135] This conceptualization of the two sentencing factors also explains why the gravity of the crime should in fact be regarded as the primary sentencing factor: It is the gravity criterion that reflects the offence's seriousness and the offender's

[133] ICC, Decision of 21 June 2016 (TC), *Bemba*, ICC-01/05-01/08-3399, para. 68; ICC, Judgment of 27 September 2016 (TC), *Al Mahdi*, ICC-01/12-01/15-171, para. 94.

[134] In this direction ICC, Decision of 23 May 2014 (TC), *Katanga*, ICC-01/04-01/07-3484, para. 85; ICC, Judgment of 27. September 2016 (TC), *Al Mahdi*, ICC-01/12-01/15-171, para. 97.

[135] ICC, Decision of 21 June 2016 (TC), *Bemba*, ICC-01/05-01/08-3399, para. 68; ICC, Judgment of 27 September 2016 (TC), *Al Mahdi*, ICC-01/12-01/15-171, para. 94.

culpability and thus indicates the degree of retributive justice appropriate, while the individual circumstances are more relevant in determining the degree of punishment needed to further preventative aims, such as the offender's rehabilitation.

The practice of the ICC to this day is disparate. The *Lubanga* Trial Chamber seems to have treated the individual circumstances as also determining the gravity of the crime.[136] The *Katanga* sentencing decision discusses personal circumstances in the context of mitigating circumstances, taking into account the age, family situation and prospects for reintegration of the convicted person as well as his 'kindly and protective disposition towards the civilians in his community', while according them very limited weight.[137] In *Bemba*, the Trial Chamber differentiated between the gravity of the crimes, Jean-Pierre Bemba's culpable conduct and his individual circumstances.[138] The judges made it clear that individual circumstances of the convicted person are those 'that do not relate directly to the crimes or his culpable conduct'.[139] They identified, 'of those factors in Rule 145(1)(c), the convicted person's age and social and economic condition' as particularly relevant factors in assessing the individual circumstances of the convicted person.[140] The Trial Chamber in *Al Mahdi* followed a similar approach, considering the gravity of the crime, the offender's culpable conduct and his individual circumstances.[141] In the section dealing with individual circumstances, the Chamber addressed 'all relevant circumstances that are not directly related to the crime committed or to Mr Al Mahdi's culpable conduct'.[142] The Chamber determined that the age and economic background of the accused were not of relevance and that the 'absence of prior convictions is a fairly common feature among individuals convicted by international tribunals and shall not [...] be counted as a relevant mitigating circumstance'.[143] The Chamber attached, however, limited weight to Al Mahdi's good behaviour in detention.[144] The judges also took into account his admission of guilt and his cooperation with

[136] 'Mr Lubanga is clearly an intelligent and well-educated individual, who would have understood the seriousness of the crimes of which he has been found guilty. This marked level of awareness on his part is a relevant factor in determining the appropriate sentence.', ICC, Decision of 10 July 2012 (TC), *Lubanga*, ICC-01/04-01/06-2901, para. 56.

[137] ICC, Decision of 23 May 2014 (TC), *Katanga*, ICC-01/04-01/07-3484, paras. 78 et seq., 88.

[138] ICC, Decision of 21 June 2016 (TC), *Bemba*, ICC-01/05-01/08-3399, para. 20.

[139] ICC, Decision of 21 June 2016 (TC), *Bemba*, ICC-01/05-01/08-3399, para. 68.

[140] ICC, Decision of 21 June 2016 (TC), *Bemba*, ICC-01/05-01/08-3399, para. 68.

[141] ICC, Judgment of 27 September 2016 (TC), *Al Mahdi*, ICC-01/12-01/15-171, para. 75.

[142] ICC, Judgment of 27 September 2016 (TC), *Al Mahdi*, ICC-01/12-01/15-171, para. 94.

[143] ICC, Judgment of 27 September 2016 (TC), *Al Mahdi*, ICC-01/12-01/15-171, para. 96.

[144] ICC, Judgment of 27 September 2016 (TC), *Al Mahdi*, ICC-01/12-01/15-171, para. 97.

the Prosecution as an indication that 'he is likely to successfully reintegrate into society'.[145]

It remains to be seen how the sentencing practice of the ICC will develop. It can be assumed, however, that the ICC will follow the interpretation advanced by the *Bemba* and *Al Mahdi* sentencing decisions, which is essentially in line with the approach proposed above: Individual circumstances are those that do not relate to the gravity of the crime or the culpability of the offender. In this context, it is important to stress, once again, that such factors can influence the sentencing decision only to the extent that the sentence remains proportionate to the crime and the culpability of the offender. An increase or decrease of an appropriate sentence with a view to special deterrence or rehabilitation is therefore only permissible if the overall outcome can still be considered as proportionate to the offender's guilt.

3 *Promoting Norm Awareness and Reconciliation*

As we have established above, positive general prevention refers to the creation and reinforcement of an international awareness of law as well as the promotion of peace and reconciliation. Positive general prevention is of crucial importance when it comes to justifying international criminal law as such.[146] However, it is difficult to determine the consequences of this purpose of punishment for the actual sentencing decision. It stands to reason, however, that neither the creation and reinforcement of an international awareness of law nor the promotion of peace and reconciliation requires anything else than a proportionate sentence that adequately reflects the harm done to the victims and their relatives, the impact that the crime had on the affected communities as well as the culpability of the offender.[147] Conversely, excessively lenient or harsh sentences could 'weaken the respect for the legal order as a whole'.[148] Similarly, a proportionate sentence will also fulfil the expressive function of international punishment as it conveys the message that the offender is held accountable for his or her crimes in a transparent, consistent and proportional and thus fair manner.[149] Accordingly, Trial Chamber III held in its *Bemba*

[145] ICC, Judgment of 27 September 2016 (TC), *Al Mahdi*, ICC-01/12-01/15-171, para. 97.

[146] Werle, 'Menschenrechtsschutz durch Völkerstrafrecht', 821; Werle and Jeßberger, *Principles*, paras. 108 et seq.

[147] Epik, *Strafzumessung*, 142, 153; Melloh, *Einheitliche Strafzumessung*, 339.

[148] ICTY, Judgment of 11 March 2004 (TC), *Češić*, IT-95-10/1-S, para. 26.

[149] On the ensuing importance of 'outreach', see the contribution by Philipp Ambach in Chapter 20.

sentencing decision: 'The objectives underlying sentencing are fulfilled with "the imposition of a just and appropriate sentence, and nothing more".'[150]

V CONCLUSION

The ICC has passed only a handful of sentencing decisions to date. However, from the very beginning, the judges have engaged with the question of which sentencing objectives the Court should pursue. Even though it is too early to draw final conclusions, the Court has quite consistently highlighted retribution, deterrence, positive general prevention and rehabilitation as relevant purposes of punishment. However, the Chambers have so far refrained from – explicitly – deducing clear sentencing guidelines from the purposes of punishment. We have highlighted some elements that could assist the Court in further developing a coherent sentencing practice, which takes into account the sentencing objectives as well as the sentencing provisions of the ICC Statute and the Rules of Procedure and Evidence. In this regard, a thorough analysis of the gravity of the crime involving considerations not only of the gravity *in concreto* but also of the abstract gravity of the relevant crime is indispensable. By demanding that the judges determine an appropriate range of sentences based on the gravity of the crime and the culpability of the offender first before taking into account further sentencing factors, the approach proposed above ensures proportionate sentencing outcomes while allowing for a certain degree of individualization. It also reduces the risk of inconsistencies as similar cases will more probably be treated alike if abstract and objective criteria, such as the gradation in seriousness between the core crimes and the individual acts within each core crime or the mode of participation of the offender, are placed at the centre of the sentencing decision. It remains to be seen, however, whether the Court will consider such an approach in the future. As highlighted above, the Chambers have shown a certain degree of reluctance to bind themselves by setting rigorous abstract criteria for sentencing. At the same time, the Court has, at this early stage of its judicial activity, established a fairly consistent scheme for its sentencing decisions that has produced legally sound sentencing decisions. Our proposed approach is, therefore, not an antithesis to the Court's sentencing practice but an attempt to highlight its potential to further predictability, proportionality and transparency in international sentencing.

[150] ICC, Decision of 21 June 2016 (TC), *Bemba*, ICC-01/05-01/08-3399, para. 11.

19

Theories of Punishment at The Hague

A Comment on the Contributions by Alex Whiting, Harmen van der Wilt and Gerhard Werle and Aziz Epik

SILVIA D'ASCOLI

Within the framework set by the first two parts of this volume, the relevance of the theories of punishment in international criminal law assumes a more pragmatic connotation in this third part devoted to the International Criminal Court (ICC). What are the effects and consequences of the 'why punish' question for the practice of the ICC?

This topic somehow closes the circle of the discussion by reconnecting theory and practice. In fact, ultimately, the relevance of the question at the heart of this volume – Why punish perpetrators of mass atrocities? – is a fundamental one not only for the purpose of building a solid theory of international punishment, but also to explore the way that such a theory can, and should, relate to the practice of a permanent court such as the ICC and the sentences imposed by it.

The three contributions that focus on the ICC in this part give unique insights into the interplay between theory and practice. Gerhard Werle and Aziz Epik discuss the sentencing decisions pronounced by the ICC to date, focusing on the approach to the purposes of punishment and distilling from these decisions elements deemed essential to a coherent sentencing approach. Alex Whiting examines the constraints and factors shaping the prosecution strategy at the ICC, as well as the theories of punishment put forward by the Office of the Prosecutor. Harmen van der Wilt reflects on the relationship between the inherent selectivity of 'situations' and 'cases' at the ICC and the purported theories of punishment. He addresses the issue of whether selectivity in international criminal law is a problem for the theories of punishment, and discusses how the constraints (legal, structural and political) that limit the ICC and the powers of the Office of the Prosecutor may have repercussions on these theories.

There are numerous interesting issues raised in these three contributions that would be worth further discussion, but I shall limit my brief contribution to a couple of points.

I RETRIBUTION AND DETERRENCE AS PRIMARY RATIONALES FOR PUNISHMENT

The question regarding the (most appropriate) purposes of international punishment, which has resurfaced in relation to the purposes that the ICC would or should apply in its sentencing practice, has occupied many scholars and practitioners (myself included), and is at the core of several contributions to this volume.

Because of the absence of specific provisions in the ICC Statute or Rules of Procedure and Evidence indicating the purposes that should inform the imposition of sentences before the Court, one has to derive these purposes from an integrated analysis and interpretation of the ICC statutory framework. In practice, this leads to what Werle and Epik described as follows: '[j]udges applying international criminal law in practice also need to conclusively determine why they are punishing an individual perpetrator for the crimes he or she has been convicted for [. . .]'.[1] This is not an ideal scenario. The objectives or purposes guiding the sentencing process should be predetermined by the relevant system and not decided by the judges on a case-by-case basis. Trial Chambers should not be the organs invested with the duty to 'establish a proper foundation for [their] sentencing decision by determining the sentencing objectives guiding the sentencing process'.[2] The purposes of punishment for an international criminal court such as the ICC should be clear from the outset. The possibility to infer such purposes from the Preamble or the larger ICC legal framework cannot be considered as the equivalent of provisions expressly prescribing a specific sentencing policy to be pursued in meting out penalties. In the absence of specific provisions, the way the jurisprudence has addressed the issue becomes even more essential. However, the expectations of practitioners and scholars have been disappointed so far.

In their analysis of the relevant provisions of the ICC Statute and Rules of Procedure and Evidence, Werle and Epik show that the traditional purposes of punishment of retribution, deterrence (both general and special deterrence) and rehabilitation are applicable by the ICC.[3] These traditional

1 See the contribution by Gerhard Werle and Aziz Epik in Chapter 18.

2 Werle and Epik in Chapter 18.

3 Werle and Epik in Chapter 18 (Section I).

purposes can in fact be deduced from specific provisions of the Statute or the Rules, and they have also been uniformly recognized by the jurisprudence. The decisions on sentence issued by the ICC so far show an overall consistent approach, with retribution and deterrence being the primary purposes of punishment[4] (even when offences against the administration of justice are concerned),[5] and rehabilitation or social reintegration playing a more limited role.[6] Thus, while there seem to be no issues regarding whether retribution and deterrence are in fact the primary purposes of punishment recognized and applied by the ICC in its sentencing decisions, what surprises (and disappoints) is: (i) the superficial and cursory manner in which these purposes are discussed, often succinctly in one or two paragraphs;[7] (ii) the repetition of language and the identical concepts used across sentencing decisions; and (iii) the unclear impact of the purposes of punishment on the actual determination of the sentences.

I will discuss this third point later on in this comment. With regard to the first two points, Sergey Vasiliev discusses these in his paper in the first part of this volume.[8] There is not much to add to his exhaustive remarks, save that it is disappointing how little the ICC jurisprudence on sentencing has so far contributed to the development of rationales for international punishment.

Further, what remains unclear is the distinction between the underlying rationales for international justice – in other words, the reasons for having an international criminal court at all – and the specific aims of sentencing and punishment. These two levels of analysis often overlap or are obfuscated in the reasoning of the Chambers in their decisions on sentence, which shows that a coherent and advanced theory of punishment specific to international criminal

4 ICC, Decision on Sentence of 10 July 2012 (TC), *Lubanga*, ICC-01/04-01/06-2901, para. 16; ICC, Decision on Sentence of 23 May 2014 (TC), *Katanga*, ICC-01/04-01/07-3484, paras. 37–38; ICC, Decision on Sentence of 21 June 2016 (TC), *Bemba*, ICC-01/05-01/08-3399, para. 10; ICC, Judgement of 27 September 2016 (TC), *Al Mahdi*, ICC-01/12-01/15-171, paras. 66–67.

5 See ICC, Decision on Sentence of 22 March 2017 (TC), *Bemba et al.* (Art.70), ICC-01/05-01/13-2123, para. 19, and ICC, Decision on Re-Sentencing of 17 September 2018, *Bemba et al.* (Art.70), ICC-01/05-01/13-2312, para. 18(i).

6 See, e.g., ICC, Decision on Sentence of 23 May 2014 (TC), *Katanga*, ICC-01/04-01/07-3484, para. 38; ICC, Decision on Sentence of 21 June 2016 (TC), *Bemba*, ICC-01/05-01/08-3399, para. 11; ICC, Judgement of 27 September 2016 (TC), *Al Mahdi*, ICC-01/12-01/15-171, para. 67.

7 See, e.g., ICC, Decision on Sentence of 10 July 2012, *Lubanga*, ICC-01/04-01/06-2901, para. 16; ICC, Decision on Sentence of 21 June 2016 (TC), *Bemba*, ICC-01/05-01/08-3399, paras. 10–11; ICC, Decision on Sentence of 22 March 2017 (TC), *Bemba et al.* (Art.70), ICC-01/05-01/13-2123, para. 19.

8 See the contribution by Sergey Vasiliev in Chapter 4 (Section II.1).

law is not yet in place. Some examples of these overlapping levels can be discerned, for instance, in the *Lubanga*[9] and *Katanga* sentencing decisions.[10]

II CONCRETE IMPACT OF PURPOSES OF PUNISHMENT ON THE DETERMINATION OF SENTENCES

Probably as a consequence of the scant analysis that the rationales for punishment have received by ICC Chambers, the actual impact that the identified purposes of retribution and deterrence exercise on the sentences is not discernible.

The question of whether the purposes of punishment inform the actual determination of sentences finds no direct answer in the jurisprudence. If we consider the first decisions on sentence of the ICC,[11] we find no indication as to whether and how the stated purposes of punishment inform the determination of the specific sentence. None of the sentencing decisions, for example, reconnect the chosen purposes of punishment to the length of the sentence imposed, or explain how the emphasis on one purpose or the other may result in different sentencing outcomes. While the purposes of punishment are mentioned at the beginning of the decisions, often in connection with the relevant principles and legal framework, there is no further mention of these purposes in the section devoted to 'determination of the sentence'.[12] Does this mean that the purposes of punishment have no discernible influence on the sentences imposed? It is likely so. In the absence of a specific link, we should

9 See ICC, Decision on Sentence of 10 July 2012, *Lubanga*, ICC-01/04-01/06-2901, para. 16, where the Trial Chamber simply recalls the two rationales of retribution and deterrence without delving into further analysis and then concludes that '[t]he ICC was established "to these ends and for the sake of present and future generations"', obfuscating the rationales for punishment in sentencing with those of the whole system of international justice/international criminal law.

10 See ICC, Decision on Sentence of 23 May 2014 (TC), *Katanga*, ICC-01/04-01/07-3484, para. 38, where the Trial Chamber states that: 'When determining the sentence, the Chamber must further ensure that, pursuant to rule 145(1)(a) of the Rules, the sentence reflects the degree of culpability while contributing to the restoration of peace and reconciliation in the communities concerned.'

11 ICC, Decision on Sentence of 10 July 2012 (TC), *Lubanga*, ICC-01/04-01/06-2901; ICC, Decision on Sentence of 23 May 2014 (TC), *Katanga*, ICC-01/04-01/07-3484; ICC, Decision on Sentence of 21 June 2016 (TC), *Bemba*, ICC-01/05-01/08-3399; ICC, Judgement of 27 September 2016 (TC), *Al Mahdi*, ICC-01/12-01/15-171; ICC, Decision on Sentence of 22 March 2017 (TC), *Bemba et al.* (Art.70), ICC-01/05-01/13-2123.

12 See, e.g., ICC, Decision on Sentence of 10 July 2012 (TC), *Lubanga*, ICC-01/04-01/06-2901, paras. 92–99; ICC, Decision on Sentence of 23 May 2014 (TC), *Katanga*, ICC-01/04-01/07-3484, paras.141–147; ICC, Decision on Sentence of 21 June 2016 (TC), *Bemba*, ICC-01/05-01/08-3399, paras.90–96; ICC, Judgement of 27 September 2016 (TC), *Al Mahdi*, ICC-01/12-01/15-171, paras. 106–111.

conclude that the reference to the purposes of punishment in the decisions on sentence amounts to nothing more than a reiteration of the relevant parts of the Preamble of the ICC Statute.

I agree with Werle and Epik that reiterating these purposes without any further analysis does not contribute to any clarification; and that – despite the constant reference to the purposes of retribution and deterrence – ICC Chambers have so far refrained from deriving any clear sentencing guidelines, including any expressed weight, from the purposes of punishment.[13]

This is not unprecedented. In the jurisprudence of the ad hoc Tribunals, we equally observed that Chambers did either not elaborate on the purposes of punishment, or did not explain the impact, if any, of the chosen sentencing objectives on the penalty imposed. I concur with the conclusion of Werle and Epik that the lack of discussion of the relevance and weight attached to each sentencing objective constitutes a missed opportunity to develop a coherent sentencing model based on the specific objectives pursued.[14]

Further, certain statements seem more the expression of a rhetorical exercise than of a real evaluation of how theories of punishment can effectively impact on the sentence. For example, the *Katanga* Trial Chamber refers to the 'inevitability' of punishment,[15] echoing Cesare Beccaria's observations recalled by the International Criminal Tribunal for the former Yugoslavia (ICTY) Trial Chamber in the *Furundzija* case.[16] It is rather clear that this is an empty statement. 'Inevitability' of punishment is not a given, and definitely not a certainty in international criminal law; quite the opposite. It is, rather, the inherent selectivity of international criminal justice that seems to be the rule.

Is selectivity an intrinsic problem for the efficacy and validity of the chosen rationales of punishment, especially retribution and deterrence? Van der Wilt and Whiting devote two very interesting papers to various aspects of this question and connected issues. They both point out how the limited resources and constraints[17] that the Office of the Prosecutor faces at the ICC have

[13] Werle and Epik in Chapter 18 (Section III).

[14] Werle and Epik in Chapter 18 (Section III).

[15] ICC, Decision on Sentence of 23 May 2014 (TC), *Katanga*, ICC-01/04-01/07-3484, para. 38: 'The punitive aspect of the sentence is therefore meant to restrain any desire to exact vengeance and it is not so much the severity of the sentence that should prevail as *its inevitability*.'

[16] See ICTY, Judgment of 10 December 1998 (TC), *Furundzija*, IT-95-17/1-T, para. 290: 'The Trial Chamber is further guided in its determination of sentence by the principle proclaimed as early as in 1764 by Cesare Beccaria: "punishment should not be harsh, but must be inevitable." It is the infallibility of punishment, rather than the severity of the sanction, which is the tool for retribution, stigmatisation and deterrence.'

[17] See, e.g., the contribution by Harmen van der Wilt in Chapter 17 (Section I).

shaped its prosecutorial strategy and the theories of punishment embraced by the Office: '[R]ather than theory dictating practice, it has been the other way around.'[18]

This leads me to my last observation, which concerns the theories of punishment relied upon by the Office of the Prosecutor of the ICC.

III THEORIES OF PUNISHMENT AND PROSECUTORIAL STRATEGY

The Office of the Prosecutor, too, has relied on the traditional purposes of retribution and deterrence in its sentencing submissions.[19] Similarly to the way Chambers have made use of these purposes, the Prosecution's references are rather cursory and formalistic. They are either limited to the statement that the Court, in its determination of the appropriate sentence, must take into account the objectives of sentencing,[20] or recall previous findings of Trial Chambers regarding purposes of punishment,[21] or mention other objectives that have also been considered by the ad hoc Tribunals, such as reconciliation, restoration of peace and rehabilitation.[22]

Once again, the references to the purposes of punishment seem to amount to nothing more than a reiteration of the relevant parts of the Preamble of the

18 See the contribution by Alex Whiting in Chapter 16.

19 See, e.g., ICC, Prosecution's Submissions on the Procedures and Principles for Sentencing of 18 April 2012, *Lubanga*, ICC-01/04-01/06-2868, para. 23; ICC, Prosecution's Submissions on the Procedures and Principles for Sentencing of 17 March 2014, *Katanga*, ICC-01/04-01/07-3444, para. 17; ICC, Public redacted version of Prosecution's Sentencing Submissions of 15 April 2016, *Bemba*, ICC-01/05-01/08-3363-Red, para. 14.

20 See, e.g., ICC, Prosecution's Submissions on the Procedures and Principles for Sentencing of 17 March 2014, *Katanga*, ICC-01/04-01/07-3444, para. 12: 'The Court is vested with the discretion to impose an appropriate sentence within the range of applicable penalties set out in the Statute. In determining the appropriate sentence, the Court must consider the objectives of sentencing, the inherently grave nature of the crimes prosecuted by this Court, any factors relevant to the gravity of the offence and any relevant aggravating and mitigating factors.'

21 See, e.g., ICC, Public redacted version of Prosecution's Sentencing Submissions of 15 April 2016, *Bemba*, ICC-01/05-01/08-3363-Red, para. 15: 'Trial Chamber II considered that the purpose of sentencing is two-fold: on the one hand, punishment, or the expression of society's condemnation of the criminal act and of the person who committed it, and, on the other hand, deterrence'; and ICC, Public redacted version of 'Prosecution's submissions on sentencing' of 22 July 2016, *Al Mahdi*, ICC-01/12-01/15-139-Red, para. 11.

22 See, e.g., ICC, Prosecution's Submissions on the Procedures and Principles for Sentencing of 17 March 2014, *Katanga*, ICC-01/04-01/07-3444, para. 17; ICC, Public redacted version of Prosecution's Sentencing Submissions of 15 April 2016, *Bemba*, ICC-01/05-01/08-3363-Red, para. 16.

ICC Statute,[23] and do not seem to inform the actual (length of the) sentence requested by the Office of the Prosecutor. In some cases, like in the *Lubanga* and *Katanga* Prosecution's sentence requests,[24] there is no mention at all of the purposes of punishment. The relevant sections devoted to the 'determination of sentence' of the Prosecution's submissions and requests mostly rely on the analysis of other elements, such as gravity of the offence, the individual circumstances of the accused, and aggravating and mitigating factors, to support the imposition of a specific sentence. The Office of the Prosecutor has used a range of arguments to advocate for severity of punishment, but the purposes of punishment do not seem to form part of the factors justifying the requested length of sentence.

In only two cases[25] has the Office reconnected the purposes of punishment, in particular deterrence, to the severity of the sentence requested. In *Bemba*, for example, the Prosecution argued that: 'A long sentence, proportionate to gravity of Bemba's culpability would also pursue the objective of deterring other military commanders from committing similar crimes.'[26] This is as far as we get in terms of connecting purposes of punishment to sentencing recommendations.

An area where the rationales of punishment have played a more prominent role is at the stage of selection of situations and cases. Whiting argues that the theories of punishment embraced by the Office of the Prosecutor in its selection of situations and cases have largely sought to justify the choices that the Prosecutor made given the limited resources and constraints faced by the Office operationally and politically.[27] In explaining the shifts that the prosecutorial strategy has taken when transitioning from the first Prosecutor of the ICC to the second (from a specific deterrence theory to more expressivist rationales and normative theories), Whiting observes how these shifts have been reactive to events and constraints, rather than being proactive and leading.[28]

[23] See, e.g., ICC, Prosecution's Submissions on the Procedures and Principles for Sentencing of 18 April 2012, *Lubanga*, ICC-01/04-01/06-2868, para. 23: 'The Statute establishes the mandate to end impunity and contribute to the prevention of crimes.'

[24] ICC, Prosecution's Sentence Request of 14 May 2012 *Lubanga*, ICC-01/04-01/06-2881; ICC, Prosecution's Sentence Request of 7 April 2014, *Katanga*, ICC-01/04-01/07-3455.

[25] See ICC, Public redacted version of Prosecution's Sentencing Submissions of 15 April 2016, *Bemba*, ICC-01/05-01/08-3363-Red, para. 126; and ICC, Prosecution Sentencing Submissions of 30 April 2018, *Bemba et al.* (Art.70), ICC-01/05-01/13-2279, para. 77.

[26] See, e.g., ICC, Public redacted version of Prosecution's Sentencing Submissions of 15 April 2016, *Bemba*, ICC-01/05-01/08-3363-Red, para. 126.

[27] See the contribution by Alex Whiting in Chapter 16 (Section I).

[28] Alex Whiting in Chapter 16 (Section II).

Another example showing that the prosecutorial strategy has been consequential to developments and occurrences rather than pre-emptive and practice-shaping in terms of sentencing policy can be seen in the initial Prosecution's proposition (quickly abandoned) of a starting point or 'baseline' to determine sentences. In fact, the very first time the Prosecution put forward its submissions 'on the Procedures and Principles for Sentencing' in the *Lubanga* case, the Prosecution urged the Chamber to adopt a 'baseline' for sentences set at approximately 80 per cent of the statutory maximum,[29] submitting that this baseline should then be adjusted in accordance with Rule 145 of the ICC Rules of Procedure and Evidence to take into account any aggravating and mitigating circumstances and other relevant factors applicable to the case.[30] In the Prosecution's submissions, this would also avoid sentence discrepancies and would ensure that the Court's sentences are sufficiently severe, thus reflecting the inner gravity and seriousness of international crimes under the ICC's jurisdiction.[31]

The *Lubanga* Trial Chamber found that the Prosecution offered no established principles of law or relevant jurisprudence under Article 21 of the ICC Statute in support of its position.[32] Leaving aside the Trial Chamber's reasons for dismissal, the '80 per cent baseline' proposed by the Prosecution would have caused a number of risks: (i) conflating different aspects of gravity: gravity of the offence and gravity of the individual criminal responsibility at hand; (ii) levelling all crimes together and eliminating potentially substantial differences between crimes of a different nature, which protects different interests; (iii) disregarding the fact that – in certain circumstances – *punishment per se* is of significance, even if not necessarily combined with the severity of sentences. This last point is well illustrated by, e.g., the *Al Mahdi* prosecution, which represented the first time that the war crime of intentionally directing attacks against religious buildings or historical monuments was the main charge of a case before an international criminal court, a standalone war crime. The significance of this prosecution,[33] which marked a timely development in

[29] ICC, Prosecution's Submissions on the Procedures and Principles for Sentencing of 18 April 2012, *Lubanga*, ICC-01/04-01/06-2868, paras. 4–5.

[30] ICC, Prosecution's Submissions on the Procedures and Principles for Sentencing of 18 April 2012, *Lubanga*, ICC-01/04-01/06-2868, para. 5.

[31] ICC, Prosecution's Submissions on the Procedures and Principles for Sentencing of 18 April 2012, *Lubanga*, ICC-01/04-01/06-2868, paras. 3–4.

[32] ICC, Decision on Sentence of 10 July 2012 (TC), *Lubanga*, ICC-01/04-01/06-2901, para. 93.

[33] At the confirmation of charges hearing, the ICC Prosecutor emphasized the importance of the charges against Al Mahdi: 'Let us be clear: what is at stake here is not just walls and stones. The destroyed mausoleums were important, from a religious point of view, from an historical point of view, and from an identity point of view. Such an attack against buildings dedicated to

the protection of cultural heritage in international justice, goes beyond the 9-year sentence of imprisonment sought by the Prosecution and imposed by the Trial Chamber.

It is understandable that, in the absence of a gravity scale and ranking of the crimes under the jurisdiction of the ICC, the Prosecution sought to emphasize and secure a certain degree of gravity for these crimes, and thus a certain severity of the sentences. However, the proposed baseline would have not achieved what only a systematization of crimes into different categories, to which different gravity and corresponding penalty ranges are associated, could achieve.[34]

After the *Lubanga* case, the Prosecution did not reiterate its position in its sentencing submissions in other cases, did not explain the reasons why it had abandoned or dismissed its initial approach, nor did it propose any other approach or solution. Perhaps akin to that phenomenon of repetition of language and notions discussed earlier, the Prosecution seemed to simply accept the Chamber's view and react to it by adapting its theories to the predominant practice of not having any starting point, baseline or ranges of penalties. I find Whiting's comment that 'rather than theory dictating practice, it has been the other way around'[35] applicable to this case as well.

What is unfortunate, in my opinion, is that the *Lubanga* Trial Chamber did not discuss in detail how and why a 14-year sentence (rather than, e.g., the 30-year sentence requested by the Prosecution) was proportionate to the crimes of which Thomas Lubanga was found guilty. Equally, it did not discuss how the sentence imposed was appropriate in light of the purposes of punishment sought and the consideration that the crimes under the jurisdiction of the ICC are 'the most serious crimes of concern to the international community as a whole'.[36] The other decisions on sentence delivered by ICC Chambers so far similarly do not discuss in detail how judges arrived at their determination of a certain length of the sentences imposed and alleged proportionality to the

religion and historic monuments falls into the category of crimes that destroy the roots of an entire people and profoundly and irremediably affect its social practices and structures. This is precisely why such acts constitute a crime under article 8(2)(e)(iv) of the Rome Statute.' See Statement of the Prosecutor of the International Criminal Court, Fatou Bensouda, at the opening of the confirmation of charges hearing in the case against Mr Ahmad Al-Faqi Al Mahdi, 1 March 2016, available at www.icc-cpi.int/Pages/item.aspx?name=otp-stat-01-03-16.

34 See S. D'Ascoli, *Sentencing in International Criminal Law* (Oxford: Hart, 2011), 303–308, 318, 321.

35 See the contribution by Alex Whiting in Chapter 16.

36 ICC Statute, Preamble paragraph 4. See also ICC, Prosecution's Submissions on the Procedures and Principles for Sentencing of 18 April 2012, *Lubanga*, ICC-01/04-01/06-2868, para. 3.

crimes at stake. Because of the lack of a uniform scale of gravity of offences and penalty ranges for international crimes, the lack of an informative reasoning on an issue as significant as the length of sentences remains problematic, especially in light of the extraordinary gravity of international crimes. Van der Wilt captures this dichotomy very effectively by referring to the 'embarrassment of *retributive theories* [...] to explain penalties that are woefully incommensurate to the enormity of the crimes [...]'.[37]

In sum, when reflecting on the impact of the theories and purposes of punishment on ICC sentencing practice and prosecutorial strategy, the end balance so far is not entirely positive or promising. Where expectations regarding the elaboration of a specific theory of punishment for international criminal justice by the ICC were high, these expectations were disappointed and met with only cursory references to the relevant parts of the Preamble of the ICC Statute, with a high degree of reiteration of previously used formulas and findings. The objectives of the prosecution of international crimes, the prevention of such crimes and the fight against impunity have not been further substantiated, and thus seemed to have remained general, almost impracticable and idealistic, especially in light of the constraints limiting the ICC and the Office of the Prosecutor, and in light of the seemingly inadequate prosecutions (in terms of exiguous number and severity of punishment).

It is arguable that selectivity, particularly when imposed by the structural and political constraints that influence and limit the spectrum of action of the ICC, weakens the retributive and deterrent effect of the international criminal justice system.[38] If this is added to the problems identified above, the whole picture appears gloomy and maybe not worth the effort of creating a complex system such as the ICC. However, the discussion regarding theories of punishment in international justice must be considered within the broader context of the role of the international community with regard to atrocities, the need for collective action against international crimes, and the relation between international justice and the promotion and maintenance of peace. In this sense, effective prevention of future atrocities requires more than just prosecutions, and thus the intrinsic selectivity of international criminal justice is not per se a problem that cannot be overcome by a synergy of instruments going beyond criminal prosecutions, and supporting such prosecutions.

[37] See the contribution by Harmen van der Wilt in Chapter 17 (Section II.1).

[38] See, e.g., M.A. Drumbl, *Atrocity, Punishment and International Law* (Cambridge: Cambridge University Press, 2007), 152; see also the contribution by Harmen van der Wilt in Chapter 17 (Section II.1 and 2).

Strengthening the rule of law in critical countries, overpowering the culture of impunity, promoting relevant training and advancing educational human rights programmes, for instance, would be key aspects in fostering the realization of those very same outcomes that the theories of punishment in international justice are meant to achieve.

The silver lining to look at is, in my view, the very existence of a permanent system of international criminal justice that can now be integrated into a broader context. Whether the ICC will make a difference in achieving a more just world is hard to tell. The system is not perfect, nor effectively functioning (yet), but it is there to grow and develop: 'babies are not born full-grown. First, they crawl, they cry, they mess up, they throw up, and they need help. [...] Eventually, with care and nurturing they grow and become useful citizens.'[39]

[39] B. Ferencz, 'The Experience of Nuremberg' in D. Shelton (ed.), *International Crimes, Peace, and Human Rights: The Role of the International Criminal Court* (Ardsley, New York: Transnational Publishers, 2000), 9.

20

From Punitive to Restorative Justice

Victims' Participation, Reparations and Theories of Punishment

PHILIPP AMBACH*

Since the inception of the international criminal justice idea in 1945/1946 with the International Military Tribunals in Nuremberg and Tokyo, the legitimacy and usefulness of international criminal justice mechanisms for international core crimes committed by individuals has been subject to discussion. With the creation and successful operations of the ad hoc International Criminal Tribunals for the former Yugoslavia (ICTY)[1] and for Rwanda (ICTR)[2] by the UN Security Council in 1993 and 1994 respectively, the retributive justice aspect clearly took the front seat, with victims' options to participate in the proceedings reduced to the witness stand. In addition, both Tribunals served as judicial ad hoc solutions to immediate threats to international peace and security. In this geopolitical climate, as an expression of a more durable justice solution for large-scale atrocities, the International Criminal Court (ICC) was a logical consequence.

Through its explicit statutory stipulation of victims' rights to participate in the proceedings in their own right (Article 68(3) of the ICC Statute), the drafters of the Rome Statute recognized victims for the first time as potential front-line addressees of international criminal justice. In addition, the reparations regime of Article 75 of the ICC Statute underlined victims' prominent role in the proceedings and the convicted person's accountability towards victims.[3]

* The views expressed in this article are the author's alone and cannot be attributed to any institutions.

1 ICTY: UN S/RES/827 (1993) of 25 May 1993.

2 ICTR: UN S/RES/955 (1994) of 8 November 1994.

3 ICC, Judgment of 3 March 2015 (AC), *Lubanga*, ICC-01/04-01/06-3129, para 69; see also C. Stahn, 'Reparative Justice after the Lubanga Appeals Judgment on Principles and Procedures of Reparation', 7 April 2015 EJIL Talk!, available at www.ejiltalk.org/reparative-justice-after-the-lubanga-appeals-judgment-on-principles-and-procedures-of-reparation. Of

A number of subsequently established internationalized 'hybrid' ad hoc criminal courts and tribunals followed this trend and included more or less comprehensive victim participation regimes. The Extraordinary Chambers in the Courts of Cambodia (ECCC), the Special Tribunal for Lebanon (STL), the Kosovo Specialist Chambers and Specialist Prosecutor's Office (KSC) and the *Cour Pénale Spéciale Centrafricaine* (CPC) all contain specific provisions on victim participation and, to varying degrees of detail, on reparations. Similarly, the African Union-sponsored Extraordinary African Chambers (EAC),[4] established to try former Chadian dictator Hissène Habré, provided for victim participation and a reparations regime subsequent to the accused's conviction.

It would thus seem that the ICC pioneered a set of new victim-centred features that every subsequent internationalized justice mechanism for crimes under international law has to some degree adopted since, at least regarding its main principles and premises. Victim participation in international criminal proceedings has become a central aspect of modern international criminal justice. Reparations for victims of crimes under international law at the end of a criminal process have likewise become a prominent feature. This notably expands the group of direct addressees of international criminal justice from what has traditionally been encompassed in general considerations of punishment for atrocity crimes. Victims are no longer a mere conceptual group of beneficiaries through retribution for past crimes and deterrence of future crimes. They are accepted as participating actors in the process, able even to shape the proceedings through a number of procedural tools at their disposition, as prominently stipulated in the ICC's governing framework; and they may receive reparative justice at the end of the process.

Seen through the victims' lense, the expanding international criminal justice regime is thus highly beneficial in two major ways, neither of which *directly* relates to the perpetrator's punishment and sentence as key factors of relief. The present contribution will briefly outline these two beneficial features and also point towards some remaining challenges.

note, the activation of the reparations mechanism attaches to the conviction of an accused person before the ICC, see ICC, Judgment of 3 March 2015 (AC), *Lubanga*, ICC-01/04-01/06-3129, para 151.

[4] See Statute of the EAC within the courts of Senegal created to prosecute international crimes committed in Chad between 7 June 1982 and 1 December 1990, available at www.hrw.org/news/2013/09/02/statute-extraordinary-african-chambers (unofficial translation of the French original).

I VICTIM PARTICIPATION

Participation of victims in the international criminal process provides redress already *prior* to the final verdict of the judges and therefore, to an extent, detached from the concept of punishment. For many participating victims, the possibility of seeing their voice heard and their story told in court already provides a degree of reconciliation, satisfaction and repair. Before expanding on this concept, the regime of victim participation shall be briefly outlined by looking at the example of the ICC.

1 *Victim Participation at the International Criminal Court*

Article 68(3) is the only provision in the ICC Statute addressing the victims' right to participate in the proceedings. It does so in rather vague terms, stipulating that '[w]here the personal interests of the victims are affected, the Court shall permit their views and concerns to be presented and considered at stages of the proceedings determined to be appropriate by the Court and in a manner which is not prejudicial to or inconsistent with the rights of the accused and a fair and impartial trial'.[5] While the words 'shall permit' cement victims' participatory status in the proceedings, the provision at the same time provides clear boundaries, most importantly the rights of the defence to a fair, impartial and speedy trial. In addition, the judges' discretion as to how victim participation is embedded in the proceedings *in fine* balances the rights of the parties – including victims – from pre-trial to appeals and reparations proceedings – and beyond.[6]

Article 68(3) of the ICC Statute also provides that victims' 'views and concerns may be presented' by legal representatives of victims as appropriate; indeed, the

[5] Other hybrid tribunals' legal frameworks have to an extent followed the example of outlining the victim participation regime in their rules of procedure and evidence rather than in their statutes. Art. 17 of the STL Statute mirrors Art. 68(3) of the ICC Statute, and the ECCC does not have a single provision on victim participation in its 'Law on the Establishment of the Extraordinary Chambers as amended', of 27 October 2004. The KSC, in contrast, are more specific already in their Law on Specialist Chambers and Specialist Prosecutors Office, Law No.05/L-053, available at www.scp-ks.org/en/documents/law-specialist-chambers-and-specialist-prosecutors-office-3-aug-2015 (see Art. 22).

[6] Also, during the implementation of reparations there may be a role of victims to litigate certain matters before the ICC; e.g., during the administrative screening of eligible beneficiaries of individual reparations by the ICC Trust Fund for Victims (see ICC Statute, Art. 79), applicants for individual reparations are able to contest a negative assessment of the Trust Fund on their eligibility before the Trial Chamber: ICC, Decision of 8 March 2018 (AC), *Al Mahdi*, ICC-01/12-01/15-259-Red2.

representation of victim groups through legal counsel in court has become the general practice at the Court.[7] Similar provisions, regulating the participation of victims through legal counsel, can be found in the legal texts of the aforementioned hybrid internationalized tribunals constituted subsequent to the ICC.[8]

The ICC Rules of Procedure and Evidence contain more detailed provisions pertaining to victims' role in the proceedings. Rule 85 of the ICC Rules of Procedure and Evidence represents a key provision in that it defines the term 'victim'; jurisprudence has filled space left by the rather wide definition entailed in the provision itself.[9] Rule 89 outlines the application process for participation of victims in the proceedings and codifies the victims' right to make opening and closing statements, as appropriate.[10] Rule 90 regulates the assignment of legal representation to victims. As to said legal representation, a number of different approaches have been approved by the ICC Chambers, including external counsel chosen by victim groups, counsel provided by the ICC Office of Public Counsel for Victims, or a combination of the two.[11]

Victims' participatory rights in the proceedings through their legal representatives are addressed in Rule 91 of the ICC Rules of Procedure and Evidence, providing for (i) participation in hearings; (ii) the right to make oral and written submissions; (iii) the questioning of witnesses, an expert or the accused (upon application to the Chamber); and (iv) the introduction of documents.[12] Yet, the exact set of participatory rights remains in the

7 ICC RPE, Rule 90(2).

8 See, e.g., Rule 86(C)(ii) of the STL Rules of Procedure and Evidence; Art. 22(6) of the Law of the KSC; Art. 14(1) of the EAC Statute; Rules 23(3), 23*ter*(1), 106(3) of the Internal Rules of the ECCC (albeit only during the trial phase and beyond).

9 Rule 85(a) of the ICC Rules of Procedure and Evidence stipulates that '"[v]ictims" means natural persons who have suffered harm as a result of the commission of any crime within the jurisdiction of the Court'. For judicial specification of this broad definition, see ICC, Decision of 21 January 2008 (TC), *Lubanga*, ICC-01/04-01/06-1119, paras. 87–94; ICC, Decision of 7 August 2012 (TC), *Lubanga*, ICC-01/04-01/06-2904, para. 194; see also in the same ICC, Decision of 11 July 2008 (AC), *Lubanga*, ICC-01/04-01/06-1432; ICC, Decision of 8 April 2009 (TC), *Lubanga*, ICC-01/04-01/06-1813. Regarding reparations see ICC, Decision of 7 August 2012 (TC), *Lubanga*, ICC-01/04-01/06-2904, paras. 194–201; ICC, Decision of 24 May 2018 (PTC), *Al Hassan*, ICC-01/12-01/18-37; ICC, Decision of 6 March 2015 (TC), *Gbagbo/Ble Goude*, ICC-02/11-01/11-800, paras. 30 et seq. (outlining also the practical aspects of victims' admission to the proceedings).

10 ICC RPE, Rule 89(1).

11 See most recently ICC, Decision of 23 May 2019 (PTC), *Yekatom/Ngaissona*, ICC-01/14-01/18-205. The Office of Public Counsel for Victims has been established to provide general support and assistance to the legal representative of victims and to victims, including importantly the representation of victims in court as common legal representative; see Regulations 80(1), 81(4) of the ICC Regulations, version of 6 December 2016, ICC-BD/01-05-16.

12 For an early discussion of the applicable legal framework to victims before the ICC see ICC, Decision of 18 January 2008 (TC), *Lubanga*, ICC-01/04-01/06-1119, paras. 20 et seq.

prerogative of the respective chamber.[13] Jurisprudence in the different cases before the ICC has carved out a rather comprehensive set of victims' participatory rights, with minor differences between the cases.[14] The guiding principle, as spelled out in Article 68(3) of the ICC Statute, has been throughout that the victims' personal interests have to be affected to invoke relevant participatory rights.[15] It is for the judges to find the just equilibrium between granting the most meaningful rights to the participating victims and, on the other hand, avoiding prejudice to the rights of the accused or to the fair and impartial conduct of the proceedings.[16]

The regulatory frameworks of other tribunals have followed the ICC's example, with some variation, in providing to victims rather comprehensive procedural tools to bring not just their own grievance to the judges' attention, but also to participate in the shaping of the case as it evolves hearing the parties' evidence, and in some instances even through the possibility of introducing their own evidence.[17]

[13] Pursuant to Rule 89(1) of the ICC Rules of Procedure and Evidence, the Chamber shall specify 'the proceedings and manner in which participation is considered appropriate', in keeping with Art. 68(3) of the ICC Statute (as 'determined to be appropriate by the Court'); see also similar language in Rule 91(3)(b) of the ICC Rules of Procedure and Evidence and Regulation 24(2) of the ICC Regulations, ICC-BD/01-01-04, as amended on 12 July 2017, ICC-BD/01-05-16 ('[v]ictims or their legal representatives may file a response to any document when they are permitted to participate in the proceedings [. . .], *subject to any order of the Chamber*' (emphasis added)). See, on the aspect of 'meaningful', also C. van den Wyngaert, 'Victims before International Criminal Courts: Some Views and Concerns of an ICC Trial Judge' (2011) 44 *Case Western Reserve Journal of International Law* 476, 489.

[14] See, e.g., ICC, Decision of 11 July 2008 (AC), *Lubanga*, ICC-01/04-01/06-1432; ICC, Decision of 18 January 2008 (TC), *Lubanga*, ICC-01/04-01/06-1119; ICC, Decision of 3 October 2012 (TC), ICC-01/09-02/11-498; ICC, Decision of 27 November 2015 (TC), *Ongwen*, ICC-02/04-01/15-350, paras. 27 et seq., ICC, Decision of 6 March 2018 (TC), *Ongwen*, ICC-02/04-01/15-1199-Red, fn. 22 and paras. 17–23, 78–83; ICC, Decision of 6 February 2015 (TC), *Ntaganda*, ICC-01/04-02/06-449 (followed up by multiple decisions further qualifying the applicable regime of victim participation); ICC, Decision of 22 January 2010 (TC), *Katanga*, ICC-01/04-01/07-1788-tENG; ICC, Decision of 22 February 2012 (TC), *Bemba*, ICC-01/05-01/08-2138, paras. 13 et seq.; ICC, Decision of 16 July 2010 (AC), *Katanga*, ICC-01/04-01/07-2288 OA11, paras. 43–48, 72, 75 and 81.

[15] ICC, Decision of 16 June 2007 (AC), *Lubanga*, ICC-01/04-01/06-925, para. 28. At trial, judges have underlined that victims' 'personal interests' may not be confused with a 'Prosecutor *bis*' role, i.e., mere attempts by victims' legal representatives to elicit evidence that aims to prove the elements of the crimes charged or the accused's role in their commission are not acceptable; ICC, Transcript of Hearing on 4 April 2017 (TC), *Ongwen*, ICC-02/04-01/15-T-65-Red-ENG, page 56 lines 3–13, cited in Public Redacted Version of Decision on the Legal Representatives for Victims Requests to Present Evidence and Views and Concerns and Related Requests, ICC-02/04-01/15-1199-Red, 6 March 2018, fn. 27.

[16] See ICC RPE, Rules 89(1), 91(2), (3)(b); ICC, Decision of 27 November 2015 (PTC), *Ongwen*, ICC-02/04-01/15-350, para. 28.

[17] See, e.g., Rules 91(H), 146 of the RPE of the STL; Rule 80*bis*(4), (5) of the Internal Rules of the ECCC; Rule 114(5) of the Rules of Procedure and Evidence before the KSC.

2 *Enhanced Ownership – Moving Away from Punitive Aspects?*

The trend seems quite clear that a purely punitive concept, as had been followed by the ad hoc Tribunals and the Special Court for Sierra Leone (SCSL), has been abandoned for 'contemporary' international criminal tribunals. There now is a general recognition of the need to provide essential elements of restorative justice through victim participation in some form or other.[18] The STL, ECCC, KSC, EAC, and the future CPC in the Central African Republic bear testimony to this. As briefly outlined above, these regimes are built on the conceptual premise that while victims' redress for crimes under international law is much more complex than 'only' retributive justice, the latter may still play a major role and become a powerful component of a victim-oriented transitional justice process. This, in turn, lends additional legitimacy to the international(ized) court in question because it responds credibly to a larger audience than only those asking for criminal punishment of the most responsible perpetrators. It is beyond doubt that a criminal conviction and punishment of an accused, and even more so of a well-known political or military leader, will have a reconciliatory and satisfying effect on those that suffered from the crimes committed by the former. Yet, the more powerful aspect is the enhanced ownership and possibility to interact during the criminal process, even if only through a proxy – the legal representative of victims in the courtroom. Victims' individual stories of how they suffered harm are documented in the case file, and so are their legal submissions on any litigated issue. Even if in the end a case would not lead to a conviction due to insufficient evidence or other reasons, victims would at the very least have had the benefit of documenting their suffering in a court of law. This feeling of ownership, largely ascribed to hybrid criminal courts operating in the country where the crimes occurred and employing national staff in the adjudication of crimes, can also be generated through a well-designed system of victim participation in the proceedings. That said, it is difficult to claim that an acquittal would be of little negative impact on participating victims; many victims would feel that the evil that has befallen them has ultimately 'won' in court, and positive effects generated through their prior participation may be heavily affected.

It can, therefore, be concluded that victim participation seems to move the criminal process away from the mere punitive aspect, thus providing victims

[18] On restorative justice, see also the contribution by Silvia Fernández de Gurmendi in Chapter 2. From a criminologist's perspective, see the contribution by Frank Neubacher in Chapter 3.

with a more comprehensive redress than just telling (part of) their story as a witness of one of the parties. Yet, the verdict at the end of the trial will have a (more or less) validating effect, and so will the punishment – or the absence thereof. Examples are manifold from international tribunals where victim communities have reacted very sensitively to unexpectedly low sentences, even though victims' grievances were documented in the judgment and subject to charges confirmed by the judges in their verdict.[19]

3 *Challenges*

The move towards a greater emphasis on restorative justice in international criminal law and the idea of providing victims with a sense of ownership over the proceedings poses new challenges to the 'design' of the international criminal process and calls for an adjustment of accompanying measures. First, the administration of international criminal justice – at least in case of the ICC – takes place far away from the affected communities and, in general, years after the crimes have been committed.[20] Second, international core crimes produce a high number of victims and not all of them will be able to participate in legal proceedings – because not all international crimes will be subject of an international criminal trial.[21] Even where a specific crime complex is dealt with by a court or tribunal rather exhaustively, not all victims of the specific crimes will have access to the proceedings. This is in most cases due to logistical reasons: victim communities may have moved on to safe(r) locations; they may live in areas that are extremely difficult to access; and means of communication may be heavily reduced. In addition, reasons of personal safety and security may often prevent victims from coming forward at all where a conflict is still ongoing. Therefore, in international criminal law, selectivity applies to both the holding to account of perpetrators on the one hand and the involvement of victims on the other. For these reasons, in

[19] J.N. Clark, *International Trials and Reconciliation: Assessing the Impact of the International Criminal Tribunal for the Former Yugoslavia* (Abingdon: Routledge, 2014), 58–82; B. Holá, C. Bijleveld and A. Smeulers, 'Consistency of International Sentencing – ICTY and ICTR Case Study' (2012) 9 *European Journal of Criminology* 539. Yet, again, these tribunals did not feature victims' participatory means in their own right.

[20] On this, see, e.g., P. Clark, *Distant Justice* (Cambridge: Cambridge University Press, 2018).

[21] At the ICC – as at the hybrid tribunals assessed in this chapter –, victim participation is tied to the charges as they are brought before the relevant chamber, i.e. in order to participate, an applicant needs to be personally affected by the crimes alleged in the charges brought by the Prosecutor. As to the ICC Prosecutor's current charging/prosecutorial strategy, see ICC Office of the Prosecutor – Policy Paper on Case Selection and Prioritisation, 15 September 2016, available at www.icc-cpi.int/itemsdocuments/20160915_otp-policy_case-selection_eng.pdf.

practice, victims' participation has proven to be challenging in rendering it meaningful and inclusive.

a) Procedural Rights

The judicial discussion of victim participation in the courtroom remains predominantly oriented towards procedural rights, i.e., how much participation may be granted? Yet, this discussion also speaks to the general quality of victim participation: should victims' 'views and concerns where their personal interests are affected'[22] be allowed to entail the presentation of new evidence or at least new aspects of evidence not yet addressed by the parties?[23] It could be argued that the more powerfully the victims' procedural rights are exercised, the more 'party-like' victims' status becomes, generating an even more onerous duty on the Chamber to keep the equality of arms between the parties in balance, as victims will generally adduce elements that also bolster the prosecution case. Remarkably, most recently, in the *Ongwen* case, Trial Chamber IX authorized the common legal representatives of victims in the case to present their own (expert) witness evidence rather comprehensively through a number of witnesses. This extended to, inter alia, issues related to children and youth, in particular former child soldiers; sexual and gender-based violence; and to the victimisation of the affected communities.[24] It will remain an important and sensitive challenge to strike the right balance between the interests and rights of all parties and participants involved.[25] Judges of the ICC – and hybrid tribunals featuring victim participation – need to dispose of a highly sophisticated skill set to juggle all these factors in the courtroom as well as in their decisions and, ultimately, the judgment on the guilt or innocence of the accused.

[22] ICC Statute, Art. 68(3).

[23] Of note, Art. 69(3) of the ICC Statute provides the Chamber with the authority to request the submission of all evidence that it considers necessary for the determination of the truth.

[24] ICC, Decision of 6 March 2018 (TC), *Ongwen*, ICC-02/04-01/15-1199-Red, paras. 31, 32, 37, 68, 69 and Disposition.

[25] See ICC, Decision of 6 March 2018 (TC), *Ongwen*, ICC-02/04-01/15-1199-Red, para. 16. ICC jurisprudence has provided some guidance as to the admissibility of evidence tendered by victim representatives: '[i]n addition to whether the personal interests of the victims are affected, the Chamber will assess whether: (i) the presentation is consistent with the rights of the accused; (ii) the hearing of evidence is appropriate and affects the issues in the case; and (iii) the hearing of evidence is necessary for the determination of the truth'. ICC, Decision of 6 March 2018 (TC), *Ongwen*, ICC-02/04-01/15-1199-Red, para. 17; ICC, Decision of 16 July 2010 (AC), *Katanga*, ICC- 01/04-01/07-2288, para. 114; ICC, Decision of 15 February 2017 (TC), *Ntaganda*, ICC-01/04-02/06-1780-Red, para. 11.

b) Access to the Court

Broadening the focus from the courtroom to more general aspects of victims' access to the court or tribunal in question, some more practical considerations can be made regarding key factors to render victims' access effective and meaningful. An initial question, also in terms of chronology, is how to reach out to victims. In order to provide victims with any benefit from criminal proceedings at an international(ized) court, there needs to be a strategy regarding how to reach out to them and explain potential benefits – be that satisfaction through acknowledgement as a participating victim in the proceedings, retribution, and/or reparations. It is fundamental for such a court to be aware of its potential partners in the field, the latter being instrumental in getting access to affected communities and getting relevant messages across. The role of (grass root) NGOs and local victim associations cannot be over-emphasized as they will be able to help where an international(ized) court's resources will often be insufficient to afford the required manpower, let alone specific regional background knowledge. A mapping of relevant actors and strong partnerships are essential to enable a representative number of victims to find their way to the relevant court and decide whether they want to engage with it.

An important next step is the organization of legal representation. Mass crime scenarios will always generate large and often diverse victim communities that may even follow partially adverse interests – think only of child soldiers and their families on one hand, and victims of the child soldiers' crimes on the other. Yet, mindful of the accused's right to a fair and speedy trial, victim groups are often bundled, also to keep the number of legal representatives in court manageable.[26] Another factor is the scarceness of funds to finance such legal representation; victim communities will in most cases lack sufficient funds to remunerate a legal representative, requiring the relevant court to step in with the disbursement of legal aid funds.[27] Common legal representation, therefore, is an inevitable reality that needs to be (i) organized in the legal framework of the relevant court, as well as by a designated section in the Registry; and (ii) communicated in an effective manner; again, designated court staff will be required to master the task, not least to manage expectations of victims who may find themselves represented

[26] As the most recent case examples at the ICC, see ICC, Decision of 23 May 2019 (PTC), *Yekatom/Ngaissona*, ICC-01/14-01/18-205; ICC, Decision of 20 March 2019 (PTC), *Al Hassan*, ICC-01/12-01/18-289-Red-tENG-Corr.

[27] See Regulations 83 et seq. of the ICC Regulations. Rule 90 of the ICC Rules of Procedure and Evidence allows for the provision of legal aid funds for victims' legal representation.

by a counsel they never chose or even heard of before. In addition, any court will need to face the fact that legal aid has become more than just an option, but rather a standard feature of modern international(ized) courts. Adequate provision needs to be made for this significant cost driver, which, however, entails a fundamental enabler for meaningful victim participation and representation in the judicial proceedings.

Related to this, the quality of legal representation needs to be guaranteed and surveyed at all times. A key task for a court's registry is to require a minimum set of qualifications for any counsel to be able to represent victims in court. These qualifications should be akin to those of defence counsel because broadly comparable skill sets and reflexes will be required.[28]

Constant outreach to victims and affected communities throughout the proceedings is key. Only if the broader public is sufficiently aware of relevant proceedings will the relevant court gain sufficient (local) standing and legitimacy, which in turn makes it easier for victims to come forward. Generally, in the absence of proper outreach and public information, any verdict will remain with little effect on the affected population. Specific to victim communities, this may generate dissatisfaction and the lack of public recognition of victimhood. In addition, the lack of continuous and well-focused information creates gaps that tend to be filled by other elements, including erroneous assumptions, allegations or even malicious misinformation about the court in question, its mandate and relevant activities. The general need for outreach has already been acknowledged by the ad hoc Tribunals as well as the SCSL.[29] Specific to victim participation, additional outreach efforts need to be undertaken to give effect to victims' active role in judicial proceedings.

When speaking about victims' access to the court, one highly relevant circumstance is often overlooked: security. A court's contact with victims

[28] For example, Rule 22 of the ICC Rules of Procedure and Evidence stipulates some fundamental minimum requirements regarding the qualifications of (defence) counsel before the ICC. Rule 90(6) clarifies that a legal representative of a victim or victims shall have the qualifications set forth in Rule 22. Pursuant to Rule 21, the Registrar is held to maintain a list of counsel that meets the criteria set forth in Rule 22 and the ICC Regulations. Regulation 67 et seq. of said Regulations outlines the details of both qualifications of counsel and the application of the list of counsel.

[29] See ICTY, Outreach – 15 Years of Outreach at the ICTY, available at www.icty.org/x/file/Outreach/15-years-of-outreach/outreach-15_en_light.pdf; P. Schulz, '"Justice Seen Is Justice Done?" – Assessing the Impact of Outreach Activities by the International Criminal Tribunal for Rwanda (ICTR)' (2015) 74 *Croatian International Relations Review* 63 et seq.; E. Ottendoerfer, 'Outreach, in-Reach or beyond Reach? Lessons Learned from Hybrid Courts', 15 March 2018, available at https://justiceinconflict.org/2018/03/15/outreach-in-reach-or-beyond-reach-lessons-learned-from-hybrid-courts.

creates risks on both ends: for the court's personnel and for the individuals/groups reached out to. Particularly in active conflict or crisis areas, it is a major challenge to provide any information to affected groups, let alone establish a two-way communication channel. Civil society and other groups connecting affected communities with relevant international(ized) courts through safe and secure ways of communication mindful of the specific (high) risk environment are absolutely essential, as is the open-mindedness by said courts to try all means of communication available.[30]

II REPARATIONS

Reparations represent a centerpiece of the restorative justice concept as it is embedded in the ICC regulatory framework, as well as in the laws and rules of the aforementioned hybrid tribunals. Reparations are quite obviously closely tied to the punitive aspects of (international) criminal justice in a technical sense because they are – at least for the ICC and other hybrid tribunals referred to in this contribution – dependent on a previous conviction of an individual. Reparation orders are usually issued *against* the convicted person, and in their amount directly linked to the criminal liability previously established by the relevant chamber in the judgment.[31] Yet, this punitive aspect may not necessarily play a central role in a victim's motivation to apply for reparations. The request to receive reparations may focus solely on the aspect that the victim seeks redress for the harm he or she has suffered; the fact of who is (ultimately) responsible may not even be known to the victim. Of note, at the ICC victims can choose whether they want to apply for participation in the proceedings, reparations, or both; in

[30] By way of example, the Victims Participation and Reparations Section of the ICC developed in 2017/2018 an online form for victims to partake in the Afghanistan-related victim representation process under Art. 15(3) of the ICC Statute and Rule 50(3) of the ICC Rules of Procedure and Evidence; in 2019, a similar approach was put in place in the *Myanmar/Bangladesh* victim representation process. Also regarding victim participation in judicial proceedings where suspects have been identified, in the *Yekatom/Ngaïssona* case (Central African Republic) as well as in the *Al Hassan* victim participation process in the Mali situation, victims can for the first time follow a fully online application process, leaving no (paper) trace at a victim's end for a successful application process.

[31] ICC, Decision of 3 March 2015 (AC), *Lubanga*, ICC-01/04-01/06-3129, paras. 65 ('reparation orders are intrinsically linked to the *individual* whose criminal liability is established in a conviction and whose culpability for those criminal acts is determined in a sentence'), 76, 118 ('A convicted person's liability for reparations must be proportionate to the harm caused and, inter alia, his or her participation in the commission of the crimes for which he or she was found guilty, in the specific circumstances of the case.')

other words, the system caters for victims that have no desire to partake in the proceedings but merely want to benefit from reparations.[32]

The ICC provides for the most comprehensive reparations regime of an international criminal court to date, particularly also in light of the wealth of relevant jurisprudence. It shall be briefly outlined in Section II(1).

1 *Reparations at the International Criminal Court*

Article 75 of the ICC Statute provides the centerpiece of the ICC reparations regime. Article 75(2) stipulates that the relevant chamber 'may make a [reparations] order directly against a convicted person specifying appropriate reparations to, or in respect of, victims, including restitution, compensation and rehabilitation'. This underlines the fundamental premise, as already mentioned, that reparations at the ICC are linked to a prior conviction. As a special feature of the ICC framework, the provision continues to regulate that the Chamber 'may order that the award for reparations be made through the Trust Fund [for Victims][...]'.[33] Reparations proceedings follow the conviction of an accused by a panel of three judges, similar to the trial proceedings at first instance.[34] In contrast to trial, during the reparations phase victims are given a more central role in the proceedings as they are potential direct beneficiaries of any reparation order.[35] Procedural rights are comparable to

[32] Rule 94 of the ICC Rules of Procedure and Evidence and Regulation 88 of the ICC Regulations; these provisions are separate from those on victim participation in the proceedings (ICC RPE, Rules 89–91) and thus underline the fact that these are in fact two separate regimes. Yet, victims are asked, to the extent that they can, 'to state the identity of the person or persons the victim believes to be responsible for the injury, loss or harm' (ICC RPE, Rule 94(1)(c); ICC Regulations, Regulation 86(2)(d)). In addition, the Court has in the recent *Al Hassan* and *Yekatom/Ngaïssona* cases followed an approach using a joint participation/reparations application form, with a view to streamlining the proceedings and guaranteeing victims' rights to make their participatory choices at the earliest stages of proceedings. See as an example of the form used at www.icc-cpi.int/itemsDocuments/appForms-yn/ynAppFormInd_ENG.pdf.

[33] ICC Statute, Art. 75(2) second sentence. The Trust Fund for Victims is established through Art. 79 of the ICC Statute by the Assembly of States Parties. It is, therefore, not an organ of the ICC and enjoys in many respects independence from the latter. See ICC, Decision of 3 March 2015 (AC), *Lubanga*, ICC-01/04-01/06-3129.

[34] ICC Statute, Art. 39(2)(b)(ii); reparations proceedings under Art. 75 are part of judicial proceedings, thus requiring a panel of three judges.

[35] See, generally as to the victims' role and relevance in reparations proceedings before the ICC: OPCV Manual for legal representatives, 'Representing Victims before the International Criminal Court', 5th edition (2019), Section 6. *Issues related to Reparations*, p. 524 et seq., at www.icc-cpi.int/iccdocs/opcv/manual-victims-legal-representatives-fifth-edition.pdf; see also Office of the Prosecutor, Policy Paper on Victims' Participation, April 2010, 18 et seq., available

those of the defence, effectively giving victims the status of parties to the proceedings.[36] Rule 91(4) of the ICC Rules of Procedure and Evidence lifts victim legal representatives' restrictions on the questioning of witnesses during hearings on reparations, and victims have a genuine right to appeal a reparation order.[37] This stands in contrast to the 'views and concerns' permitted during trial proceedings, where the onus remains on the prosecution to prove the guilt of the accused.[38] At the reparations stage, questions regarding the accused's guilt and mode(s) of criminal liability are no longer at issue. In addition, Trial Chambers hearing reparations are vested with the possibility that they can 'appoint appropriate experts to assist [the judges] in determining the scope, extent of any damage, loss and injury to, or in respect of victims, and to suggest various options concerning the appropriate types and modalities of reparations'.[39] ICC Chambers have done so already in two out of four reparation proceedings to date, namely in *Al Mahdi* and in *Bemba*.[40]

2 *Some Challenges*

One of the fundamental challenges relating to reparations is one that spans across all participatory rights of victims in the criminal process: If an institution provides for these rights in its governing framework, it needs to ensure that these rights can be meaningfully exercised.[41] Great expectations are being raised through this novel feature of international criminal justice mechanisms, and the impact among the affected communities may be extensive in both directions: positive, if funds are available and well distributed; negative, if

at www.icc-cpi.int/NR/rdonlyres/9FF1EAA1-41C4-4A30-A202-174B18DA923C/281751/PolicyPaperonVictimsParticipationApril2010.pdf.

36 See ICC Statute, Art. 75(3) (see infra); ICC RPE, Rules 94 et seq. See also ICC, Decision of 13 June 2007 (AC), *Lubanga*, ICC-01/04-01/06-925, para. 28; ICC, Decision of 3 March 2015 (AC), *Lubanga*, ICC-01/04-01/06-3129, para. 86. See also ICC, Reparations Phase Calendar of 29 September 2016 (TC), *Al Mahdi*, ICC-01/12-01/15-172, addressing the victims' legal representative and the defence as 'parties', paras. 2 et seq.

37 ICC Statute, Art. 82(4).

38 On victims' rights to provide evidence and relevant disclosure obligations, see ICC, Judgement of 11 July 2008 (AC), *Lubanga*, ICC-01/04-01/06-1432, para. 3.

39 ICC RPE, Rule 97(2).

40 ICC, Decision of 19 January 2017 (TC), *Al Mahdi*, ICC-01/12-01/15-203-Red; ICC, Decision of 2 June 2017 (TC), *Bemba*, ICC-01/05-01/08-3532-Red.

41 ICC, Decision of 6 March 2018 (TC), *Ongwen*, ICC-02/04-01/15-1199-Red, para. 51; ICC, Decision of 6 February 2015 (TC), *Ntaganda*, ICC-01/04-02/06-449, paras. 26, 53; ICC, Decision of 3 October 2012 (TC), *Ruto and Sang*, ICC-01/09-01/11-460, para. 59; see also L. Moffett, 'Meaningful and Effective? Considering Victims' Interests Through Participation at the International Criminal Court' (2015) 26 *Criminal Law Forum* 255 et seq.

there are insufficient funds, if existing funds are inappropriately distributed, and if the relevant tribunal's outreach is deficient in communicating this early enough. That latter point, effective outreach and expectation management, also needs to address the often extensive time lapse between a victim's request for reparations (usually even before the commencement of trial proceedings[42]) and the implementation of reparations, the latter occurring years after the commencement of trial. Part of the respect and recognition that any international criminal justice mechanism can demonstrate to victim communities is encompassed in transparent and frequent communication. If victims receive clear indications up-front and during the judicial process of what they can expect and when, expectations can be successfully managed and potential re-traumatisation prevented. Courts and tribunals need to take this task seriously and have a powerful victim outreach strategy that reaches affected communities comprehensively and with well-calibrated messages. Sufficient funds need to be made available from the very beginning. This is particularly so for hybrid courts that have a limited life span and need to establish their legitimacy among the affected population as of the commencement of its activities.

The absence of funds that the convict could be ordered to make available for reparations can be countered in the case of the ICC through its Trust Fund for Victims; the latter has the capacity to implement reparation orders through its own funds received through voluntary contributions of states and other benevolent parties. Yet, current realities show that the Trust Fund's resources thus obtained are insufficient to cover relevant reparations orders by Trial Chambers. For example, in *Katanga*, the Chamber set Germain Katanga's liability for reparation at USD 1,000,000.[43] In *Al Mahdi*, the Chamber set Ahmad Al Faqi Al Mahdi's liability for reparations at € 2.7 million.[44] In *Lubanga*, the Chamber held that USD 10 million are required to express Thomas Lubanga's overall liability.[45] The Trust Fund's reparations reserve of presently € 7.7 million[46] will not suffice to complement all the presently

42 See ICC RPE, Rule 94(2).

43 ICC, Decision of 24 March 2017 (TC), *Katanga*, ICC-01/04-01/07-3728, para. 264, and Disposition at page 118.

44 ICC, Decision of 17 August 2017 (TC), *Al Mahdi*, ICC-01/12-01/15-236, para. 134, and Disposition at page 60.

45 ICC, Decision of 21 December 2017 (TC), *Lubanga*, ICC-01/04-01/06-3379-Red-Corr, para. 281.

46 ICC, Report to the Assembly of States Parties on the projects and the activities of the Board of Directors of the Trust Fund for Victims for the period 1 July 2017 to 30 June 2018, ICC-ASP/17/14, 23 July 2018, para. 12, available at https://asp.icc-cpi.int/iccdocs/asp_docs/ASP17/ICC-ASP-17-14-ENG.pdf.

standing awards in full. The Trust Fund's limited capacity in this regard carries a strong risk of frustrating many victims' expectations. This problem is exacerbated for hybrid courts that merely refer victims to national compensation programmes, with the convicting judgment as a 'title' enabling these victims to claim compensation; in many cases, such national programmes will not provide sufficient redress, if any at all.[47]

III CONCLUSION

For victims of atrocity crimes, international criminal justice can be a powerful tool to receive satisfaction and redress. The point of punishment still takes a prominent role in this context, as even victims that participate in the proceedings will often do so not only to tell their own story, but also to identify their suffering with the person perceived as most responsible (or at least the accused standing trial before them) and benefit from the retributive value of conviction and punishment. Yet, victim participation also shifts potential satisfaction and redress into the trial hearing stage, thus amplifying potential beneficial effects for victims by an important feature.

In particular, the reparations idea can be a powerful one that entails a much stronger restorative justice element than is the case for victim participation, in that harm can be quite figuratively repaired through relevant reparation measures. The relevance of the criminal conviction of an accused may shift gradually into the background, as does the punishment of the individual, the former remaining a technical condition *sine qua non* for a reparations order and subsequent implementation of reparations. This is where the traditional objectives of international criminal justice are most visibly altered – or rather: *enhanced* – to include the restorative justice component as a concluding chapter to the criminal process *by institutional design* (see, e.g., Article 75 of the ICC Statute; Article 22 of the KSC Law; and Rule 23 of the ECCC Internal Rules).

Yet, many challenges attach to the new victim-related features of the ICC and more recent hybrid internationalized courts and tribunals. It starts with victims' access to the respective court and the challenge for the institution to render victims' participation meaningful despite the often large geographical distance and the need for representation of victims in

[47] See, e.g., regarding potential state-governed compensation activities for victims of the previous regime under dictator Hissène Habré: Human Rights Watch, Chad: Court Order, but No Cash, for Ex-Dictator's Victims, 24 March 2016, available at www.hrw.org/news/2016/03/24/chad-court-order-no-cash-ex-dictators-victims.

court through counsel – as opposed to direct and personal interaction with the judges. The exact procedural status and rights are another important factor to manage well. Judges need to find the just equilibrium between victims' interests and rights of the Defence, requiring their constant vigilance in the courtroom, and in their rulings. In addition, the general security situation in the country may be a heavily determining factor of victims' possibility of accessing relevant proceedings – a factor that remains largely outside a court's control.

For a meaningful reparation mechanism, the availability of funds will be essential. If the system is properly funded and if victim redress projects are well chosen, the system can work. It is often underestimated with how little money meaningful projects can be carried out that make a real difference to victim communities.

Communication is another key factor that actually spans beyond reparations and will play a key role in the judicial mechanism's legitimacy among affected communities and have a restorative and reparative impact in the longer term.

If victims are provided access to international criminal justice as a direct actor, addressee and beneficiary, one needs to be serious about making that access to justice meaningful. A key component in this is to actively control the system and measure the impact as perceived by the participating victims. Negative feedback should not lead to doubts about the system but rather encourage ideas on how to improve it. Every situation requiring an international criminal justice solution will have its own, unique victim-related challenges; the ICC as the only permanent international criminal court is producing a wealth of different possible approaches, jurisprudence, lessons learnt, and thus an important tool kit. This has two main benefits: first, it allows the ICC to steadily improve and learn from challenges and mistakes; second, other (hybrid) international(ized) justice mechanisms can conceptualize their own victim features in view of ICC lessons learnt, and start off with the best possible system in place, tailored to the specifics of the situation. This will help the ICC, other international(ized) courts and their respective victim-centered features to become what is indeed a key word for the entire modern international criminal justice idea: meaningful.

21

Concluding Remarks

Dimensions of 'Why Punish?'

FLORIAN JESSBERGER AND JULIA GENEUSS

Since Nuremberg, international punishment for mass atrocities is pervasive, as an idea and as a practice. In fact, many observers regard the institutionalization of international punishment – i.e., the incarceration of perpetrators of genocide, crimes against humanity and war crimes – as a progress and as a promise: The international community, by and large, seems to have, at least rhetorically, agreed that criminal punishment rather than impunity or, e.g., summary executions, is the adequate reaction to mass atrocities.

But *why* do we punish perpetrators of mass atrocities? The institutionalization of international punishment as such does not inform us of the reasons why we punish. The 'why punish' question goes to the heart of the theoretical foundation of international criminal law. At first sight, this question seems rather odd: Why *not* punish perpetrators of mass atrocity? If criminal punishment is a common reaction to 'ordinary' crime in every domestic legal system, then why should there be any different reaction towards those who violate the laws of war and basic human rights on a massive scale and in a systematic manner?

The question of purposes of punishment has been discussed in the domestic context for centuries. There is a vast number of different theories and subtheories, often rooted in different penal cultures. Therefore, it does not come as surprise that the discussion continues beyond the pure domestic context and seems to be even more complicated when it comes to international punishment. International criminal justice, as a social practice and as an academic discipline, is, by its nature, pluralistic and multi-disciplinary – and equally diverse is the group of those who reflect upon the 'why punish' question. Not surprisingly, perspectives vary from practitioners to theorists and criminal philosophers, from international lawyers to criminal lawyers. Obviously, the answer to the 'why punish' question depends on whom you ask.

In this conclusion, we do not aim to repeat what has been said before, but to offer some subsequent and more general deliberations on the subject at hand. Our modest aim is to identify and briefly discuss some recurrent themes and issues that have been touched upon by the authors of the present volume and that seem to be important in conceptualizing and addressing the question 'Why punish perpetrators of mass atrocities?' – in theory as well as in practice. This way we hope to carve out at least some of the multiple dimensions of a theory of international punishment.

I THE VARIOUS WHYS

First of all, as has been emphasized by a number of authors in this volume, it is important to disentangle the various aspects of the 'Why punish perpetrators of mass atrocities? ' question. There seem to be at least four subquestions that, albeit having multiple inter-relations, need to be distinguished:

The first fundamental question is why (and whether) *criminal law* is the appropriate response to collective and systematic mass atrocities. Why is criminal punishment as such the agreed upon reaction to international core crimes? What is, and what should be, the general role of criminal law in situations of mass violence? What overall goal is meant to be achieved with the establishment of a criminal justice system for the prosecution of international core crimes? It should be noted that these questions apply to both the domestic justice systems prosecuting international core crimes and the international criminal justice system. In this regard, a distinction must be made between those who argue that criminal law should be abolished altogether in any context and those who argue that criminal law is no adequate reaction to situations of mass atrocities only. The latter, however, would have to explain why they believe that perpetrators of 'ordinary' crimes should be punished while those who take part in international core crimes should be treated differently. While international criminal punishment of core crimes has been regarded as a progress in the so-called 'fight against impunity', critiques of the 'international punitive justice model' have been growing louder in recent years. For example, it is argued by some that punitive justice is too narrow, too selective and too exclusive, that its asymmetrical enforcement perpetuates international power relations, that its limited perspective does not and cannot grasp the wider complexities of the conflict situations and blurs the involvement of actors from the Global North in the crimes. Before this background, some authors call for an international (or internationalized) restorative justice model that turns away from international punishment. Others emphasize the elements of restorative justice *within* the current system of international criminal justice, such as the participation of victims and reparations.

The second question, which is closely linked to the first one but includes a different dimension, relates to the establishment specifically of *international institutions* as agents of criminal punishment. What are the specific goals set for the establishment of international criminal courts and tribunals? What are the institutional mandates and socio-political objectives that were meant to be achieved by their establishment? This question includes the aspect of the legitimacy of the system of international criminal justice, the issue of the *ius puniendi* without a state raised by some authors, and the justification of international punishment vis-à-vis the individual, mentioned by others.

The third question, which is the one this volume primarily intends to address, accepts criminal justice in general and international punishment in particular as a reaction to mass atrocities, and is concerned about the *purposes* of punishment for international core crimes in the narrower sense. We punish perpetrators of mass atrocities, but why? What are the purposes of punishment for international core crimes? Given the explanation of international crimes and their collective dimension, the question of 'why punish' is closely related to the question of 'whom to punish'. The natural starting point for this debate is a 'domestic analogy': Is it possible to transfer the purposes of punishment applied in the domestic context (for ordinary crimes) to the punishment of international core crimes? Yet, this narrow dimension of the 'why punish' question also seems to be relevant for the domestic punishment for international crimes, at least when based on universal jurisdiction. Or are there different purposes of punishment depending on whether international punishment *stricto sensu* or domestic punishment for international crimes is concerned?

Finally, the fourth and last dimension of 'why punish' refers to the question of *how* to punish perpetrators of international core crimes. What is of interest in this regard is the relationship between the purposes of punishment and the *sentencing* process and outcome (i.e., the type and severity of punishment). If and how do purposes of punishment influence the determination of the sentence? Can and should they give any guidance?

II ON DOMESTIC ANALOGIES, OR: HOW SPECIAL IS INTERNATIONAL CRIMINAL LAW?

It seems intuitively right that our perception of international criminal justice and punishment is based on our understanding of 'ordinary' criminal law, i.e. domestic criminal punishment for 'ordinary' crimes. Indeed, the way we see domestic criminal law shapes our understanding of why, whom, and how to punish. Therefore, when discussing the 'why punish' question, the so-called domestic analogy forms a natural starting point. In our context, the reference to the term 'domestic analogy' is a shortcut to the question of whether the purposes of punishment can be transferred from the domestic realm without further ado to the punishment of international core crimes, or whether a different set of new or at least modified purposes of punishment should apply. To put it differently: Should purposes of punishment derive from what operates at the national level for ordinary common crimes? While, again, at first sight the question might seem odd – why would the discussion be different only because the crimes are committed systematically and on a larger scale? – some authors argue that international core crimes and their (international) prosecution and punishment is so fundamentally different that a transfer of rationales is impossible. Thus, the domestic analogy issue basically boils down to the question of: 'How special is international criminal law?'

An important set of arguments that speaks against a simple transfer of the purposes of punishment, as has already been mentioned in the Introduction and discussed extensively in a number of contributions to this volume, relates to the explanation of international core crimes, their nature and quality, which, arguably, makes them categorically different from ordinary crimes. In particular, international core crimes are typically committed in the context of an overall disturbed society – with the actions of the perpetrator often being at least socially non-deviant – and by and against a collective. The latter – the fact that international core crimes are usually committed against a collective – may explain the (strong emphasis on the) active role of victims in international criminal proceedings and, ultimately, the stronger focus on elements of restorative justice. It points to the importance of having a forum where victims can speak and be heard and 'own' the process of reconciliation – a perception that puts the trial proceedings at the centre and that seems to be accommodated easily within a framework of expressivist theories of punishment. The former – the fact that international core crimes are usually committed *by* a collective – results in (and requires!) different layers of explanation for international core crimes, the macro-, meso-, and micro-levels, connected to the system, the group and the individual. On the other hand, if it is true that international criminal courts and tribunals are meant to 'complement' domestic criminal courts, which have failed and still fail to prosecute international core crimes, there does not seem to be any objection against the domestic analogy. The practical problem here, of course, is that international punishing institutions, enforce international criminal law in a highly selective, disrupted and arguably politicized way.

Most authors seem to agree that while there are important differences between ordinary and international crimes and their respective enforcement on the domestic and the international level, these differences should not be exaggerated. Therefore, there does not seem to be an objection against the domestic analogy *per se* – to learn from and to be guided by domestic experiences. However, when borrowing and importing concepts from the domestic context, one must avoid the simple repetition of the domestic – at times confusing and at times self-referential – discussion on purposes of 'ordinary' punishment. It is important to carefully analyze and keep in mind the specificities of international core crimes, international criminal law and justice, and its enforcement.

III FROM THEORY TO PRACTICE – OR FROM PRACTICE TO THEORY

As was explained in the Introduction, it is an important aim of this volume to link the theoretical debate on the purposes of punishment to its practical consequences. Yet, we must concede that the discussion on purposes of international punishment is and remains predominantly academic. As we have learnt from a number of contributions, the 'why punish' question is rarely genuinely discussed in the jurisprudence of international courts and tribunals. It largely seems to be a 'non-question' for both, the judges who render the verdict and mete out the sentences, as well as for international prosecutors in their decision on which situations to investigate and which cases to prosecute. As regards the former, we see ritualism and a 'hypnotic repetition' of the domestic criminal law discussion, without questioning the suitability of these arguments in the international criminal law context. As regards the latter, the multi-dimensional limitations of international criminal courts and tribunals, in particular the ICC, rather than theoretical considerations on institutional goals and purposes of punishment are relevant. We share the observation that practical concerns shape the agenda and that theory is only secondary. We also share the concern emphasized by several authors in this volume that if there is no theory of international punishment, if international punishment is not grounded on some theoretical considerations, then there is no principled way to guide the prosecutors and judges, and there is no way to systematically critique their actions.

When it comes to the purposes of punishment, we believe that retribution, prevention, as well as expressivism, have their legitimate part to play in the international criminal law context. As in the domestic discussion, different authors argue in favour of different theories, or a combined theory with different emphasis on the one or the other rationale, specifically adapted to the international context. At the same time, all purposes of punishment are subject to criticism. What seems to be important is to move beyond the 'ordinary' counter-arguments, e.g., the existence of a deterrent effect, and carve out the purely international criminal law related criticisms, if any, against specific purposes of punishment.

IV EXPRESSIVE THEORIES OF INTERNATIONAL PUNISHMENT: WHAT'S THE MESSAGE?

Several authors determine a 'trend' towards expressivism in international criminal law, either in the scarce statements of international criminal courts and tribunals or in the academic discourse. And indeed, expressivism seems to be a plausible rationale for international punishment. However, expressivist theories, notwithstanding their variations in detail, seem to be rather vague and flexible, and, ultimately, form a 'catch-all rationale' that can work as an agreeable minimal consensus. Expressivism is broad enough to encompass any message and seems to work as a theoretical 'cloak'. While this flexibility is appealing, scholarship needs to develop an in-depth definition and a clear concept of expressivism in international criminal law, specify the messages that are to be communicated, identify their addressees and determine the relationship of expressivism with retribution and deterrence. However, reading through the contributions of this volume, it becomes apparent that we are far from there.

First, there seems to be different views regarding the relationship between expressivism and other purposes of punishment, in particular retribution and deterrence. Some authors (and courts) want to integrate retribution and deterrence into an expressive theory of punishment. Others understand expressive theories of punishment as being similar to positive general prevention (also referred to as integrative prevention). Second, authors have different positions on what messages are and should be communicated through international punishment. Is international punishment a didactic exercise? Does it include elements of communicating the historical truth? Does it strengthen the (international) rule of law? Is it meant to communicate solidarity with the victims? Or is international punishment just an expression of faith that reinforces the normative belief system of international criminal prosecutions?

V FROM WHY TO HOW: PURPOSES OF PUNISHMENT AND SENTENCING

Another topic that has been touched upon in several contributions of the present volume relates to the relationship between the 'why punish' and the 'how to punish'. While it has been argued that the sentencing process bears no or only little relation to the 'why-punish' question, a convincing argument has been made that the method and outcome of the sentencing exercise and the enforcement of sentences are indeed (or at least should be) influenced by the theoretical question of the purposes of punishment. The question why we punish is connected to the criteria that need to be taken into account during sentencing as well as the outcome. This, however, does not only concern the severity of the punishment, but also the type of sanction. It is not clear what guidance judges draw from rationales of punishment during the sentencing process. The lack of a structured and transparent sentencing practice makes it even more difficult to understand the reasons for imposing punishment and the objectives it is meant to achieve.

Finally, it may be argued that, as in the domestic context, it is necessary to discuss alternatives to incarceration, e.g., social work, in the international criminal justice system. Similarly, the issue of enforcement of punishment – how? where? – that is connected most clearly to the rationale of rehabilitation, as well as post-trial justice in general, and the question of reduction of sentences in particular, received very little attention.

Select Bibliography

Akhavan, Payam 'Beyond Impunity: Can International Criminal Justice Prevent Future Atrocities?' (2001) 95 *American Journal of International Law* 7–31.

Amann, Diane Marie 'Group Mentality, Expressivism, and Genocide' (2002)2 *International Criminal Law Review* 93–143.

Ambos, Kai 'Punishment without a Sovereign? The *Ius Puniendi* Issue of International Criminal Law' (2013) 33 *Oxford Journal of Legal Studies* 293–315.

Arendt, Hannah *Eichmann in Jerusalem: A Report on the Banality of Evil* (New York: Viking Press, 1963).

Damaska, Mirjan R. 'What Is the Point of International Criminal Justice' (2008) 83 *Chicago-Kent Law Review* 329–365.

D'Ascoli, Silvia *Sentencing in International Criminal Law: The UN Ad Hoc Tribunals and Future Perspectives for the ICC* (Oxford: Hart, 2011).

deGuzman, Margaret M. 'Choosing to Prosecute: Expressive Selection at the International Criminal Court' (2012) 33 *Michigan Journal of International Law* 265–320.

deGuzman, Margret M. 'Harsh Justice for International Crimes?' (2014) 39 *Yale Journal of International Law* 1–35.

Drumbl, Mark A. *Atrocity, Punishment, and International Law* (Cambridge: Cambridge University Press, 2007).

'Victims Who Victimise' (2016) 4 *London Journal of International Law* 217–246.

Duff, Anthony *Punishment, Communication, and Community* (Oxford: Oxford University Press, 2003).

'Process, not Punishment: The Importance of Criminal Trials for Transitional and Transnational Justice' (2014) *University of Minnesota Law School Legal Studies Research Paper Series*, Research Paper No. 14–03.

Epik, Aziz *Die Strafzumessung bei Taten nach dem Völkerstrafgesetzbuch* (Tübingen: Mohr Siebeck, 2017).

Feinberg, Joel 'The Expressive Function of Punishment' (1965) 49 *The Monist* 397–423.

Doing and Deserving: Essays in the Theory of Responsibility (Princeton: Princeton University Press, 1970).

Fletcher, George *The Grammar of Criminal Law: American, Comparative, and International* (Oxford: Oxford University Press, 2007).

Gierhake, Katrin *Begründung des Völkerstrafrechts auf der Grundlage der Kantischen Rechtslehre* (Berlin: Duncker & Humblot, 2005).

Golash, Deirdre 'The Justification of Punishment in the International Context' in Larry May and Zachary Hoskins (eds.), *International Criminal Law and Philosophy* (Cambridge: Cambridge University Press, 2010) 201–223

Greenawalt, Alexander K.A. 'International Criminal Law for Retributivists' (2014) 35 *University of Pennsylvania Journal of International Law* 969–1044.

Günther, Klaus 'Crime and Punishment as Communication' in A.P. Simester, Antje Du Bois-Pedain and Ulfrid Neumann (eds.), *Liberal Criminal Theory, Essays for Andrew von Hirsch* (Oxford: Hart, 2014) 123–139.

Haque, Adil Ahmad 'Group Violence and Group Vengeance: Toward a Retributivist Theory of International Criminal Law' (2005) 9 *Buffalo Criminal Law Review* 273–328.

'Retributivism: The Right and the Good' (2013) 32 *Law and Philosophy* 59–82.

Harmon Mark B. and Fergal Gaynor, 'Ordinary Sentences for Extraordinary Crimes' (2007) 5 *Journal of International Criminal Justice* 683–712.

Harrendorf, Stefan 'How Can Criminology Contribute to an Explanation of International Crimes?' (2014) 12 *Journal of International Criminal Justice* 231–252.

Hart, H.L.A. *Punishment and Responsibility* (Oxford: Oxford University Press, 1968).

Hassan, Farooq 'The Theoretical Basis of Punishment in International Criminal Law' (1983) 15 *Case Western Reserve Journal of International Law* 39–60.

Henham, Ralph The Philosophical Foundations of International Sentencing, (2003) 1 *Journal of International Criminal Justice* 64–85.

'Developing Contextualized Rationales for Sentencing in International Criminal Trials' (2007) 5 *Journal of International Criminal Justice* 757–778.

Holá, Barbora, Catrien Bijleveld and Alette Smeulers, 'Consistency of International Sentencing – ICTY and ICTR Case Study' (2012) 9 *European Journal of Criminology* 539–552.

Holá Barbora and Joris van Wijk, 'Life after Conviction at International Criminal Tribunals – An Empirical Overview' (2014) 12 *Journal of International Criminal Justice* 109–132.

Jäger, Herbert *Makrokriminalität: Studien zur Kriminologie kollektiver Gewalt* (Frankfurt: Suhrkamp, 1989).

Jo, Hyeran and Beth A. Simmons 'Can the International Criminal Court Deter Atrocity?' (2016) 70 *International Organization* 443–475.

Karstedt, Susanne 'Contextualizing Mass Atrocity Crimes: The Dynamics of "Extremely Violent Societies"' (2012) 9 *European Journal of Criminology* 499–513.

Ku, Julian and Jide Nzelibe, 'Do International Criminal Tribunals Deter or Exacerbate Humanitarian Atrocities?' (2006) 84 *Washington University Law Review* 777–833.

Luban, David 'Fairness to Rightness: Jurisdiction, Legality, and the Legitimacy of International Criminal Law' in Samantha Besson and John Tasioulas (eds.), *The Philosophy of International Law* (Oxford: Oxford University Press, 2010), 575–588.

Malamud-Goti, Jaime 'Transitional Governments in the Breach: Why Punish State Criminals?' (1990) 12 *Human Rights Quarterly* 1–16.

McAuliffe, Pádraig, 'Suspended Disbelief? The Curious Endurance of the Deterrence Rationale in International Criminal Law' (2012) 10 *New Zealand Journal of Public and International Law* 227–262.

Meernik, James 'Sentencing Rationales and Judicial Decision Making at the International Tribunals' (2011) 92 *Social Science Quarterly* 588–608.

Mégret, Frédéric 'The Anxieties of International Criminal Justice' (2016) 29 *Leiden Journal of International Law* 197–221.

Minow, Martha *Between Vengeance and Forgiveness: Facing History after Genocide and Mass Violence* (Boston: Beacon Press, 1998).

Mulgrew, Róisín *Towards the Development of the International Penal System* (Cambridge: Cambridge University Press, 2013).

Mulgrew Róisín and Denis Abels (eds.), *Research Handbook on International Penal System* (Cheltenham: Edward Elgar, 2016).

Nemitz, Jan C. 'The Law of Sentencing in International Criminal Law: The Purposes of Sentencing and the Applicable Method for the Determination of the Sentence' in Avril McDonald et al. (eds.), *Yearbook of International Humanitarian Law 2001* (The Hague: T.M.C. Asser Press, 2004) 87–127.

Neubacher, Frank 'How Can It Happen That Horrendous State Crimes Are Perpetrated? An Overview of Criminological Theories' (2006) 4 *Journal of International Criminal Justice* 787–799.

Ohlin, Jens David 'Towards a Unique Theory of International Criminal Sentencing' in Göran Sluiter and Sergey Vasiliev (eds.), *International Criminal Procedure: Towards a Coherent Body of Law* (London: Cameron May, 2009) 303–404.

Osiel, Mark J. 'Why Prosecute? Critics of Punishment for Mass Atrocity' (2000) 22 *Human Rights Quarterly* 118–147.

Rawls, John *A Theory of Justice*, revised ed. (Harvard: Harvard University Press, 1999).

Raz, Joseph *The Authority of Law*, 2nd ed. (Oxford: Oxford University Press, 2009).

Reuss, Vasco *Zivilcourage als Strafzweck des Völkerstrafrechts. Was bedeutet positive Generalprävention in der globalen Zivilgesellschaft?* (Münster: LIT Verlag, 2012).

Schabas, William A. 'Sentencing by International Tribunals: A Human Rights Approach' (1997) 7 *Duke Journal of Comparative & International Law* 461–517.

Sloane, Robert D. 'The Expressive Capacity of International Punishment: The Limits of the National Law Analogy and the Potential of International Criminal Law' (2007) 43 *Stanford Journal of International Law* 39–93.

Sloane, Robert D 'Sentencing for the Crime of Crimes: The Evolving "Common Law" of Sentencing of the International Criminal Tribunal for Rwanda' (2007) 5 *Journal of International Criminal Justice* 713–734.

Smeulers, Alette and Roelof Haveman (eds.), *Supranational Criminology: Towards a Criminology of International Crimes* (Antwerp: Intersentia Press, 2008).

Tallgren, Immi 'The Sensibility and Sense of International Criminal Law' (2002) 13 *European Journal of International Law* 561–595.

von Hirsch, Andrew and Vivian C. Schorscher, 'A System of International Criminal Justice for Human Rights Violations: What Is the General Justification for Its Existence?' in Julian V. Roberts and Lucia Zedner (eds.), *Principles and Values in*

Criminal Law and Criminal Justice (Oxford: Oxford University Press, 2012) 209–223.

Werkmeister, Andreas *Straftheorien im Völkerstrafrecht* (Baden–Baden: Nomos, 2015).

Wippman, David 'Atrocities, Deterrence, and the Limits of International Justice' (1999) 23 *Fordham International Law Journal* 473–488.

Wringe, Bill 'Why Punish War Crimes? Victor's Justice and Expressive Justifications of Punishment' (2006) 25 *Law and Philosophy* 159–191.

Index

www.ingramcontent.com/pod-product-compliance
Lightning Source LLC
LaVergne TN
LVHW052025200926
848481LV00005B/1584
* 9 7 8 1 1 0 8 4 6 5 8 9 2 *